Borderlines

BORDERLINES

GENDERS AND IDENTITIES IN WAR AND PEACE, 1870–1930

Edited by BILLIE MELMAN

ROUTLEDGE
NEW YORK   LONDON

Published in 1998

Routledge
29 West 35th Street
New York, NY 10001

Published in Great Britain by

Routledge
11 New Fetter Lane
London EC4P 4EE

Copyright © 1998 by Routledge, Inc.

Printed in the United States of America on acid-free paper.

Library of Congress Cataloging-in-Publication Data

Borderlines : genders and identities in war and peace 1870–1930 /
    edited by Billie Melman.
        p.   cm.
    Includes bibliographical references and index.
    ISBN 0–415–91113–3. — ISBN 0–415–91114–1 (pbk)
    1. Sex role—History—19th century.   2. Sex role—History—20th
century.   3. Women in politics—History—19th century.   4. Women in
politics—History—20th century.   5. Feminism—History—19th
century.   6. Feminism—History—20th century.   7. Gender identity—
History—19th century.   8. Gender identity—History—20th century.
I. Melman, Billie.
HQ10/5.B67   1997
305 3—dc21   97–12078
                                                        CIP

For Yotam D. Melman, and Daria L. Melman,
who was conceived and born with this volume

Contents

Prologue   ix

List of Illustrations   xi

Introduction   *Billie Melman*   1

Part I Gendering the Nation: Definitions and Boundaries   27

The British Imperial State and the Construction of
     National Identities   29
       Pat Thane

From Empire to Nation: Images of Women and War in
     Ottoman Political Cartoons, 1908–1923   47
       Fatma Müge Göçek

Men and Soldiers: British Conscripts, Concepts of
     Masculinity, and the Great War   73
       Ilana R. Bet-El

Family, Masculinity, and Heroism in Russian
     War Posters of the First World War   95
       Karen Petrone

Re-Generation: Nation and the Construction of Gender
     in Peace and War—Palestine Jews, 1900–1918   121
       Billie Melman

Taking Risks for Pictures: The Heroics of Cinematic
     Realism in World War I   141
       Sonya Michel

Part II Borderlands: Identities and Sexualities   161

Fin-de-Siècle Theatrics: Male Impersonation and
     Lesbian Desire   163
       Martha Vicinus

Lesbians before Lesbianism: Sexual Identity in Early
     Twentieth-Century British Fiction   193
       David Trotter

Spectacles and Sexualities: The "Mise-en-Scène" of the
    "Tirailleur Sénégalais" on the Western Front, 1914–1920   213
    Annabelle Melzer

"Objects to Possess and Discard": The Representation
    of Jews and Women by British Women Novelists
    of the 1920s   245
    Phyllis Lassner

Part III Dissent and Acquiescence: War, Feminism, and
    Female Action   263

Challenging Traditions: Denominational Feminism in
    Britain, 1910–1920   265
    Jacqueline R. deVries

Religion, Emancipation, and Politics in the Confessional
    Women's Movement in Germany, 1900–1933   285
    Ursula Baumann

Ideological Crossroads: Feminism, Pacifism, and Socialism   307
    Amira Gelblum

The Politics of Female Notables in Postwar Egypt   329
    Beth Baron

Part IV Moving Boundaries: Work, Gender, and Mobilization   351

Public Functions, Private Premises: Female Professional
    Identity and the Domestic-Service Paradigm in Britain,
    c. 1850–1930   353
    Anne Summers

Emily Goes to War: Explaining the Recruitment to
    the Women's Army Auxiliary Corps in World War I   377
    Doron Lamm

Work, Gender, and Identity in Peace and War: France
    1890–1930   397
    Françoise Thébaud

Class, Ethnicity, and Gender in Post-Ottoman Thessaloniki:
    The Great Tobacco Strike of 1914   421
    Efi Avdela

Contributores   439

Index   443

PROLOGUE

The title of this collection comes from a scene in Pat Barker's 1993 novel *Regeneration*, the first in her Great War trilogy. In this particular scene Rivers, the writer's construction of the famous neurologist and social anthropologist, and Prior, a fictive creation and Rivers's most difficult and least placeable case, hold a brief conversation about the Great War, social difference, and the borders of social identities.

> "All right. How did you fit in?"
> Prior's face shut tight. "You mean did I encounter any snobbery?"
> "Yes."
> "Not more than I have here."
> Their eyes locked. Rivers said, "But you did encounter it."
> "Yes. It's made perfectly clear when you arrive that some people are more welcome than others. It helps if you've been to the right school. It helps if you hunt, it helps if your shirts are the right colour. Which is a **deep** shade of khaki, by the way."
> In spite of himself Rivers looked down at his shirt.
> "Borderline," said Prior.
> "And yours?"
> "Not borderline. Nowhere near . . ."

"Borderlines" denotes much more than the shade of uniform. It stands for the color of difference among classes, between genders and sexualities. And it also signifies the borders that mark sanity from insanity—the latter identified with war. The two men have undefined sexualities—Prior being bisexual and Rivers asexual. Their very genders are ambiguous. As officers, both act maternally towards their men. The geography of their war experience is indefinite. Front and home, soldiers' 'no man's land' and the terrain of civilians strangely merge in the two men's nightmares. In Rivers's and Prior's neurotic world the trench is the domesticated habitat of feminized soldiers, and the streets and factories of Britain's cities a masculinized women's territory.

The idea of a collection on the borderlines of genders and identities in a period of transformation from peace to war and again to peace, first came about in 1992, in a six-month, advanced-studies' seminar on gender and the First World War held at the Wiener Library at Tel Aviv University. Papers delivered at a conference held in March of that year became the nucleus of the collection. My residence and Norman Freehling Fellowship at the Institute for the Humanities at the University of Michigan in 1994–95 were instrumental in turning *Borderlines* from a Eurocentric (and strongly Anglo-American) project into a broader comparative study. Most of the pieces covering Southern European and colonial ground are the result of fruitful exchanges with historians of Russia, the Balkans, and the Middle East during my year at the Institute.

My first and longest-standing debt is to Shulamit Volkov, my co-chair at the Wiener Seminar, who extended this project hospitality, intellectual support, and unfailing encouragement. I am deeply grateful to her. I am also grateful to those participants in the seminar and conference whose work could not be accommodated within the confines of the collection. I especially wish to thank Ute Frevert, Karen Hausen, Margaret R. Higonnet, Avner Offer, Jane Lewis, and Jay Winter for their contributions to the seminar and unstinting support for the project.

A number of colleagues and fellow-historians patiently answered my queries, discussed with me their own unpublished work on World War I, and commented on drafts of the Introduction. I am particularly indebted to Dan Diner, Laura Lee Downs, Geoff Eley, Tom Laqueur, Rudiger Lautmann, George L. Mosse, Susan Pedersen, Michelle Perrot, Mary Louis Roberts, Anita Shapira, and the late Raphael Samuel. The staff at the Imperial War Museum in London, and in particular Nigel Steel, Deputy Keeper of Documents, deserve special mention for their equanimity throughout my research trips to the Documents department. Ina Stasker has been the most assiduous and devoted research assistant I could have wished for.

The completion of this collection was made possible by grants and fellowships from the Institute for the Humanities at the University of Michigan, The Institute for German History, the Chair for Comparative History, and the faculty of the Humanities at Tel-Aviv University.

At Routledge I am indebted to Brendan O'Malley, Brian Phillips, and Ken Wright for their devoted efforts, in uneasy times, to the production of this book. Finally, I wish especially to express my profoundest appreciation to Philippa Shimrat, the collection's copyeditor and the most intelligent of readers. It is to her that I owe my survival as editor and that *Borderlines* owes its very appearance.

Billie Melman
Tel Aviv, 1997

LIST OF ILLUSTRATIONS

1. "Long Live Free Turkey," cartoon in *Musavver Papağan*
   4 December 1908   57

2. "The Reason Why Peace Comes So Late and So Hard,"
   cartoon in *Akbaba*, 12 April 1923   58

3. "The Bridal Party," cartoon in *Akbaba*, 23 July 1923   58

4. "Let Go of Me . . . I'm Leaving," A Greek Soldier Fleeing
   One of the Defenders of Anatolia, cartoon in *Aydede*,
   30 March, 1922   61

5. "My Dear Pasha, Do Not Forget Your Old Mistress."
   Greece Seeking Peace, After the Turkish Victory in 1923,
   cartoon in *Karagöz*, 12 March 1923   62

6. "In Response to the Sufferings of the Wounded Homeland."
   Cosmopolitan Turkish Women Betray their Country,
   cartoon in *Alay*, 6 March 1920   63

7. " May God Protect Your Child, Sister, Is It a Boy or a
   Girl?" cartoon in *Kalem*, 22 April 1910   65

8. A Conversation Between an Anatolian Mother and
   Mustafa Kemal, Commander of the Turkish Forces,
   cartoon in *Karagöz*, 27 December 1922   66

9. "The Tragicomical Capture of a German Officer or the
   Cowardice of the Germans," Russian war poster   103

10. "Parade," Russian war poster   105

11. "The Old Woman is not a Blockhead. She Can Capture
    an Airplane." Russian war poster, 1915   106

12. "A Pair of Bay Horses," Russian war poster, 1915   107

13. " About Turkish Cowardice and [Russian] Boldness,"
    Russian war poster   108

14. "Conversation Near Constantinople," Russian war poster   110

15. "War with the Turks in the Transcaucasus," Russian
    war poster   112

16. "The Heroic Exploit of Private Katz," Russian war poster   113

17. Sarah Bernhardt as "Black Hamlet" (1899)   170

18. Sarah Bernhardt as the Duke of Reichstadt in *L'aiglon*
    (1900)   171

19. Natalie Barney as a Hamlet-Like Page   174

20. The Marquis of Angelsey as the Duke of Reichstadt,
    The Sketch, January 1, 1902   175

21. Radclyffe Hall, ca. 1910   177

22. Ethel Smyth with her Dog Pan   181

23. "The Suffragette" from "A Series of Present Day Types,"
    Bystander, 31 December, 1913   182

24. "'Ya bon," "Smile with the Big Teeth," a French drawing
    of a tirrailleur senegalais (1917)   221

25. "Cri séditieux—Vive les Teutons!" "Seditious Cry: Long
    Live the Teutons [the 'boob']!" French postcard illustrated   223

26. Karl Geotz, "The Black Shame Medallion," depicting
    the rape of the Rhineland by black Senegalese troops   229

27. "Voilà les Turcos: Gare aux fesses!!!" "Here Come the
    Turcos, Cover your Asses!!!" French postcard illustration
    (1915)   232

28. Recruitment of the WAACS by Month   379

Introduction

Billie Melman

Across Borderlines: Mary Ann Brown's Itinerary

On a scorching July 11, 1917, temperatures in the hospital base in Kirkee in India reached 121°F in the shade. Mary Ann Brown, staff nurse in Queen Alexandra's Imperial Nursing Service (Reserve) (QUAMNS[S]), entered them in her diary, in which she punctiliously monitored the traffic in her ward: "head strokes [sic] coming by the dozen" and "several deaths already . . . 9 buried." On July 15, when temperatures soared to the mid-120s, strokes continued to pour in, and Brown was busy preparing bodies for burial. In her sparse prose she noted that most patients found it easier to drop out.[1]

The war took Brown across many borders. Her itinerary included its theaters in the Mediterranean, Mesopotamia, and India. From aboard a series of hospital ships, river boats, and paddle steamers she watched the spectacle of evacuation in the Dardanelles, Cape Helles, and Thessaloniki, the Serbian exodus from the Balkan hinterland to the Albanian coast, the last of the Mesopotamian campaigns of Kut and Basra, and the ravages of climate and epidemics upon the remnants of the Allies' and Central Powers' armies. In one rare moment of irony she described herself as a "Kitchener tourist." The evocation of Britain's imperial icon seems appropriate: the floating hospitals in which Brown spent most of World War I were microcosmic empires, carrying a multinational and multi-ethnic cargo between ports of call that were also imperial outposts. Her "cases"—never "men"—included British men and officers, Australians, Serbs, Greeks, Turkish POWs, and Indian troops.

Mary Ann Brown's experience of World War I may seem atypical of a woman of her origins and class, or, for that matter, of a nurse serving abroad.[2] Yet her biography is a lesson in the geography of that war, both the physical geography and the cartography of gender identity. The war was a global and colonial affair—altering borders and shifting people, and sometimes whole ethnic and national groups—as much as it was a European one. Brown's biography also conveys a sense that gender identities did not develop discretely, solely within the framework of class or nation, but in confluence with imperial and ethnic identities. War marked a great change in her life. It propelled her out of rural Sutherland (in Scotland) and offered her, the eldest of ten children, a career in nursing and a life away from Britain. It gave her considerable independence and the ability to challenge the hierarchies of gender and class. Travel, however, did not eliminate the borderlines of color or those of ethnicity. Mary Ann Brown's vocabulary rigidly preserves imperial hierarchies. Using the nurse's impersonal tone (which Susan Kingsley Kent and Margaret Darrow have traced in the records of nurses), Brown reserved a familial and distinctly maternal idiom for British patients of the North of the Isles (her "boys"), a nationalist idiom for the "brave" Serbs, and a paternalist colonial colloquialism for colonials ("poor men," often "helpless"). Jews were given short shrift as "Jippies." Officers, regardless of nationality and color, are mentioned in her diary by rank, and accorded bravery in battle and a child's helplessness in a hospital ward.[3]

This collection is concerned with the intersections of femininities and masculinities and women's and men's lived experiences of modern global war. World War I serves both as a focal point and a crossroads in the discussion of the associations among gender, change, and war. We have sought to place the war in the longer continuum of 1870–1930 and to assess these associations from a multinational perspective that is neither exclusively nor discretely Western European. This seemed appropriate for two reasons: In the first place, the Great War involved colonial societies in the West and in Asia, Africa, and Australasia. It marked the apex of the age of High Colonialism (1878–1940) and of a global "culture of imperialism."[4] Postwar "reconstruction" was not only about the economy and politics within Western Europe, but also about the reallotment of colonial territories, the resettlement of colonial borders, and the reformulation of relations among victors, vanquished, and their colonial territories, as well as the realignment of indigenous nationalist movements across these territories. The second reason for the emphasis on multinationalism was methodological. Although our perspective of the relationship between World War I and gender has been enormously broadened by comparisons between societies during that war, it has been largely limited to Western and Central European industrialized nation-states, which, even before the war, had controlled the technologies of destruction that produced the unprecedented devastation and mass death during the war.[5] By comparing gender systems in these societies with those in less industrial and mobilized (or nonindustrial) ones, which represent diverse forms and stages of nationalism and national mobilization, we hope to reconsider some assumptions about the relations between gender and war. Was there a gender-specific experience of war that cut across borderlines in Europe and across boundaries between "West" and "non-West," or was such an experience national and local? Was discourse about gender, and specifically about women, everywhere, the privileged discourse that specific studies of national cultures have shown it to be? Put differently, was the debate on women, in effect, a debate about the changes wrought by the war? And what exactly was the space they could and were allowed to occupy in relation to a national and a colonial war? How did the period of societal breakdown before 1914 affect the changes in the gendered space—within both the state and civil society? Did women's incursions into the polity and into armies have real significance or did their activity as soldiers and nurses and in the auxiliary service merely enhance their exclusion from war?[6] Were women "of" war and "in" war or, as Margaret Darrow recently put it, outside of war and the myth of war experience?[7] To answer all or some of these questions completely or satisfactorily would seem crazily ambitious, especially as the present collection does not cover all colonial societies touched or influenced by the war such as Australia.[8] But by including in our comparison societies that became subject to different kinds of dislocation, including repatriation and sometimes organized persecution and mass systematic extermination (in Armenia, for example), we question some assumptions of the "experience of war" and the "myth of the experience of war" as *per definitio* masculine.[9]

THE BOUNDARIES OF WAR

Borderlines' geography of war impinges upon the war's chronology and, more broadly, on periodization and the distinction between "total war" and peace. East of the Rhine, a clear-cut division between the Great War and postwar is problematic. In Germany, war was followed by revolution, and the combined effect of both, as Ursula Baumann and Amira Gelblum demonstrate, had special bearing on how women experienced dislocation and responded to it. In Russia, war, the October Revolution, and the civil war that followed it also make it difficult to dissect war from non-war. In Southern Europe and throughout the eastern Mediterranean, notably in those territories formally attached to the Habsburg and Ottoman Empires, the shifts from non-war to war, then to peace and colonial and national reconstruction, were even less clearly marked, as World War I was a phase in at least a decade of political instability, and, in some cases, collapse of state and civil society. The break-up of parts of the Ottoman Empire during the extended war decade (1908 to1923) which is examined here from the vantage point of gender, well demonstrates the limits of standard periodization. Outside Western Europe the extended war was accompanied by the rise of national movements which utilized, constructed, and in turn were reconstructed by gender. Suffice it to mention here the role of gender in the construction of Greek nationalism and national identity, during the series of wars that led to the Hellenization of Macedonia (studied by Efi Avdela) and Turkey's transformation from empire to a nation—a transformation in which gender served as an index for inclusion in, and exclusion from, the new nation (described by Müge Göçek).

The multinational and gendered perspective may also modify and extend current definitions of "war" and "war experience" in relation to gender. Historians have repeatedly (and justifiably) argued that from the late nineteenth century the very concept of war was related to gender in what George L. Mosse has described as "the Myth of War experience," a myth that was, above all, masculine.[10] The war, runs the argument, was experienced and conceived as a project of remasculinization (or disillusionment with such remasculinization). Both the material experience of the war and its representation are still largely seen in relation to a divide between a war zone (forbidden to women) and its rear, or the home front, the place of both genders, but mainly of women. Subsequently, much of the recent study of women "in" or "during" the war has been devoted to the closest female equivalents to the combatant man: military nurses, munitions workers, and women who served in armies in a variety of auxiliary roles.[11] Of course the special type of warfare and the trench experience that evolved on the Western Front was a distinctive feature of this particular war,[12] but this was not the sole experience, nor always the predominant one. Once we acknowledge that the war involved not only the varying degrees of mobilization of the Western home front, but also occupation, the dislocation of civilians, and degrees of persecution—both random and systematic—we realize that women were not excluded from the experience of war and its so-called myth, and that the impact of the war on entire populations blurred the borderlines between "front" and "rear" in their gendered perspective. The example of Belgium is the most documented one. Less studied are the experiences of men and women in Italy, the Balkans, Greece, Turkey, Syria, and Palestine. The militarization of the civilian rear was evident to contemporaries and dominated national discourses and rhetoric.[13]

Borderlines may also help reconsider the relationship among the war, gender, and change. Indeed, the question whether World War I changed gender relations and systems has become the central conundrum in the historiography. As formulated by Margaret Randolph Higonnet and Patrice Higonnet, the issue to be addressed by historians of wars and gender has been "when is change change?" Did the war materially change the status of women? Did it enhance change in gender relations, or merely precipitate or accelerate trends already on the move in society, social production, and culture? Or, did the war in effect buttress existing gender inequalities and hierarchies?[14] Crucial to the change conundrum has been the very longevity of the effects of war with "short-term" changes weighed against "long-term," "real" ones. Historians adopted three positions on change, which, by and large, constituted three consecutive phases in the historiographic debate on the Great War. It may be useful to consider them briefly in order to situate the present volume in the debate on gender and World War I.

THE CHANGE CONUNDRUM AND THE DEBATE ON GENDER AND THE WAR

In the first phase, historians emphasized war's emancipatory effects on the position of women. This early "ameliorative" and, to borrow from British historiography, "optimistic" approach toward social upheaval was criticized in the second wave of studies and eventually replaced by a "revisionist" interpretation which Sylvia Walby aptly described as "the new Feminist pessimism."[15] Partly as a reaction to the triumphalism of the earlier historians, the second and, by far, longest-standing position in the debate on gender and World War I, stressed the absence of "real" and meaningful change. Changelessness was instanced in the swing from women's war work to domesticity or domestic service, the stagnation of feminism into quiescence, and an acceptance of a non-oppositional maternalist politics (both in places where women had been granted the vote *and* in others where it had been delayed). True, the revisionist or "neopessimist" interpretation of the war did concede that it had brought about material improvements for women, such as welfare benefits and a rise in standards of health and living (comparable to those for working-class men). However, the second-wave, revisionist assessment of change discounted its significance "in the long term," the last term usually denoting the interwar era.[16] In chronological terms feminist debate shifted from the war (and the years immediately following it) to a longer durée, covering the *fin de siècle* to World War II, sometimes seen as one long continuum. This reduced changes to temporary shifts, sometimes to aberrations, which, historians insisted, lasted solely "for the duration" of the war. By implication "total" wars served to enhance the ways gender worked in societies. Of course the Great War, as Michelle Perrot, Françoise Thébaud, and

Steven Hause have shown for France, and Gail Braybon for Britain, enhanced persisting discourses, or structures of "patriarchy" (the last Braybon's term).[17] For some historians, the war marked an impasse and the beginning of a "regress," seen to characterize postwar gender relations, the attitude of the state toward women, and, most pronouncedly, postwar feminism.[18] There are, of course, variations within the revisionist model, as it does not preclude that the war made women aware of the possibilities of liberation beyond the domestic space and signaled "the possibility to take on new responsibilities, to be independent and to widen their horizons. . . ."[19] The revisionist effort has been vital and hugely benefited our understanding of World War I, of gender and of wars in general. The different participants in *Borderlines* are indebted to it in different ways, and some have represented stages in its development, as well as a commitment to the long-term approach.[20] However, they too would concur that the change/progress conundrum, and particularly the sense that in wars "plus ça change plus c'est la même chose," may make historians lose sight of contemporaries' sense of change in gender relations and of the locus of gender in the cultural and political discourse about change during the war and the extended decade of the twenties. As Mary Louise Roberts, Angela Woollacott, Ute Daniel and I have pointed out, it was through discourse about gender experience and identity that contemporaries made sense of a web of related social, political and economic changes. Some of the "long-term" historiography of the war and gender has tended to belittle this privileging of gender and subsequently its centrality in the "project" of general and global war.[21] Moreover, emphases on changelessness, on war's inherent "conserving" force (of gender relations), may well run the risk of essentialism and perpetuate some of the assumptions of the incompatability between women and war.[22]

Evidently, the present collection does not surrender the study of the "long term" for close-up shots at an intense moment of discourse on gender during the war and its aftermath. We do, however, concur that the historiography of gender and World War I, and of wars in general, should proceed beyond the debate of the significance to posterity, or posterities, of change, "regression," or non-change in the position of women. In its stead we propose to take stock of the mutations in the borderlines of femininities and masculinities and between them, mainly in relation to two other components of the modern identity: nation-ness and an ethno-colonial identity. How did these three components interact in an era of changes within nationalism and colonialism? And how did class and social production and the organization of work relate to them? As our work on this collection progressed, it became clear to most of us that between the 1870s and the 1930s male and female subjects and masculine and feminine identities were formed, contested, re-formed, and reshaped in relation to the national component of the modern subject, or modern identity. It also became clear that the national gendered subject was inextricable from the colonial or imperial one.

The juncture of gender, nationalism, colonialism, and war clearly is one of time, as well as a structural one. The era of gender instabilities (often described in the literature on sexuality and identity in terms of "flux") was also one of instabilities in the nation and the imperial state and society.[23] The decades between 1870 and the outbreak of World War II were marked by national and ethnic tensions, by the break-up of multi- or supra-national empires, and the emergence of national units and movements. It has been cogently argued that after 1870 nationalism became increasingly ethno-linguistic and that national identities became increasingly removed from, or even bypassed, the "older" post-Enlightenment notion of territoriality connected to statehood and of citizenship based upon social contract and hence "voluntary" and rational.[24] The break-up of the multinational Austro-Hungarian and Ottoman Empires and the upsurge of Irish, Balkan, Arab, and Jewish nationalisms are obvious examples of the new type of nationalism. More significantly, ethno-linguistic definitions of the national identity mark the "older" type of the nation-state, incorporating larger-than-ever segments of a politicized citizenry, yet, at the same time, excluding entire groups from "the nation" on account of ethnicity, culture, and gender.[25] Indeed, the combination of cultural or ethno-linguistic nationalism *and* the expanding nation-state is particularly pronounced in Britain, where the liberal state (which, at least from the 1870s, had made incursions into civil society), also cemented definitions of subjecthood and formal identity which were firmly based in racial notions of "stock." These were becoming increasingly gendered. Women, literally the "reproducers of the nation," were perceived as the site of the ethnic nation, of its continuity and well-being.

Nation is recognized to have been inextricably linked with Empire, a link marked by the formalization of imperial control into juridical and military forms and by the insurgence of indigenous movements for decolonization. The war mobilized the manpower and economic resources of India, Egypt, Palestine, and Africa, parts of whose male populations were shipped to the theaters of fighting. By late 1918, for example, 190,000 West Africans had been forcibly recruited into the French army and fought in battalion-force units on the Western Front. Indian regiments fought in France and Belgium and in the Mesopotamia campaigns. Additionally colonials, notably Chinese and Indo-Chinese, were shipped to Western Europe to substitute, together with Western women, for Western male conscripts. Tensions generated by the presence of colonials in Europe—both on the battlefields *and* within the labor force—erupted in a debate that focused on gender. Here too, popular images of masculinity and femininity stood for much more than gender. These images helped make sense of the apparent shifts within colonial and interracial relationships between European and non-European societies. Of course, as the expanding scholarship on colonialism and gender has shown, discourse on the empire—at least from the 1870s—had been intimately related to the debate on femininity and sexuality.[26] However, the war, which brought the colonies into Europe as never before, seemed to have challenged the borderlines of color, to have threatened the stability of masculinity and whiteness. As Annabelle Melzer's study of French trench journalism and performance on the Western Front demonstrates, the presence of Senegalese (a term covering a heterogenous group of West African ethnic groups) on that front stretched definitions of Frenchness, of the identity of colonizer and colonized, and of maleness. Moreover, the Senegalese were always defined in relation to French women—whom the former were seen to have pursued and satisfied. Anxieties about gender and the purity of the French nation precipitated the removal of colonial battalions from France to Germany, where they were seen and presented as a racial and sexual danger. Here again, women, as well as colonial men, were the site of a broader concern with the larger topic of defeat and postwar reconstruction.

Notwithstanding the many intersections between constructions of gender and nationalism, interest in these "irreducible components" of the modern identity remained separate from, or peripheral to, our understanding of peace and the Great War. "General" classical studies of the modern national subject, such as Benedict Anderson's, arguing that World War I, its memory and symbolic representation produced the "most arresting emblems of the modern culture of nationalism," have omitted women.[27] George L. Mosse's seminal studies of nationalism and sexuality and of the myth of war experience also interpret the war in terms of the "remasculinization of the nation." Feminist interest in the structural connections between gender identity and nationalism also remains peripheral to the study of gender and the war. This interest has largely assumed the subsumption of the interests of women in those of the nation— thus accepting that women's activity within national movements, or the nation-state, were subordinated to them. Notable exceptions include Angela Woollacott, David Sibley, Janet Korbin Watson, Marilyn Lake, and Afaf Lutfi Al-Sayyid Marsot.[28]

INTERSECTING BORDERS: GENDER AND NATIONAL IDENTITY

The studies in the present collection suggest that the relationship between participation in the nation and the discourse about women and the nation is complex and may not be reduced to "subordination" models. Gender, we contend, framed the very terms in which national identities were comprehended and constructed, as well as the "narrations of nation."[29] This relationship changed in accordance with time, class, and notions of sexuality. Nevertheless, a few characteristics loom large and appear across borders and cultures. First, the "new" cultural or ethno-linguistic nationalism seems to have expanded possibilities for action for both genders, but notably for women (who had been excluded from older notions of the nation-state). Women's inclusion usually did not draw on notions of gender equality and was sometimes detached from their right to political citizenship. Nationhood was invested upon them on account of their ethnicity, or on account of a gender-specific social production (maternity), or as producers of culture. This kind of inclusion typifies the Southern European and Middle Eastern nationalism studied here and was noted in studies of "new" nationalism in Western Europe such as the Irish.[30] However, identification between women and race and culture does appear in the "older" type of nationalism, typified by Britain for example. Studies of gender and welfare in Britain demonstrate the relations between maternalist legislation and outlook and the notion that women of British "stock" were the conduits of race and a British culture.[31] On the other hand, as Pat Thane points out, nationality could be withheld precisely on the same basis of ethnic or cultural purity—from women and alien men (Jews or colonials).

A second multinational saliency is that national identities were not and may not be regarded solely as "constructions" superimposed on women and men. True, nation-states, old and new, as well as national movements, mobilized both. However, the present collection makes clear the centrality of individuals and groups as active agents, influencing states and movements and actively interpreting their nationality and ethnicity. Moreover, we suggest that the war was not merely a "force" recruiting and mobilizing individuals, but rather that it presented for many women opportunities of negotiating their status and place. Doron Lamm's study of recruitment to the WAAC (Women's Auxiliary Aid Corps) is an object lesson in the interaction between state and army on the one hand, and the economic needs and patriotic ambitions of women recruits of the working and lower-middle classes on the other. As Lamm demonstrates, women often frustrated national economic needs created by the drain on manpower and acted in accordance with their own interests. In places where central government broke down due to the war or colonial processes (the Ottoman Empire being an example), women's action channeled itself to the societal space of voluntary, but professional or semi-professional work—the plethora of nationalist organizations that mushroomed in Turkey and in some of its colonial outposts (notably Egypt), which Müge Göçek and Beth Baron study, present this case. As both emphasize, these nationalist (and sometimes non-feminist) organizations developed a gender solidarity which, far from submerging gender in the nation, stressed women's interests. The national gendered identity was constantly negotiated between states or movements on the one hand, and agents on the other.

A third feature is the perception and interpretation of World War I as a sexual war. This sexualization of contemporary discourse has been noted in feminist scholarship *and* in studies of nationalism and sexuality.[32] However, the former did not probe the discourse of sexuality from the angle of nationalism, and the latter focused on masculinity. What emerges from the studies of war iconography, popular culture, and propaganda in the present volume is the ubiquity of certain feminine and masculine symbols of sexuality. Most pervasive is the figure of the sexually violated woman as a symbol for national degeneration and impurity: the iconic image of Belgium and the less familiar figures of Serbia, Turcia, Germania, and Zion (embodying the Jewish diaspora in Eastern Europe and Palestine Jews).[33] Another is Franz Werfel's representations of violated Armenian women in his 1932 novel *Die Vierzig Tage Des Musa Dagh*, a forceful (and at the time internationally influential) rendition of the Armenian uprising in Cilicia, in the wake of the genocide of Ottoman Armenians in 1915. Anxieties regarding sexual impurity often took the form of attempts to control female sexuality—attempts which usually aborted. For example, in the winter of 1916–17 the British Foreign and Colonial Offices, together with army representatives from Britain and the U.S., held a series of conferences on venereal diseases. The conference, which sought to protect overseas forces from contamination, deliberated on the possibility of a renewed enforcement in Britain of the long-repealed Contagious Diseases Acts, the subject of a fierce feminist campaign in Britain during the 1860s and 1870s and well into the 1910s in the Empire. Most participants in the conferences stressed that the control of women's sexuality was unrealistic precisely because of the change in moods and in the status of women.[34] However, the very fact that the subject was debated reflects deeply rooted anxieties. Other salient examples include the establishment of a female factory inspectorate in France and Britain, aiming to regulate, amongst other things, the conduct and morality of women munitions workers, and the Women's Police Force in London (a descendant, according to Anne Summers, of the female vigilant associations of the 1880s and 1890s).[35]

Sexual images of violation and impurity, or their reverse—the equation between sexual and national purity—did not focus solely on women. Quite the contrary. Male purity—identified with heterosexuality, masculinity, and valor in battle—was central to the propaganda and popular iconography of all belligerent powers. Virtually all depicted the enemy as feminized, and in some cases presented him as the subject of sexual violation (violent sodomization). War propaganda in Imperial Russia presented the Germans and Turks as effeminate males; at the same time Turkish propaganda represented the Greeks as violated women. In French official propaganda, but more forcefully in trench journalism and performance, Germans and colonials were depicted alternately as sexual violators and as violated women. This image was not limited to depictions of the enemy. Soldiers' performance, especially cross-dressing in all its manifestations, seems to reveal more than a feminization anxiety. They indicate that the borderlines of genders and between sexual identities, as well as among genders, were becoming increasingly blurred.

Let there be no misunderstanding. By foregrounding the relationship between nationalism, gendered identity, and experience, the collection does not seek to play down, or bypass, other determinants of femininity and masculinity. Quite the contrary. We concur that class was crucial to the ways in which women and men experienced and made sense of change during the war, and that social production—especially as instanced in the mobilization of work—was determined by gender and, at the same time, further influenced gender divisions. We also concur that World War I had a special bearing on the relationship between the private and the public. Since both subjects have received ample attention, it suffices to point to some of their multinational aspects that are highlighted here.

THE ORGANIZATION OF PRODUCTION

Work and, in particular, women's work, has had a privileged place in the debate on war, peace, and change. In contemporary discourse about the Great War, the working woman was seen as the harbinger of social and cultural change and treated as an emblem of the modern age and, sometimes, of the dislocation wrought by the war in gender relations.[36] Historians have regarded work as a crucial, perhaps the most crucial, index of change and/or continuity in the Western gender system. This is partly because of an interest in labor and gender but, mostly, as Françoise Thébaud points out, because women's work has been seen as an "observatory" through which, or from which, it is possible to scan shifts in gender systems during transformations from peace to national emergency.[37] In Western societies, at least from the second half of the nineteenth century, the woman worker was a material "presence" as well as the discursive construction and "problem," discussed by Joan Wallach Scott.[38] During and after the war, discourse related to this "problem" erupted, disclosing age-old notions of gender yet, at the same time, signs of change regarding the organization of social production, domesticity, and the very definition of work by gender. Studies of women's work outside Western Europe are still scarce. But from the few cases presented here it seems that mobilization—albeit in limited form—of the female labor force was a multinational phenomenon and that it typified both "developed" and highly mechanized industries and the agricultural sector. Indeed, as the studies of France and Egypt by Thébaud and Baron respectively show, agriculture absorbed significant numbers of women and remained feminized after the war. Regardless of the form of the economy and the degree of central organization, within the period 1870–1930, the extended war decade presented, at one and the same time, an expansion and contraction of opportunities for women. Demobilization, as Lamm shows, preceded the end of war, and in that sense women's work may be taken to represent not the culmination of a trend toward a (temporary) expansion, but the beginning of a long-term demise. However, women, particularly working-class women, moved into the new modern industries and, in some cases, the tertiary sector and were able to take advantage of changes in perceptions of women's mobility and "freedom" ushered in during the war.

Not least among these notions is the blurring of the borderlines between a public space and the "private." Of course, these terms are Western and should be relativized and applied with caution to societies outside Europe, where domesticity and interiority were identified with both femininity *and* with masculinity and political authority.[39] Yet several changes in the relationship between spaces that contemporaries considered as "womanly" and "domestic" or "masculine" and "military" register everywhere. First, during World War I, the state, everywhere, made inroads into areas considered as domestic and "private." With increasingly developed apparatuses of propaganda, it also, unprecedentedly, sought to define a feminine and a masculine "subject." The studies of propaganda in Russia, Great Britain, and Turkey all show the variegated ways in which the intervening state mobilized its citizenry along lines of divisions by gender. Yet parallel to state intervention in civil society (or the domestic space), the decades of war and revolution also witnessed incursions of a domestic and "feminine" sphere into politics, the public workplace, and, sometimes, into the war zone itself. As Anne Summers shows, as far as women's work was concerned—even during the war—premises about domesticity and female hierarchy were transposed, almost intact, to public areas, most notably to "public" and semi-military work. Rather than being imposed on women by masculine organizations, these premises were preserved by women of the upper and middle classes. In gender-segregated societies like those of urban Egypt and Turkey, or of multinational and multi-religious Macedonia, national or colonial wars legitimized the invasion of public spaces by women of all classes. In some cases it was war that made these women visible. Their action did not end segregation, but rather feminized the public sphere, thereby blurring the borderlines of the domestic and non-domestic. The last, but by no means least, of changes is the shift in the borderlines of the war zones. As already argued, the involvement of large civilian populations in the war casts doubts on some assumptions about the exclusion of women from the battle zone and the myth of war experience. The essays, by Efi Avdela, Müge Göçek, Beth Baron, and Billie Melman, on women in colonial areas which became theaters of battle or were militarized zones, show that these women were "in the war" and "of it," as much as the men. Furthermore, women on the moving front line were not merely victims, but agents, who negotiated their place in the dislocated society and economy (though in different ways from working women in the West). The evidence gathered in these essays is strongly supported by that recently amassed by Margaret Higonnet in her panoramic survey of women's testimonies of their experiences during the Great War.[40] Moreover, even within the world of the trenches, gender became ambiguous. Combatants questioned the status and definition of their masculinity. Of course, misogyny on the front was rampant, but so was the sense of many combatants that the war feminized them, not only because it gave women so many opportunities, but also because the war zone itself and its emblem the trench were limiting and imprisoning, quite like the domestic space. As Pat Barker's Dr. Rivers puts it: "The war that had promised so much in the way of 'manly' activity had actually delivered 'feminine' passivity."[41]

BORDERLINES: ORGANIZATION AND STRUCTURE

The essays are divided into four sections, according to the organizing themes discussed above: the relationship between nationalism and gender; the shifting of the borderlines of sexualities; female and feminist action in, and interpretations of, the public and societal space; and the moving borderlines of societal production. Such a division may seem too tidyminded for a volume whose main theme is the shifting of borderlines. There are, of course, many overlappings between the sections: the gendering of national identities and narratives and, indeed, the centrality of nation building for the "Bildung" of gender, runs through the majority of articles. Efi Avdela's essay on the 1914 tobacco workers' strike in Thessaloniki—an epochal event in Greek labor and gender relations—is as much about the construction of Greekness as it is about the gendering of work. The essay by Phyllis Lassner on the construction of borderline sexualities of fictional British Jews touches on the subject of exclusion from the national and imperial identity in wartime and postwar Britain, as well as discussing the instability of heterosexual masculinity. The slicing of the material is intended primarily to serve readers, and bring into focus the distinct themes and concerns of this volume.

GENDERING THE NATION: DEFINITIONS AND BOUNDARIES

Gendering the Nation: Definitions and Boundaries offers studies, from different aspects, of the shifting relationships between the evolution of national identities and narratives of the changing nation, and parallel developments of gender identity. Gender, it is argued, was used as an index of, or for, nation-ness, serving both to include women and men in the nation and to exclude them from it. The gendering of the nation was ubiquitous and manifested itself in the action of the expanding state, in propaganda, and popular iconography and in the construction of the memory of the Great War (cf. p.16). One important feature of the process of nation gendering is its relation to a new type of expanding, imperial state, that appears around the 1870s. As Pat Thane argues, assumptions about the state's roles in setting boundaries between it and the "subject," as well as between different groups of subjects, was at the heart of political discourse that changed its contours as a result of the war. The state defined the boundaries of British and imperial identity, decided who possessed this identity (and who did not), and increasingly related identity to "rights" (of welfare, for example) and citizenship. Both were, of course, gendered and racialized. Thus the state that sought to enhance the national stock by promoting the welfare and fitness of women denied them an inherent nationality. The Nationality Acts that were passed after 1869, but in particular that of 1914, denationalized British wives of aliens and hence deprived them of citizenship and welfare. In the same vein, the Treaty of Versailles stipulated that the savings of the wives or widows of Germans would be confiscated to pay Germany's war debt. The Nationality and Status of Aliens Acts, drawing on the same criteria of "stock" and "culture" that served to exclude women, also denied the status of subject and citizenship to Jews.

However, the state never operated as sole agent of change, imposing an identity from above on passive "subjects." Indeed, Thane and others demonstrate that identity was the result of an ongoing negotiation between, on the one hand, the state and the official apparatus of propaganda and, on the other, groups or individuals who resisted such impositions, protested against them, and modified them.

The discourse of inclusion and exclusion intensified at moments of transition or transformation in national politics during the extended war decade. During such periods the ambivalence of national narratives allowed both genders, but particularly women, a space within the nation at the same time that it withheld various freedoms from them. Such transformatory moments are studied by Müge Göçek, Karen Petrone, and Billie Melman. Göçek and Petrone, who both focus on visual representations of the nation—official and popular—show that in Turkey and Imperial Russia the borderlines of gender were stretched to expand the definition of the nation. During Turkey's transition from empire to a (secular) nation-state, an uninterrupted fifteen years of colonial, global, and civil wars (1908–23), Turkish women were incorporated in, yet at the same time constricted within, the evolving nation. Drawing on the notion of the ambivalence of national narratives—as both "subordinating, fracturing, diffusing," and "producing," Göçek points to the dissonance between Turkish women's actual participation in the wars and their representations. Participation that significantly defined and transformed women's identities was "narrated into" national stereotypes that served to constrict women. Karen Petrone discusses the construction of masculinity within Russian imperial nationalism during Imperial Russia's moment of political disintegration. While Western notions of masculinity during World War I stressed male sodality and the brotherhood of combatants, Russian concepts of manhood stressed the solidarity of fathers and sons yet, at the same time, considerably modified the patriarchalism that had been so central to Russian society and national culture. More signifi-

cantly, war necessitated the national mobilization of all men, regardless of ethnicity and religion. Jews, Georgians, and other non-
Russians were thus accommodated within a multinational vision of
a masculine Imperial Russia.

It was within the new linguistic and "cultural" nationalism that
women were given—and elected to assume—roles, mainly as the
producers of a new national culture and identity. The various Balkan
nationalisms, Irish, and Jewish nationalisms all represent comparable cases of the centrality of gender and, sometimes, the feminization of ethno-linguistic revival. Zionism probably represents one of
the most radical attempts to construct an "imagined" national community. The Zionist Revolution, whose formative decades span the
period studied here, was not solely about the colonization of a territory, but also about the construction of a new Jewish man and a new
Jewish woman—opposed to the European Jew. Billie Melman studies
the national discourse in its most formative era (1881–1920) and
within its constituting group—the first generation of Hebrew speakers—analogous with the generation of 1914. For this generation, the
war redefined their gender and politicized it, mainly by opening up
possibilities of national resistance and the practice of force—formerly at odds with Jewish Bildung and character.

As virtually all students of World War I have realized, its memory—the diverse ways in which that war was recalled, recorded, reclaimed, and commemorated—shaped the identity and kind of
cognizance that are commonly dubbed "modern." Recently J.M.
Winter challenged the assumptions that the catastrophic events of
the Great War engendered modern memory and modernist forms of
understanding and representation. He argued instead that the cata-
strophe that befell (Western) culture was comprehended in traditional terms, using traditional forms of recall, whose strength lay in
their power to heal bereaved men and women. This turn away from
the "modernism-interpretation" and towards "tradition," is crucial
precisely because it re-places the war in the social and cultural history of the twentieth century. World War I is understood here not as
sui generis, the very first collective modern experience, but rather as
the last of "old" wars—devastating, but comprehensible and, by implication, more "human."

It is significant that as with the general debate on nationalism and
colonialism, so with that on modernism against tradition, the study
of gender had remained peripheral to the more general one of memory. To be sure, cultural historians and feminist critics (mostly literary ones), have noted that the remembrance of the experience of war,
both by individuals and through collective ritual, was a gendered and

gendering process. As the latter argued, the "modern memory" discussed by Paul Fussell (and to a large extent by Modris Eksteins, Samuel Hynes and George L. Mosse) was constructed by the male literary elites consisting of volunteers, who grafted their sexual and class identities upon the collective memory, to the exclusion of other identities.[42] Ilana Bet-El and Sonya Michel examine elisions from, and the manipulation and shaping of, collective memories of the war. Both consider the borderlines of masculinity and heroism. Bet-El examines what possibly is the greatest elision from the national memory of the Great War *and* the historiographic debate on war and identity, that of Britain's 2.5 million conscripts. In Britain, which was the last European power to conscript its male population, soldiering and active citizenship were equated with volunteering, and both constituted a culturally dominant notion of masculinity. Subsequently the conscripts' experience of war and identity became wholly submerged in a unifying elite notion of masculinity. An examination of conscripts' records indicates the limits of such interpretations of the masculine identity as Paul Fussell's, which focus solely on the writings of literary volunteers. It also critiques feminist literary historiography on the Great War "masculinity crisis." Conscripts' writing lacks the homoerotic undertones described elsewhere as a part of the camaraderie of the trenches. Sonya Michel, too, takes stock of some of the work on the construction of masculinity and the collective memory. The war, she argues, generated not only the "ironic" mode identified with a modern identity, but a realism, highly typical of documentary war cinematography. This mass-produced artefact depicted a masculine heroism that was distinctly American (and Midwestern) and which it exported abroad. Representation substituted the heroism of the producer of art—the war photographer—for that of real soldiers, hence eliding the mass of infantrymen from the war's memory and celebrating older national notions of masculinity.

BORDERLANDS: IDENTITIES AND SEXUALITIES

"Borderline" figures, notes Martha Vicinus, and, one might add, borderline identities, remained peripheral to the study of World War I. "Borderline" may be taken here to mark sexual and gender identities, which, even before the war, had gained a political significance, and which, in the eyes of contemporaries, deviated from and threatened gender relations. The term covers both deviant gender roles (mannish women and effeminate men, suffragettes and single-career women) and deviant sex roles (self-confessed lesbians and homosexuals). Aliens in the national and imperial culture, such as the West Africans

and Jews, whose representations are studied here, were also borderline figures, whose gender and sexuality threatened national or social
homogeneity and who were often represented as deviant. Yet the four
essays in this section show that a borderline position signifies more
than marginality. Borderline figures fascinated and disturbed contemporaries by demonstrating that sexual or gender identity was not
fixed and that the war endangered the clear-cut distinctions between
and among the feminine and masculine and, sometimes, between
homosexuals and heterosexuals. Of course, no discussion of borderline figures during the fin-de-siècle and the war decade can be complete without a study of homosexuality. The present volume touches
on the subject only marginally, in relation to the widespread anxieties in the armies regarding sodomy. The lesbian identity before and
during the war is studied in greater detail by Martha Vicinus and
David Trotter. Both stress that there had been a language of lesbianism and lesbian identity before "lesbianism" *and* that both had been
created through the agency of individuals, rather than being "determined" or "constructed" by the sexologists' discourse or by a cata-
clysmic fissure wrought by the war and suddenly releasing female
desire. Both criticize discourse and performance theories of identity
as manifested by some gay theorists and in historicist literary studies
of the war.[43] Vicinus studies the theatricalization of women's sexual
and political identities. The upper-class Anglo-American expatriates,
male impersonators (including Sarah Bernhardt), and suffragettes she
considers created their own sexual self-image and identity, thus a
new defining category—believing that "one was born a lesbian,
which gave one a specific responsibility to express this unique sexual
identity."[44] Trotter traces a feminist genealogy of the New, Newer,
and Newest Woman, a genealogy which he offers as a process of identity development through "partial imitation." A circulation of identities between these generations may be described as a "reciprocal
gaze" that modified the feminist and lesbian identity along a "movable borderline of partial resemblance." Melzer's article on representations of colonial combatants in trench performance may be read
together with Vicinus's, for it too is about the theatricalization of desire, in this case male desire and front-line misogyny and racialism.
Melzer shows that the colonial constituted a borderline figure, the
site of conflicting masculine identities, both colonial and sexual.

DISSENT AND ACQUIESCENCE: WAR, FEMINISM, AND FEMALE ACTION

In recent debate the war has been predominantly presented as having
effectively demobilized feminist radicalism and subordinated feminist ideology and agenda to national ones, while postwar reconstruc-

tion has been depicted as feminism's era of "quiescence." It is precisely on the juncture of war, feminism (or female public action), and nationalism that the four essays in this section focus. All seem to further stress the point made in the first section, that national emergency brought a simultaneous expansion and contraction in the scope of opportunities for action. Furthermore, feminists and women activists—within both pacifist and nationalist movements—practiced tactics and adhered to ideologies that were oppositional and dissenting while, at the same time, signifying acquiescence with dominant gender relations. The discursive tension between quiescence and dissension is attributed here mostly to the specific nationalist contexts of the movements, as well as to national politics during the war and reconstruction. That most of these movements seem, in retrospect, conservative or even reactionary, does not mean that they were interpreted as such by contemporaries—feminists and non-feminists alike. To ignore the oppositional potential of some of the movements discussed here would be to de-historicize them.

Two of the essays examine the political potential of religion in mobilizing feminists in Britain and Germany. Jacqueline deVries considers the British denominational suffrage movements—Anglican and Catholic (CLWS and CWSS, respectively)—and Ursula Baumann their German counterpart, the mass women's confessional organizations of Deutsch-Evangelischer Frauenbund (DEF) and Katholischer Deutscher Frauenbund (KDF). Both the German and British movements were aligned to the churches' male hierarchies. But while in Britain the war gave denominational feminists a sense of purpose and defined their national and feminist identities, in Germany national defeat, which, combined with a socialist republic, brought about the emancipation of women, disoriented confessional feminists. There are also differences among Catholics and Protestants. While in Britain Anglican identification with the national political culture made women confident and militant (British Anglicans fought for reform, including the ordination of women, as a means of political and national regeneration), German Protestant feminists rejected the Weimar Republic and identified with conservative nationalism. These attitudes were reversed within the two countries' Catholic feminist organizations. British Catholic women were empowered by the war, but their status of double marginality, within a hierarchical church and the national culture, inhibited their drive for reform. In Germany it was precisely the minority status of Catholic feminists and the existence of a Catholic political culture *and* identity that empowered women. In both cases, opposition and quiescence moved along divides within the nation.

Public action for, or in relation to, the nation had somewhat dif-

ferent meanings and ramifications in colonial contexts where the
public and private divide had been quite distinct from the Western
European one. Beth Baron explores the role played by Egyptian
women during the country's national, anti-British rebellion and the
ways in which they created for themselves a public and political
identity that was gender-specific. As in Turkey and Greece, the war,
interpreted as a colonial war, politicized women and catapulted
them into a public place in which they were visible, but in which
they kept the divide between the domestic and feminine and the
masculine. The demonstrations of veiled women in Egypt's urban
centers were internationally publicized precisely because the veiled
nationalist activist became an emblem of the fragility of borderlines
between genders and between colonial identities.

Moving Boundaries: Work, Gender, and Mobilization

It is in relation to the mobilization of labor and the organization of
production that borderlines may seem to have been the least movable. The four essays on work and gender stress the persistence, even
during national emergency and social unrest, of longstanding assumptions, widely shared across classes about gender and labor and
especially about women's work. Such assumptions, argues Anne
Summers, proved remarkably tenacious. The domestic paradigm of
labor relations was transposed to public occupations—notably factory work and army service. This paradigm was supported by notions of class, which hinged upon the assumed subordination of
working-class to middle-class women. Domestic service became the
site of a system of female hierarchy that, in contradistinction to
male hierarchies, resisted processes of professionalization and the
modernization of association in the workplace. Doron Lamm's consideration of the recruitment of women to the British army (in the
WAAC) enhances Summers's point. Army recruitment policies reflected the assumptions of a class hierarchy. (The army sought domestic servants for ordinary WAAC jobs and middle-class women
for positions of control and for professional jobs.) However Lamm,
like Françoise Thébaud, concurs that the war did make a difference,
since it widened the opportunities of working-class women whom
an expanding war economy helped make mobile and gave experience
in negotiation of employment and status. Finally the essays demonstrate how diffuse the borders between domestic and non-domestic
work became during the war. Not only was the workplace feminized, but work itself was the subject of a discourse about femininity. The experience of the war, especially the control of the labor

force, standardization, and, later, automatization, was related to the feminization of the labor force. At the vanguard of modernization were those new industries such as engineering, touched on here by Thébaud and discussed elsewhere by Downs, which were the "carriers" of automatization, control methods (Taylorism and Fordism), and the harbingers of a discourse of work that drew on gender rather than on skill.[45]

To return to the opening metaphor of travel, the itineraries that the different essays outline are not the only ones which individuals and groups made before the war, during the "long war" decade and its aftermath. It is possible that they are not the most important ones. However, these itineraries point to the relationship among gender, national culture, and experience, the culture of empire, and the war. They also indicate that during the "long war" the borderlines of masculine and feminine identities were altered and that itineraries were not simply imposed on women and men by constructs like the nation, state, empire, class, or "civil society," or determined by the war. Identities were charted by individuals. We hope that our studies will help expand the cartography of gender identity in these decades of war and peace.

NOTES

1. Imperial War Museum (IWM), 88/7/1/ Miss M. A. Brown, Diary, vol. 3.

2. Brown (1883–1968), a professional nurse, who served as an officer in QAIMNS and in the rank of Sister. Her travels during the war were of much wider scope than those of most professional nurses and VAD volunteers serving on-board hospital ships. The most publicized experience is that of Vera Brittain, which is hardly representative. For a nurse's record comparable to Brown's see I. Haigh, IWM.

3. IWM, 88/7/1. For perceptive readings of nurses' records see Susan Kingsley Kent, *Making Peace: The Reconstruction of Gender in Interwar Britain* (Princeton, 1994), Margaret H. Darrow, "French Volunteer Nurses and the Myth of War Experience in WWI," *American Historical Review* 101 (Feb. 1969): 86–125.

4. All European powers and most of the European states were involved in the war, with the exception of Spain, Portugal, Holland, and the Scandinavian countries. On degrees of involvement see Eric Hobsbawm, *Age of Extremes: The Short Twentieth Century, 1914–91* (London, 1994). For the culture of imperialism see Edward Said, *Culture and Imperialism* (New York, 1994), and Nicholas B. Dirks, *Colonialism and Culture* (Ann Arbor, MI, 1992).

5. On the globalization of war and the specificities of warfare, see Ian

F.W. Beckett, "Total War," in Colin McInnes and G. D. Sheffield, eds., *Warfare in the Twentieth Century: Theory and Practice* (London, 1988), 3–9; Lawrence Freedman, ed., *War* (Oxford, 1994); Raymond Aaron, *The Century of Total War* (Garden City, NY, 1954). For comparative studies of the war and gender see Margaret Randolph Higonnet et al., eds., *Behind the Lines: Gender and the Two World Wars* (New Haven, 1987); Françoise Thébaud, "The Great War and the Triumph of Sexual Division," in idem, ed., *Towards a Cultural Identity in the Twentieth Century*, vol. 5 of *A History of Women* (Cambridge, MA, 1994), 21–76. For cross-cultural comparisons of the effect of wars generally on gender, see Miriam Cooke and Angela Woollacott, eds., *Gendering War Talk* (Princeton, 1993), and Helen M. Cooper, Adrienne Auslander Munich and Susan Merrill Squier, eds., *Arms and the Woman: War, Gender and Literary Representation* (Chapel Hill, NC, 1989). See also Eva Isaksson, ed., *Women and the Military System* (New York, 1988).

6. For "proper" military service, see A. S. Senin, "Zhenskie batal'ony i voennye komandy v 1917 godu (Women's battalions and military detachments in 1917)," *Voprosy istorii* (Russian), no. 10 (1987): 176–82; Julie Wheelwright, "Flora Sandes: A Military Maid," *History Today* 39 (Mar. 1989): 42–48. For women's military service, see also Müge Göçek's essay in this volume, and Lettie Gavin, *American Women in World War I: They Also Served* (Boulder, 1997).

7. Darrow, "French Volunteer Nurses."

8. On Australian participation in the war and gender construction see Marilyn Lake, "Mission Impossible: How Men Gave Birth to the Australian Nation-Nationalism, Gender and Other Seminal Acts," *Gender and History* 4, no. 3 (1992): 305–22; Annabel Cooper, "Textual Territories: Gendered Cultural Politics and Australian Representations of the War of 1914–18," *Australian Historical Studies* 25, no. 100 (1993): 403–21.

9. For Armenia, see Vahakn N. Dadrian, *The History of the Armenian Genocide: Ethnic Conflict From the Balkans to Anatolia to the Caucasus* (Berghahn Books, 1995).

10. George L. Mosse, *Fallen Soldiers: Reshaping the Memory of the World Wars* (London, 1990).

11. Gail Braybon, *Women Workers in the First World War: The British Experience* (London, 1981); Darrow, "French Volunteer Nurses"; Kingsley Kent, *Making Peace*; Angela Woollacott, *On Her Their Lives Depend: Munitions Workers in the Great War* (Berkeley, 1994); Claire Culleton, "Gender-Charged Munitions: The Language of World War I Munitions Reports," *Women's Studies International Forum* 11, no. 2 (1988): 109–16, and Lettie Gavin, *American Women in World War I*, for women in the U. S. Army.

12. Tony Ashworth, *Trench Warfare 1914–1918* (London, 1980); Jay. M. Winter, *The Experience of World War I* (London, 1988). On this particular kind of experience and identity see Eric J. Leed, *No Man's Land: Combat and Identity in World War I* (Cambridge, 1979).

13. For Italy see Diego Leoni and Camillo Zara, "I Ruoli Sconvolti: Donna E Fagmilia A Volano Nel Trentino Durante La Guerra Del Quindici," *Movimento Operaio E Socialista* 5, no. 3 (1982): 421–38. For Russia and the

Middle East, see the essays by Karen Petrone, Müge Göçek, Beth Baron, and Billie Melman.

14. Margaret Randolph Higonnet and Patrice L. R. Higonnet, "The Double Helix," in *Behind the Lines*, 31–51.

15. The early historiography is best represented by Davis Mitchell, *Women on the Warpath: The Story of the Women of the Great War* (London, 1966); Arthur Marwick, *Women at War* (London, 1977), and the parts on women in his *The Deluge: British Society and the First World War* (London, 1979). "Revisionist" is used by Penny Summerfield in "Women, War and Social Change: Women in Britain in World War Two," in Arthur Marwick, ed., *Total War and Social Change* (New York, 1988), 95–118. "Feminist pessimism" is used by Sylvia Walby, *Patriarchy at Work: Patriarchal and Capitalist Relations in Employment* (Cambridge, 1986), 156. For a shrewd analysis of the historiographic turn see Woollacott, *On Her Their Lives Depend*, 14–15. See also Françoise Thébaud's essay.

16. The best examples include Braybon, *Women Workers*, and Christa Hemmerle, "'Wir Stricken und Nähen Wasche Soldaten . . .' Von der Militarisierung des Handarbeiten im Ersten Weltkrieg," *Homme* 3, no. 1 (1992): 88–128.

17. Braybon, *Women Workers*, and the essays by Michelle Perrot and Steven Hause in Higonnet, *Behind the Lines*, 51–61, 99–114.

18. Kingsley Kent, *Making Peace*.

19. Françoise Thébaud, *La femme au temps de la Guerre de 14* (Paris, 1986), 296; Dominique Desanti, *La femme au temps des années folles* (Paris, 1985), 119.

20. Especially Anne Summers and Françoise Thébaud; also Doron Lamm and David Trotter.

21. Woollacott, *On Her Their Lives Depend*; Mary Louise Roberts, *Civilization without Sexes: Reconstructing Gender in Postwar France, 1917–1927* (Chicago, 1994); Billie Melman, *Women and the Popular Imagination in the Twenties: Flappers and Nymphs* (London, 1988), and Ute Daniel, *War from Within: German Women in the First World War* (Oxford, 1997). Two recent examples of a useful consideration of the war within the "long term" are: *Christine Bard, Les Filles de Marianne, histoire des féminismes (1914–1940)* (Paris, 1995) and Sian Reynolds, *France Between the Wars. Gender and Politics* (New York, 1996).

22. See Darrow, "French Volunteer Nurses." See also Nancy Huston's much earlier "The Matrix of War: Mothers and Heroes," in Susan Rubin Suleiman, *The Female Body in Western Culture* (Cambridge, MA, 1985).

23. Examples of considerations of the fluidity in definitions of gender and gender hierarchy after 1870 are Elaine Showalter, *Sexual Anarchy: Gender and Culture at the Fin-de-Siècle* (New York, 1990); Bram Dijkstra, *Idols of Perversity: Fantasies of Feminine Evil in Fin-de-Siècle Culture* (Oxford, 1986). For an analysis of gender relations in terms of sexual war, see Sandra M. Gilbert and Susan Gubar, *No Man's Land: The Place of the Woman Writer in the Twentieth Century*, vol. 1, *The War of the Words* (New Haven, 1988). For war and flux see their second volume, *Sexchanges* (New Haven, 1988).

24. Ernest Gellner, *From Nations to Nationalism* (Oxford, 1983); Eric Hobsbawm, *Nations and Nationalism since 1780: Programme, Myth, Reality* (Cambridge, 1990); John Hutchinson and Anthony D. Smith, eds., *Nationalism* (Oxford, 1994); Smith, *The Ethnical Revival* (Oxford, 1981).

25. Tom Nairn, *The Break-Up of Britain: Crisis and Neo-Nationalism* (London, 1977).

26. On the structural relations between the debate on women and colonial discourse, see Nupur Chudhuri and Margaret Strobel, *Western Women and Imperialism: Complicity and Resistance* (Bloomington, IN, 1992); Billie Melman, *Women's Orients: English Women and the Middle East, Sexuality, Religion and Work*, 2nd ed. (London and Ann Arbor, 1995); and idem, "Under the Western Historian's Eyes: Eileen Power and the Early Feminist Encounter with Colonialism," *History Workshop Journal*, 42 (Fall 1996): 119–40.

27. Benedict Anderson, *Imagined Communities: Reflections on the Origins and Spread of Nationalism* (rep., London and New York, 1992), 10–11.

28. For Britain and patriotism, see Woollacott, *On Her Their Lives Depend*, and the papers delivered to the American Historical Association in Atlanta in 1996, esp. Jane S. Korbin Watson, " 'Nothing a Woman Could Help the Country More in Doing': Gender, Class and Attitudes to Women's War Work, 1914–1918," and David Sibley, "Their Graves Like Beds: Working Class Enthusiasm for War, 1914–18." For Australia, see Marilyn Lake, "Mission Impossible: How Men Gave Birth to the Australian Nation - Nationalism, Gender, and Other Seminal Acts," *Gender and History* 4, no. 3 (1992): 305–32. For India and, more generally, the "subsumption" model, see R. Radhakrishnan, "Nationalism, Gender, and the Narrative of Identity," in Andrew Parker et al., eds., *Nationalisms and Sexualities* (New York, 1992), 77–96.

29. Homi Bhabha's phrase in his *Nation and Narration* (New York, 1991).

30. C. C. Innes, *Women and Nation in Irish Literature and Society* (Athens, GA, 1994).

31. For example, in Seth Koven and Sonya Michel eds., *Mothers of the New World: Maternalist Politics and the Origins of Welfare States* (New York, 1993).

32. Susan Kingsley Kent, *Making Peace*; George L. Mosse, *Nationalism and Sexuality* (New York, 1985).

33. For Belgium see *Report of the Committee on Alleged German Outrages* (London: HMSO, 1915); *Official Book of the German Atrocities* (London, 1915); James Morgan Read, *Atrocity Propaganda 1914–19* (New Haven, 1941). For Turkey see Yves Trenon, *Le Génocide des Arméniens* (Brussels, 1983).

34. Public Record Office, Foreign Office, 230125 (3 Dec. 1917), 234109 (10 Dec. 1917), 23419 (19 Dec. 1917).

35. For the female factory inspectorate see Laura Lee Downs, *Manufacturing Inequality: Gender Division in the French and British Metalworking Industries, 1914–1939* (Ithaca, 1995); Angela Woollacott, "Maternalism,

Professionalism and Industrial Welfare Supervisors in World War I Britain," *Women's History Review* 3, no. 1 (1994): 19–56.

36. See Roberts, *Civilization without Sexes*.

37. See, for example, Ute Daniel, *Arbeiterfrauen in der Kriegsgesellschaft* (Göttingen, 1989). For work, class, and gender identity, see Kathleen Canning, "Gender and the Politics of Class Formation: Rethinking German Labor History," *AHR* 97, no. 3 (1994): 736–68. See also Wall and Winter, eds., *The Upheaval of War*, especially the essays by Ute Daniel and Deborah Tom, and their recent works: Daniel, *War from Within* and Tom, *Nice Girls and Rude Girls: Women Workers in World War I* (1997).

38. Joan W. Scott, "The Woman Worker," in Thébaud, ed., *Towards a Cultural Identity in the Twentieth Century*, 399–427; idem, "'L'ouvrière! Mot impie, sordide . . .': Women Workers in the Discourse of French Political Economy, 1840–1860," in *Gender and the Politics of History* (New York, 1988).

39. See, for example, Erika Friedl, "Political Roles of Aliabad Women: The Public-Private Dichotomy Transcended," in Nikki Keddie and Beth Baron, eds., *Women in Middle Eastern Society* (New Haven, 1991), 215–33.

40. See above p. 4–5. Margaret Higonnet, *Lines of Fire: Women's Visions of World War I* (forthcoming New York, 1998).

41. Pat Barker, *Regeneration* (London, 1992), 107–8.

42. Jay M. Winter, *Sites of Memory, Sites of Mourning: The Great War in European Cultural History* (Cambridge, 1996), Winter and Emanuel Sivan, *War and Remembrance* (forthcoming, Cambridge). Other essential works on memory include: John Gillis, *Commemoration: the Politics of National Identity* (Princeton, 1992), Paul Fussell, *The Great War and Modern Memory* (Oxford, 1977). See also Mosse, *Fallen Soldiers*; and Samuel Hynes, *A War Imagined: The First World War and English Culture* (London, 1990). Leed, *No Man's Land*, and Modris Eksteins, *Rites of War: The Great War and the Birth of the Modern Age* (New York, 1989), certainly broaden the scope of the modern identity, but interpret the "modern" broadly as "masculine." Hynes's recent *The Soldier's Tale, Bearing Witness to Modern War* (New York, 1997) includes women's visions of war, but does not focus on World War I. For an early criticism of the deletion of women from the meaning of war, see Clare M. Tylee, *The Great War and Women's Consciousness: Images of Militarism and Womanhood in Women's Writings, 1914–64* (London, 1990).

43. For these interpretations, see Judith Butler, *Gender Troubles: Feminism and the Subversion of Identity* (New York, 1990). For interpretations in historicist studies of the period, see Caroll Smith-Rosenberg, *Disorderly Conduct: Visions of Gender in Victorian America* (New York, 1985); and Gilbert and Gubar, "'She Meant What She Said': Lesbian Double Talk," in *Sexchanges*; and Marjorie Garber, *Vested Interests: Cross-Dressing and Cultural Anxiety* (New York, 1992).

44. Vicinus, p. 25.

45. Downs, *Manufacturing Inequality*.

PART I
GENDERING THE NATION
DEFINITIONS AND BOUNDARIES

THE BRITISH IMPERIAL STATE AND THE CONSTRUCTION OF NATIONAL IDENTITIES

PAT THANE

INTRODUCTION

World War I wrought fundamental shifts in the British state and society. Although Britain emerged from the war weaker in international terms, both politically and economically, in domestic affairs the state had become bigger and more active as a result of the needs of the war. It is notable that the Liberal-controlled British state was able to be effectively interventionist during the war, despite its previous preference for a minimal central bureaucracy and reluctant intervention.[1] The flexible capacity of the British state to adjust to the exigencies of the severe test of this war was in marked contrast to the lumbering failure of the supposedly stronger and certainly much larger German bureaucracy.[2]

From the later nineteenth century, the role of the state—and citizens' expectations of it—had been growing steadily. Thus, the war in fact pushed Britain further and faster along a path it was already following. At the heart of political discourse and political thought from at least the 1870s to the 1940s was the assumption that the role of the state was expanding. From this perception flowed a range of views about the desirable boundaries of this expansion and the role, in relation to it, of the expanding body of citizens, as first all adult men and then all adult women acquired the vote between 1867 and 1928.[3] It is worth noting that in 1914 Britain was still among a handful of European countries that did not have full manhood suffrage. The 40 percent of excluded adult males were enfranchised only in 1918, along with the majority of women aged over thirty.

This was an Imperial state, and an essential theme in the discourse about the relationship between the state and its "subjects" concerned that between the metropolitan state and the colonies. The term "subject" was preferred in British official discourse, which applied the term "citizen" to republics such as France or the United States. The contours of this theme also were changed by World War I. The British Empire was expanded to its largest size ever by the postwar settlement as it took over from the defeated powers responsibility for such territories as Palestine and German West Africa. But the demands of colonies for independence were also growing as never before, most insistently by the end of the war from Ireland (which achieved partial independence in 1921) and India (which had to wait until after World War II).

Such issues became prominent in the later nineteenth century for reasons that were international as well as internal to Britain and the Empire. Within Britain, previously excluded groups were demanding participation in decision making that affected their lives, and a larger share of the visibly increasing national wealth that they helped to create; just as groups of people in certain colonies (e.g., Ireland, Australia, Canada, and South Africa) wanted greater control over decisions concerning their territories and their inhabitants. The final third of the nineteenth century was a period of mounting international competition, above all for markets and for territory. Competition among nations sharpened or created ideas of national difference: of national identity, and racist ideas as to who did not belong within the nation. It enhanced the concern not only with defining the membership and characteristics of the "stock" of each nation (in the farmyard term favored by the English), but also with whether the numbers and physical and mental capacities of that "stock" were adequate to stand up to military and economic competition from other nations. Hence the alarm in Britain and elsewhere from around the 1870s about the declining birthrate and the assumed "physical deterioration" of the population.[4]

For Britain, these fears were peculiarly focused by the experience of the second Anglo-Boer war of 1899–1902, which was the greatest threat to the integrity of the Empire since the American breakaway of 1776. Inhabitants of the colonies of South Africa, who were not of British origin but Afrikaners of Dutch extraction, sought independence in the Cape and Transvaal. That it took thirty months and much expenditure to foil this attempt exposed the weaknesses of the British imperial army. The physical unfitness of many volunteers for the army (Britain had no system of conscription) seemed to confirm fears about "physical deterioration," though it is unlikely that volunteers were physically inferior to those at any time in at least the previous half-century. Some who feared Britain's decline grasped the opportunity for propaganda for their cause, and the numbers of unfit rejects from the services were widely publicized.

After the war, one response of the British state to this shock was to seek to increase the British-born population of South Africa. Men who had fought there were granted plots of land. But men alone could not raise good British "stock" in South Africa. A series of articles in *The Nineteenth Century* in 1902 on "The Needs of South Africa" argued that:

> The emigration of women to South Africa has become a question of national importance. If that country is in the future to become one of the great self-governing colonies of the British Empire, warm in sympathy and attachment to the mother country it must be peopled with loyal British women as well as British men. . . .
>
> Without that home-life settlers will bring with them none of the peaceful influence which will be the surest means to bring about reconciliation with their Boer neighbours and fellow subjects.

For:

> As a rule the Boer women of South Africa are devoid of many of the qualities which are essential to make a British man's home happy and comfortable. Cleanliness is a virtue too often foreign to the Boer character and it is not infrequently replaced by an ignorance of the laws of hygiene which produces habits of slovenliness both injurious to health and distasteful to British ideas. . . .
>
> It is women of high moral character possessed of common sense and a sound constitution who can help to build up our Empire.[5]

Women were given official encouragement to migrate to South Africa, thereby also helping to diminish the "surplus woman problem," the excess of women over men in the British population, which was depriving women of the opportunity to marry and, it was thought, encouraging their demands for equal rights.[6]

Fears about race and Empire created a rhetoric that more explicitly than before identified women with the role of preserving, perpetuating, and enhancing the physical quality, and the numbers, of the race in their role as mothers and, more mystically, embodying the essence of each race as its physical conduit to the next generation. As Dr. Elizabeth Sloan Chesser declared in 1914, in a pioneering psychology text, "every girl has a duty to the race":

> For she is the vase of life; she has in her body the power of handing on and on the life-force which has come to her through millions of years. It is a very sacred and serious thought—is it not?—that your life is so vital a matter to others yet unborn, that by your conduct you can help to keep the life-stream pure, help to uplift the race; that, on the other hand, you can hinder the great forces of evolution.[7]

An important role of the growing British state was to define a British national and imperial identity, to define who possessed that identity, to integrate them into the Empire, and to enhance their physical condition.

THE STATE AND WELFARE

In the years following the Anglo-Boer war, the British state sought to support and encourage women in their role of improving the physical condition of the population, through a series of state welfare measures. Its expanding welfare role was a central feature of the increasing activity of the British state before 1914, which was especially evident under the Liberal governments in office between 1906 and 1914. These initiatives were cautious and not costly. It is fashionable to play down their importance, but this is to underestimate the shift in the role of the state that was in process.[8] In a number of important ways, these welfare measures grew directly out of, or intersected with, the national and international issues with which influential actors in the state were concerned. Most obviously, they were intended to assist the enhancement of national and imperial physical, economic, and military efficiency; equally importantly they were designed to integrate significant groups of the excluded and actually or potentially politically restless into a sense of full participation in the state.[9] They played an important role in defining who had the full rights of a British "subject."

In providing new forms of social benefit, the state conferred new rights and had to decide who merited those rights. In the absence of a written constitution, who was British, and what rights British subjects possessed were shaped by statute and common law and by government practice. In important ways, through welfare and other measures, the British state helped shape the identities of inhabitants of Britain and the Empire.

For centuries, the main form of publicly funded provision for the needy had been the Poor Law. Receipt of poor relief had always brought exclusion from civil rights, above all from the right to vote, which by the nineteenth century poor people often possessed in local elections. The test of need for poor relief was simply destitution. New state initiatives of the later nineteenth century had relatively unambiguous qualifications: e.g., for state education there was an age limit. For many of the new welfare benefits of the early twentieth century the state was either unable or unwilling to set such unambiguous boundaries. In particular, it faced a problem of defining eligibility for cash payments. The only direct cash payments previously made to the needy from public funds were through the exclusionary Poor Law. The new measures were intended both to aid and to *include* the recipient as a full member of the British community. This raised new questions which were anxiously debated. Who was to be included in the new old-age pensions and health-insurance benefits? All of the aged poor and the working-class sick, or only some? If the latter, where were the boundaries to lie?[10]

The Old Age Pensions Act of 1908 provided the first state old-age pensions following a thirty-year campaign by social reformers and working people on behalf of a group demonstrably suffering severe poverty. Despite pleas for a universal pension for which the only qualification was age (55, 60, and 64 were all proposed) government economic stringency dictated that it should be targeted by means test upon the poorest above the high age of 70. But poverty alone was not deemed a sufficient qualification. This would not differentiate the pension from poor relief. The pension was intended not merely to relieve destitution but also to increase the sense of security and of inclusion within the state of the deserving "subject" after years of labor and acceptable behavior. The status of full subject was denied to those guilty of "habitual failure to work according to his ability, opportunity or need, for his maintenance or that of his legal relatives," to those imprisoned for any offense, including drunkenness, during the ten years preceding the claim, and to those who were not paupers, "aliens or the wives of aliens."[11] For those who failed these tests, the Poor Law remained as the penitentiary of the excluded.

The Pensions Act also created, as the Poor Law had never done, a new, clear, and stringent definition of the boundary between old age and younger ages (though 70 was much protested as an unrealistically high limit dictated by the government's desire to cut costs) as the education system had previously defined youth. As the role of the state grew, it divided its population with ever more complex boundaries.

An important achievement of the Liberal social welfare program was the National Insurance Act of 1911, which introduced health and unemployment insurance. The health-insurance scheme differed from the wholly tax-financed old-age pensions in that it was partially funded by contributions from workers and employers. The scheme was open to most manual workers, and payment of contributions conferred a right to benefit. The right was not absolute, and could be withdrawn for disreputable behavior such as feigning illness. Unemployment benefit was restricted to a limited number of trades.[12] Health insurance introduced a new matrix of rights and obligations between state and subject. It was designed to improve the health and sense of security and inclusion of the average manual worker, rather than to relieve poverty.

Who qualified for this benefit? In practice, the poorest casual workers were excluded because irregular pay precluded the necessary regular weekly contributions. Low and irregular pay also excluded the great majority of women. As discussed below, an attempt was made again to exclude "aliens." Included were the great majority of respectable working men, those most likely to threaten the status quo by supporting a trade union or the Labour Party.

Most of the other welfare measures of this period before World War I provided services to easily definable groups such as school-children, and were explicitly designed to reverse "physical deterioration." The Midwives Act of 1902 was one of a number of measures designed to reduce infant mortality, in this case by improving midwives' training.[13] From 1906, a succession of measures provided free school meals for needy schoolchildren and, first, free medical inspection, then free medical treatment for schoolchildren. In 1914, local authorities received government grants for maternal and child welfare services.[14] Improving health by improving the environment was also a motive for the Housing and Town Planning Act of 1909, which insisted upon minimum density and sanitation standards for new housing.

The war came too soon for these measures to have a noticeable effect upon the quality of the recruits now required. The rediscovery of the poor physical quality of volunteers (from 1916 conscripts) and consciousness of the need to replace men killed in the war if there were to be enough workers and fighters in the next generation, led to increased government expenditure on infant and maternal welfare during the war. Even before the war, women's groups took advantage of this unusual concern in influential circles with conditions of childbirth and childrearing to campaign for improvements that they conceived of as primarily benefiting women rather than the future of the "race." An important role in this campaign was played by the Women's Co-operative Guild, the largest working-class women's organization of the period. In 1916, to promote the cause, it published *Maternity*, a collection of letters by its members about their, often distressing, experiences of childbirth and childrearing. The volume was introduced by Herbert Samuel, the Liberal President of the Local Government Board (the Ministry responsible for most social welfare). He wrote:

> There are few now who do not see that the high death rate is due, in large measure, to a bad environment . . . it is the duty of the community, so far as it can, to relieve motherhood of its burdens, to spread the knowledge of mothercraft that is so often lacking, to make med-

ical aid available when it is needed, to watch over the health of the infant. And since this is the duty of the community, it is also the duty of the State. The infant cannot indeed be saved by the State. It can only be saved by the mother. But the mother can be helped and taught by the State.

Action is necessary also because, for the lack of it, the nation is weakened. Numbers are of importance. In the competition and conflict of civilizations it is the mass of the nations that tells. Again and again in history a lofty and brilliant civilization embodied in a small state has been borne under by the weight of a larger state of a lower type. The ideals for which Britain stands can only prevail as long as they are backed by a sufficient mass of numbers. It is not enough to make our civilization good. It must also be made strong, and for strength, numbers are not indeed enough without other elements, but they are none the less essential. Under existing conditions we waste before birth and in infancy a large part of our population.[15]

This was an especially clear expression of the fears that drove the actions of the British state at this time and of the importance of social welfare among them. One outcome was the introduction at the end of the war, in 1918, of a wide-ranging Maternity and Child Welfare Act, which funded a major extension of publicly funded provision.

The British state played an important role in defining through welfare measures what were the desirable characteristics of the British, in seeking to promote these, and in defining who did or should possess them. At the same time, by other means it defined still more directly who did and did not qualify to be British.

WHO WAS BRITISH?

Women?

As nation-states defined themselves in the later nineteenth century, they had to define who belonged to them. They decided that this was determined by gender as well as by geographical or "racial" origin. In Britain from 1870, by statute, any British-born woman was deemed on marriage to take the nationality of her husband and, should he not be British, to lose her British nationality and with it all rights associated with that nationality. Previously in Common Law, she had retained the citizenship with which she was born, though this had been increasingly challenged. It had been impossible for men or women to renounce British nationality, even if they took up that of another country. This was causing increasing problems in international law with respect of men, women, and the children of cross-national marriages. The nationality of married women came to matter as nationality itself mattered more and as, unevenly across national boundaries, women acquired more independent rights. These rights raised new problems in international law. What if, as was increasingly the case, women possessed independent property rights, rights to custody over children, or rights to divorce in their country of origin, but not in that of their husbands? This conflict was most readily resolved, at a time when women could not vote against a change in the law, by enshrining in statute a woman's obligation to take her husband's nationality upon marriage.

The question of national status was considered by a Royal Commission on the Laws of Naturalization and Allegiance in 1869. This recommended that the practice whereby "the allegiance of a natural-born British subject is regarded by the Common Law as indelible" was "neither reasonable nor convenient" and should be abolished in respect of British subjects who became naturalized abroad and British-born wives of aliens. Women of foreign birth who married British men might, at the discretion of the Home Office, acquire British nationality.

The essential reason given for the change was that British law could not in practice enforce its obligations with respect to people who left its jurisdiction for long periods and "it conflicts with that freedom of action which is now recognized as most conducive to the general good as well as to individual happiness and prosperity."[16] That this was indeed conducive to the happiness of women married to "aliens" was so wholly taken for granted that the recommendation that they adopt their husband's nationality was stated rather than discussed or justified by the Commissioners. No fundamental objections were raised in the brief debates in the Houses of Lords and Commons when these recommendations were translated into law in 1870. Two members of the Commons objected on the grounds that separated wives of husbands who adopted another nationality would also lose their British status, without being allowed the opportunity offered to widowed and divorced women to apply for re-naturalization as British. Mr. Kinnaird was "surprised that at a time when the rights of women were so loudly advocated, the House should seem determined to curtail them." The government felt that such cases would be too few to merit special provision in law.[17] It was later to defend the treatment of married women's nationality on the grounds that they were simply conforming "to the practice of the whole civilized world," though the United States did not adopt the practice until 1907.[18]

This law became an ever greater problem for women as the rights associated with formal national identity increased with the growing activity of the state. As we have seen, as state welfare provision expanded, access to it was confined to British citizens. The British-born wife of an "alien," even if living in Britain, did not qualify for the old-age pension. Nor did she gain the vote when other women did. Upon marriage, she lost the right that a number of women had, to vote in local elections.[19] In Britain and elsewhere after World War I, under the terms of the Treaty of Versailles, the savings of women legally married to (or widows of) Germans were confiscated as security for the payment of the German war debt, sometimes causing real hardship.

In 1914, before the war, this principle of married women's nationality was extended to the entire British Empire by the British Nationality and Status of Aliens Act. This act is normally discussed for its treatment of foreign immigrants and for its definition of Imperial citizenship. It was important in both respects (see below), but at the time it aroused most opposition in the exclusively male House of Commons for its treatment of married women. The shift from the casual treatment of this topic in 1870 suggests how much consciousness of women's rights had increased by 1914.

The attack was led by a Liberal, Mr. Booth, who emphasized how women resident in Britain but married to unnaturalized "aliens"— for example, the not infrequent case of the non-Jewish woman married to a Jewish immigrant—found themselves excluded from the local vote and the old-age pension. He insisted:

> Those who can conceive and defend an idea of this kind are hopelessly behind the times and they are voicing the condition of an eastern harem . . . it is perpetuating the idea that a woman is a slave and chattel of a man as soon as she is married to him.[20]

A fellow Liberal, Mr. Edmund Harvey, protested:

> I for one feel that we are not justified, men elected by men, in barring out from their rights in the citizenship of the Empire a large number of our fellow subjects.[21]

The Secretary of State for the Colonies defended it as "the practice of the whole civilized world . . . very grave questions arise as to domicile, taxation and other matters if you have a dual nationality of husband and wife."[22] The protest continued, another Liberal arguing that now that a woman "has her individuality with regard to all questions of holding property, she should have it also in this respect."[23] MPs pointed out that the child whose father changed nationality could, upon attaining majority, revert to the nationality of his or her birth by making a simple declaration. They asked why this could not also apply especially to widows, who, under current law, could revert to British nationality only after five years of widowhood, by paying a fee and obeying the normal laws of naturalization. The Home Secretary this time protested that he had to "exercise discretion and he has to be satisfied that she is of good character." Pressed as to why, he replied, "I should have thought it was unnecessary to argue the point. There are cases in which Englishwomen have married foreigners who are spies, and they may be very undesirable persons to have as British subjects."[24] The government was forced to back down sufficiently to grant that widows of "aliens" might revert to British nationality immediately on widowhood.

Men and women carried on the battle through the interwar years against the notion that women had no inherent nationality. The issue was an object of national and international women's campaigns, especially targeted upon the League of Nations through such organizations as the International Council of Women and the International Women's Suffrage Alliance.[25] In 1922 the law was changed in the U.S. to give women "independent nationality," as international women's organizations were demanding; i.e., women could keep their nationality unless they chose to change. For women of other countries who married Americans this caused new problems. A woman from Britain, or any country with similar laws, who married a U.S. citizen lost her original nationality without automatically acquiring a new one.

The clause of the 1914 Act relating to married women had passed the Australian legislature where women had the vote, only with great difficulty. In 1933 the Parliaments both of Australia and New Zealand enacted that women marrying aliens might retain the right to be treated as British subjects within those countries, though they would not be so treated in Britain or elsewhere in the Empire, or Commonwealth as it was increasingly called.[26]

The law was changed, for Britain and the Commonwealth, only in the 1948 British Nationality Act, when the Labour government put the change through without fuss. In the lengthy debates only two maverick imperialists opposed the change.[27] They were outnumbered by warm supporters.

Jews?

About 250,000 mostly poor Jews migrated into Britain between c.1880 and 1914, escaping from persecution in Central and Eastern Europe. They were the largest non-colonial immigrant group to enter Britain in modern history. In 1826, legislation restricting immigration during the Napoleonic wars was repealed and thereafter immigration into Britain was unrestricted. Naturalization could be acquired reasonably easily on payment of about three pounds, plus often an agent's fee.

There were no significant calls for renewed restriction until April 1886, when a public meeting, attended by 1,500 people, asking for statutory restriction was held in the East End of London. The immigration that was thought problematic was that of Jews, who had settled in large numbers in the East End. Then, and for two more decades, Jews were accused of taking jobs and homes from native English people and contributing to the deterioration of living standards and of the national "stock" by reason of what was represented as their physical feebleness. Britain's lack of restriction upon immigration was contrasted unfavorably with the limitations imposed by her leading economic rivals, the U.S. and Germany, and cited as one reason why Britain appeared to be losing out to economic competition. Parallels were drawn with Britain's preference for free trade, while her rivals flourished behind tariff barriers. But until after 1900, immigration was not a major issue, even in East End politics.

After 1900 it became so, due in part to the desire of a floundering Conservative government to woo votes. The first restrictions upon immigrants were introduced by this government in the Aliens Act of 1905. The rhetoric of East End politics again stressed jobs, homes, and the disruption of established communities. That of members of the government pointed to the damage inflicted by the immigrants upon the nation's health and efficiency. Prime Minister Arthur Balfour informed the House of Commons: "We have the right to keep out everybody who does not add to the strength of the community— the industrial, social, and intellectual strength of the community."[28] The Aliens Act required immigrants to demonstrate that they were able to support themselves and their dependents "decently." Criminals, the insane, and anyone thought likely to become a pauper due to disease, age, or infirmity were excluded. The parallel with those excluded from old-age pensions is evident. The burden of proof in case of appeal was placed upon the immigrant. At the last moment asylum was also extended to immigrants seeking to escape "persecution involving danger of imprisonment or danger to life or limb, on account of religious belief."[29] The numbers of immigrants entering Britain declined sharply.[30]

Also in 1905 the terms on which naturalization could be granted were altered to exclude those who could not "speak, read or write English reasonably well." Previously, it had been sufficient for the applicant to pay taxes, obey the law, and pay the fee.[31] This change was embodied in a Home Office circular of 1912 (which determined administrative practice) rather than in the statute. It explained that:

> The practice is founded on the principle that, save in very exceptional circumstances, a person can have no claim to be invested with the full rights of British nationality in the United Kingdom if he has not identified with the life and habits of the country to the extent of becoming reasonably proficient in the language; and a man can hardly be said to be reasonably proficient if he cannot read the language. . . . Mere conversational facility when he meets a Gentile does not suffice to show that a Jew is identifying himself with English life. On the contrary, if the only newspapers he can read are Jewish ones the likelihood is that his ideas are kept widely apart from those of the ordinary English citizen.[32]

This practice became statutory in the British Nationality and Status of Aliens Act of 1914. Second to the exclusion of married women, this was the aspect of the Bill that aroused the greatest protest from MPs. The Home Secretary defended it as "existing practice" and almost repeated the words of the 1912 circular:

> . . . every applicant for British nationality in this country shall show that he or she has the intention to associate himself or herself with British institutions, and we say that as a first evidence of that intention a man or woman who comes to live here must learn the English language.[33]

The exclusion of "aliens" from old-age pensions caused little comment in the Commons during the passage of the Act. Jews were better prepared when it was attempted to exclude them from National Insurance. In the original Bill, aliens were explicitly excluded. A memorandum explained:

> Aliens over the age of 16 are excluded from the benefit of the Government grant and from the right to join approved societies [which administered the benefits]. There is no reason why the government should contribute, for to do so would be to encourage the immigration of aliens.[34]

Jews, supported by politicians of all parties, pointed out among other things how many immigrants were too poor to pay for naturalization whilst being law-abiding, hard-working taxpayers. Lloyd George conceded the right of "aliens" to join approved societies, but initially refused them the state's 2d per week contribution to the benefit, for "there would be a great deal of criticism if that exceptional benefit were given to a man who did not care to take over the full responsibility of citizenship."[35] In the end he agreed to include aliens who had been in the country for five years, the period necessary to qualify for naturalization. The Jews had successfully represented themselves as meriting participation in rights conferred by the British state despite their "alien" status. Also in 1911, following protest, the Old Age Pensions Amending Act allowed widows, but not wives, of "aliens" to receive the pension.

Colonials?

In Common Law since at least the seventeenth century, British nationality extended to the whole Empire. The "Common Code" stated that allegiance to the Crown was "the link which bound the whole Empire together." Anyone born within the Empire was a British subject of the Crown and shared British nationality and identical rights. All British subjects had the right to enter the United Kingdom, to reside and to hold property, to take up employment, to vote (if suitably qualified), and were equal before the law.[36]

This appears to have become problematic only at the very end of the nineteenth century as certain colonies began to wish to define their own idea of nationhood and whom to exclude and include within it. These were colonies with powerful white elites, mainly of British origin, who did not wish to give identical rights to all who were born within their boundaries, to accept as residents people born anywhere in the Empire, or necessarily to accept British rules of naturalization.

In the early years of the twentieth century the issue "caused doubt, difficulty and discussion, and . . . seemed insoluble."[37] It was first discussed by a British Interdepartmental Committee in 1901 whose recommendations were discussed at the Imperial Conference in 1907. A further committee produced revised proposals, which were discussed at the Imperial Conference of 1911. The outcome was a draft Bill that was circulated around the Dominions (as the largely internally self-governing white-controlled colonies were now called). It took until late 1913 for a compromise to be reached. This was embodied in the British Nationality and Status of Aliens Act of 1914, which for the first time placed on the Statute Book the principles of the Common Code: "that much desired affirmation—that a British subject anywhere is a British subject anywhere," but with important concessions to the demands of the Dominions.[38] Those born within the Empire retained, in principle, full rights of nationality within Britain and the right to British protection anywhere else in the world, unless, as we have seen, they were women married to "aliens." But there were important provisos. Each Dominion was "left free to grant legal nationality on such terms as its legislature thinks fit" and "nothing now proposed would affect the validity and effectiveness of local laws regulating immigration or the like, or differentiating between classes of British subjects."[39]

In practice, the Dominions did not, as Britain expected, simply adopt the British legislation, but rather enacted their own similar, but not identical, statutes. Thereafter, as the Attorney-General pointed out in 1948, "the whole system started to break down."[40] Australia was free to develop a "white Australia" policy, which refused settlement to British subjects who were not defined as "white," and to exclude its Aboriginal population from the Australian "nation," as the Canadian government excluded North American Indians and the South African government progressively excluded its black and Indian inhabitants.

At least in public, British officials appeared to avoid discussion of exactly how "British" were the "native races" (as they were routinely called) of the Dominions and of the directly controlled (mainly black-populated) Crown Colonies. Since few such people yet traveled to Britain, the issue could be evaded in 1914, though it was the movement of, in particular, Indian and Chinese workers around the Empire which in part brought about the raising of racial barriers in some of the Dominions.

Through the first half of the twentieth century, Britain sought with increasing desperation to preserve the fiction of a unified Imperial nationality, to symbolize to the world the continuing unity of an Empire which in reality was crumbling. This struggle led to more and more compromises. When the Irish Free State achieved partial independence within the Empire/Commonwealth in 1921, its citizens retained all their previous rights, including voting rights, if they resided in Britain. The extension of welfare rights in the interwar years, including the significant extension of unemployment benefits, raised questions about the eligibility of the Irish and of British subjects from other countries of the Empire. It was decided that they were eligible on the same terms as native-born British.[41]

But there were limits to the inclusion of the Empire-born as full British citizens. The status of the "native races" was tested as more of them came to Britain as merchant seamen and settled. While demand for seamen was high during World War I, few questions were asked about the actual place of birth of, for example, African, Asian, or Arab seamen, and they were readily accepted as Empire-born British subjects. With the onset of unemployment in 1920 and the emergence of open racial hostility in some British ports, many of them found their nationality questioned by police, port, and immigration officials. Fears that if unemployed they would be charges on the British taxpayer, and the reality that some of them in employment were demanding improvement of their normally atrocious pay and conditions, intensified pressures and moves to restrict their rights. Since few of them carried evidence of their place of birth, it was difficult for them to prove that they were indeed "subjects of the Crown" and not "aliens." Under pressure from employers and others, the Home Office in 1925 introduced the Coloured Alien Seamen's Order, which effectively enabled all "coloured" seamen to be treated as "aliens" unless they could prove otherwise, as few could. Despite protests, this and similar barriers to "coloured" immigrants from the Empire/Commonwealth to Britain claiming British nationality remained and intensified throughout the interwar years.[42]

Such actions of the British state and a variety of restrictive measures introduced by Dominion governments rendered increasingly evident the fragility of the British identity of "every person in the British Commonwealth and Empire who owes allegiance to the King."[43] The last attempt to preserve this symbol of Commonwealth unity and British pre-eminence was the British Nationality Act of 1948. In struggling to hold on to the semblance of common nationality throughout the Empire, Britain made maximum concessions to Commonwealth nations. Each could now "confer its own citizenship, and through citizenship of a country—and through citizenship alone—will a person become a British subject."[44] They did not even now have to describe themselves as British subjects, but could choose the term "Commonwealth citizen" and, in law, the expressions "shall have the same meaning."[45] The boundaries of the British subject/Commonwealth citizen became still more porous in 1949 when the Republic of Ireland left the Commonwealth and its citizens retained the rights they had held within it.[46]

The British state played an important role in defining identities in Britain and the Empire, but never as a wholly free agent. Throughout the first half of the twentieth century, it was forced to negotiate, from an ever weaker position, as women, Jews, white, and then black colonials enforced compromise and awareness of their definitions of their rights.

NOTES

1. Pat Thane, "Government and Society, 1750–1914," in F. M. L. Thompson, ed., *The Cambridge Social History of Britain, 1750–1950* (Cambridge, 1990), 3:1–61.

2. Gerald Feldman, *Army, Industry and Labour in Germany, 1914–18* (Princeton, 1966); Pat Thane, "Women in the British Labour Party and the Construction of State Welfare, 1906–1939," in Seth Koven and Sonya Michel, eds., *Mothers of a New World: Maternalist Politics and the Origins of Welfare States* (London, 1993), 343–77.

3. José Harris, "Political Thought and the Welfare State, 1870–1940: An Intellectual Framework for British Social Policy," *Past and Present*, no. 135 (May 1972); idem, "Society and the State in Twentieth Century Britain," in Thompson, ed., *Cambridge Social History*, 3: 63–118; idem, "Political Thought and the State," in Simon J. D. Green and Richard C. Whiting, *The Boundaries of the Modern State* (Cambridge, 1996), 15–28.

4. José Harris, *Private Lives, Public Spirit: A Social History of Britain, 1870–1914* (Oxford, 1993), 41–60; Maria-Sophia Quine, *Population Politics in Twentieth Century Europe* (London, 1996); Bernard Harris, *The Health of the Schoolchild* (Milton Keynes, 1995); Deborah Dwork, *War Is Good for Babies and Other Young Children* (London, 1987); Daniel Pick, *Faces of Degeneration: A European Disorder c. 1848–1918* (Cambridge, 1989).

5. The Hon. Mrs. Evelyn Cecil, "The Needs of South Africa II: Female Emigration," *The Nineteenth Century* (Apr. 1902): 683.

6. A. James Hammerton, *Emigrant Gentlewomen* (London, 1979).

7. Dr. Elizabeth Sloan Chesser, *From Girlhood to Womanhood* (London, 1914), 125; Jane MacKay and Pat Thane, "The Englishwoman," in Robert Colls and Philip Dodd, *Englishness: Politics and Culture, 1880–1914* (London, 1986), 191–229.

8. Pat Thane, *The Foundations of the Welfare State* (London, 1982).

9. Pat Thane, "The Working Class and State 'Welfare' in Britain, 1870–1914," *Historical Journal* 27 (1984): 877–900.

10. Pat Thane, "Non-contributory *versus* Insurance Pensions, 1878–1908," in idem, ed., *Origins of British Social Policy* (London, 1978), 84–106.

11. Ibid., 103.

12. Thane, *The Foundations of the Welfare State*, 91ff.

13. Jane Lewis, *The Politics of Motherhood* (London, 1980), 141–42.

14. Bernard Harris, *The Health of the Schoolchild*, 48–69.

15. Margaret Llewellyn Davies, ed., *Maternity: Letters from Working Women* (London, 1916), preface.

16. *Report of the Royal Commissioners for Inquiring into the Laws of Naturalization and Allegiance. Parliamentary Papers*, 1868–69, vol. 25.

17. *Hansard*, House of Commons, vol. 200, col. 1740, 25 Apr. 1870.

18. *Hansard*, House of Commons, vol. 512, col. 1466, 13 May 1914.

19. Patricia Hollis, *Ladies Elect: Women in English Local Government, 1867–1914* (Oxford, 1986).

20. *Hansard*, House of Commons, 1914, vol. LXII, col. 1211.

21. Ibid., col. 1464.

22. Ibid., col. 1466.

23. Ibid., vol. LXV, col. 1498.

24. Ibid., col. 1481ff.

25. Carol Miller, "Lobbying the League: Women's International Organizations and the League of Nations" (Ph.D. diss., Oxford University, 1992).

26. *Hansard*, House of Commons, 1947–8, vol. 453, col. 497, 7 July 1948.

27. Ibid., col. 418 (Viscount Hinchingbrooke); col. 457–58 (Mr. Pickthorn, MP for Cambridge University and History don, who accurately described himself as "on the Blimp side in the controversy"). Kathleen Paul, "'British Subjects' and 'British Stock': Labour's Postwar Imperialism," *Journal of British Studies* 34, no. 2 (Apr. 1995): 237 n. 10, singles out the comments of the latter; they were far from typical.

28. Quoted in David Feldman, *Englishmen and Jews: Social Relations and Political Culture, 1840–1914* (New Haven, 1994), 287. This section is much indebted to this book.

29. Ibid., 290.

30. Ibid., 355.

31. Ibid., 371.

32. Quoted in ibid., 372.

33. *Hansard*, House of Commons, 1914, vol. LXV, col. 1477, 13 May 1914.

34. Feldman, *Englishmen and Jews*, 272.

35. Ibid., 376.

36. Ann Dummett and Andrew Nicol, *Subjects, Citizens, Aliens and Others: Nationality and Immigration Law* (London, 1990); Paul, "'British Subjects' and 'British Stock'," 236–37.

37. *Hansard*, House of Commons, 1914, vol. LXII, col. 1197, 13 May 1914.

38. Ibid., col. 1201.

39. Ibid., col. 1199.

40. *Hansard*, House of Commons, 1947–8, vol. 453, col. 496, 7 July 1948.

41. For the extension of welfare rights, see Thane, *The Foundations of the Welfare State*, 163ff. For information on Irish nationality, I am indebted to my research student, Carole Hanson.

42. Laura Tabili, "The Construction of Racial Difference in Twentieth Century Britain: The Special Restriction (Coloured Alien Seamen) Order, 1925," *Journal of British Studies* 33, no. 1 (Jan. 1994): 54–98.

43. *Hansard*, House of Commons, 1947–8, vol. 453, col. 386, 7 July 1948.

44. Ibid., col. 388.

45. 11 and 12 Geo. 6. Ch. 56.1 (2) British Nationality Act 1948.

46. Paul, "'British Subjects' and 'British Stock'," discusses the 1948 Act at length.

FROM EMPIRE TO NATION

IMAGES OF WOMEN AND WAR IN OTTOMAN POLITICAL CARTOONS, 1908–1923*

FATMA MÜGE GÖÇEK

The concept of ambivalence in representation—the constant fluctuation between depictions of actual life experiences and their idealizations in cultural narratives—is strikingly reflected in the images of women and war found in political cartoons. This fluctuation creates ambiguities as the lines between the idealized and the actual begin to blur; it becomes difficult to determine exactly the role of women and the impact of war, since the same formulations are used both to legitimate existing relations and, at the same time, to challenge them. The new interpretations of women and war become both liberating and confining. Still, even though political cartoons as a form tend to distort and embellish the traits of all social groups and events, they favor or disfavor some groups and events at the expense of others. All too often, women's actual experiences become trivialized and/or compartmentalized, and war's terrible ravages lose their edge. The ultimate puzzle is how and why these interpretations have come to prevail over others.

What causes lie behind this selective interpretation? The response to this question, I would contend, needs to be sought in the specific social and historical context within which political cartoons come into being. In the case of the early twentieth century, national struggles fought in the name of the citizenry provided the specific context within which cultural forms were replaced, produced, and reproduced around the idea of the nation. Edward Said remarks upon the ambiguities contained in this idea as the nation becomes "an agency of ambivalent narration that held culture at its most productive position, as a force for subordination, fracturing, diffusing, reproducing, as much as producing, creating, forcing, guiding."[1] The ambivalent narration surrounding the nation thus creates a new space beyond

---

*I would like to thank Naomi Galtz and Şükrü Hanioğlu for their feedback on this article. Needless to say, all remaining errors are mine.

existing formulations, one that has the potential to create new syntheses and reproduce old ones.

The early twentieth-century Ottoman transformation from empire to nation, from the vantage point of women and war, provides an excellent setting within which to approach the concept of ambivalent narration. My analysis of the portrayal of women and war in the political cartoons of this period indeed reveals an ambivalence between the idealized images and actual experiences of women and of war, one occurring almost always at the expense of the actual experiences. For instance, even though women's actual participation in society is consistent throughout this period, their perceived participation fluctuates among three contradictory images of women as asexual heroines, as immoral vixens, or as stolid mothers. I argue that this ambivalence, this fluctuation between actual life experiences and idealized representations, controls the emancipation of women and accounts for the checkered trajectory of their gains during the transformation from empire to nation. Hence, ultimately, in the case of women and war, the new space created through the ambivalent narration surrounding the nation fails to challenge and alter existing gender relations.

ACTUAL PARTICIPATION OF OTTOMAN WOMEN IN THE TRANSFORMATION FROM EMPIRE TO NATION

The brief fifteen-year period from 1908 to 1923 contained constitutional reform, wars, rebellions, and the dissolution and replacement of an empire by a nation-state. 1908 marked the beginning of a new political era in Ottoman history as a group of officers mobilized the army and deposed Sultan Abdülhamid II, reestablished the Ottoman assembly, and reinstated the constitution. During the same year, however, capitalizing on the Ottoman domestic turmoil, Bulgaria declared independence, Crete announced its unification with Greece, and the Austro-Hungarian empire annexed Bosnia and Hercegovina; the Albanian and Yemeni rebellions followed a year later. In 1911, Italy invaded Libya, occupying the Twelve Islands on the Aegean the following year. The Balkan countries declared war on the Ottoman Empire in 1912; the outbreak of World War I soon followed in 1914. When the Ottoman Empire, an ally of the Central Powers during the War, was defeated and occupied by the Allied Forces, a group of officers commanded by an Ottoman general, Mustafa Kemal, escaped in 1919 to Asia Minor to start the Turkish War of Independence. There were two governments on central Ottoman lands for the next four years, as the sultan continued to rule under the guidance of the Allied Forces in Constantinople, and Mustafa Kemal established a national assembly in Anatolia for the same purpose. The divided allegiances of the people between the Ottoman Empire and the emerging Turkish nation-state endured until the final military victory of the Turkish nationals against the Allied Forces in 1922. The Turkish Republic was established on October 29, 1923.

Women participated in this transformative period in many ways; they provided medical and social care to the vast numbers of refugees and soldiers, joined the workforce during World War I, and served as orators, care providers, and soldiers during the War of Independence.[2] Yet this actual participation was not adequately presented in the media, and Ottoman political cartoons represented the participation of women through a set of three stock, self-contradictory images: asexual heroine, immoral vixen, and stolid mother. The ambivalence created by the disjuncture between these images and the actual participation of women often reinforced the constraints on women's position in the transformation from the empire to the nation-state.

The mobilization of Ottoman women through participation in the labor force and in voluntary associations was a very significant factor in defining and transforming women's identities, and therefore warrants a detailed analysis.[3] The middle- and upper-class women maintained a strong presence in the new Western-style schools and in women's journals, and mobilized to establish voluntary aid associations to assist in the war efforts throughout the extended period of wars after 1908.[4] The first of these voluntary aid societies, founded in 1908, was the Aid Society (Cemiyet-i İmdadiye), which provided winter clothing to Ottoman soldiers fighting in the Balkans. During the same year, the Union and Progress Committee, which led the Ottoman constitutional reform, established a Women's Branch (İttihat ve Terakki Kadınlar Şubesi) in order to enlist women's political support in this endeavor. In addition, the Society for the Elevation of Women (Teali-yi Nisvan Cemiyeti) was established to improve the knowledge and culture of Ottoman women, and the Ottoman Women's Compassionate Philanthropic Society (Osmanlı Kadınları Şefkat Cemiyet-i Hayriyesi), to aid the needy. Hence women's efforts to support the war, the Ottoman political transformation, and the needy went hand-in-hand with their attempts to educate and improve women's social standing. Similarly, in 1909 women founded two organizations: the Protection Society (Esirgeme Derneği), to provide assistance to wives and children of the war martyrs and refugees from the Balkans, and the Women's Ottoman Philanthropic Society (*Osmanlı Cemiyet-i Hayriye-i Nisvaniye*), to arrange sewing courses, literacy seminars, and schools for women.

As the Balkan unrest continued in 1910, Ottoman women founded yet another society to aid the army, the Women's Society for the Betterment of the Ottoman Nation (*Teali-yı Vatan-ı Osmani Hanımlar Cemiyeti*), which assisted the Red Crescent—the Muslim equivalent of the Red Cross—raised money for the donation of a warship to the Ottoman army, and established workshops, schools, and birth clinics for women. Once again, women's attempts to aid and ameliorate the conditions of the needy, and their attempts to strengthen the social positions of other women, coincided. In 1912, on the eve of the Balkan wars, three women's organizations were founded, including the Women's Philanthropic Society to Encourage the Use of Domestically Manufactured Goods (*Mamulat-ı Dahiliye Kadınlar Cemiyet-i Hayriyesi*), which also established textile and carpet-weaving workshops for women; the Women's Branch of the Naval Society (*Donanma Cemiyeti Hanımlar Şubesi*) to raise funds for the Ottoman navy, and the Women's Central Committee of the Ottoman Red Crescent (*Osmanlı Hilal-ı Ahmer Cemiyeti Hanımlar Heyet-i Merkeziyesi*) to collect donations and supply volunteer nurses for those wounded at the Balkan wars. This central committee also published annually a 250-page almanac that included information on social and economic issues, etiquette, practical ideas, and numerous epigrams emphasizing the worth and education of women and continually reinforcing the idea that "the position of women is the indicator of a nation's level of civilization."[5]

Other women's associations to aid the Balkan wars followed in 1913 with the establishment of the Ottoman Women's Society for National Defense (*Müdafaa-yı Milliye Osmanlı Hanımlar Cemiyeti*), which ran a series of conferences for and by women. During these conferences, Ottoman women mobilized and acquired an identity as a social group. For instance, they employed a recent technological medium to dispatch three groups of telegrams—one to the Ottoman army on behalf of all the women to demonstrate their support; another to the Muslim women of India, Turkistan, and Russia asking for their financial support; and yet another to the wives of influential European leaders requesting their social and political support in international affairs. One could conjecture that these interactions with other, distinct groups also helped Ottoman women shape their own identity as a group. The conferences also formed the rallying grounds for soliciting donations in gold, jewelry, and fur coats to aid the national defense, the employment of the term "national" in this endeavor also signaling the nascent political realities. Of the two other organizations founded in 1913, the Union for Aid to the Families of War Martyrs (*Şehit Ailelerine Yardım Birliği*) provided financial and educational assistance to this group, while the Society for the Defense of Women's Rights (*Müdafaa-yı Hukuk-ı Nisvan Cemiyeti*) was founded with three explicit aims: to reform women's public dress, to promote women's economic employment and social presence, and to enlighten women through the establishment of private schools, newspapers, books, and conferences. The activities of the society were thoroughly covered by the media; especially noted were the successful struggle of Belkis Şevket to become the first Ottoman woman to fly in a plane, and that of Bedri Osman to apply for, and gain, employment in a telephone company.[6]

The outbreak of World War I marked the establishment of the Women's Society for Aiding Soldiers' Families (*Asker Ailelerine Yardım Hanımlar Cemiyeti*). Then, in 1916, the Hearth for Knowledge (*Bilgi Yurdu*) was established, providing courses for women in foreign languages, arithmetic, history, and pedagogy. Yet the most significant society founded in this period to expand women's participation in the economic sphere was the Muslim Society for Women's Employment (*Kadınlar Çalıştırma Cemiyet-i İslamiyesi*), which aimed at finding jobs for women and providing legal and social protection for employed women; it also established and managed three manufacturing plants that employed approximately sixty thousand women.

Ottoman working-women's participation in the labor force during this period was also significant. According to one estimate, in 1908 women, mostly of working-class origin, comprised about thirty percent of the Ottoman labor force of 250,000.[7] During the war, Ottoman women, like their sisters in Europe, were employed in government offices and manufacturing plants because of the labor shortage. A law passed in 1915 by the Ministry of Trade instituted a form of mandatory employment swelling the ranks of women workers.[8] The Ottoman female employees often worked in separate rooms and were demobilized after the war, even though some petitioned to stay at their jobs and mobilized the media in support of their petitions by arguing that "women worked more enthusiastically than men."[9] Thousands of Ottoman women were also employed throughout Anatolia as workers in manufacturing plants ranging in type from textiles to tobacco and chemical products; some also worked as hairdressers, merchants, and artisans.[10] After the war, these women lost their jobs to men in most sectors except, for example, the textile industry, where they were able to keep their wartime jobs because of the low pay.[11]

After the Ottoman defeat in the war and the subsequent Allied occupation of Ottoman lands, the role of Ottoman women in the public sphere became even more textured as middle- and upper-class women became orators and resistance organizers. Leading the public protests against the occupation, one Ottoman woman, Sabhat Hanım, gave an impassioned speech on May 20, 1919 against the Greek occupation of Smyrna; she emphasized how "we women will be the leaders in this holy war for our rights and constantly put our curses upon those who are the hypocrites of civilization." Similarly, in another protest which occurred ten days later, another woman, Şükufe Nihal, swore allegiance to the homeland, stating, "O noble homeland, you provided us with our cradles, and you shall also be our tomb [if necessary]."[12] The societies that were established in the wake of these public protests now linked their cause with the Anatolian, Muslim homeland: the Muslim Women's Society of Kasaba (Kasaba İslam Kadınları Cemiyeti) was founded to resist the occupation of Smyrna, and the Women's Branch for the Defense of National Rights (Müdafaa-i Hukuk Kadınlar Şubesi) rallied to the "defense of the homeland."[13]

In the subsequent mobilization for the War of Independence, women encouraged the resistance fighters through passionate editorials and persuaded the able-bodied men at the imperial capital to join the resistance in Anatolia. The most significant organization, founded on November 26, 1919 on the eve of the War of Independence, when many national defense organizations were formed throughout Asia Minor, was the Anatolian Women's Society for National Defense (Anadolu Kadınları Müdafaa-i Vatan Cemiyeti) led by Melek Reşit Hanım, the wife of the Ottoman governor of Sivas.[14] Soon thereafter, many branches of this society were established throughout Anatolia, including the cities of Sivas, Amasya, Kayseri, Kastamonu, Eskişehir, Erzincan, Niğde, Aydın, Yozgat, Burdur, Konya, and Kangal.[15] They wrote letters against the Allied Forces and the Ottoman government in Constantinople, sent congratulatory notes to those who had left the capital to join the War of Independence in Anatolia, and raised money and supplied goods to the National Army in Anatolia. The letters they sent on January 17, 1920 included, for instance, telegrams to the wives of the French President Poincaré and the American President Wilson asking them to "influence their husbands on behalf of giving political rights to the Turkish nation," and appealing to them first as women "through their hearts, which are undoubtedly filled with compassion because of being women," then as "mothers who know how much suffering warfare causes," and finally as "wives demanding righteous and just behavior from their husbands."[16] This active participation of women in aiding society both during the empire and at the time of the nascent nation-state was not, however, recognized in Ottoman cartoons.

THE EMERGENCE OF OTTOMAN POLITICAL CARTOONS

Political cartoons became a very significant form of visual rhetoric in nineteenth- and twentieth-century Europe when they were coupled with emerging public opinion and the nascent "imagined community" of the nation. Especially during World War I, political cartoons were used as a mode of propaganda to mobilize the population both morally and intellectually, explain setbacks, confirm belief in the superiority of the fatherland, and proclaim the hope of final victory.[17] The development of Ottoman political cartoons occurred within this historical context; the first Ottoman cartoon appeared in 1867 in the journal *İstanbul*, approximately thirty years after the publication of the first Ottoman official gazette, *Takvim-i Vekayi* (Chronicle of Events), and fifteen years after the appearance of the first picture in a newspaper and the publication by an Ottoman Armenian, Hovsep Vartanyan, of the first humor gazette. The satirical gazettes in the Ottoman Empire were published monthly, bimonthly, weekly, or daily, often by a well-educated class of men whose affairs included both literature and politics. Even though there were occasional gas- or steam-run presses in the empire, most journals were still hand-pressed in 1908. A four-page, black-and-white format was the most common form for these gazettes: only after World War I did color print come into common use. The run of these gazettes ranged from ten thousand to 25,000 issues. As in Europe, the development of censorship clauses and laws in 1877 closely followed the emergence of the medium.[18]

In 1877, Sultan Abdülhamid II closed the Ottoman parliament, abolished the constitution, and increased censorship further. When this period ended in 1908 with a military coup, in that year alone, ninety-two satirical gazettes began publication in Constantinople. Once again, censorship followed closely thereafter as 1909 marked the beginning of a press law, based on the French legislation limiting the freedom of the press. Most of these satirical gazettes had shut down by the eve of World War I, due to financial reasons, while the few surviving ones were censored, as in Germany, by the Ottoman military government during the war and then by the Allied Powers that occupied Constantinople until the end of the War of Independence in 1922.[19] Printing blank pages where a cartoon was to have appeared (but had been censored) was a common mode of resistance in the Ottoman context, as in many European countries.[20] Even though most of the press sided with the War of Independence fought in Anatolia, there were certain newspapers that advocated a pro-Allied stand.[21]

The symbolism employed in these political cartoons to convey the message is of particular interest. The images depicted in Ottoman political cartoons were either symbols adopted from the West or reinterpreted traditional images of Ottoman popular culture. In portraying the Western concept of liberty, Ottoman cartoonists often replicated the European image of a woman draped in a loose-fitting Greek garment with a laurel wreath on her head. Political cartoons attempting to capture tradition or the emerging theme of national identity centered instead on "indigenous" characters such as the shadow-play figures Karagöz and Hacivat, who were known for their simple, but astute, wisdom in interpreting life, or popular rebels like Köroğlu, who were famous for devoting their lives to give voice to the sentiments of the populace.[22] A third pattern of adoption entailed the interpretation of European symbols within the Ottoman context as, for instance, in the caricatures of Münif Fehim, where the traditional Ottoman miniature aesthetic was employed in the cartoon form.[23] Reference to the Ottoman past was a significant means for legitimating the message of the cartoon, and thereby co-opting "a slice of eternity."[24] While reference to the Hellenic era often underscored the historical heritage of European civilization in European political cartoons, the Ottomans imagined two contradictory pasts: one, the immediate past, in which they were subordinated to Europe, and the other, the distant past when the ruling sultan represented power, justice, and imperial glory.[25]

In this article, I analyze Ottoman political cartoons between 1908 and 1923 in relation to their depictions of women and war. I specifically undertake a content analysis of the most popular humor gazettes of the period, *Cem* and *Kalem*, which catered to an elite audience at the Ottoman capital; I complement this analysis with a survey of all the existing anthologies of Ottoman and early Republican cartoons, which also featured the less popular humor gazettes in both the capital and the provinces, and with a review of the very limited secondary literature on the topic. I argue that the combination of these three sources captures the transformation from empire to nation: the two most popular humor gazettes portray the images of the empire during the transformation, whereas the anthologies exhibit the emerging nationalist representations, which mostly occur outside the capital. The eight cartoons analyzed in detail in this article illustrate shifts in perceptions of gender and war during the transformation from empire to nation.

WOMEN IN OTTOMAN CARTOON SPACE

In both Western and Ottoman contexts, depictions of women in cartoons often contained contradictory elements. Cartoons either idealized women and set humanly unattainable standards of purity, or debased and delegitimized them by portraying them as the root of evil, dragging them down to inescapable depths of depravity.[26] Even though women often appeared as ideal, allegorical figures representing the symbolic order, these representations were immediately trivialized when references were made to actual life-situations where women appeared predominantly as mothers, or, more negatively, as vixens. Women's portrayal as judges, statesmen, soldiers, philosophers, or inventors were extreme idealizations that only occurred to emphasize the remoteness of women from these professions.[27]

Sexuality was employed both in Europe and the Ottoman Empire to reinforce the impact of this portrayal; the presence or absence of sexual desire in the images of women was used to suggest approval or condemnation for what they represented in the cartoon. Implications of virginity, promiscuity, or elderly maturity each conveyed a set of messages: The ideal depictions of women were usually of untouched, young virgins with long hair and white, free-flowing, "natural" garments, alluding to a Greek past. These virgins easily metamorphosed into decadent vixens by the addition of trendy, avant-garde (in the Ottoman case, Western) clothing; in this transformation, the figure also gained another fifteen years in age (and experience) to insinuate the possession of dangerous carnal knowledge. The image often contrasted a curvaceous body with sharp heels and pointed jewelry to heighten the sense of danger. The garments became much more conservative and culture-bound when the cartoon reference was to the symbol of the nation—in the Ottoman case, the outfit often alluded to the "folkloric" women's costume of scarf, shirt, and harem pants.[28]

A study on the representation of Ottoman women in cartoons during the 1908–1911 period indeed demonstrates that women were depicted as four types: "as the heroic figure of Türkiye (the mythic female figure of the nation) . . . as the collaborator, representing Ottoman womanhood sacrificed on the altar of European culture . . . as the citizen-patriot, the non-mythic counterpart of Türkiye . . . and as the old nag in the figure of the public, as everywoman."[29] When I extended my analysis to the 1908–1923 period, I discovered that this representation persisted in modified form: the differences became more polarized so that the everywoman represented by the old nag and citizen-patriot coalesced in the stolid mother figure of the emerging nation-state. Women thus became depicted primarily as asexual heroines, immoral vixens, or mothers. The gendered nature of the concept of citizenship also aided this depiction; even though in theory both sexes were legally recognized as citizens, in practice men exercised the emerging rights almost exclusively and often at the expense of women. As these rights homogenized around a male-centered conception of Turkish citizenship, women's position became articulated more and more as the "mother" of the nation. Such an idealization justified women's removal from the presumably polluted everyday practice of the civic duties of citizenship. It also countered the earlier cultural construct centered on the sultan as the father of the empire—the anonymous mother of all citizens thus replaced the now alienated, aloof, and elite father of all Ottoman subjects.

Ottoman Women as Asexual Heroines. The idealized portrayal of women frequently found in Western European cartoon art was also translated into the Ottoman context. In the European press, such female figures were used to personify abstract concepts "such as the cardinal virtues (Prudence, Temperance, Justice, and Fortitude), theological virtues (Faith, Hope, and Charity), the liberal arts, and Philosophy."[30] America, Britannia, Germania, Democracy, Justice, Liberty, and Victory became recognizable descendants of mythical figures in the visual language created by political cartoons. Importantly, these figures also established a code of significant symbolic differences; while America, for instance, often appeared in Western European literature as a naked, "uncivilized" Indian princess figure, Europe emerged as matronly in some contexts and virginal in others, most often clad in ancient Greek clothing, which signified the origins of Western civilization. These symbolically differentiated figures were then adapted in non-Western contexts, some argue, in an instance of the non-Western "internalization of Western blueprints in the name of progress, modernization, industrialization and internationalism."[31] The Ottoman case represents just such an internalization to support this argument.

Figures 1–3, spanning the years 1908–1923, depict Liberty and Peace as women. In 1908, after the restoration of the Ottoman constitution, Liberty is depicted in her Western form, wreathed, wearing classical Greek garb and riding a Roman chariot pulled by lions, on

Figure 1. Cartoon drawn immediately after the restoration of the Ottoman constitution is subtitled "Long live free Turkey." The building on the left is entitled "The National Assembly." On the flag are the following notations: at the top "justice," on the right "freedom," and on the left "equality;" the word next to the parrot (the symbol of the satirical gazette) is "long live." Artist unknown, in *Musavver Papağan* 14 (4 December 1908): 2–3 (Çeviker 1988: 46).

her way to the reopened Ottoman assembly building (Figure 1). Similarly, Peace appears as a young maiden during (Figure 2) and after (Figure 3) the signing of the Treaty of Lausanne—between the Allied Forces and the Turkish national army—that led to the establishment of the Republic in 1923. What is significant in the two depictions of Peace are the differences in modes of dress. Peace appears unclothed on April 12, 1923 before the signing of the Treaty, fearfully treading blindfolded on the tips of bayonets. The naked figure heightens the fragility and vulnerability of the female body. On July 23, 1923, upon the endorsement of the treaty, Peace becomes transformed into a modest bride, fully clothed, solidly treading on the ground, married to a man symbolizing the Turkish Republic (possibly referring to İsmet Pasha, who represented the nation at the European meeting). The wedding dress she wears approximates the women's fashion of the time in Europe with some discrepancies and, in accordance with Western European conventions, she is carrying an olive branch and wearing a wreath.[32]

Figure 2. Cartoon drawn after the Turkish War of Independence during the peace negotiatons between the Allied Powers and Turkey subtitled "The reason why peace comes so late and so hard" by Ismail Hakkı in *Akbaba* 37 (12 april 1923): 4 (Çeviker 1991: 41).

Figure 3. Cartoon drawn on the occasion of the signing of the Treaty of Lausanne on 23 July 1923 between the delegates from the new Turkish Republic and the Allied Powers, subtitled "The bridal party: let those who love God utter Godspeed" by Ratip Tahir in *Akbaba* 66 (23 July 1923): 1 (Çeviker 1991: 241).

All three figures also contain indigenous elements drawn from Ottoman society. In the case of the depiction of Liberty in 1908, the numerous flags bearing the star and crescent represent sovereignty. The audience also contains a soldier following and guarding the chariot accompanied by a bearded religious scholar, who probably signifies the support of Islamic religion; the figures surrounding the chariot dressed in different religious attire represent the communal leaders of the Ottoman minorities, which include Greeks, Armenians, and Jews. The persons on the extreme right, who are playing the drum and the double-reed instrument (*davul* and *zurna*), represent the traditional folk players who celebrate festive occasions and accompany proclamations on the streets to draw people's attention to them. The children and the street dog running around at the edge of the illustration are figures that could be seen at celebrations on the streets of the imperial capital—these common elements may also signify the depth of support among the populace for the restoration of the constitution. The parrot featured in this cartoon—originally of Australian origin and now adopted as the symbol of the satirical gazette in which the cartoon appeared—conveys the gazette's favorable stand toward this occasion. The various symbols on the cartoon are marked in both Ottoman script and French, demonstrating the cosmopolitan nature of the empire and its capital. Hence the 1908 representation predating the wars displays a pluralistic, inclusive identity, one that tends to disappear during the wars and with the emergence of the Turkish Republic.

The portrayal of unclothed Peace on April 12, 1923 does not seem to contain any Ottoman elements except, of course, for the signature of the caricaturist İsmail Hakkı in Arabic script and the Ottoman subtitle explaining that Peace has arrived so late and with so much difficulty because she had to tread on bayonets. As a cartoon, it could have appeared in any journal in Western Europe. Once Peace loses her elusive and fragile characteristic and becomes domesticated in the cartoon on July 23, 1923, she becomes surrounded by Turkish figures, all men who are dressed in the fashion of the times, wearing either black hats (referred to as *kalpaks*, which were the symbol of the national fighters in Anatolia), or the traditional fez (often worn by the westernized urban men). The male figures may refer to specific characters involved in the independence movement as well. Once again, musicians celebrate the occasion with the drum and double-reed instrument, playing the tune to which all the others dance the traditional folk dance, holding hands and waving handkerchiefs.

What is particularly noteworthy in all three figures is the asexual character of the young women; each heroine faces away from the viewer, intent on lofty and honorable missions. These figures are highly idealized and, unlike the common men who are ever present in the cartoons, do not at all depict the actual women of the empire or their real presence at such occasions. In the next set of figures, this image of the inaccessible heroine is replaced by its antipode, which is used to frame political issues surrounding the Turkish War of Independence that was waged against the Allied powers in general, and the Greeks in particular.

Ottoman Women as Immoral Vixens. The inclusion and exclusion of groups and identities define the boundaries of a newly forming nation.[33] In the case of the Ottoman transition from empire to nation-state between 1919 and 1922, it was specifically through the exclusion of urban cosmopolitan women and foreign Greek elements that the Turks started to redefine their national identity. This exclusion signaled two significant transformations: Ottoman minorities such as the Greeks had always peacefully coexisted with the Ottoman Muslim majority of the empire; they had the sultan's protection and license to regulate their internal affairs in return for the payment of taxes. This arrangement started to collapse with the advent of nationalism as the Ottoman Greeks aspired to equal citizenship in both rights and responsibilities, an aspiration that proved unsustainable in an imperial framework. When their demands were not satisfied, the Ottoman Greeks protested, only to find themselves excluded by the developing nationalist identity among the Ottoman Turks. Similarly, the cosmopolitan nature of the Ottoman capital and, in particular, the emergence of women who oriented their gaze to European modes of behavior and did not adhere to the norms and values "indigenous" to Ottoman society became less tolerable under the growing influence of nationalism. The exclusion of urban cosmopolitan women from the future vision of society ensued.

This process is reflected in cartoons that appeared in this period, when the previous image of the virtuous heroine gives way to the image of a feminized Greek enemy and a female enemy at home. In a cartoon that appeared toward the end of the war, on March 30, 1922 (Figure 4), the Greek enemy is depicted as a woman running away from a Turkish soldier; in Figure 5 the Greek commander, dressed as a vixen, offers flowers to İsmet Pasha while hiding a dagger behind his back. Another negative image, drawn on March 6, 1920, refers to an earlier period, to the Allied occupation of Ottoman lands and the War of Independence, during which urban cosmopoli-

Figure 4. Cartoon drawn during the Turkish War of Independence against the Greeks who occupied Asia Minor. The conversation noted on the left of the cartoon is between a Greek soldier who is saying: "Let go of me . . . I'm leaving," and a Turkish soldier who responds: "No way, how can I do [carnal] business then?" Drawn by Ahmet Rıfkı in *Aydede* 26 (30 March 1922): 1 (Çeviker 1991: 24).

tan women, rather than supporting the war, immorally drink and toast the Greek commander (Figure 6).

War is often portrayed as an opportunity to prove one's manhood, and sexuality is employed to heighten the impact of this visual message. In the case of Ottoman political cartoons between 1919 and 1922, when the Ottoman lands were under Allied occupation and the War of Independence had started in Anatolia, gender language and symbols were enlisted to help dramatize the tension-filled relations. Life in Constantinople during the Allied Occupation of 1919 to 1922 was chaotic, with military automobiles rushing through the city, cocktail receptions hosted for and by the foreigners, and an influx of thousands of Muslim refugees from the Balkan wars, as well as Russian White Army refugees. About 1,650,000 refugees were estimated to have arrived in the imperial city between 1919 and 1922. During the last years of the War of Independence fought in Anatolia against the Greeks, the corpses of both men and horses could be seen in Constantinople, being transported through the Bosporus to the Black Sea.[34]

Although Ottoman women were in fact very active in raising

Figure 5. Cartoon drawn immediately after the Turkish War of Independence when Greece, upon defeat, started to seek peace. The Greek commander Venizelos, portrayed in a woman's outfit carrying a peace bouquet
in one hand and a dagger hidden behind in the other, coaxed by the English, French, and Italians, approaches the Turkish representative Ismet
Pasha and states "My dear Pasha, do not forget your old mistress! Put your
arm forward so we can make peace!" The response is not by the pasha but
by the traditional shadow theater figure Karagöz representing the populace: "You rascal of a lover! What is on your tongue and what is in your
hand? You are not even aware of your condition and seek peace! Don't
come too close or I'll take what is in your hand and pierce your brain with
it!" Artist unknown, in *Karagöz* 1581 (12 March 1923): 1 (Çeviker 1991: 235).

money and providing services to deal with the crises, as they had
been before and during World War I,[35] cartoons portrayed them as
immoral vixens, employing images of female sexuality to depict
women at the imperial capital as the enemy at home.[36] The figure of
the vixen epitomizes the pervasive image of these women as totally
alienated from the nation, concerned only with their own pleasures,
gleefully toasting the enemy in the company of degenerate Ottoman
men who were either rich and fat from hoarding basic goods during
the occupation, or senselessly drunk. All were portrayed as engaged
in the pleasures and privileges of living in the cosmopolitan capital,
thereby unaware of, and immune to, all the pain and suffering of the
resistance movement in the provinces.

The Greeks, against whom the War of Independence was being
fought, formed the other enemy. Even though that war was fought
against all the Allied powers, including France, Britain, and Italy, it

Figure 6. Cartoon, drawn during the War of Independence to criticize and chastise those urbanites of the imperial capital who do not support the movement, entitled "In response to the sufferings of the wounded homeland." The scene depicting six men and two women in a drunken stupor is subtitled with a stanza: "Let us imbibe (alcohol) with love and forget the tomorrows/After all, no one commended this false world to our care." Drawn by Ulvi Kazım in *Alay* 9 (6 March 1920): 1 (Çeviker 1991: 204).

was the Greeks, who had joined the war at a late stage, who were the most frequent objects of ridicule in Ottoman political cartoons. The feminization of the enemy, their depiction as "anthropomorphized and naturalized into a woman," was a method frequently employed for derision.[37] The Greeks were the ones most caricatured in feminine form, rather than demonized, because they posed the most immediate threat: they aspired to invade the Ottoman Empire and establish the former Byzantine Empire; this "megalo idea," coupled with the swift invasion of Asia Minor, the heartland of the Ottoman Empire, produced immense animosity on the Ottoman side. Since Greece also had been an Ottoman province, the Ottomans could not conceive it as being strong enough to confront them. Hence the Turks' confidence in their own superiority may have led them to feminize, rather than demonize, an enemy they held in contempt rather than fear. In the symbolic construction of power, the Greek enemy was endowed with the "womanly" qualities of a former mistress: cowardice, fickleness, and indecency. The portrayal of the Greek soldier in Figure 4 mocks his traditional fighting gear, which resembles a skirt. The Turkish soldier, dressed properly in a manly fashion with pants and boots, is pulling the skirt-like garment of the Greek soldier, who wears tight, white pants and a hat with a sash that suggests the long hair of women—the outfit is completed with shoes that look like women's harem slippers. In Figure 5, the Greek commander is the only one drawn as a woman wearing a revealing diaphanous slip of a dress and high-heeled shoes. The other occupiers of the Ottoman lands, the Italians, French, and English on the side of Greece, are portrayed as males in their ceremonial military costumes, as is the figure probably indicating Soviet Russia, standing next to the Turkish commander. The body language of the Allied Powers represents their positions on the matter; the Englishman is coaxing the Greek commander to make peace, while the Frenchman, standing with folded arms, obviously does not approve. The Italian merely observes the situation, his hands in his pants pockets, not willing to get involved. The two characters placed in the background, the traditional Ottoman shadow-play figures of Hacivat and Karagöz, comment on this scenario and warn the Turkish commander to beware of the Greek trap.

Ottoman political cartoons often coupled the feminization of Greeks with the suggestion, and justification, of violence against them. It was the Greek threat of invading the body politic that led to their association in Ottoman perception with unruly women against whom force had to be wielded in order to control them. Indeed, the image of the escaping Greek soldier in Figure 4 suggests violence, perhaps even rape. The Turkish soldier, his legs firmly on the ground, is pulling the Greek soldier's skirt from behind toward his lap; the vertical dagger and the shoe of the Turkish soldier insinuate the subsequent course of events. In Figure 5, the feminized Greek commander treacherously hides his dagger behind his back, in full view of the Allied Powers, thus making them complicit in the process. Yet it is the written message that reveals the intensity of the envisioned violence: The threat of the Turkish populace, as voiced by Karagöz, is that he "would take what is in the commanders' hand and brain him with it." Hence, these figures depict the enemy at home and outside as the immoral vixen who deserves the violence coming her way. Yet, in contrast to these negative portrayals, a different, very favorable image of women also emerged during the War of Independence: that of the stalwart mother who could do no wrong.

Ottoman Women as Stolid Mothers. During periods of war, the image of women was often used as a national symbol, as the guardian of the continuity and immutability of the nation and the embodiment of its respectability. This image of respectability also desexualized women and depicted them in an idealized form. It was no accident that in these periods of war, visions of nationhood were articulated that highlighted women "as important images of a national morality, born to nurture new relationships in the shifting terrain of the nation."[38] Women came to embody all the qualities that the masculine men who formed the nation did not possess: they were the nurturers, producers, and reproducers of the nation as mothers.[39] Yet one can argue that the nationalist discourse, by seeking to define the permanent features of national identity in these gendered terms, consigned women to the role of wives and mothers and forced these roles upon them with a sense of morality and integrity women could not escape.

In this vein, the Ottoman images of patriotic women took the form of the wise peasant mother or the traditionally dressed wife, all looking up to and nurturing the males and the nation. The cartoon in Figure 7, drawn on the eve of the Balkan wars on April 22, 1910, elaborates the constructive significance of gender in war. It depicts three women dressed in the traditional—unfashionable and non-

Figure 7. Cartoon drawn on the eve of the Balkan wars depicting two traditionally dressed women conversing with the mother of a child in the cradle wearing a fez with a crescent and carrying a rifle: "May God protect your child, sister, is it a boy or a girl?" "By God's grace, it is a soldier." Drawn by Pahatrekas (probably an Ottoman Greek) in *Kalem* 85 (22 April 1910): 5 (Çeviker 1988: 356).

decadent—garments, standing erect, self-contained, and self-confident and conversing with one another in a very supportive manner.
Inside the elaborate cradle lies the subject of the conversation, the
infant, who is holding a rifle and wearing a fez with a crescent to represent the Ottoman nation. The fact that the sex of the infant is not
known is not an issue in the cartoon since, as the mother notes,
what is significant at this time of limited humanpower is the birth
of another able-bodied soldier to fight the enemy. Even though the
cartoon suggests that gender constrictions are lifted during wars, it
is telling that it is not the three women who are mobilizing for war,
but the infant of unknown gender—a revealing slip that may illustrate the often invisible boundaries of patriarchy. The cartoon in Figure 8, drawn on December 27, 1922, immediately after the War of
Independence, depicts the patriotic mother as a peasant woman. Surrounded by her two sons, the soldiers who liberated Anatolia from

Figure 8. Cartoon drawn after the Turkish War of Independence upon the
delays faced in drawing up a peace treaty. The conversation, listened to on
the right by Hacivat and Karagöz, the two traditional shadow theater figures, takes place between "the woman of Anatolia" and Mustafa Kemal,
the commander of the Turkish forces, referred to as the "thunderbolt:"
"Dear Pasha, my sons (the soldiers) seized Smyrna in two weeks; these
European diplomats are such weird people, it has been a month and we
still could not seize a word from their mouths." The response by the pasha
is "Your brave sons are strong enough to make those diplomats sing like
nightingales, Grandma! Don't you worry, look I haven't taken off my stir-
rups yet!" Artist unknown, in *Karagöz* 1542 (27 December 1922): 1 (Çeviker
1991: 231).

the Greeks, she is older than the women in the previous figure as if years of fighting have matured her. Dressed in a peasant's costume, she also indirectly criticizes and delegitimizes the elitism of the imperial capital. Located in the background are, once more, the figures of Hacivat and Karagöz. Yet the most significant message of the figure in gender terms is that the peasant woman-mother is able to engage the leader of the Turkish forces in conversation as an equal, commenting on the current political situation.

This imagined gender equality of the Turkish nation-state did not, however, always translate successfully into action. The emerging Turkish nationalist movement promoted equality for women—in the words of its ideologue Ziya Gökalp, the new republic aimed at restoring the "Turkish feminism" and gender equality that had existed in pre-Islamic central Asian Turkic tribes—but what was promised and what was actually delivered were rather different. For instance, the 1923 Family Law turned out to be much more conservative in tenor than the 1917 one.[40] Even though the new woman of the republican era became an explicit symbol of the break with the past, and women's legal emancipation was part of a larger political project of nation-building and secularization, the Republic's rhetoric on gender equality did not translate into action for all women. Women's autonomous political initiatives, such as the petition to authorize the foundation of the Women's People's Party in June of 1923, were actively discouraged as "untimely and divisive"; women were asked to form an association instead.[41]

I conjecture that the persistent patriarchal patterns in society were not eliminated by the ambivalent narration of the nation; in the case of Turkish women, they produced limitations on actual participation in the public sphere. Indeed, the notion of citizenship, to which women now had to adhere, was based on the "fraternity of men," which severely hindered the possibility of the restitution of women's rights.[42] Thus, even though the image of the Ottoman women changed throughout the 1908–1923 period independent of their actual experience, and even though the periods of war and the emerging nation-state contained within their discourse ambivalent narration, this ambivalence did not result in the elimination of gender inequality. The ambivalent narration had briefly eroded the legitimacy of the empire and the institutions supporting it, and had helped to create a new political space that ultimately led to the emergence of the nation-state. Yet these new political structures were based on a male-centered conception of citizenship that marginalized women's participation. Women could have seized the same space to redefine their position in society, but the inherent male-centered structures of citizenship hindered, and still hinder, a complete acknowledgement of women's actual roles and the subsequent emancipation of women in all spheres of life.

NOTES

1. Quoted in Homi Bhabha, "Narrating the Nation," in J. Hutchinson and A. Smith, eds., *Nationalism* (London, 1994), 308–9.

2. For instance, Halide Edip became the highest-ranking woman in the Turkish army, a corporal; Asker (soldier) Saime also fought in the war and later served the Republic as a teacher; Kılavuz (navigator) Hatice led the occupying French forces to an ambush; Tayyar Rahmiye commanded a military detachment against a French garrison and was martyred in the ensuing successful siege; Kara Fatma fought on many fronts throughout Anatolia; and Binbaşı (Major) Ayşe joined the Anatolian forces after the death of her husband at the Caucasian front, formed and equipped a band of brigands, and engaged in guerilla activity against the Allied forces. Many other women supported the War of Independence as they harbored nationalist fugitives, tilled the lands for provisions for the soldiers, and manufactured and transported ammunition to the battlefield. See Ayşegül Yaraman-Başbuğu, *Elinin Hamuruyla Özgürlük* (Turkish women's search for freedom) (Istanbul, 1992), 121–27; Şefika Kurnaz, *Cumhuriyet Öncesinde Türk Kadını (1839–1923)* (Turkish women before the Republic, 1839–1923) (Ankara, 1991), 121–24.

3. This study is the first to focus on Ottoman women's mobilization; the material presented here likewise represents the first systematic attempt to research existing sources in order to generate information on women's participation in society during this period.

4. The issue of the Western-style education of Ottoman women had come to the forefront in the mid-nineteenth century following political reforms; schools were opened to educate women as future teachers. Legal reforms, including the abolition of slavery and concubinage, equal inheritance rights, and the ability to marry foreign men were introduced at the same time. Many women's journals and associations were also founded by women during this period. See Kurnaz, *Cumhuriyet Öncesinde*, 4–34, 78–95. See also Serpil Çakır, *Osmanlı Kadın Hareketi* (Ottoman women's movement) (Istanbul, 1993), 22–78; Yaraman-Başbuğu, *Elinin Hamuruyla Özgürlük*, 93–158.

5. Kurnaz, *Cumhuriyet Öncesinde*, 81.

6. Women's efforts toward establishing societies and founding journals continued until the end of the war. During the last year of World War I, women founded three organizations: the Women's Society for Music Appreciation (*Musiki Muhibbi Hanımlar Cemiyeti*), the Hearth for Sewing (*Biçki Yurdu*) to train women in sewing skills, and the Society of the Alumna of the Women's College (*İnas Darülfünunu Mezuneleri Cemiyeti*) to organize conferences and seminars on topics pertaining to women. During the same

period, twenty-one women's journals established at the capital focused exclusively on issues concerning women and ranging from the pedagogic to the practical. See Çakır, *Osmanlı Kadın Hareketi*; Aynur Demirdirek, *Osmanlı Kadınlarının Hayat Hakkı. Arayışının bir Hikayesi* (A story of the Ottoman women's search for Rights) (Istanbul, 1993); Deniz Kandiyoti, "End of Empire: Islam, Nationalism and Women in Turkey," in idem, ed., *Women, Islam and the State* (Philadelphia, 1991), 26–27. It is interesting to note that these journals also provided information on the women's suffrage movements in England, stating that these movements "ought to be taken as role models for the Ottoman women." Demirdirek, *Osmanlı*, 86.

7. Yaraman-Başbuğu, *Elinin Hamuruyla Özgürlük*, 98.

8. The scope of this law in particular, and the Ottoman state policy with respect to the possible mobilization or conscription of laborers in general, have not yet been studied. See Kandiyoti, "End of Empire," 30–31.

9. Kurnaz, *Cumhuriyet*, 96–97. For the similar experience of French and British women during and after the war, see Laura Lee Downs, *Manufacturing Inequality: Gender Division in the French and British Metal-Working Industries, 1914–1939* (Ithaca, 1995).

10. Kurnaz, *Cumhuriyet*, 101–103.

11. Yaraman-Başbuğu, *Elinin Hamuruyla Özgürlük*, 99. In the capital, women's participation in the workforce continued sporadically; in 1920, there were eight women employed in banks, two in the municipal utility company, and forty-eight in the telephone company in the Ottoman capital. See Kurnaz, *Cumhuriyet*, 96–97.

12. Ibid., 109.

13. Ibid., 115–20.

14. Bekir Sıtkı Baykal, *Milli Mücadele'de Kadınları Müdafaa-i Vatan Cemiyeti* (The Anatolian Women's National Defense Organization during the War of Independence) (Ankara, 1986).

15. Yaraman-Başbuğu, *Elinin Hamuruyla Özgürlük*, 120.

16. Baykal, *Milli Mücadele'de*, 30–33.

17. For more information on the history of the development of political cartoons in Europe, see Arthur Bartlett Maurice and F. T. Cooper, *The History of the Nineteenth Century in Caricature* (New York, 1970); Charles Press, *The Political Cartoon* (Rutherford, NJ, 1981); Richard Godfrey, *English Caricature, 1620 to the Present* (London, 1984); Roy Porter, "Seeing the Past," *Past and Present* 118 (1988): 186–205; and Alice Sheppard, *Cartooning for Suffrage* (Albuquerque, 1994). For the employment of cartoons during World War I in Europe, see Gabriel P. Weisberg, "Propaganda as Art: The Dreyfus Affair as Popular Exhibition," *Arts Magazine* 62, no. 4 (1987): 36–41; William Coupe, "German Cartoons of the First World War," *History Today* 42 (1992): 23–31; Eberhard Demm, "Propaganda and Caricature in the First World War," *Journal of Contemporary History* 28 (1993): 163–92; Norman L. Kleeblatt, "Merde! The Caricatural Attack against Emile Zola," *Art Journal* 52, no. 3 (1993), 54–58; and Sherwin Simmons, "War, Revolution, and the Transformation of the German Humor Magazine," ibid. 52, no. 1 (1993): 46–54.

18. Turgut Çeviker, *Gelişim Sürecinde Türk Karikatürü: Tanzimat Dönemi 1867–78 ve İstibdat Dönemi 1878–1908* (The evolution of Turkish caricature: The Reform, 1867–78, and Autocracy, 1878–1908, periods) (Istanbul, 1986) (Hereafter Çeviker 1986), 17, 61; idem, *Gelişim Sürecinde Türk Karikatürü: Meşrutiyet Dönemi 1908–1918* (The Evolution of Turkish caricature: The Constitutional period, 1908–1918) (Istanbul, 1988) (hereafter Çeviker 1988), 37, 101; Palmira Brummet, "New Woman or Old Nag: Images of Women in the Ottoman Cartoon Space" (working paper, 1994), 4–5; and idem, "Image and Imperialism in the Ottoman Revolutionary Press" (book manuscript, 1995), 16, 27.

19. Çeviker 1988, 17, 50, 61–64. During this period, many caricaturists tried to avoid censorship by creative measures, such as sending erasable drawings for approval and then replacing them with more politically provocative material. See Çeviker, *Gelişim Sürecinde Türk Karikatürü: Kurtuluş Savaşı Dönemi 1918–1923* (The Evolution of Turkish caricature: The period of the War of Independence, 1918–1923) (Istanbul, 1991) (hereafter Çeviker 1991), 58–59.

20. The replacement of a forbidden caricature with a mostly blank page, often accompanied by a denunciation of the government's action and sometimes a detailed written description of the banned drawing, was the most frequent technique of resistance employed in nineteenth-century France; the other was the publication of the obviously mutilated caricature with blank spaces for the parts that had been censored. See Robert Justin Goldstein, "The Debate over the Censorship of Caricature in Nineteenth-Century France," *Art Journal* 48, no. 1 (1989): 15.

21. Çeviker 1991, 27–28.

22. Köroğlu was a folk hero who fought successfully to protect the rights of the downtrodden against powerful oppressors. His exploits were immortalized in many songs and poems that were often recited throughout the empire by minstrels.

23. Münif Fehim, a caricaturist and painter whose life spanned the transformation from empire to nation, was renowned for employing contemporary art techniques to depict historical themes and motifs. A similar development is found in the history of Chinese political cartoons. It was argued that "to create a genuine national art, artists must attempt to adopt the Western use of perspective and of human anatomy into Chinese traditional ink-and-brush painting." See Chang-Tai Hung, "The Fuming Image: Cartoons and Public Opinion in Late Republican China," *Comparative Studies in Society and History* 36, no. 1 (1994): 134.

24. George L. Mosse, *Nationalism and Sexuality: Respectability and Abnormal Sexuality in Modern Europe* (New York, 1985), 15.

25. Palmira Brummet, "Imagined Communities and Invented Traditions in the Late Ottoman Empire" (working paper, 1993), 6.

26. For instance, female representations were used in American World War I propaganda both "as Protecting Angel standing for the conventional feminine values of nurturance and the home, i.e., for the preservation of cherished traditions," and "as Militant Victory as the winged conqueror and

Amazon warrior, reflecting the unrelenting and compelling masculine forces of progress, expansionism, and domination, i.e., a female transcending the mortal and thereby unleashing her superhuman power." Sheppard, *Cartooning for Suffrage*, 58. According to Carl Jung, the polarization by men of women's characteristics into the good/bad dichotomy lies in the male experience of the female as the Good Mother during his infancy and the devouring Great Mother during his youth; according to Freud, it reflects men's unconscious fears of their own drives and weaknesses. Ibid., 58–59, 62.

27. Marina Warner, *Monuments and Maidens: The Allegory of the Female Form* (New York, 1985), xx.

28. This set of clothing was supposed to approximate the outfit worn indoors by Ottoman women in general. Still, the flowing gauze shirts, silk scarves, and broadcloth pants that cartoonists draw portray the dress of urban, middle-class Ottoman women, and not of the much coarser, much repaired outfits of their peasant sisters.

29. Brummet, "New Woman or Old Nag," 6.

30. Sheppard, *Cartooning for Suffrage*, 57.

31. R. Radhakrishnan, "Nationalism, Gender, and the Narrative of Identity," in A. Parker et al., eds., *Nationalisms and Sexualities* (New York, 1992), 86.

32. These discrepancies are noteworthy since they may indicate the consequences of Ottoman decontextualization: European fashion at the time did not include a clearly drawn waistline or such a long hemline. Ottoman cartoonists thus seem to have paid little attention to the finer details of European fashion.

33. Partha Chatterjee, "National History and Its Exclusions," in Hutchinson and Smith, eds., *Nationalism*, 209.

34. Vera Dumesnil, *İşgal İstanbul'u* (Istanbul under siege) (Istanbul, 1993), 12, 82, 93–94.

35. Ibid., 60–61.

36. This sexuality was often portrayed as ambiguous and fickle, in order to justify men's continuing patriarchal control; along with the emergence of both the American and British women's rights movements, negative visual images of women activists began to appear in the popular press, often showing them as "aggressive, overbearing shrews who neglected their children and forced their menfolks into domestic drudgery." Elisabeth Israels Perry, "Image, Rhetoric, and the Historical Memory of Women," in Sheppard, *Cartooning for Suffrage*, 3. The women in the imperial capital had also been satirized on other occasions. Cartoons satirizing their sense of fashion had accompanied the westernization process, often commenting on the new straight posture gained by rigid corsets, the capes that replaced the traditional outer clothing that covered them completely, and the large underskirts that doubled the circumference of a woman's skirt. See Nora Şeni, "Fashion and Women's Clothing in Constantinople as Depicted in Late Nineteenth-Century Cartoons" (in Turkish), in Ş. Tekeli, ed., *1980'ler Türkiye'sinde Kadın* (Women in Turkey of the 1980s) (Istanbul, 1990), 43–67.

37. Susan M. Morrison, "The Feminization of the German Democratic Republic in Political Cartoons, 1989–90," *Journal of Political Culture* 21, no. 1 (1992): 35–51. See Çeviker 1991, 23;

38. Martha Lampland, "Family Portraits: Gendered Images of the Nation in Nineteenth-Century Hungary," *East European Politics and Societies* 8, no. 2 (1994): 288.

39. Nationalism "has typically sprung from masculinized memory, masculinized humiliation and masculinized hope." Cynthia Enloe, *Bananas, Beaches and Bases: Making Feminist Sense of International Politics* (London, 1989), 44.

40. Kandiyoti, "End of Empire," 34–38.

41. Ibid., 41. See also Milüfer Göle, *Modern Mahrem* (The forbidden modern) (Istanbul, 1992).

42. Carol Pateman, *The Sexual Contract* (Cambridge, 1988). This follows from the proposition that only when women are seen as both producers and reproducers of a nation can they gain equal footing with men. See Nira Yuval-Davis, "Gender and Nation," *Gender and Ethnic Studies* 16, no. 4 (1993): 627.

Men and Soldiers

British Conscripts, Concepts of Masculinity, and the Great War

Ilana R. Bet-El

The Deepest part of a man is his sense of essential truth, essential honour, essential justice. This deepest self makes him abide by his own feelings, come what may. It is not sentimentalism. It is just the male human creature, the thought-adventurer, driven to earth.

—D. H. Lawrence, *Kangaroo*

I'm asleep at present—I've signed on to be & I'm not allowed to be anything else. I sit in clubs & estaminets with my own poor uniformed self in hundreds. We say & do the same silly things. We've got to.[1]

On July 1, 1991, the seventy-fifth anniversary of the Battle of the Somme, the British newspaper *Independent on Sunday* carried a large photograph of an Allied war cemetery near a battlefield in northern France. The brief text accompanying the picture summarized the event as "one of the most traumatic battles of the First World War," in which by the end of the first day "20,000 British volunteers were dead and 40,000 wounded"—not men, not soldiers, but *volunteers*. This statement reiterated in the bluntest possible manner one of the most enduring myths of the Great War: the Myth of the Volunteer, which maintains that all British soldiers who participated in that war were volunteers.[2]

According to this myth, the British soldier in the Great War was a man who enlisted in a spirit of intense patriotism: a brave knight who took himself off on a crusade of chivalry and sacrifice; who fought for liberty and the innocent population of women he left behind in "Good Old Blighty." Ultimately it is this glorious image of the heroic volunteer—a creation of the earliest days of the war—that has survived in the national culture to this day.[3] However, it is an image that is confounded by fact: fifteen months of voluntarism gave way to three years of conscription, which commenced in January of 1916, and out of the five million wartime enlistments in Britain, over half were conscripts.[4] Indeed, by the Allied summer advance of 1918, a majority of the men fighting in the British Army were conscripts, and it was this force that won the war. Yet these men have been excluded from the image of the heroic British soldier and subsumed within the Myth of the Volunteer, which has become part of the collective British memory.

British civilians may have constructed fantasies about the glories of military heroism in the Great War, but the reality of military endeavor remained far removed from them—as did the reality of daily soldiering. Within the public arena therefore, the terms "volunteer," "conscript," and "hero" expressed civilian rather than military conceptions. Indeed, it is the contention of this essay that the image of the Great War soldiers, both during the war and in subsequent years, originated not in the experience of battle, but rather in accordance with a particular public construction of masculinity that was based upon a series of equations: a real man = a patriot = a volunteer = a soldier. In other words, it was the rigid correlation between patriotism and voluntarism that excluded the conscripts from the prevailing imagery of both masculinity and soldiering—though, as will be shown, there is no evidence to suggest that conscripts were unpatriotic—and also redefined the soldier, a traditional male role common to all societies, as a volunteer. Nonetheless, conscripts *were* soldiers and men, and as such they undoubtedly functioned within a certain construction of masculinity, albeit one that differed from the public construction of the gender.[5] While conscripts were not necessarily devoid of ideology, it did not appear to constitute a major component of their conception of their maleness. Instead, it was survival—both physical and emotional—that became the central tenet of their being as both men and soldiers. What British civilians saw, however, was only the act of volunteering or the abstention from it, and it was in the public domain that the demarcation was made between volunteers and conscripts, and the image of the Great War soldier was determined.

The power of public opinion, and the awareness of failing to conform to it, may be gauged by the conscripts' own failure to participate in creating the imagery of the war. Very few conscripts contributed to the flood of war memoirs and autobiographical novels that appeared from the late 1920s and that were immensely influential in establishing the imagery of the Great War and its soldiers within the postwar collective memory.[6] Although in itself the reticence of such a large population gives pause for thought, the issue has never come under consideration. Indeed, the conscripts have been consistently ignored in historiography, except for the minority of approximately 16,500 Conscientious Objectors among them who have been widely discussed. By contrast, the regular soldiers and the volunteers have been thoroughly documented throughout the past eighty years.[7] Moreover, scholarship in recent decades, which has focused on the literary output of the war—the vast majority of which was written by volunteers—has also contributed to enhancing the image of the volunteer as the representative soldier of the war. The most outstanding and influential examples of this trend are the works of Paul Fussell, Eric J. Leed, and George Mosse, who employ the equation of soldier and volunteer not only as a premise of their studies, but also as a tenet in their analyses of the construction—and crisis—of masculinity during the war. All three focus upon the disillusionment of the volunteers when confronted with the harsh reality of war and the compensation they sought in male comradeship on the front line, elevated to concepts of homoeroticism verging upon homosexuality.[8]

Feminist scholarship has also largely accepted the equation of volunteer and soldier, and the ensuing construction of masculinity, in its discussions of both women and men.[9] Sandra M. Gilbert has postulated that the liberation of women during the war, along with the crisis of masculinity, emerged from the premise of the volunteer in search of fulfilled manhood: "Paradoxically, in fact, the war to which so many men had gone in hope of becoming heroes ended up emasculating them." She then goes on to quote Eric J. Leed, who suggests that the symptoms of shell shock may be compared to those of hysterical disorders normally attributed to women. Building upon these theses, Elaine Showalter, in her discussion of male hysteria, argues that shell shock was a form of protest against prevalent notions of male heroism and masculinity. Hence the "most masculine of enterprises," the Great War, the "apocalypse of masculism" feminized its conscripts by taking away their sense of control.[10]

Most conscripts, however, like the majority of soldiers in the ranks, were not public school boys, even though they may have been raised no less within the Victorian and resultant Edwardian images of masculinity and heroism. Moreover, within public cognizance, conscripts were excluded from these images by definition: since volunteering was probably the most publicly gendering activity a man could undertake, the failure to volunteer was a stigma the conscript carried, regardless of his subsequent military service and the dangers he faced or overcame.

I would suggest that conscripts experienced a distinct crisis of masculinity as a result of their own construction of gender. This was both a *public* crisis of masculinity, which arose from their deviation from the socially accepted construction of the gender; and a *personal* crisis of survival, engendered not by a shattered heroic male ideology, but by the harsh realities of life and death on the front line for which they were ill-equipped, both mentally and physically. This essay draws on a large unpublished collection of personal papers written by conscripts (such as diaries, letters, and accounts) and a wide selection of recruiting posters and contemporary journalism to examine these soldiers as men trapped in a double bind of image and reality, within which they confronted their own masculinity.

THE HEROIC CONSTRUCTION OF MASCULINITY

Recruiting stations were probably the most vital locations in wartime Britain, in which the public status of men was decided, and the image of the soldier was established. It was there that men exhibited their self-motivation, which was the issue underlying any perceived difference between volunteers and conscripts, the dividing line between activity and passivity. The volunteer was deemed active by virtue of his own positive motivation for the sake of the ideological goal of victory, and thus he was portrayed in the wartime public arena: "Go to the nearest Post Office or Labour Exchange. There you will get the address of the nearest Recruiting Office, where you can enlist."[11] The conscript, on the other hand, was the passive subject of a bureaucratic act. The Military Service Acts, which regulated conscription made this situation very clear: the applicable groups of "male British subjects" were "deemed as from the appointed date to have been enlisted in His Majesty's regular forces for general service with the Colours or in the Reserve for the Period of the war, and have been forthwith transferred to the Reserve."[12] The conscript's subsequent appearance at a recruiting station on a given date would thus be the result of a summons, a "call-up" notice, rather than any individual initiative.

On the level of personal experience, there was also a clear difference between volunteers and conscripts. A man who volunteered in September of 1914 described the process that led to his enlistment as follows: upon seeing ambulances full of wounded men, "I determined to join up that same evening. I went home, had a hasty meal, smartened up and duly presented myself at the HQ of the 24th London Regiment." In marked contrast is the diary entry of a man conscripted in February 1917: "Received calling up notice from Croydon Recruiting Office." The element of passivity is striking in another account: "In the December of the year 1916, I reached the age of 18. In the following March I was duly enlisted."[13]

Just as volunteers were not always motivated by altruistic patriotism, so conscripts did not necessarily lack motivation. Men volunteered for a variety of reasons, ranging from concepts of patriotism and duty to social pressures and economic need, as apparent even among the better-known volunteers.[14] C. E. Carrington (a.k.a. Charles Edmonds), for example, stated that he enlisted "when the issues were clear, when men had no doubts about the duty that lay before them." Robert Graves was clearly impelled to volunteer by the force of ideology: "I was outraged to read of the Germans' cynical violation of Belgian neutrality." Yet at the same time, he also acknowledged the more personal, pragmatic consideration of delaying his entrance to Oxford, which he dreaded. The poet Isaac Rosenberg clearly had no interest in volunteering: "I feel about it [enlisting] that more men means more war,—besides the immorality of joining with no patriotic convictions." Yet only weeks after writing those words, Rosenberg enlisted in October of 1915: "I could not get the work I thought I might so I have joined this Bantam Battalion."[15]

The same ambivalence was apparent also among conscripts. Thus Alfred M. Hale, a minor composer, exemplified the "classic" conscript in his lack of motivation. He awaited the "dreaded calling-up notice" after the passing of the Military Service Acts; and after attempting to fight it, and failing, decided to "go to the recruiting office next morning and give myself up, as it were, then and there." Another conscript, Harry Adams, did not necessarily lack positive motivation when he was conscripted, being a patriotic young man, but as he was also deeply religious, fighting "had always been abhorrent to me . . . [and] it was with very mixed feelings that I left the homestead to join the army." By contrast, A. J. Abraham actively wanted to enlist. He, too, was called up in 1917, but his parents arranged for him to be placed in a reserve occupation in order to keep him out of the army. However, as he "was not willing to hide behind this," he resigned his job and went to the local recruiting office. "There I explained my position to an old sergeant, who gave me a peculiar look and said he would see if something could be arranged for me." Within days he was enlisted in an infantry unit.[16]

The public perception of men who presented themselves at the recruiting stations was reinforced by the conscription legislation of 1916. Before that date, they were volunteers; after it, conscripts. In the eyes of civilians, far removed from the battlefield, it was the method by which a civilian was transformed into a soldier that defined him as either masculine hero or failed man. The volunteer not only actively professed a willingness to become a soldier, an acknowledged masculine role that encompassed a contextual world of sacrifice, adventure, and chivalry, but also expressed his commitment to the nation and sanctioned the commonly approved cause of war, thereby ennobling his act. In other words, by virtue of this single public act of self-motivation, the volunteer became equated with an ideal of masculinity and elevated to the status of hero—regardless of any subsequent military performance in the army. Within such a construction, achievement in battle, far from the public gaze, was of no importance; but this also implied that one who did not volunteer would be denied the public definitions of masculinity and heroism. A conscript was such an individual.

This construction was based upon the two interconnected concepts of soldiering and masculinity that had evolved throughout the nineteenth century. But whereas the latter was rooted in the reality of middle-class life and slowly became imposed upon ever-widening social strata, images of soldiering were based largely upon ignorance. The absence of any sustained interaction between the army and civilians, such as conscription, engendered an artificial notion of soldiering in the minds of the vast majority of British people. While this distance from the army did not contradict the existence of militarism in various forms within civilian society or the creation of part-time or quasi-military organizations such as the Volunteer Force or the Boys' Brigade,[17] it was a sanitized and carefully staged image of the army that was observed and eagerly consumed by civilians, whether in glamorous state-sponsored parades and military spectacles or in the theater, popular songs, magazines, and books. The army thus acquired a very alluring image, as did the soldier who was endowed with a certain glamour, infused with civilian notions detached from the reality of warfare.[18] Indeed, wars were largely deemed to be events enacted by British soldiers far from civilian eyes, or as John Galsworthy put it, the "Boer wars, and all those other little wars, Ashanti, Afghan, Soudan, expeditionary adventures, professional affairs far away."[19]

Yet these distant wars also assumed growing importance as national and cultural focal points, re-created for popular consumption through the various media. And just as a glittering exterior image of the army was created, so war became for many a glorious event in which the soldier in action was imbued with concepts such as adventure, bravery, sacrifice, and heroism.[20] These were notions adopted from the medieval code of chivalry, which gained new currency in the nineteenth century and laid great emphasis upon honor, justice, duty, personal commitment, and fighting: A knight fought a duel or went into battle in the name of a sacred, just cause, and in so doing exhibited his nobility of spirit—regardless of the outcome of his endeavor. The act itself was sanctified, often in isolation from the context in which it was performed.[21] The renowned Charge of the Light Brigade is an excellent case in point: only 673 men took part in a badly planned attack, of whom 157 were killed—out of a total of twenty thousand war dead. By contrast, the Heavy Brigade's much more successful charge on the same day was deleted from the collective memory: as a well-planned and -executed battle between evenly matched forces, it evidently did not constitute a knightly endeavor.

The knightly ethos served not only to create military legend, but also to promote middle-class ideals of masculinity, within all ranks of society, as derivatives of heroic endeavor, duty, patriotism, physical strength, and strict morality. According to Samuel Smiles's *Self Help* (1859), which had sold 250,000 copies by the turn of the century, "the glory of manly character" depended upon the "honest and upright performance of individual duty," under the premise that "life, too, is 'a soldier's battle'," while national decay resulted from "individual idleness, selfishness and vice."[22] Lord Baden-Powell, the founder of the Boy Scouts Movement, promoted a similar philosophy of masculinity in his *Scouting for Boys* (1908). Scouts were defined as "strong and plucky, ready to face danger . . . accustomed to take their lives in their hands, and to risk them without hesitation if they can help their country by so doing."[23] Under a section titled "Chivalry," three chapters dwelt upon such subjects as the medieval code of knights, duty, and religion. Alongside the general moralizing tone of the work, the last chapters were specifically devoted to physical endurance as dependent upon an upright character. In addition to countering the masculine image of smoking and drinking, the author deemed masturbation the most ruinous vice, which "tends to lower both health and spirits. . . . if you have any manliness in you, you will throw off such temptation at once."[24]

This linkage among the ideas of nation, masculinity, and morality, in its bourgeois guise of respectability, was used by the middle classes to transform a socioreligious issue into one of national strength, based on the notion that all impurity, both private and public, had to be rooted out.[25] To this end, the sexuality of both genders became the focus of interest, in keeping with emerging notions of respectability as the defining framework of both private and public spheres.[26] The family was promoted as the imperative social unit for the formation and preservation of ideal gender constructions, according to which physical and moral strength and self-restraint were seen as the bases of masculinity. The vices deemed most ruinous to the image of moral masculinity were, of course, those of the flesh: a real man was one who curbed his desires regarding prostitutes and masturbation, whilst the laws governing both prostitution and homosexuality were tightened a number of times.[27] Much effort was invested throughout the nineteenth century in educating boys and young men to these traits of gender, whether through formal schooling or, as in the case of the lower classes, through religious organizations and voluntary associations such as the YMCA. Voluntarism was therefore central to the concept of Victorian and Edwardian morality, as an ethos boys imbibed not only within the masculine image of chivalry, but also as a socioreligious tenet.[28]

This concept of morality wrought a certain stratification—or hierarchy—within the notion of respectable masculinity. Pride of place was occupied by the married man, not only because of the mantle of family responsibility he assumed, but also because the status implied regulated and approved sexual activity. He was closely followed by the industrious Christian bachelor and the boy who embodied all the virtues of the scout. Beneath these was the idle male of lax morality; or, as Baden-Powell told a youthful audience, "wishy-washy slackers without any go or patriotism in them."[29] And finally there was the homosexual, who was beyond the normal social conceptions of masculinity, an "other" who served, in his publicly charted image of disgrace, as a caution to the overall male population.[30]

THE WARTIME CONSTRUCTION OF MASCULINITY: THE VOLUNTEER

It took the Great War to put the image of masculinity, with its strict moral stratification, to the service of the state. The outbreak of hostilities was promoted as the long-awaited opportunity to realize all the concepts imposed upon the glittering façades of the army and the soldier, as the embodiment of national strength and manhood. It was now up to the men of the nation to seize the opportunity and prove themselves equal to it: to volunteer. And even if, as noted above, men volunteered for a variety of reasons, the overriding imagery of fulfilled masculinity and citizenship encompassed them from the moment they presented themselves at a recruiting station; for this was how their personal act was daily defined by the recruiting propaganda, at recruiting rallies, on stage and screen and, above all, in millions of posters, newspapers, magazines, pamphlets, and postcards.[31]

The posters probably made the greatest impact of the campaign, with slogans such as "Your Country Needs You!" and "Daddy, What Did You Do in the War?" plastered over every conceivable surface in the land. However, while such messages obviously inspired guilt and a sense of duty, a close examination of the 160 posters issued by the Parliamentary Recruiting Committee (PRC) reveals that they were the outcome of a structured campaign that promoted volunteering as a cause in itself, no less than recruitment.[32] The parameters within which both issues were defined corresponded almost exactly to those by which the meaning of masculinity had been defined and stratified in the decades before the war. Thus, the most fundamental theme of the PRC recruiting posters was the equation of the soldier with masculinity. However, the posters re-created this equation by emphasizing two further elements: the individual as moral subject, and the romantic civilian conception of the masculine ethos. The posters presented not the battlefield, or even the army, but the image of the male and the soldier. The recruiting campaign subtly and inextricably combined these two factors into a single message, which differentiated between a male and a man, with only one route of transformation from the former into the latter: If one was born a male, one became a soldier, and one became a soldier only by volunteering.

On a depictive level, this message was conveyed by presenting the war as a moral event—with slogans such as "Can Britons Stand By While Germany Crushes an Innocent People?" "Take Up the Sword of Justice" and "Avenge This Devil's Work"—and also as an event collectively sanctioned by state and society: "Thousands Have Answered the Nation's Call," "Make Us As Proud of You As We Are of Him!"[33] The construction of femininity is also of interest in this context: on the one hand, women were presented as the embodiment of patriotism, whose role was to send men out to war: "Women of Britain Say - 'Go'!" "Go! It's Your Duty Lad";[34] but on the other hand, and within the same construction, women were also portrayed as the obstacle to men in their search for true masculine fulfillment: "Some of your men folk are holding back on your account. Won't you prove your love for your country by persuading them to go?"; "When the war is over and someone asks your husband or your son what he did in the Great War, is he to hang his head because you would not let him go? Won't you help and send a man to join the army today?"[35] The underlying assumption in these messages was that men were by nature volunteers according to their own conception of masculinity, inhibited only by their sense of moral responsibility to their dependants. These posters thus placed the moral commitment to nation above the moral commitment to family by making the latter dependent on the former: "Do you realise that the safety of your home and children depends on our getting more men <u>NOW</u>?"[36]

Concepts of chivalry were evoked by appealing to the image of women and children as defenseless targets, with constant references to duty, honor, and noble conduct: "Your rights of citizenship give you the privilege of joining your fellows in the defence of your Honour and your Homes"; "Show Your Appreciation by Following Their [the volunteers'] Noble Example."[37] Moreover, by implying that their targeted audience was potentially in opposition to the moral values they urged, these posters challenged the moral character of each man: "There Are Three Types of Men: Those who hear the call and Obey, Those who Delay, and—The Others. To which do you belong?" "Be honest with yourself. Be certain that your so-called reason is not a selfish excuse."[38] The appeal to enlist—as a volunteer—was thus endowed with moral significance: the recruiting posters shifted the emphasis of the campaign from the soldier needed for war, to the narrow act of enlistment—from the purpose of the campaign to the initial point of transformation from civilian into soldier. As a result, the traditional masculine role of soldier-as-warrior came to be redefined as soldier-as-volunteer. The thrust of the PRC posters evolved into a campaign against those men who did not voluntarily enlist, establishing them in the public eye as lacking both morality and masculinity: "Every Fit Briton Should Join Our Brave Men at the Front"; "Does the call of Duty find no response in you until reinforced—let us say superseded—by the call of compulsion?"[39]

It was the repetition of these messages over fifteen months on millions of posters that left the conscripts who enlisted after the campaign bereft of public support in their transformation into soldiers. This image of the volunteer was further enhanced by the commemorative efforts surrounding the fallen, mostly by the upper classes of society. Death gave the final seal to the notion of supreme, self-sacrificing heroism exhibited by young, single, upper-class knights, best embodied in one such as the poet Rupert Brooke, but reflected also in many memorial tributes to soldiers throughout the land. A pamphlet in memorium of a Lt. Warneford, aged twenty-three, for example, published by a little-known organization called "The Patriot's League," chronicled his life and bravery, followed by a specially composed poem:

WHAT DID HE DO? Why, the whole world knows
    The foeman he fought alone,
And to save the lives of children and wives
    He gallantly risked his own.

Since Cressy the blood has been just the same
    And that is the reason why
THIS NATION LIVES ON—for her gallant sons
In a cause that is JUST WILL DIE![40]

If any doubt still existed as to the moral and masculine superiority of the volunteer over the conscript, the last months of the campaign were used to quash them systematically: "Do not force your country to force you to fight, but come of your own free will."[41] This poster was issued during the Derby Scheme, which commenced in October 1915 and in which men were canvassed in their homes as to their willingness to enlist—a system that basically undermined the premise of volunteering as a self-motivated act. However, the Scheme was promoted as a last chance for voluntarism as the sole honorable option: "Will You March Too or Wait Till March 2?"—the date on which the January 1916 Conscription Bill was to be enforced; "The new Military Service Bill need not apply to you if you ENLIST NOW under the Group System" promoted by the Derby Scheme; "Your duty is to fight the COMMON FOE and to get your comrades to join you."[42] The implication was clear: there was another foe, within British society, that did not do its duty: the non-volunteer, who very shortly was to become the conscript. A number of posters presented this message in slogans such as "Forward!" and "An Appeal To You!" which directly targeted the civilian onlooker.[43] "Are You In This?" portrayed a young civilian, hands in pockets, on the side of the enemy and in opposition to symbolic figures representing the national effort. This poster, which was conceived and drawn by Baden-Powell, reflected the definition of immoral and unmasculine young men he had made in a prewar speech, as "loafing about with your hands in your pockets, doing nothing to keep it [the Empire] up."[44]

Hence not only the imagery, but also the stratification, of masculinity within the prewar moral code was expressed and reinforced in the wartime drive for volunteers and used to isolate the non-volunteers. Lord Derby himself presented the Derby Scheme as resting entirely upon the premise of morality:

I believe the moral effect of showing to our enemies that England is perfectly determined by the voluntary method to put into the field all that could be got by the compulsory method will be such that it will bring the war to a far quicker conclusion."[45]

However, since such a sweeping condemnation of non-volunteers threatened to stigmatize a large number of men—precisely those who were earmarked for conscription—the moral stratification of masculinity was again invoked to reduce the size of the scorned population. Thus the married non-volunteers were set apart from the unmarried through the acknowledgment of family responsibility. This hierarchy was reflected both in the Derby Scheme, which promised to take single men first, and in the public discourse of the period. *The Times*, for example, published many letters concerning the plight of the "young professional married man who is entirely dependent for the support of himself and his family upon what he can earn by his own personal exertions." Pointing out that the separation allowances would be totally insufficient for such men, this letter asked: "Are they unpatriotic if they say 'No'? Have they no right to expect that the unmarried men with no responsibilities should be taken first?" The populist *Daily Mail* highlighted this issue with screaming headlines such as, "Meanwhile the single slackers wait to be fetched," and articles stating that "there are still in the London area alone 750,000 young unmarried men."[46]

The recruiting campaign thus sanctified the prewar moral hierarchy of masculinity: At the top were the married volunteers—men who resolved the moral conflict between duty to family and duty to nation entirely through their own self-will. They shared pride of place with the single volunteers, endowed with the idealized image of masculinity coupled with noble youth. Beneath these two came the married non-volunteers—men deemed to have self-motivation, yet lacking the salient tenet of commitment to nation in their own construction of masculinity. And finally, there were the young, single non-volunteers: the despised "other," perceived as neither moral nor masculine, or, as *The Cornish Post and Mining News* from November 11, 1915 put it, the men who "remained impervious and cold" to the recruiter, who had appealed "to your cupidity, your patriotism, your manhood and your selfishness, all with small success."

THE CONSCRIPT AS SOLDIER

The conscripts were thus stigmatized and isolated, as social deviants from the combined ideals of masculinity and nation. In the words of one young conscript: "things started to get awkward, women and girls were handing out white feathers, even the girls in the store were looking a little askance at me."[47] If, as we have seen, volunteers enlisted out of a desire to realize accepted images of the heroic soldier, conscripts were faced with the task of constructing themselves as soldiers and as men in defiance of preconceived images. Indeed, this may have been to their advantage since it meant that their self-perception as soldiers was founded in reality rather than in abstract notions. While all soldiers had to contend with the problem of survival on the front line, volunteers had the additional problem of correlating their actual experience as soldiers with their shattered masculine preconceptions of soldiering.

Indeed, in the reality of army life, there was no discrimination between volunteers and conscripts: both encountered the army's fundamental demands for physical ability and discipline in the basic training they underwent before being sent out to fight. Discipline essentially nullified the issue of motivation, which had been central to the recruitment campaign and sanctified by civilians, while the only criteria deemed important in the line were the abilities to operate in combat and survive life in the trenches—as an officer serving in the Somme sector late in 1916 dispassionately observed:

> Whether Volunteers, Derbyites or Conscripts, the average physique was good enough, but the total included an astonishing number of men whose narrow or misshapen chests, and other deformities or defects, unfitted them to stay the more exacting requirements of service in the field. . . . Route marching, not routine tours of trench duty, made recurring casualties of these men.[48]

It was sheer physical ability, not motivation, that was the most salient aspect of any military conception of masculinity, a fact well reflected in the writings of conscripts who found themselves physically transformed by their basic training: "My girl and the folks at home were surprised how I had filled out, put on weight and looked disgustingly fit and well."[49] This sentiment was expressed in all the types of writings examined here, which highlights both its importance to the conscripts themselves, as well as their general physical condition as a population.[50]

Physical ability may also have been reflected in the sexual activity of these men. Yet this issue cannot be easily gauged, since it would not be deemed an acceptable subject either to write home about or to recall in a memoir written for an audience of strangers. Such references were made only during the period of training, in regard to prostitution, a fact that reflects both the prewar heterosexual conception of masculinity and the image of the soldier. Alfred Hale wrote that many men in his camp were "carrying on . . . to the extreme point of sexual intercourse . . . [with] girls of the prostitute class."[51] Another man claimed more coyly that next to the factory building in which his unit was billeted was the house "of a notorious female, 'The Black Diamond,' [who] was so attractive to one eighteen-year-old, that . . . he married her, who was old enough to be his mother."[52] Another eighteen-year-old conscript expressed his distaste for such behavior, rejecting it as a framework for his own masculinity: "to be a 'real' soldier I was told that I must get syphilis or some such disease . . . I was determined never to become a 'real' soldier."[53]

Comradeship, so central to the constructed image of the volunteer, was another matter; it certainly existed among conscripts, but it was often of a passing nature. The varied composition of this population made initial contacts somewhat difficult, as A. J. Abraham reflected: "I shared a tent with two ex-convicts, a man who had been a butler, another a gardener, another a farmer."[54] The absence of any common interest in soldiering also tended to inhibit the formation of any deep friendships, especially in training. A post-office sorter from London made friends with another sorter, "who if anything hated the life more than I did . . . I had no other real chums—fellow soldiers—yes, but companionship under conditions like ours was not really possible."[55] However, by the end of training, the shared destiny of these men as soldiers undoubtedly created a bond that enabled easier association:

> I met a dozen of our fellows on Waterloo & we all came down together [from embarkation leave] . . . We had a fine journey down. Everyone packed his troubles in his old kit bag & we were very cheerful.[56]

The departure to France completed the first phase of soldiering experienced by all recruits, in which they became externally transformed into soldiers and versed in the basic rites of fighting and fellowship. But for conscripts it was also the culmination of the initial cycle of gender construction within a military image, which would be put to the test in the harsh existence of the front line. By mid-1916, when the conscripts began arriving in France, they faced not only a territory devastated by war, but also a military organization drained by two years of battle and dependent upon a deteriorating economy. The nature of the army in France became progressively more functional, even occasionally haphazard, with drafts suddenly sent out to the front and men despatched between units in the line in response to an unexpected attack or an initiative that had failed and left behind many wounded and dead. A conscript still in training in August of 1917 described this situation well:

> There is a proper wind up in camp to-day. A big draft sent out last night
> . . . and to-day another big draft has been picked out for Sunday: every
> available man has been raked out—the barber, cooks, officers, servants
> and so on. Due of course to big battle in Flanders [the Third Ypres].[57]

The first encounter with the front line and combat quickly exposed the conscripts to the daunting realities of their new life:

> Hundreds of men were lying about in distorted attitudes, with battered, mutilated bodies and blackened faces and hands . . . the effect
> upon us new men was, to say the least, depressing. Silently still, and
> looking and feeling rather like ghosts ourselves . . . we sat down just
> where we could and became occupied in deep thought, experiencing a
> strange feeling of desolation, as if completely cut off from the world
> we had left behind us.[58]

Any man would have been shocked by such gruesome spectacles, but as this conscript put it, his "desolation" also stemmed from an awareness that his civilian perception of himself had included no image of a soldier in battle. Moreover, the soldier on the front line had to contend not only with the danger of battle, but also with the abysmal living conditions. Over two years of shooting had reduced the terrain to a series of holes filled with water and mud, which made daily life a constant struggle:

> [It] made our dugouts almost intenable [sic], for we entered them
> through openings only two feet high. When crawling into them on
> hands and knees over the threshold of wet mud, our overcoats soon
> became so thickly coated that some of us cut wide strips from the bottom, to lighten the load, roughly hemming round the new edge at our
> later leisure.[59]

Dugouts were the prevalent form of accommodation on the front line, and it was up to the men to create them. But behind the lines the situation was often not much better:

> Our camp was composed of all sorts of shanties rigged up of wood &
> canvas. It seems that the army authorities did not seem to think artillery men required any sort of housing while on active service so
> they supplied nothing. In consequence the men had to make shift the
> best way they could to provide shelter for themselves. This they managed to do by stealing or to use the army word "scrounging" anything
> that may come in handy for the purpose. Those who were lucky had at

sometime or another been able to annexe a sheet from a motor lorry or railway wagon & this would make a tidy bivouac for 4 or 5 men; others not so fortunate rigged up shelters about the size of a dog kennel which they had to creep into on their hands & knees.[60]

Supplies were also often delayed and inadequate when they arrived, with rations reduced a number of times in the latter two years of the war, making hunger a common predicament, especially on the front line.[61] In 1917, for example, a conscript who was meticulous in recording his meals, began the year by commenting that "Food awful. Breakfast 1/2 slice of bread (bacon or cheese). Din. 1 mug of soup. Tea 2 biscuits (jam, butter)." Apart from a short period between April and July, in which the food was "a lot better," he consistently complained of shortages, ending up on a pitiful note: "food is awfully scarce we are all weak and faint through hunger were with[out] food at all for two days."[62] As a result, men became very adept at scrounging, "in other words 'pinching'" at every opportunity. In some cases this meant raiding potato fields or "confiscating" bars of chocolate from a store, but at other times it entailed acts of desperation. A conscript on the march noted "a couple of soldiers sitting beside a fire warming a tin of food, one got up to go . . . [and] the other turned his head and in a flash I grabbed the tin and bolted between our column . . . To what lengths hunger will drive a man."[63]

Survival—whether in battle or daily life—was thus the central tenet of being experienced by the conscripts at the front, and often also in the reserve lines. The fear of death, the unexpected orders for movement of individuals or units, the constant struggle against mud, rain and cold, and the shortage of food made any other consideration largely redundant. Comradeship was also perceived within this context, as part of their survival at any given time, rather than as a deep and meaningful masculine bond. Describing the awful retreat of March of 1918, in which men marched for days with neither food nor sleep, a conscript noted that no one would aid some artillerymen whose horses were caught in barbed wire: men were "not only too full of their own troubles . . . they were also afraid of losing touch with the little parties to whom they had attached themselves."[64] But even in less dire circumstances, friendship was often firmly rooted in survival, as apparent in a conscript's diary:

26.11.1917   Ian Downe is a champion scrounger, keeps us well supplied with coke, sugar, candles etc.
30.11.1917   Ian Downe has gone on leave & we miss him very much. I am afraid stores will run low now.[65]

Thus mutual reliance was often the true expression of friendship among conscripts, although this is not to deny the existence of a strong fellowship among some men, or even their awareness of being *men* thrown together in an isolated situation. But given the diffuse nature of the army by this point, as an organization that gave them a framework but little support, these were not brave bands of soldiers realizing a fantasy of masculinity. These were not men who sought consolation in homoerotic comradeship after being disillusioned by the war or by the absence of opportunity for personal feats of bravery. In other words, these were men who were suffering not a crisis of masculinity, but rather a crisis of existence; they were not interested in whether they performed within a masculine image, but whether they would live to perform.

In this situation a hero was a man who survived battle: not necessarily one who led a charge or shot more Germans than anyone else, but simply one who participated in battle and lived to tell of it:

> I have achieved the utmost respect for the infantry since I came out here. It's really one of the few stirring sights of the war to witness a remnant battalion of silent tommies plodding back laden like Atlas - & into rear billets - (and <u>such</u> rest billets!) - which spell heaven and sanctuary to them after a bout in the impossible trenches.[66]

* * *

In her discussion of the modern male myth, Marina Warner has noted that "myths define enemies and aliens and in conjuring them up they say who we are and what we want, they tell stories to impose structure and order. Like fiction, they can tell the truth even while they're making it all up."[67] Such an assessment is undoubtedly true of the British image of the Great War, whereby conscripts were first isolated and stigmatized in public consciousness and finally excluded from the collective memory. For it was the Myth of the Volunteer that told a good story of wartime Britain: a story in which patriotic ideology was the only reason men went out to fight; a story in which the grotesque death toll made some sense because those who died had volunteered to do so; a story of self-sacrifice. The conscripts told another story, one of passive patriotism, which became active through the force of law; one in which men were sent out to fight and were thus possibly sacrificed. Such a story did little to alleviate the civilian populace's pain of bereavement, to explain a war that had shattered life for over four years, or to substantiate the notion of moral masculinity. Thus the memory of the conscripts was elided, sacrificed to the Myth of the Volunteer, which was essentially a fantasy of nineteenth-century masculinity.

NOTES

All unpublished manuscript sources are reproduced with the permission of the authors' families and the Trustees of the Imperial War Museum (hereafter IWM).

1. E. Blore, letter of Jan. 10, 1917, IWM 86/36/1.

2. For a discussion of the main myths of the Great War and their sources, see John Terraine, *Myths and Anti-Myths of War, 1861–1945* (London, 1980), chap. 5.

3. The autobiographical poetry and literature of the Great War, which began emerging in the 1920s and has never lost its appeal, is a major reason for the focus upon the volunteer as the generic soldier, largely because a vast majority of authors were volunteers. The pervasive influence of this imagery may be seen in various media representations of the event in the last thirty years. Thus the twenty-six-part TV documentary *The Great War* (1964) dwells upon the immense expansion of the British army exclusively through the recruitment of volunteers; while in the popular drama series from the early 1970s, *Upstairs Downstairs*, set in the first two decades of the century, both master and footman volunteer with the outbreak of war, thus reflecting the common cause of all strata of society—and the common monolithic image of the volunteer soldier. See Ilana R. Bet-El, "Experience into Identity: The Writings of British Conscripts 1916–1918" (Ph.D. diss., University of London, 1991), chaps. 8–10.

4. Under the voluntary system, 2,466,719 men enlisted between August 1914 and December 1915; Between January 1916 and the end of the war, 2,504,183 were conscripted. *Statistics of the Military Effort of the British Empire During the Great War* (London, 1922), 364.

5. As the psychologist Robert Stoller noted in his discussion of maleness, the "awareness *I am a male* . . . [is] the essentially unalterable core of gender identity." *Sex and Gender* (New York, 1968), 40. For a succinct summary of opinions on the creation of masculine identity, see Phyllis Tyson, "Male Gender Identity: Early Developmental Roots," in R. M. Friedman & L. Lerner, eds., *Toward a New Psychology of Men: Psychoanalytic and Social Perspectives*, special issue of *The Psychoanalytic Review* 73, no.4 (1986): 1–22. The entire volume offers interesting insights into the ongoing process of gender construction—and crisis—throughout a man's life.

6. The few that are known are: F. Gray, *Confessions of a Private* (Oxford, 1929); F. A. Voigt, *Combed Out* (London, 1929); Paul Fussell, ed., *The Ordeal of Alfred M. Hale* (London, 1975) (hereafter *Hale*); F. A. J. Taylor, *The Bottom of the Barrel* (London, 1978); W. V. Tilsley, *Other Ranks* (London, 1931).

7. This article was researched for and written before the publication of Joanna Bourke's *Dismembering the Mlae: Men's Bodies, Britain and the Great War* (London, 1995). Also on the conscripts is Ian F. W. Beckett, "The Real Unknown Army: British Conscripts 1916–1919," *The Great War* 2, no.1 (Nov. 1989): 4–13. For a discussion of conscription as a purely political issue, see for example R. J. Q. Adams & P. P. Poirier, *The Conscription Con-*

troversy in *Great Britain 1900–1918* (London, 1987). For a comprehensive list of publications and sources on the Conscientious Objectors, see Thomas C. Kennedy, "An Essay on Sources," in *The Hound of Conscience: A History of the No-Conscription Fellowship 1914–1919* (Little Rock, Arkansas, 1981), 303–16. For a summary of bibliography based upon the Regular and Volunteer experience, see Brian Bond, ed., *The First World War and British Military History* (Oxford, 1991), esp. "Chronology of Publications on the Military History of the First World War," vii–x, and the essays in Part 4, "The Great War Rediscovered," 261–314.

    8. Paul Fussell, *The Great War and Modern Memory* (New York, 1975); Eric J. Leed, *No Man's Land: Combat and Identity in World War I* (Cambridge, 1979); George L. Mosse, *Fallen Soldiers: Reshaping the Memory of the World Wars* (New York, 1990).

    9. Claire Tylee and Sharon Ouditt, for example, examine women's consciousness and identity during the war as a correlative of the volunteer soldier, without questioning the representativeness of this image in regard to both men and women. See Claire M. Tylee, *The Great War and Women's Consciousness: Images of Militarism and Womanhood in Women's Writings, 1914–64* (London, 1994); Sharon Ouditt, *Fighting Forces, Writing Women: Identity and Ideology in the First World War* (London, 1994).

    10. Sandra M. Gilbert, "Soldier's Heart: Literary Men, Literary Women, and the Great War," in Margaret Randolph Higonnet et al., eds., *Behind the Lines: Gender and the Two World Wars* (New Haven, 1987), 223; Elaine Showalter, "Male Hysteria: W. H. R. Rivers and the Lessons of Shell Shock," in *The Female Malady: Women, Madness and English Culture, 1830–1980* (London, 1987), 173.

    11. Parliamentary Recruiting Committee, Poster no. 33.

    12. Military Service Act (No. 2), 1916, in *Public General Acts*, 5 & 6 George V, chap. 104. This first Act applied only to single men between the ages of eighteen and forty. It was extended to married men in May 1916, and in July 1917 another Act was passed, concerning the conscription of British subjects abroad and Allied citizens residing in Britain. The third and final Military Service Act, of February 1918, raised the age limit to fifty, with a proviso for a further extension to fifty-six, and the application of conscription to Ireland, to which the law had not yet been applied. The first section of the Act, regarding attestation, was identical in all the Acts.

    13. E. J. O. Bird, undated letter, IWM BBC/Great War Series; W. D. Tonkyn, Diary, IWM / Con Shelf; E. C. Barraclough, unpublished account, IWM 86/86/1, p.1.

    14. See Peter Simkins, *Kitchener's Army: The Raising of the New Armies* (Manchester, 1988), 168–75; Denis Winter, *Death's Men* (London, 1978), chap. 1.

    15. Charles Edmonds, *A Subaltern's War* (1929; London, 1984), 16; Robert Graves, *Goodbye to All That* (1929; Harmondsworth, 1979), 60; Ian Parsons, ed., *The Collected Works of Isaac Rosenberg* (London, 1984), 219.

    16. *Hale*, 32, 37; H. L. Adams, IWM 83/50/1, p.1; A. J. Abraham, IWM P.191, p.4.

17. For discussions of British militarism and associated organizations before 1914, see: Hugh Cunningham, *The Volunteer Force* (London, 1975); Scott Hughes Myerly, "'The Eye Must Entrap the Mind': Army Spectacle and Paradigm in Nineteenth-Century Britain," *Journal of Social History* 26, no. 1 (1992): 105–31; John Springhall, Brian Fraser & Michael Hoare, eds., *Sure and Steadfast: A History of the Boys' Brigade 1883 to 1983* (London, 1983); Anne Summers, "Militarism in Britain before the Great War," *History Workshop Journal*, no. 2 (1976): 104–23.

18. This was largely the image of the dashing officer rather than that of the soldier in the ranks, since soldiering was deemed a despised profession among the lower classes throughout much of the nineteenth century, due to the excruciating terms of service which mainly attracted men who could find no other employment. For discussions of the recruitment problem until 1914, see for example: Correlli Barnett, *Britain and Her Army, 1509–1970* (Harmondsworth, 1974), chaps. 12–15; Brian Bond, "The Late Victorian Army," *History Today* 11 (1961): 616–24. On working-class perceptions of soldiering both before and during the war, see D. Englander and J. Osborne, "Jack, Tommy, and Henry Dubb: The Armed Forces and the Working Class," *The Historical Journal* 21, no. 3 (1978): 593–621.

19. John Galsworthy, "Soames and the Flag, 1914–1918," in *On Forsyte Change* (1930; Harmondsworth, 1991), 266.

20. For discussions of this imagery in popular culture, and especially among the lower classes, see Hughes Myerly, "The Eye Must Entrap the Mind." On the influence of this imagery upon the perception of the Great War soldier, see Mark Girouard, *The Return to Camelot: Chivalry and the English Gentleman* (New Haven, 1981); Mosse, *Fallen Soldiers*, chap. 7; Tylee, *The Great War*, chap. 1.

21. For a discussion of this issue, see Girouard, *The Return to Camelot*, chap. 1.

22. Samuel Smiles, *Self Help, with Illustrations of Character and Conduct* (London, 1859), v, 4, 152.

23. Robert Baden-Powell, *Scouting for Boys: A Handbook for Instruction in Good Citizenship* (1908; London, 1963), 1.

24. Ibid., 199.

25. See George L. Mosse, *Nationalism and Sexuality: Respectability and Abnormal Sexuality in Modern Europe* (New York, 1985); idem, "Masculinity and the Decadence," in Roy Porter and Mikulas Teich, eds., *Sexual Knowledge, Sexual Science: The History of Attitudes to Sexuality* (Cambridge, 1994), 251–66. Emanating from Mosse's work, yet with different emphases, is Andrew Parker, et al. eds., *Nationalisms and Sexualities* (New York, 1992). For an interesting discussion of late nineteenth-century middle-class conceptions of masculinity in Britain, see Seth Koven, "From Rough Lads to Hooligans: Boy Life, National Culture and Social Reform," in ibid., 365–91.

26. The vast subject of Victorian morality and sexuality has been discussed extensively, both as an issue in itself and as part of analyses of related interest. For two excellent general surveys, see Frank Mort, *Dangerous Sexualities: Medico-Moral Politics in England since 1830* (London, 1987); and

Jeffrey Weeks, *Sex, Politics and Society: The Regulation of Sexuality since 1800* (London, 1981). For the emergence of morality as a defining social force, see for example: Leonore Davidoff and Catherine Hall, *Family Fortunes: Men and Women of the English Middle Class, 1780–1850* (London, 1987), esp. chaps. 2, 9, 10; and F. M. L. Thompson, *The Rise of Respectable Society: A Social History of Victorian Britain, 1830–1900* (London, 1988), esp. chap. 8.

27. For a discussion of the legislation governing issues of morality, see Weeks, *Sex, Politics and Society*, 96–117; and Mort, *Dangerous Sexualities*, 63–150. The homosexual came to be imaged as a despised "other," not only out of moral revulsion, but also, as Mosse notes, in order to maintain an approved ideal of masculinity, since "nationalists felt that the line between normal and abnormal had to be tightly drawn if the nation was to be protected against its enemies." *Nationalism and Sexuality*, 33.

28. On the importance of voluntarism within middle-class social thought, especially in relation to the concept of duty, and as an ethos to be imparted to the lower classes, see Stefan Collini, *Liberalism and Sociology: L. T. Hobhouse and Political Argument in England, 1880–1914* (Cambridge, 1979), esp. chap. 1; Jane Lewis, *Women and Social Action in Victorian and Edwardian England* (Stanford, 1991); Melvin Richter, *The Politics of Conscience: T. H. Green and His Age* (London, 1964), esp. chaps. 8–10.

29. Quoted in Springhall, Fraser, and Hoare, eds., *Sure and Steadfast*, 101.

30. Cf. Michel Foucault, *The History of Sexuality: An Introduction* (Harmondsworth, 1984), 43.

31. For a discussion of the war propaganda, see Peter Buitenhuis, *The Great War of Words: British, American and Canadian Propaganda and Fiction, 1914–1933* (Vancouver, 1987); Cate Haste, *Keep the Home Fires Burning: Propaganda in the First World War* (London, 1977); Nicholas Reeves, *British Film Propaganda in the First World War* (London, 1986); Michael Sanders and Phillip M. Taylor, *British Propaganda during the First World War* (London, 1982).

32. The discussion of British war posters is based upon the collection in the Department of Art at the Imperial War Museum. Further images and analysis are based upon J. Barnicoat, *Posters: A Concise History* (London, 1972, repr. 1988); M. Hardie & A. K. Sabin, eds., *War Posters: Issued by Belligerent and Neutral Nations, 1914–1919* (London, 1920); P. Paret, B. I. Lewis, and P. Paret, *Persuasive Images: Posters of War and Revolution from the Hoover Institution Archives* (Princeton, 1992); Maurice Rickards, *Posters of the First World War* (London, 1968).

33. PRC 7 / IWM 5083; PRC 111 / 0409; PRC 91, 92 / IWM 5163, 5127; PRC 94 / IWM 5143; PRC 119 / IWM 4887.

34. PRC 75 / 0313; PRC 108 / IWM 0408;

35. PRC 55 / IWM 4884.

36. PRC 69 / IWM 5118; ibid. (Emphasis in the original.)

37. PRC 144 / IWM 5063; PRC 120 / IWM 5051.

38. PRC 103 / IWM 5041; PRC 127 / IWM 5068.

39. PRC 84 / IWM 5111; PRC 113 / IWM 0309.

40. The pamphlet is part of the collection of T. Hardman IWM 84/1/1. The capitals and italics appear as such in the original.

41. PRC 140 / IWM 5043.

42. PRC 151, 152, 157 / IWM 5253, 5052, 5021; PRC 129 / IWM 3527; PRC 142 / IWM 5054.

43. PRC (no number) / Peter H. Liddle, *Voices of War: Front Line and Home Front* (London, 1988), 71; PRC 88 / Paret, Lewis, and Paret, *Persuasive Images*, 53.

44. Quoted in Springhall, Fraser, and Hoare, eds., *Sure and Steadfast*, 101.

45. Mansion House speech of Oct. 19, 1915; *The Times*, Oct. 20, 1915.

46. *The Times*, Oct. 28, 1915; *Daily Mail*, Sept. 14, 1915 and Oct. 18, 1915.

47. Lt. P. Creek, IWM 87/31/1, p.19.

48. Capt. J. C. Dunn, *The War the Infantry Knew, 1914–1919* (1938; London, 1989), 245.

49. Taylor, *The Bottom of the Barrel*, 34.

50. In the early months of voluntarism, the prewar medical standards were still in use, and only the fittest men were taken. As the war progressed, and the need for men intensified, standards were dropped and medical examinations were often cursory. By the end of 1916, only 6.5 percent of new recruits were rejected, and approximately 50 percent of those taken were placed in the highest grade, A. See J. M. Winter, *The Great War and the British People* (London, 1986), 52, passim. The process of examination and classification was revised and extended in the autumn of 1917, however the general perception remained that military need usually overrode medical opinion, and thus many unfit men were both taken into the army and placed in combat units.

51. *Hale*, 107.

52. A. J. Jamieson, IWM 88/52/1, p.5.

53. Barraclough, p.1.

54. Abraham, p.4.

55. W. Cobb, IWM 73/188/1, p.4.

56. B. Davies, IWM 83/31/1, letter of Apr. 11, 1917.

57. W. L. Fisher, IWM 85/32/1, diary entry of Aug. 3, 1917.

58. R. D. Fisher, IWM 76/54/1, p.14.

59. Ibid., 24–25.

60. F. R. Jolley, IWM/Department of Documents vd, p. 14.

61. For a description of the organization and quantity of food, see: "Supply Services during the War (August 1914–March 1919); Note by the Quartermaster-General to the Forces," in *Statistics of the Military Effort*, 841–43.

62. E. D. Bishop, IWM 77/111/1, diary entries of Jan. 28, 1917, Apr. 13, 1917, Nov. 25, 1917; passim.

63. E. Holdsworth, IWM 73/147/1, p.6; A. Hynd, IWM WWI 78/4, letter of May 24, 1918; Creek, p.41.

64. R. D. Fisher, p.57.

65. W. L. Fisher.

66. E. Blore, letter of Jan. 10, 1917.

67. Marina Warner, *Six Myths of Our Time* (New York, 1994), 28.

FAMILY, MASCULINITY, AND HEROISM IN RUSSIAN WAR POSTERS OF THE FIRST WORLD WAR*

KAREN PETRONE

If middle-class Europe seemed to be suffering from a "crisis of masculinity" in the first decade of the twentieth century,[1] both Russia's elite and peasantry experienced instead a crisis of "patriarchal authority." After 1905, the patriarchal authority of the Tsar and his government was undermined by revolution, and the authority of fathers in peasant households was increasingly challenged by their sons. When Russia declared war on Austria-Hungary in August of 1914, the tsarist government faced significant challenges on numerous domestic fronts: demands for political participation among elites, the strains caused by the multi-ethnic nature of the Empire, and rising social unrest, especially among urban workers.[2] To counteract this threat of fragmentation, the Russian mobilization for war emphasized the unity of the peoples of the Russian Empire as one nation. Despite the cracks that had already begun to appear in this image, the dominant metaphor of the Russian army—and by extension the Russian Empire—at the beginning of the war, was still that of a family united in battle for Tsar and Fatherland.

Did rapid social and political change and the trauma of war lead to transformations in the age-old definitions of family, nation, and hero? This essay focuses on the representations of the Russian Empire as family in Russian World War I broadsides, literary sketches,

*This research was made possible by grants from the Institute for the Humanities at the University of Michigan and a University of Kentucky Summer Faculty Research Fellowship. Many thanks to Carole Leadenham and Sondra Bierre of the Hoover Institution Archives, who assisted me in identifying and reproducing the posters used in this essay. I am grateful to my colleagues in the History Department of the University of Kentucky for their many helpful suggestions when I presented an early draft of this work at the History Department Colloquium in November of 1994. Special thanks to Billie Melman and Ken Slepyan, who carefully read, and thoughtfully commented on, several drafts of this essay.

posters, and participant autobiographies—prime examples of Russian popular iconography and commercial literature for the masses in the early twentieth century[3]—and examines how gender and race distinctions structured meaning in the wartime vocabulary of masculinity, heroism, and cowardice. It is based on a study of over six hundred Russian World War I posters in the Hoover Poster Collection, which provide a rich and variegated source for analyzing Russian ideologies of war and the ways in which the Russian government both represented and sought to motivate its men in arms.[4] These posters have attracted the attention of relatively few scholars.[5] The chronology of posters in the collection corresponds to the fortunes of the Russian Empire during the war. The vast majority of the posters that I studied were printed in the first year of the war, primarily in the fall of 1914 and the winter of 1915. These posters illustrate the early victories of the tsarist Empire. As the war progressed and both Russian society and the Russian military disintegrated, the publication of this type of poster practically ceased. The heroic and satirical posters and postcards were replaced by sentimental scenes and Western-style war-loan and charity posters. This article is, therefore, a study of the images of the mobilization for war and early optimism regarding victory.[6]

Artists and writers articulated class, hierarchy, and racial and religious difference through representations of inclusion and exclusion from the tsarist family and through contrasting depictions of heroes and cowards. The representation of Russia as a family was a central tenet of the Russian imperial ideology. While the definition of the Russian Tsar as "the Father of the Fatherland" had existed since the time of Peter the Great, the explicit articulation of a patriarchal ideology of family occurred during the reign of Nicholas I (1825–1855). When he ascended to the throne, Nicholas's personal image was that of a "loving husband and caring father."[7] His doctrine of Official Nationality, with its three intertwined principles of Orthodoxy, Autocracy, and Nationality, affirmed that "the entire past of the nation was based on the great institution of the family."[8] Historian Mikhail Pogodin (1800–1875), for example, asserted that Russia was "a single family in which the ruler is the father and the subjects the children." This patriarchal relationship was divinely sanctioned and had a uniquely harmonious character because both father and children adhered to the tenets of Russian Orthodoxy. The familial ties that bound the nation together allowed, somewhat paradoxically, for both the "complete authority" of the father, and the "full freedom" of the children. Pogodin believed that the familial model ought to hold sway throughout Russian society: "The military commander must be the father of his soldiers, the landlord must be the father of his peasants." In this doctrine, Russianness was defined as the innate devotion of the Russian people-children to their Tsar-father. The most dedicated children of all were the Russian soldiers.[9]

The centrality of patriarchal relations existed not only in official ideology, but also in the social relations of the peasants who constituted the vast majority of the population. Supreme authority in the peasant household resided in the *bolshak*, or eldest male member, who ruled over an extended household made up of his sons and their wives and children.[10] Thus the identification between fatherhood and authority had a basis in day-to-day social relations as well as in state doctrine and the philosophical outlook of the elite.

However, in the decade before World War I, the "familial" solidarity of the Russian army was challenged both by a military debacle and by political unrest. The crushing defeat of the Russian Imperial Army in the Russo-Japanese War and the turmoil of the Revolution of 1905 made tsarist leaders profoundly aware of the need for reform within the officer corps, and of the potential for mutiny because of the strained relationships between officers and the overwhelmingly peasant soldiers.[11] The main difficulty in officer-soldier relations was the "manifold outward marks of social distance imposed by regulations and by society at large." One of the most significant social distinctions was reflected in speech. The soldier was obliged to use elaborate honorific addresses and speak to the officer using the formal second-person pronoun *vy*. The soldier was addressed by the officers in the informal *ty* and was forbidden to smoke in public, ride trams, or go to parks, restaurants, and theaters.[12]

The mobilization for World War I in Russia was characterized by the uniting of various layers of Russian society behind the war effort, which was strongly supported even by some of the socialist parties. Many members of the elites and educated urban dwellers became army officers. The peasant recruits who made up the army in overwhelming numbers, however, were in very different material and social circumstances and were much less enthusiastic about going to war. For those peasant families who had only one adult male laborer, the effect of conscription could be catastrophic. At many mobilization points, drunken rioting occurred. Other peasant recruits responded to mobilization with "sullen resignation."[13] Despite the fact that the soldiers and their officers came from distinct social worlds, the posters and literary sketches created an ideal image of one family that included both soldiers and officers and denied their conflicting goals and needs.

During World War I, the newly recruited peasant soldiers experienced the social distinction between soldier and officer through regulations, personal forms of address, and in terms of privileges. One Polish officer in the Russian army explained, "If for instance, there were a puddle of water, a piece of mud and a wet stone for three people to lie on, the officer got the wet stone, the sergeant got the mud and the soldier lay down in the water."[14] While peasants became junior officers in great numbers as front-line officers fell, these new officers tended to be as disaffected from the war as the soldiers they led. Many of these men were radicalized in 1917.[15] The war posters analyzed in this article, however, were produced before most peasant-officers were trained and promoted. When the Russian army met defeat due to lack of weapons and ammunition, soldiers and junior officers were quick to blame their superiors for needless casualties and for sending peasant troops to their death while they remained in safety.[16]

While it is difficult to ascertain the influence that these posters had on the armed forces and the general public, it is clear that publishing houses, municipal government, and other institutions used posters to attract the attention of the broad public and, in the case of private publishing houses, to earn profits from the sale of images of the war. Many posters were printed in the style of the *lubok* (pl. *lubki*) or the traditional peasant broadside. Little research has been done on this topic, but one contemporary analyst, Vl. Denisov, who published a book entitled *The War and the Lubok* in 1916, asserted that at the beginning of the war these pictures were in great demand and that "new publishing houses are coming into being and there is competition among them."[17]

Ever since the war of 1812, *lubki* had been published by the government and private firms, affirming the intentions of individual Russian heroes to be "ready to die for the Tsar and for Russia."[18] The publishing houses that produced World War I posters in this style attempted to attract a broad viewership by presenting their messages in a familiar form. Denisov argued that peasants hung the *lubki* in their homes in the icon corner next to images of saints because they saw the war as a "worldwide cosmic event sent by God."[19] World War I posters drew on satirical images of Napoleon's defeat to mock Kaiser Wilhelm, and used modern versions of the centuries-old image of a saintly hero astride his white steed to denote heroism and create the image of a just war.[20] The public also had personal access to several of these images, since a number of the posters were reproduced in the form of postcards that, like the *lubki*, were hung on the walls of people's homes in both the city and village.[21]

In 1914 and 1915, publishing houses also produced collections of short stories or literary sketches about the war. Like the posters, these one- or two-page descriptions of the war's people and events pursued the theme of heroism by highlighting the actions of the Russian military in battle and by focusing on individual events and heroism in a form that was easily accessible to the common soldier. Many were devoted to the very same events and heroes portrayed by posters.[22] In conjunction with the posters, these sketches reveal Russian ideals of heroism, masculinity, and honor.

At least some posters were successful in capturing the notice of the Russian public and the military, even if they did not necessarily mobilize these groups to action. Leonid Pasternak, the father of the novelist, drew a poster of a wounded Russian soldier entitled "Help for War Victims" that was so popular that "crowds in Moscow gathered before it, and women burst into tears."[23] Russian military officials made sure that soldiers were exposed to posters and broadsides about military exploits and heroes. The cavalry officer Vladimir Littauer remembered that, shortly before World War I, the walls in the barracks of the soldiers he commanded were covered with "framed pictures depicting the heroic deeds of Russian soldiers." These pictures included "Major Gortalov dying on Turkish bayonets; Private Riaboff in the process of being executed by the Japanese for refusing to divulge information . . . Private Osipov blowing up a powder magazine and himself with it."[24] Military officials thus exposed soldiers to images of martyrdom for the sake of Russia. Unlike Pasternak's depiction of the wounded soldier, these pictures singled out individual soldiers to be remembered by name, and presented the dead as men to be admired and not pitied. These remembered deeds were meant to inspire other soldiers to perform such heroic acts so that they too could be remembered by name.

THE GREAT MILITARY FAMILY

Russia's participation in World War I, like its engagement in the Napoleonic wars, was termed "otechestvennaia voina," a patriotic war. As in Latin, the Russian word for "patriotic" was connected with the idea of protecting the Fatherland (otechestvo). Military order was modeled on the institution of male power that had controlled Russian life for centuries: the hierarchy of the patriarchal family. Within the family, many Russian men (especially peasants) had complicated relationships with their senior male relatives, whom they both respected and feared.[25] The notion of fatherhood was very important in Russian military culture. Russian World

War I posters depicted military events as taking place within a
closed all-male society within which many of the relationships were
based on familial associations. In the Nicholas Cavalry School, for
example, first-year students were "nephews," and second-year students "uncles."[26]

While authority was represented as paternal throughout the nineteenth century, in World War I propaganda, the relationship between
the father-commanders and the son-soldiers changed. Nineteenth-
century *lubki* had often portrayed commanders in the foreground
with row after row of identical, stylized soldiers marching in the
background.[27] World War I propaganda created a new image of filial
respect and obedience by focusing on the personal relationship between the individual soldier and the commander. The commander
no longer held authority over dozens of identical soldiers; instead he
engaged in a fatherly relationship with each of his subordinates.
World War I publications idealized the familial relationship between
superiors and their soldiers. One sketch published during the war,
entitled "Father-Commanders," described the attitude of a certain
General Ivanov to his soldiers: "General Ivanov is not only the chief
commander, but a friend to all of the soldiers; he worries about his
soldiers as much as a father worries about his own children. Wherever he is, and he is everywhere, any soldier in trouble or sorrow
finds comfort." This panegyric suggests how the idealized military-
familial contract of authority might work: in return for the care and
concern of their father, the son-soldiers were to obey his authority
and "follow him through fire and through water."[28]

This notion of patriarchal fatherhood in wartime was quite distinct from the Western European representations of wartime relations between men. According to George Mosse, the dominant trope
of the war myth among Western European combatants was an emphasis on male camaraderie and communalism that drew the nation
together and transcended class divisions.[29] By creating male camaraderie, the war was an antidote to the "crisis of masculinity" that
middle-class Europe faced. Unlike the Western European myth, the
notion of benevolent hierarchy and the emphasis on fatherhood remained major aspects of Russian representations of war. Thus, one
of the many popular biographies of the Cossack war hero Koz'ma
Kriuchkov begins with Kriuchkov's grandfather telling him stories
of fighting for Russia in 1877 during the Russo-Turkish War. The
grandfather recounts his friendly interaction with his commander,
General Skobelev, who "smiled and jokingly slapped [him] on the
shoulder" as he bade farewell to the detachment.[30] The model of authority depicted here is one of intimacy in which Kriuchkov's grand-

father and General Skobelev have a similar relationship to the one that Kriuchkov enjoys with his grandfather. The emphasis on the military service of Kriuchkov's grandfather turns fighting for Russia into a familial obligation for Kriuchkov, as well as a political or national duty.

In literary sketches, heroic soldiers returning from battle were not only praised for valor and sacrifices for their country, but also for showing respect toward their own fathers. In a sketch entitled "Two Sons and a Father in the Ranks," a wounded son returning from battle meets his father going off to war and gives him two revolvers, a bayonet, and a helmet that he has captured from the enemy as keepsakes.[31] Another sketch reported that Koz'ma Kriuchkov gave his fifty-four-year-old father the lance with which he had defeated eleven Germans. The father took the lance with him when he himself joined the war against Turkey.[32] In each of these cases, the heroic warriors show their respect not only to their military-commander fathers, but also to their own fathers. Both fathers and sons go into battle, but these fathers each have the special weapons provided to them by their valiant and respectful sons. The realities of military life were often very far from this ideal representation of filial love and respect. Both officers and enlisted men endured a cruel process of hazing that served as initiation into their military family. Like the elders of a peasant family, the elders of the military family (the commissioned and non-commissioned officers) had the power to punish its junior members physically for any breach in discipline, but also arbitrarily.[33] The difficulty that officers had in maintaining good relations with soldiers, even under the egalitarian conditions of trench warfare, was one of a number of causes that led to the disintegration of the Imperial Army in a matter of months after the October Revolution.[34] General Anton Denikin, who became the Chief of Staff in May of 1917, admitted after the Revolution that "Heartfelt solicitude, touching care of the men's needs, simplicity, and friendliness— all these qualities of the Russian officers, who lay for months on end in the wet, dirty trenches beside their men . . . were marred by an occasional roughness, swearing, and sometimes by arbitrariness and blows."[35] Denikin describes the ideal officer in much the same terms in which the father-commander was described above, but admits that even the ideal officer lapsed into cruelty and brutality in his dealings with his soldier-sons.

Russian propagandists minimized social divisions in the army by defining hierarchy through terms of filial respect and love. These depictions of father-son relations were traditional in their emphasis on family, yet they also created a more egalitarian image of family based on love and affection, rather than on fear and respect. One poster, entitled "Russian Soldier," depicted the heroic deed of Private David Vyzhimok, who "under heavy fire searched for his wounded officer and carried him six versts."[36] Vyzhimok, who is depicted as the prototypical Russian soldier, is young, quite handsome, clean-shaven except for a neat moustache, and has stylized Russian features. This image of the Russian hero is taken from late nineteenth-century *lubki* of mythic warrior heroes from Russia's medieval past such as the *bogatyr'* Il'ia Muromets.[37] Vyzhimok's body seems disproportionately large and dwarfs that of the wounded officer. In the world of the poster, there was no antagonism between soldiers and officers. Instead, Vyzhimok revered his officer and risked his own life in order to save him. Unity as part of the all-male military family overcame class and cultural differences.

The theme of officer-soldier relations was also used by propagandists in their characterizations of the enemy's army. One poster, entitled "The Tragicomical Capture of a German Officer or the Cowardice of the Germans" (Figure 9), illustrates the disregard of German soldiers for their commanding officer. In this poster, German soldiers hear Russian gunshots, panic, and run away, abandoning their officer who is answering the call of nature behind a haystack. The captured officer declares that "all of the soldiers who abandoned him would be shot without fail."[38] This scene first and foremost attacked the dignity and status of the German officer, who is pictured as a ridiculous figure, open-mouthed in surprise, pulling up his pants. It also implied the German soldiers' lack of respect for their officers and the officers' callous and brutal behavior toward their soldiers. In propaganda, an idealized Russian familial relationship was contrasted to the hatred and indifference of the Germans, while in reality the relationship between officers and soldiers was a serious problem in both countries.[39]

Traditional Russian definitions of heroism were also put under pressure by the changing conditions of modern warfare. The culture of Russian officers before and during World War I placed great importance on the honor (*chest'*) of the individual officers and of the regiment. This focus on honor within a closed and extremely hierarchical brotherhood of men was extremely difficult to maintain during wartime conditions. The Russian Hussar ethos that harkened back to the Napoleonic wars—"when the time came we would charge [with swords drawn] and, if necessary, die with glory"—had become obsolete. Russian cavalry units were well trained in hand-to-hand combat, but in the age of artillery, they could not get near enough to the Germans to employ their skills.[40] Nevertheless, a sig-

Figure 9. "The Tragicomical Capture of a German officer or the Cowardice of the Germans," kind permission of the Hoover Institution on War, Peace and Revolution, Stanford University.

nificant number of Russian propaganda posters portrayed the Russian cavalry charging toward its enemy with swords and lances drawn, and engaging in hand-to-hand combat. These posters sought to preserve the image of a traditional battle in which the warrior's reward was the preservation of manly honor. They glorified the old ways even as they introduced a new style of hero.

The Cossack Koz'ma Kriuchkov became the prototypical image of Russian heroism, appearing in more posters than any other individual figure, including Nicholas II. Kriuchkov was the first World War I soldier to be awarded a St. George Cross for a skirmish with the German Cavalry on August 12, 1914 in which, according to the propaganda legend, he single-handedly defeated eleven German officers although he and his horse suffered sixteen and eleven wounds, respectively.[41] The ways in which the deeds of Kriuchkov were depicted in posters ranged between the heroic and the mythic. While a "realistic" poster of Kriuchkov hailed him as the "valiant son of the quiet Don," who upheld the "military glory of Russian Cossacks," a *lubok*-style poster by Dmitrii Moor, who was later to become one of the most prominent Soviet poster artists, pronounced Kriuchkov to be a *bogatyr'*.[42] The more realistic poster detailed how he defeated the eleven Germans: "The Germans struck with lances and first he repulsed them with his rifle, when his rifle gave out, then he began to fell them with his saber, and then he wrested a lance from a German and put it to use." The *lubok*-style poster features a highly imaginative rendition of the scene with Germans skewered on lances, still grimacing in pain, and Kriuchkov victoriously holding a lance with two Germans spiked on it. The heroic Kriuchkov, whose fame was based on real events, was thus turned into a supernatural mythic hero, in much the same way as the socialist realist heroes of the Soviet Union would be portrayed in the 1930s.

The many accounts of Kriuchkov's valor failed to identify his rank, referring to him only as "Cossack." The Cossacks, who were an ethnically mixed group of Ukrainians, Russians, and Tatars, had created self-governing communities in the south and southwest of Russia in the sixteenth and seventeenth centuries, performing military service for the Tsar in exchange for political autonomy. As Russia expanded in the seventeenth and eighteenth centuries, the Cossacks gradually lost their autonomy and became the loyal servants of the centralized Russian state, renowned for their horsemanship and for their allegiance to the Tsar. They were assimilated and welcomed into the Imperial family as "Russian" Cossacks in the late eighteenth and early nineteenth centuries. Kriuchkov's identification by caste instead of rank suggests that he was not a commissioned officer. Nonetheless, his fame spread throughout the country in songs, poems, and stories, which suggests that even military men of higher rank were expected to emulate him. This praise of a hero from the people is further evidence of the loosening of the strict hierarchy of the military family as the war progressed.

The Racial and Gendered Nature of Cowardice

A major theme in the war posters was the intimate connection between courage and masculinity, a connection that was etymologically reinforced by the fact that in the Russian language the word "courage" (*muzhestvo*) is derived from the root "man" (*muzh*) and has connotations of manliness. Representations of cowardice, associated with unmanliness, thus had a significant gender component, which was reflected in portrayals of the enemy. For example, a poster entitled "Parade" depicted the officers of Kaiser Wilhelm's and Franz Joseph's armies as little boys playing with war toys under the supervision of their nursemaids (Figure 10).[43] The message that any nursemaid could deal with Kaiser Wilhelm created a gendered

Figure 10. "Parade." Kind permission of the Hoover Institution.

juxtaposition between a female nursemaid and a real, male, Russian warrior, implying that the Germans were so lacking in manliness that they were weaker even than women.

The *lubok*-style poster "The Old Woman Is Also Not a Block-head—She Can Capture an Airplane" (Figure 11) shows a group of peasant women advancing on the crew of a landed Austrian plane with sticks and rakes.[44] The text explains that even when the Austrians threatened them with revolvers, the women continued to advance, and succeeded in spanking the Austrians. The Austrians are portrayed as both ridiculous and unmanly for allowing themselves to be beaten by a group of women with farm implements. The words "old woman" (*baba*) and "blockhead" (*churban*) suggest to the viewer that since the Austrians were beaten by uneducated and unarmed peasant women, they could be easily defeated by the real, male, Russian warriors of the Imperial Army.

A lurid, satirical poster entitled "A Pair of Bay Horses" depicts Kaiser Wilhelm, Franz Joseph, and a personification of Turkey in a relationship with a different kind of female image (Figure 12). Germany is personified as an obese and ugly woman with enormous

Figure 11. "The Old Woman is not a Block-head—She can capture an Air-plane." Kind permission of the Hoover Institution.

breasts spilling out over the top of her dress, greedy for food, money, and sex. In exchange for fighting the war, Wilhelm and Franz Joseph give her money and food, while the scrawny Turk is caught grotesquely in her massive embraces. While Germania is hugging the Turk, she manages to pick his pocket.[45] The result of Germania's obesity, greed, and prostitution is her death. Parodying the many European and American World War I posters that employed the image of a mythological woman to represent the purity and honor of the nation, this poster underscores the corruption of Germany by representing the enemy nation as a disgusting and sinful woman.[46] Once again, Russia's enemies are ridiculed in relation to a female figure, though in this case it is a female whom they "have their way with" and ultimately destroy.

As in much war propaganda, the portrayals of cowards and heroes varied according to nationality and ethnicity. While Austrians and Germans were depicted as ridiculous, inept, and weak in specific battle situations, Turkish cowardice was generalized in accordance with the tradition of Russian *lubok* and popular literature, which created racialized images of the enemy such as the "slant-eyed devil" of the Russo-Japanese War of 1904–1905.[47] These stereotypi-

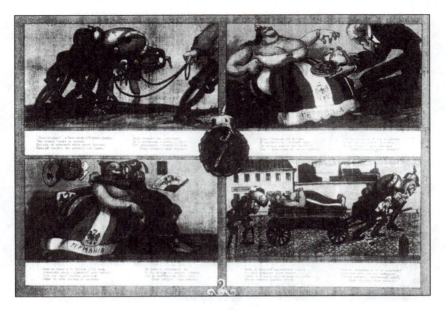

Figure 12. "A pair of Bay-Horses." Kind permission of the Hoover Institution.

cal negative images were more impervious to change than the images of positive heroes whose creation led to a reworking of the concept of the Russian Imperial family. The poster "About Turkish Cowardice and Spirited Boldness" (Figure 13) sets up a binary opposition between a heroic Russian cavalry officer and a Turkish soldier, who is fleeing toward the viewer as if to escape outside of the frame of the poster.[48] This image of the cowardly Turk dominates the composition of the poster and is drawn to be as ethnically distinct from the Russian horseman as possible. Like Vyzhimok in "Russian Soldier," the smartly uniformed horseman is handsome and clean-shaven except for a characteristic moustache. The Turk is dressed in stereotypical oriental clothing: a large red fez, flowing red pantaloons, and dainty black slippers. His facial features are quite exaggerated: he has a very long and pointed nose, swarthy skin, an unkempt goatee and moustache, jet-black hair, and bushy eyebrows. His terrified eyes stare out at the viewer and his hands, with long fingernails, are held up in resignation and fear. In addition to creating an image of the ethnic other, the flowing pants and eastern clothes feminize the Turks.[49]

The text of this poster is in the form of a *chastushka*, a traditional Russian folk rhyme which was often used in the late nineteenth-

Figure 13. "About Turkish Cowardice and [Russian] Boldness." Kind permission of the Hoover Institution.

century *lubki* to contrast, for example, the "foolish military formation" of the Turks with the bravery of Orthodox Russian warriors.[50] The verses in this poster both accentuate the religious and ethnic differences between Russians and Turks and systematically denigrate the Turks as thieves rather than warriors. They convey the message that it was the Germans who "instigated" the Turks to fight against the "Orthodox land," thus robbing the Turks of their independence, and clearly define the Turks as an inferior "other": "There are the wide pants/ He is also wearing a fez/'I,' yells the war hero/ 'have already fired off my mouth'." The poster implies that the only noises that this Turkish soldier can make in battle are his screams as he runs away. The ironic application of the term "war hero" to the fleeing Turk suggests that there is a fundamental contradiction between the two. By presenting the exalted status of war hero as a Russian and manly attribute, this stanza both invokes the ethnic particularities of the Turks and denies their status as worthy opponents in war. The final stanza assures the viewer that the outcome of this encounter between Turk and Russian was the victory of the Russian on horseback and the humiliation, if not the annihilation, of the Turk.

Another poster, "Conversation near Constantinople," with verses by M. Petrov (Figure 14), contrasts the giant figure of a handsome, young, ethnic Russian and a miniature Turk, who barely comes up to the Russian's knee.[51] Demonstrating the difference in character between the two races, the Turk impotently stamps his foot on the ground, while the Russian sits placidly smoking a cigarette. The text is also written in the form of a *chastushka*. The Turk marvels at the recent Russian victory and asks, "Where did you get so much strength?" The derisive reply is couched in the colorful style and language of traditional peasant insults and repartee:

> Oh my friend—though you're a Turk
> And look like you're good at darting blows,
> As for such a mind as yours,
> It seems as if there's nothing there.
>
> With my strength to fight against you,
> You'll never be able to get even.
> And your Turkish guns,
> Can't even reach me.
>
> Many different foreigners,
> I've beaten and will beat again.
> I've pounded Austrians and Germans,
> But on you I . . . sneeze.[52]

The Russian soldier establishes a hierarchy in which the Austrians and the Germans are considered to be enemies who merit serious attention, while the Turks are not. The ellipses in the last line, before the word "sneeze," suggests that the poet is inviting viewers to substitute other words for that verb—indeed, since many Russian verbs end with the same syllable, there are a number of obscene or scatological alternatives that would preserve the rhyme. Petrov thus encouraged the primarily male viewers of the poster—peasants and soldiers—to magnify the insults against the Turks by employing the rich Russian peasant-culture of swearing.[53]

The Russian soldier uses language that suggests that the Turk is not masculine, or even human. The adjective "darting" (*iurkii*) is one that would be applied to mice scampering away from a cat. The derisive comment on the capabilities of the Turk's gun can be seen as a metaphorical reference to the Turk's phallus, striking to the quick of Turkish masculinity. The Turkish guns, which are too weak even to reach the Russians, render the Turks impotent against the superior and more virile Russian forces. Visual mockery of the Turks' weaponry also occurs in another *lubok*-style poster entitled "To the

Figure 14. "Conversation near Constantinople." Kind permission of the Hoover Institution.

Bloody Battle, Forward with Glory."[54] Here the Turkish guns are drawn as tiny cannons on strings like children's toys. These visual depictions and insults both infantilize and emasculate the Turks.

While Allied propaganda against Germany and Austria tended to focus on the atrocities of the uncivilized and dehumanized Hun,[55] Russian propaganda often depicted the Germans as fools and as the inferiors of Russian women. In the racial and gendered hierarchy of the other, Germans were granted the status of men, albeit weak men. The Turkish anti-hero in the posters was far feebler than the Germanic one: he was defined both as a racial other and as a despised female.

THE CHANGING IMPERIAL FAMILY

While World War I depictions of the Turks invoked the racist images of previous wars and a firmly nineteenth-century notion of otherness, posters and literary sketches portrayed non-Russian and non-Orthodox "sons" of the Imperial family in a positive light, reflecting the needs of a multi-ethnic Empire that relied on all of its citizens to wage war. The chaos of war thus led to transformations in the boundaries and structure of the great military family.

An example of this new image of the Empire is a poster entitled "War with the Turks in the Transcaucasus," which is drawn in a relatively realistic style, depicting a Caucasian soldier from the Russian Imperial Army about to overpower a Turkish guard, while Russian soldiers fight by his side (Figure 15). The text proclaims: "Russia is again at war with her ancient enemy—the Turks" and confidently announces that "this war will be the last and will complete the expulsion of the Turks from Europe."[56] The poster articulates a model relationship among the three ethnic groups: the Russian conquerors, the Caucasian citizens of the Russian Empire, and the enemy Turks. In past wars, the Russians had rescued the Orthodox Caucasians from Turkish rule. Now, as loyal subjects of the Russian Empire, these Caucasians were to fight side by side with the Russians in what was supposed to be the definitive battle to eliminate Turkish influence on the borders of the Orthodox land. Like other posters discussed above, this poster presented a heroic-ethnic image of a Russian soldier, but the face of the Caucasian hero is turned away from the viewer, maybe to conceal the fact that its features had more in common with the Turkish enemy than with the archetypal ethnic Russian. Here, the artist has sidestepped the problem of a hero who did not conform to the ethnic Russian mold.

Other posters also glorified the efforts of non-Russians in the Imperial Army. One series, entitled "Guard-Heroes," depicted Ossetian and Circassian guards pursuing and firing at their Austrian attackers.[57] Another poster showed Circassian cavalry attacking German soldiers as they ate in an outdoor cafe.[58] Thus, the symbolic relationship of Russians to non-Russians in the Empire was transformed during the war from one of strict hierarchy, in which the Russians were superior, to one that affirmed equality and unity. The Russian Imperial "family" welcomed outsider-heroes into its ranks in an unprecedented way, even expanding to include Jews, who suffered from repressive tsarist policies both before and during the war. On the one hand, over 600,000 Jews fought against the Germans in the Russian Imperial Army, demonstrating their loyalty to the Empire; on the other hand, the Jews near the front were treated as potential traitors, and many were forcibly resettled by the Russian army.[59] Nonetheless, posters explicitly identified Jewish heroes as well as Caucasian ones.

A poster celebrating the exploits of a Jewish soldier, Private Katz, revealed how the Imperial family expanded to embrace non-Russians; it also showed the flexibility of a family hierarchy in which a

Figure 15. "War with the Turks at the Transcaucasus." Kind permission of the Hoover Institution.

valorous son could become a "father" and leader of other soldiers. "The Heroic Exploit of Private Katz" describes how this daring Jewish soldier discovered the Germans' position, fired on it, and sent a report to his commanding officer (Figure 16). After his ammunition ran out, Katz attacked the enemy with his bayonet and was wounded. Just as he lost consciousness, Katz heard the "Russian 'Hurrah'" and knew that "his own" had arrived. For this deed, Katz was awarded a St. George Cross and was promoted to Second Ensign.[60] This account emphasizes both that Katz was Jewish and that he was an active member in the Russian Imperial military family who considered the Russians to be "his own" people. While the popular literature of earlier wars had frequently denigrated Jews,[61] this poster, along with another honoring Katz, "The Exploit of Private Katz," affirmed the Jewish soldier as a full-fledged military hero in the same language used for Russian heroes.[62] The message was clear: Under battle conditions, the army valued merit over social position or religion, and status could be gained through appropriate deeds.

Various collections of heroic stories about the war that were produced by Russian publishing houses and geared to the broad Russian public also included the exploits of Jews. The story "Letter of a Vol-

Figure 16. "The Heroic Exploit of Private Katz." Kind permission of the Hoover Institution.

unteer," for example, features a Jewish soldier writing to his parents to apologize for enlisting without their permission. His filial piety toward the Empire was greater than that toward his parents and his religion, and he had joined the army to "fulfill his patriotic duty."[63] The literary sketch "Hero-Jew with Two St. George Crosses" describes the battle experiences of a Jewish scout who overhears the conversation of some German soldiers and, employing his excellent knowledge of German, warns the rest of his scouting party about the Germans' plan. As a result, the scouts drive away an entire German detachment and capture a Howitzer with ammunition.[64] Both of these stories emphasize the voluntary nature of the Jewish soldiers' service. In the first, the Jewish soldier voluntarily enlists in the Imperial Army, while in the second, the Jewish soldier volunteers for the dangerous task of gathering information in enemy territory. These sons of the Fatherland show their loyalty by their willingness to risk their lives as active members of the Russian military family. In the second story, the soldier's knowledge of Yiddish, which ordinarily marked him as a despised "other" in the Russian Empire, is the very skill that saves the day. Here, ethnic diversity within the Imperial family is presented as leading to success on the battlefield.

In addition to posters and literary sketches, films, such as *The Jewish Volunteer* and *The War and the Jew*, by Jewish directors, presented the achievements of Jewish soldiers in the Imperial Army to the public. A new journal, also called *The War and the Jew*, which was produced by the Moscow publisher D. Kumakov, was established with the specific purpose of celebrating the accomplishments of Jews who served the Russian Empire on the battlefield.[65] Large numbers of Russian citizens, therefore, had access to these images of Jews as an integral part of the Russian Imperial family. In similar vein, a pamphlet entitled *War and the Georgians*, published in 1915 by the government printing-house in Petrograd, highlighted the heroic deeds of Georgians in the Russian Imperial Army. This pamphlet proclaimed that "on the battlefield the hearts of all [people] of Russia beat in unison" and "the blood of Russians, Poles, Lithuanians, Latvians, Jews, Armenians, Tatars and Georgians is mingled."[66] This officially sponsored description of the relationships between the different peoples of the Empire, be they Slavs, Turks, or Caucasians, be they Catholic, Orthodox, Muslim, or Jewish, points to an emerging wartime redefinition of Empire. In this new relationship, the hearts of all peoples of the multinational Empire beat in unison and unanimity. As blood was spilled for Russia, the diverse peoples of the Russian Empire became true blood brothers.[67]

* * *

Through the rhetoric of family, Russian propagandists explored how to encourage discipline and a respect for authority in a way that would make them acceptable to the troops of the Russian Empire. Through the notion of hero, they presented an idealized image of one nation that would inspire all nationalities of the Empire to fight for Tsar and Fatherland. Both hierarchy and nation were articulated through masculine exemplars, while the opposite of this ideal masculinity, the cowardice and weakness of "the other," was expressed through a gendered notion of impotence. The ferment of the war also created new images of family and hero that coexisted with traditional ones. The family expanded to include non-Russian nationalities such as Caucasians and Jews, and representations of heroes sometimes reordered the hierarchy of the military family.

World War I propaganda was thus a syncretic mixture of rigid nineteenth-century images of a patriarchal and hierarchical nation, and twentieth-century democratic and inclusive visions of the national community. Propagandists employed stereotypical racist images of the infidel enemy Turks, while valorizing heroic Jews and Caucasians who served the Russian nation. They projected an outdated image of the hand-to-hand combat of valiant *bogatyr'* heroes and, at the same time, celebrated aviation and other aspects of modern warfare. Posters and literary sketches affirmed the legitimacy of paternal authority while granting "sons" a more significant role in the defense of the nation. Although these images ultimately failed to mobilize the subjects of the Russian Empire, they show that the Russian wartime government and society were cognizant of the need to create a more inclusive and modern vision of the nation. This symbolic image of the nation was successfully created only in the Soviet Union.

Notes

1. Michelle Perrot, "The New Eve and the Old Adam: Changes in French Women's Condition at the Turn of the Century," in Margaret Randolph Higonnet et al., eds., *Behind the Lines: Gender and the Two World Wars* (New Haven, 1987), 51. For a discussion of the testing of the myth of masculinity during the war, see Elaine Showalter, "Rivers and Sassoon: The Inscription of Male Gender Anxieties," in ibid., 63–65; George L. Mosse, *Fallen Soldiers: Reshaping the Memory of the World Wars* (New York, 1990), 63–64.

2. For a discussion of polarization in Russian society, see Leopold H. Haimson, "The Problem of Social Stability in Urban Russia, 1905–1917," *Slavic Review* 23, no. 4 (1964), and 24, no. 1 (1965).

3. For a discussion of Russian popular literature, see Jeffrey Brooks, *When Russia Learned to Read: Literacy and Popular Literature, 1861–1917* (Princeton, 1985).

4. The collection at the Hoover Institution on War, Peace, and Revolution, Stanford University, contains over eight hundred Russian World War I posters, including variants of approximately 650 different posters. These posters were most likely collected by Frank A. Golder of the Hoover Library while he was participating in the American Relief Administration's mission to Russia in 1921–1923. Because of the Hoover Library's commitment to preserving the legacy of World War I, it seems likely that Golder obtained as wide a sample of World War I posters as he could. See Peter Duignan, ed., *The Library of the Hoover Institution on War, Revolution and Peace* (Stanford, 1985), 30–31.

5. A recent exception is the work of Hubertus F. Jahn, *Patriotic Culture in Russia during World War I* (Ithaca, 1995). As Stephen White has pointed out, despite the similarity between World War I and Soviet posters in terms of style, the subjects portrayed and the artists involved, Soviet analysts have overlooked or minimized the participation of artists who were influential in creating Bolshevik posters in the production of World War I posters: *The Bolshevik Poster* (New Haven, 1988), 3.

6. See Jahn, *Patriotic Culture in Russia*, 62–63. The posters from the initial period of the war can be broken down into four categories: (a) (by far

the largest) battle scenes from the various fronts of the war (273 posters, of which sixty-one depict battles with Turkey, and the rest with Germany and Austria); (b) individual Russian soldiers and officers who performed heroic deeds, images of generals, and images of groups of heroes (108 posters); (c) caricatures of the enemies and their atrocities (107 posters); (d) the Allies, fund-raising for war causes, and other non-military issues (the rest).

7. Richard S. Wortman, *Scenarios of Power: Myth and Ceremony in Russian Monarchy*, vol. 1 (Princeton, 1995), 64, 254.

8. Nicholas V. Riasanovsky, *Nicholas I and Official Nationality in Russia, 1825–1855* (Berkeley, 1959), 93.

9. Ibid., 118–19, 121.

10. See Steven L. Hoch, *Serfdom and Social Control in Russia: Petrovskoe, A Village in Tambov* (Chicago, 1986), 91–132.

11. See John Bushnell, *Mutiny and Repression: Russian Soldiers in the Revolution of 1905–1906* (Bloomington, 1985).

12. Allan K. Wildman, *The End of the Russian Imperial Army: The Old Army and the Soldiers' Revolt (March–April 1917)* (Princeton, 1980), 35.

13. Ibid., 77–78.

14. Richard Boleslavski with Helen Woodward, *The Way of the Lancer* (New York, 1932), 13.

15. Wildman, *The End of the Russian Imperial Army*, 101.

16. Ibid., 88–89.

17. Vl. Denisov, *Voina i lubok* (Petrograd, 1916), 28.

18. Brooks, *When Russia Learned to Read*, 314.

19. Denisov, *Voina i lubok*, 3.

20. Compare "Parad" (Moscow: Tipo-lit. E. F. Chelnokova, n.d.), Hoover Institution on War, Peace and Revolution, Stanford University, Poster Collection (hereafter Hoover), RU–SU 705; and I. I. Terebenev, "Retirada frantsuzskoi konnitsy," in M. A. Nekrasova, *Otechestvennaia voina 1812 goda i russkoe iskusstvo* (The Patriotic War of 1812 and Russian art) (Moscow, 1969), illustration 34.

21. Postcards were produced by a publishing house in Moscow, "The Contemporary *Lubok*," and private firms such as that of I. D. Sytin. See White, *The Bolshevik Poster*, 3, 131, n. 25; Denisov, *Voina i lubok*, 33.

22. The battle near Lvov was depicted in the poster "Razgrom avstriiskoi armii pod Lvovom" (The rout of the Austrian army near Lvov) (Moscow: Litografiia T-va I. D. Sytina, no. 20, 1914), Hoover RU–SU 468; and the sketch, "Pod Lvovom" in *V ogne: Boevie vpechatleniia uchastnikov voiny* (In the fire: Battle impressions of participants in the war) (Petrograd, 1914), 10. The exploit of a regiment commander who was wounded in both legs and led his men into battle on a stretcher was immortalized both in the poster "Geroiskii podvig komandira polka" (The heroic exploit of a regiment commander) (Moscow: Litografiia T-va I. D. Sytina, no. 102, 1915), Hoover RU–SU 310, and the literary sketch "Geroi-polkovnik," in *Nashi chudo-bogatyri v voine 1914 goda* (Our heroes in the 1914 war) (Petrograd, 1915), 94.

23. White, *The Bolshevik Poster*, 14.

24. Vladimir Littauer, *Russian Hussar: A Story of the Imperial Cavalry, 1911–1920* (Shippensburg, PA, 1993), 50.

25. See Reginald Zelnik, "Introduction," in *A Radical Worker in Tsarist Russia: The Autobiography of Semën Ivanovich Kanatchikov* (Stanford, 1986), xvii–xix, for a discussion of Kanatchikov's relationship with his father. See also Cathy Frierson, "*Razdel*: The Peasant Family Divided," in Beatrice Farnsworth and Lynne Viola, eds., *Russian Peasant Women* (New York, 1992), 81–85, for a discussion of sons seeking independence from their fathers.

26. Littauer, *Russian Hussar*, 13.

27. See, for example, "Khrabryi Kul'nev General Maior," in V. Bakhtin and D. Moldavskii, eds., *Russkii lubok XVII–XIX vv.* (The Russian *lubok* in the seventeenth–nineteenth centuries) (Moscow/Leningrad, 1962), illustration 51.

28. "Ottsy-komandiry," in *Nashi chudo-bogatyri*, 92. The epithets of "father who worries about his people" and "friend to all" were later used to describe Stalin.

29. Mosse, *Fallen Soldiers*, 64–69.

30. Khristofor Shukhmin, *Slavnyi podvig Donskogo Kazaka Koz'my Kriuchkova* (The glorious exploit of the Don Cossack Koz'ma Kriuchkov) (Moscow, 1914), 5. General Skobelev was himself the subject of military *lubki* in the 1880s for his bravery in undergoing a medical operation on the battlefield. See the collection *Russkii narodnyi lubok* (Moscow, 1887–1889), Slavonic Division of the New York Public Library.

31. "Dva syna i otets v stroiu," in *V ogne*, 39–40.

32. V. D. Davydov, *Slavnoe Kazachestvo vo Vtoruiu otechestvennuiu voinu* (The glorious Cossacks in the Second Patriotic War) (Novocherkassk, 1915), 40.

33. See Viktor Shklovsky, *A Sentimental Journey: Memoirs, 1917–1922*, trans. Richard Sheldon (Ithaca, 1984), 7–9, for officer-soldier relations.

34. For an excellent discussion of the disintegration of the Russian army, see Wildman, *The End of the Russian Imperial Army*; for the war on the Eastern Front, see Norman Stone, *The Eastern Front, 1914–1917* (New York, 1975).

35. A. I. Denikin, *The Russian Turmoil. Memoirs: Military, Social, and Political* (New York, n.d.).

36. "Russkii soldat" (Moscow: Litografiia T-va I. D. Sytina, no. 57, 1914), Hoover RU–SU 337; a verst is about two-thirds of a mile.

37. "Sil'nyi Khrabryi Bogatyr' Il'ia Muromets" (Moscow: Litografiia Vasil'eva, 1887), in *Russkii narodnyi lubok*.

38. "Tragikomicheskii plen germanskogo ofitsera" (Moscow: Tipo-lit. Chelnakova, Russkoe slovo no. 228, n.d.), Hoover RU–SU 75.

39. See Dennis E. Showalter, *Tannenberg: Clash of Empires* (Hamden, CT, 1991), 114–17; Martin Kitchen, *The German Officer Corps 1890–1914* (Oxford, 1968), 182–86.

40. Littauer, *Russian Hussar*, 4–5, 78, 91.

41. In the Hoover collection there are twenty-eight posters featuring

Kriuchkov and only nine of Nicholas II. The most often pictured anti-hero was Kaiser Wilhelm, who appeared on twenty-three posters.

42. "Geroiskaia bor'ba kazaka Koz'my Kriuchkova s 11 nemtsami" (The heroic struggle of the Cossack Kuz'ma Kriuchkov with eleven Germans") (Odessa: Knigoizdatel'stvo M. S. Kozmana, 1914), Hoover RU–SU 162; "Bogatyrskoe delo Koz'my Kriuchkova" (The *bogatyr'*-like deed of Koz'ma Kriuchkov) (Moscow: Litografiia T-va I. D. Sytina, no. 13, 1914), Hoover RU–SU 134.

43. Hoover RU–SU 705 (see n. 20 above).

44. "Baba tozhe ne churban—mozhet vziat' aeroplan" (Moscow: Litografiia T-va I. D. Sytina, no. 17, 1914), Hoover RU–SU 852.

45. In other posters, the money in the German-Turkish relationship flowed in the other direction. They showed how the Germans paid the Turks for their war effort against Russia, thereby demonstrating Turkey's lack of independence. See, for example, the *lubok*-style poster, "Nemets kurit trubku, Turka kliuet krupku" (The German smokes a pipe, the Turk pecks at groats) (Petrograd: Izdanie V.F.T., no. 1, n.d.), Hoover RU–SU 8.

46. For images of mythical women in Allied posters, see "Joan of Arc Saved France," in Walton Rawls, *Wake Up America* (New York, 1988), 217; for an Italian example see Maurice Rickards, *Posters of the First World War* (New York, 1968), illustration no. 26.

47. Brooks, *When Russia Learned to Read*, 314.

48. "Pro trusost' turetskuiu da pro udal' molodetskuiu" (Moscow: T-vo Tipo-Lit. I. M. Mashistova, 1914), Hoover RU–SU 147.

49. For a discussion of European images of "the Orient," see Edward Said, *Orientalism* (New York, 1979).

50. "Soldatskaia pesnia" (Moscow: Sytin, 1889), in *Russkii narodnyi lubok*.

51. "Beseda pod Tsar'gradom" (Moscow: Tipo-lit. t. d. E. Konovalova i ko., no. 5, n.d.), Hoover RU–SU 46.

52. I am grateful to Igor Sopronenko, Lexington, KY, for assisting me with the transcription and translation of these verses.

53. See Olga Semyonova Tian-Shanskaia, *Village Life in Late Tsarist Russia*, ed. David L. Ransel (Bloomington, 1993), 29.

54. "Na boi krovavyi vpered s slovoi" (Petrograd: Izdanie V. T., n.d.), Hoover RU–SU 36A.

55. "Remember Belgium—Buy Bonds, Fourth Liberty Loan" in Rickards, illustration no. 182, is a symbolic depiction of the rape of Belgium: a young girl is abducted by a brutish German soldier. "Destroy this Mad Brute" in Rawls, *Wake Up America*, 66, shows a giant gorilla wearing a German army helmet, armed with a bloody club marked "culture" and carrying off a helpless woman.

56. "Voina s turkami v Zakavkaz'e" (Moscow: Litografiia T-va I. D. Sytina, no. 79, 1915), Hoover RU–SU 346. Earlier, non-Russian officers of the Empire, such as the Georgian General Bagration, had been heroized as individuals. Groups of Kirghiz cavalrymen were depicted during the

Napoleonic era because of their exotic nature. See Nekrasova, *Otechestvennaia voina 1812 goda*, illustrations. 14, 16, 46.

57. "Velikaia evropeiskaia voina," nos. 167, 171: Strazhniki-geroi" (Moscow: Lit. t. d. A. P. Korkin, A. V. Beideman i ko., n.d.), Hoover RU–SU 275, 276

58. "Cherkessy v Chenstokhove" (Circassians in Chenstokhova) (Grodno: Tipo-lit. "T-va S. Lapina s s-mi," n.d.), Hoover RU–SU 455.

59. Salo W. Baron, *The Russian Jew under Tsar and Soviets*, 2nd ed. (New York, 1987), 156–60.

60. "Geroiskii podvig riadovogo Katsa" (Odessa: Knigoizdatel'stvo M. S. Kozmana, 1914), Hoover RU–SU 319.

61. Brooks, *When Russia Learned to Read*, 316.

62. "Podvig riadovogo Katsa" (Grodno: Tipo-lit. "T-va S. Lapina s s-mi", n.d.), Hoover RU–SU 258. Although posters depicting Jewish heroes may have been produced by Jewish publishing houses, they nevertheless had to gain the approval of the military censor and therefore can be seen only as officially sanctioned images of war heroes.

63. "Pis'mo dobrovol'tsa," in *V ogne*, 17–18.

64. "Geroi-evrei s dvumia georgievskimi krestama," in *Nashi chudobogatyri*, 72–73.

65. Jahn, *Patriotic Culture in Russia*, 113.

66. D. Chiabrov, *Voina i Gruziny* (Petrograd, 1915), iii–iv.

67. The concepts of unity among the peoples of the Russian Empire— and their blood relationship to one another—reemerged in the 1930s in the slogan of the "friendship of peoples" and in the representations of the eleven Soviet republics as brothers or sisters. See Karen Petrone, "Life Has Become More Joyous Comrades: Politics and Culture in Soviet Celebrations, 1934–1939" (Ph.D. diss., University of Michigan, 1994), 275–79.

Re-Generation

Nation and the Construction of Gender in Peace and War—Palestine Jews, 1900–1918

Billie Melman

A generation is not merely a demographic fact. It is not any "whole body of persons" born about the same time, but a cultural construct, evolving in relation to a real or an assumed shared social experience and hence responding to certain collective needs.[1] These three related meanings of "generation" have figured prominently in discussion of World War I—both the contemporary and scholarly one—in which the "generation of 1914" occupied a privileged place and was elevated to a symbol of the disruptive effects of war. The best-known notion of this generation probably is that of loss and useless sacrifice—as in the "lost generation"—and of disillusionment with war.[2] At the same time, this notion has also had another constitutive meaning that is embedded in "generation"—that of reproduction and re-creation. As has been noted, in certain circles the war was welcomed as an opportunity for a regeneration of the nation and of a decaying civilization.[3]

However, the generation that came of age in 1914 still remains peripheral to the study of national identity and gender. This is mainly because considerations of this particular sociocultural group suffer from two elisions. In the first place, they tend to ignore gender and—with very few exceptions—are limited to men and an androcentric experience of the war,[4] and second, they tend to play down the relationship between the construction of that generation to the evolution of national identities. As Benedict Anderson has noted, this relationship is central to nationalism and was especially manifest during World War I, for the sense of belonging to a nation succeeded in converting war's fatality into a sense of continuity, expressed in the idea of the re-generation of the nation.[5] I would like to elaborate upon what Anderson implies but also to contest it. Implicit in his notion of the notion as an imagined community is that of a family with distinct roles of gender and age grafted onto the construct of "generation." Men and women are active members of this family that may be seen as extending both horizontally and vertically, that is, as including both the living generation and those yet to be born. I would argue instead, that the "familial" definition of the nation was open to interpretations, not only by national movements, but also by individual women and men, who negotiated their respective roles within the new, ethno-linguistic, national communities. Women in particular challenged the role prescribed to them as "mothers of the nation" and, in times of war, stretched the borderlines of femininity and masculinity. I consider the generation that matured around 1914 as the site of this national and colonial identity in flux.

A discussion of Zionist constructions of gender and the nation serves the purpose of this study because Zionism presents one of the most radical and concerted efforts to redefine gender in relation to the very perception of national regeneration. The Zionist revolution was not only about the resettlement and colonization of Palestine and a radical change in modes of life. Resettlement after 1881 also involved, and should be studied as, an attempted revolution in constructions of gender. Furthermore, Zionism and, in particular, Zionist colonization in Palestine present the case of the "invention" of a new man and woman, in opposition to Jewish models in Europe (both religious and secular).[6] Central to all varieties of Zionist discourse is the notion of the "first generation" of Jews, natives of Palestine (*yelidei ha-aretz*), who spoke the Hebrew language and whose life and social productivity embodied the nation.[7] This first generation was conceived as the locus of a modern Jewish national identity, defined in terms of gender that were dynamic and negotiable.

Notwithstanding its centrality to a "native" Zionist identity, this generation has been neglected and marginalized in Zionist historiography. This is partly for reasons of periodization and methodology, but mainly because the ideology and outlook of this particular generation did not fit in the mainstream, labor-oriented narrative of resettlement. With very few exceptions, recent attempts to recover this generation for history ignore gender. Moreover, some efforts to situate this early native identity and culture flounder because of the attempt to employ them as a basis for an alternative right-wing Zionist tradition.[8] My purpose here is to examine the invention of and negotiation over the national gendered identity of men and women born in Palestine during the formative decades of the Zionist Revolution between 1880 and 1920. I am particularly interested in how individuals defined their loyalties, not only to the Zionist project, but also to the colonial powers active in Palestine before and during World War I. I focus on the native Jewish elite in relation to the national and linguistic revival before the war. I then move to the war, to trace changes in the gendered national discourse and relate them to anti-Ottoman resistance. The war erupted and redirected the process of formation of Jewish "nation-ness." Stateless, Jews were forced to define their loyalty to the nation-state, a definition that was complicated by their marginal status in it. In Palestine—a part of the Ottoman Empire—this choice was further complicated by issues like citizenship and proximity to the war zone. Here I focus on the discourse of activists within the nationalist elite (mostly members of the Jewish anti-Ottoman espionage network, known within British Intelligence as "A Organization" and locally as "Nili"), and which was active between the spring of 1915 and its capture and liquidation in October of 1917. Nili received enormous coverage, not least because it was coordinated by a woman, Sara Aaronsohn (1890–1917), of the colony of Zikron Yaakov.[9] However, as has been noted, these studies are partisan and focus on "spying" and elide its larger national cultural (not to mention gendered) contexts.

THE GENDER OF NATION: INTERPRETATIONS OF "GENERATION" BEFORE 1914

The conventional view in recent, gender-centered studies of the Zionist project of regeneration is that it was largely one of remasculinization, that the new Jewish identity was androcentric, that it excluded women from the process of "normalization" and renewal of the nation (unless in traditional, family-centered roles), and that women's exclusion matched their removal from representation and power in a patriarchal colonial community.[10] The status of the native generation seems to have duplicated Central and Eastern European Jewish patterns of power and authority, thus confirming the premises of current scholarship. The first wave of immigration to Palestine (First Aliya, 1881–1904) settled mostly in families. Social production and the division of labor were familial, with women increasingly limited to domestic production (and reproduction). Labor became increasingly stratified according to age. Within the community, access to land and local power (and later in civil, self-governing bodies) was limited to heads of families. Indeed, lack of access to resources is often used as an explanation for the intra-generational tension that so often destabilized the agricultural settlements (moshavot) and few urban centers (in Tel Aviv and Jerusalem, for instance).[11] Tension erupted in the plethora of youth organizations that thrived in the pre-war decade. Semi-military organizations, like the Gideonites (1913), aimed at organizing Jewish self-defense but also at achieving participation in community politics, excluded women, and advertised themselves as male sodalities. The numerous "new generation" societies and associations for the revival of Hebrew, which mushroomed in agricultural settlements and in urban centers with large student communities, were mixed and indeed gave women space for action. Examples include The Generation of Hope, founded in the colony of Zikron Yaakov in 1903, The Young Generation, founded in Petah Tikva during the war, and the national students' associations and bodies actively agitating for national education in Hebrew, notably The Young Generation Association, later to be merged in the Students' Union and the smaller Executive Association, which organized the studentship of the first Hebrew gymnasium in Jaffa (Gymnasia Ivrit Herzelia [GIH]) in a self-governing and autonomous body in which women in their mid- and late-teens were active. These organizations have been justifiably seen as examples of a native national youth culture.[12]

The sociopolitical marginalization of youth in Palestine was complicated by their iconic place in the Zionist ethos, for there certainly was a discrepancy between the experience of the native generation within the familial agricultural community and their discursive construction as an elite and as the site of a new Jewish nationalism. The discrepancy is specially apparent in the status of men who came of age around the outbreak of World War I. For the Zionist ideal of a new Jew, apotheosized—in theory—in the new generation, was a construction of masculinity. Indeed, in Hebrew the very term "generation" (dor, from the Aramaic dar) seems to exclude women. The first Hebrew dictionary, the repository of the revived and modernized language and the life project of philologist Eliezer Ben-Yehuda (Perlman, 1858–1922), defines "generation" as "Histories born one of the other, which are one to the other as generations: the father, the son and the son of the son are three generations." Ben-Yehuda's impressive array of Biblical and Talmudic quotations stresses a patrilinear notion of a nation "fathered" by men.[13] Ben-Yehuda was reiterating the notion of the new man as the progenitor of the renewed nation, a notion familiar from the enormously popular national poetry of Saul Tschernikovsky (1875–1943) and laureate Chaim Nachman Bialik (1873–1934). In the former's popular rhymes, a generation "will live, act, do/ a generation on the land indeed lives/ not in the future—in heaven," while a phrase in Bialik's epic "The Dead of the Desert" became a household term: "We are the last generation of the enslaved and the first of the redeemed."[14]

Zionist models of masculinity and its embodiment in a native generation were constructed in diametric opposition to the diaspora

Jew, both the traditional Jew of Eastern Europe and the emancipated and assimilated (and secularized) Jew of Central Europe. Much has been written about the versus nature of the "new" Jew model, as well as about Zionism as an effort toward a reconstruction of a masculinity that was distinctly manly and heterosexual. Its staple characteristics—physical prowess, commitment to physical labor, and more generally, a "productive" way of life and a closeness to nature—were opposed to bodily weakness, a life that was not socially productive, and to an alienation from nature, all of which were seen as marks of the "old" Jew.[15] Both models reveal a critique of gender and of the relationship between Jewish nationalism and sexuality, which has scarcely been noted. Powerlessness—in the very physical sense—of the "old" type of Jew compromised Jewish honor, that is, the purity and respectability of the Jewish family, upheld by the sexual virtue of Jewish women. Impure families stood for an impure and degenerate nation. Of course, the analogy between men's honor—as a guarantor of women's purity—and the honor of the nation is a staple in nationalist mythologies. In Zionist discourse, however, the relationship between nationalism and sexuality was particularly significant, for after 1881, organized and large-scale anti-Semitic persecutions became part of the Jewish experience in Eastern Europe and particularly in Russia. The waves of organized *pogroms* in 1881, 1902, and 1905 became a spur to emigration and, at the same time, an index of the Jewish condition.[16] The pogroms occupied a central place in a collective memory in which the violated Jewish woman and her corollary, the impotent Jew unable to defend her, became predetermined metaphors for the degeneration of the nation. As long as Jewish men were unable to guarantee the purity of the "daughter of Zion" (hence their honor), she (the woman/nation) would remain desecrated. The theme of the rape of the nation was exploited by writers as politically different as Zionist leader Yehuda Leib Lilienblum (1843–1914), novelist and essayist Yosef Chaim Brenner (1881–1921), and the "native" polemicists like Absalom Feinberg (1889–1917). Thus Brenner, in a "Long Letter," published in London in 1906, refers to: "A definite complete development: the eighties—the blowing of feathers [of pillows and bed covers—a symbol of the pogroms] and of brains in the hundreds: the beginning of the [twentieth] century—the torture of virgins and the killing of souls by the thousands."[17]

In the writings of members of the new generation who did not themselves experience persecution, the symmetry of male impotence and female degradation is even more prominent. This is precisely because the new masculine identity evolved by pitting itself against, and denying, traditional models of masculinity. One striking example is the correspondence of Absalom Feinberg following the 1905 pogroms. Feinberg, dubbed "the first native-born Jew," who constructed himself, and was constructed by his milieu, as a new Hebrew, offers an explicitly sexualized interpretation of the national condition, in which he relates sexuality to force and violence. This particular relationship and his peculiar aesthetics of blood are possibly traceable to French Catholic and ultra-nationalist influences such as Charles Péguy's (1874–1914). Feinberg's apparently "irrational" and uncanny rendition of the recent history of Jewish humiliation is actually a self-conscious literary construct. Significantly, his most outspoken statements on nationalism and force are in his vast correspondence with women, notably with Sonya (Alexandra) Belkind, prominent gynecologist and physiologist and one of Palestine's first female doctors.

Imagining himself as a crow, a symbol of desolation and, in biblical imagery, carrier of bad news—Feinberg envisions the white wilderness of a Russian winter and a Russian landscape criss-crossed with streams of Jewish women's blood watering a human flora of dismembered bodies. His eye/I roves over shrubs and hedges budding with female eyes, heads, amputated breasts, and bellies slit open and filled with birds' feathers. In this horrific landscape, unnatural sexual acts take place, as Jewish women of all ages are raped by members of the anti-Semitic "black hundreds." Over the entire scene presides a voluptuous red Venus.

> I distinctly see them, these girls and women who knew how to be grilled for a God stupid and wild, these girls of a hoard, which calls itself a people . . . Damnation! Thy daughters Israel shall be on the loose and . . . thou shall not be blamed Jacob![18]

This bloody orgy is concluded with a cry for revenge and sacrifice— not Christ's sacrificial and passive death, but a violent and heroic one that involves killing. "If I could have communicated the rage which consumes me to all their men, how will they take their revenge!!! Oh well, a new Christ in my fashion . . . but no. Not Christ! I want the kingdom of Earth!"—a kingdom to be gotten solely by force. For historic models of violent death for national purity, Feinberg draws on Balkan national movements and on biblical examples.[19] His probably is one of the earliest formulations, in Palestine and elsewhere, of the idea that the ability to kill is the ultimate test of the new Jewish masculinity and a necessary component of the new Jewish national identity.

The demand for activism manifested itself in the well-studied organizations for self-defense that appeared in Russia from the turn of the century, and in paramilitary and semi-legal bodies for the defense of property in the colonies founded in Palestine, such as Bar-Giora (1907), Ha-Shomer (1909), and the Gideonites. Although women were admitted to, and participated in, most of these organizations, they were excluded from the ultimate practice of physical force, the right to kill. Women *did* practice force, and there is ample evidence of gender-specific active resistance in the agricultural settlements, to Ottoman soldiers, for example (mainly to Ottoman attempts to tear down illegal buildings). But this kind resistance did not affront Jewish or, for that matter, Ottoman notions of femininity, and were accepted and even sanctioned.[20] There were models of female activism and use of arms, available from Russian revolutionary and anarchist tradition, but these were limited to activists of the second wave of immigrants (Second Aliya, 1904–1914), notably to such activists as Ha-Shomer members Manya Vilboshevitz Shochat (1879–1961) an ex-anarchist, and Rachel Lishanski Ben-Tzvi (1886–1972), rather than to members of the native generation who refuted both the revolutionary *and* the socialist tradition of their contemporaries. Women of the native generation are routinely characterized as active and physical and as mastering horsemanship. They conventionally celebrate their physicality, sometimes in terms that blur the borderlines between the genders and indeed between the male and female bodies. Feinberg's younger sister Zila (see below) and female members of his extended Feinberg-Belkind "clan" and of his milieu exemplify this type of physical culture. Another rather typical example is Yehudit Harari (1886–1979), their contemporary, whose fictionalized autobiography includes a number of references to her horsemanship, physical force, and resort to arms. She often compares herself to a young male Bedouin.[21] A few other women, notably Sara Aaronsohn, had had access to arms, which they used before the outbreak of war. More significantly, in the national education system, notably in secondary schools and teachers' academies, girls received physical education and also flocked to the national sports' organizations.[22] Nonetheless, there seems to have remained one immovable borderline between the new kind of Jewish man and woman: the ability to kill in self-defense or to avenge violations of Jewish honor.

REGENERATION AND LANGUAGE

Both genders, however, had access to another component of nationness: native birth, or a "right of birth," conferred by the mastery of the "native" language—Hebrew. Significantly, such knowledge was "natural" and experiential rather than being an intellectual process. Here, indeed, the model new national woman enjoyed an advantage, for the maternalist approach to women in Judaic and Zionist traditions qualified them as the re-generators of a national language. A true Hebrew man is one who speaks (rather than reads or writes) Hebrew—argued Ben-Yehuda, and his son Ittamar (1885–1961), "the first Hebrew child."[23] Women were even truer Hebrews. They were seen as ideal practitioners of the language, and better teachers precisely because of maternity. Ben-Yehuda maintained that mothers—hence all women—were more important than fathers to the Hebrew renaissance. The former were the producers of a generation and hence could transform Hebrew from a merely literary language to a living national tongue. They were, literally, a "national asset . . . the basis of our national wealth . . . our national fund"[24] Ben-Yehuda was writing in 1903, at a time when the number of Hebrew-speaking women among the immigrants themselves was insignificant, and indeed when education was not yet "nationalized," and Hebrew had not yet been made the first language. The Hebrew transformation would occur only in the second, native generation, certainly among women of the elite. The point, however, is the representation of women as the conduits of the future nation. This point was taken further by women publicists, teachers, and writers such as Ben-Yehuda's wife Chemda (1873–1951), a journalist, popular writer, and editor of the first women's magazines in Palestine. "Would you know who could do more [towards national regeneration]? The maidens. You could not imagine the effect of a Hebrew-speaking woman, a woman who is at the vanguard of a national movement, a woman who speaks from the pulpit."[25] This was, according to her, a rare enough apparition. In similar fashion, Chava Hirschenzohn (1861–1932), a member of an old-settlement rabbinical family and a convert to the idea of female Hebrew revival, argued for a national education for women, in her biweekly *Beit Yaako* (House of Jacob), published in German Jewish (Hebrew Teitch) for the uninitiated. Hirschenzohn's transliteration was well-grounded in a long tradition that transcribed religious texts—notably prayers—in Jewish (Yiddish) especially for women. The tradition was vehemently rejected by nationalist feminists like writer and polemicist Nehama Puchachevsky (1863–1935), who denounced rabbinical attempts at constructing a "woman's language," as the main hinderance to female participation in the language renaissance.[26] The insistence that women too be taught (and teach others) "Hebrew in Hebrew" informed the activities of female language associations like Debora (founded 1902) and the mixed organizations for a national Hebrew education mentioned earlier (see p 24).

Outside religious circles, women's access to language—hence their national potential as the conduits of nationality—was not contested. Moreover, precisely because Hebrew was a new and "artificial" construct, it was a discursive field in which access to power and roles were negotiable. Thus women and men negotiated their relative places as the "producers" of language, hence of the national identity. This flexibility is important, for the early construction of Hebrew—and, by implication of nationalism—does not seem to represent the case of a textual operation in which only the powerful are active, and in which the "voices" of the powerless—on account of their gender—are muffled. Women defined their own access to language/nation differently than men. The latter usually tended to perceive the study of Hebrew by women as a domestic operation that was essentially maternalist. Women tended to "naturalize" their national role and detach it from maternity. In Feinberg's correspondence with women, their linguistic and national roles are prominent issues, which he and his correspondents approach quite differently. Thus Feinberg to Zila Feinberg:

> . . . nature made you a woman. Be, sister, what nature made you. A true woman. Those we lack. The Hebrew women who, when fifteen and in school will school their brothers, when twenty their spouses, and when twenty-one—at home—their children. With her small, weak hands, woman will knead and mould that giant generation, the generation which will create your homeland. Women will weave our future life, in a word that creature who will console in work, will encourage in war, and celebrate victory in singing . . . when your brother will become a strong man you shall become a strong woman . . . Little Zila, show yourself to be a great Hebrew mother and a great Hebrew woman.[27]

Feinberg's admonitions may be taken to represent his lack of confidence in his own manhood. His sister and her generation of educated women made the newly acquired Jewish masculinity seem precarious. "Little Zila" had been far removed from standard ideals of femininity. She continuously flaunted decorum by publicly challenging definitions of gender: cross-dressing, shaving her head to protest a sister's wedding and, the most publicized gesture, literally dropping the skirt that female students were obliged to wear in physical education classes—a public act that achieved for Jewish women in Palestine the right to exercise in shorts. More significant, whereas Absalom's formal education was never completed, Zila embarked on the complete course of female national education. She attended the first Hebrew kindergarten in Jaffa and at six entered, together with five other girls, the first class in the first Hebrew high school, GIH, which in 1913 she matriculated in Hebrew and Turkish. She then studied science in the University of Berlin and became a botanist and agronomist. After her return to Palestine in 1921, she joined the country's first feminist organization, Hebrew Women's Union for Equal Rights in Eretz Israel (Histadrut Nashim Ivriot le-Shivion Zekhuiot be-Eretz Israel).

The Feinbergs' debate, like the broader discussion within their milieu, was familial, both literally and metaphorically. The trajectory of the nation under construction was debated within and among the number of families that constituted the elite, occasionally between parents and children, but more typically within the native generation, among siblings, or among relations bound by blood and social and economic attachments. Four of the six Aaronsohns of Zikhron Yaakov—Sara, Rifka, Aaron, and Alexander repeatedly returned to the subject, which they also debated with their peers, members of the Feinberg, Belkind, Chankin, and Vilbushevitz families. Conventionally enough the nation was represented as a family, and families literally as the site of the nation. But significantly, in the writings by women, the nation is detached from the conjugal family. As is also evident from recent studies of women's literature of the First Aliya, they tended to represent families as sites of discord between genders. Indeed, these writers presented the national family not as the site of the nation, but as a patriarchal construct that excludes mothers from it. Puchachevsky's fiction is a case in point.[28] The notion of historical and ancestral family that is detached from marriage and childbearing is also apparent on the level of daily discourse. One example is the correspondence between Sara Aaronsohn, her eldest brother Aaron, and her fiancé, the affluent Constantinople merchant Moshe Abraham, concerning Sara's dowry—in land—which she refused to change into cash. Sara's priorities were her land, nation, and ancestors, not her future husband: "What made you, an eager Zionist Jew, you first of the Maccabees, prefer cash to the soil wet with the sweat of the pioneers, the tilled soil of the colony given you by the father of the girl you marry . . . the land of my colony, burial place of my mother . . . where after a hundred years my family will lie . . . Is your love such that when you marry a daughter of the colony you wish to cut her off from her homeland?"[29]

WAR AND REGENERATION

The outbreak of war threw open the definition of the young elite, forcing individuals to take stock of their place both as colonial subjects and as members of a national community vis-à-vis the global and international upheaval. Of course, for Jews generally, the conflict of identity and loyalty was acute, but among Jews in Palestine and especially within the native generation, loyalty and identity acquired a special significance for two reasons: First, the choice between Turkey and the Allies was intricately connected to the definition of citizenship and Jewish participation in the future government of Palestine. Second, the options for men's and women's participation in the war were intertwined with their self-definition as new Jews. As will be shown below, both participation and identity were debated and represented in terms of gender. Put differently, gender was used to make sense of the dislocation wrought by the war. Furthermore, images of gender and sexuality came to be the site of the changes—both local and international.

Turkey's declaration of war—and its decision to join the Central Powers—in the autumn of 1914—forced all inhabitants of Palestine either to take Ottoman citizenship actively or to renounce it and be expelled. The war abruptly ended the centuries-old capitulation and indemnity system that allowed non-Ottoman subjects of the empire to be under the protection of foreign consulates. Since about a half of the country's 89,000 Jews were citizens of foreign colonial powers— mainly of the Alliance and predominantly Russia, war meant Ottomanization or dislocation.[30] Ottomanization was gender-specific. Naturalized males were forced to enlist into the army (which formally had been open to them since the Young Turks Revolution in 1908), while those refusing Ottomanization were under threat of deportation or had to desert. For women, Ottoman subjecthood was optional—and in a number of cases they chose it. The question of Ottomanization was connected (albeit not causally and automatically) to the age- and gender-specific experience of dislocation, particularly in the period from the British occupation of the south of Palestine in 1917, to the completion of their campaign in 1918.

From the outset, the youth of the "native" elite adopted a pronouncedly activist and nationalist position with regard to the war. Initially they opted for Ottomanization as a conduit to a full-fledged Jewish "citizenship," understood as civil and political participation in the Ottoman Empire and as a means towards national regeneration and possibly degrees of self-government. As Baruch Ben-Yehuda, a graduate of the GIH class of 1914 and an activist campaigner for national education and a leader of the Young Generation association put it:

> We were a handful of thirty or forty young men and women, graduates
> of the first two classes of GIH, who determined destiny: to stay on the
> land! A minority amongst us born Ottomans, natives of the land from

Gedera to Metula, most of us new Ottomans, enthusiasts of Ottomanization in theory and practice . . . We included boys and girls
with a home and a family but many of us were alone, with no home
nor parents . . . Our national education implanted in us all the hopes
for a first "generation to redemption" [. . . and] the deep sense of a
unique historical vocation . . .[31]

Technically, Ben-Yehuda was not a "native," and in contradistinction to the second generation of agricultural colonists like the
Aaronsohns, he identified with Socialist Zionism and its ideology of
labor. But he properly belonged to the emerging urban nationally educated, "civil" elite (as distinguished from "labor," this last distinction being commonly used in the historiography). Unlike other
members of his class and school, Ben-Yehuda did not enlist but took
advantage of the year's postponement granted to high-school graduates by the Ottoman authorities. His "national service" (Ben-
Yehuda's term) was teaching Hebrew to the members of the
commune of Degania, the prototype socialist and communal settlement of the Second Aliya. The tensions between the urban and civil
type of nationalism and its socialist counterpart are evident both in
Ben-Yehuda's rejection of the manly model of the settler and in his
utterly secular and "naturalist" attitude to Hebrew.[32]

Ben Yehuda's peers who enlisted in the Ottoman army soon suffered a crisis of loyalty. This was partly caused by the deteriorating
conditions in the army, but mostly by the military's discrimination
against non-Muslim volunteers. In Palestine such volunteers were
attached to the Fourth Army's auxiliary forces, notably to the labor
battalions (*Tabur Amaliah*). Subsequently nationalist volunteers
like the members of the paramilitary organization of the Gideonites,
who had initially interpreted military service as an exercise in nationalism, began to regard this service as a humiliating experience,
both to their Jewishness and to their manhood. Cadets in the military schools recorded similar experiences.[33]

Women interpreted and exercised loyalty (and in some cases citizenship) quite differently from men, not least because Ottoman attitudes towards gender and femininity excluded women from active
public service in capacities other than maternal. Thus women who
did not serve in the army were not required to actively Ottomanize.
But as Rachel Lishanski Ben-Tzvi reports, a number among them
chose to claim their citizenship publicly. Moreover, women rendered Ottomanization a specifically national Jewish interpretation,
using "this occasion [to] change their foreign family names into Hebrew ones. Our appearance at the Serail took by surprise Turkish and

Arab officials who had not been used to seeing women address [them] on matters of documents."[34]

Claim of a passive citizenship, and sometimes service in the army's auxiliary or in emergency services for civilians, were acceptable—both to the Ottoman military and among Jews—secular as well as Orthodox. Indeed, nurses who served in Turkish, Austrian, and German hospitals were seen to be quite indispensable, and the number of women professionals who practiced as paramedics or doctors in urban centers and the moshavot were met with public approval. Alexandra Chankin, the district physician in Haifa, and Helena Cagan, the first Jewish doctor of the Jerusalem municipality, were described as "national" prodigies.[35] Such autonomous public roles in the wartime economy did not challenge maternalist politics. Indeed, the discourse about female devotion and women's role as healers coexisted with another "traditionalist" discourse, which cast them in their role as the victims of war, and which interpreted the war itself as a sexual conflict.

ARMENIA AND ZION: METAPHORS OF DEGENERATION AND SEXUALITY

As the war progressed, nationalist discourse became increasingly sexualized. In this discourse, women figured as the site of the nation and were elevated to a metaphor for the fate of the whole of the occupied Jewish population in Palestine. Of course, the sexualization of the discourse on the war, and especially the analogues between sexual dangers for women and dangers to the nation, were universal. The displaced and violated woman was perhaps one of the war's most potent and mobilizing metaphors: one has only to recall the tremendous impact of the so-called Belgian Atrocities, in which the allegedly raped Belgian women were identified with violated Belgium.[36] In Hebrew discourse, the overdetermined metaphor of the woman as a victim of war had particular meanings and national usages. This metaphor was distinctly orientalist, for violent sexuality was seen as a trait of all Muslim men but especially of Ottomans: it was the Ottoman victors, and not their allies the Germans or Austrians, who were depicted as dangerous to the women of Palestine and, by implication, to Palestine's Jews.[37] The role of aggressor, then, was transplanted from the Russian to the Turk (formally an ally—as the Zionist movement and establishment, as well as the formal leadership in Palestine kept their neutrality until at least early 1917). Memoirs and private histories of the war, such as Mordechai Ben Hilel Hacohen's *War of the Nations*, repeatedly invoke images of female weakness and the vulnerability of women during the war, a vulnerability that allegedly the Ottomans were not sensitive to.[38] Similarly, memorialists of the colony of Zikron Yaakov—the scene of anti-Ottoman activity—obsessively detail attempts of the Ottoman soldiery and officialdom to violate women and the emotionally charged reaction of Jewish men in defense of their honor.

It was, however, the nationalist and activist circles, which from 1915 identified themselves as anti-Ottoman, who most politicized the symbolic language of sexuality. Members of the pro-British Nili organization exploited the rape metaphor in publications and records that targeted Jewish audiences in the West and particularly the U.S. and Germany, as well as British Intelligence. Absalom Feinberg's *Report to Henrietta Szold* (1915), (a Zionist American leader and member of the board of the Agricultural Experiment Station, which was the base for the organization's intelligence activity) swarms with sexual images of the war. In one account of the army's acts of requisitioning supplies, he describes "heaps and heaps of women's underwear, of fine silk stockings and napkins and who knows what else," which the Ottoman Fourth Army expeditionary force carried away on their Suez Campaign to be used for dressing the wounded. Worse, the army even requisitioned gynecological and obstetrics equipment: "Women and mothers suffer—to no avail—and the instruments will be lost in the sands of the desert . . . This is how requisitioning is done in Turkey."[39] Elsewhere the report multiplies examples of attempts to harass women in the Jewish colonies, and of the abduction and violation of Christians.

What rendered the sense of sexual danger especially powerful was the systematic massacre of the Armenians, perpetuated by the Ottoman government and military between April and November 1915. The massacre of a minority, singled out for its ethnic and religious identity, was interpreted as an object lesson in the politics of war: disloyalty on the part of Jews would visit upon them a calamity similar to that of the Armenians. When the Ottoman military uncovered A Organization, there were widespread fears of a "second" Armenian massacre in Palestine. The network leader Aaron Aaronsohn (1882–1918) and his organization used the same massacre as a major explanation for the transfer of loyalty to Britain.[40] In both the "neutral" and anti-Ottoman, West-oriented renditions of the massacre, its gendered character is central. Armenian men, incapable of defending the womanhood of their nation, were systematically murdered; Armenian women and girls were systematically violated, sold, and abused. In intelligence reports of the massacre, the deportation of Armenians from their center at Van, through the Syrian

Desert and to "labor camps," Aaron Aaronsohn repeatedly notes the destruction of the Armenian family, the enslavement of Armenian women, the systematic abuse of girls by Turks of all classes, and large-scale (enforced) prostitution.

> The purity of [the Armenian nation's] family life is destroyed, its manhood is killed, its children boys and girls, enslaved in the private Turkish homes and for vice and debauchery, that is what the Armenian race in Turkey has come to.

And that, implies Aaronsohn—and others state outright—is what an unregenerated Jewish race would also come to.[41]

SARA: NARRATIVES OF FEMALE HEROICS

Notwithstanding its mobilizing power, the image of the woman as the victim of the war was not the only or most potent one in the national discourse. That discourse also contained the notion of female nationalist activism which, in itself, redefined the borderlines of gender. This coexistence is best manifest in the activity of the women members of Nili and their immediate milieu, most notably in the activity and writing of Sara Aaronsohn. From late 1916 until her capture and death in October of 1917, she coordinated the activities of the organization—the largest pro-British network in the Middle East—in Palestine and the Lebanon area, handling Nili's larger network of supporters and occasional informers and the organization's finances. Additionally she liaised with both the Ottoman authorities and the representatives of the hostile local community of her native Zikron Yaakov. Her leadership was partly familial, drawing on her position as the sister of the powerful Aaron Aaronsohn. But there is ample evidence that neither the other members of the underground nor members of her community, nor Turkish and British intelligence representatives regarded her as a strong man's sister and proxy.[42] There is, however, a revealing disparity between Sara Aaronsohn's construction as a national hero and her own self-representation. In contemporary and later biographical accounts of her, mainly in those by her brothers and co-workers, she is feminized. Her brand of heroism and sacrifice are seen as manifestations of an innate femininity.[43] For example, her conversion to the national cause, and transfer of loyalty to Britain are represented as an emotional reaction to the victimization of Armenian women and children. Her domesticity, too, is stressed. However, Sara Aaronsohn's few extant records reveal her to have been acutely conscious of the instability of gender.[44] A highly "feminine" woman, whom contemporaries marked out as sexually active, she nevertheless was described as manly. She often refers to herself and her work as masculine and occasionally attributes manliness to women outside the network, on whose cooperation she sometimes relied. More significantly, she seems to have been acutely aware of gender reversals. One striking example is her rendition of her cross-dressing in the traditional Purim costume party in March of 1916:

> We well turned the world upside down. I as a man and Tova [Gelberg, another underground member] . . . I in Absa[lom's] suit, a new grey habit which he brought from his last trip . . . it suited me well. Tova as a man in Aaron's tuxedo . . . we danced and turned the world upside down, till we put in danger quite a few women, the wretched fell for us . . . If you ever achieve something how happy you will feel yourself to be. Try to be merry as long as you are a free child and are given the chance.[45]

Gender reversal in the traditional Jewish theatricals of Purim was permissible and may be regarded as a carnivalesque act. As such, women's masquerading as men during Purim did not transform gender in the "real" world but possibly confirmed gender hierarchy. But to reduce Aaronsohn's act to mere performance is to ignore her broader criticism of contemporary notions of the borderlines between feminine and masculine sexuality and identity. The evidence in her writings clearly suggests that she rejected the attempts to interpret her lifestyle and authority in "traditional" terms of a desexualized and saintly femininity. As she wrote to one member of the organization, regarding his journal essay on sacred and profane female love, "With you everything is erected upon fantasies and hallucinations . . . I am all too real . . . and must accept life as it is . . ."[46] Her attempted suicide on October 5, 1917 (she died on October 8) after her capture and torture by the Turks is—as I have shown elsewhere—the very first instance of a voluntary death, by a woman, for a national (and secular) cause in Palestine. Moreover, Aaronsohn's staged and public act constitutes a break away from the paradigm of religious martyrdom available to Jewish women, as well as the passive resistance of the victimized female colonial subject. As presented in her suicide note, this was an active choice, even an act of defiance out of scorn of what she viewed as the weakness of her people. Significantly, she feminizes the Jewish people by naming the young women who betrayed her to the Turks.[47] This instance of her rejection of passive femininity may not be reduced to the mere adoption of male rhetoric, just as her conduct cannot be presented solely as that of an "emergency man." Like the suicide note, all her writing manifested detachment from the rhetoric and style of the men around her. Sara Aaronsohn's writing is sparse and austere, and her Hebrew self-consciously simple. In contradistinction to the other Aaronsohns and Feinberg, she is markedly self-effacing, a feature she attributes to a lack of "a knack for writing and an expression of the word . . ."[48] Taciturnity, the concealment of emotion, and indeed the repudiation of outward displays of emotion, have been repeatedly noted as characteristics of the ideal native Jew. Recently they have been marked out as central features of the first native generation in Palestine. However, the rhetoric of nationalism of the women considered here suggests that it was less emotionally charged than that of their male contemporaries. The former, regardless of their education and literariness (or lack of it) seem to reject the bathos and effusion so characteristic of Feinberg, the Aaronsohn men, and Ben-Yehuda. Significantly it is the men who employ Hebrew in a manner which the language revivalists of the earlier generation regarded as feminine. The women seem to detach themselves from the dominant style.

The notion of a native generation accommodated notions of masculinity and femininity, each flexible and negotiable enough to contain within itself contradictory images, and each changing its contours during the war. The new native Jewish man's main trait seems to have been the ability to exercise force—to defend women and thus the family/nation. However, this Jew's very masculinity (hence his national identity), was unstable, not least because of the emergence of the new generation of new nationalist women. Thus while Zionist discourse cast women as victims, mothers, or as cultural producers of the nation/language, women of the native elite detached themselves from these maternal models, and instead developed new ones for a female national activity. Theirs was a notion of a national family as a sodality of siblings. They also neutralized the rhetoric of nationalism, thus traversing the borderlines between genders.

NOTES

1. *Concise Oxford English Dictionary* (1982), 411; A. B. Spitzer, "The Historical Problem of Generations," *American Historical Review* 78 (1973): 1353–85; H. Moller, "Youth as a Force in the Modern World," *Comparative Studies in Society and History* 10 (1967): 237–60.

2. Robert Wohl, *The Generation of 1914* (Cambridge, 1979); J. M. Winter, "The Lost Generation," in *The Great War and The British People* (London, 1985), 65–76; George L. Mosse, *Fallen Soldiers: Reshaping the Memory of the World Wars* (Oxford, 1990), 63–64.

3. Mosse, *Fallen Soldiers*; Samuel Hynes, *A War Imagined: The First World War and English Culture* (London, 1990), 3–25.

4. Vera Brittain, *Testament of Youth* (rep., 1993) and dedicated to both women and men of her generation is one example. For a more recent consideration see Mary Louise Roberts, *Civilization without Sexes: Reconstructing Gender in Postwar France, 1917–27* (Chicago, 1994).

5. Benedict Anderson, *Imagined Communities: Reflections on the Origin and Spread of Nationalism*, rev. ed. (London and New York, 1991), 9–12.

6. On the invention of the new man, see George L. Mosse, "Max Nordau: Liberalism and the New Jew," in idem, *Confronting the Nation: Jewish and Western Nationalism* (Hanover, Massachusetts, 1993), 161–76; Rachel Elboim-Dror, "Gender in Utopianism: The Zionist Case," *History Workshop Journal* 37 (1994): 99–116. See also Michael Berkowitz, *Zionist Culture and West European Jewry before the First World War* (Cambridge, 1993), and especially Ch. 4, "Zionist Heroes": 91–118. On the state of studies of Zionist culture and gender see Billie Melman, "From the Periphery to the Center of Yishuv History: Gender and Nationalism in Eretz Israel," *Zion* (forthcoming, vol LXIII, no. 3 [1997]).

7. Itamar Even Zohar, "The Emergence and Crystallization of Local and Native Hebrew Culture in Eretz Israel, 1882–1948" *Cathedra* (July 1980): 165–90; Jaffa Berlovitz, *Inventing a Land, Inventing a People: Literature and Culture During the First Aliya* (Tel Aviv, 1997). I am grateful to Berlovitz for letting me read her manuscript before publication.

8. Anita Shapira, "A Generation on the Land," *Alpayim-A Multidisciplinary Publication for Contemporary Thought and Literature* (in Hebrew) no. 2 (1990): 178–203. For the attempt at an alternative and probably right-wing narrative, see Rachel Elboim-Dror, "'He is come, from amongst us he is come the first Hebrew': On the Youth Culture of the First Waves of Immigration," ibid., no. 12 (1996): 104–136.

9. See for example Eliezer Livneh, Yosef Nedava, Yoram Efrati eds., *Nili, Toldoteha shel He'aza Medinit* (Nili, the history of political audacity), (Tel Aviv, 1980). For a critical review of the literature on Nili see Yigal Shefi, "Intelligence in the British Occupation of Palestine, 1914–18" (Ph.D. diss., Tel Aviv University, 1993). For a discussion of Nili see pp. 181–95.

10. Deborah Bernstein, ed., *Pioneers and Homemakers: Jewish Women in Pre-State Israel* (New York, 19), especially Ran Aaronsohn, "Through the Eyes of A Settler's Wife: Letters from the Moshava," 29–49; Margalit Shilo "The Transformation of the Role of Women in the First Aliya 1882–1903," *Jewish Social Studies, History, Culture and Society* 2, no. (Bloomington, IN, 1996), Yossi Ben-Artzi, "Between Farmer and Laborer: Women in Early Jewish Settlements in Palestine (1882–1914)," in Yael Atzmon, ed., *Eshnav le-Hayim shel Nashim be-Hevrot Yehudiot* (A view into the lives of women in Jewish societies: Collected essays) (Jerusalem, 1995), 309–25. For literary feminist critique see Berlovitz, "Literature of Women of the First Aliya: The Aspiration for Women's Renaissance in Eretz Israel," in Bernstein, *Pioneers and Homemakers*, 49–75, and "The Melancholy Voice as the Voice of Protest: A Study of the Writings of Nehama

Puchaczewski, One of Palestine's First Women Story Tellers" in Atzmon, *A View*, 325–37.

11. Rachel Elboim-Dror, *Ha-Hinukh ha-Ivri be-Eretz Israel* (Hebrew education in Eretz Israel), vol. 2, *1914–20* (Jerusalem, 1990), 311–83.

12. Elboim-Dror and Barouch Ben-Yehuda, *Sipura shel ha-Gymnasia Herzelia* (The story of Gymnasia Herzelia) (Tel Aviv, 1970), 69–83.

13. Eliezer Ben-Yehuda, *Milon ha-lashon ha-Ivrit ha-Yeshana ve-Hahadasha (A Dictionary of Ancient and Modern Hebrew)* (Jerusalem, 1910), vol. 2, pp. 900–901.

14. Saul Tschernikovsky, "I Believe," *Poetry* (Tel Aviv, 1948); Chaim Nachman Bialik, *Selected Poems*, bilingual edition, (Jerusalem, 1981), 112.

15. See Mosse, "Max Nordau"; Even Zohar, "The Emergence and Crystallization of a Native Culture"; Elboim-Dror, "Gender in Utopianism," and Daniel Boyarin, *Heterosexuality and the Invention of the Jew* (Berkeley, 1997).

16. Anita Shapira, *Land and Power: The Zionist Resort to Force, 1881–1948* (New York, 1992).

17. Yosef Chaim Brenner, *Mikhtav Arokh* (A long letter) in *Works*, vol. 6 (Tel Aviv, n.d.), 42. See also "Hu Amar La" ("He said to her,") ibid., 29–34.

18. Absalom Feinberg to Sonya (Alexandra) Belkind, Aaronsohn House Archives, Zikron Yaakov (hereafter AHA), Absalom's Records, 2.

19. For the Balkans, see Feinberg to Mendel Chankin, Jan. 18, 1909, and to Israel (Lolik) Feinberg, Oct. 14, 1907, AHA, Absalom's Records, 4.

20. See Berlovitz, *Inventing a People*, 46; Yehudit Harari, *Isha va-Em be-Israel* (A woman and mother in Israel) (Tel Aviv, 1959), 240; Moshe Smilanski, *Rehovot* (Rehovot, 1950), 25–26; Yaakov Yaari Polskin, *Sefer ha-Yovel li-Mlot Hamishim Shana le-Yisud Petah Tikva* (Petah Tikva Jubilee Book) (Tel Aviv, 1939), 530–31; Ever Hadani, *Sefer Hadera* (Hadera Book) (Jerusalem, 1951), 125–26.

21. Yehudit Harari, *Bein ha-Kramim* (Among the vineyards) (Tel Aviv, 1947), 18, 34.

22. Elboim-Dror, *Hebrew Education* 2:21.

23. Ittamar Ben Avi, *Im Shahar Atzma'utenu: Zikhronot Hayav shel ha-Yeled ha-Ivri ha-Rishon* (Memoirs of the first Hebrew child) (Tel Aviv, 1961).

24. Eliezer Ben-Yehuda, *Hashkafa* (Jerusalem), 19 (1903).

25. Chemda Ben-Yehuda, "The Progress of Hebrew," ibid., 10 (1903).

26. For Hirschenzon, see David Tidhar, *Encyclopedia le-Halutzei ha-Yishuv u-Bonav* (Encyclopedia of pioneers and builders) (Tel Aviv, n.d.), 4:1167; Berlovitz, *Inventing a People*, 66.

27. Absalom Feinberg to Zila Feinberg, June 15, 1910, AHA, Absalom Records, Additional Papers from Feinberg/Shoam Archives.

28. Berlovitz, *Inventing a Land*, 65–73.

29. Sara Aaronsohn to Haim Abraham, n.d., AHA, Sara Records, 2.

30. Jacob Markowitzky, "Conflict of Loyalties: The Enlistment of Palestinian Jews in the Turkish Army" (in Hebrew) in Mordechai Eliav, ed., *Ba-Matzor u-va-Matzok* (Siege and distress: Eretz Israel during the First World War) (Jerusalem, 1991), 97–111.

31. Archives of Hebrew Herzelia Gymnasium, Tel Aviv (hereafter GIH), Ben-Yehuda, "Degania Journal."

32. GIH, "Degania Journal."

33. On students' experience of the army, see *The Story of Gymnasia Herzelia*, 181–202. On the experience of the army outside the officer class, see Markowitzky, "Conflict of Loyalties."

34. Rachel Yanait Ben-Tzvi, *Anu Olim* (We make Aliya) (Tel Aviv, 1961), 111.

35. See Mordechai Ben Hilel Hacohen, *Milhemet ha-Amim* (The war of the nations) (Tel Aviv, 1929), 3:86–87.

36. See my Introduction above.

37. For Hebrew orientalism, see Yitzhak Laor, *Anu Kotvim Otakh Moledet* (Narratives with no natives: Essays on Israeli literature) (Tel Aviv, 1995), 77–79.

38. Mordechai Ben Hilel Hacohen, *The War of Nations*, 3:36–37, 148, Yirmiyahu Yaffe, "Journal," Zikhron Yaakov, April 1917–1918.

39. Aaron Amir, ed., *Absalom* (Absalom: The writings and letters of Absalom Feinberg) (Haifa, 1971), 275.

40. On attitudes to the Armenian massacres, see Vahakn N. Dadrian, *The History of the Armenian Genocide: Ethnic Conflict from the Balkans to Anatolia to the Caucasus* (Berghahn Books, 1995); Yair Auron, *Ha-Banaliut shel ha-Adishut* (The banality of indifference) (Tel Aviv, 1995), 151–203.

41. Aaron Aaronsohn, "Pro Armenia," AHA, Aaron Aaronsohn Records, 6, Articles, 26/13.

42. The Journal of Yirmiyahu Yaffe, AHA, Nili Records, 1; Anthony Verrier, ed., *Agents of Empire, Anglo-Zionist Intelligence Operations 1915–19: Brigadier Walter Gribon, Aaronsohn and the Nili Spies* (London, 1995).

43. Alexander Aaronsohn, *Sara Shalhevet Nili* (Tel Aviv, 1962), 11–12; Yehuda Yaari Polskin, *Nili Book Four: Sara* (Tel Aviv, 1940), 142–43.

44. Ibid., 83, 86.

45. AHA, Sara Aaronsohn Records.

46. To Lioba Shneorsohn, quoted in Yaari Polskin, *Nili*, vol 4: *Sara*, 73. On the new model of active death for the nation see Melman, "From the Margins to the Center of Yishuv History."

47. See Livneh et al., *Nili*, 312.

48. Livneh, 73.

Taking Risks for Pictures

The Heroics of Cinematic Realism in World War I*

Sonya Michel

"But it is extraordinary, monsieur, that you should take such risks for pictures. You may in all probability get shot."

"Possibly, sir . . . but to obtain genuine scenes one must be absolutely in the front line."[1]

At the turn of the nineteenth century, American men were feeling besieged. The closing of the frontier, the rise of corporate bureaucracy, and tightening of industrial discipline, and the spread of political machines, coupled with women's growing authority in the family and assertions into the public sphere, had eroded the traditional foundations of men's independence, political status, and masculinist prerogatives. It is not surprising, then, that American men, who, like those elsewhere, had been bred on the legends of past wars, looked to the coming conflict as an opportunity to redefine and reclaim their manhood.[2] It would be, in Theodore Roosevelt's words, "a great adventure."

What the "Doughboys" encountered instead was the tedium and intermittent deadliness of modern warfare and a rationale for the conflict that was beyond the comprehension of most.[3] Though their battle stints turned out to be brief, and their casualty rate far lower than that of the other belligerents, American soldiers returned disappointed and disillusioned.[4] According to literary historian Paul Fussell, their feelings, like those of their long-suffering British counterparts, were registered in a cultural language of irony—a language that belied the heroics and patriotism that are usually associated with men at war.[5]

With instabilities of gender masked as existential complaints, but still close to the cultural surface, one might expect that gender

---

*The perceptive comments of John Whiteclay Chambers II, Janet Gray, Billie Melman, and Elizabeth Young helped sharpen the focus of this essay.

values in the two societies would be dramatically reconfigured. Yet, soldiers' anxieties notwithstanding, World War I disturbed but did not bring down masculinist hegemony. It survived, in part, because the ironic mode, though unmistakable, was but one aspect of Anglo-American culture, and it was confined largely to high literary modernism. Popular culture, particularly movies, continued to uphold traditional manly qualities such as courage, stoicism, and daring. Though literary consumption was, as Fussell explains, widely dispersed during the war, particularly in Britain, moviegoing was arguably even more popular and probably more effective in shaping values and the way people saw the world.

According to literary historian Samuel Hynes, "by the end of 1916 there was a new realism in the ways in which some English men and women thought about the war. . . . It was the motion picture that made the war imaginable for the people at home."[6] The same was true in the U.S.[7]

Movies were not only more compelling than literature, but their messages were different. While poetry, fiction, and essays expressed men's doubts and anguish, much of what appeared on the screen—both dramatic "photoplays" and documentary news and military footage—upheld conventional norms of masculine behavior and emotions. Thus while modernist literature revealed a destabilized gender system, film (a less sophisticated medium) remained a site for the reproduction of male domination.

Different film genres did this in different ways. Photoplays, for example, tended to perpetuate the rather traditional images of masculinity and femininity that were borrowed, along with narrative conventions, from Victorian and late nineteenth-century drama and melodrama.[8] Newsreels and documentaries, by contrast, initially took as models theatrical reenactments—known as "actualities"—of significant public events, which were less obviously gendered. Their gender neutrality gradually changed, however, as documentary filmmaking about the war not only focused primarily on men and their activities, but also established conventions of production that were coded as masculine. Moreover, the films themselves created new criteria for what constituted (or came to be taken for) cinematic realism—criteria that were also linked to masculinity.[9]

Masculinity and realism were joined in the person of the wartime cinematographer, who, as the war went on, faced ever-greater dangers in pursuit of "genuine scenes." More dashing and adventurous, and usually less constrained by military discipline, than the humble *poilu* (French front soldier), Tommy, or Doughboy, cinematographers (who were almost all men) reportedly risked their lives to capture vivid images that could convey to the civilian population the "true" experience of the war. The press helped turn the experiences of such men into instant legends. When George Ercole, a Pathé cameraman, was wounded at the first Battle of Przemysl, the American trade paper *Motion Picture News* reported that "he kept turning the crank" and was decorated by the Russian government "for his bravery."[10] Similarly, according to Homer Croy's *How Motion Pictures Are Made* (1918), a French filmmaker's camera continued to roll after he was shot dead at the Battle of Verdun.[11]

Cinematographers were the original participant observers, living cheek by jowl with the troops and undergoing the same risks and hardships. Yet their images somehow escaped the irony that marked their more mundane counterparts, probably because they managed to achieve their goals with only minimal loss of life and limb.[12] Theirs, moreover, was a story of creation, not destruction, of an attempt to preserve on film the nation's experience of war, its blood and flesh. Their search for "the truth" came to be read as a form of patriotism which, because detached from the killing and maiming, emerged as pure, free of the cynicism that suffused perceptions of the war itself, and all the more laudable because most of the men performing these heroic feats were civilians—ordinary men.[13]

Still in its fledgling state at the outset of the war, news and documentary filmmaking advanced dramatically as those involved in production (of whom front-line cinematographers were only the most visible) faced and resolved unprecedented technical, practical, logistical, and political problems. Cinematographers, like other journalists, were barred from the battlefront until May 1915, when France became the first nation to relax its regulations; Britain and Germany soon followed.[14] Though many countries sent camera crews, the war so disrupted production that by 1917 the United States was, for all intents and purposes, the only country still getting movies out to the public.[15]

Once at the front, cinematographers had to face many technical challenges. In addition to avoiding bodily harm, they had to devise ways to accomplish their tasks under difficult, often dangerous, conditions. These included finding equipment that could be easily carried on ten-mile marches and in battle. Most early motion picture cameras weighed around one hundred pounds (the average infantryman carried only seventy), required hand-cranking, and were designed to be operated on tripods.[16] Cameras protruding "over the top" made easy targets, so one ingenious cinematographer, Donald Thompson, learned to start up his electric-powered model, mount it on a pole, and use a periscope to aim it.[17] Even with such devices, modern trench warfare, vast and unpredictable, was elusive and hard to capture on film.

Though, in theory, either men or women with sufficient determination could meet such challenges, war cinematography became masculinized early on. This was evident in the press's treatment of Jessica Borthwick, one of the few women who tried to enter the field. At age twenty-two, Borthwick, the daughter of a British general, spent a year filming the war in the Balkans. In a 1914 interview with the trade magazine *Moving Picture World*, she spoke of finding her equipment awkward and unwieldy (as did most male cinematographers) and also alluded to personal danger: "During the Serbian war in Macedonia, my tripod was smashed by a shell, and although the camera was intact, the film . . . got hopelessly jumbled up. . . ."[18] Borthwick herself dismissed the idea that her gender interfered with her work, but the magazine seemed bent on presenting her as someone who had stumbled into situations—and a profession—that were "no place for a lady." With few other women following in her footsteps, the ranks of war cinematographers became marked as male, and the veracity of wartime footage was inextricably linked with the skill and bravado (and therefore the gender) of those who "got" the pictures.

"THE REAL THING"

The demand for firsthand battle footage came from film producers and exhibitors eager to satisfy a public that was hungry for information and images (nowhere more so than in the U.S., both before and after entering the war), and from governments seeking to mobilize support for the war. When fresh footage was unavailable, producers used stock footage or faked battles and other events.[19] Though many scenes were (to the modern eye) obviously staged or recreated (glimpses of both production personnel and spectators at the margins of a frame were not unusual), viewers did not initially object.[20] Their cinematic expectations had been formed by "actualities"—frank reenactments of events from the Boer and Spanish-American Wars, when cameras were also barred from the battlefront and filmmakers had to manufacture their own footage, even resorting to staging naval battles in bathtubs.[21] The results were hardly seamless, but anti-Spanish jingoism was so strong that the mere sight of the U.S. military on the screen, coupled with the novelty of the medium itself, was enough to set off waves of patriotism among American audiences.[22]

Moviemakers had another advantage: while the public tended to suspect journalism of bias, they accepted the veracity of film at face value. As a contemporary film critic put it, "The only real and incorruptible neutral in this war is . . . the film. The moving-picture camera is convincing beyond the peradventure of a doubt. . . . It is utterly without bias and records and reports but does not color or distort."[23] "It is hard to convey the ingenuousness of the motion picture audiences of 1914," film historian Kevin Brownlow has concluded. "They believed the camera could not lie, and that the photographic image represented undistorted reality."[24]

Reality, however, was an unstable category. With each technical innovation, each step closer to the lines of battle, the criteria changed. "As the war churned on," film historian Michael T. Isenberg notes, "outright fakes proved unacceptable to seasoned audiences."[25] Producers themselves sharpened the demand; an ad for *The German Side of the War* (1915) told exhibitors, "You must give your patrons the real thing. Substitutes will not do. You cannot get away with it very long. There is no doubt that all others are cheaper. But the public is wise. . . ."[26]

The availability of photography, and especially cinematography, radically transformed popular perceptions of war during these years. The Great War was, in Samuel Hynes's words, "not only the great military and political event of its time, but . . . also the great imaginative event," and filmed images had much to do with shaping the "imaginative version" of the war and turning it toward a "new realism." With cinematic images so ubiquitous, it seemed that for many civilians the war existed only insofar as it was represented on screen. Films, says Hynes, "clearly . . . appealed to audiences eager for a glimpse of the real thing."[27]

Yet on the screen, footage of actual events was often disappointing; it tended to be monotonous and lacked the dramatic power of scenes shot in studios.[28] Contemporary critics tried to defend "honest" films on patriotic grounds. Reviewing *America's Answer* (1918), a movie made by the U.S. Committee on Public Information that focused mainly on behind-the-lines activities, the *New York Times* demurred, "Scenes representing this side of war may not be as exciting as those made in sight of No Man's Land," but they demonstrate America's contribution to the war effort.[29] Audiences, however, according to film historian David Mould, "expected the real war to be as colorful and exciting as the fictional one. . . ."[30] In many films, the most memorable scenes turned out to be those that were actually staged.[31]

Thus filmmakers found themselves in a quandary: Should they continue to fake scenes or rely only on "genuine" footage? Most, according to Mould, resorted to a mixture of the two, and this, in turn, established new criteria for cinematic realism.[32] For our purposes, the question of whether or how much footage was actually faked is important not in itself, but only insofar as it reveals the level of audience demand for "realism," which, in turn, put pressure on cameramen to produce footage that was both exciting *and* looked authentic. Filmmakers could try to do this in a studio, or they could risk going to the front to obtain "genuine scenes."

GUARANTEES

One way to certify authenticity was to inscribe the cinematographer himself within the text of the film. Whereas in earlier newsfilms, glimpses of cameramen or even spectators had occasionally slipped in, now the inscriptions were deliberate, drawing attention to the effort made to obtain a particular shot or scene. Cameramen might be shown loading equipment or embarking for the battlefront;[33] Donald Thompson's *War As It Really Is* (1916) opens with a shot of Thompson reading a telegram: "cable story what war really is." Donning a scarf and helmet, he boards a plane and takes a series of aerial shots of the harbor at Salonika.[34] Cameramen also inserted their personalities into the visual text by commenting on their own responses to events; in an intertitle at the end of *The German Side of the War* (1915), cinematographer Edwin Weigle assesses the emotional toll of his experience: "Having the horrors of war indelibly inscribed in my memory . . . I sailed to America. . . ."[35]

References to the conditions under which particularly striking scenes were shot or the techniques used, also pointed up the feats of the cameramen. One segment of *War As It Really Is*, "In the Jaws of Death: French Fighting As It Really Is," shows soldiers ducking as enemy fire comes toward them *and* toward the camera, which is apparently positioned behind the Allies' trench. French soldiers light rockets to be fired back, and eventually—in close-up—go "over the top," shouting "Vive la France" as they charge. Underscoring the visual information about the location of the camera (and the cameraman), an intertitle notes that in some places the trenches were only forty feet apart and claims, "Donald Thompson risked his life many times to photograph this attack."[36]

Cameramen's presence in specific scenes was often confirmed through the mode of direct address—figures looking straight into the camera. Considered transgressive in fiction films (where, to preserve the illusion of verisimilitude, visual references to the camera are avoided), this device occurs fairly often in newsreels and documentaries (whether deliberately or coincidentally), where it calls attention to the presence of the camera and thus, by implication, of the camera *operator*.[37] There are several examples of direct address in another Thompson film, *Somewhere in France* (1915). In one scene, where live ammunition rounds are being traded between the French and the Germans, several French soldiers turn and stare into the lens, while in another, one German prisoner glances at the camera while another makes a cranking motion with his hand.[38] The use of direct address reminded audiences that the cinematographer was being exposed to the same dangers—live gunfire, hand-to-hand combat—that he was filming, and thus simultaneously confirmed his bravery as gripping scenes of battle rolled by.

Masculine qualities also became linked to authenticity in movie advertising and promotion, which made authenticity a major selling point for wartime films. A trade ad for *The Battle and Fall of Warsaw* (1915) proclaimed, "These pictures are not imaginary, they are REAL. They were not staged."[39] To support their claims, promoters and exhibitors cited cameramen's courage and daring as signs that footage had actually been made on the site of battle.[40] Exploiting the association between risk and authenticity to the fullest, in 1917 the owners of the Strand Theatre in New York went so far as to re-edit *Battle of the Somme* and claim that four of its fourteen cameramen had been killed in the course of filming—this while the two men who had actually shot the movie, Geoffrey Malins and J. B. McDowell, were both still very much alive and continuing to make films.[41]

Emphasis on the heroic qualities of cameramen served to distract audience attention from the ghastliness of the war itself. For instance, the trade magazine *Reel Life* regaled readers with the exploits of Leon Crabier, a cameraman for the newsreel *Mutual Weekly*, who was filming in the Vosges in 1915:

> Of a sudden the air is alive with bursting shells. Men are falling, dead and dying, many of them within but a few rods of the lens, the undaunted photographer having brought his camera right into the heat of battle. Then comes the charge through the snow, where the men are mowed down by hundreds. Rescue of the dying and injured and recovery of as many of the dead as possible are clearly depicted in all their horror, together with scores of other thrilling scenes and incidents of battle, making this set of pictures by far the most wonderful of their kind ever obtained.[42]

While the courage of the "undaunted photographer" and the "thrilling scenes" are celebrated, the dead and dying become reified—"mowed down," "depicted in all their horror," and finally captured by the camera's lens. The ignominious loss of identity on the part of numberless and faceless soldiers is to be recuperated by the hypermasculinity of the cameraman.

CRITICAL INTERVENTIONS

Film critics and entertainment reporters in the trade and popular press also collaborated in the marketing of heroic realism by celebrating the footage obtained through extraordinary means. A *Moving Picture World* review of *The Battle of Przemysl* (1915) lavishly praised the results of cameraman Albert K. Dawson's courage: "Dawson frequently risked his life in the making of this picture, and for a crowning achievement photographed an actual battle—the capture of a town. It seems safe to say that these scenes . . . have never been equalled."[43] Writing in a similar vein in *Picture-Play Magazine*, critic Roger Packard emphasized the risk-taking implicit in Merl LaVoy's *Heroic France* (1917):

> In contrast to most war pictures shown in this country which have been taken rather remote from the firing line, these pictures were almost invariably taken under the muzzles of the guns. Here you see the French artillery batteries swinging into line for one of the big "punches" on the Verdun front. In another scene are shown the ambulance corps men tending wounded under fire. . . ."[44]

Packard's piece was provocatively entitled "The Movie Machine Gunner."

Praise for heroic realism was found not only in popular and trade magazines but also in the elite press. Lauding *How Britain Prepared: The Retreat of the Germans* (pt. 4) (1917) for providing "in perpetuity a picture history of the struggle in its various phases," a *New York Times* reviewer explained why, over only a few months' time, the quality of war films had risen by ninety-five percent:

> The art of taking battle pictures is one that improves by practice and in this case, the lessons have been paid for in the blood of venturesome men who have taken all risks to procure for the great public at home good pictures of what modern war means and how it is waged today. So there is plainly shown "the real thing" as our own troops will see and share it in the era now beginning.[45]

Once again, we have "the real thing," this time associated with the suffering and sacrifice not of the troops, but of the cameramen.

Critics further underlined what was at stake in battle films by dismissing as frivolous many of the commercial films released during these years. The *New York Times* critic, for example, delivered a scathing review of a seemingly innocuous 1918 photoplay, *The Venus Model*, in which a working girl saves her boss from business failure by designing an ingenious style of bathing suit.[46] In wartime, the preference was clearly for dramatic films that depicted women as sober and self-sacrificing. Though wartime settings expanded women's cinematic roles beyond the usual wife-mother-sweetheart (sometimes they got to be nurses or canteen workers, or even spies), female characters were expected to remain subordinate to a dominant plot that was driven by the actions or situations of the male characters.[47] The only movies in which women were central featured "narratives of beset womanhood."[48]

CINEMATOGRAPHER AS HERO

Eventually, the personae of the cinematographers, both individually and collectively, took on lives of their own. One of the most flamboyant figures, a star in his own right, was Donald Thompson. *New York World* writer Alexander Powell recalled,

> Of all the horde of adventurous characters who were drawn to the continent on the outbreak of war . . . I doubt if there was a more picturesque figure than a little photographer from Kansas named Donald Thompson. . . . He blew into the consulate [in Ostend] wearing an American army shirt, a pair of British officer's riding breeches, French puttees, and a Highlander's forage-cap, and carrying a camera the size of a parlor phonograph. No one but an American could have accomplished what he had, and no one but one from Kansas. He had not only seen the war, all military prohibitions to the contrary, but he had actually photographed it."[49]

Thompson first gained notoriety by defying the French prohibition against cameras at the front. Arriving in Paris, he set out for the trenches on bicycle. At Mons he marched with a regiment of Highlanders, coming under barrage for a week. Though he was arrested several times and wounded more than once, he managed to obtain "some of the most remarkable pictures of the entire war"—pictures (film footage) he had to smuggle out of the country.[50]

When he returned to Kansas in 1915 with his movie *Somewhere in France*, the *Topeka Daily Capital* referred to Thompson as a "Topekan globetrotter and daredevil war photographer, who has snapped his camera on the battlefields of Europe along every front and photographed some of the most stirring scenes of the great conflict."[51] His native city rolled out the red carpet, celebrating his visit with displays of his paraphernalia, National Guard drills, and regimental band concerts.

Thompson himself was at least partly responsible for creating his "daredevil" image. In an interview with the *Daily Capital*, he described the experience of being in a Russian trench for three days while shooting another of his films, *With the Russians at the Front* (1915). "There were charges and counter-charges from each side," he recalled. "The Germans nearly got to us. I got my action all right, and pretty nearly lost my life."[52] His films were shot from close up, not from ten miles away like other war films. Using a by-now familiar phrase, he announced to audiences, "I'm going to show you the real thing." The *Daily Capital* dubbed Thompson "the photographic hero of the war. He is known on every front. . . . They have seen him risk his life to get a good picture."[53]

Thompson also made sure that his reputation carried well beyond Topeka. When *War As It Really Is* opened at Wurlitzer Hall in New York City, he was on hand to claim authorship and vouch for the film's realism. *Moving Picture World* obliged by commenting, "The most impressive feature of Mr. Thompson's pictures is their authenticity. Nothing is faked. The photographer was under fire repeatedly, and scene after scene was taken at the risk of his life."[54] Moving on to Washington, D.C., he screened his film at the Army and Navy Club, where, according to the trade paper, "The officers were astounded when shown the pictures, as scenes never before exhibited were incorporated in the reels."[55]

With his freewheeling independence and irreverence for authority, Thompson was the very antithesis of the ordinary footsoldier. Yet his Midwestern origins, brashness, and ingenuity marked him as quintessentially American. Even before the United States had entered the fray, Thompson and his films seemed to be pointing a way out of the morass, a means by which a seemingly hopeless and endless war could still be made to yield a new notion of heroism.

A number of other cinematographers also stood out as individuals, their reputations the product of a shrewd combination of promotion and self-promotion. Captain F. E. Kleinschmidt, an American cameraman who worked with the Austrian army, wrote in *Exhibitors Trade Review*:

> We were very fortunate, not only in obtaining these pictures, but many times in escaping with our lives. When the shrapnel burst near our aeroplane, the concussion deafened us for several days, although none of the flying fragments struck either the machine or ourselves. I believe that we have pictures which no other cinematographer has equalled.[56]

Kleinschmidt and Thompson had their British counterpart in Lt. Geoffrey Malins, the "official British kinematographer" who made *The Battle of the Somme*. In his popular memoir, *How I Filmed the War*, Malins "depicted himself as a kind of death-defying comic-book hero."[57]

The image of the cinematographer-as-hero became generic in Francis Collins's 1916 book *The Camera Man*. Without always focusing on specific individuals, he contributed to the general process of lionization with his graphic depictions of filming under dangerous conditions. Typical of his anecdotes was one about a cameraman who was traveling with Austro-Hungarian forces on the Eastern Front when they mistakenly calculated that they were out of range of Russian guns. When it turned out they were wrong, Collins reported:

> The gunners nevertheless stuck pluckily to their guns, and the movie man stuck no less bravely to his camera. When a shell struck within range of his lens, he swung his camera in position and turned the crank. His films show great masses of earth, tons of it, leaping into the air. . . . So close were many of these shots that the camera man was sprinkled with falling earth. . . . The films at times show the dismembered bodies of the gunners hurled into the air. In one film the picture is actually shaken by the explosion which occurred less than one hundred feet away. . . .[58]

Such experiences were not unusual, according to Collins:

> Many films are exposed with the bullets literally flying about the camera man's head. It is a common experience for the cameras to be shot away or smashed by the impact of an exploding shell. Several of the operators have fallen beside their instruments, and a number have been decorated for conspicuous bravery.[59]

In societies that still lived at least partly by the written word, cinematographers' exploits sold books as well as movie tickets. Yet unlike the literary genres that form the basis of Paul Fussell's interpretation, contemporary writings both by and about the cinematographers were devoid of ironic self-reflection; rather, the dominant mode seemed to be one of self-vaunting triumphalism.

While the most explicit hero-creation occurred in commercial films and the culture surrounding them, traces of it could also be found in straightforward government documentaries such as those produced by the U.S. Signal Corps, the unit assigned to film all aspects of American military participation in the war. The scenario of a typical documentary of an airborne unit shows flyers checking their equipment, boarding planes, and performing aerial acrobatics. In *Photographic Activities of the Signal Corps, AEF, 1917–1918*, however, a camera is mounted on the side of a plane; the pilot, sporting a trademark leather helmet and flowing scarf, climbs in; the plane takes off. A few seconds later, it crashes—but the pilot survives. He climbs out, unloads the camera, and demonstrates it functioning.[60]

In the same film, by contrast, soldiers performing the more mundane tasks involved in post-production are feminized. Rolling film onto reels, splicing and editing it, checking and packing prints, and typing labels for shipment, they work in small office cubicles or factory-like settings and dress in conventional uniform.[61] Their clearly hierarchical work settings and mechanical, repetitive motions would have reminded contemporary viewers of office or factory workers, whose ranks, due to the war, were largely made up of women. Indeed, the cones of film lined up for shipping could easily be mistaken for the upturned shells, waiting to be filled with gunpowder, that often appeared in photographs and films of wartime munitions factories.[62] The contrast between these two sets of images indicates that it was not filmmaking in general, but frontline cinematography in particular, that took on heroic dimensions in wartime.

CINEMA AS METAPHOR

Cinematographers became heroes not only for the civilian population but for the troops as well. Just as the filmed version of the war came to stand for reality in the minds of civilian populations, it also helped shape the perceptions of the troops, with the cameraman performing the function of witness or enabler, someone who could find a means of expression to which the ordinary soldier had no access. Too, there may have been a comforting sense of distance, even control, in watching on the screen the horrors they had experienced, dumbstruck, firsthand. As historian Modris Eksteins suggests:

> If the past had become a fiction and if all was indeed flux, then perhaps the cinema, some witnesses felt, was the only appropriate vehicle for capturing the movement to the abyss. It is striking how often references to the cinema appear in the letters, diaries, and reminiscences of soldiers. The newness of the medium and the excitement aroused by its development are part of the explanation for the frequent references, but there does seem to have been a genuine feeling among some par-

ticipants that what was happening belonged somehow on the screen rather than in life.[63]

Soldiers had greater access to movies than might be supposed from reading literary studies like Fussell's. Numerous makeshift cinemas were set up just behind the lines, and their benches were always crowded with men recently rotated out of the trenches.[64] The fascination with movies was evident in soldiers' everyday speech; trenches were referred to as "picture house tea rooms," machine guns became "cinema cameras," and gunners were ordered not to open fire but "turn the crank." An offensive was a "show"; dugouts were dubbed "Vitagraph Village" and "Keystone Kottage," and "the pictures" was used as a metaphor for theaters of operations.[65]

Films themselves also blurred the distinction between fighting and "shooting" by depicting the functions of the fighter pilot and the aerial cinematographer as virtually interchangeable. In the Signal Corps film *Activities of the 90th Aero Squadron* (1917–1918?), flyers preparing for a mission are shown loading film into a camera and then mounting it on a plane. The parallels between camera and gun, cinematographer and fighter/pilot, are made tangible as a machine gun is removed from the nose of the plane, and a camera installed in its place.[66] Thus subsumed under the sign of the military, the cinematographer was assured his medal of valor.

THE MYTH PERPETUATED

In 1925, King Vidor's *The Big Parade* was named one of the ten best films of the year. The *New York Times* praised it for presenting "a real man for a character, a man who ducks when he hears the hiss of a shell, a man who gets covered with mud, who sneers, who is vengeful and a man who comes back and marries his French sweetheart."[67] Both the plot of the film and its reception indicate that an anti-heroic mode had set in; the explicit admission of fear, prohibited in wartime (hence the resort to irony), was now permitted. The ultimate expression of such sentiments was, of course, Erich Maria Remarque's 1929 novel *All Quiet on the Western Front* and the 1930 movie that was based on it. Yet, though rejection of war had found its way into much postwar popular cinema, it was not all-pervasive. Films like *Wings* (1927), the winner of the first Academy Award for best picture, not only perpetuated the heroic mode but, in celebrating planes and pilots, created a modern image for the hero.[68]

Postwar movies also helped sustain the heroism of the wartime cinematographer. In *The Big Drive*, a 1933 compilation of Great War

footage assembled by Albert L. Rule, a narrator replaces the interti-
tles, but the terms of certification are familiar: "These pictures were
taken by cameramen who were soldiers and risked their lives."[69] The
description of the filmmaking process becomes almost formulaic:

> Remember also, the cameramen were soldiers and had to do as in-
> structed. If they were told to go into a trench and take pictures of
> hand-to-hand fighting, they'd better come out with the scenes. Other-
> wise they'd be court-martialed for disobeying orders and probably
> shot. And many of the cameramen were killed, of course. The cam-
> eramen carried side arms like officers and NCOs—and often they
> would use their guns with one hand while cranking their cameras
> with the other.[70]

The narrator's voice is heard over a close-up of an American soldier
struggling with a German. The American stabs the German with a
short sword and the German falls back, gagging. In the next shot,
two soldiers engage in hand-to-hand combat. As the German glances
at the camera (another instance of direct address), his helmet falls directly in front of it.[71]

Films such as *The Big Drive*, in combination with memoirs and
journalists' accounts, kept alive the image of the cinematographer-
as-hero. This is apparent in the memories of those who had been involved in the war. In the 1970s, Bertram Brooks-Carrington, one of
the last surviving Great War cameramen, told Kevin Brownlow that
when he and his colleagues got caught up in the action, they forgot
about danger. "I've been afraid several times in my life, but if you've
got a camera in your hands and you know there's a picture to be got,
you just get it, and you forget all about fear."[72]

Veterans contributed to the process of lionization as well. P. J.
Smith, an American World War I veteran, told Brownlow, "Some of
these chaps went over the top with the rest of us, starting the camera as they went, perhaps running off the whole magazine without
stopping. They had guts, did those chaps."[73] Though his memory
might be faulty or exaggerated, it reveals an indelible association between cameramen and heroism.

The image of the cinematographer cannot be separated from the
cinematic record of World War I. His inscribed presence not only
guaranteed the authenticity of specific films, but saturated representations of the war with masculinity. Men not only fought the
war, but also preserved and communicated it, enabling its transformation into history. Indeed, film footage was often the only thing
that could be salvaged from otherwise horrific and mutually destructive episodes of slaughter.

At the same time, the heroics of wartime realism provided a distinct and important counterpoint to what has heretofore been taken as the dominant mode of wartime culture, that is, irony and disillusionment. If high literary culture threatened to feminize the experience of war and those who participated in it, popular documentaries and newsreels offered another perspective on the war by foregrounding the daring and courageous persona of the cinematographer-as-hero. The cultural impact of literary modernism cannot be discounted, but throughout the war and the decades that followed, it has had to contend with a deeply entrenched popular belief that some men risked their lives not only to save democracy, but also to find and preserve the truth.

NOTES

1. Lieut. Geoffrey H. Malins, O.B.E., *How I Filmed the War: A Record of the Extraordinary Experiences of the Man Who Filmed the Great Somme Battles*, et cetera (New York, n.d. [1920]), 6–7.

2. President Woodrow Wilson, announcing the draft, invoked "the old spirit of chivalric gallantry." As the war began in Europe, the immediate point of reference for Americans was the Civil War, which was often recalled in a language of knighthood and chivalry; see Michael C. C. Adams, *The Great Adventure: Male Desire and the Coming of World War I* (Bloomington, 1990), chap. 5. Excellent discussions of gender during the Civil War itself may be found in Catherine Clinton and Nina Silber, eds., *Divided Houses: Gender and the Civil War* (New York, 1992). For an overview of the history of American men and masculinity prior to the Great War, see E. Anthony Rotundo, *American Manhood: Transformations in Masculinity from the Revolution to the Modern Era* (New York, 1992), esp. chap. 10 and Epilogue. For a feminist critique of the notion of using war as a means of achieving manhood, see Claire Tylee, *The Great War and Women's Consciousness: Images of Militarism and Womanhood in Women's Writings, 1914–64* (Iowa City, 1990); also Sharon Ouditt, *Fighting Forces, Writing Women: Identity and Ideology in the First World War* (London and New York, 1994).

3. See David M. Kennedy, *Over Here: The First World War and American Society* (New York, 1980).

4. The British lost over 600,000 men in battle, the French more than a million, the Germans two million, and the Americans (out of a total of two million enlisted men), 83,000; Lawrence Stallings, *The Doughboys: The Story of the AEF, 1917–1918* (New York, 1963), 367.

5. Paul Fussell, *The Great War and Modern Memory* (New York, 1975).

6. Samuel Hynes, *A War Imagined: The First World War and English Culture* (London, 1990), 120–21. Having said this, Hynes then discusses film only briefly and quickly returns to fiction and drama.

7. See Kevin Brownlow, *The War, the West, and the Wilderness* (New

York, 1979); and David Mould, *American Newsfilm 1914–1919* (New York and London, 1983).

8. On melodrama and other forms of popular American culture that served as paradigms for early dramatic films, see Robert C. Allen, *Horrible Prettiness: Burlesque and American Culture* (Chapel Hill, NC, 1991); David Grimsted, *Melodrama Unveiled: American Theatre and Culture, 1800–1850* (Chicago, 1968); and Bruce McConachie, *Melodramatic Formations: American Theatre and Society, 1820–1870* (Iowa City: University of Iowa Press, 1992).

9. Early film audiences tended to be less gender-segregated than they later became. Thus women as well as men were exposed to the hypermasculinity of wartime documentary and newsreels.

10. "Pathé Camera Man Decorated for Work at Przemysl," *Motion Picture News* (hereafter *MPN*), Apr. 17, 1915, 38; quoted in Mould, *American Newsfilm*, 89.

11. Homer Croy, *How Motion Pictures Are Made* (New York, 1918).

12. The casualty rate among war cinematographers was low; Brownlow, *The War, the West*, 128. Casualties in the U.S. Signal Corps, the military's own film unit, included only one death and several other serious injuries.

13. British film historian Rachael Low writes: "The job was a new one, evolved by the initiative and courage of men with few precedents to guide them. It can hardly have seemed reasonable for non-combatants to risk their lives carrying heavy cameras into dangerous hiding places thirty yards or so from the German snipers, filming soldiers running out into no-man's land, falling, lying in heaps or returning with bleeding, limping prisoners." *The History of British Film, 1914–1918* (London, 1950), 154–55; quoted in Mould, *American Newsfilm*, 99.

14. Brownlow, *The War, the West*, 6–7; Mould, *American Newsfilm*, 179. Some cinematographers were commissioned as officers, some belonged to special units like the U.S. Signal Corps, others remained free-lance.

15. See Larry Wayne Ward, *The Motion Picture Goes to War: The U.S. Government Film Effort during World War I* (Ann Arbor, MI, 1985), 6.

16. Mould, *American Newsfilm*, 17, 97; Brownlow, *The War, the West*, 66–68. One camera, the Aeroscope, was lighter and could be hand-held, but they were hard to come by; Hynes, *War Imagined*, 126. The montages in D. W. Griffith's *Birth of a Nation* (1915) were a brilliant attempt to approximate something of the chaos of battle.

17. Louis Tenny, "Filming the Trail of the Serpent," *Picture-Play Magazine*, Mar. 1918, 114; cited in Mould, *American Newsfilm*, 129.

18. *Moving Picture World* (hereafter *MPW*), Sept. 19, 1914, 1617; quoted in Brownlow, *The War, the West*, 4. Borthwick reported that she was motivated by curiosity and found that her father's position (as advisor to army of Eastern Rumelia) gave her entree to the front. She had had no previous photographic experience. At the time of the interview, she had returned from the battlefront and planned to open a sanitarium in the Arctic.

19. Stephen Bottomore, "The Biograph in Battle," in Karel Dibbets and

Bert Hogenkamp, eds., *Film and the First World War* (Amsterdam: Amsterdam University Press, 1995), 21; Mould, *American Newsfilm*, 48.

20. Ibid., 10, 26–28; Bottomore, "The Biograph." For a discussion of realism, see Michael T. Isenberg, *War on Film: The American Cinema and World War I, 1914–1941* (Rutherford, NJ, 1981), 59. Isenberg points out that because of film's naturalizing tendencies, early filmgoers tended to be unaware of distortions.

21. See Miriam Hansen, *Babel and Babylon: Spectatorship in American Silent Film* (Cambridge, MA, 1991), 30–31; also David Levy, "Re-constituted Newsreels, Re-Enactments and the American Narrative Film," in *Cinema 1900–1906: An Analytical Study* comp. Roger Holman (Brussels, 1982), 1: 243–58.

22. Mould, *American Newsfilm*, 9–14; Bottomore, "The Biograph," 30.

23. W. Stephen Bush, "War Films," *MPW*, Sept. 19, 1914, 1617; quoted in Mould, *American Newsfilm*, 142. Moreover, as long as still photographers and sketch artists were also barred from the front, movies remained the public's primary source of visual information about the war.

24. Brownlow, *The War, the West*, 6.

25. Isenberg, *War on Film*, 231 n. 38.

26. *MPW*, 13 Nov. 1915, 113.

27. Hynes, *A War Imagined*, ix, 120. See also Laurent Veray, "Montrer la guerre: La photographie et le cinématographe," *Revue d'histoire* 171 (special issue: *Guerres mondiales et conflits contemporains*): 111–22.

28. Film historian Pierre Sorlin argues that because few contemporary filmmakers actually captured the stench and misery that marked the everyday experience of the war, "there remained an unbridgeable gap between film and reality"; "War and Cinema: Interpreting the Relationship," *Historical Journal of Film, Radio and Television* (New Series) 14, no. 4 (1994): 361.

29. *New York Times* (hereafter *NYT*), July 30, 1918, 9:3.

30. Mould, *American Newsfilm*, 147.

31. Hynes, *A War Imagined*, 125. Viewing the film from a more rarified aesthetic stance, he finds *The Battle of the Somme* "a powerful and convincing image of the reality of the war. This reality is more than a matter of real soldiers in actual trenches; it is expressed in the very structure of the film"; there is no coherent narrative, but there is tedium, confusion, and inexplicable action. Faces are dirty, "taut with anxiety or nervously grinning." There is no climax; nothing much happens; the enemy is never seen except as prisoners or corpses (124). Nevertheless, Hynes asserts, "The Somme film changed the ways civilians imagined the war" (126).

32. Mould offers a useful test: "It is possible to make an educated guess by putting oneself in the position of the camera operator and asking: could this shot have been obtained from this angle? Although some cameramen had more nerve than sense, shots taken from positions that appear to be directly in the firing line should be regarded with scepticism." *American Newsfilm*, 52.

33. Ibid., 81. In *The German Side of War* (1915), an intertitle explains

that the cameraman, Edwin Weigle, filmed exploding shells from 3,000 feet, using a telephoto lens.

34. *War As It Really Is* (1916), cinematography by Donald Thompson, U.S. National Archives, reel 1.

35. Quoted in Mould, *American Newsfilm*, 82.

36. *War As It Really Is*, reel 6.

37. As film analysts Ine van Dooren and Peter Krämer put it: "The full reality of what the newsreel or documentary cameraman aimed to capture quite naturally included their own presence in the scene. Unlike the self-contained diegesis of the feature film, this reality was understood by the people in front of the camera, the filmmakers and audience, to be a world on display." "The Politics of Direct Address," in Dibbets and Hogenkamp, eds., *Film and the First World War*, 104. The use of direct address and other inscriptions of the filmmaker were, of course, a trademark of the *cinéma vérité* films of the 1960s; here, however, I would argue that the purpose was somewhat different. While in both instances the inscription is deliberate, in the earlier films the intent was relatively straightforward: to establish the presence of the filmmaker on the scene, whereas later it serves an epistemological purpose by becoming a form of self-reflexivity.

38. *Somewhere in France* (1916), cinematography by Donald Thompson, U.S. Library of Congress, reels 1 and 2.

39. Mould, *American Newsfilm*, 192: advertisement for *The Battle and Fall of Warsaw* from *MPN*, Oct. 16, 1915: 95. Though government films were often shaped to extract maximum propaganda value from them, they were prized by exhibitors and audiences who felt that their "official" imprimaturs guaranteed straightforward filming. Hansen also notes that the emphasis on realism was part exhibitors' effort to reach a higher class of spectator. Hansen, *Babel and Babylon*, 68–69.

40. Universal Pictures started the trend in 1914, when *Moving Picture World* published a letter from Universal's London representative, John D. Tippett, to the company president, Carl Laemmle, stressing the risks involved in trying to film the war: "It just means a man's life to take any pictures over there at present . . . I do not care what the American papers print, it is twice as terrible. . . . To get even small photographs is a most daring exploit." "All War Pictures Fakes," *MPW*, Oct. 3, 1914, 50; quoted in Mould, *American Newsfilm*, 63.

41. The producer Charles Urban, an American working in Britain, was reportedly furious about the incident; Brownlow, *The War, the West*, 54.

42. "Facts and Figures and Such," *Reel Life*, May 8, 1915: 6; quoted in Mould, *American Newsfilm*, 92.

43. Lynde Denig, *MPW*, Aug. 14, 1915, 1175. Brownlow doubts the authenticity of the battle scene and argues that it was staged; again, this does not really matter for our purposes; the important thing is that Dawson's bravery was publicly highlighted.

44. *Picture-Play Magazine*, Sept. 1917, 62,

45. *NYT*, Aug. 16, 1917, 9:3. The critic's comments also remind the au-

dience that while the war is destructive, filmmakers create something permanent.

46. Ibid., June 17, 1918, 11:3.

47. Mould, *American Newsfilm*, 200.

48. For an analysis of *Birth of a Nation* as the archetype of such narratives, see Sonya Michel, "The Reconstruction of White Southern Manhood," in Norbert Finzsch, ed., *Different Reconstructions: Germany and the United States* (Berghahn, forthcoming); see also Hansen's discussion of "fantasies of rescue" in *Babel and Babylon*, chap. 10. An example of a narrative of beset womanhood set in the period around World War I would be *The Captive* (1915) (U.S. Library of Congress), in which the central female character is shown as being plucky and resourceful, but ultimately vulnerable to the predations of enemy soldiers.

49. Quoted in Ward, *Motion Picture Goes to War*, 27.

50. Mould, *American Newsfilm*, 103: quote from *MPW*, Nov. 6, 1914: 46.

51. *Topeka Daily Capital*, Dec. 19, 1915, 1; quoted in Mould, *American Newsfilm*, 113–14.

52. *Topeka Daily Capital*, Dec. 27, 1915: 6; quoted in Mould, *American Newsfilm*, 114.

53. *Topeka Daily Capital*, Dec. 21, 1915: 14; quoted in Mould, *American Newsfilm*, 123.

54. "Real Thrills in Battle Pictures," *MPW*, Nov. 11, 1916, 857; quoted in Mould, *American Newsfilm*, 125–26.

55. *MPN*, Nov. 8, 1916, 3126; quoted in Mould, *American Newsfilm*, 125–26.

56. *Exhibitors Trade Review*, Feb. 10, 1917, 675; quoted in Mould, *American Newsfilm*, 87; see also Brownlow, *The War, the West*, 20–22.

57. Mould, *American Newsfilm*, 96.

58. Francis Collins, *The Camera Man* (New York, 1916), 10, 13.

59. Ibid., 8–9.

60. U.S. Signal Corps, *Photographic Activities of the Signal Corps, AEF, 1917–1918*, National Archives, reel 1.

61. Ibid., reel 2.

62. See, for example, *The Munitions Makers*, part of an official three-part British serial on the war, released in 1917. On women in other wartime films, see Mould, *American Newsfilm*, 200.

63. Modris Eksteins, *Rites of Spring: The Great War and the Birth of the Modern Age* (Boston, 1989), 223. Hynes, *A War Imagined*, 126, suggests that all soldiers were not equally credulous about what they saw on the screen; he quotes some who doubted the authenticity of certain battle scenes and thought they had been staged, though they conceded that casual scenes seemed lifelike. (This distinction may be a question of timing; he cites only one source for the skeptical position, Raymond Asquith, who was writing a letter from the front just before being killed at the Somme; those who were less dubious were writing later, in retrospect.)

64. Mould, *American Newsfilm*, 42. Films were also used in training; up to 1,500 were screened weekly for various purposes, including propaganda and target practice. See "Ways in Which Motion Pictures Are Playing a Big Part in the War," *Current Opinion* 64 (June 1918): 403–4; and "Canned Recreation for Boys in Khaki: Presentation of Motion Pictures at Military Camps an Important Part of Nation's War Activities," *Dramatic Mirror* 77 (Sept. 8, 1917): 11. Films contributed by the Commission on Training Camp Activities and the YMCA were shown as often as four nights a week; Stanley W. Todd, "Entertaining Our Soldiers in Training: How Moving Pictures Are Helping to Make the Boys Happy in Uncle Sam's Training Camps," *Motion Picture Magazine*, July 15, 1918, 76, 78, 111.

65. Mould, *American Newsfilm*, 46. Cinematic metaphors seem to have vied with or in certain instances even displaced the sports metaphors that were ubiquitous at the outset of the war. See Tylee, *The Great War*, 34.

66. U.S. Signal Corps, *Activities of the 90th Aerial Squadron*, National Archives, reel 1. See for comparison another Signal Corps film, *Activities of the 94th Aero Squadron*, National Archives.

67. *NYT*, Jan. 10, 1926, VII, 5:1.

68. Ibid., Aug. 13, 1927, 10:4

69. Albert Rule, *The Big Drive* (1933), U.S. Library of Congress, reel 3.

70. Ibid., reel 6.

71. Historian John Whiteclay Chambers II suspects that these scenes were re-enactments (personal communication to the author, June 13, 1996). If so, it is not clear whether they were done during the war or made especially for The Big Drive.

72. Brownlow, *The War, the West*, 78.

73. Ibid., 22, 59, 73.

PART II
BORDERLANDS
IDENTITIES AND SEXUALITIES

Fin-de-Siècle Theatrics
Male Impersonation and Lesbian Desire*

Martha Vicinus

Although the European fin-de-siècle lesbian is a well-known figure for anyone who researches the history of medicine or the history of sexuality, she has remained peripheral to the study of feminism, peace, and war. A few literary critics have noted the presence of the perverse single woman in World War I novels, but she remains strangely absent from discussion of "borderline" figures.[1] In the understandable efforts to recover lost women who were involved in the many institutions of peace and war, we have neglected European women whose sexual preferences complicate categories of class, occupation, or political beliefs. Indeed, those who publicly insisted upon their homosexuality worked to create a new defining category, that of sexual identity. The years 1880–1920 are especially important in any recuperation of the modern lesbian identity because they mark an important shift from conceptualizing homosexual practices in terms of deviant gender roles (mannish women or effeminate men capable of deviant sex acts) to deviant sexual roles (a deviant lifestyle characterized by same-sex object choice).[2] Not surprisingly, the two definitions overlapped at the time and still do; indeed, for many, gender deviance signified (and still signifies) sexual deviance. To look or behave mannish is to be a lesbian. This definition, seemingly so straightforward in its implications, has a complicated history that has yet to be fully unraveled. My project here is narrower: I examine the theatricalization of women's sexual and political identities at the beginning of the twentieth century. I explore the decision of individual upper-class women to wear mannish clothing, in public or among friends, in order to call into question longstanding female behavior. I explore how and why male impersonation became

*Portions of this essay appeared previously in "Turn-of-the-Century Male Impersonation: Rewriting the Romance Plot," in Andrew H. Miller and James Eli Adams, eds., *Victorian Studies/Victorian Sexualities* (Bloomington, 1996). I am indebted to the National Endowment for the Humanities for a fellowship that enabled me to research and write on male impersonation.

the means to assert a specifically female desire, whether sexual or political.

In the first part of my essay, I look at a group of wealthy Anglo-American women who used cross-dressing to embody their sense of sexual distinctness—of being defined by their lesbian identity. They were among the first women who could insist upon sexual identity as a defining characteristic. I explore the ways in which these pioneering homosexuals created a "borderline" culture through a self-conscious playing against contemporary theater's popular *travesti* role. But they did not control the circulation of images. During the early years of the twentieth century, at the peak of the suffrage movement, mannishness became identified with abnormal political demands, as well as aberrant sexual desires. The two deviancies were elided by social commentators eager to undermine the credibility of the suffrage movement. This identification of female political aggression with sexual deviancy briefly pushed both lesbian sexuality and feminism to the center of twentieth-century political discourse. In the second part of this essay, I examine the theatrical images and behavior of militant suffragists. The dramatic, law-breaking tactics used by the militants emphasized their demand for sexual independence from men, as well as participation in the political affairs of state through the vote. Without theatrical display, women would remain unnoticed and ignored; with it, they could be stereotyped as hysterics and deviants. It is this double bind I explore through two different examples—the Parisian lesbian circle of the wealthy American—Natalie Barney, and the militant suffragists, who attracted the mannish composer, Ethel Smyth.

By the end of the nineteenth century, the growing numbers of educated single women who rejected marriage and motherhood for jobs and friends appeared to threaten normative gender roles.[3] Larger social fears about the spinster focused on the mannish woman. Masculine behavior or appearance, whether in dress or political action, was defined as unwomanly. Comic, lower-class female soldiers and sailors seemed to be walking off the popular stage and ballad page and into life in the form of the aggressive, middle-class woman. Because she seemed to imitate male behavior and wore parts of male clothing, this "New Woman" was construed as anti-feminine. As Carroll Smith-Rosenberg has pointed out, the German sexologist Richard von Krafft-Ebing did not focus on the sexual behavior of deviant women, but on their public behavior and appearance.[4] For him and other medical men, "mannishness" was not a temporary comic aberration but a socially threatening condition to be guarded against. Sexologists defined the feminine solely in biological terms, namely motherhood, but enforced its "naturalness" by heightening long-standing cultural assumptions about its moral and emotional centrality for all women. If the only true women were mothers, then spinsters, and especially outspoken feminists, lacked an essential characteristic that signified sexual—and social—maturity. Only after World War I do we find a consistent image of the mannish woman as a sexual deviant, and even then sexologists disagreed about whether her appearance was biological or pyschological in origin. The psychoanalytic paradigm competed with several other sexual paradigms about women's sexual subjectivity.[5] But by the 1920s the theories of the medical sexologists had permeated large sections of society, so that a specific deviant gender role—the mannish woman—came to represent a deviant sexual role.[6]

Historians have assumed that the years 1880–1920 were dominated by the sexologists' definitions of so-called deviant sexuality, but homosexuals themselves remained largely impervious to the medicalization of desire. Not until the 1920s, and then only among one strand of homosexuals, did Krafft-Ebing, Havelock Ellis, and Sigmund Freud become defining forces. The larger society, and especially the middle class, condemned homosexuality, but urban sophisticates were well attuned to its many semi-public manifestations. An elaborate code of recognition, amidst concealment, existed.[7] By performing—costuming—homosexual desire, it was made visible for those in the know, and then gradually for the general public. Imitation, parody, and play were the means through which homosexuals could rewrite and partially control pre-existing sexual scripts, rather than depending exclusively on the theorizing of the medical men of the day. It was not necessary to identify oneself in public in order to be recognized. Women could also select their own fashion, "mannish" or otherwise, from a range of visual imagery that suited particular occasions; illustrations of turn-of-the-century New Women show many wearing a practical small hat, tweed jacket, blouse, and tie or brooch. These were fashionable signifiers that could be worn with flirtatious dash among friends. Women could—if they so wished—"pass" as either homo- or heterosexual.

Upper-class homosexuals created their own self-image out of a bricolage of reworked classicism, popular theater, decadent art, and poetry.[8] Visual imagery, however, became especially important for coteries of wealthy women intent upon the expression of female sexual subjectivity. These privileged women did not invent a new script, but seized one that had characterized a specific deviant gender role, the male impersonator. Both music-hall and theater stars were expanding the roles played by this favorite character. Although predominantly a satiric commentator on male foibles, s/he could also be a sympathetic representative of thwarted desires. The music-hall dandy in evening dress, and the theater's *travesti* heroes were refashioned as androgynous champions of the marginal. Specific plays, theatrical fashions, and the personae of favorite stars all provided materials from which to construct a lesbian identity. The frame of reference one hundred years ago differed from today: wearing theatrical clothes was not a performance of one's sexual identity, but a revelation of it; cross-dressing was either a temporary erotic statement or a disclosure of one's true nature. So-called feminine and masculine lesbians both turned to the male impersonator as representative of their sense of displacement, of being in some subtle sense androgynous. Self-conscious lesbians of the turn of the century created a private borderline culture based upon the mannish woman, but altered for their own purposes.

In looking at the multiple meanings that adhered to the figure of the male impersonator, I argue against both Judith Butler and Marjorie Garber. Butler's influential arguments about the performative nature of all sexual identities have encouraged many to see sexual object choice as unstable, playful, and most of all, a constantly changing performance. She asserts that no one can be defined by, or limited to, a single gendered identity; even the process of speaking as a lesbian is, in her words, "a production . . . an identity which, once produced, sometimes functions as a politically efficacious phantasm," but which, as an "identity category" suggests "a provisional totalization."[9] For Butler, the performance of gender, and especially present-day butch/femme and drag, offer a more viable politics in our postmodern world than identity-based politics, which depends upon privileging one identity over another.[10] I want to turn this argument on its head, and suggest that we historicize lesbian images, which then seem both less fluid and more fixed than Butler's paradigm suggests. To argue that our subjectivity is constructed through discourse, as she does, is to evade the question of how this discourse itself comes about. We know that there was a language for sexual deviancy before the sexologists, but not one of sexual identities. How this linguistic and attitudinal change occurred cannot be answered by recourse to metaphor or abstraction, but only through careful historical analysis. I examine here a group of upper-class lesbians during the years immediately before World War I who believed firmly that one was born a lesbian, which gave one a specific responsibility to create a culture suitably expressive of this unique sexual identity. Even those who refused such a precise label as "lesbian," such as the composer Ethel Smyth (1858–1944), felt they had a distinct nature.

They were not separate from, but participants in and creators of, an ongoing discourse about sexual roles and identities. For them, the discourse was fluid, but not their identities.

Their belief in an intrinsic lesbian identity also undermines Marjorie Garber's constructed cross-dressed homosexual. In *Vested Interests*, Garber argues that critics repeatedly "look through rather than at the cross-dresser, to turn away from a close encounter with the transvestite, and . . . instead to subsume that figure within one of the two traditional genders."[11] Her insistence forces us to look directly at what we see, rather than comfortably remaining within the pre-existing categories of male or female. But her focus on the "reality" of the third gender does an injustice to the complex responses to, and uses of, the cross-dressed figure, and the wide range of often contradictory readings and recuperations that s/he makes possible. Fin-de-siècle lesbians were never less than women, whatever their outward appearance; their androgynous costumes were an imaging of a desire that found no viable expression within the narrow confines of upper-class femininity. By making visible this desire, whether at home in their transvestic theatricals or abroad in their jackets and ties, these women insisted upon their sexual subjectivity. Their adoption of various male symbols was a means of self-representation, rather than any exclusive medicalized definition of a third gender.[12] While Garber privileges the cross-dresser's own interpretive strategies, I focus here on the ways in which this particular figure was reinterpreted and realigned by homosexuals at the turn of the twentieth century. This essay is an initial effort to trace the ways in which homosexuals drew from contemporary cultural materials to fashion images that recast longstanding stereotypes. Although they were only partially successful in their efforts at self-creation, this does not negate the importance of their actions.

1. HOMOSEXUAL THEATRICS

During the 1890s several wealthy American and English lesbians settled in Paris, including the American heiress, Natalie Barney (1876–1972), and the upper-class Renée Vivien (1877–1909), who became one of Barney's lovers. Barney and Vivien systematically set about creating their own version of lesbian culture; both, but especially the former, believed in living a public life as a sexually free woman. They learned Greek in order to read Sappho in the original, and in 1904 they visited the isle of Lesbos. In 1909, when she moved to 20 rue Jacob, Barney began her Friday evening salon, to which she invited artists and writers. These cultural events, attended by some of the most famous men of the day, also attracted lesbian and bisexual women whose self-confidence and style have become legendary. These included the portraitist Romaine Brooks, Oscar Wilde's lesbian niece Dolly Wilde, and novelists Radclyffe Hall, Gertrude Stein, Vita Sackville-West, Violet Trefusis, Dorothy Bussy, and French writers Colette, Rachilde, Adrienne Monnier, and Marguerite Yourcenar.[13] Barney had a genius for friendship, bringing together ex-lovers and American exiles, including Eva Palmer, Winnaretta Singer Princess de Polignac, Lucie Delarue-Mardus, and the Duchess of Clermont-Tonnerre. Among this circle of wealthy lesbians, Vivien was the most determined to embody her particular version of lesbian desire. She transformed herself from the upper-class Anglo-American, Pauline Tarn, to be Re-née, or re-born, to a new life as a French-writing lesbian.

Natalie Barney and her artistic mother, Alice Pike Barney, adored theatricals, and staged presentations that included music, dance, and mime at their summer home. Barney continued this tradition in Paris, encouraging her friends at her afternoon women-only salon to dress up and role-play.[14] She and her various lovers celebrated lesbian passion by photographing themselves in costumes that ranged from nudity in the woods of Maine to the britches and ruffles of eighteenth-century pages and the flowing gowns of Sappho's Greece. For Barney, cross-dressing was an erotic embellishment of lesbian play, and not the embodiment of her special nature; passing as male was bad form. Indeed, one of her lovers roundly declared in her memoirs, "I shall never understand that kind of deviation: wanting to look like a man, sacrificing feminine grace, charm and sweetness. . . . And cutting off one's hair when it can be a woman's most beautiful adornment! It's a ridiculous aberration, quite apart from the fact that it invites insult and scandal."[15] A theatrical persona was not to be confused with one's self, but it was a means of revealing that self's specific sexual nature.

In contrast, Renée Vivien took their acting more seriously, attempting in her fiction and life to manifest the perfect lesbian figure. In her games with Barney, she was a mysteriously handsome page, refusing to look at the camera, unlike her self-confident lover.[16] She wrote openly of lesbian desire in decadent poems and fiction, and gained cult status by her eccentric behavior. Mourning the loss of two lovers, Vivien refashioned her body, starving herself into a wraith-like representative of deviancy. In her only novel, *Une femme m'apparut* (1904), her heroine is the self-contained androgynous artist, San Giovanni. The move from a gender role to a sexual role turned upon both looking and being androgynous, rather than masculine. But for Vivien, androgyny was also infinitely superior to the dull, ordinary sensibilities of heterosexuals. In decadent fashion, it was also anti-bourgeois and anti-liberal; the artist is invariably misunderstood by society, but her art remains supreme. Theatrics in life and fiction were an expression of Vivien's artistic soul, as well as her deviant desire; indeed, her desire made possible her artistry, and her art was expressive of that desire.

The sources of Barney's theatrical lesbianism can be traced biographically to her youthful masquerades, but when she moved to Paris, she feasted on the theater of Paris. Her circle of friends all admired Sarah Bernhardt (1845–1923), the best-known actress in Europe and America. This French-Jewish actress had revolutionized the French theater with her unconventional interpretations of the female leads in such famous French plays as *Phèdre, Hernani, La Dame aux camélias*, and *Théodora*. In the 1870s and 1880s she had taken Paris, London, and New York by storm; she never retired, bringing her lavish productions year after year to English-speaking audiences; the spectacle of this famous woman was sufficient to overcome any language barrier. Her well-publicized slim beauty, curly red hair, personal extravagance, and sexual liaisons thrilled admirers everywhere; photos, postcards (including pornographic versions of her most famous roles), card games, commemorative plates, and other mementos of the most famous actress of her time can still be found in antique markets. Bernhardt never feared controversy, publicly fighting with the Comédie Française, actively supporting Dreyfus, and openly praising the suffrage movement. She also included in her intimate circle the mannish artist, Louise Abbéma.[17] Moreover, she lived her life in public, courting the admiration or criticism of her fans by flaunting her liaisons with a series of young leading men.

In her fifties, at a time when most actresses retired or took supporting roles, Bernhardt shifted from her famous *femmes fatales* to portray a series of tragic male heroes. In the first thirty-two years of her career, she appeared in nine *travestis*; in the final twenty-seven, in eighteen.[18] Bernhardt worked to extend the possibilities of the *travesti* role, beyond comedy or satire and into tragedy. She chose her roles carefully, specializing in men who had "a strong mind in a weak body," claiming that only an older woman was mature enough to interpret thought-wracked young men.[19] Her best-known roles, labeled after the color of their uniforms, were her self-consciously lighthearted "black Hamlet" (Figure 17) in Shakespeare's play (1899) and her vacillating, idealistic "white Hamlet," (Figure 18), as she dubbed the title role of Duke of Reichstadt, son of Napoleon Bonaparte in Edmond Rostand's *L'Aiglon* (1900). The young Duke, forced by Metter-

Figure 17. Sarah Bernhardt as "Black Hamlet" (1899). Author's collection.

nich to live with his mother in Austria, had died at seventeen of tuberculosis. His utterly blank life gave Rostand the opportunity to create a patriotic melodrama of failed revolt. *L'Aiglon* was never popular outside France, but there it became a modern classic. French audiences, still smarting from the defeats suffered during the Franco-Prussian War, reveled in the patriotic sentiments expressed by the frail but chivalrous Duke and his faithful retainers. At the same time, Rostand's play provided a counter-Napoleonic version of patriotism. He upstaged the legend of brutal masculinity and ambition with a fantasy of chivalric concern for women and futile dreams of military

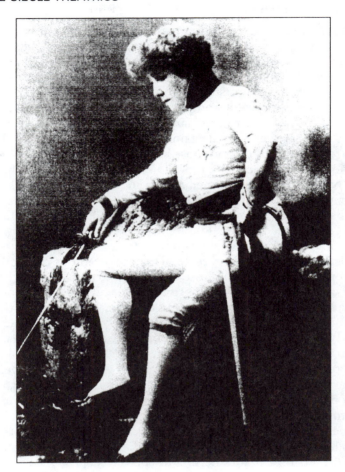

Figure 18. Sarah Bernhardt as the Duke of Reichstadt in *L'aiglon* (1900). Author's collection.

action.[20] The femininity and ineffectiveness of Napoleon's son is made into an appealing heroism. Bernhardt's *travesti* roles spoke to the inchoate idealism and thwarted ambitions of the era, while her theatrical life offstage embodied sexual and political courage.

Bernhardt's fans idolized her. On one occasion she agreed to meet with a French girl who had refused to consider any of the presentable young men her parents introduced her to because none looked like Bernhardt's Duke of Reichstadt. Bernhardt persuaded the girl to forget her stage-hero by receiving her "in her oldest dressing-gown, no make-up, wrinkles and hollows showing up horribly."[21] The shocked

young girl readily agreed to her parents' choice after this incident.
But Bernhardt knew she could not always control how her fans interpreted her roles. Nor was she always so successful offstage in persuading young women to mend their ways. She may have enjoyed
the flattery of the mannish Abbéma in her inner circle, but she expected a level of decorum from her family that had not characterized
her own life. The courtesan, Liane de Pougy, gossiped in her memoirs, "Sarah Bernhardt tried again and again to tear a beloved niece
away from those circles and those habits, she reasoned with her, she
gave her an allowance, she took her to America, she put her into
plays. Nothing worked. Dinner jackets and love nests, short hair and
the style of an invert."[22] The very casualness with which de Pougy
describes the characteristics of "an invert" indicates its well-estab-
lished base on the theatrical figure of the male impersonator. A bor-
der culture, in the process of formation, took a star at the very center
of Parisian cultural life and remade her most famous characters for
their own purposes. For homosexuals, the beloved *L'Aiglon* became
a kind of touchstone, representative of their own idealism and powerlessness; self-loathing and fears of discovery dwindled in the face
of the Duke's profound patriotism and early death. They admired
not only Bernhardt's interpretation of her thought-wracked character, but also her grandiloquent acting style. Artificiality and acting
characterized the lives of contemporary homosexual men and
women, not the natural. Just as Renée Vivien had chosen to write
poetry in an affected style, so too did many see flamboyance as truer
to themselves. The increasing popularity of a quiet "realistic" style,
practiced by the Italian actress Eleanora Duse, seemed emotionally
flat and bourgeois in comparison with the many tempestuous heroines and histrionic heroes Bernhardt chose to depict. As a theatrical
figure, in both senses of the word, Bernhardt seemed almost irresistible to countless admirers, whatever their sexual preferences.
Cabaret parodies of Bernhardt's most famous roles were legion—and
so too were private responses to her.[23]

Barney and her coterie took Bernhardt's tragic heroes and turned
them into romantic exponents of lesbian love. Barney addressed a
poem to Bernhardt after seeing her in *L'Aiglon*. The tubercular
Duke, confined to his bedroom by poor health and politics, seemed
to represent the confined world of women. The poem was published
in 1900 as part of a collection of lesbian verse; as if to highlight her
close identification with the Duke, Barney included a portrait of herself as a page. Liane de Pougy published a *roman à clef*, *L'Idylle
saphique*, in 1901, describing her tumultuous affair with the young
Barney. In one scene, clearly drawn directly from their relationship,

the two lovers watch Bernhardt play Hamlet. Rather than falling in love with her Hamlet, as so many heterosexual women did, they identified with him. The Natalie-figure compares the frustrations of women with Hamlet's impotent rage against tyranny, "For what is there for women who feel the passion for action when pitiless Destiny holds them in chains? Destiny made us women at a time when the law of men is the only law that is recognized."[24] The staginess of this speech echoes Bernhardt's own grandiose style of expression. But Barney did not see Hamlet only as an embodiment of her own feminist frustrations. She also found his feminine masculinity, as portrayed by Bernhardt, expressive of a desire that could not be identified as wholly male. She ordered a dark green velvet suit similar in style to Bernhardt's Hamlet, for a series of self-portraits that turned an indecisive adolescent boy into the epitome of the self-confident lesbian. Her Hamlet includes a provocative garter, as if to draw attention to the erotic nature of her costume (Figure 19). A beautiful actress playing a man represented lesbian desire, rather than a specifically male character acted by a man.

But Bernhardt was also a cult figure among male homosexuals. Her theatricality is redoubled, for a passionate woman playing an ineffectual man becomes a means of speaking the effeminate desire of the male homosexual. The amateur actor, the Marquis of Angelsey, was photographed as the Duke of Reichstadt (Figure 20) in "a romantic pose and appropriate costume" in the gossip column of *The Sketch* in January of 1902.[25] H. Montgomery Hyde describes the Marquis as "the most notorious aristocratic homosexual" immediately following the Wilde trial; he was "an extreme example of the effeminate transvestite type, and was a gifted female impersonator."[26] What did it mean that he was also an impersonator of a female playing a male role? The Marquis probably found the femininity of Bernhardt's characterization of the Duke of Reichstadt representative of his own homosexuality. Within six years of coming into his inheritance, the Marquis had to declare bankruptcy and flee to Monte Carlo. The music-hall male impersonator, Vesta Tilley, added to her male wardrobe by buying "dozens" of waistcoats of "delicately flowered silk" at the sale of his personal effects.[27] Her stage dandies personified an extreme fashionableness that tipped into the recognizable signs of male homosexuality. We have no surviving commentary by male homosexuals about Tilley, but surely some in her audience noticed a mimickry of effeminate masculinity in her flowered waistcoats and soprano voice. In the 1930s the lead role in *L'Aiglon* was taken over by a well-known homosexual, Jean Weber.[28] Weber was proud of his ability to play roles that had previ-

Figure 19. Natalie Barney as a Hamlet-like page. Courtesy of George Wickes.

ously been exclusively *travesti* parts. He continued the tradition of exaggerated emotionalism and gender ambiguity in his portrayal of the Duke of Reichstadt, if a surviving publicity still is any guide. The amateur Marquis and the professional Weber both found permission to act out their effeminacy by playing Bernhardt's roles.

Bernhardt's fame as an androgynous hero transcended class lines, demonstrating the power of specific mainstream theatrical images and figures to be reinterpreted by members of marginal subcultures. In 1892, during a New York trial for sexual solicitation, a witness testified that one man called himself Sarah Bernhardt, "had his hair

Figure 20. The Marquis of Angelsey as the Duke of Reichstadt, *The Sketch* Jan. 1, 1902. Courtesy of the British Library.

bleached in tissue red," and "carried the illusion as far as he could imitating her, wearing bangles and bangs and dance shoes. I was told he wore corsets and chemise." Another effeminate man emphasized "her" propriety, informing the witness, "'Sarah' wasn't hustling, she was being 'kept . . . in a house on 32nd Street.'"[29] The red-haired, cross-dressed Sarah serviced only well-to-do men. Surviving pornographic postcards, sold in sets to tell a tale, were also aimed at this same clientele of sexually privileged men. They portray robust prostitutes in various stages of undress, preparing to act in *L'Aiglon* or another Bernhardt play. Brandishing swords and bosoms, these women make no pretense of imitating Bernhardt's androgynous heroes, but rather rehearse a familiar pornographic trope of lesbian kisses as a preamble to heterosexual intercourse. Our knowledge of this subculture of male and female prostitutes remains fragmentary and dependent upon police records, in contrast with the notorious antics of the Marquis and of Barney. Nevertheless, evidence points to a widespread adaptation of mainstream cult figures as homosexual icons.

We might well ask why homosexuals were so attracted to Bernhardt's vacillating and weak heroes, who came dangerously close to fulfilling the stereotype of the ineffectual male homosexual. The answer to this question may be obvious: they liked her artificiality, her daring refusal to be who she was—a plump, aging woman whose acting style and dramas were rapidly becoming outdated as Ibsen and naturalistic acting swept across Europe. Homosexuals refused to accept the definition of failure that adhered to her ineffectual protagonists, and instead made them into successful figures, worthy of imitation. The Duke of Reichstadt may have been the embodiment of thwarted patriotism for the mainstream theatergoer, but for homosexuals he could also be an ideal image of imprisoned desire. This doubling interpretive strategy underscores the difficulty in labeling the political stance of this generation of homosexuals. Many upperclass homosexuals loftily ignored politics for art, but then discovered that their sexuality contained political implications that could not be ignored. While some were fiercely conservative in their economic and social attitudes, they could also take courageous stands for peace and sexual freedom.[30] Barney, for example, believed that war, central to male culture, was irrelevant to women. Since she did not consider lesbians as flawed men, she never felt compelled to identify with male ideals. She steadfastly refused to succumb to the emotionalism of World War I.[31] Hamlet's refusal to act in this context becomes a refusal to accept the dictates of masculine political imperatives.

It is not surprising to find a dense web of cross-references between the theater and homosexuals. If the Parisian lesbians of Barney's circle eschewed cross-dressing in public, others did not. Mirroring the resplendent effeminacy of the Marquis of Angelsey, some women appeared as very stylish mannish women. Colette's lover, the Marquise de Belbeuf, was a notorious male impersonator on stage and off; in her memoir of her years with "Missy," Colette noted the popularity of flowered vests among lesbians.[32] Radclyffe Hall (1880–1943), following the formulation of the German sexologists, felt that she had been born with a male soul trapped in a female body. From a very early age, she began to wear men's jackets and ties, and in 1920 she cut her hair short, but she continued to wear skirts until the 1930s, when trousers became socially acceptable. By purchasing many of her clothes from a theatrical costumier's, she wore her homosexuality as a stylized, imaginary masculinity. She shared with the English Marquis and the French Marquise a taste for flowered silk. This flamboyant signifier, along with loosely knotted ties, represented sexual deviancy among both male and female homosexuals. Since Hall (Figure 21) strongly disapproved of women who passed as men, she had to make visible her femininity as well as her masculinity. The result was the same kind of captivating vulnerability that Bern-

Figure 21. Radclyffe Hall, ca. 1910. Courtesy of the Henry Ranson Humanities Center, University of Texas, Austin.

hardt embodied in her Hamlet. Hall, dressed in a dinner jacket and tie, and her partner, Una Troubridge (1887–1963), cut a dash at opening nights in London during the interwar years. (Troubridge, like many upper-class girls, saw Bernhardt play and later reminisced about her nursery theatricals, dressing as one of her *travesti* heroes).[33] As Figures 21 and 19 show, no one would mistake Radclyffe Hall or Natalie Barney for men; both are obviously costumed in the sense of wearing nontraditional clothes that draw attention to themselves. But each portrays a different version of mannishness—one earnest and erotic, the other playful and sexy. One was designed for private pleasure, the other as a public statement. Drawing on the theater, both women transformed the mannish gender role into an expression of a new sexual role.

2. POLITICAL THEATRICS

In this section, we move to a different social class and to a different venue to examine the "mannish" as a political statement. Male impersonation for the wealthy Parisian lesbians was a masquerade to be played among friends. Barney and her friends throughout their lives spurned public display, mocking Radclyffe Hall and others who insisted on dressing in an openly mannish fashion; they were equally indifferent to suffrage. As George Wickes says of Barney, "She was never one to pay attention to what was happening in the street."[34] The suffrage movement could not afford such aristocratic indifference, for it had to use the streets to make an impression. Only public drama could bring the needed press coverage. Each of the major organizations had its own colors, banners, costumes, uniforms, and other insignia. Wearing the colors of suffrage and openly avowing one's beliefs blatantly contradicted the norms of respectability, whereby a woman did not draw attention to herself. For little over a decade (1903–1914), women orchestrated public demonstrations that took the phrase "making a spectacle of themselves" and turned it into brilliantly organized displays of political theatricality.[35] The various suffrage organizations were extraordinarily successful in creating a wide range of collective images and rituals in which conventions from the theater, including the male impersonator, were crucial.

The militant movement began with a theatrical gesture: individual women attended Liberal Party meetings and at question time rose and asked, "Will the Liberal Government give women the vote?" This question was repeatedly asked, leading to the forcible removal of the women. Courting notoriety everywhere brought publicity—and a steady stream of young volunteers.[36] With the help of the Actresses' Franchise League (AFL), plays, pageants, and parades all brought "the cause" to the attention of the general public. In addition, Actresses' Franchise League members donated time to teach women how to speak on the hustings, including how to project their voices and how to handle hecklers. Most of the members worked in the legitimate theater and longed for an opportunity to test their skills in serious drama; they favored the new Ibsenite naturalism in their portrayals of the legal inequities women faced. But they soon found that traditional nineteenth-century farce was more effective than tragedy.[37] For example, *How the Vote Was Won* (1909) comically illustrates the catastrophic effects of a women's general strike, in which women quit their jobs and demand that their nearest male relative support them. In the final scene, the anti-suffrage Horace, surrounded by female relatives, becomes an ardent suffragist. Mainstream popular theater images and plots, altered by feminists, became the principle means of popularizing suffrage among ordinary people. What had been a marginal political movement for nearly fifty years—women's suffrage—quickly became one of the most widespread and controversial movements of the pre-World War I period.

After years of organizing, home meetings, and petitions to Parliament, women moved decisively into the public sphere. The very act of claiming the streets was revolutionary in the eyes of some; shocked male onlookers saw their streets being taken over by political women. When respectable women sold newspapers or stood on a soapbox and spoke in public, traditional male privileges were called into question. Unescorted upper-class women on the streets spoke of political and sexual independence—and made a woman fair game for lewd jostling and obscenities.[38] Maud Arncliffe-Sennett was followed during a 1908 pageant by a man who kept saying, "I'm ashamed of you, I'm ashamed of you and you all belong to the Street." She hated the experience but concluded that she and other women were fighting, "to purge from these minds the connection of Women and the Street."[39] Men wanted to literalize the actions of political women—by walking the streets, these women were streetwalkers, low-class prostitutes.

The suffragists were determined to define what was womanly and unwomanly, even at the cost of being labeled by their foes as sexual deviants. Both men and women had long admired the sexual independence of the tuxedoed impersonator, strutting across the stage without a care; her stylish swagger and natty appearance were widely imitated. Young suffragettes preferred the sprightly determination of the music-hall dandy to the languid passivity of Bernhardt's heroes. Style and actions were to be assertive, indicating a new independence from men; if this was "masculine" behavior, so be it. The rank and file who sold suffrage newspapers on the street dressed in tweed suits, sturdy boots, and neat bow ties. Music-hall male impersonators had appropriated specific male symbols as shorthand for masculinity; they liked to sport such obvious phallic accouterments as a cigarette or cigar, sword or walking stick, or, at the very least, a tie. Now suffragists all seemed to be wearing a version of a man's tie. Photos and illustrations of suffragettes invariably include a woman with a tie (Figure 22). The clothing that Radclyffe Hall had considered a daring statement became commonplace among feminists. (A similar change was to occur in the 1920s; Stephen, the heroine of her *The Well of Loneliness*, looked too slim-hipped and masculine before World War I, but epitomized postwar refinement.) Activists sought a sartorial elegance that would represent their sexual independence from men, as well as their political steadfastness. Although the dominant image created by leaders of the militant Women's Social and Political Union (WSPU), such as Emmeline Pankhurst, her daughter Christabel, and Emmeline Pethick-Lawrence, was of unimpeachable femininity, their followers adopted a more practical, more masculine, dress.

The composer Ethel Smyth (1858–1944) was a bridge between the Parisian lesbians and the suffragettes. The daughter of a general, Smyth was as politically conservative and socially radical as Natalie Barney. She had had to make her way alone in the musical world, and therefore projected a kind of determined independence that shrugged off gossip and criticism. She was the classic mannish woman (Figure 23) among her upper-class friends, too openly admiring of women and too personally independent. For a time, Smyth was frequently in Paris, pursuing the Princesse de Polignac, one of Barney's closest friends. It was not a happy affair, so perhaps both sides wished to bury many of the details. Barney and Smyth each maintained a discrete silence, but they must have known each other. Like Barney and her friends, Smyth had been indifferent to politics, but unlike them, she "converted" to suffrage at the age of fifty-two in 1910, and proceeded to devote two years full time to the WSPU. She also fell in love with Mrs. Emmeline Pankhurst, the leader of the organization.

Barney and her friends were fascinated by Bernhardt's *travesti* heroes because they were larger-than-life figures, drawn not from the natural world, but from an imagined past. The outspoken Ethel Smyth better fit the self-image of the militant suffragette. She had

Figure 22. Ethel Smyth with her Dog Pan. Author's collection.

dressed in a mannish style as early as the 1870s; in the 1900s her pragmatic clothing became common, though not fashionable. Smyth's strong predisposition toward performance chimed with the militant suffrage movement's keen awareness that only through staged activities, well covered by the press, could they succeed in capturing the attention of the general public. As a composer of operas, Smyth had long recognized the importance of the theatrical as a weapon for change.[40] By temperament she was attracted to the resplendent colors, songs, and ceremonies staged at rallies of the WSPU. She threw herself into teaching as many suffragists as possible her freshly composed "March of the Women." Unwilling to do less than the leaders of the WSPU, Smyth successfully sought arrest during their 1912 window-smashing campaign. Her old friend, Sir Thomas Beecham, managed to combine masculine condescension with humorous approval in publicizing Smyth's zeal. He describes her as "beaming approbation from an overlooking upper window, beat[ing] time in almost Bacchic frenzy with a toothbrush" while

Figure 23. "The Suffragette: Number 1 in a series of Present Day Types."
Bystander, 31 Dec. 1913. Courtesy of the Mansell Collection.

her compatriots marched in the courtyard, "singing lustily their war-chant."[41] Publicity—so long an anathema to respectable women—was the movement's single most effective tool. But it brought to the fore the eccentric and marginal, such as Smyth, providing anti-suffragists with ammunition against the Cause.

Indeed, Smyth's androgynous appearance was too real and not sufficiently theatrical for many of her contemporaries in the movement. When she dressed for the occasion, so to speak, it only drew attention to her ill-concealed deviancy. According to Sylvia Pankhurst (Christabel's younger sister, a fellow suffragette and, from 1913, a critic of WSPU elitism), in her history of the suffrage movement:

Ethel Smyth was a being only these islands could have produced. In-
dividualized to the last point, she had in middle age little about her
which was feminine. Her features were clean cut and well marked,
neither manly nor womanly. . . . Wearing a small, mannish hat, battered and old, plain-cut country clothes, hard worn by weather and
usage, she would don a tie of the brightest purple, white and green, or
some hideous purple cotton jacket, or other oddity of the W.S.P.U.
colours, she was so proud of, which shone out from her, incongru-
ously, like a new gate to old palings.[42]

Male impersonation, or even the adoption of a few male characteristics did not threaten; but to *be*, rather than *act*, androgynous sent a
perceptible *frisson* through allies and enemies of suffrage. At about
this time, Ethel convinced Radclyffe Hall, her younger contemporary, to support the suffrage movement. But Hall, ever the traditionalist, never accepted militancy. Moreover, her identification with
men, like Barney's acceptance of the perquisites of wealth, made her
recoil from the strong female bonds of the movement; for her they
may have represented the cloying, sentimental side of Victorian life
that she had escaped only with great difficulty.[43] And she may have
realized that suffrage women would have been less tolerant of her
masculinity than they were of the famous composer's.

Ethel Smyth, through seven volumes of autobiographical writings, never referred to herself as a lesbian, even though she foregrounded her passionate *cultes*, as she called them, for aristocratic,
mothering women.[44] Emmeline Pankhurst fit this mold, and was the
subject of Ethel's adoration during her years of activism. As a late
Victorian Smyth was able to move between the casual romantic
friendships of an earlier generation and the more self-consciously
lesbian behavior of Barney and her circle. Defiantly boyish well into
middle age, she wore her masculinity easily and naturally, while still
strongly identifying with the female world. In her memoir of Mrs.
Pankhurst, she speaks fondly of their time together in adjoining
prison cells. The two months included, however, a characteristically
revealing action on Smyth's part, guaranteed to embarrass the leader
of the WSPU. Each prisoner was to prepare an (illegal) decoration for
the prison-yard wall. Smyth chose

the fabrication of a pair of prisoner's half-breeches, cut in two identical pieces by captives in the tailoring department so that you could
not tell back from front. These pieces I sewed together all around, on
the apple-pie-bed principle, and hung them up in the exercise court together with the legend: 'A Mus. Doc.'s notion of small clothes.' But

Mrs. Pankhurst thought the joke undesirable, so I had to remove this
exhibit and do some unpicking.[45]

The grotesque prison underclothes were meant to remind the authorities of their distinguished female non-voter. Instead, the public
joke backfired: the underwear seemed to lay bare a concealed sexual
deviance best left unmentioned and unseen. In contrast, Hall and
Barney, born twenty years later, wore their masculinity openly as a
sexual statement—as a signifier of a lesbian sexuality they wanted
recognized. Their construction of a specific identity was both enabling and constricting. For the Victorians, Smyth was an egregious
upper-class eccentric; for the Edwardians, she was an eccentric with
something unmentionable added. Her musical fame and class position did not prevent the voicing of suspicions. For her younger contemporaries, her assumption of an androgynous gender role signified
her deviant sexual role.

Smyth's awkward hats and ties were converted into attractive
practicality by two leaders of the AFL, Cicely Hamilton and Edy
Craig. Both were known for their lesbian proclivities; they sported
tweed skirts, shirts, jackets, and flowing bow ties.[46] Their stylish-
ness bears some resemblance to the pantsuit of the 1970s, drawing
attention to a sexual independence from men, without tipping into
Smyth's mannishness. Both women contributed their theater expertise to the cause, writing and producing suffrage plays, training volunteers for numerous events, and masterminding the vast and
colorful pageants, exhibitions, and marches. These events, as well as
local plays and celebrations, gave the rank and file opportunities to
dress up and to play the part of a hero. The massive pageants, in
which women represented historical heroines and present-day professions, included a range of publicly active, masculinized women.
Cicely Hamilton's *Pageant of Great Women* in 1909 (produced by
Craig) included famous eccentric women, including the mannish
French artist, Rosa Bonheur (played by Craig). Participants fought
over who could play Joan of Arc, who usually headed the long procession through the streets. Almost as coveted was the role of her
page or courtier, a demotic echo of Renée Vivien's favorite role.

The Parisian homosexuals had taken the ineffectual warrior, symbolized by the Duke of Reichstadt, as their representative hero. Suffrage activists, in contrast, took Joan of Arc as their representative
heroine. Her virginal patriotism may seem a long way from Bernhardt's character, but both embodied idealism, chastity, and loyalty.
(Bernhardt played Joan several times during her long career.) That
British Protestants so frequently turned to Catholic (and Jewish)

France for its cultural icons is only one of the many cultural ironies of the time. Joan shared with Hamlet a historical remoteness and vagueness as to the details of her life. As such, she could mean different things to different people, under the broad heading of spiritual and military leadership. And unlike such living heroines as Ethel Smyth, her masculine attire represented not a suspect sexual nature, but rather martyrdom. A symbol of persecuted womanhood, Joan of Arc transcended the limitations of her sex to exemplify spiritual militancy.[47] Marginalized women took high art, popular stage trappings, and mainstream history and reworked them for personal or political purposes.

So too did the enemies of suffrage. The anti-suffrage movement and its journalist allies reworked theatrical symbols largely drawn from comedy and pantomime. Anti-suffragists took the whimsical asexuality of male impersonation and turned it into a savage burlesque of the militant suffragist. The female impersonator's comic dame, usually portrayed as an aging, fat woman of uninhibited sexual desire, was transformed into a voracious destroyer of young women, rather than men. Lisa Ticknor has described how long-standing iconographic shorthand, familiar from *Punch*, the music halls, and comics, was used to portray the suffragist as an older, unattractive spinster—a frustrated music-hall dame with either a vindictive or excitable nature.[48] Young, attractive women in particular needed male protection, lest they fall victim to a coarse, man-hating virago. The womanly woman could be saved only by the intervention of paternal authority. As Figure 23 shows, this could be an open attack on the suffragist, portraying her as a hefty, ugly dame, in danger of leading astray the vulnerable boyish girl in the background. Reporters willfully refused to see the main point of the pageants, namely the long history of effective leadership and social responsibilities carried out by women from Joan of Arc to the present. No matter how often Edy Craig put the most attractive young women at the head of the pageant, the press re-presented them as victims of their man-hating leaders. Ethel Smyth's outspoken mannishness was no longer comic, but instead dangerous.

In the eyes of male journalists, medical men, and most politicians, suffragists were assumed to be usurping male power, both in the bedroom and in Parliament. Some of the anger expressed by male onlookers may have come from their outrage at what they saw as the desecration of traditional symbols of patriotism and loyalty, but misogyny gave them permission to speak the previously unmentionable. Since Woman was *the* sex, her political behavior could only be sexualized. Lesbian innuendo was pervasive. Rumors abounded about Emmeline Pankhurst's close relationship with Ethel Smyth. Commentators spoke darkly of the undue influence of the "female celibate pedagogue," and medical men warned against the contagion of inversion.[49] To outsiders, suffragists seemed to flaunt their sexual preference; Smyth was simply the most egregious example. The popular novelist, Marie Corelli, dismissed the suffragists with the comment "No man likes to be libellously caricatured and a masculine woman is nothing more than a libellous caricature of an effeminate man."[50] Laurence Senelick, in his examination of the American female impersonator Bert Savoy, points out that his "large-boned masculinity bloated the androgynous ideal into hermaphroditic freakishness." His straight man, by way of contrast, was small and "ladylike."[51] Onstage, these characters might defuse social fears; offstage, they embodied sexual anarchy. What an earlier generation of writers had left implicit was now explicit: the ravening lesbian harridan (Figure 23) and the effeminate male homosexual (Figure 20) endangered society. Sexual deviancy was defined by these two figures, brought together a generation earlier under the sexologists' heading of the "third sex."

The viciousness of the attacks on suffrage women in Parliament, the press, and cartoons is a reminder that the positive expression of women's sexual desire, and specifically lesbian desire, was a dangerous, imaginative act with potentially explosive political and personal consequences. Early twentieth-century lesbians and suffragists successfully recuperated mannishness as an expression of sexual independence, but they did so at a price. The wealthy lesbians who frequented Barney's soirées could afford to ignore momentary notoriety, but suffrage women—homosexual or heterosexual—found themselves unable to control negative publicity. The fashionable elegance of their leaders was not sufficient to overcome the widespread fear that when women demanded male political prerogatives, they became like men and desired women. Women were given partial suffrage in 1918, and the WSPU renamed itself "The Woman's Party," but it never gained a single seat in Parliament, and its leaders drifted into obscurity. A new generation of postwar political women shifted their political demands to foreground motherhood. Low-key pressure groups through lobbying and journalism kept alive the spirit of feminism, while eschewing the theatricality of militancy. The implicit demand for sexual subjectivity made by the prewar militants did not disappear, and public fears of women's sexual deviancy became more explicit. By the 1920s some legislators were calling for the criminalization of lesbian acts.[52]

The theater has always been a refuge for the sexually suspect; the drive for respectability within the profession marginalized the homosexual, the divorcée, and the mistress, but did not eliminate them. Theater professionals openly spoke against the moral degeneracy of homosexuality. The Edwardian star and AFL member Violet Vanbrugh, warned would-be actresses in her 1920 *Dare to Be Wise*:

> I must write a word of warning against those whose instinct is abnormal and perverted. Those poor wretches—unnatural and morally unhealthy themselves—they contaminate all who come within their influence. You must shun their companionship. Their principles and practices are vile. If ever through your own folly or by some misadventure you should find yourself in such a set, or even on its outskirts, don't hesitate or delay. Cut yourself adrift.[53]

Vanbrugh's vehement warning echoes a larger public concern about sexual deviancy, but it also indicates a shift to more rigid sexual roles, both on and off the stage. By 1920, when she wrote, the polymorphous possibilities of cross-dressing had become increasingly déclassé, and live entertainment specialized in upper-class sophistication. Ibsenite realism of a sort triumphed on stage, while movies replaced the music hall. Although female impersonation remained popular among amateurs, by the 1930s the male impersonator survived largely as a nostalgic remnant of a more innocent past, rather than as a central theatrical role.

The hardened attitudes toward mannish women in the postwar years may have led the novelist Radclyffe Hall to create Stephen, a noble character who assumes she is damned in the eyes of the general public. Certainly the lesbians in *Well of Loneliness* (1928) suffer far more ostracism than Hall herself. During the interwar years, Hall lived in Sussex, socializing with Edy Craig and her friends as well as several prominent male homosexual writers and artists, including the playwright Noel Coward. Barney continued to avoid politics, holding her famous salon as if neither the Great War nor the Depression had occurred. The elderly Ethel Smyth, too deaf to compose, turned to letter writing and autobiographical essays, solidifying her reputation as an unconventional phenomenon. Visibility did not mean damnation, however hard journalists and social commentators tried to damn. But the playful theatricality of the prewar years disappeared, and the sexologists' definition of deviance as same-sex desire triumphed. Inappropriate gender behavior became the single most important indicator of sex role deviance. The stereotype of the mannish *femme damnée*, so eloquently portrayed in Bernhardt's weak heroes, became the dominant public image of the lesbian. Theatricality was not considered a choice by the medical establishment, but an intrinsic characteristic of the deviant woman; a fondness for stylish, masculine clothing and exaggerated gestures defined the twentieth-century invert.

Notes

1. See, for example, Shari Benstock, *Women of the Left Bank, Paris, 1900–1940* (Austin, 1986); Sandra M. Gilbert and Susan Gubar, "'She Meant What I Said': Lesbian Double Talk," in idem, *No Man's Land: Sexchanges* (New Haven, 1989), 215–57, and Jane Marcus's afterward to Helen Zenna Smith's 1930 novel, *Not So Quiet . . .* (New York, 1989).

2. For a discussion of these taxonomic confusions in the context of a single infamous case, see Lisa J. Lindquist, "Images of Alice: Gender, Deviancy, and a Love Murder in Memphis," *Journal of the History of Sexuality* 6, no. 1 (July 1995): 30–61.

3. These developments are discussed in my *Independent Women: Work and Community for Single Women, 1850–1920* (Chicago, 1985).

4. See Carroll Smith-Rosenberg's important analysis of the role of the early sexologists in defining female sexual deviance, "The New Woman as Androgyne: Social Disorder and Gender Crisis, 1870–1936," in her *Disorderly Conduct: Visions of Gender in Victorian America* (New York, 1985), 270–71.

5. The wide variety of competing sexual ideologies are embodied in the last Sexual Reform Congress held before Germany was taken over by the National Socialists. See the Proceedings for the Third Congress of the World League for Sexual Reform, published as *Sexual Reform Congress, London 8–14: IX: 1929*, ed. Norman Haire (London, 1930).

6. Mary Louise Roberts explores the ways in which the post-World War I young, unmarried woman, smoking cigarettes and bobbing her hair, came to represent a wide range of political, eugenic, and cultural fears in France. See her *Civilization without Sexes: Reconstructing Gender in France, 1917–1927* (Chicago, 1994).

7. For American male homosexuals, see Laurence Senelick, "Lady and the Tramp: Drag Differentials in the Progressive Era," in Laurence Senelick, ed., *Gender in Performance: The Presentation of Difference in the Performing Arts* (Hanover, 1992), 26–45; and George Chauncey's introduction to his *Gay New York: Gender, Urban Culture, and the Making of the Gay Male World, 1890–1940* (New York, 1994).

8. My essay, "The Adolescent Boy: Fin-de-Siècle Femme Fatale?" *Journal of the History of Sexuality* 5, no. 1 (July 1994): 90–114, looks at one representative homosexual figure in literature.

9. Judith Butler, "Imitation and Gender Insubordination," in Diana Fuss, ed., *Inside/Out: Lesbian Theories, Gay Theories* (New York, 1991), 13–15. The running head to this article gives a better sense of its contents than the title: "Decking Out: Performing Identities."

10. See not only "Imitation and Gender Subordination," but also her

Gender Trouble: Feminism and the Subversion of Identity (New York, 1990). See also Sue-Ellen Case, "Toward a Butch-Femme Aesthetic," Henry Abelove, Michèle Aina Barale, and David M. Halperin, eds., *The Lesbian and Gay Studies Reader* (New York, 1993), 297–306.

11. Marjorie Garber, *Vested Interests: Cross-Dressing and Cultural Anxiety* (New York, 1992), 9.

12. In this interpretation I disagree with Esther Newton, who privileges the sexologists for enabling turn-of-the-century lesbians to speak their sexual desire. See her "The Mythic Mannish Lesbian: Radclyffe Hall and the New Woman," in Martin Duberman, Martha Vicinus, and George Chauncey, Jr., eds., *Hidden from History: Reclaiming the Gay and Lesbian* (New York, 1989) (hereafter *Hidden from History*), 281–93.

13. See Benstock, *Women of the Left Bank*, 37–64, and Lillian Faderman, *Surpassing the Love of Men: Romantic Friendship and Love Between Women from the Renaissance to the Present* (New York, 1981), 369–73.

14. George Wickes, *The Amazon of Letters: The Life and Loves of Natalie Barney* (New York, 1976), 88–99 describes Barney's theatricals and the various participants.

15. Liane de Pougy, *My Blue Notebooks*, trans. Diana Athill (London, 1979), 111.

16. The biographical information in this paragraph is based on Wickes, *The Amazon of Letters*, and Karla Jay, *The Amazon and the Page: Natalie Clifford Barney and Renée Vivien* (Bloomington, 1988).

17. The details of her life are best found in Gerda Tarnow, *Sarah Bernhardt: The Art within the Legend* (Princeton, 1972). Biographies of Bernhardt are legion. In addition to Tarnow, see Arthur Gold and Robert Fizdale, *The Divine Sarah: The Life of Sarah Bernhardt* (New York, 1991). For an analysis of her theatrical innovations and influence, see John Stokes, "Sarah Bernhardt," in John Stokes, Michael R. Booth, and Susan Basnett, *Bernhardt, Terry, Duse: The Actress in her Time* (Cambridge, 1988).

18. Tarnow, *Sarah Bernhardt*, 211.

19. The critical response to Bernhardt's numerous *travesti* roles are recounted in many biographies. The best summary is ibid., 210–27. Bernhardt's description of her Hamlets as strong minds in weak bodies comes from her *The Art of the Theatre*, trans. H. J. Stenning (London, n.d. [1929]), 141.

20. I am indebted to Billie Melman for pointing out to me the ways in which this mainstream play questions the dominant French patriotic heritage.

21. May Agate, *Madame Sarah* (London, 1945), 124.

22. De Pougy, *My Blue Notebooks*, 110–11.

23. Tarnow, *Sarah Bernhardt*, 221, cites nine parodies of *L'Aiglon* alone, with at least a dozen more based on her other successes.

24. Quoted and translated in Wickes, *The Amazon of Letters*, 40.

25. See *The Sketch* (Jan. 1902): 403. *The Sketch* does not identify who the Marquis is imitating, but theatergoers of the day would never have missed the visual reference.

26. H. Montgomery Hyde, *The Love That Dared Not Speak Its Name* (Boston, 1970), 153–54. He had married his cousin, Lilian Chetwynd, who left him on their honeymoon and received a decree of nullity.

27. Lady De Frece [Vesta Tilley], *Recollections of Vesta Tilley* (London, 1934), 125. According to Hyde, *The Love That Dared Not Speak Its Name*, 154, the sale of his jewelry and clothes (mostly women's or, like his vests, effeminate) raised £88,000 for his creditors, but he had debts of over £500,000.

28. Gilles Barbedette and Michel Carassou, *Paris Gay 1925* (Paris, 1981), 66. See also the illustration of Weber in costume, opposite p. 255.

29. I am indebted to Jonathan Ned Katz for sharing this material with me, drawn from his work-in-progress on an 1892 trial.

30. A full discussion of the political beliefs of the Parisian lesbians is not possible here. For an introduction to the complexities, see Shari Benstock, "Paris Lesbianism and the Politics of Reaction, 1900–1940," in *Hidden from History*, 332–46.

31. See Wickes, *The Amazon of Letters*, 141–44 for a description of Barney's behavior during World War I.

32. For a colorful account of Colette's years with the Marquise, see Michèle Sarde, *Colette: Free and Fettered*, trans. Richard Miller (New York, 1980), 195–235. See also Colette, *The Pure and the Impure*, trans. Herma Briffault (New York, 1966), 67–68 and passim.

33. At fourteen, Bernhardt was "her 'number one' theatrical idol." Richard Ormrod, *Una Troubridge: The Friend of Radclyffe Hall* (London, 1984), 28.

34. Wickes, *The Amazon of Letters*, 104, in reference to May of 1968, when the Paris streets were filled with protesting students, and Barney continued to hold her salon as if nothing were happening.

35. See, for example, the description of the National Union of Women's Suffrage Society's June 13, 1908 procession in Lisa Ticknor, *The Spectacle of Women: Imagery of the Suffrage Campaign 1907–14* (Chicago, 1988), 80–91. This was one of the most successful and characteristic pageants in its size, organization, speakers, banners, and costumes. Ticknor describes the range and brilliance of the suffrage art, theater, and pageantry during these years.

36. These early days are described in Andrew Rosen, *Rise Up Women! The Militant Campaign of the Women's Social and Political Union, 1903–1914* (London, 1974), 49–57. He also documents the WSPU's move toward greater and greater acts of disruption in order to continue to receive publicity.

37. The range and effectiveness of the suffrage theater is discussed by Julie Holledge, *Innocent Flowers: Women in the Edwardian Theatre* (London, 1981), 49–72. See also the essays in Vivien Gardner and Susan Rutherford, eds., *The New Woman and Her Sisters: Feminism and Theatre, 1850–1914* (Ann Arbor, 1992); none deals specifically with suffrage plays, but they document the range of possibilities available for women in the theater at the turn of the century.

38. Policemen often stuck their nightsticks up women's skirts, both to

expose them and to hurt them. These and similar incidents are described in Vicinus, *Independent Women*, 262–68.

39. Quoted in Ticknor, *The Spectacle of Women*, 88. She also noted that opposition from the public had decreased in comparison to the previous year's march.

40. See Elizabeth Wood's analysis of the relationship between Smyth's music and her lesbian sexuality, "Lesbian Fugue: Ethel Smyth's Contrapuntal Arts," in Ruth A. Solie, ed., *Musicology and Difference: Gender and Sexuality in Music Scholarship* (Berkeley, 1993), 164–83, and her "Sapphonics,"in Philip Brett, Elizabeth Wood and Gary C. Thomas, *Queering the Pitch: The New Gay and Lesbian Musicology* (New York, 1994), 27–66.

41. Quoted in Christopher St. John, *Ethel Smyth: A Biography* (London, 1959), 155.

42. E. Sylvia Pankhurst, *The Suffragette Movement: An Intimate Account of Persons and Ideals* (London, 1931), 377.

43. Michael Baker, *Our Three Selves: The Life of Radclyffe Hall* (New York, 1985), 48–49, describes the few known facts about Hall's involvement with the suffrage movement, which culminated in an anonymous letter to the *Pall Mall Gazette* on March 4, 1912, attacking the suffragists for their agitation during a miners' strike.

44. Louise Collis interprets this refusal as a sign that Smyth was "a chaste woman and also emotionally immature," *Impetuous Heart: A Biography of Ethel Smyth* (London, 1984), 73. But see the nuanced readings of her life by Elizabeth Wood and Suzanne Raitt, "'The Tide of Ethel': Femininity as Narrative in the Friendship of Ethel Smyth and Virginia Woolf," *Critical Quarterly* 30, no. 4 (Winter 1988): 3–21.

45. Ethel Smyth, *Female Pipings in Eden* (London, 1934), 210–11. Smyth had been awarded an honorary Doctor of Music by the University of Edinburgh a few years before she became a suffrage activist.

46. See Cicely Hamilton's unrevealing autobiography, *Life Errant* (London, 1935); *Edy: Recollections of Edith Craig*, ed. E. Adlard (London, 1949); and J. Melville, *Ellen and Edy: A Biography of Ellen Terry and Her Daughter, Edith Craig, 1847–1947* (London, 1987). Edy and her partner were friends with Radclyffe Hall and her partner during the interwar years. Craig "claimed to have belonged to at least eight different suffrage societies . . . and to have ended up organising for all of them." (Ticknor, *The Spectacle of Women*, 24).

47. Ticknor, ibid., 209–12, discusses the ideological and symbolic instability of Joan of Arc, who was co-opted by militants and non-militants.

48. Ibid., 162–74. See especially her astute discussion of the hysteric.

49. Ethel Colquhuon, "Modern Feminism and Sex-Antagonism," *Quarterly Review*, no. 219 (1913): 155; and Walter Heape, *Sex Antagonism* (London, 1913), 206–14. See also the infamous Sir Almroth E. Wright, *The Unexpurgated Case Against Woman Suffrage* (London, 1913), which argues that women could not lead the country because they suffered temporary monthly insanity.

50. Quoted from Marie Corelli's *Woman,—or Suffragette?* in Ticknor, *The Spectacle of Women*, 198.

51. Senelick, "Lady and the Tramp," 39. He outlines the increasingly public denunciations of effeminate men after World War I, as well as arrest of Mae West for her "camp" imitations of Savoy.

52. Jeffrey Weeks, *Coming Out: Homosexual Politics in Britain, from the Nineteenth Century to the Present* (London, 1977), 106–07.

53. Quoted in Holledge, *Innocent Flowers*, 20.

Lesbians before Lesbianism

Sexual Identity in Early Twentieth-Century British Fiction

David Trotter

Towards the end of Radclyffe Hall's *The Unlit Lamp* (1924), the heroine, Joan Ogden, who has grown miserably old in a small provincal town, overhears two young women discussing her. She recognizes them as women of the same "type" as her: unattached, independent, sexually ambiguous. They dress like her, and wear their hair cut in a similar style. But they seem to inhabit a different world: *their* lamps have very definitely been lit. Unlike her, they are aggressively intelligent and purposeful, "not at all self-conscious in their tailor-made clothes, not ashamed of their cropped hair." At once envious of, and terrified by, their success, Joan has to acknowledge that she belongs to another age: Her place in the evolution of feminism is that of the "pioneer" who "got left behind." She is, as one of her tormentors puts it, "what they used to call a 'New Woman.'"[1]

It's a powerful scene because it notices both the anguish of the old New Woman, the superseded pioneer, and the boldness of the really new New Woman, who would not be half so formidable were she not so determined to put the past behind her. When they identify her as a superseded pioneer, Joan Ogden's tormentors bring to bear on the development of feminism an intricate genealogy whose scope and function are no longer self-evident. They define themselves in relation to their feminist precursors, rather than in relation to an understanding of the development of British society as a whole. This genealogical habit has, to date, attracted little attention. I believe that the habit merits attention, not because it will deliver a ready-made account of the development of modern British feminism, but because it offers a unique insight into the ways in which early twentieth-century British feminists imagined their opportunities and purposes, that is, the ways in which they created an identity for themselves.

One might begin to reconstruct that genealogy, in very rough terms, by positing three "waves" of feminist activity. The first, consisting of women born in the 1860s and 1870s, peaked in the 1890s. Its concern with education, and with the economic and sexual emancipation of women inside (and sometimes outside) marriage, found a focus in the New Woman novels of the 1890s, and their successors, the "marriage problem" novels of the Edwardian era.[2] The second wave, consisting of women born in the 1870s and 1880s, peaked in the 1900s. Its concern with the economic and political destinies of women who had chosen not to marry found a focus in campaigns to improve living and working conditions, and to secure the vote.[3] These, one might call the Newer Women. New and Newer Women sometimes came under the suspicion of lesbianism, as we shall see, but did not necessarily think of themselves as lesbians, and were not necessarily thought of as lesbians. The third wave, peaking in the 1920s, divided from their precursors by the abyss of World War I, and conscious that some of the political and economic battles had been at least half-won, found a focus in androgynous modernity and in the emergence of a lesbian subculture.[4] These were the Newest Women of all. The opportunities and purposes I have sketched were not, of course, the only ones available to feminists. But some women did recognize them, and by that recognition instituted a genealogical habit whose outcome was a radically made-over identity: an identity constructed genealogically, in relation not to what wholly resembles it, or wholly opposes it, but to what partly resembles it.

New Historicism, the form of analysis currently dominant in literary and cultural studies, has tended to attribute to "discourse" a decisive function in the determining of identity, and to rupture or crisis—a decisive function in the determining of social change.[5] Current explanations of the emergence of a lesbian subculture in the 1920s thus favor a crisis (World War I) and a discourse (the classificatory schemes of the new sexology). For example, Sandra Gilbert and Susan Gubar argue that the war made possible an "unprecedented transcendence of the profounder constraints imposed by traditional sex roles": they instance the "erotic release" experienced during it by lesbian writers like Radclyffe Hall, Amy Lowell, Gertrude Stein, and Vita Sackville-West.[6] Other scholars have argued that an identity of any kind, sexual or otherwise, cannot be known until it has been articulated. Thus, it is said, Victorian feminists could not or would not alter their "romantic vocabulary" so as to incorporate desire for another woman; later generations, however, maturing after 1920, found themselves able to "discuss their sexual identity in a new sexual language."[7] That language was provided by the male sexologists (e.g., Richard von Krafft-Ebing, Havelock Ellis, and Edward Carpenter) who invented the category of the third sex: "inverts" concealing the soul of a man in a woman's body. Radclyffe

Hall, by appropriating and revaluing the stereotype of the "mannish lesbian" in *The Well of Loneliness* (1928), became the first British writer to articulate female homosexuality.[8]

There is evidence to support both arguments. "And then again the war made everything different!" is the refrain of Marie Belloc Lowndes's *Lilla* (1916), and of a great number of other novels and memoirs: the things made different included sexual attitudes and behavior. Hall said that the war's death-dealing had finally given a "right to life" to women like Stephen Gordon, the lesbian heroine of *The Well of Loneliness*.[9] Similarly, a right to life could also be claimed by appropriating, and transvaluing, the classifications of the sexologists. In 1915, the feminist Frances Wilder wrote to Carpenter to tell him that she had at once recognized herself in his account of an "intermediate" sex, part male, part female. Wilder attributed her "strong desire to caress & fondle" a female friend to a "dash of the masculine" in her own temperament.[10] Clearly, both war and sexology made some difference (a big difference) to some women who were beginning to think of themselves as lesbians. But all the difference to all such women? Did the strong desires experienced by women like Frances Wilder always have to be categorized and named before they could be known?

A number of recent studies have shown that the scope of lesbian self-awareness in Britain, both before and after World War I, vastly exceeded the scope of sexological knowledge.[11] If we are to do justice to that self-awareness, we will have to discard or refine the preoccupations—with crisis, with discourse—engendered by the New Historicism. It is at this point that the genealogies sketched by a writer like Radclyffe Hall may prove of some assistance. In particular, they may help us to rethink the question of agency. The crisis-model of personal and social change tends to obscure agency. Thus when Gilbert and Gubar claim that to literary women "the soldier's sacrifice at times seemed to signal a cultural wound or fissure through which radically new social modes might enter," it is hard to be sure who is doing what to whom, and how, and exactly when.[12] The discourse-model does address the question of agency, but in somewhat static terms. Thus sexology is said to create a position (that of "invert," say) that can then be occupied, by the woman who desires other women, and in the occupation revalued. The genealogical model, by contrast, envisages a process of partial imitation, a continual adjustment of sameness and difference within a shared history. Joan Ogden is strictly speaking a Newer Woman who partially resembles the New Women who befriend and teach her: like them, she does not wish to marry; unlike them, she is interested in politics. Her young rivals misidentify her as a New Woman, brusquely conflating the categories of New Woman and Newer Woman in order to emphasize their difference from all that has gone before them. The circulation of identities does not stop there, however. For Joan's response to the Newest Women's emphasis on difference is to make herself more like them, to dress as they dress. Her imitation of them, in turn, were they ever to notice it, would show them to themselves in a new light. The play of reciprocal gazes, of reciprocal fantasies, continually modifies identity along the movable borderline of partial resemblance. And the novel itself actively contributes to the circulation of identities by exploring the sameness within the difference upon which the Newest Women insisted too rigidly. It reestablishes, in its account of Joan Ogden's youth and early adulthood, the very distinction between New and Newer Women, which they have, for their own genealogical purposes, collapsed. That account imagines homosexual identity as a choice made, or entered into, over a period of time and within some quite punitive constraints, between the erotic possibilities available in a society that did not as yet contain a recognizable lesbian subculture.

This essay has been written, like *The Unlit Lamp*, from Joan Ogden's point of view. It tries to reconstruct some of the social and erotic possibilities available to women who had not read Edward Carpenter, in prewar and wartime Britain. My main focus will be on the fiction of the period ("Newer Woman" fiction, if you like), which I believe constitutes a dense and varied historical resource, and one which, by comparison with the New Woman novel of the 1890s or the Modernist writing of the 1920s, has received very little attention.[13] I shall look first at a number of notably serious-minded feminist writers, including Rose Allatini (c.1890–c.1980) and "Cicely Hamilton" (Cicely Mary Hammill: 1872–1952), then at a prolific author of best-selling romances, L. T. Meade (1854–1914). Some, but not all, of these writers might have regarded themselves as lesbians. Some, but not all, of the "odd" women they portray might have been regarded as lesbians. What matters is that, in a period without prominent sexual or literary subcultures, both polemical and mass-market fiction sustained a range of narratives in which women desired and were desired by other women.

Such narratives tell us more about collective fantasy than they do about individual behavior. Of course, it is hard to establish how they might have been read at the time. Although my main concern here is with the fiction and the collective fantasies it might be said to articulate I will approach the question of readerships by discussing, in the third and final section of the essay, an openly lesbian writer,

"Christopher St. John" (Christabel Marshal: c.1875–1960), who published before Radclyffe Hall but nonetheless clearly hoped and expected that she would be read by lesbians.

The point of examining fiction published in the first two decades of the century is not simply to fill a gap in the historical record. In a curious way, the scandalous homosexual couples of the 1920s, real and fictional, echo the scandalous heterosexual couples of the 1890s, real and fictional. Both arrangements established in and through the very form of renegade partnership an alternative to social and sexual norms. In both cases, two people unite against the world, and find in their union a cultural politics. The arrangement, and the thinking that surrounds it, are essentially dyadic: in that respect, they mirror, or even reproduce, the social and sexual orthodoxy to which they are opposed in most other respects. The world against which two people unite is itself made up of couples. But the lives and the writings I shall discuss here tell a different story. During the 1900s and the 1910s, the advantages and disadvantages of singleness became a major issue. Single women flourish in the fiction of the period in a way they rarely did before, and have rarely done since. Furthermore, in radical life as well as in radical books, the renegade couple found powerful rivals not only in the solitary woman, but also in the group of women, and even, on occasion, the female threesome. What we find in the lives and the books of the Newer Women is a range of possibilities which in some respects exceeds those available both to the New Women and to the Newest Women. Indeed, the monadic and triadic thinking they articulate remains as provocative today as it must have been when it was originally formulated.

INDEPENDENT WOMEN IN PREWAR AND WARTIME FICTION

Rose Allatini's *Despised and Rejected*, published in 1917 under the pseudonym A. T. Fitzroy and immediately banned on the grounds that it was likely to prejudice the recruiting of persons to serve in His Majesty's Forces, and their training and discipline, is a novel about homosexuality and about pacificism. In a Europe polarized by military conflict, pacificism offered Allatini an analogy for the sexual "intermediacy" that was one self-definition by then available to gay men and women. When war breaks out, Dennis Blackwood and his male lover both become conscientious objectors and are duly arrested and charged. It is clear that Allatini, like Frances Wilder, had been reading Edward Carpenter. A journalist friend of Dennis's claims that men who stand "mid-way between the extremes of the two sexes" are the "advance-guard" of a more enlightened civilization.[14] The novel's understanding of male homosexuality, in short, justifies the stress some historians have put on the efficacy of scientific discourse.

One of Dennis's closest allies is Antoinette de Courcy, whose life has been shaped by her passion, now extinguished, for an older woman, Hester Cawthorn. Hester, with her "masculine-looking" walking stick and the brim of her felt hat turned down to shade her "thin, sombre face," fascinates Antoinette from the moment of their first meeting, in a drearily conventional family hotel. The walking stick, the felt hat, and the sombreness are all there is to see, or to know, about Hester. Yet for Antoinette this is enough. Hester's violations of the codes governing dress and manner represent a microscopic tear in the uniform fabric of bourgeois life. Her singleness, among men and women whose main business is to be or to become a couple, represents another microscopic tear. If those men and women notice Hester at all, they notice her as an oddity, a lack (or the sign of a lack). But the lack acquires, in and through this very neglect and the vague unease it sometimes provokes, a definite moral and erotic charge. Hester's "fierce reserve," the "sensitiveness" lying behind a "brutally direct manner," give her in Antoinette's eyes a "compelling and magnetic dignity." Eroticism, here, is the call of one singularity to another. It is genealogical: the ambiguous acknowledgement of a pioneering Newer Woman by someone still young enough to become in due course one of the Newest. Antoinette feels that no "irritation or annoyance" can ever touch her as long as she wraps herself around with memories of Hester: the "world of men" will always prove disappointing by comparison.[15]

Antoinette's love for Hester, though no more than a prelude to the main action, is the novel's most memorable event. And this despite a distinct shortage of explanatory contexts. Dennis Blackwood may define himself as a member of the "intermediate sex," but neither Hester nor Antoinette does; and while his struggle with the military authorities provides a political analogy and support for his newly affirmed sexual orientation, it does nothing for Antoinette. The cultural fissures opened by war do not bring her erotic release. How, then, are Hester and Antoinette able to ackowledge one another? How do we recognize them for what they are? Some of the book's first readers would have recognized Hester, I believe, and through Hester the nature of Antoinette's love, because they had already encountered her like in Newer Woman fiction.

The conventions of domestic realism, dominant in the nineteenth-century British novel, insisted the marriage of hero and heroine in the final chapter should complete both their identities and the

narrative. Edwardian women writers sometimes modified those conventions so as to incorporate a minor character whose uncompromising independence the heroine admires but does not in the end
want for herself. These characters are superfluous, both in social
terms (they never marry) and in narrative terms (they fade away as
the wedlock plot sweeps hero and heroine on to their own and the
novel's resolution). Yet they often stay in the mind rather longer
than the happy pair. Their unfulfillment is both a dead end and a
new beginning, since some readers might imagine for them, under
different circumstances, another story, an alternative resolution.
They inhabit a virtual narrative that might be said to exist in the
minds of readers for whom the wedlock plot has little or no interest.

In that virtual narrative, deprivation and lack acquire a positive
charge. For these superfluous women are by no means unlit lamps.
Elspeth Macleod, in Alice Stronach's *A Newnham Friendship* (1901),
expresses a view as familiar then as it is now when she encourages
Carol Martin, who lives with a random assortment of secretaries,
journalists, and landscape gardeners in a "Women's Barracks" in the
East End of London, to marry. "Don't be one of them, dear friend.
Don't be a neutral."[16] Neutrality—a failure to commit oneself, and
therefore a failure to be anything—is, Elspeth Macleod suggests, the
fate of the unmarried. But if neutrality is the result of a conscious
decision, it cannot be understood as mere lack, or inadvertence. The
choices it makes possible, the choices that reproduce it in everyday
life, of allegiance and self-image, are choices not available to a married woman. Decisions made speak, genealogically, to decisions in
the making.

Carol Martin has chosen to live in the women's barracks, and the
preference creates her new identity. Edwardian writers had a great
deal to say both about the institutions that have since been described by social historians (women's colleges, settlement houses),[17]
and about the more loosely defined communities of the boardinghouse and the informal club. Their novels gave independent working women not only a physical presence, but also an address. Hilda
Forester, in Olive Birrell's (1848–1926) *Love in a Mist* (1900) wants
the heroine to live with her and a journalist friend in their Bloomsbury flat, which serves as both home and meetingplace; Jehane
Bruce, in Violet Hunt's (1862–1942) *The Workaday Woman* (1906),
throws Bohemian parties in *her* Bloomsbury flat, at which the relations of the sexes are "a little altered," and the women gain character at the expense of the men.[18] Bloomsbury, in central London, was
free-lance territory, a place where things were a little altered. Dolf
Wyllarde's (d. 1950) *Pathway of the Pioneer* (1906), set in a Blooms-

bury boardinghouse, describes an informal society called "Nous Autres," whose members include a free-lance journalist, an actress, a typist and shorthand clerk, a post office clerk, a music teacher, and a musician who plays in the Ladies' Catgut Band. Sally Richards, the wartime typewriter girl in Violet Tweedale's (1862–1936) *The Heart of a Woman* (1917), may have given her woman's heart, in the traditional fashion, to the man who employs her, but she also belongs to a club whose membership consists "entirely of free lances, unmarried working women of advanced opinions and pronounced celibacy."[19] The very pronouncement of the pronounced celibacy gives it its compelling and magnetic dignity. These young free lances have heard the message of the pioneering Newer Women.

It is important to recognize that "Nous Autres" could be reconfigured as an audience, and their attitude to narrative thus made explicit. In "A Conjugal Episode," a late and rarely noticed short story by one of the most successful New Woman novelists, George Egerton (Mary Chavelita Dunne: 1859–1945), the narrator, visiting Paris, takes a room in a house owned by a woman separated from her husband, and so enters a female community consisting of the landlady, the landlady's two sisters, and her closest friend. In the husband's absence, the women fantasize, momentarily, about becoming men, about dressing in men's clothes. When he reappears, the community disperses. But this account of the triumph of heterosexuality is framed in an interesting way: the narrator tells her story, in London, to three friends, all working women, gathered in the Bloomsbury apartment belonging to one of them. The framing narrative recalls the many occasions in fin-de-siècle fiction when male listeners assemble to hear a tale brought back from the unknown: Kipling's soldiering stories, Wells's *The Time Machine* (1895), James's *The Turn of the Screw* (1898), Conrad's *Heart of Darkness* (1899). These occasions at once threaten the men assembled, by disclosing the uncanny, and confirm them in their privileged access to a knowledge forbidden to women. The occasion of "A Conjugal Episode," by deliberate contrast, confirms women in their access to a knowledge forbidden to men, and so challenges the male reader in his narrative rather than his sexual pride.[20] What the three friends witness, and by witnessing make actual, is the actualization of a narrative which normally remains virtual: the story of the homosocial and homoerotic fantasies threaded through the triumph of heterosexuality.

Again, this was a challenge renewed by the next generation of writers. In G. B. Stern's (1890–1973) *Children of No Man's Land* (1919), a group of working women (a secretary, a chauffeuse, two caterers, and a biologist) debate the impact of the war on the "sex problem." These free lances see themselves as belonging to a "transition period," and they are certainly revisers of femininity (one of them crops her luxuriant hair while they talk). As in "A Conjugal Episode," the occasion of the debate matters as much as its content. While the women discuss the sex problem, a group of men, lubricated by whiskey and soda, gathers to discuss *them*. Male clubland still goes about its traditional business; but it has met its match (or its mirror image).[21]

One answer to the heterosexual couple was the group or club. Another was the defiant singularity adopted by such as Hester Cawthorn. The one thing which unites Joan Ogden and her detractors, in *The Unlit Lamp*, is the knowledge that femininity can be redefined by the conscious manipulation of social symbolism: dress, bodily styling, gesture. There was much to be gained, as well as lost, by these tiny violations of custom. Joan's first instinct, after the shock of humiliation has worn off, is to head straight for the outfitter and buy some properly masculine neckties, a gray flannel suit, and a soft felt hat.[22] Neckties were a feminist issue.

No one was more aware of the defining qualities of social symbolism than the actress and writer Cicely Hamilton. Hamilton was initially attracted to the suffrage movement because it looked set to "shake and weaken the tradition of the 'normal woman.'" But she lost faith when she discovered that its leaders were intent on preserving the normal woman. They insisted too much, for her taste, on "the feminine note": "In the Women's Social and Political Union the coat-and-shirt effect was not favored; all suggestion of the masculine was carefully avoided, and the outfit of a militant setting forth to smash windows would probably include a picture-hat." The picture hat frames the militant even as she breaks a frame. Hamilton's feminism involved, among other things, the disruption, not of political meetings, but of the 'costume-code' that defined traditional femininity.[23] The two forms of action may well have reinforced each other's effect. A character in Beatrice Harraden's (1864–1936) *Interplay* (1908) mistakenly identifies a fellow passenger as a suffragette on the basis of her red tie and "severe hat."[24] The Pankhursts might not have been amused.

The coat-and-shirt effect was one to which a number of writers gave imaginative substance. The narrator of Katherine Mansfield's (1888–1923) "The Avanced Lady" is appalled when prim German feminists denounce women who smother their femininity under what one calls the "English tailor-made" and another the "lying garb of false masculinity." Discreetly masculine garb adorns a long line of neutrals from the protagonist of Menie Muriel Dowie's (1866–1945) *A Girl in the Karpathians* (1891) through to Edith Haynes, in Hamilton's war novel *William—An Englishman* (1919), a "tall young woman in tweed coat and skirt," as fiercely reserved, and as compelling, as Hester Cawthorn.[25]

If tweed, with its connotations of masculinity, was one way to disrupt the costume-code, then color, particularly bright or discordant color, was another. Joan Ogden learns nonconformity from older feminists like Beatrice Lesway, a schoolteacher who lives in Bloomsbury. Beatrice's untidiness and garish clothes make her almost, but not quite, a figure of fun. "Her whole appearance left you bewildered; it was a mixed metaphor, a contradiction in style, certainly a little grotesque, and yet you did not laugh."[26] Mixture and contradiction make her hard to interpret, but easy to distinguish. The extraordinary clothes worn by the artist Yvonne Irdwine, in Margaret Legge's (1872–1957) *The Rebellion of Esther* (1914), "purples and greens and scarlets and yellows all mixed anyhow," give her, too, a distinctive illegibility. Equally striking is the "singular effect" of the mackintosh, golf cap, and dogskin riding gloves worn by Anne Yeo, in Ada Leverson's (1862–1933) *Love's Shadow* (1908).[27] Leverson contrasts Anne's passionate, prickly devotion to Hyacinth Verney with the boredom of marriage and the banality of adulterous intrigue. When Hyacinth decides to marry, Anne retires to a Bloomsbury boardinghouse. What makes these women compelling (more than a joke) is that the decision they have taken, to be odd, affects every aspect of their lives. Colorfulness and tweed, overstatement and understatement, set in motion a genealogical "reading." They are the point from which a well-informed and well-disposed contemporary reader might have embarked upon a virtual narrative.

Woman to Woman: L. T. Meade and the Fantasy of Seduction

L. T. Meade married when she was twenty-five, and had three children. She was not, as far as I know, a lesbian. But her innumerable, and in most respects entirely conventional, romances return again and again to the portrayal of women whose compelling and magnetic dignity is overtly erotic, and therefore the site of virtual narrative. These women are utterly imperious, unlike the free lances of the Newer Woman novel, whose love for them sometimes serves as a measure of their imperiousness. They dominate the narratives in which they appear. Meade began to publish in the 1870s, and made her name in the 1880s as an author of school stories. Thereafter, she was prolific both in that genre and in many others. A discussion of two books published in 1898, one a New Woman novel, the other a terrorist novel, will show how she adapted the conventions of disparate genres to the portrayal of a new type of heroine.

The Cleverest Woman in England develops the sensational aspects of the New Woman fiction so popular during the first half of the 1890s. Dagmar Olloffson, the child of an unhappy marriage, dedicates herself to the campaign for the emancipation of women, both as a writer and as a public speaker. She falls in love with Geoffrey Hamlyn, a staunch conservative and bitter opponent of women's rights. They strike a bargain: neither will interfere with the other's convictions. Dagmar becomes an assiduous wife and mother, while continuing to speak and write on behalf of the "Cause." She converts half their Bloomsbury house into a shelter for battered and fallen women. She continues to speak and write on behalf of the "Cause," and at the same time converts herself into the perfect wife and mother. She is, as she herself puts it, a "contradiction."[28] Tragically, one of the women she has rescued from distress brings smallpox into the house, and Dagmar dies. The novel celebrates her as a pioneer, while at the same time emphasizing, luridly, the dangers of political commitment.

Meade dramatizes Dagmar's divided loyalty by contrasting her love for her husband with her more ambiguous feelings for Imogen Pryce, a suffragette whom she has long befriended. The marriage comes as a shattering blow to Imogen, whose jealousy thereafter irradiates the action. Geoffrey huffily tells Imogen that, although they both love Dagmar deeply, they should not put themselves in "the same category." But the palpable strength of Imogen's feelings makes it hard to put her in any other category. The very closeness of the names by which Dagmar calls her husband and her friend (Geoff, Genny) suggests that one might quite easily be substituted for the other. "I do not love you as I ought," Imogen tells Dagmar.[29] The expression of these feelings, which ought not to be, is the book's most vivid event.

Scenes between husband and wife quickly fall into the same pattern: a disagreement about politics, followed by an embrace. The embrace, however, has little erotic charge. "He knelt by her, she laid her head on his breast. A moment later she had dropped asleep." Although her affection for Geoffrey is genuine, and frequently reiterated, she does not appear to desire him passionately. Dagmar and Imogen make the more promising couple. "Now I—sometimes I think I am too big, there is too much of me; but you are *petite*, Imogen, altogether the sort of woman that a man would fall in love with." Their encounters, punctuated by false moves and eruptions, are suffused with an ambiguous eroticism.

> "Sit down by me, Imogen, for a moment."
> Imogen obeyed. Dagmar kept her hands folded lightly in her lap. Imogen, who was always fond of touching those she loved, tried to take possession of one of the hands, but Dagmar very decidedly repulsed her.
> "What did you do that for?"
> "I don't want you to hold my hand. I have told you before that it is terribly effeminate."
> "Ah, you can little guess what I feel for you."

It is the indeterminacy of Imogen's feelings that unsettles Dagmar and provokes her to uncharacteristic abruptness. The only description she can find for them is "effeminate," an affectation as repellent to her in a woman as it would be in a man. Imogen determines the rhythm of these encounters: her caress elicits from Dagmar no more than a gesture of rejection; but that very rejection, whose abruptness acknowledges her desire, emboldens her to declare herself.

> Imogen stood behind her friend, pushing back her soft hair, and laying her cool fingers on the white broad forehead.
> Dagmar submitted to the caress in utter weariness, then irritation, altogether foreign to her nature, seized her, and she sprang up.
> "Oh, don't touch me just now, Genny, I can't quite bear it, I have gone through a good bit. The fact is, I am in a dilemma, and only you can put me straight."
> "Then I will, darling, to my heart's blood."[30]

That irritation, so foreign to Dagmar's nature, is, by its very foreignness, an intenser feeling than any to which Geoffrey moves her. His desire remains unacknowledged. Dagmar knows that Imogen is a lesbian, even if she cannot, or will not, say as much. Addressed, implicitly, as a lesbian, Imogen responds with a declaration, with her "heart's blood." Although the novel holds her indirectly responsible for Dagmar's death, it never portrays her as a monster or a joke. Imogen's desire measures Dagmar's imperiousness.

The Cleverest Woman in England is sober stuff, however, by comparison with one of the six other novels Meade published that year, *The Siren.* Vera, the siren in question, is half English, half Russian (Dagmar Olloffson is half English, half Swedish). A brutal public flogging received in Siberian exile converts her to Nihilism. Her mission is to secure the fortune of her wealthy English father, Colonel Nugent, then assassinate him and the Tsar with bouquets of poisoned roses. In England, she proves an immense success, and eventually learning to love and respect her father, longs to exchange Russian magnetism for English respectability. But the memory of the flogging keeps her loyal to the cause. There can be no compromise between a daughter's love and a terrorist's dedication. She commits suicide.

By far the most compelling passages in this routine thriller concern her arrival in English society and her mass seduction of Colonel Nugent's household. First to go is Frank Norreys, the fiancé of Nugent's niece, Wilmot. He is soon followed by Wilmot, and her mother, Lady O'Brien. Vera's mission requires her to exercise her "powers of fascination" to the full: "walking over hearts," she calls it. However, whereas Nugent and Norreys submit instantly, the two women put up a fierce resistance, and their capitulation, when it comes, is thus the more heartfelt, the more charged. Lady O'Brien is struck immediately by Vera's wonderful eyes: "when they look at you they make you feel queer." Vera's frank avowal of will-to-power finally overwhelms her.

> She kissed Lady O'Brien as she spoke. That kiss thrilled through the widow almost as if it had been bestowed by a lover. She took one of Vera's hands and held it tightly.

The kiss widows Lady O'Brien more effectively than her husband's death, obliterating heterosexuality. Wilmot, too, aware of Norreys's fascination with Vera, hates her power. But Wilmot's hatred fades mysteriously on the eve of her wedding.

> "If you will I should love it; and yet sometimes, Vera, I hate you so much—so much."
> "No, no, Wilmot, you cannot hate me."
> "I do not now; I love you with passion. Oh, yes, come and sleep with me."
> "I will come to you soon after midnight, not before. Now I must go."[31]

Vera's terrorist mission, like Dagmar Olloffson's commitment to women's rights, expresses her imperious will. That imperiousness provides a context in which the writer can imagine the seduction of one woman by another.

Meade remained extraordinarily prolific. By the Edwardian period, she was averaging about ten books a year. Although the bulk of her output is dull stuff, her taste for the lurid did allow her to develop extensive fantasies about powerful women. Lady Darnley, for example, in *A Maid of Mystery* (1904), a standard crime story, has compelling reddish-brown eyes that are "not nice," and holds the

heroine's hand in "a sort of caressing manner which I could not escape from without marked rudeness."[32] The caress, as urgent in its
way as Imogen Pryce's, creates a degree of excitement for which bur-
glary may provide the occasion, but surely not the cause. There is no
possible connection between Meade's novels and the "new sexual
language" elaborated at more or less the same time by Edward Carpenter. But they, too, I would suggest, made lesbianism visible.

ANOTHER STORY: CHRISTOPHER ST. JOHN AND HER CIRCLE

The suffragette, journalist, and author Christabel Marshal became,
on the title pages of her books and in the memoirs of her friends,
Christopher St. John. In 1899, when she was in her mid-twenties,
she met and fell in love with Ellen Terry's daughter Edy Craig. St.
John and Craig lived together, at first in London, then in Small Hyth
in Kent, until the latter's death in 1947. During World War I, they
were joined in Small Hyth by Clare Atwood, a painter. Bernard Shaw
encouraged St. John to write a history of that "unique" *ménage à
trois*. She never did. But Vita Sackville-West's "Triptych" is an informative beginning.[33]

   The lesbian trio dissimulates lesbianism. It preempts any suspicion of "marriage," of coupling. To that extent, it may seem, and
may well have been, a defensive measure, possibly a self-denial. But
it also creates possibilities, ways of thinking and acting, which were
to be foreclosed by the lesbian couples of the 1920s. The presence of
a third ensures that the love between women cannot settle into an
imitation of heterosexual marriage, a fixed distribution of masculinity and femininity. According to Sackville-West, three "strong personalities" had managed to live at "close quarters" for many years
without overshadowing each other.[34] St. John and Atwood played
full parts, as writer and designer, in the plays and pageants directed
by Craig, who has been seen as the model for Miss La Trobe in Virginia Woolf's *Between the Acts* (1941).[35] It is hard to be sure, without
further biographical research that would exceed the scope of this
essay, whether the arrangement was a strategy or a happenstance.
But the testimony of Sackville-West and Shaw does suggest that it
was regarded at the time as distinctly, and richly, unorthodox.

   St. John was a writer, and avowed her lesbianism in her writing.
The semi-autobiographical *Hungerheart* was published in the same
year (1915) and by the same publisher (Methuen) as D. H. Lawrence's
The Rainbow. While *The Rainbow* was banned, largely on account
of its depiction of a lesbian affair, *Hungerheart* attracted little attention, although far more radical in its representation of homosexual

desire. It is a first-person narrative, set in the final decades of the nineteenth century, and describes the emotional and spiritual development of a young woman (a Newer Woman, in my classifiction), Joanna Montolivet. Joanna, also known as John and John-Baptist, notices that while men have both a male life and a life as a human being, women have been expelled from "common humanity" and become "merely females." Rejection of the "merely female" life shaped by marriage and maternity frees her to love women.[36]

Joanna's first overwhelming passion is for Lady Martha Ladde, who inspires "heroic, erotic, infantine, splendid" daydreams, and on whose pillow she leaves red roses and poems. Lady Martha's appeal lies not only in her beauty, but, more interestingly, in her "insolent, off-hand manner." Social status has liberated her from convention. She wears whatever she likes ("a rose-coloured felt hat and rough tweed clothes of a masculine cut"), and behaves as she pleases.[37] This is, if you like, the Newer Woman's crush, the Newer Woman's genealogical passion. It mixes two images from the fictional repertoire: free lance and siren, femininity played down and femininity played up. Young Joanna finds the combination of the free lance's felt hat and tweed with the siren's imperiousness utterly irresistible.

After Lady Martha, Joanna falls for a succession of opaquely exotic or refractory women who both grant and withhold, recognize and disavow, thus enabling her to desire them along the borderline of partial resemblance. "It was *to love* I yearned more than to *be loved*, and I was entirely free from sexual instincts." To define sexuality as an instinct is to relegate it to the impersonal, the array of sexological categories, and at the same time to reclaim for the personal (the crucially formative, the moral, the political) a range of ambiguously fantasized erotic feelings. What connects Joanna's lovers is that they are all the same as her, and yet different. Identity emerges in the circulation of sameness and difference. The ones who arouse the strongest emotions are Lady Martha and the stormily compelling Giovanna Ludini, who reaches to her "innermost part." Giovanna recognizes Joanna's desire, and disavows it. "Perhaps she has withheld herself from me because she is contaminated with innumerable unknown loves. Yet how fair and innocent is her white forehead! I caress it despairingly with my fingers."[38] Giovanna has been touched, as another siren, Dagmar Olloffson, had been touched, but she, too, will not touch others. In fact, the two women touch in name only, their desire announcing itself through the echo of Joanna in Giovanna and of Giovanna in Joanna.

The novel never resolves the tension between sameness and difference. Indeed, it finds in that irresolution a structure for lesbian eroticism. Joanna eventually becomes a Catholic. The "insupport-able rapture" produced by a vision of the Virgin Mary displaces the supportable (if barely so) raptures produced by heroic-erotic day-dreams.[39] However, Joanna's relation to the nun who is her spiritual adviser reproduces her relation to all the other women in her life. Spiritual conversion seems less like the climax towards which the narrative has always been moving than one more rapture in a se-quence of raptures. The structure of this *Bildungsroman* is serial rather than developmental. Each new lover is introduced abruptly, with a minimum of context, and disappears as soon as the rapture dies down: the rhythm of Joanna's life is the rhythm, or a-rhythm, of serial eroticism.

Sameness and difference circulate not only within the text, but also between the text and its readers. It is surely St. John speaking through Joanna when she addresses a particular kind of reader, dif-ferent from her, and yet the same. "Brotherly minds of mine, ne-glected in the study of womanhood, this was written for you!"[40] *Hungerheart* makes actual the virtual narrative of Newer Woman fiction. Homosexual desire is no longer a subordinate clause within the sentence of the wedlock plot or melodrama. It is itself a sen-tence: or, rather, a series of clauses, a parataxis.

Hungerheart was St. John's only novel. Thereafter, she turned to biography, writing lives of two prominent New Women: Christine Murrell, the first woman to be elected to the Council of the British Medical Association (1924) and to the General Medical Council of Great Britain (1933); and the composer Ethel Smyth (1858–1944).[41] Published long after the era of the Newer Woman, both books fall outside the scope of this essay. But they contain some significant emphases. In both, St. John casts herself as the Newer Woman who both resembles and differs from the New Woman. She remembers Murrell as the kind of mixed metaphor that Joan Ogden, in *The Unlit Lamp,* sees in Beatrice Lesway: "a woman of massive frame, a virile woman, whose irreproachably feminine clothes seemed in-congruous." Similarly, the imperious Smyth "usually wore a rough tweed coat and skirt, a cap of the same material, or a 'boater.'"[42] Like Lady Martha Ladde, these are women who both understate and over-state femininity.

Neither had much time for dyadic thinking and living. Murrell lived for thirty years, in a succession of London flats and a house in Surrey, with Honor Bone. Both were graduates of the London School of Medicine for Women, and they established a joint practice in Bayswater in 1903. Their "professional partnership" could be said to have set the pattern for their personal partnership. Murrell, how-

ever, proved too energetic for the semi-invalid Bone, and in 1925
Marie Lawson came to live with them in their Surrey house: this
time, the friendships were based on "chemical," rather than professional affinity.[43] Again, the decision to form a *ménage à trois* is sug-
gestive, although there is even less biographical evidence here than
in the case of St. John, Craig, and Atwood. Smyth, by contrast,
claimed in her memoirs that she had given up heterosexuality for
work. The space cleared in her life by that renunciation filled with
passionate "engouements," with a serial eroticism comparable to
Joanna Montolivet's. Smyth's *engouements*, like Joanna's, often involved women of high social standing. Her "almost insane passion"
for the Princesse Edmond de Polignac, for example, turned on her
beloved's aristocratic insouciance. "Grave, natural, don't-care-ish,
the soul of independence—in short, all the things I like."[44]

St. John's biographies of Christine Murrell and Ethel Smyth constitute a genealogical testament: the Newer Woman's last word on
the New Woman. They demonstrate that, for one early twentieth-
century British feminist at least, genealogy had become not only a
habit, but an article of faith. St. John moved towards, and into, homosexual identity by living and writing along the borderline of partial resemblance.

Notes

1. Radclyffe Hall, *The Unlit Lamp* (London, 1981), 284–85.
2. For New Woman novels, see, inter alia: A. R. Cunningham, "The
'New Woman Fiction' of the 1890s," *Victorian Studies* 17 (1973): 177–86;
Gail Cunningham, *The New Woman in Victorian Fiction* (London, 1978);
Kate Flint, *The Woman Reader 1837–1914* (Oxford, 1993), 294–316. For the
Edwardian "marriage problem" or "sex" novel, see David Trotter, *The En-
glish Novel in History 1895–1920* (London, 1993), 197–213.
3. Martha Vicinus, *Independent Women: Work and Community for
Single Women 1850–1920* (Chicago, 1985). For novels about working
women and about the suffrage campaigns, see Trotter, *English Novel*, 44–48.
4. For representations of the Newest Woman, see Mary Louise
Roberts's wide-ranging and incisive account of *la femme moderne (la
garçonne)*, in *Civilization without Sexes: Reconstructing Gender in Post-
War France, 1917–1927* (Chicago, 1994), 19–87.
5. In literary studies, New Historicism is still associated primarily with
the description and analysis of Renaissance literature. For an anthology of
representative approaches, see Richard Wilson and Richard Dutton, eds.,
New Historicism and Renaissance Drama (London, 1992). Its spread to
other fields is charted in Jeffrey N. Cox and Larry J. Reynolds, eds., *New Historical Literary Study: Essays on Reproducing Texts, Representing History*
(Princeton, 1993).

6. Sandra M. Gilbert and Susan Gubar, *No Man's Land: The Place of the Woman Writer in the Twentieth Century*, vol. 2, *Sexchanges* (New Haven, 1989), 299–300.

7. Carroll Smith-Rosenberg, *Disorderly Conduct: Visions of Gender in Victorian America* (London, 1985), 284. For a similar analysis, see Jeffrey Weeks, *Sex, Politics and Society* (London, 1981), 115.

8. Esther Newton, "The Mythic Mannish Lesbian: Radclyffe Hall and the New Woman," in Martin Bauml Duberman, Martha Vicinus, and George Chauncey, eds., *Hidden from History: Reclaiming the Gay and Lesbian*, (New York, 1989), 281–93. See also Sonja Ruehl, "Inverts and Experts: Radclyffe Hall and the Lesbian Identity," in Rosalind Brunt and Caroline Rowan, eds., *Feminism, Culture and Politics* (London, 1982); Jean Radford, "An Inverted Romance: *The Well of Loneliness* and Sexual Ideology," in idem, ed., *The Progress of Romance: The Politics of Popular Fiction* (London, 1986); and Jonathan Dollimore, *Sexual Dissidence* (Oxford, 1991), 48–52.

9. Marie Belloc Lowndes, *Lilla: A Part of Her Life* (London, 1916), 159; Radclyffe Hall, *The Well of Loneliness* (London, 1982), 275.

10. Quoted by Newton, "Mythic Mannish Lesbian," 286. See Ruth F. Claus, "Confronting Homosexuality: A Letter from Frances Wilder," *Signs* 2 (1977): 928–33.

11. Terry Castle, *The Apparitional Lesbian* (New York, 1993); Suzanne Raitt, "Charlotte Mew and May Sinclair: A Love-Song," *Critical Quarterly* 37 (1995): 3–17; Martha Vicinus, "Fin-de-Siècle Theatrics: Male Impersonation and Lesbian Desire" in the present volume.

12. Gilbert and Gubar, *No Man's Land* 2:309.

13. On gender and female Modernism, see Suzanne Raitt, *Vita and Virginia: The Work and Friendship of Vita Sackville-West and Virginia Woolf* (Oxford, 1993); and, more generally, Bonnie Kime Scott, ed., *The Gender of Modernism* (Bloomington, 1990). Jane Eldridge Miller's *Rebel Women* (London, 1994) is exceptional in the attention it gives to female Modernism's Edwardian precursors.

14. A. T. Fitzroy, *Despised and Rejected* (London, 1988), 348. On Feb. 25, 1919, Virginia Woolf recorded in her diary that Allatini had been to tea with Lady Ottoline Morrell: "she almost fainted & had to be fed on bath buns, which Ottoline had by her—& confided, of course, the story of her unhappy love, which made it necessary for her to be fed on Bath Buns." *Diary*, ed. Anne Olivier Bell, vol. 1 (Harmondsworth, 1979), 246.

15. Ibid., 12, 44, 51, 65–66, 69.

16. Alice Stronach, *A Newnham Friendship* (London, 1901), 385.

17. Vicinus, *Independent Women*.

18. Olive Birrell, *Love in a Mist* (London, 1900), 228, 247; Violet Hunt, *The Workaday Woman* (London, 1906), 35.

19. Violet Tweedale, *The Heart of a Woman* (London, 1917), 225.

20. "A Conjugal Episode" was published in *Flies in Amber* (London, 1905).

21. G. B. Stern, *Children of No Man's Land* (London, 1919), 226–52.

22. *The Unlit Lamp*, 285.

23. Cicely Hamilton, *Life Errant* (London, 1935), 65, 75.

24. Beatrice Harraden, *Interplay* (London, 1908), 131.

25. Katherine Mansfield, *Short Stories* (New York, 1983), 105; Menie Muriel Dowie, *A Girl in the Karpathians* (London, 1891), 17; Cicely Hamilton, *William—An Englishman* (London, 1919), 153. "The Advanced Lady" was published in *In a German Pension* (London, 1911).

26. *The Unlit Lamp*, 200.

27. Margaret Legge, *The Rebellion of Esther* (London, 1914), 35; Ada Leverson, *Love's Shadow* (London, 1950), 299.

28. L. T. Meade, *The Cleverest Woman in England* (London, 1898), 19.

29. Ibid., 25, 116.

30. Ibid., 217, 18, 161, 243.

31. L. T. Meade, *The Siren: A Novel* (London, 1898), 129, 112, 105, 137, 144–45.

32. L. T. Meade, *A Maid of Mystery* (London, 1904), 162.

33. The essay appeared in Eleanor Adlard, ed., *Edy: Recollections of Edith Craig*, (London, 1949), 118–25, together with further recollections by St. John, Cicely Hamilton, Sheila Kaye-Smith, and others. See also Julie Holledge, *Innocent Flowers: Women in the Edwardian Theatre* (London, 1981), chap. 8.

34. *Edy*, 123.

35. In an unsigned article, "Some Sources for *Between the Acts*," *Virginia Woolf Miscellany* 6 (1977).

36. Christopher St. John, *Hungerheart* (London, 1915), 58.

37. Ibid., 61–62

38. Ibid., 88, 248–49.

39. Ibid., 283–84. On lesbian converts to Catholicism, see Joanna Glasgow, "What's a Nice Lesbian like You Doing in the Church of Torquemada: Radclyffe Hall and Other Catholic Converts," in Joanna Glasgow and Karla Jay, eds., *Lesbian Texts and Contexts: Radical Revisions* (New York, 1990), 241–54.

40. *Hungerheart*, 98.

41. Christopher St. John, *Christine Murrell, M.D.: Her Life and Her Work* (London, 1935); *Ethel Smyth: A Biography* (London, 1959).

42. *Christine Murrell*, xvii; *Ethel Smyth*, 42.

43. *Christine Murrell*, 35, 102.

44. Quoted by St. John in *Ethel Smyth*, 123–24.

Spectacles and Sexualities

The "Mise-en-Scène" of the "Tirailleur Sénégalais" on the Western Front, 1914–1920

Annabelle Melzer

Staging "Les Idées Noires": Black Thoughts

> Dear little girl: I haven't the pleasure of knowing you, but allow me to tell you here, how much joy, in its charming simplicity, your letter, which accompanied a pair of woolen socks and which a tirailleur* received, brought me, so that I now respond to it. Surely, while you knitted with your nimble fingers, you never thought that they would warm the feet of a black . . .[1]

November 1, 1916. A letter from the Western Front initialled M.T., appears in the trench journal of the 44th Senegalese Battalion, *Les Idées noires*, one of hundreds of newspapers written and edited by soldiers for soldiers—this one published at the isolated "black forces" camp at Corneau in the Gironde. A black soldier has received a pair of woolen socks from a young French girl. He realizes they were not intended for him, but is grateful nonetheless, and writes.

Wrong. M.T.'s letter is in the grand tradition of the theatrical reversal, the *supercherie*, where what one thought was, was not, and in my own first reading, thinking I had found that rare first person "utterance-marking,"[2] the "I" of the black soldier, I was completely fooled. *Les Idées noires* is, in fact, "écriture blanche,"[3] a trench journal for the "troupes noires" written by its white colonial officers—there was no note, no young girl—just an editorial "excuse" for a lesson in colonial ambition which begins, of course, with geography:

> Have you ever opened your geography book to the map of Africa? If not, we'll look at it together. The simple contours of this continent are arranged to please schoolchildren who usually draw badly. You see there a large area shaded pink. The legend will tell you that this color represents the possessions of France and your young patriotic heart will rejoice, seeing that on the map of Africa, this pink holds a very respectable place and that from Algeria to Chad and along the Atlantic

---

* Literally: "rifleman." The term was used to describe the colonial infantryman.

coast it is uninterrupted. No foreign colonies can erase or threaten the pink area which represents our African colonial empire.

So! This pink which strikes your young eyes, you owe to the fathers of these *tirailleurs* who fight today on the soil of France, brought here by the Faidherbes, Galliénis, Mangins and a few other no less glorious names. This is a handful of tireless men trained by leaders of whom they were worthy, who, for us, conquered the Sudan and Chad.

The *tirailleurs sénégalais*, whose selective history is here recounted by their white officer, were battalion-strength black units of the French infantry, founded by decree of Napoleon III on July 20, 1857. In 1914 they numbered thirty thousand, which number the French, openly anxious about what they saw as the widening demographic imbalance with Germany (giving Germany a potentially insurmountable military advantage), rapidly increased by an extensive and brutal recruiting policy to 63,000 in early 1918, and 190,000 by the summer of that year.[4]

Colonialism found its political, ideological, and cultural expressions heightened in the setting of the theater of World War I. It is not surprising, therefore, that M.T's letter is, alongside its cult of the military personality and its championing of the geographic strongarm tactics of French colonial practice, a site of that gendering so prominent in the colonialist discourse of discovery: the classic mating of colonizer and feminized land, intruded upon by the presence of the third leg to the adulterous triangle: the black male *indigène*—native. The coziness of colonial conquest, with its metaphors of mastering and deflowering a feminized space, is, as Peter Hulme writes, "inevitably disturbed by the unfortunate presence of the other parties who were there beforehand and who could only be seen as, at best, recalcitrant fathers or brothers holding back the lovematch, at worst already the husbandry to the 'virgin' land."[5]

M.T., stationed at the black camp at Corneau, is well aware of these "other parties," as he writes to his "dear little girl" the letter whose *coup de théâtre* is guarded until its conclusion:

> Do not regret then, little schoolgirl, that your contribution to the soldiers went to please a *tirailleur*. You must love and admire them. But let not your affection and your admiration restrict itself to the limited category of the *tirailleur*. Let it carry over as well to those heroic Europeans who abandoned all: home, loved ones, comfort, health to serve where we maintain a colonial empire. Do not, therefore, do as so many of your older sisters—not even want to glance past the *tirailleur* to see the white who has the difficult task of civilizing them.

Just what is it that older sisters do with "uncivilized" *tirailleurs* that "little girls" do not yet do? Here is the second triangulation: the white *colon*/soldier, the black native *tirailleur sénégalais*, and the French "woman." Two partake of a natural depravity and loose character necessitating the controlling presence of the third—a male European overlord. His is this letter, a monologue recited by a phallus to a virgin, before it (with its passion to fill a great blank space) penetrates her rose-colored geography—colonized female land and virgin girl conflated. Here is France reproducing "himself" in Africa. The "white" colonial officer's words not only address, but also give voice to his white soldier-readers, while simultaneously representing and effectively silencing two "others." For it is not only the maidenhood of Africa that is to be forced (fulfilling the historic destiny of the white colonizer by planting blotches of miscegenated culture on the perceived-as-blank black continent), not only the *indigène* soldier to be abducted and "civilized," projected, represented and feminized, but perhaps, above all, it is the Frenchwoman to be mastered in this unique joining of war and colonial campaign. It is the young French schoolgirl, her older sister, French women, the category "Woman," who, through hostility, distrust, contempt, and desire, will be the *colon*'s/soldier opponent in a gendered struggle of mastery, authority and will.

Yet M.T.'s letter, despite its seemingly confident cartographic impulse, expresses a lurking malaise. It is not only the generalized uneasiness that is a hallmark of imperial culture, needing continually to confirm and reconfirm itself to and for itself, but also the much more insidious, fear-laced desire of the *poilu* at the front, a fear that crossed over lines of class and rank to be expressed again and again in the combatant "trench scripts" (texts written by soldiers to be performed by soldiers for an audience of soldiers):

> There's a question that's been on the tip of my tongue since you showed up. Is it true that our wives at the home front, aren't behaving quite up to par, that they're flirtatious, frivolous, that . . . that . . . that in fact (he makes the sign of the cuckold at his temples).[6]

The topic of sexual conduct was, at the front, a point of convergence for a multiplicity of discussions, among them gender, ethnicity, nationality, and social stratification. The clearest place from which the soldier's voice could be heard on this complex subject was the warfront stage, and the trench scripts are one of the rich, neglected sources for his voice. Significantly less official than the trench journals, these sketches, rude and crude in their world of men-for-men, often (as we see above) describe or imply gesture as well as leaving open for conjecture the unrecorded and therefore uncensorable area of improvisation in performance. Soldier performance in war is one more ancient male-created and performed theater—a performing space designed so that men could talk to themselves about themselves in a public forum, while representing, enacting, and appropriating their "others"—especially "woman." *Poilu* performance took advantage of the special status of the stage as a "safe place" in which one could both voice fears and play dangerous games. There was almost no talk about the first fear—dying. Instead, what moved into first place was "woman," and to talk about her, the soldier did what men have done since time immemorial: he put on a dress and mounted the stage.[7]

Gender is, among other things, performance, and soldier-dressed-as-woman is an especially complex construct, a boundary transgression, both catalyst and testing of the limits of indecorous and disorderly behavior. The one constant in each and every trench script is the cross-dressed soldier, and though the "mistress of ceremonies" in the soldier-sketch with the cuckolded husband will attempt to assuage the sexual anxiety of the *poilu*, the "lady" doth protest too much:

> It's a lie. The French woman has remained the most worthy and charming of women in the world. She patiently awaits her dear *poilu*, composed and hopeful, dividing her time between the household tasks and her small children. Here, once again, is a scheme of the Germans who spread their perfidious rumors to break your morale, to weary you of the war, and to make you give up. Don't believe a word of it.

M.T.'s letter and the soldier "travesty" must be heard in their contexts. The value of these texts is that they are filled with local knowledge, man to man, in the world of men-at-war, and the mistress of ceremonies' response, as he/she graced the war-front stage in drag, was performed with gestures filled with sexual innuendo and greeted by the loud and raucous laughter of the all-soldier audience. Soldier-drag marked a trouble spot which, as 1914 moved towards 1918, became quite clear. What the *poilu*-woman realized was that what he had thought was rock solid, his "manliness," was frighteningly disintegrating. To talk about this, he put on "her" dress and trod the boards.

To appear on stage is to display one's body to strangers. The erotic pervasion of theatrical space encouraged the displaying and framing of soldier-bodies, tantalizing an all-male audience with more potent inscriptions of gender than daily life condoned. The gender signals and gender issues beamed from the war-front stage were especially powerful and dynamic. Though to cross-dress on stage at the front between 1914 and 1918 was hardly a challenge to the hegemonic heterosexual regime; even as the declared object of desire remained "woman," gender switching through parodic transvestism barely masked a homoerotic *frisson*. This was risky business, especially in a world in which gender identity itself was on very shaky ground. As a soldier who signs himself "Epsilonn" writes in a trench newspaper of 1916:

> The war or rather the death of too many *poilus* during the war has created a major economic problem: "The replacing of men by women in industry and commerce etc. . . ." Far from being jealous (we love them too much for that) at learning that women will replace us in many fields, we are, on the contrary, delighted. We fully support this project and we look with the greatest pleasure at the prospect of the beautiful sex replacing us completely in all our careers. . . .[8]

"Oui chères lectrices . . ." ("Yes, dear readers . . . ,") the front-line author continues, addressing his buddies in the feminine. Indigenous usage is always correct (and significant) in its own setting.

With the outbreak of war, the ongoing dialectical process of identity formation, in which the male is mirrored in a complementary female form, this engendering through the "other," undergoes fundamental mutations. It is this whole area to which so much recent critical attention has been paid—war as a gendering activity, how men and women have been marked by this "men's business."

As Eric J. Leed writes:

> . . . in setting aside the chief engendering institution, the patriarchal family, warfare engenders the genders homoerotically and narcissistically. . . . [With] biological reproduction bracketed out . . . [for the duration of the war] the genders map their relations to the "other" along an erotic-aggressive continuum, relating to each other through nonreproductive sexuality ("sex proper") or through the reigning gendering activity—violence.[9]

Having little, no, or strange-for-him sex, the soldier (no matter what side he was on), while worrying about what his own woman was doing in bed, sang of taking the women of the enemy.

> But that day, it will come
> (And that day is at hand)
> When we'll pay you court, all
> Lady-*boches* in your land
> Not one trick need we pull
> All the beds will be full
> Set the *boche* up to fall
> And we'll cuckold them all.[10]

The colonial soldier had additional options in the colonies. In *Les Idées noires* of November 1, 1916, J.C. writes erotically of his wife Fula:

> The sun as it plays in your eyes filled with fire
> Your golden soft skin of the African clime
> Your haughty demarche, with its majestic height
> Make you preferable by far to the rest, virgin mine.
> Thousands of games, your naive rashness invented
> Where our lascivious flesh grew ever wetter,
> And faint with the pleasure of loving kisses
> In the darkness and cool of our home made of clay.
> Your hot excitable body, I loved to caress it
> So childlike and supple, like a tropical vine
> Which quivers with life in the depths of the forest . . .

Here, as in M.T.'s geography lesson addressed to the "little girl," the *supercherie* reigns: the wife is black, the husband gone-native white! Within the sexual dynamics of colonial power, the native woman will continue to play her role as magnificently "other," literally embodying her nation. The narrator's awareness of sun and climate, his seduction by the triumphant gait of his statuesque and golden but "juvenile" and "naive" woman, are all products of the colonizing gaze, a sexuality very differently weighted, very differently experienced than indigenous descriptions that employ proverbial wisdom ("The old people used to say: a woman is like the skin of kabundi, there is room in it [for one person only]")[11], mockery ("Like impotent chiefs who hide shriveled fruit between their legs before their moist young wives, like stolen horses they cannot ride"), or elemental and visceral images, products of a primal interaction between man and nature.

Nothing this carnal appeared in any French trench journal written to a French (read: white) wife; nothing, in fact, written to any wife at all.[12] Although letters of sexual innuendo appear to one's "marraine,"[13] the curtain descends on any intimate sexual dialogue between the French soldier and his wife. The only things written on this subject are "fictionalized" accounts, usually narrated in the third person, about the betrayal of one's trench-buddy by his wife, a betrayal which is never with another soldier but with a home-front draft dodger (*l'embusqué*), or with a soldier of the *"force noire."* The black "wild man" became the screen onto which the white soldier projected his darkest and most compelling fantasies of wantonness and perverse sexuality. These the black-male "animal" wore as a threat, while the black female carried them as a disturbing allure.

Black Africa, though less eroticized than the Islamic Orient, was nonetheless a place where white men hoped to find sexual experiences unobtainable in Europe. J.C.'s boldly narrated sexuality is a ritual possession in the State's name—a conspicuous assertion of lordship by the casual use of the body of a native African woman— the rape of native land and the rape of native women going hand-in-hand. Printed in a trench newspaper and read by his fellow white officers (and subservient black soldiers as well), J.C.'s erotic exhibitionism is one more way he will assert his power over the *indigène*—through his Fula, given him by the local *emir* in the time-tested practice of "alliance through matrimony," or, as it played itself out in the colonies, "colonization through bed."[14] Here is sex as patriotism, an ideologically meaningful (and overdetermined) act of violence (and its narration), impelled by and confirming the imperatives of appropriation, possession, and domination that characterize the colonial project in general.

The bravado potency in the *poilu*'s song of taking the German women, and the bold eroticism of J.C.'s "ode to miscegenation" has, however, its mirror in feared impotence: ". . . one no longer knows how to talk to women." The war had made the recent past, the recalled "normality" of the home front, seem peculiar, and women, by their absence, began more and more to bear an aura of unalterable strangeness. Woman/"other" and native/"other"—with little difficulty, the familiar tropes used to describe women—became the tropes conveniently used for the *indigène*/primitive. Here, colonizer/colonized, soldier-civilizer/native-savage, front-line combatant/home-front or front-line female carnavalesquely changed partners—all those on the left side of the line remained male, all those on the right were, or "became," female.

Still, the white soldier-at-war, despite his overdetermined sexual anxiety, was capable of shouting strong answers to the question "Who are you?"—a perception of self and the limits of his community. It is just this self-description, this self-definition, that is so desperately lost to us for the black troops. In *Culture and Imperialism*, Edward Said describes those "broken narratives" that come into play when representation overwhelms the represented. In this situation, a group is unable to represent itself, not because its members cannot speak or have no stories, and not even because they have been repressed (although that is often also the case). Nor is it even chiefly a question of their lack of access to the means of distribution of the "narrative" (although at the front this was true).[15] They cannot represent themselves because they are already represented, and that representation is so strong that they are scarcely perceived as capable of having stories, their stories are unimaginable, they have no "Permission to Narrate."[16] The *tirailleur* remained, so it would seem, inarticulate, eerily invoking the repeated fantasy that colonized people were without speech, while the French *poilu/colon*, his collective voice urging him on, the means of distribution of his "narrative" at his disposal, proceeded to stage his black brother-in-arms in prose, drawing, and performance, using the *tirailleur* as he used the woman's dress, to talk about himself.

The *tirailleur sénégalais* was over-represented on the Western Front. The idea of representation is a theatrical one. "Us," "we," and "ours" incorporate a fantasized enemy whose costumes, facial features, gestures, and language are not ours; an "other" onto whom the unthinkable is projected, that which arouses and exceeds civilized desire—a "savage." As French colonial General Charles Mangin wrote, "One is always somebody's barbarian."[17] Most importantly, this "barbarian's" expressions of sexuality and ritual (performance/religion) are not ours. The French soldier's *mise-en-scène* of the *tirailleur* is a stunning demonstration of the *colon*'s/soldier exercise of power alongside cultural difference. It will be the product of a crude and anxious misogynistic projection, a powerful conjunction of the savage/sexual ("savage tribes," "issues of barbaric races," "innate aggression," "a material penchant for war"), in which the topic of land is dissimulated by the topic of sex and savagery (a shift characteristic of all narrations of the colonial encounter), and the child-like/feminine ("docile," "blind obedience," "infantilism," "simple souls," "reduced nervous system").[18]

"Monstrosity," "anthropophagy," the *topoi* in the discourse of savagery are common, familiar since Herodotus's investigations of Greece's "barbarian" neighbors, or Marco Polo's accounts of "man-eating savages," and present in the oral texts that precede them both.[19] Here was the earliest popular vocabulary for constituting "otherness." War, however, seems to complicate the binary notion of "otherness," often presenting us not merely with representations of an enemy facing us, but troubling soundings on the enemy-other within. For the Germans, then, to describe the *tirailleurs* as cannibals, drawing them in *Lustige Blätter* eating German prisoners or brandishing the "coupe-coupe," the huge combat knife used for "beheading," is long-standing fair game in colonialism and war. However, for the French to do the same, drawing the *tirailleur*, their brother-in-arms, with a necklace of German ears for his wife, or gathering German helmets with the bloody heads of the Germans still dripping inside, is more problematic and encourages recourse to the defensive "you-did-it-so-we'll-do-it-too" position—you Germans cut off the ears of children (part of the widely disseminated anti-German propaganda describing fabricated German atrocities in Belgium in 1914), you carried back rings for your wives with the fingers still inside. Your barbarity had no excuse; our "barbarians" are (and here, of course, the French are in trouble) "out of Africa." The barest indication that the French are aware that there is a problem here is evident in one complexly composed French postcard illustration showing a *tirailleur sénégalais* guarding his German prisoners, turning to ask the family of local French villagers out for a Sunday stroll, "You've come to see the savages?" Here is the French soldier's displacement of anxiety about his own accusations of *indigène* savagery, through the illustration of condescension, as the question of just who the savages are hangs in the air. One may choose to read the naivete of the *tirailleur* in his assuredness that there is only one savage group at the fence. Or one may shift to the continually reiterated conviction of France's "civilizing mission," which would allow the French soldier/artist to raise even the lowest of the ranks within the colonial troops, the *force noire*, to a level above the savagery of the *boche*.

Figure 24: "'Ya bon," "Smile with the Big Teeth," a French drawing of a tirailleur senegalais (1917). Collection: *Bibliothèque de Documentation Internationale Contemporaine et Musée d'Histoire Contemporaine—BDIC*, Paris. Archipel Copyright Spaden.

In the heyday of pre-World War I French colonialism, the French described their black recruits as "half-savages with barbaric faces and eyes that move with the look of hunted animals, with intelligence that yet sleeps." "They cannot understand, they are monkeys."[20] In 1911, Charles Mangin wrote, "The nervous system of the black man is much less developed than that of the white. All the surgeons have observed how impassive the black is under the knife."[21] When sketched by the French in the landscape of his own country, the *tirailleur's* country is no place, emptier than a desert, a "null" with no history, no civilization. From this nothingness, a domesticated *tirailleur* is re-created. In his European uniform, he becomes more familiar, his perennial "smile with the big teeth" (Figure 24) drawn as a red-lipped-coon-grin, working to neutralize his savagery (though it merely reinforces that lack of self-consciousness associated with his rampant sexuality). Exotic, he is astonished at seeing his first snow. Enormous infant, it is a drawing of his face that in 1917 is selected for the wrapping of the cocoa powder "Banania," with his singular pidgin French "Ya bon" ("It's good") inscribed on the label.

The contemporary French trench newspapers, trench scripts, and postcards are filled with racist language and iconography. Most striking, however, are the blatant sexual narratives and illustrations as the weapons of choice. Though in the cuckolded husband's script the potential partner of the betraying French woman is not specified, in M.T's letter this person is clear. Two major candidates "outside-the-community" appear continually, ready to sexually serve the French woman: the draft dodger on the home front (with whom I will not deal in this essay) is one; the *tirailleur sénégalais*, the other.

Though it is classic to represent the enemy-other as the violator of "our" women, it is unheard of to represent one's comrades-in-arms as such violators. I have not come across one single account, not one narration or illustration of a French soldier, a trench-buddy, accused of sexual involvement with the woman of his friend (though we may well suppose that this did occur). Here silence reigns. Here, the community closes the circle tightly around itself and from its entrenchment, projects, formulates, and communicates its unique soldier, and in this case *colon*/soldier, ethnography: its "study" of those who do not live by one's own rules. The "draft dodger," the *tirailleur sénégalais*, and the French woman are the unique subjects and objects of this "field-court" of soldier-ethnographers—a court convened in the mud, the cold and the wet, a court that received and recorded testimony from all but the "accused" themselves and pronounced sentence on them. The evidence against the guilty is staged again and again, as in the postcard illustration (shown in figure 25) the *tirailleur sénégalais*, caught in a moment of his free, licentious sexuality, his lascivious ape-hands cupping the breasts of the French maid, is striking as a staging of the oriental-as-sexual-demonic-exotic. What is unique here is the attachment of the demeaning bestial caricature, not to an enemy, but to a much more intimate enemy—the native black soldier. The ironic text reads, "Seditious cry: Long Live the Germans" (a pun: also "the boobs"). Most seditious (and accused), the French woman, though merely a maid, is enjoying it thoroughly! (Figure 25).

Problemed "manliness" such as existed for the soldier at the front, compounded with colonialist racism, is a hard combination to

Figure 25: "Cri séditieux—Vive les Teutons!" "Seditious Cry: Long live the Teutons [the 'boob']!" French post card. Collection: *Bibliothèque de Documentation Internationale Contemporaine et Musée d'Histoire Contemporaine—BDIC*, Paris. Archipel Copyright Spaden.

beat. The projection of natural depravity, unharnessed sexuality, and loose character onto the black soldier and the French woman alike was a correlative of the complex bond between power and pleasure, sensuality and cruelty, that is so much a part of both imperial domination and man-at-war. The "older sister" and the black collective "other" are both immensely serviceable alibis for aggression. The "primitive," "sexual," black "enfant/sauvage," was photographed, drawn, and narrated by the *colon*/soldier so that he could write upon him, enhancing his supremacy through representation.[22] Africa's submissive, or at least indifferent, presence in his life allowed the French soldier to pursue his projections with a seemingly unchallenged intensity.

FRANCE ON TOP—POSITIONAL SUPERIORITY AND THE STAGING OF SEXUALITY

The culture of war has its own unique exclusions. First among these is women. "Pas de femme," goes the French soldiers' chant:

> "There'll be no women, and no girls"
> Says the colonel and he's rough!
> "Not a woman, not a girl"
> And he means it and he's tough![23]

War has traditionally been considered the quintessential proving ground for masculinity—a masculinity achieved through rituals of bodily pain, sacrifice, and violence and defined as a flight from the feminine. But like some specter, "woman" hovers over the front, for to make a man remains that ancient dyad: to send him to war and to have him "make a woman"—to go from the embrace of bodies to the embrace of battle. For in battle violence becomes the reigning gendering activity and women, (with their swampy triangle), by their (and its) absence and exclusion, become more and more *unheimlich*—uncanny—in the sense that Freud spoke of female genitals, the entrance to that *heim* (home) where everyone dwelt in the beginning, as an *unheimlich* place.[24]

Women's growing unfamiliarity and the painful intensity of the soldier's desire will cause him to represent them, fragmented or whole, endlessly sketched on the walls of abandoned village houses, sculpted in muddy trenches and on sandy beaches. It will raise up as well frenzied fantasies of seduction and betrayal, in which the male partner will most often be the *tirailleur sénégalais*. In a trench journal drawing of 1917, a metropolitan lovely is in bed, propped up against the pillows, her nightgown dropped to just above her nipples. Her black companion is fast asleep beside her. The caption reads: "The Paris nights are so black! I didn't notice he was a nigger!"[25] In a trench newspaper of 1916, a short tale entitled "Black Style" presents a nude *tirailleur* arriving to satisfy a roomful of home-front women:

> An old maid has a fine Senegalese as her pen-pal. Once when our nigger was on leave, his *marraine* invited over a number of her friends to celebrate with the *poilu* . . . It's dinner time, the door opens and what do we see? The darky, radiant, but naked as the day . . . "Bonjour Mamzelle," he says bowing, "to honor you, I came in "civvies." Party time for the *marraine* and her lady friends.[26]

Sandra Gilbert has addressed "the unmanning terrors of combat [that] lead not just to a generalized sexual anxiety but also to an anger directed specifically against the female."[27] The gap between men-at-war and women is pervasive and profound. Women are actually and metaphorically "behind the lines," resented for their absence, their safety, scorned for their ignorance of the "real" and really masculine experience of battle—an experience that women will never understand: "And I shudder with that shiver which I've known throughout the war, no woman will share my suffering."[28]

In his anger, the soldier draws and narrates his woman—the war having gone straight to her ovaries—copulating at home. His projected partner for her is the *tirailleur*, and he stages the lascivious couplings of their miscegenation from a position of powerful enti-

tlement—"on top," alternately co-opting the authority of the ethnographer, the dramatist, the storyteller. Positional superiority was
his, and exaggeration and caricature boldly characterize his representations. There are no real people here, no real woman, no real
tirailleur. As staged by both *poilu* and elite officers, functioning
within a long tradition of military/colonial memoirs and exposi-
tions, the *tirailleur sénégalais* will be exhibited as were the Ashanti
in the Vienna Prater in 1896,[29] as male "primitives," imported ex-
otics, icons of extreme sexuality possessed of a vital masculinity and
phallic power. "Samba Bana always gets women . . ."[30] He and his
fellow black soldiers will "with a victorious demeanor . . . fill the
three or four cafés . . . then when their pockets are empty . . . they
[will] walk in the streets . . . making love to women seduced by their
triumphal gait and soldierly boldness."[31] The courting style of the
tirailleur is impulsive, instinctive, and occasionally brutal, which
only adds to his virile "primitive" charm. As an anonymous soldier
describes them in *Les Idées noires*, no. 2, in December of 1916,
speaking in the voice of the Frenchwoman, with more than a small
hint of the homoerotic: "ils sont rudement bien montés . . ."
("they're incredibly well hung").

The group strategy in the projection of brute sexuality onto the
tirailleur is but one expression of the complex erotic bond which
united front-line soldiers. The sexual life of soldiers and "the sexual
life of savages" (as Bronislaw Malinowski called his ethnographic
study of 1929) joined. The significant difference was that only one
party was writing about both.

> We shall follow several [of the villagers] in their love affairs . . . we
> shall have to pry into their domestic scandals and take an indiscreet
> interest in their intimate life . . . taking an increasingly detailed view
> of native love-making . . . [observing] the dalliance of lovers at close
> quarters.[32]

Such soldier (and ethnographer) projection, a privileged excuse for
oneself—and fuel for aggressive action—worked exceedingly well just
because it was largely unconscious. This allowed the *colon*/soldier to
deny, unjustly, but with perfect sincerity, any harboring of belliger-
ence, woman-lust, or (most problematic of all) homoerotic excitement. Transposing these feelings from oneself to one's "other"
promoted a drama of sexual voyeurism, racism, and misogyny, which
assumed centerstage at the front. As Sartre wrote in his preface to
Frantz Fanon's *The Wretched of the Earth*, "the European has only
been able to become a man through creating slaves and monsters."[33]

The *tirailleur*, invented sideshow performer at the crazy carnival
of war, was staged as "mating" with many varieties of French

women: maids with prominent breasts, old surprised *marraines* and svelte seductive young ones, nondescript wives, "older sisters," and nurses (especially nurses). Nurses received the brunt of a rampant misogyny directed at women who found their way to the front. As early sexologist Dr. Magnus Hirschfeld wrote in his classic study *The Sexual History of the World War*, "it was quite clear that a considerable portion of the female nurses were impelled to nursing by quite other than patriotic and humanitarian motives."[34]

To stage the hospital scene, then, first the *tirailleur* had to be represented as wounded (weakened, fragile, vulnerable), yet potent ("Where are you wounded," she asked with concern. "All over, but not in the cock!"[35])—a very black Senegalese being cared for by a young, attractive, and very white nurse. The nurse was represented as looking up at him with intense solicitousness, supporting him as his wounded weight leaned on her encircling arm, presenting us with a figure-ground paradox where one is constantly blinking to readjust the figure foregrounded. The tendency in the little that has been written about these black-and-white images has been to foreground the representation of the black.[36] The French soldier however, foregrounded the nurse, feeling as Céline's Ferdinand Bardemu did, in only one of his many damning statements in *Journey to the End of the Night*: "The nurses, the bitches, . . . their only thought was to go on living . . . and to copulate thousands and thousands of times."[37] Klaus Theweleit documents again and again the soldiers' perception of the front-line nurse as aggressor, recruited from the ranks of women whose "true profession" was clear from the start—prostitute.[38] With whores "costumed" as nurses, "attending to" men could mean only one thing: "doing it."

And so we find the soldier "Joseph Blanche," a stand-up-comedy specialist in "the monologues of Senegalese soldiers"—an expert on the musings of "these simple-hearted souls which his tour of duty in the colonies had exposed him to." Writing in the trench newspaper *Rigolboche* of January 30, 1917, in the pidgin "petit nègre" French of the *tirailleur* (one more unfamiliar language converted into a mocking racist idiom so much the butt of *poilu* humor that it attained both a name—"talking *tirailleur*,"—and a dictionary to go with it[39]), he presents a black who, in his naiveté, cannot understand how the French nurse can "attend to" the German enemy whom just yesterday he tried to kill. The Senegalese here serves as the "fool"—allowing the *poilu* to speak what otherwise he may not, and in language he may not—his own rage at the healing of the German soldier, the "boche," at the nurse who will do it and then "attend" to the *tirailleur* as well. Here is the triangulation once more: white soldier,

black primitive *tirailleur*, and French woman. The piece is, of
course, called "Idées noires":

> Madame Red Cross, my dear *colon*
> Has done much good for Sambali
> This Madame's there for blacks, that's good
> But there is something not as it should.
> I saw it not so long ago
> You bastard, you, and its quite vile.
> D'you understand your Mamadou?[40]
> This mam' Red-Cross, is she mad or what?
> For yesterday she was with a *boche*.
> Yes, a filthy *boche*, like on a spit.
> The madame, she was bandaging "it."
> This vermin, yeah, this dirty swine,
> Now that's no way to go, you see,
> You split their throat, you fuck their ass,
> And after that, its too commode
> Madame Red Cross, just mends 'em right.
> So then, ole pal, when the doc came round
> I said my piece, let's cut the crap!
> If Mam' Red-Cross, she heals 'em hear?
> Me, Mamadou, I'm out of here.

In a hospital bed, Mohammed Ben Miloud is cheered up by his
wounded French companion, who shows him an illustrated cata-
logue from the big Parisian department store Galeries Lafayette:
"Look at the beautiful women, Mohammed," he tempts him. And
Mohammed, who does know how to read, but only painfully, deci-
phers the text: "Corsage de . . . mi . . . con . . . fec . . . ti . . . o . . . nné.
Prix: tren . . . te cinq francs," forming out loud the syllables which
indicate the price of the clothing. "My God, thirty-five francs," he
exclaims, "that's astonishing! My friend, so cheap, the women of
France . . . I swear I'll marry here old pal. With my soldier's compensation, I'm in the money!"[41]

While the Senegalese is presented as barely literate, and not very
smart at that, the real message is in the French soldiers' displaced
voice, saying, "so cheap, the women of France. . . ." This sentiment
is astonishingly reiterated by a high-ranking functionary in the
Colonial Ministry who, in 1917, expressed his great concern that
the native soldiers not take home with them "too bad an opinion of
the women of France."[42]

At the end of 1915, the French Undersecretary of State for affairs
of health in the military, Justin Godart, cautioned nurses to guard

against excessive "attentions" or "largesses" accorded the *tirailleurs* and "dangerous" correspondence carried on with them. "Regrettable endearments" and the exchange of photographs, which then passed from hand to hand among the *tirailleurs*, causing "joy and derision," were seen as especially pernicious. When, by March of 1916, these warnings proved insufficient, the medical services of the military recommended hospitalizing the Senegalese in segregated hospitals to which access would be strictly limited to authorized personnel and in which the *tirailleurs* would be serviced totally by male nurses and orderlies.[43]

In the spring of 1919, as the first Senegalese regimental units numbering some ten thousand troops moved in to occupy the Rhineland,[44] the following tale appeared in the trench journal *Bellica*:

> "It's you the nigger . . ." [continued]

> One of our most charming little towns in the Midi, situated between Montpellier and Narbonne, had the good fortune to bivouac a regiment of Senegalese during several months of the winter of 1915. One of them, Don Juan of Dakar, knew how to satisfy the wife of a local dignitary who was spared the draft for reasons among which senility played a role. At first all went well . . . but after several months, the conquest of our "Boudou badabou" understood that Senegal had assumed such a place of importance within her that she was about to provide France with a defender whom she felt was not white. What should she do? She set out to find the local druggist and confided in him the story of her affair, imploring him to at least whiten her shame, if it was impossible to make it disappear completely.

> And do you know what the druggist advised her?

> To drink milk; to drink it so outrageously that it would sweat out of her pores.

> This is a true story, whose ending we unfortunately do not know, but its quite possible that the little "hot chocolate" which should have been made with water was made with milk.[45]

What is striking in this clichéd "café au lait" joke, is the intensity of contempt for the woman, the story narrated through the clenched teeth of degradation: the symbolic blond beast having invited the gorilla embrace of a nigger.

One of the less-discussed reasons for the French transfer of "force noire" troops into the Rhineland, was to decrease their presence in France.[46] The accepted view on the presence of black troops in France at the end of the war is that they were considered "popular" in the villages. French villagers, however, responded to the stationing of the

Senegalese in their midst, crying, "we can no longer let our little girls walk the roads among these savages. We ourselves will no longer dare go out alone to thresh or cut wood. Just think of it! if one were to be taken by these gorillas."[47] As the soldiers saw it, village popularity polls were to be read as female popularity polls, for who else had passed the war in the villages but women, children, old men, and draft dodgers? After the armistice, there were sufficient male voices raised in favor of sending the "force noire," if not back to its own villages, then "pas chez nous"—and choosing what was an anathema to the Germans—sending the "force noire" *chez eux*—which was killing two birds with one stone.[48] The war may have been over, but the psychological war was surely not—not against Germany, and not against women. As Colonel Auroux, a representative of the French Ministry of War described it, "The Moroccans on the Rhine were doing marvelously; the Germans are very much afraid of them."[49] It was in fact the French use of Moroccan troops as their advance guard in occupying Frankfurt in April of 1920 that set the stage for a German-instigated international "cause célèbre." Describing the black troops (all North Africans were seen as "blacks") as both subhuman and superhuman, the Germans launched an intense propaganda campaign against the stationing of the "force noire" on their soil.

In 1920, German sculptor Karl Goetz created "The Black Shame" medallion, in which a fully erect black penis, its bulging testicles clearly sculpted, assumes center stage. (Figure 26) Its helmeted glans creates an instantaneous personification of "soldier." Bound to "him" is naked Germany—the object of conquest, as always, positioned as female, claimed and about to be possessed.[50] The impact is enormous: penis and captive woman foregrounded at the center of the visual

Figure 26: Die Schwarze Schande. The Black Shame—German medallion designed by Karl Goetz, 1920. Collection: *Bibliothèque de Documentation Internationale Contemporaine et Musée d'Histoire Contemporaine—BDIC*, Paris. Archipel Copyright Spadem.

field so that there is no escape from looking. The soft curves of the woman's body, the sensuality of her firm belly, thighs and breasts, the sexuality of her erect nipples and her flowing hair, the slight sway of the erect phallus—for a moment all speak more of an act of desire than an act of rage. That this commemorative object, with its sensuous relief, not only solicits touch but will in fact be handled, makes it even more perverse. Here are the basic ingredients of the proto-colonialist fantasy/nightmare: the crude, misogynist coupling of the black savage and the white female—miscegenation.

France's allies were no less opposed than the Germans to the use of black troops as an occupying force. If E. D. Morel, a well-known British radical who had for many years fought the exploitation of African natives (especially by Belgium), could rant on about those who "thrust barbarians—barbarians belonging to a race inspired by Nature . . . with tremendous sexual instincts—into the heart of Europe," and British General Allen could be publicly dubious about the wisdom of using troops of a "lower civilization" for duty in Europe, there is little reason to be so surprised at the Goetz medallion.[51] Raising the subject of destroying the race by the contamination of blood and bastardization was, however, not the prerogative of Germany alone. On November 4, 1914, barely three months into the war, the first French trench journal to appear, *L'Echo d'Argonne*, published "La Nymphe de l'Argonne: Ode au Petit Colonial." "To you," my unit "le Petit Colonial," the anonymous author addresses his love poem, personifying his collective comrades in the nymph of the title. This female lover of the title, however, only momentarily displaces the actual male lover of the text, for "he" and "she" are actually "he" and "he": two combatant comrades who have killed and kissed ("before my lip gives you the kisses I promised") and pleasured each other in the war-"bed of Atilla." Here is misogyny, homoerotic sex, and aggression, the typical war-cocktail that the soldier-author continues to stir up: "you've never shown the *boche* your ass . . . so now let's go pay him a real visit . . . to drink his wine . . . to fuck his daughters." But who exactly will bed with his daughters but "a Senegalese" or his British counterparts—"a Sikh or . . . a Gurkha," planting their seeds for a bastard of mixed blood, who will be born to the "Gretchens" (German maidens), thus contaminating the German race "who for a month have been swarming over the Argonne."

Looking at the medallion once more, one cannot help but see another "face": the sexual intertwined with the excremental, as the penis assumes the shape of a turd, the medallionist working to elicit a level of arousal and disgust designed to offend all social decency.[52] Here is the clear staging of conquest—the sculpted memory of the most ancient of political performances, where in the presence of the favored deities (the medallion's all-seeing eye of Gnostic iconography), allies and hostile rulers witnessed ritual pageants of song, dance, orgy, and human sacrifice. The significance of these performances went beyond the conventional politics of terror to the basis of mimesis in sympathetic magic: the belief that in some way or another one can protect oneself from evil spirits or damn them by portraying them, by performing them. In these political pageants, such as the Aztec "flower wars," the performance-text linked aestheticism to imperial expansion and militarism, as power, sexuality, fecundity, and beauty joined terror in a staged tournament whose goal was not to kill the enemy, but to take captives for sacrifice. Here the warrior became an artist-of-empire as ritual rape was performed on captives of the greatest and most violent empire ever seen in the New World.[53] In the Aztec rituals however, these captives were male, and a strong part of the *frisson* of the ritual was homoerotic. When one looks once more at the Goetz medallion, it is hard to deny an adoration alongside the dread of the black phallus.

A French postcard illustration of 1915 shows *tirailleurs* overrunning a German-occupied trench. The caption reads, "Here come the Turcos [originally North African troops, but used as a generic name for all colored troops], cover your asses!!!" (Figure 27) The well-rumored threat of sodomization by the black forces was so successful that in one French account of Germans attacked by Senegalese forces, the Germans "raised their hands, they were terrorized. Their corpsmen waved the Red Cross flags, yelling 'protektion sanitat.' The prisoners . . . are so scared that they even tried to climb over the top [of the trenches] while keeping their hands raised at all times."[54]

There is a complex strategy at work here. On the one hand, the feminization of the enemy by representing them as the recipients of an act of sodomy; and in the French war-front illustrations, the Germans—Kaiser and officers as well as the common soldier—are sodomized again and again by anything from bullets to trumpets. But never is the sodomizer a white French soldier. The only soldier to be drawn or described as sodomizing the enemy is the *tirailleur sénégalais*. This, though it still leaves him in the male position (penetrating rather than being penetrated), raises again the issue of the "unnatural" sexual practices of the black "other," with its implication of homosexuality, a marker for a power imbalance between col-

Figure 27: "Voilà les Turcos: Gare aux fesses!!!" "Here come the Turcos. Cover your Asses!!!" French post card. Collection: *Bibliothèque de Documentation Internationale Contemporaine et Musée d'Histoire contemporaine—BDIC,* Paris. Archipel Copyright Spadem.

onizer and colonized.[55] The effeminization here, then, of both "others," Germans and *tirailleurs,* is also a way of asserting the masculinity of the "conqueror" in a world of men in which, while women have been marginally erased, "femaleness" has been transformed into a masquerade forced on both the enemy and the colonized male. In the drawing, as "fireworks" break in the sky between French village and dense, menacing "Schwartzwald," the *tirailleurs* carnivalesquely dance their way toward the German trench, incompetently holding their bayoneted rifles in any way but the appropriate one. Conforming to no military discipline or training, one *tirailleur* breaks ranks to race not only toward the German soldier whose head barely remains in the illustration's lower frame, but toward us as well.

The performing of war in war, the performing of capture, rape and sodomy, the performing of ritual war dances at the front, the excesses and reversals in these representations and performances, the paradoxical doubleness of the sexual and the scatological, colonized performing before colonizers, defeated before the victors, all designate a fertile and neglected terrain for the study of men at war. There will, I think, emerge a startling resemblance between the conditions eliciting the scene "performed" on the Goetz medallion, and certain aspects of *tirailleur sénégalais* performance at the front, both Germans and *tirailleurs* performing in the presence of their oppressors. The abuse directed at the oppressor, however, creates a complex dynamic. If the "filth" in the Goetz medallion is directed at the French by the Germans, it still must be swallowed by the Germans. If the "filth" in *tirailleur* performance is directed at the French by the *tirailleurs*, it is still swallowed by the *tirailleurs*. As Stephen Greenblatt writes:

> The gesture of insult is at the same time an acknowledgment of defeat, for the satiric humor of the oppressed, no matter how telling it may be, always assumes the condition of oppression, perhaps even reinforces that condition, both by releasing aggression non-violently through laughter and by confirming in the minds of the conquerors the impotence of the conquered.[56]

Yet this duality may not be the most important point, for such ritual is conceived as powerful medicine. The seemingly paradoxical dialectic of aggression and submission somehow blend in the pestle of sympathetic magic, and powerful "native medicine" will continue, at the front lines of the white man's war, its fight to ward off not only the attacking enemy, but also the most deadly encounters with white civilization.

SPECTACLES OF RESISTANCE

The *tirailleur* camp at Corneau in the Midi contained thousands of men recruited from throughout France's African colonies. There were, for example, Fulas, Mandinkas, Jurankos, Yalemkas, and Bambaras. This cultural diversity was exhibited in a variety of activities ranging from music, dance, and athletic contests to folk tales and divinations. What these soldiers wanted of rites and ceremonies was what your basic village wants: that in its tales, its chants, and its spectacles, its existence be shown to be credible, continuous, and true to life. What life, then, we may ask, was it true to?

Long before the coming of the "white man," the black races of French West Africa, among them the Peuhls, Bambaras, Fulas, Wolofs, Serères, Malinkés, and the Tukulors, lived their lives with bards, "jeli" or (in French) "griots," oral chroniclers who left no written records for succeeding generations. As the renowned Malian scholar Amadou Hampâ té Bâ said, "with the death of each old man, a library is burnt."[57] Mute in written lore, only one black who served in World War I, Bakare Diallo, has left the historian any written material from which to work.[58] It is a history, therefore, seen almost uniquely through French eyes, the vision and the version of the colonizers, despite the fact that over 300,000 black men and many more of their parents, wives, lovers, and children were affected by the French recruiting agent.

How little one needs to set it all in motion, recruiting "à l'aimable": a "headcount" agreement with village chiefs so as not to intrude upon custom. The chiefs brought the men; the French washed their hands of it. Next to a small, metal folding table precariously balanced on the ground, a folding chair, one pith-helmeted, white-suited officer, and rows of barefoot, brown men lined up for the privilege of being killed.

Les Idées noires of November of 1916 features the first installment of a tale about one "Tourmané, tirailleur," who lived in his village where "it sufficed him to care for his flock of sheep, enjoying the long siestas and exciting tam tam drums." If his ancestors had once been bellicose, he recalled none of that:

> His soul was simple, his thoughts few, his ambitions modest, his dreams immense and vague. But one day, without having even known that the war had broken out in the country of the "whites", Tourmané became a *tirailleur* . . .

Here is that displaced modern pastoral, so often informing ethnographic writing and photography, endowing the *tirailleur*/subject with certain idealized characteristics within a pristine, relatively unchanging "scene." Staging a "native" in shepherd's clothing, the *colon*-soldier-author/photographer, speaking through the textualized person of the narrator (or the camera's lens), "can enjoy relations suffused with a tender courtesy that appear to transcend inequality and domination."[59]

Recent research, emphasizing the oral testimony of *indigène* veterans, has made it difficult to see the scaffolding of the French recruiting system as functioning from anything other than a base of something akin to slavery to something not far from forced conscription and labor—with treatment hardly better than that customarily dealt "retarded" races. It was the Moroccan crisis of 1906 that indicated to the French the viability of using Senegalese troops to pacify their Northern Africa territories, driving home the fact that France's population was significantly less than Germany's and that in a conflict she would be severely outnumbered. To maintain order in Morocco, two black battalions were sent from St. Louis, the French-Senegalese stronghold at the mouth of the Senegal River. These troops clearly demonstrated how well blacks might replace French forces, enabling the latter to defend France's own frontiers.

The implications from this early mobilization for World War I were clear and immediate.

> ... he never again saw his village, traveled down the river, became one of those tiny dots in the long line, column or convoy which wended its way through the bush. He was transported by boat, by train, knew many cities, passed through many villages, before arriving at the camp where he had to put on his uniform.
>
> For many weeks, he lived a dream. He wore the uncomfortable clothes, handled delicately an enormous quantity of strange objects for unclear purposes, learned many words which made no sense to him, contorted himself into innumerable positions whose purpose and usefulness evaded him, suffered long explanations which he couldn't succeed in translating into clear thoughts, constantly received orders and obeyed them endlessly. It was a complete world—the military world—unsuspected, which discovered itself to him, and which he accepted blindly, a bit bewildered, a bit dazed. Since resignation was his way, Tourmané accepted his new lot in life. He was given a rifle and, the first time, he went mad with joy, like a child . . . then he got a hold of himself, took up his chattering once more, his smiles and his dances . . .

The *tirailleurs* conscripted into the French army were, to use Céline's phrase, "virgins in horror."[60] Thousands fled to avoid conscription and among the Bambara, the Scriba, and the Mossi, the headcount was so severe that by 1917 there were protracted, though isolated, revolts against French authority.

For these soldiers, war still came out of the living's obligation toward the ghosts of the slain in a community, a community that was their world, which nurtured them. You don't go out to die for what is not your world, for what does not nurture you. Nature, culture, and the supernatural urged fidelity to one's ancestors, and a strong ritual/performance tradition, integrating movement (gesture/dance), oral narrative (recitative/chant), drumming, and music, served as a continual reminder of the prowess of these ancestors in battle. In the collective memory of the *tirailleur* there was imparted wisdom about war:

> War may give to some, my father
> Although it be not theirs
> War may take from some
> Although it be their own.
> If there be no war,
> Men of power would not be known.[61]

There were tales of tribal military valor and theatricality in combat, instances of magnificent madness, fought against those same French (and recorded by them) who would now ferry them in the awful rowing toward the white man's war—instances such as a native horseman daring, against all odds, to plant his banner some twenty paces from the French: "[he] dismounted and continued to fire until he was killed, facing us alone . . . there were a few horsemen of insane gallantry who paraded under our bullets, slowly turning their long rifles."[62]

There was the insult hurled at Gourang, King of Baguirimi, when he moved to support the French, "Gourang, you are a woman,"[63] and the account of the Sudanese "marabout" facing an assault of French infantry, shouting (in the tradition of verbal insult as part of attack) until he was silenced: "Fali toubabo! Fali toubabo!" (White pigs, you are all white pigs).[64] These moments of bravery were linked to no concept of nation, no definition of empire or state so clear to Europeans by the early 1900s. The Sahel of the Western Sudan, or the North African models, admitted a flexible organization based more on people than on land—a migratory "state" with its scribes, soldiers, courtiers—an "army" faithful to its leader (chief, sheik), an infinity of communities, some nomadic, a diversity and fluidity of political, ethnic, and religious combinations that would prove favorable, as the conquering, feminizing, and colonizing image has it, to French "penetration."

The almost unique resistance of the indigène soldier was a prise-de-parole, a self-description through the transplanting of his ritual, oral, and performative tradition to the front, though we cannot know exactly which or how many griots were present to perform the praise songs, to recount the genealogies; just what dancing, drumming, and chanting it was that invoked the strength of the community, functioning as a cleansing, binding, recreative force. In his paternalistically titled book of 1922, Nos Sénégalais pendant la Grande Guerre, Maurice Dutreb "records" a war chant of the Peuhls, one of the communities among the Senegalese. The chant relates to an incursion by Boukari, Mossi emperor of Ovaagadougou in the Djilgodi, in about 1890, during which the Peuhl pushed back Boukari's forces near the pond of Djibo.

At Djibo there is a pond.
Those with good intentions can quench their thirst and bathe there.
Those with evil intentions will sate their thirst for blood there.
It was surrounded with stallions.

God keeps watch from night to morn, and the spears keep watch from
morn to night.
Its banks will be covered with bowels, they will no longer be covered
with the loincloths of women.
Around the pond, hedges of thorny mimosa were set out.
Treacherous spears are in the pond, there are arms in the pond
On them one will plant the heads of the dead, one will no longer plant
the water-lilies.
Boukari Koutou has surrounded us
He has surrounded us with thousands of stallions, he has arranged in
a circle, dugouts filled with rifles.
Let every man who has come here with anger, go!
Let him leave the birds of the pond in the pond!
Kyendé-Kyendé, great son of Mossi!
It is not Kyendé-Kyendé we want, it is Millamilla who pleases us.[65]

This war chant, performed and transcribed at the Western Front, is a
valuable, if problematic, text. Following the Western privileging of
the written text, the chant has been entirely removed from its performance context and from the authority of its *griot* or communal
"reciter[s]" within the site of performance. Not only does it appear
in Dutreb's French translation, but this transcription also becomes a
"best," "correct," or "primary" version, printed and invested in its
singularity, denying multiplicity and the ability of story and teller,
through improvisation, to absorb, reflect, criticize, and transform
contemporary life at the front in relation to the sustaining myths
and values in the primary tale. Still, what we have here is one of the
precious few "recordings" of the *tirailleur* voice at the front. Sustaining communal memory with pride and defiance, the *indigène*
soldier was, through his spectacles, "performing back," *in medias
res* of war, the tribulations of uprooting and displacement, of loneliness and alienation, seeking out the strength of the evocative passage of the race, its constant thread and continuity. There is a kind
of knowledge here that can be represented—made present—only
through action, enactment, or performance.

In the complex and problemed comradeship-in-arms of the French
colonizer-soldier and the *tirailleur sénégalais*, the French arranged
their absence from *tirailleur* storytelling and chant, stifling the doc-
umenting of any *tirailleur* response to their military/colonial presence. An old colonial pattern is at work here, the "colonized" or
"appropriated" object being Bambara, or Wolof, or Bardes, or Peuhl
culture. And so the war chant of Samba, son of Galadieghi, was

recorded, stripped of any relation to contemporary events if such existed in the war-front performance, leaving it, and its *tirailleur séné-galais* performers conveniently "timeless" and "traditional."

Notes

1. All translations from the French are my own.

The problematic choice of epithet for the black soldier is made evident in a handbook published in 1923 for the use of metropolitan NCOs and officers sent to work with Senegalese recruits garrisoned in Europe. It spelled out that the cadre "will forbid that they [the *tirailleurs*] be called 'nègres'," a name that the blacks heard as "sale nègre" ("dirty nigger"). A footnote explained that the black soldiers did not object to being called "noirs."

2. The term is Michel de Certeau's.

3. I borrow Roland Barthes's description of Albert Camus's style in Barthes' *Le Degré zéro de l'écriture* (1953; Paris, 1964), 10.

4. Until World War I, the *tirailleurs sénégalais* were essentially a mercenary army unit, its soldiers both the object of scorn ("captives of the whites") and envy among tribal blacks. Royal slaves, prisoners-of-war, and soldiers purchased by "rachat," the re-purchase system in which indentured slaves were "sold" to the army by their masters who received the "rachat" (later called the"enlistment bonus fee," to color slightly its moral reprehensibility), made up the largest part of the force which, by 1910, numbered about thirteen thousand men. Those who did volunteer were attracted by the incentives of food, regular pay, adventure, prestige, and the promise of booty, especially slaves and women. Still, by 1912, the colonies were having difficulty supplying even five thousand volunteers a year. On February 7, 1912, therefore, the French government initiated its first colonial system of partial conscription, incited by Charles Mangin's description of black Africa as "an almost inexhaustible reservoir of men," whom he saw as, by nature and history, ideally suited for military service (Charles Mangin, *La force noire* [Paris, 1910]). This black force, which numbered thirty thousand as World War I began, was quickly deployed: some of its soldiers to conquer German Togoland, some for the occupation of Madagascar, Algeria, and Morocco, some sent immediately to the Belgian front. In the face of the continuing massive French losses on the Western Front, black recruitment was raised to the level of mass levees. By 1917, the Clemenceau government, weighing the risk of economic ruination of the colonies (the short supply of labor in a still traditionally subsistence-based economy had already caused desperate food shortages accompanied by massive demoralization) or even armed revolt (in Upper Senegal and Niger, and Dahomey) in protest of its now extensive and brutal recruiting policies, still opted for recruiting. As thousands of men fled the recruiters, to British West Africa, the French ordered the largest levy of the war—fifty thousand men—eventually drafting 63,000 by early 1918. By the summer of 1918 that number had catapulted to 190,000, 134,000 of whom were transported to the Western and Bulgarian

fronts and the Dardanelles. Though the "tirailleurs sénégalais" were a major component of the French Colonial Army, other largely segregated units included the Malagasy (Madagascar) Tirailleurs, the Algerian Tirailleurs, and the Moroccan Tirailleurs. The Senegalese themselves were not one "race" and did not speak one language, numbering among them Wolofs, Bambaras, and Tokolors, to name but a few. The most thorough study of the black forces in World War I is Marc Michel's *L'Appel à l'Afrique: Contributions et réactions à l'effort de guerre en A.O.F., 1914–1949* (Paris, 1982), and his "Les Troupes Noires, La Grande Guerre et l'Armée Française." in Janos Riesz and Joachim Schultz, eds., *"Tirailleurs sénégalais": zur Bildlichen und Literarischen Darstellung Afrikanischer Soldaten im dienste Frankreichs [Présentations littéraires et figuratives de soldats africains au service de la France]* (Frankfurt am Main/Paris, 1989), 11–20, from which sources I take my figures. See also Myron Echenberg, *Colonial Conscripts: The tirailleurs sénégalais in French West Africa, 1857–1960* (Portsmouth, NH, 1991).

5. Peter Hulme, *Colonial Encounters: Europe and the Native Caribbean 1492–1797* (London and New York, 1992), 159.

6. Roger Tanniers, *Les Algériens aux tranchées*, a revue in one act and three tableaux written by Sergeant Roger Tanniers of the 1st Zouave Regiment and performed for the first time at Médéa, at the Theater of the Zouaves, on July 14, 1917 (text published in Algiers, May 1917).

7. My article on soldier cross-dressing at the front is forthcoming in *The Drama Review*.

8. Epsilonn. "Féminisme," *Le Camouflet*, no. 6, Sept. 1, 1916.

9. Eric J. Leed, "Violence, Death and Masculinity," *Vietnam Generation* 1, nos. 3–4 (Summer–Fall 1989): 175–76.

10. Grémillet, *À la marrocaine. Revue d'actualitée de la D.M.* in one act and twenty tableaux. Artistic troupe of the 8th Zouaves, Jan. 1917.

11. Proverbial saying quoted in Johannes Fabian, *Power and Performance: Ethnographic Explorations through Proverbial Wisdom and Theater in Shaba, Zaire* (Madison, 1990), 277.

12. This resounding silence of the French soldier facing his wife is the subject for an essay in itself.

13. The "marraine," or female penpal, played a much more important role for the front-line soldier than the term "penpal" suggests. Correspondent, sender of packages, source of contact with the home front, woman to visit on one's home leave, and in well-documented narratives and illustrations, potential lover, the "marraine" was a state-encouraged "institution" and a soldier-supported fantasy.

14. Village chiefs offered a certain number of their younger or unmarried females to French officers, thereby ensuring their own preferential treatment. These "marriages" between metropolitans and West African women were temporary unions, consummated without ceremony, and sanctioned in a French manual of 1902 addressed to colonial military and administrators departing for the African colonies by the following explanation: "The European who has no native wife is not well regarded by the soldiers, ser-

vants and married natives placed under his orders, who are always afraid that he will abuse the power given by his position." Dr. Baret, *Guide pratique de l'Européen dans l'Afrique Occidentale* (Paris, 1902), 206–9, quoted in John C. Balesi, *From Adversaries to Comrades in Arms: West Africans and the French Military, 1885–1918* (Waltham, MA, 1979), 47. General Faidherbe's own illegitimate son, fathered with a Khassonké concubine, eventually became an *indigène* officer in the French army.

15. Marc Michel, in his *L'Appel à l'Afrique*, 382, 392, describes the official corps of "translators/letter writers" provided to the *tirailleurs*. These were instructed to "favorably influence" the soldiers' letters home, which they then effectively censored.

16. Edward Said. "Permission to Narrate," London *Times Book Review*, Feb. 29, 1984.

17. Mangin, *La force noire*, 123.

18. For an in-depth study of the deep structure underlying the projection of the both attractive and threatening cultural fantasies of sexuality and race onto an "other," see Sander L. Gilman, *Difference and Pathology: Stereotypes of Sexuality, Race, and Madness* (Ithaca, 1985).

19. See J. B. Friedman, *The Monstrous Races in Medieval Art and Thought* (Cambridge, Mass. 1981); Margaret T. Hodgen, *Early Anthropology in the Sixteenth and Seventeenth Centuries* (Philadelphia, 1964); Peter Hulme's "Columbus and the Cannibals: A Study of the Reports of Anthropophagy in the Journal of Christopher Columbus," *Ibereo-Amerikanisches Archiv*, N.F., 4 (1978): 115–39; R. Wittkower, "Marvels of the East: A Study in the History of Monsters," *Journal of the Warburg and Courtauld Institutes* 5 (1942): 159–97.

20. Respectively: Captain Marceau, *Le Tirailleur Soudanais* (Paris, 1911), 20; Lucie Cousturier, *Des inconnus chez moi* (Paris, 1920), 45.

21. Charles Mangin, "Caractères physiques et moraux du soldat nègre," *La Revue anthropologique*, no. 10 (1911): 10.

22. Though the few researchers who have been interested in looking at these representations have sometimes attempted to present a more balanced or ambivalent portrait of the *tirailleur* from their evidence, Balesi speaks of "positive paternalism" in his *From Adversaries to Comrades in Arms*, 38), there is little they can do to ameliorate what remains an abominable portrayal. Laurent Gervereau, in his "De bien trop noirs dessins" (in Riesz and Schultz, eds., *"Tirailleurs Sénégalais"*, 111–19), is honest enough to write, "In fact French and Germans maintained a very similar attitude towards the colonial troops."

23. [Anon.] *Clemence! Couches-Toi*, revue in three tableaux, Dec. 1915.

24. Sigmund Freud, "The Uncanny," in *The Standard Edition of the Complete Psychological Works of Sigmund Freud*, trans. and ed. James Strachey, in collaboration with Anna Freud, 24 vols. (London, 1953–1974), vol. 17.

25. *Le Ver Luisant*, 3ème Année, no. 17, Organe de la 223 Section d'Autos-Projecteurs de Campagnie, 21ème Génie [1917].

26. *Le Mouchoir*, no. 17, Mar. 5, 1916.

27. Sandra M. Gilbert, "Soldier's Heart: Literary Men, Literary Women, and the Great War," in Sandra M. Gilbert and Susan Gubar, *No Man's Land: The Place of the Woman Writer in the Twentieth Century*, vol. 2, *Sexchanges* (New Haven and London, 1989), 260.

28. Drieu de la Rochelle, *La comédie de Charleroi*.

29. See Peter Altenberg, *Ashantee* (Berlin, 1897). Magnus Hirschfeld, editor of *The Sexual History of the World War* (New York, 1941), recorded "the queer predilection for Ashantis that for a while raged in Vienna" among the Viennese women who would "approach these negroes under different pretexts" for sexual encounters. Hirschfeld also noted, writing of women's attraction to the "other," that even "in peacetime, the fair sex had manifested an inclination for Senegalese, Bedouins, and other colonials" (p. 47).

30. Louis Gustave Binger, *Une vie d'explorateur: Souvenirs extraits des Carnets de Route ou notes sous la dictée par son fils Jacques Binger* (Paris, 1938), 57.

31. Marie-Étienne Péroz, *Au Niger, récits de campagne, 1891–1892* (Paris, 1899), 350–51. Péroz writes as well: "The raid of spahis in Bafoulabé brought pandemonium. . . . This morning quite a few awoke in the cabins of women who obviously were not their wives. . . . One of the spahis Sergeant Soumare, thrashed, they say, a half-dozen disturbed husbands and proved to their better halves that his valor was complete in all types of action" (p. 355).

32. Bronislaw Malinowski, *The Sexual Life of Savages: An Ethnographic Account of Courtship, Marriage and Family Life among the Natives of the Trobriand Islands, British New Guinea* (1929; New York, 1987), 14, 281, passim.

33. Jean-Paul Sartre, Preface to Frantz Fanon, *The Wretched of the Earth*, trans. Constance Farrington (1961; New York, 1968), 26.

34. Hirschfeld, ed., *The Sexual History of the World War*, 53.

35. Louis-Ferdinand Céline, *Journey to the End of the Night*, trans. Ralph Manheim (1934; New York, 1983), 71.

36. See Nicolas Bancel, Pascal Blanchard and Laurent Gervereau, *Images et colonies: Iconographie et propagande coloniale sur l'Afrique française de 1880 à 1962* (Paris, 1993); Gervereau, "De Bien Trop Noirs Dessins"; Hugh Honour, *L'image du Noir dans l'art occidental de la Révolution Américaine à la première guerre mondiale* (Paris, 1989); Marie-France Latour, *Blackness and the Articulation of Racial Difference in French Advertisements for Hygienic Products, 1890–1930* (Cambridge, MA, 1992); Jan P. Nederveen-Pieterse, *White on Black: Images of Africa and Blacks in Western Popular Culture* (New Haven, 1992); and Sander L. Gilman, *Difference and Pathology*.

37. Céline, *Journey to the End of the Night*, 73.

38. Klaus Theweleit, *Male Fantasies*, vol. 1, *Women, Floods, Bodies, History*, trans. Stephen Conway (Minneapolis, 1987), 79–90, passim.

39. *Le français tel que le parlent nos tirailleurs sénégalais* (Paris, 1916).

40. "Mamadou" (the slight linguistic shifting of "Muhammad") became one of the generic names used by French soldiers for the *tirailleur*.

41. From the soldier newspaper, *La Greffe Générale*, Organe des Blessés de la Face, Val de Grace, Feb. 1, 1918.

42. Charles Regismanset, "La Croisade Coloniale," in *Questions Coloniales* (Paris, 1917), 57, quoted in Michel, *L'Appel à l'Afrique*, 390.

43. See ibid., 389.

44. The Malagasy troops were the first to arrive in April 1919, followed by the Senegalese in May. By the spring of 1920, 42,000 "force noire" troops were stationed in the Rhineland, and in the spring of 1921, 45,000. Most of these were Algerians, Moroccans, and Tunisians, but as the Germans liked to point out, many of the North Africans were so "black" as to be indistinguishable from the "niggers." Gilbert Hitchcock, Democratic Senator from Nebraska, could only agree, arguing that "there is no need to make a distinction [between the Senegalese and the Algerian and the Moroccan]. They are men of an inferior, half-civilized race. They are brutes when stationed among white people, as the evidence shows." Quoted in Keith L. Nelson, "The 'Black Horror on the Rhine': Race as a Factor in Post-World War I Diplomacy," *Journal of Modern History* 42, no. 4 (Dec. 1970): 623.

45. From the trench newspaper, *Bellica*, no. 5 (Apr.–May 1919).

46. For the policy, opinions, and reactions surrounding the posting of "force noire" troops to Germany, see the following: Nelson, "The 'Black Horror on the Rhine'"; Hans-Jürgen Lüsebrink, "'Tirailleurs Sénégalais' und 'Schwarze Schande': Verlaufsformen und Konsequenzen einer deutsch-französischen Auseinandersetzung, 1910–1926," in Riesz and Schultz, eds., *"Tirailleurs Sénégalais"*, 57–71; Robert C. Reinders, "Radicalism on the Left: E. D. Morel and the 'Black Horror on the Rhine,'" *International Review of Social History* 13 (1968): 1–28.

47. Quoted in Cousturier, *Des inconnus chez moi*, 12–13.

48. The American responses are no less startling: "Do you not think that in having black troops in your army of occupation . . . you run some danger . . . ? One or two cases of rape, committed by your blacks on the German women, well advertised in the southern states of America, where there are very definite views with regard to the Blackmen, would likely greatly reduce the esteem in which the French are held" (Major Paul H. Clark to General Pershing, June 5, 1919); and "thoughtful persons in America and throughout the world are horrified by the victimization of German women and girls by half-savage African troops" (Dudley Field Malone to Woodrow Wilson, Oct. 18, 1920). Over two years later, a correspondent of Senator William E. Borah remembered that "I was in the midst of the presidential campaign in Connecticut, when the word went along that Mr. Harding should be voted for because he would do his best to get those niggers out of Germany." All quotes are from Nelson, "The 'Black Horror on the Rhine,'" 610, 618.

49. Colonel Auroux, May 22, 1920. Minutes of the Interministerial Conference. Mangin papers, quoted in ibid., 613.

50. It is difficult to avoid seeing a striking resemblance between the German medallion and the Roman, "IVDAEA CAPTA" commemorating the conquest of Judea: the cowed Jewish colony, represented as a woman, at the base of the phallic tree. The erect Roman soldier, his left foot on a helmet,

one hand encircling his staff, the other clasping a short sword, has mastered the prone, nude woman. One might speculate that the famous Roman medallion was not unknown to Goetz.

51. Morel in a letter to *The Nation*, Mar. 27, 1920; Allen quoted in Nelson, "The 'Black Horror on the Rhine,'" 623.

52. Through Goetz's pushing what Norbert Elias has called "the threshold of shame and embarrassment" (*The Civilizing Process*, trans. Edmond Jephcott [1939; New York, 1978] past the periphery, the medallion exhibits one crucial part of what Mikhail Bakhtin, in *Rabelais and His World* (Cambridge, MA, 1968), designates as the "grotesque body"—the penis, exceeding its limits, abusive, unbounded. Goetz's sculpted penis may be seen as well like Rabelais's "fine faecal matter to swell up inside her!"—a form best understood within the context of festive ritual and performance. See François Rabelais, *The Histories of Gargantua and Pantagruel*, trans. J. M. Cohen (Baltimore: Penguin), bk. 1, chaps. 4–6, pp. 47–53.

53. See David Damrosch, "The Aesthetics of Conquest: Aztec Poetry Before and After Cortès," in Stephen Greenblatt, ed., *New World Encounters* (Berkeley, 1993), 139–58.

54. F. Ingold, *Les Troupes noires au combat* (Paris, 1940), 70, cited in Balesi, *From Adversaries to Comrades in Arms*, 110.

55. That the existence of "homosexuality" as a social category within Western discourse has made it virtually impossible for post-colonial African writers to write about male/male sexual intimacy in their societies without constantly crashing against this "foreign" term, is but a small indication of just one of the myriad of problems in "reading" the homoerotic scene "then" at the Western Front. See Chris Dunton, "Wheything Be Dat? The Treatment of Homosexuality in African Literature," *Research in African Literatures* 20, no. 3 (1989): 422–48.

56. Greenblatt, "Filthy Rites," in idem., ed., *New World Encounters*, 65.

57. Quoted in Lilyan Kesteloot, "The West African Epics," *Présence Africaine* 30:58 (1966): 202.

58. Diallo, an illiterate Fulani shepherd from Senegal who enlisted in the colonial army in 1912, fought and was seriously wounded on Nov. 3, 1914 at Sillery (Marne). Remaining in France, he received French citizenship at the war's conclusion. Diallo, educated by and in the army, published his war memoir *Force bonté* ([Paris, 1926] Nendeln: Kraus Reprints, 1973) to little interest in its time, except from the cadres of the French colonial powers whose prejudices on blacks, and their position within the Empire, it confirmed. Today, the book is considered, within the growing body of work on African literature, with no small measure of embarrassment as, at best, a naive panegyric; at worst, the act of collaboration of a flatterer, or it is not considered at all.

59. I am indebted to Renato Rosaldo's stimulating essay, "From the Door of His Tent: The Fieldworker and the Inquisitor," in James Clifford and George E. Marcus, eds., *Writing Culture: The Poetics and Politics of Ethnography* (Berkeley, 1986), 77–97, for my own reading of this *colon*/soldier "tale." Quote from p. 97.

60. Céline, *Journey to the End of the Night*, 9.

61. *The Epic of Son-Jara: A West African Tradition*, text by Fa-Digi Sisòkò, notes, translation and new introduction by John William Johnson (Bloomington, 1992), lines 1091–96. This famous epic, which celebrates the exploits of the legendary founder of the empire of Old Mali some 750 years ago, is still widely recited by *griots* among the Mandekan-speaking peoples of West Africa. This text was collected on Mar. 9, 1968 in the city of Kita in Western Mali, in a performance lasting roughly four hours.

62. Recorded in Charles Mangin, *Lettres du Soudan* (Paris, 1930), 71, 82.

63. Part of songs collected by the sons of Rabah, interviewed by Dr. J. Décose, *Du Congo au Tchad: La Brousse telle qu'elle est, Les gens tels qu'ils sont* (Paris, 1906), recorded in Pierre Gentil *La conquête du Tchad*, 3 vols. (Paris, 1971), 1:101.

64. Recorded by Edouard Thiriet, a lieutenant in the "spahis soudanais" in his *Au Soudan français: Souvenirs: 1892–1894* (Paris, 1932), 155.

65. Maurice Dutreb, *Nos Sénégalais pendant la Grande Guerre* (Metz, 1922), 86.

"Objects to Possess or Discard"

The Representation of Jews and Women by British Women Novelists of the 1920s*

Phyllis Lassner

Although British literature in the interwar period is rife with stereo-typical images of Jews, there was scant analysis of these images until after World War II. In the last twenty years, interest in marginalized "others" has coincided with the growth in scholarly studies of Jewish representation. Coupled with the compelling challenges of studying the Holocaust, it has become impossible to ignore representations of the Jew as a racialized literary subject. Recent studies have stressed connections between literary-historical contexts and prevailing cultural and political ideologies. This approach has shown that British literary images of the Jew are not equivalent to mythic, transhistorical anti-Semitic icons, but highly ambivalent, histori-cally particular projections of complex attitudes towards British na-tional and cultural identity. This research, however, focuses on male writers as representing the range of approaches to Jewish portraiture, and therefore does not address the relationship between a gendered and racialized narrative discourse.[1]

To recover the racialized narratives of women writers raises new questions about the representation of the Jew, of national identity, of the literary history of British women writers, and the implications of gender in the discourse of ethnicity and race. If we link these ques-tions to women's interwar novels, we are in a better position to un-derstand how their gendered representations of cultural and national identities are related to their literary projections of the Jew.

For British women writers, the interwar period is fraught with is-sues of national and cultural identity, especially as they debate the gains and losses that mark the aftermath of the Great War.[2] Women writers of the period depicted a middle-class society desperately seek-ing normalcy as it adjusts to stressful change. The pains of the ad-justment are often found in both female and Jewish characters; the

---

*Quote in title taken from Phyllis Bottome, *Old Wine* (London, 1924), 156.

marginalized position of Jews within larger British society could easily have made them seem appropriate analogues for women. Like Jews, women were placed in a double bind by society by being branded as exceptional. Like the Jews, women were romanticized, indeed sentimentalized, and yet criticized for their differences, and even though there were exceptions, by and large both Jews and women were denied access to complete social and economic equality.

Only instead of an anti-Semitic or racialist discourse, women confronted a discriminating discourse of gender. At a time when Britain's recovery from the Great War was complicated by the revisioning of traditional social relationships and roles, the nation, having lost a generation of its male heirs, found women's reproductive capacity necessary for its regeneration and yet labeled them as "surplus."[3] Women who had performed various work roles during the war found their new freedom subverted by demands for a newly domesticated sexuality.[4] If women assumed the shape of boys in their new bobs and flattened breasts, they were also encouraged to fill the human losses of the grim war years by succumbing once again to romance and marriage plots.

In response to contradictory social demands, several interwar women writers questioned the social and cultural constructions of selfhood and identity by foregrounding the gendered, cultural, and ethnic nature of "Englishness." While the fictional plight of the middle-class Englishmen is often made to resemble that of the Jews, the Jews' fates are constructed very differently. The women's roles and struggles for self-definition are illuminated through their relationship to Jewish characters and/or through the fates of Jewish characters, but the Jew ultimately serves as a contrast, not as an analogue. Unlike English heroines, who, even when they struggle against the social grain, are assimilated into the mainstram of society, Jews in many interwar fictions remain on the periphery or are made to disappear entirely. In novels of the early twenties, *The Happy Foreigner* by Enid Bagnold (1889–1981), *Potterism* by Rose Macaulay (1881–1958), *The Constant Nymph* by Margaret Kennedy (1896–1967), and *Old Wine* by Phyllis Bottome (1882–1963), the fortunes of women and Jews are linked to the larger questions of postwar recovery. These novels dramatize the nation's adjustment to peace as related to fears of continuing loss that were exacerbated by economic turbulence and women's shifting social roles. These fears, in turn, are related to the emerging postwar identity of the nation by centering on a destabilized masculine pride. In each of these novels, masculine pride is threatened by young women who assert a sense of independence, and a Jew who fails to fully integrate with the values and images that constituted middle-class English masculine identity.

The introduction of the Jew challenges binary categories of difference and "the other" by asking: How is it possible to negotiate between the stereotypical images of Jews and the complexities of their social and historical experience? These writers respond to such questions in a tantalizingly similar way. Whether they are central to the plot, marginal, or even absent, their fictional Jews are marked by destabilized gender identities, the effects of which challenge the distinctiveness of English national identity. Portrayed as noble, feminized men and victimized, masculine women, these fictional Jews uncannily prefigure the emergence of what in the next war would emerge as the gendered terms of fascist anti-Semitism. As Jews in these novels are either marginalized or killed off, they represent a marked absence, not only in fictional plots of Britain's post-World War I recovery, but as uncanny signs of their actual vulnerability barely twenty years later. It is in this sense that these fictional Jews are an especially haunting presence for today's readers.

The novels I consider coincide with a post-World War I yearning for both social stability and change. Jewish characters, who are identified with both the stability of a continuous identity and the historic contingency of persecution and assimilation, carry the weight of the postwar period's sense of itself as dislocated and decentered. Indicative of their cultural and historical instability, Jewish characters are made to carry their questionable genders like the baggage representing their status as immigrants, no matter how long they have resided in Britain. The writers I consider confront self-consciously such cultural and gender role displacements by scrutinizing the literary tradition of the romance and marriage plot in relation to the theme of rebuilding the postwar nation. By destabilizing the marriage plot, they test the possibility that gender roles and the social fabric of the nation may be permanently altered, indeed in a state of permanent flux. Instead of destroying the cohesiveness of the nation, however, this plot turn restores faith and mutual accommodation between English men and women when a scapegoat is discovered in the figure of the Jew. As they develop relationships between Jewish men, middle-class women, and those men who represent political and social power, these novels suggest that prevailing social codes of masculinity and femininity may inhibit both recovery and reform. Either a second-generation Englishman or European immigrant, these Jewish figures are sacrificed in the narrative effort of revising traditional definitions of masculinity and femininity. And as these novels strain to accommodate such revisions to the need for recovery, they cannot integrate Jews, for, as aliens, Jews defy myths of the nation's continuity and stability, the combination of which is needed to restore the nation's faith in itself.[5]

Although individual Jewish characters represent their people's brutalized lives in Europe, they are also constructed by narrative strategies to embody the entire history of the Jews. This embodiment signifies a collective identity that ironically questions, and therefore threatens, notions of cohesive nationhood and Britain's national identity. Their status as outsiders, however, also reinscribes these mythic notions. After all, compared to Jewish history, a turbulent England seems normative and cohesive. The end result of these ironies is a kind of narrative ambivalence in which the Jew must be both present and evicted. A persistently unintegrated presence, these fictional Jews are a stark reminder of differences that exacerbated English xenophobia as World War I broke out, and that found expression in the jingoistic propaganda against all foreigners. Whatever their origins, the Jews in these novels—with their desire to remain different even after the war—threaten the notion of a pristine Englishness unsullied by foreign influence. Britain might be able to sustain its image as a political and cultural island in fictional depictions of the postwar period, but the presence of the Jew invariably suggests that its cultural dominance was vulnerable.[6] Whether or not writers such as Margaret Kennedy, Phyllis Bottome, Rose Macaulay, and Enid Bagnold knew of the Aliens Act of 1919, which made it easy to deport foreign-born Jews, their novels enact debates about the nature and goals of English national identity, differences between particularist views of "little England" and a diverse Britain with a role in the future of Europe.

* * *

A minor character in a postwar novel by Enid Bagnold embodies Britain's anxiety about its national identity at the very moment of victory. The problem is that national identity may become diffused as a result of sharing victory with European allies. Bagnold's 1920 novel, *The Happy Foreigner*, traces the war's effects on the identity boundaries of culture and gender through the escapades of a young Englishwoman serving as driver to military personnel assessing the war's dammage in France. As critics have noted, the novel follows a pattern of destruction and regeneration as Fanny's journey through mud-caked fortresses and battlefields coincides with a healing love affair with a French soldier.[7] Although their romance is fleeting, it conveys the sense of laying a ritual cornerstone to a bridge between stalwart Britain and the unstable Continent. If the lovers are separated ultimately by their different cultural allegiances, they have been united by their discovery of underlying harmonies. What cannot be integrated into this reconciliation is the figure of the Jew. Where Bagnold expresses sympathy for the defeated, and now impoverished, former enemy, affection for the uncouth Americans and Italians, she reserves a kind of difference for the Jew that identifies him as unassimilable to her vision of Britain's regeneration. Sweet, kind, and otherwise sympathetic, the "Jew boy, Reherrey," is marginalized by being feminized. Having helped Fanny choose fabric for her party dress, he is then positioned in competition with her by having him appropriate her femininity: "He had wound the black stuff . . . so cleverly round his slim body that he seemed no fatter than a lacquered hairpin."[8]

This depiction does not represent cross-dressing as a liberatory act. The Jew's effeminacy not only undercuts his role as soldier, but also makes him ineligible to compete on the field of Bagnold's heterosexual love plot. Heightening his dismissal is the fact that Reherrey spends more affable time with Fanny than her French lover does. But their compatibility makes quite another point about postwar social relationships and codes. More of a "woman" friend, Reherrey also draws attention to Fanny's own gendered development. With feminist sensitivies, Bagnold removes her heroine from the temptations of English domestication and allows her to find romance while functioning in roles that look nostalgically back to women's liberating war work. However this strategy may validate women's changing social roles, the novel also expresses a nostalgic yearning for a more traditional England. What allows the novel to balance these countermoves and yet point to the dangers of destabilization is the figure of the Jew. Fanny can be granted an indeterminate future so long as her European adventure does not turn into exile, and she is restored to her Englishness. Although she and her French lover must therefore be separated, he can keep his romantic aura and retain the integrity of a European ally so long as the threat of the alien is embodied in another "other"—the Jew. Reherrey's effeminacy makes him an alien twiceover, suggesting a kind of sterile narcissism that denies him both the restorative possibilities of the romance plot and participation in the story of England's regeneration.

Unlike Bagnold, Rose Macaulay took a more jaundiced view of Britain's postwar future.[9] Macaulay was known throughout her career for the caustic wit she deployed in scathing satires of Britain's best intentions, which remain critical documents of postwar debates about social change. Her 1920 novel *Potterism* is dedicated "To the unsentimental precisians in thought, who have, on this confused,

inaccurate, and emotional planet, no fit habitation."[10] The global instability suggested by the dedication also identifies the place of this
novel within the postwar critical discourse on the nation's sense of
its political and social direction, and therefore issues of national
unity and identity. Within the plot, those who embody "the unsentimental precisians in thought" are identified as a group of young
people at Oxford before the Great War who form an alliance opposed
to prejudice, sentiment, and romantic cant. The object of their opposition is represented by the mass media of the time: *The Daily
Haste*, a newspaper owned and operated by Percy Potter (probably
inspired by the real *Daily Express*) and the popular romance novels
of his wife, Leila Yorke. The plot focuses on the twin children of the
Potters, Jane and Johnny, who with their Jewish friend Arthur
Gideon found the Anti-Potterism League. The novel follows the
younger generation through the war years and afterwards, when
their own convictions are tested by the social and political vicissi-
tudes of recovery. Stymied by their misdirected emotional lives, at
the end Jane Potter and Arthur Gideon sacrifice their newly acknowledged love to his search for personal and political identity.

In a novel where the narrator confirms the characters' political
and social cynicism, the Jew, Arthur Gideon, is made even more of
an outsider by his historically grounded, but transformative, outlook. Unlike his sardonic friends or the complacent Potterites,
Gideon looks to the past for meaning, while searching for a way out
of the moral and cultural stasis he finds in his friends' attitudes. The
past that he researches, however, is not one to which the elder Potters subscribe—a mythically stable, imperial prewar Britain—but an
historic epic of political oppression and turbulence. If Percy Potter
can build himself "a lordly mansion" and earn a title by shaping his
dreams to fit the public's, Gideon is the perennial alien who defies
all hope for assimilation and affirmation by reclaiming his Jewish
identity.[11] The grandson of Russian Jews massacred in an Odessa
pogrom, Gideon was meant to be an Englishman by dint of his immigrant father marrying an Englishwoman and assimilating. Until
the age of twenty-one, Arthur's "cynical dislike" of Jews, Russians,
and Britons situates him at the center of English intellectual life, but
when he reverts to his father's Jewish name, he sets himself apart
and his character is destabilized. When war begins, he declares himself neither pacifist nor patriot, insisting on the need to defeat Germany as well as the "mess" of war.[12]

Though Macaulay was generally opposed to war, and had become
a pacifist because of World War I, she questioned her own pacifism
as early as 1920. Her Jewish character's marginal position represents

her ambivalences about ideologies that uphold either pacifism or war. Gideon's approach resonates with her cynical distrust of the hierarchies of power implicated in political ideologies and institutions. In such fashion he refuses to distinguish between the abuse of "his nation" by Christians and by Christianity as an ideology. The latter, he finds, may be "well-meaning but a failure" because its unresolved tension between claims for universal love and true faith leads to persecutions of "others."[13] That Macaulay's views are historically grounded and not universalized is evinced by Gideon's response to the outbreak of the Great War:

> What makes me angriest is the reasons [the Potterites] vamp up why we're fighting. For the sake of democracy, they say. Democracy be hanged. It's a rotten system, anyhow, and how this war is going to do anything for it I don't know how. If I thought it was, I wouldn't join. But there's no fear. And other people say we're fighting "so that our children won't have to." Rot again. Every war makes other wars more likely . . . why can't people say simply that the reason why we're fighting is partly to uphold decent international principles, and mainly to win the war— to be a conquering nation, not a conquered one, and to save ourselves from having an ill-conditioned people like the Germans strutting all over us. It's a very laudable object, and needs no camouflage.[14]

Gideon's critique marks him as outsider not only from the world of the Potters, but from postwar debates about the war's aims and costs. He refutes not only the government war propaganda, but the pacifist view that war for any cause, and by any means, is wrong.[15] But Gideon does not merely position himself along the spectrum of British politics. His internationalism is antagonistic to the rhetoric expounding Britain's sense of itself as both island-nation and expansionist or as a liberal democracy and reformist. Indeed, his political agenda and historically grounded personal identity speak to a different fate. He not only declares, but also embodies, "his nation," which is subject not only to Britain's domestic and foreign affairs, but also to the Jews' status as a particular conquered people, regardless of whether it is the Germans or Christians who are "strutting all over us." When the narrator announces the intention of dwelling on the "more cheerful aspect" of "the worst period of" Europe's experience, the story of history's grimmer contingencies is left to the Jew.[16] Gideon emerges from the war in constant physical and psychological pain, reflecting the war's incalculable losses and chaos as well as the continuous sense of loss and decenteredness he feels as a British Jew. And while his friends begin the process of rebuilding their nation, he is obsessed with rediscovering the roots of his dislocation. Searching for his complex historical and cultural identity, he decides to travel to Russia, his family's most recent origins before emigrating to Britain. While Gideon's British friends have begun to heal, he is killed for "defending some poor Jewish family." His fate is to be buried in his "nation's" historic story.[17]

Gideon is victimized not only by historic oppression, but also by the narrative pressure Macaulay creates. The pressure derives from the novel working towards an ethical model that represents an alternative to its otherwise totalizing disenchantment. True to her analysis of Britain's ambivalences towards the place of its Jews, Macaulay depicts Gideon's idealism as inexpressible because it implies a rejection of the culture it would revise. The narrative plotting thus rejects Gideon's idealism even as it valorizes it. Gideon may be "temperamentally Christian" in living "for causes and beliefs and ideals," but in its persistent difference, his Jewish identity questions the possibility that Christian spirit and "dogma" and British pragmatism and cultural nationalism could reconcile.[18] In his victimization, Gideon is a romantic hero of good causes, but not in love. As his own narrative reveals, both his newspaper, *The Weekly Fact*, and his love for Jane Potter mark him as a romantic quester while expressing dismay at Britain's postwar pragmatism. The irreconcilable tension between these impulses also signals his inescapable status and inability to survive as one of "an outcast people."[19]

No matter how Macaulay deplores this state of affairs, her own ambivalences resonate in the contrast between Gideon's fate and that of his beloved. Jane's unambivalent cynicism—compatible with the reformist anti-Potterists and the self-satisfied opportunism of Potterism—becomes a survival strategy within the narrative pitfalls of a bad marriage and the death of her lover. What Gideon disdains as her "profiteering" registers a pragmatism that implicates and validates her place in a masculinist value system where she can perform as wife, mother, and lover, and subscribe to a "damnable" war by wanting to fight in it.[20] The Jew's death, predicated on his continuing the history of his people, frees the English heroine from romance and marriage plots and leaves her fate open.

Because of his intensely committed ideals and passions, Gideon may be the novel's most compelling male character, but his romanticism also marks him as less fit for English constructions of masculinity than his lover. Ultimately, he has "no fit habitation" in the plot that will reestablish a pragmatic society. Because *Potterism* does not offer an alternative to the despair embedded in its satire, it upholds the plot of British cultural hegemony. Thus the child of Gideon's sister and her Jewish husband is no "throw-back to a most degraded Russian-Jewish type," as Jane's mother fears Gideon might spawn, but rather her golden delicacy is a sign that it "was Manchester and Birmingham that persisted, not Palestine or Russia."[21]

Despite the Jews' bodily disappearance from novels of Britain's postwar recovery, they remain a significant, if ghostlike, presence in its cultural history. In Macaulay's 1923 panoramic novel of England from 1879, *Told by an Idiot*, there are no Jewish characters, but their haunting absence represents a contested site of cultural power. One character, upon reading "Recessional," Kipling's poem written for Victoria's Jubilee, is piqued by a pompous celebration of British imperialism that invokes the "days of Israel's glory." But even more grating for this Englishman is the presence in this invocation of "Those Jews!" for "How their influence lasts!" and, as a result, calls the very essence of Englishness into question. By proclaiming the origins of Britain's cultural power and glory in the Jews' foundational text, the empire's poet laureate has marginalized the English as other: Are we then Jews, and not "Gentiles"?[22]

In other novels of the twenties, the Jew's presence is required as an agent of British postwar recovery. Margaret Kennedy's 1924 blockbuster, *The Constant Nymph*, begins in the Austrian Alps, a timeless, pristine setting that suggests denial of the war as well as recuperation. When the primary characters return to England, and it becomes clear that the setting is prewar, the narrative nonetheless evokes a theme of postwar dislocation and recovery as the domestic conflicts at its dramatic center are played out in the shadow of a persistently disturbing European presence. When the Europeanized children of Albert Sanger, an errant English composer, are brought back to England, efforts to assimilate them are akin to the process of healing the nation. It is as though the emphasis on English values and tradition will insulate the nation's children, and therefore its future, from external danger.

Recovery and danger are represented in the novel by a Jew. Although Jacob Birnbaum is stereotyped as a garish dabbler in international finance, he is also the novel's one stable male presence, generously committed to his friends' and family's welfare. This paradox is complicated by another—ridiculed as being too fat to be manly, Birnbaum is nonetheless accused of sexual coercion. He refigures the wartime rapist of innocence by transferring the terror of the Hun onto the postwar invader—the Jewish émigré. But Birnbaum is restored to favor when his victim admits to taking him as her lover under the influence of champagne, and that she loves and will marry him because she is also moved by pity and guilt over his love for her.[23] In contrast with Birnbaum and with *Potterism*, the romantic quester in this novel, Lewis Dodd, is not only not Jewish, but also apolitical, volatile, and committed only to his musical gifts, much like his English mentor, Sanger. As an agent of emotional and social chaos, Dodd's fate is to leave England. In its prewar setting and reflection of postwar recovery, the novel portrays Dodd as threatening the nation's desperate hold on stability and continuity in the twilight before war and its equally intense need to recuperate from war and survive the changes it would bring. Dodd can be absorbed by Europe because its history of turbulence mirrors his character while showing that it can survive it and represent a fantasy of timelessness.

England's place in historic time—its stability and recovery—is then paradoxically left to the Jew. In his archetypal roles of prophet and healer, Birnbaum predicts the chaos Dodd will produce, and then acts as healer. He offers to support and educate the Sanger children and thus integrate them into their national identity. Despite his commitment, the society that needs his nurturing capacities continues to excoriate him as one of those "building Jerusalem in England's green and pleasant land, and doing well out of it."[24] The prewar narrative thus positions itself in the postwar politics of national recovery as closing ranks against the invasion of values that would deconstruct English codes of masculinity and femininity. Birnbaum's caregiving is devalued because it is associated with the maternal, while his business acumen is impugned because he is a Jew. It is thus no wonder that he sees himself reflected in a mirror-lined space as "an infinitely long row of gentlemen carrying offerings to an unforgiving past."[25]

The historical circumstances that constitute the "unforgiving past" are dramatized and analyzed by Phyllis Bottome in her 1924 novel *Old Wine* about the aftermath of World War I in Austria. The novel is startling in its prescience of the coming of World War II and the destruction of the Jews. The Jewish healer in this novel, Dr. Jeiteles, is lauded for salvaging Europe's future by ministering to its children, while other, hapless Jews are imprisoned years before Hitler appears.[26] One major character, an Austrian princess whose work with the Jewish doctor signifies a rejection of her old, supremacist order and its imperial nationalism, observes that Jews bear "the fruit of race hatred and pet nationalities";[27] in this novel they are defiled and destroyed by a decayed civilization for which they represent regeneration. With the collapse of the Austro-Hungarian Empire, the Princess's cousin, Count Otto Wolkenheimb, faces the loss of his ancestral privilege. His only salvation is a business and sexual sell-out to a Jewess he finds repellent: Elisabeth Bleileben. In turn, Elisabeth's lust for Otto is as fierce as her craving for money and social status. But just as her passions are stifled by Otto's aristocratic diffidence, his salvation becomes damnation in her hands. Their marriage can thus only be described as a mutually hostile takeover. As despicable as they both are, however, in the end their losses make them equally pitiable.

A narrative balancing act like this one interrogates any model of literary and gender analysis that casts women as victims, and men as aggressors, in a transhistorical and pancultural sexual battle. The end of Bottome's novel exposes a conflict that can only be understood in its particular historical and cultural contexts—the relationship between the English writer, her construction of a fallen post–World War I European civilization, and the figure of the Jew, whose marginalized presence is now even more destabilized. In the final scene, while Otto remains ensconced in his Hapsburg mansion, albeit "alone . . . with his defeated ghost," Elisabeth finds herself being led outside on its cold, marble steps—in effect, back to the margins.[28] While sufficiently dramatic in its execution, the scene also raises provocative questions about the representation of the Jew and a woman at a moment in a literary text calling for moral regeneration. Has the Jewish woman been led back to the margins because she has been masculinized by her mantle of aggression? Perhaps, on the other hand, it is because she is another kind of "other," and here we are reminded of what Bottome said of her Jewish friend Alfred Adler, the prominent psychologist, who gave up his Jewish identity because under threat of persecution: the Jews are "forced to get the better of their opponents by flattery or undue persistence."[29]

How do we sort out the rhetorical and ideological moves of texts that express outrage against the oppression of women and the tragic fate of European Jews, that point the finger of blame at a fallen European civilization, when they also represent the Jew either as a despicable woman or as a noble healer who resembles a Christian more than a Jew?[30] The character of Elisabeth Bleileben complicates these questions by collapsing under the weight of its grotesque stereotyping and then leaving a narrative space where she can be rescued by the historical and literary discourses that victimize her. In contrast to the feminized Jewish man, Elisabeth is defeminized. Her ruthless ambitions and sexual drives constitute powers typically associated with men. Her scheme to profit from a Red Cross milk delivery to starving children demonizes her not only as a Lilith who rejects motherhood, but also as a female conflation of Shylock and Fagin, the latter an exploiter and poisoner of children. The combination makes her a phallic woman, marking her not only as a perversion of the feminine, but also as a parody of European anti-Semitic cartoons of the inherently depraved Jewish man. It is his circumcision, according to Sander Gilman, that marks the Jew as either castrated as "a version of female genitalia . . . or oversexed and a carrier of disease."[31] The masculinized woman is an object of disgust on several counts, and her exit into the cold signals the fumigation of a rarified aristocratic space.

Ultimately, however, Elisabeth is saved by her monstrous portrait. Because her appetites are omnivorous and crude, they are far less appealing, and therefore less seductively lethal, than the polished decadence of her beloved adversary, Count Wolkenheimb. Moreover, her ruthlessness betrays an intelligence struggling against assigned dependency roles that restrict its expression. The ameliorating resolutions of marriage and romance plots cannot accommodate the Jewish woman who, by birth and social construction, stands outside their social codes. Our last view of Elisabeth challenges that of Wolkenheimb, who represents the ghostly remnant of a politics of racial purity.

Bottome's portrait of postwar Austria and the position of the Jews is based on her experiences living there and in Germany after World War I. Throughout the interwar period, she was concerned that postwar recovery was hindered by the revival of old supremacy myths as a defense against social change, and she continued to depict this concern in her fiction as a retrogression signaled by persecution of the Jews. She and her husband left Munich in "May 1933,   was no longer possible to live there without witnessing the cruel persecution of our Jewish friends, or ourselves refusing to make terms, however passively, with the controlling gangsters."[32] Her judgment, however, indicts not only Austria or Germany, but also "the easy nonchalance of London."[33] *Old Wine*'s portrait of a decayed civilization reflects Bottome's concern that Britain was also endangered by the resurgence of myths promoting insularity and isolation. At the postwar moment of social upheaval, such myths promote a cohesive national identity that, in her view, would deny the nation's responsibility to "others." *Old Wine* thus reconstructs the history of postwar Europe by implicating Britain in its moral fate and judging it as having made "too little progress," especially as Bottome holds Britain's political complacency about the security of the Jews responsible for it.[34]

* * *

In each of their novels discussed above, Bottome, Kennedy, and Macaulay work towards taking responsibility and implicating themselves in the social and cultural myths that reconstruct postwar English national identity. The many-faceted roles and gender identities of Jews in these novels expose equally complex ambivalences about the reconstruction of postwar British national identity. Along the range of their responses, these writers also reject much of the past. As their Jewish characters represent critical perspectives on the fates of their female protagonists, it appears that whatever possibilities might be available to the women survivors are linked to questions about the fates of the Jews with whom their lives intersect. Whether man or woman, healer or witch, the figure of the Jew is made to incorporate all that represents the best, as well as the worst, that derives from English moral, political, and social codes. Paradoxically, the Jew comes to represent both the possibility for change and the victim of intransigent codes. For women writers, this embodiment suggests a narrative space in which they can continue to negotiate the agency and subjectivity of the character of the Englishwoman.

For the Jewish characters, there is no negotiable space. As though in perpetual exile from a place in which to become agents of their own fates, they function in these novels as prophets of the fates of others. They warn of the dangers of destabilized gender and cultural identities, but they also represent what the nation needs in order to transform itself to become more hospitable to its own and to the others it would absorb if only these outsiders would allow it. As the twenties drew on into the thirties, and social and political upheaval intensified—especially with fascist and Nazi developments—these novels stand as warnings about the end of safe boundaries—between the Continent and Britain, alien and self, and internal and external enemies.

NOTES

1. Until recently, scholars assumed that stereotypes coincided with a cultural anti-Semitism that transcended historical change and place. Edgar Rosenberg, in *From Shylock to Svengali: Jewish Stereotypes in English Fiction* (Stanford, 1960), Harold Fisch, in *The Dual Image: A Study of the Jew in English Literature* (London, 1971), and Esther Panitz, in *The Alien in Their Midst* (Princeton, 1981), use archetypal models to distinguish negative Jewish stereotypes from historical reality. Bryan Cheyette identifies an ideological bind in images of the Jew as redemptive and degenerate, in *Jewish Representations in English Fiction and Society 1875–1925: A Study in Semitism* (Cambridge, 1992); Andrea Loewenstein, in *Loathsome Jews and Engulfing Women* (New York, 1993), uses psychoanalytic theory to link Jewish figures to expressions of writers' defensive system; and Michael Ragussis, in *Figures of Conversion* (Durham, NC, 1995), shows such writers as Maria Edgeworth and Charles Dickens making reparations in later novels

for their early anti-Semitic portraits. With the exception of studying George Eliot, whose novel *Daniel Deronda* offers a map of ambivalences, research focuses on male writers as representing the range of approaches to Jewish portraiture, and therefore does not address the relationship between a gendered and racialized narrative discourse.

2. For discussion of these debates, see essays in Harold L. Smith, ed., *British Feminism in the Twentieth Century* (Amherst, MA, 1990), and Jane Lewis, *Women in England: 1870–1950* (Bloomington, 1984).

3. Arthur Marwick discusses such postwar turbulence as soldiers' demobilization riots and mass unemployment in *Britain in the Century of Total War* (Boston, 1968), 146–213. Angela Ingram argues that women's writing that was critical of social policies and pressures "to replace the millions killed or maimed courted . . . censorship": "Un/Reproductions: Estates of Banishment in English after the Great War," in Mary Lynn Broe and Angela Ingram, eds., *Women's Writing in Exile* (Chapel Hill, NC, 1989), 331. The novels I discuss depict these pressures in relation to postwar constructions of national identity.

4. For social contexts of the newly domesticated sexuality, see Lewis, *Women in England*, and Lesley Hall, "Uniting Science and Sensibility: Marie Stopes and the Narratives of Marriage of the 1920s," in Angela Ingram and Daphne Patai, eds., *Rediscovering Forgotten Radicals: British Women Writers, 1889–1939* (Chapel Hill, NC, 1993), 118–36. Sharon Ouditt argues that private grief implies "women's interiorization of the war" and rejection of public roles, but a bifurcated analysis ignores the fictional representation of how each is contained in the other: *Fighting Forces, Writing Women* (London, 1994). Nicola Beauman explores fictional tensions between postwar women's emergence from Victorian social codes and remaining domestic constraints. Her writers, like mine, are middle-class: *A Very Great Profession: The Woman's Novel 1914–1939* (London, 1983). Sandra Gilbert's and Susan Gubar's study insists that the war produced an embattled literature marked by men's and women's angry and defensive projections deriving from different wounding experiences. Their focus on gender without cultural distinction allows them to consider neither ideological concerns nor other "others": *No Man's Land: The Place of the Woman Writer in the Twentieth Century*, vol. 2, *Sexchanges*, and vol. 3, *Letters From the Front* (New Haven, 1989, 1994, resp.). Alison Light adds important complexity to analysis of interwar British women writers by identifying a conservative modernism that rebelled against the past while building a "culture of privacy" where women could flourish: *Forever England: Femininity, Literature, and Conservatism between the Wars* (London, 1991), 12.

5. Mary Cadogan and Patricia Craig survey interwar British writers disillusioned with "the ethics of nationalism" in *Women and Children First: The Fiction of Two World Wars* (London, 1978), 134. Paul Rich shows the British Right defending against "massive economic and social change," with an ideal "homogeneous nature of English society" in "Imperial Decline and the Resurgence of English National Identity, 1918–1979," in Tony Kushner and Kenn Lunn, eds., *Traditions of Intolerance: Historical Perspectives on*

Fascism and Race Discourses in Britain (Manchester, 1989), 37. That these issues crossed ideological lines is apparent in the ambivalent responses of many British women writers.

6. David Gervais has studied how English writers of the twentieth century (all male) use the novel to understand the nature and inheritance of England and English cultural and national identity, from elegiac notions of the green isle to alienation: *Literary Englands: Versions of 'Englishness' in Modern Writing* (Cambridge, 1993). The 1917 Balfour Declaration on establishing a Jewish state in Palestine merged conflicting attitudes towards the Jews, and implicitly represented a debate on English national identity in relation to the Empire. While many saw such a state as preserving the People of the Book, H. G. Wells among others blamed anti-Semitism on Zionism as an example of Jewish insularity, while the *Daily Express* reported from Palestine that before the arrival of "pushful, grasping and domineering" Jews, there had been peace and quiet (Loewenstein, *Loathsome Jews*, 22). For analysis of pressures on English Jews to assimilate, see Todd Endelman, *Radical Assimilation in English Jewish History, 1656–1945* (Bloomington, 1990). David Feldman argues that the forms of ongoing debates about English national identity "determined the terms of Jewish integration in England": *Englishmen and Jews: Social Relations and Political Culture 1840–1914* (New Haven, 1994), 381.

7. Enid Bagnold, *The Happy Foreigner*, in *The Girl's Journey* (London, 1929). The novel is based on Bagnold's experience driving an ambulance in France. See Arthur Calder-Marshall's forward to this edition, and Claire Tylee, *The Great War and Women's Consciousness: Images of Militarism and Womanhood in Women's Writing, 1914–1964* (Iowa, 1990), 231.

8. Bagnold, *The Happy Foreigner*, 98.

9. Samuel Hynes finds that "as a Christian, and as a woman," Macaulay "expected less of humankind" at the end of the war; she and H. G. Wells, to whom he compares her, "saw the loss of faith and the loss of momentum in the nation at war as realities." *A War Imagined* (New York, 1990), 135.

10. Rose Macaulay, *Potterism* (New York, 1920). Renewed interest in Macaulay challenges Samuel Hynes's judgment that the "exact particulars" of novels "[located] in public time . . . are restraints that confine the novels to their historical moments, and restrict meaning and suggestion" (*A War Imagined*, 135). Macaulay's historically based questioning of conventions of war and gender is of compelling interest to today's critics; see Squier, "Rose Macaulay," in Bonnie Kime, ed., *The Gender of Modernism* (Bloomington, 1990), 252–74; Gloria Fromm, "The Worldly and Unworldly Fortunes of Rose Macaulay," *The New Criterion* (Oct. 1986): 38–44. D. A. Boxwell sees Macaulay questioning stereotypes of pacifism as a "purely feminist ideology" in "The (M)Other Battle of World War One: The Maternal Politics of Pacifism in Rose Macaulay's *Non-Combatants and Others*," *Tulsa Studies in Women's Literature* 12 (Spring 1993): 95. The addition of ethnic identity to the particulars of the historically depicted moment expands "meaning and suggestion" even more, especially as it expands our understanding of

the relationship between what Hynes identifies as a focus of *Potterism*, "the problems of war and historical change" (*A War Imagined*, 334).

11. Macaulay, *Potterism*, 3.

12. Ibid., 19.

13. Ibid., 60.

14. Ibid., 22.

15. For the range of British women's attitudes towards peace in the post-World War I period, see Susan Kingsley Kent, *Making Peace: The Reconstruction of Gender in Interwar Britain* (Princeton, 1993).

16. Macaulay, *Potterism*, 23.

17. Ibid., 226. Alice Benson views Gideon as "a tool against anti-Semitism. His courage in the war . . . make[s] him initially sympathetic to readers who would tend to be antagonistic to his views": *Rose Macaulay* (New York, 1969), 72. Angela Woollacott's stress on class differences as related to women's World War I memorialization and identification with their brothers opens the way towards recognizing that the lack of grieving for Gideon probably relates towards his being an unassimilable "other": "Sisters and Brothers in Arms," in Miriam Cooke and Angela Woollacott, eds., *Gendering War Talk* (Princeton, 1993), 128–47.

18. Macaulay, *Potterism*, 174.

19. Ibid., 66.

20. Ibid., 20.

21. Ibid., 191, 198.

22. Rose Macaulay, *Told By an Idiot* (New York, 1922), 174–75.

23. Margaret Kennedy, *The Constant Nymph* (London, 1986). Billie Melman notes that Kennedy used obesity as a sign of "lasciviousness" in Sanger's character, but only the Jew must be rescued from the charge of rape by being excessively generous: *Women and the Popular Imagination in the Twenties* (London, 1988), 82.

24. Kennedy, *The Constant Nymph*, 181.

25. Ibid., 160.

26. Phyllis Bottome, *Old Wine* (London, 1924). Bottome's critique of British and European politics always views the fate of the Jews as a moral template. Her 1938 letter to the Archbishop of Canterbury, entitled "J'accuse," held him "culpable" in his "joy over the German military occupation of Austria" for the fate of "the race from which the Founder of his own religion sprang . . . Can any Christian accept lightly the fate of the 200,000 Jews in Vienna who are being systematically pillaged and tortured?" The letter was printed in *The New Republic* after "several liberal-minded weeklies in Great Britain refused it with regret" (Dec. 28, 1938, 232).

27. Bottome, *Old Wine*, 110.

28. Ibid., 287.

29. Bottome's biography of Alfred Adler, *Apostle of Freedom* (London, 1939), attributes his abandonment of his Jewish identity to an oppressive history, 25.

30. I show how such questions are self-consciously addressed in the World War II novels of several British women writers in "A Cry for Life:

Storm Jameson, Stevie Smith, and the Fate of Europe's Jews," in M. Paul Holsinger and Mary Anne Schofield, eds., *Visions of War: World War II in Popular Literature and Culture* (Bowling Green, 1992), 181–90.

    31. Sander Gilman, *The Jew's Body* (London, 1991), 127.

    32. Phyllis Bottome, *The Goal* (New York, 1952), 207.

    33. Ibid., 258.

    34. Ibid., 129.

PART III
DISSENT AND ACQUIESCENCE
WAR, FEMINISM, AND FEMALE ACTION

Challenging Traditions

Denominational Feminism in Britain, 1910–1920

Jacqueline R. deVries

The impact of World War I on the progress of women's emancipation in Great Britain has been the subject of much scholarly attention.[1] The standard interpretation has emphasized that the war, while the occasion of women's achievement of the vote, ushered in a period of quiescence in feminist organizing. Susan Kingsley Kent, for example, has argued that within the postwar climate, suffragettes demobilized their "sex war," succumbed to public anxiety about women's political and economic emancipation, and ceased to challenge the dominant gender ideology of separate spheres.[2] Other scholars have argued that the postwar emphasis on maternalist values was neither necessarily a concession to the ideology of separate spheres nor inherently antifeminist.[3] These interpretations, however, tend to focus on feminist attitudes toward such issues as politics, employment, and the family, and include little analysis of postwar (or, for that matter, prewar) feminist attitudes toward religion. Yet, as Sheila Fletcher's biography of the prominent Anglican suffragist A. Maude Royden suggests, the postwar period was characterized by unprecedented progress for women within religious contexts and witnessed the rise of the movement for women's ordination to the Anglican Church.[4] When the category of religion is included in the analysis of the British women's movement, postwar feminism begins to look less quiescent.

This essay will attempt to sketch out the ways in which religious beliefs and contexts helped to shape feminist identity and action before, during, and immediately after World War I. I begin with a general consideration of the place of religion within the context of the prewar suffrage movement as a whole. I then move on to a more specific analysis of feminist activism within the contexts of the Anglican and Roman Catholic Churches. Finally, I consider the ways in which World War I reshaped national attitudes toward religion and consequently sparked new confidence and provided fresh opportunities for those women who advanced their feminist ideals through organizations affiliated with specific denominations. I refer to these women as "denominational feminists"; conversely, I use the term "nondenominational feminist" to refer to those women who worked for the vote exclusively through secular suffrage organizations, even though these women may have considered themselves religious and been members of specific denominations.

BRITISH FEMINISM AND PROTESTANT CULTURE BEFORE 1914

The linkages between religion and national identity have been well established for the British context. Protestantism, as embodied in the Anglican Church, traditionally functioned as a key component in the formation and preservation of British national consciousness and, through its staunch opposition to "foreign" Roman Catholicism, served as a powerful force for national integration.[5] As David Hempton has argued, well into the nineteenth century this "shared Protestantism and Anti-Catholicism did not, of course, dissolve the cultural and historical divisions of the British peoples, but it did offer an easily available and deeply felt principle to rally around."[6] By the late nineteenth century, Anti-Catholicism was in swift decline, in part because the growth of Anglo-Catholicism had discredited the Church of England as a bastion of Protestantism, and in part because of the decline of religion more generally.[7] But Anti-Catholicism did not decline at the same pace among all social classes in all parts of the British Isles.[8] Nor did it affect men and women in the same ways.

The British women's movement was shaped within this ever-changing, but still deeply rooted, context of the Protestant nation-state. The earliest participants in the nineteenth-century women's suffrage movement were drawn largely from the Protestant middle classes. Many were strongly influenced by evangelicalism, which as the work of Leonore Davidoff and Catherine Hall has demonstrated, "offered women a life work, which, while subordinate, carried dignity and moral weight."[9] Women who joined the movement rarely chose to reject religion wholesale, and in fact frequently attributed their political work to the expression of devout religious belief.[10] The few women who did leave traditional churches turned most often to alternative forms of religious practice, such as spiritualism or Theosophy, rather than to agnosticism or atheism.[11] Whether orthodox or unorthodox, participants in the nineteenth-century women's movement tended to see religion not only as compatible with feminism, but also as a very real, or at least a potential, catalyst for women's emancipation as they defined it.

By the late nineteenth century, the women's movement in Britain had become increasingly focused on the campaign for women's suffrage at the national level and had begun to attract a membership from a broader social spectrum. Growing numbers of working-class women joined suffrage societies after 1900, drawn in by the efforts of Emmeline Pankhurst and her daughters, Christabel and Sylvia, in the slums of Manchester.[12] Catholic and Jewish women also became active in the suffrage movement, although their numbers initially remained small and were drawn mainly from the middle and upper classes. The movement's increasing class and religious heterogeneity inevitably brought varying perspectives and vocabularies. Many Protestant middle-class suffragists, for example, expressed their demands for the vote in strikingly evangelical terms.[13] Suffrage rallies were consciously modeled after the revivalist meetings popularized by Victorian evangelists, the Salvation Army, and the Labour Church, and thus drew on language and styles that may have been unfamiliar to non-Protestant women.

Nevertheless, the evangelical style of the movement did not prove to be a major stumbling block to cross-denominational suffrage cooperation. As I have argued elsewhere, the spiritual language of the Protestant middle-class suffragists served as a common metaphor, unifying suffragists and suffragettes from diverse class and religious backgrounds in a shared struggle for national regeneration.[14] Yet, differences of perspective remained. Protestant middle-class suffragists, for example, largely took for granted their affinity with British political culture and saw the vote as a means by which they could, by virtue of their gender, make important contributions to national life. In contrast, Catholic women, and women from other dissenting groups, saw the vote as a potential victory for both themselves, as women, and for their minority confessional communities.

In an attempt to express these differences, groups of suffragists and suffragettes established their own denominational suffrage leagues between 1909 and 1912. Representing the Anglican, Free Church, Catholic, Scottish Presbyterian, and Jewish traditions, these suffrage societies strove to articulate their unique perspectives on the suffrage question, as well as to persuade more members of their denominations to support the suffrage cause. In contrast to the religious women's organizations in France and Germany, which were distinctly antisuffragist,[15] each of the religious suffrage leagues was committed to securing political rights for women on an equal basis with men. All apparently were inspired by the militancy of the Women's Social and Political Union (WSPU) and (with the possible exception of the Quakers' Friends' League for Women's Suffrage) saw themselves as sharing common goals with the "fighting women."

Furthermore, the religious leagues recognized commonalities in their "religious perspective" on suffrage, and they frequently held joint demonstrations and sponsored educational meetings under the collective known as the "United Religious Leagues."

CHOOSING BETWEEN RADICALISM AND RESPECTABILITY: ANGLICAN AND CATHOLIC SUFFRAGISTS

The two most active and long-lasting suffrage leagues were the (Anglican) Church League for Women's Suffrage (CLWS) and the Catholic Women's Suffrage Society (CWSS). Both were established in the midst of the suffrage agitation and remained vital organizations after the vote was granted in 1918 to women over the age of thirty. A comparison of these two leagues is particularly useful because, while they were both feminist organizations within male-dominated, hierarchically organized churches, they each had a very different relationship to the predominantly Protestant British national culture. As members of the national church, Anglican feminists struggled to define a place for themselves within a hierarchical church, but they also enjoyed greater security and latitude for action than did Catholic feminists. Consequently, Anglican feminists became much bolder than the Catholics in demanding expanded roles and positions of authority for women within their church's structure. Catholic feminists also worked hard to overcome opposition and apathy within their own confessional community, but they faced the additional challenge of overcoming prejudice toward their religion within the wider English population. Consequently, Catholic feminists shaped their organization into more moderate and respectable directions.

The CLWS was the largest of the religious leagues. In the years between 1909 and 1914, the CLWS attracted more than 5,700 men and women members, representing ninety-one branches across England, Scotland, Ireland, and Wales.[16] The league was democratically organized, with regular annual meetings and a governing structure that allowed all members to vote on policy and strategy. Initially, the guiding force of the CLWS was a group of individuals—Gertrude and Claude Hinscliff, Henry Scott Holland, Margaret Wynne Nevinson, and Mabel and Percy Dearmer—who had been strongly influenced by the Christian Socialist movement of the 1880s and 1890s. They brought to the CLWS a strong belief in the potential of combining progressive social action with Christian faith, as well as the conviction that the Anglican Church was to be the main force in the regeneration of British society.[17] These leaders attracted similarly reform-minded Anglicans, particularly those who had drifted from, or become increasingly critical of, the Anglican Church, but had not entirely given up on organized Christianity. Margaret Nevinson, who had dabbled in spiritualism and explored Christian Socialism in the 1890s, commented that the CLWS drew "back to the church of their baptism many wanderers from the fold."[18] The CLWS also attracted a few aristocratic and more orthodox members, who saw it as a respectable alternative to the more militant societies. Louise Creighton, widow of Bishop Mandell Creighton and formerly a prominent suffrage opponent, publicly announced her support for women's suffrage shortly after the formation of the CLWS. To her, the CLWS offered a much-needed counterbalance to the "wild performances" of the suffragettes.[19] More than five hundred clergy also joined the CLWS. Such prominent figures as the Bishops of Lincoln, Hereford, and Kensington agreed to sit on the executive committee; Bishop Gore of Oxford, Bishop Winnington-Ingram of London, and Bishop Paget of Stepney frequently spoke on CLWS platforms; and the editor of the CLWS monthly newspaper, *The Church League for Women's Suffrage* (hereafter *CLWS*), launched in January of 1912, was the Rev. F. M. Green, Vicar of St. Mark's in north London.[20]

The main aim of the CLWS was to persuade both clergy and laity that a suffrage victory for women would benefit both the Anglican church and the nation as a whole. Leaving to nondenominational leagues the work of lobbying the government, the CLWS concentrated its efforts on influencing attitudes among Anglicans. The organization sought to win over critics who believed that public—and, more specifically, political—roles for women were against God's will.[21] Echoing a point made frequently in the wider movement, CLWS members claimed that women's emancipation and Christianity were both compatible and fundamentally intertwined. Through their work, CLWS members hoped the league would model a broad, socially active form of Anglicanism.

Many who joined the CLWS also saw it as a means through which to achieve more general, and not always exclusively feminist, reform within the Anglican Church. Some hoped, for example, that the CLWS would help facilitate greater lay participation in church governance. Among the chorus of enthusiastic clerical members of the CLWS, some advocated women's suffrage less for its own sake than for the benefits it might bring to the Church and the nation. They equated the advancement of women more with the promotion of public morals and national well-being than with women's own rights and needs. Logically, such an argument would weaken if women did not prove themselves worthy of this lofty goal. Indeed, among some Anglican clergy, support for women's suffrage waned as suffragette militancy made national headlines. The Archbishop of Canterbury, Randall T. Davidson, for example, withdrew his support for the suffrage movement after the WSPU began to foment violence, claiming doubts about women's suitability for participation in national politics. As the head of England's national church, Davidson insisted he could not promote a group of women whose views and actions might have a negative effect on the nation's moral tone.[22] By extension, Davidson was reluctant to support the CLWS, which never formally condemned suffragette militancy.

Some Anglican women were unhappy with the CLWS's male-centeredness and timid policies and sought a more confrontational approach. In 1912, Alice Kidd organized the Suffragist Churchwoman's Protest Committee, which bypassed the CLWS's "educational methods" and encouraged the boycott of churches whose clerics were openly opposed to women's suffrage.[23] The Protest Committee's initial efforts predictably caused much consternation among more conservative CLWS members and especially the clergy. Kidd asserted that the Protest Committee's goal was to demonstrate that women were not merely permanent and submissive members of the Church of England.[24] Some women believed the church boycott was still too passive, and formulated another strategy: they attended worship services but walked out immediately before the sermon, or, even more dramatically, interrupted the sermon with shouts of "votes for women." Introduced in 1913, this tactic was particularly successful in drawing publicity and was soon co-opted by other denominational and nondenominational suffrage leagues. The CLWS executive committee officially distanced itself from these actions, preferring to address suffrage opponents directly (and moderately) on the pages of the *CLWS*.

Like the CLWS, the Catholic Women's Suffrage Society attempted to fashion itself as a feminist organization within a male-dominated, hierarchically organized church. But, in contrast to the CLWS, the CWSS was an all-woman society, free from the constant control of the Catholic hierarchy. The society was adamantly in favor of equal suffrage rights and tried not to let the opinions of the Catholic clergy openly influence its aims or methods. Yet, despite its attempts at autonomy, the CWSS could not escape the implications of its status as a Catholic organization within a predominantly Protestant nation. By the end of the nineteenth century, anti-Catholic prejudices were losing ground in Britain, in part because of the examples of social activism and civic leadership provided by prominent Catholic leaders.[25] By 1910, augmented by both new converts and Irish immigrants, the Catholic community in England was no longer a tiny minority. Nevertheless, many Catholics continued to feel that they occupied a secondary status within the Protestant British nation.[26] The CWSS responded to the uncertainties of this position by guarding the integrity of the Catholic tradition and attempting to champion a model of Catholic political activism.

The CWSS was begun in November of 1910 by two young, single, Catholic women who were sympathetic to the militant suffrage movement but concluded that it did not satisfactorily express the vision of Catholic feminists.[27] Few Catholic women of any class background had joined the nondenominational suffrage societies, and Gabrielle Jeffery and May Kendall hoped that the CWSS would provide Catholic women with a respectable way of becoming active in the suffrage battle. In its early years, however, the CWSS remained small and exclusively middle-class. The seven original members of the CWSS executive council were mostly in their twenties, single, and well-educated, and they tended to attract members from similar backgrounds. The CWSS drew some members from the Catholic social and cultural elite—including the acclaimed poet Alice Meynell and the well-known convert Mrs. Virginia Crawford, who was also a London County Council member. But it largely failed to interest and, at least before the war, remained comfortably aloof from the bulk of working-class Catholic women.[28]

The CWSS executive council and the majority of its members preferred to advance the suffrage issue quietly through uniquely Catholic "religious and educational" methods. Members were asked to say one "Hail Mary" and the invocation "Blessed Joan of Arc pray for us" every day. The CWSS colors were selected to signify their loyalty to their tradition: blue, in homage to Mary the Mother of Jesus, and the papal colors of white and gold, to honor their allegiance to the Catholic Church. Only Catholic speakers were to appear on CWSS platforms. According to one pamphlet, the CWSS defined its purposes as, first, "to uphold the definite Catholic teaching on points connected with the position of woman legally, socially and politically" and, second, "to carry on an active propaganda on [women's suffrage], which being political cannot be mentioned in the pulpit."[29]

The official Catholic stance toward the CWSS was one of ambivalence, sometimes bordering on hostility. When first organizing their society, the CWSS women asked Archbishop Bourne of Westminster his opinion on women's suffrage. When he refused to offer one, they interpreted his silence as tacit approval and continued with their plans.[30] Few members of the Anglo-Catholic hierarchy

were openly supportive of the suffrage cause, and at times some attacked it outright. In 1912, for example, the CWSS found itself an
unwitting target of suspicion and hostility from many segments of
the Catholic community after the Jesuit Father Henry Day delivered
a series of sermons condemning women's social and political emancipation as "immoral," "a blasphemy," and "anti-racial," by which
he meant that the vote would lead to the decline of the British
birthrate and consequently the weakening of the Anglo-Saxon race.[31]

Within this uncertain climate, the CWSS struggled to define its
feminist vision. In response to Father Day's attacks, for example, one
CWSS member, Alice Abadam, retaliated with her own series of
speeches in which she defended suffrage militancy as "righteous"
and berated Father Day as "a politician."[32] But the CWSS executive
was uncomfortable with Abadam's bold style and strident rhetoric,
believing that patience and fortitude were the best responses to attacks such as Father Day's. In a private letter, the CWSS press secretary Blanche Smyth-Piggot admitted to her friend Mildred Tuker
that she believed Father Day was wrong, yet she also thought that
"the safest pose for the Catholic Suffrage Society is that of defending
the Church and not exposing it, especially to outsiders." The
Catholic hierarchy was not infallible, she readily admitted:

> [But] in the case of us Catholics, we must be so absolutely certain of
> our facts which is not always possible. One has to be on guard against
> one's own colouring and prejudices, for a time at any rate we must
> convince the priests rather than set them all against us.[33]

Smyth-Piggot's comments reveal the underlying lack of confidence
that pervaded the CWSS before World War I. Unsure of their place as
feminists within the Catholic tradition, CWSS leaders were not prepared to push too far or too confidently their claim that women's
emancipation was the fulfillment of Christian ideals—a claim that
would require some to rethink their conservative Christian beliefs.
Wary of latent Anti-Catholicism, the CWSS was reluctant to openly
criticize the opinions of other Catholics. The CWSS never confronted the Catholic Church in the manner of the Anglican Alice
Kidd. The vast majority of CWSS members did not challenge the
Catholic hierarchy, nor did they work to change church polity in
order to expand women's roles. The evidence here suggests that their
moderation was at least in part a product of their consciousness of
minority status within the Protestant state. The women of the
CWSS were aware of their church's vulnerable position and, envi-
sioning themselves as representatives of Catholicism, strove to protect it from outside attack rather than to reshape it from within.

NATIONAL MORALITY AND MORAL PATRIOTISM:
THE IMPACT OF WORLD WAR I ON CHRISTIAN FEMINISM

World War I brought many changes to the CLWS and the CWSS. Like the larger suffrage societies, they pledged their support for Britain's war effort and ceased most of their suffrage campaigning; and like other British suffrage organizations, they too lost some membership and funds during the 1914–18 conflict. Unlike their secular counterparts, however, members of the CLWS and CWSS emerged from the war years with a greater sense of confidence and purpose, largely because of the war's impact on the place of religion in national public life.

For Anglican feminists, progress came in part because of a crisis of (male) authority within the Church of England. While World War I certainly did not begin the drift away from the Church of England, it revealed—more than ever before—the alienation of a majority of the English male population from the life and practice of the nation's established religious institution.[34] At the same time, however, the war spurred greater concern for spiritual issues, as individuals sought hope and sustenance in the face of an often meaningless situation.[35] Because of this increasing interest in spirituality, which was generally perceived as a "feminine" aspect of religious practice, Anglican feminists found widening opportunities and encountered greater interest in, and respect for, their participation in, and reform of, the Church of England.

The high degree of disillusionment with the Church resulted, in part, from disappointment with Anglican leadership on the home front. When war first broke out, many Anglican clergy had responded with enthusiastic support and used their pulpits to appeal for recruits. But by 1916, war weariness had set in, and ordinary people began to regard the Church of England as both hypocritical and complicit with the government in the war's mismanagement.[36] The gap between clergy and lay members was further exacerbated by the clergy's exemption from the draft.[37] In 1916, in an attempt to reclaim the church's waning influence in the everyday lives of the British people, the Archbishop of Canterbury launched the "National Mission of Repentance and Hope." Plans were laid for revival-style retreats and conferences "through all the cities and towns and villages of the land."[38]

Members of the Council of the National Mission, which included A. Maude Royden, believed that the Mission should take a broad view of the nation's "spiritual needs" and speak forthrightly on the issues that had divided the nation before the outbreak of war. In July of 1916, they adopted a resolution on "Relations with the Women's

Movement," which declared in unequivocal terms that "underlying this movement there are moral and spiritual elements which demand the frank recognition and close sympathy of the Church." The statement went on to claim that the women's movement had introduced a "new moral consciousness," which doubtlessly would bring "conflict with such laws and customs, habits and traditions, in the social regime inherited from the past," but which deserved the firm support of the Church.[39] This remarkable document signified a new willingness within the Anglican hierarchy to consider women as valuable members of the Church and nation. But this attitude was not shared by the ultra-cautious Archbishop Davidson, who suppressed the statement because of its apparent partisanship on a "political" issue.

Nevertheless, interest in women's moral leadership remained strong among the Council members. As preparations continued for the National Mission, and the Council faced severe shortages of clergy to help with preparation and speaking at the parish level, it began to consider the possibility of using women to lead local prayer and instructional meetings. News of these deliberations leaked out and provoked a wide public discussion of the propriety of female Anglican priests. Critics asserted a "slippery-slope" argument that the use of women speakers during the Mission would inevitably begin a movement for the ordination of women to the priesthood. In the face of such opposition, several Council members reversed their original support for women speakers and allowed the proposition to die. However, the final decision was reached in such a bumbling fashion that many Anglican parishioners were left confused about the Church's official position toward women speaking and teaching in church.[40]

Within this atmosphere of renewed interest in women's leadership roles (but confusion over the specific parameters), advocates of women's ordination saw their opportunity. The CLWS, which during the first two years of war had largely demobilized its suffrage campaign and redirected its organization toward patriotic work, began to concentrate its efforts on expanding women's influence on Anglican Church policy. The organization revived an effort begun before the war to secure women's representation on Anglican lay church councils and, although it initially avoided an official position on women preachers, the CLWS leadership encouraged individual members to consider the issue prayerfully.[41] By the time the vote came in February of 1918 to women over the age of thirty, the CLWS had lost most of its clerical members to war service; of the remaining membership, most were middle-class women, and many were advocates of women's ordination. They knew their goals for the CLWS extended beyond the franchise victory.[42]

In a symbolic gesture, members voted in January of 1919 to re-name the organization the "League of the Church Militant" (LCM) to protest that the Church was "not half militant enough" (an inter-esting choice of words in light of the recently ended war).[43] The LCM also pledged to work for the "spiritual equality" of men and women, a term which proved hard to define. Rev. F. M. Green, for example, who continued as editor of the CLWS journal, now renamed *The Church Militant*, understood "spiritual equality" to mean that no differentiation of function should exist in lay Church work.[44] Other LCM members defined "spiritual equality" to include non-lay work—that is, the right of women to preach and teach from Angli-can pulpits. In May of 1919, the General Council of the LCM voted to make women's ordination to the priesthood a central goal: "We repudiate 'subordination' just as earnestly as we repudiate 'inferior-ity'; we deny that upon man there is conferred according to the di-vine intention a permanent and essential headship."[45]

As the LCM attempted to chart a course into the male-dominated territory of the ministry, it tended, at first, to adopt an equivocal tone. Both positive and negative opinions (some claimed too many) on women's ordination were included in *The Church Militant*. The LCM executive explained: "Though we are indignant we are not dis-loyal . . . and though indignant we are not unreasonable."[46] They did not, for example, urge Bishops to ordain women on their own re-sponsibility, nor did they put pressure on Parliament to vote on An-glican polity. Instead, the LCM appealed directly to church members in the hope that "the truth will prevail." But after mid-1919, when Anglican women were granted the right to equal representation on each of the newly reorganized lay councils, the LCM grew bolder in its campaign for women's ordination. LCM members led study groups and public debates and initiated an educational campaign in schools, colleges, and training colleges, to appeal to the "young, well-educated, and thinking class of women" about the position of women in the Church.[47]

Interestingly, as the war-torn nation struggled to rebuild, the issue of women's ordination drew significant public attention. While some LCM members departed in protest, the organization drew more support than it lost. The number of subscriptions to *The Church Militant* in 1920 was four times larger than in 1914, al-though donations never regained prewar levels, which suggests that while many were interested in the issue of women's ordination, fewer were willing to give it their wholehearted support.[48] The issue

did attract the attention of some prominent suffragists, including
Millicent Garrett Fawcett and Emmeline Pethick-Lawrence, who
served on a women's ordination advisory committee. Public discussions of women's ordination drew large crowds. "Hundreds" had to
be turned away from a debate on women's ordination in June of 1919
between the Rev. A. V. Magee and A. Maude Royden held in the
Church House in Westminster.[49]

Interest in expanding women's leadership roles in the Church also
came from official quarters. In February of 1920 the Lower House of
the Canterbury Convocation defeated by a single vote a statement
that would have allowed women to preach at non-liturgical services.
Several church newspapers resoundingly condemned the failure to
pass the motion.[50] The issue of women's ordination came to a head
at the July of 1920 meeting of the Lambeth Conference of Anglican
bishops, where, after some discussion, Church leaders avoided an explicit statement condemning women preachers. Instead, the bishops
reaffirmed the office of deaconess as the sole order of ministry for
women "with apostolic approval," but also indicated that women
could, on occasion, be allowed to speak and lead prayer in unofficial
capacities.

The war years had changed the contexts of action for Anglican
feminists. The National Mission had left the door slightly ajar to the
possibility of women preaching in church with official sanction.
Such an opportunity, the LCM clearly recognized, would allow
women to begin to influence church policy and Christian theology
at the highest levels. Throughout the 1920s, the LCM would continue to work toward this goal with energy and conviction.[51]

Like the Anglicans, members of the Catholic Women's Suffrage
Society emerged from the war years with a broadened sense of purpose and a clearer understanding of their feminist position within
their own tradition. The war offered Catholic feminists an opportunity to articulate more clearly their identity as feminists, Catholics,
and British citizens. Throughout the war, CWSS members worked
hard to demonstrate loyalty to Britain through patriotic service. As
the war continued, Catholic feminists benefited from a gradual decline in anti-Catholic attitudes and an increasing recognition of the
important contributions Catholics could make to national public life.

At the beginning of the war, the Roman Catholic Church became
a target of much British frustration and outrage. In August of 1914,
Pope Pius X had died, and his successor, Benedict XV, remained
silent on the war until November of 1914, when he issued a statement that called simply for the war's speedy end. The Pope's failure
to place guilt for the war squarely on Germany was regarded by

many in England as "studied nullity" and "moral supineness," and rumors circulated that the Holy See was secretly allied with Germany.[52]

Within this uncertain climate, the CWSS began to carve an independent voice for itself. Shortly after the outbreak of hostilities in Belgium, the CWSS issued a statement declaring the war a "calamity." Despite their reluctance to applaud Britain's war effort, CWSS members quickly began patriotic work, believing that support for their country was a moral duty. Initially their war service involved mainly relief work among the Catholic poor. While focused along denominational lines, these activities helped to awaken a sensitivity among the predominantly middle-class CWSS membership to the needs of working-class Catholic women.[53]

The CWSS made a big step toward greater self-definition when it launched in January of 1915 a monthly newspaper, *The Catholic Suffragist*, under the editorship of Leonora de Alberti, a talented writer who worked part-time in the Public Record Office. The paper had been in the planning stages since the end of 1913, but had been delayed by various financial difficulties. The CWSS executive saw the war as a crucial moment to begin a suffrage newspaper representing the Catholic perspective. In the opening essay of the first issue, Catholic author Alice Meynell underscored what the CWSS saw as its unique perspective:

> The production in war time of a new paper dedicated to the cause of Votes for Women should remind us that though thousands are suffering acutely, splendidly, and conspicuously, millions are suffering chronically, inconspicuously, and with little hope, evils against which the whole Suffrage movement has set its face. Crime has been lessened by the War, we hear; but we cannot hope that sin has been lessened. And the difficult and arduous work of the women reformers is essentially and fundamentally a moral work. A Catholic suffragist woman is a suffragist on graver grounds and with weightier reasons than any other suffragist in England.[54]

CWSS women believed that Catholicism provided them with a moral framework within which to exercise their civic and patriotic duties in a way that transcended narrow wartime partisanship. CWSS members continually highlighted the kinds of contributions that Catholic women could make to the moral well-being of the British nation. Through the pages of *The Catholic Suffragist*, the CWSS began to articulate its demand for women's suffrage as a kind of moral patriotism.

Indeed, as CWSS members turned their attention to nursing

orphans and visiting the sick, they became more—not less—committed to their feminist ideals. Early in 1915, CWSS Executive member Miss Christopher St. John observed that the country had slid into a "rather primitive state of things. Men are fighting, women are nursing and knitting and enduring." She saw this as particularly worrisome because it was coupled with increasing government restrictions on women's liberties.[55] To combat these slippages, the CWSS began to join with nondenominational women's organizations more readily than it had before the war. When the Plymouth Watch Committee proposed to re-enact the Contagious Diseases Acts, for example, the CWSS joined other suffrage organizations to protest these measures.[56] Such willingness to participate in cross-denominational feminism signaled a bolder attitude among CWSS members and enabled them to widen the range of their feminist interests and involvement.

By 1918, anti-Catholic attitudes in Britain had eased. On the war front, religious differences between Protestants and Catholics had faded in importance as British soldiers fought side by side with French and Belgian Catholics, against a Protestant foe. In a gesture of confidence in Catholics' central place within the British nation, the CWSS changed the name of its newspaper to *The Catholic Citizen* in late 1917, when the vote for women seemed assured. In January of 1918, while many suffrage leagues were dissolving, the CWSS voted to continue its work "for the further extension of the franchise to women on the same terms as it is, or may be, given to men; to establish the political, social and economic equality between men and women; and to further the work and usefulness of Catholic women as citizens."[57]

The CWSS clearly felt empowered by the deepening concern in postwar Britain for public morality and by a growing recognition of the contributions that women—especially religious women—could make to cleaning up the public sphere. CWSS members were also encouraged by evidence of increasing support among their own confessional community for a Catholic society of feminist women. In February of 1917, for example, the Archbishop of Glasgow declared in a pastoral letter that, since witnessing women's war service, he had reconsidered his views on women's "place and value . . . in the world" and concluded that their public roles were "in harmony with the practice and teaching of our religion." He charged women to rise "to the heights of your great vocation" and to work "to purify and ennoble the world," either through childrearing or government service.[58] While in retrospect we can see that more women in the postwar period chose the route of childbearing than of government service, such statistics do not diminish the reality that the CWSS emerged from the war years with a greater sense of its purpose as a Catholic women's society devoted to women's leadership within both the Church and the nation. Significantly, the organization enjoyed the longest existence of any of the religious suffrage leagues, becoming the St. Joan's Social and Political Alliance in 1923, and later in the 1920s expanding into the St. Joan's International Alliance, the name under which it continues today.

CONCLUSIONS

Before World War I, both Anglican and Catholic feminists had found themselves shackled by the largely conservative interests of their constituencies. As a result of the war's impact on attitudes toward religious belief and practice, as well as toward the relationship between religion and national public life, denominational feminists found expanding opportunities and greater popular interest in their reform agendas. Both the CLWS and CWSS emphasized the expansion of women's moral influence in national public life. While these two organizations clearly drew from a legacy of Victorian ideals about women's natural moral superiority, they reshaped this legacy and applied it in dramatically new ways. The LCM's postwar campaign for women's ordination to Anglican orders aimed at deeply embedded, culturally rooted, gender stereotypes. Similarly, the CWSS's decision to continue their work furthering Catholic women's citizenship activities constituted a clear victory over both their own doubts and wider prejudices toward British Catholics.

Although Anglican and Catholic feminists may be charged with being overconfident and overly impressed by changes in public attitudes that would ultimately prove "evanescent"—after all women's ordination into the Anglican Church was not achieved until November of 1992—the progress they made during the war in defining their feminist vision was certainly not illusory.[59] Particularly in the case of the Anglicans, the war years weakened the clergy's hold on the CLWS and created spaces for Anglican women to assert their independent voices. While they were not immediately successful in securing women's access to the highest offices of the Church of England, the mere fact that the LCM attempted to do so represents a significant development in Anglican feminists' understanding of the cultural sources of women's subordination. Catholic women did not reach the same conclusion as readily, in part because their position as Catholics within a Protestant nation required them to focus more immediately on defining Catholic citizenship, rather than on challenging their church's structure and doctrine. But the continuing vitality of the CWSS demonstrates that, at least among denominational feminists, the British women's movement was far from "quiescent" after World War I.

Notes

1. See, for example, Sandra Gilbert, "Soldier's Heart: Literary Men, Literary Women, and the Great War," in Margaret Higonnet et al., eds., *Behind the Lines: Gender and the Two World Wars* (New Haven, 1989); Susan Kingsley Kent, *Making Peace: The Reconstruction of Gender in Interwar Britain* (Princeton, 1993); and Susan Pedersen, "Gender, Welfare, and Citizenship in Britain during the Great War," *American Historical Review* 95, no. 4 (1990): 983–1006.

2. A succinct statement of Kent's argument can be found in her article, "The Politics of Sexual Difference: World War I and the Demise of British Feminism," *Journal of British Studies* 27 (July 1988): 232–53. For a sharp critique of Kent's work, see Jo Vellacott's review of *Making Peace* in *The American Historical Review* 100, no. 3 (June 1995): 903–4.

3. See in particular Seth Koven and Sonya Michel, eds., *Mothers of a New World: Maternalist Politics and the Origins of Welfare States* (London and New York, 1993), who argue that maternalist rhetoric and politics did not originate during the war.

4. Sheila Fletcher, *A. Maude Royden: A Life* (Oxford, 1989).

5. For an introduction to these ideas, see Linda Colley, *Britons* (New Haven, 1993); David Hempton, *Religion and Political Culture in Britain and Ireland* (Cambridge, 1996); Keith Robbins, *History, Religion and Identity in Modern Britain* (London and Rio Grande, 1993); and John Wolffe, *God and Greater Britain: Religion and National Life in Great Britain and Ireland, 1843–1945* (London, 1994).

6. Hempton, *Religion and Political Culture*, 147.

7. D. G. Paz, *Anti-Catholicism in Mid-Victorian England* (Stanford, 1992).

8. Hempton, *Religion and Political Culture*, 150.

9. Leonore Davidoff and Catherine Hall, *Family Fortunes: Men and Women of the English Middle Class, 1780–1850* (London, 1987), 111.

10. See, for example, Barbara Caine, *Victorian Feminists* (Oxford, 1992); Philippa Levine, *Feminist Lives in Victorian England: Private Roles and Public Commitment* (Oxford, 1990), 31. Josephine Butler is the most prominent example.

11. Diana Burfield, "Theosophy and Feminism: Some Explorations in Nineteenth-Century Biography," in Pat Holden, ed., *Women's Religious Experience* (London, 1983), 27–55; Alex Owen, *The Darkened Room: Women, Power and Spiritualism in Late Victorian England* (Philadelphia, 1990).

12. Jill Liddington and Jill Norris, *One Hand Tied Behind Us: The Rise of the Women's Suffrage Movement* (London, 1978).

13. Andrew Rosen, *Rise Up, Women! The Militant Campaign of the Women's Social and Political Union, 1903–1914* (London, 1974), 199–200; Martha Vicinus, "Male Space and Women's Bodies: The Suffragette Movement," in idem, *Independent Women: Work and Community for Single Women* (Chicago, 1985). For the rather different gender ideals among England's immigrant Jewish population, for example, see Rickie Burman, "'She Looketh Well to the Ways of Her Household': The Changing Role of Jewish Women in Religious Life, c.1880–1930," in Gail Malmgreen, ed., *Religion in the Lives of English Women, 1760–1930* (London, 1986).

14. Jacqueline R. deVries, "'A New Heaven and Earth': Feminism, Religion and the Politics of Identity in England, 1890–1925" (Ph.D. diss., University of Illinois at Urbana, 1996), esp. chap. 3. The term "suffragist" is commonly used to describe nonmilitant suffrage campaigners, while "suffragette" is reserved for those who used militant methods or belonged to a suffrage society that advocated them.

15. Steven Hause with Anne Kenney, *Women's Suffrage and Social Politics in the French Third Republic* (Princeton, 1984); see also Ursula Baumann's essay in this volume.

16. *Church League for Women's Suffrage Fifth Annual Report* (Mar. 1915), i. Little has been written about the CLWS. The most comprehensive account can be found in Brian Heeney, *The Women's Movement in the Church of England, 1850–1930* (Oxford, 1988).

17. Edward Norman, *The Victorian Christian Socialists* (Cambridge, 1987).

18. As quoted by Claude Hinscliff in "The Story of the CLWS," *Church League for Women's Suffrage*, Oct. 1913, 299–300.

19. Louise Creighton, *Memoir of a Victorian Woman: Reflections of Louise Creighton, 1850–1936*, ed. James Thayne Covert (Bloomington, 1994), 145–46.

20. The most complete list of clerical CLWS members can be found in the CLWS *Fourth Annual Report* for 1913, 45–53.

21. See Brian Harrison, *Separate Spheres: The Opposition to Women's Suffrage in Britain* (London, 1978).

22. See, in particular, Randall T. Davidson's letter to Agnus Gardiner, Mar. 1, 1907, Papers of Randall T. Davidson, Lambeth Palace.

23. Suffragist Churchwoman's Protest Committee flier, Arncliffe-Sennett Collection, Volume 21, British Library.

24. Alice M. Kidd, letter to the *CLWS*, Dec. 1912, 133; Alice M. Kidd, letter to Archbishop Randall Davidson, Mar. 25, 1912, Papers of Randall T. Davidson, Lambeth Palace.

25. Edward Norman, *The English Catholic Church in the Nineteenth Century* (Oxford, 1984); Owen Chadwick, *The Victorian Church, Part II*, 2nd. ed. (London, 1972), 411–22.

26. Chadwick, *The Victorian Church, Part II*, 401ff; Norman, *The English Catholic Church*, 16ff. Between 1851 and 1911, the Catholic population in England and Wales had grown from approximately 900,000 to 1,710,000. Robert Currie, Alan Gilbert, and Lee Horsley, *Churches and Churchgoers:*

Patterns of Church Growth in the British Isles since 1700 (Oxford, 1977), 153–54.

27. The one scholarly account of the CWSS is Francis M. Mason's "The Newer Eve: The Catholic Women's Suffrage Society in England, 1911–1923," *The Catholic Historical Review* 72, no. 4 (Oct. 1986): 620–38. Two other, rather anecdotal accounts of the CWSS are Leonora de Alberti, "A History of the Catholic Women's Suffrage Society," *Catholic Citizen*, Oct. 15, 1928, 77; and Nancy Stewart Parnell, *A Venture in Faith* (London, n.d.).

28. Parnell, *Venture in Faith*, 6. In late 1913 the CWSS had attracted about one thousand members, representing thirteen branches across England and Scotland.

29. "Why do we want a Catholic Suffrage Society?" (CWSS pamphlet, n.d., Fawcett Library, London).

30. Parnell, *Venture in Faith*, 5.

31. Day's sermons were widely publicized in both the Catholic and secular press. See, for example, *The Tablet*, Oct. 26, 1912 and Nov. 2, 1912. Day uses the term "race" to denote nationality.

32. For the conservative Catholic response to Abadam's speeches, see "The Abadamites," *Universe*, Dec. 20, 1912.

33. Blanche Smyth-Piggot to M. A. R. Tuker, Dec. 30, 1912, M. A. R. Tuker Papers, Fawcett Library, London.

34. Alan Wilkinson, *The Church of England and the First World War* (London, 1978); Alan Marrin, *The Last Crusade: The Church of England and the First World War* (Durham, NC, 1974).

35. J. M. Winter, "Spiritualism and the First World War," in R. W. Davis and R. J. Helmstadter, eds., *Religion and Irreligion in Victorian Society: Essays in Honor of R. K. Webb* (London, 1992), 185–200.

36. Wilkinson, *Church of England*, 131.

37. In March of 1918, after the all-out German offensive, the clergy exemption was abolished; but six days later the Government reversed this decision. Ibid., 39–40.

38. Ibid., 72.

39. These statements can be found in *National Mission Paper No. 11: Women and the National Mission* (London, 1916).

40. For one account of the haphazard decision-making process, see Fletcher, *A. Maude Royden*, 145–51.

41. Since its inception in 1903, women were denied the right to sit on the Representative Church Council, the Church of England's body of lay representatives. Women's sole official means of influencing church policy was through attendance at the annual Church Congresses. These bodies, however, were non-authoritative—no votes were taken, or decisions made, on any ecclesiastical issues. See Heeney, *The Women's Movement in the Church of England*, 94ff.

42. Membership figures in the postwar period are elusive. Twenty-one of the more than ninety CLWS branches dissolved, and only one new branch was begun, during the war. But the remaining members appeared more

tightly organized and committed to advancing feminist reform within the Church of England.

43. "Title and Objects," *The Church Militant*, Feb. 1919, 12.

44. Rev. F. M. Green, "The Functions of Women as Lay Members of the Church," ibid., Nov. 1918, 109–111.

45. "Women and the Priesthood," ibid., May 1919, 36.

46. Ibid.

47. "Educational Campaign," ibid., Dec. 1919, 91.

48. "Annual Report of the Executive Committee," published in *The Church League for Women's Suffrage*, Mar. 1915, and *The Church Militant*, Jan. 1921.

49. For a full transcript of the debate, see "Women and the Priesthood," *The Church Militant*, July 1919, 50–56.

50. Including *The Guardian*, *The Church Family Newspaper*, and *The Challenge*. *The Church Times* withheld comment, which might be interpreted as a silent protest.

51. In 1928 the LCM dissolved itself, leaving advocacy of women's ordination to the "Anglican Group for Bringing the Subject of the Admission of Women to the Priesthood Before the Next Lambeth Conference" (which occurred in 1930).

52. Marrin, *The Last Crusade*, 223–24.

53. For example, the CWSS's Liverpool branch assumed leadership of a club begun by the Women's Patriotic League, through which CWSS members provided relief, entertainment, and educational classes for wives of soldiers and sailors. "Suffrage Work in War-time," *The Catholic Suffragist*, 15 Sept. 1915, 76–77.

54. Alice Meynell, "The Catholic Suffragist," ibid., 15 Jan. 1915, 1.

55. Christopher St. John, "Sursum Corda!" ibid., 15 Feb. 1915, 9–10.

56. The original Contagious Diseases Acts had been passed in Britain in the 1860s to establish regular health inspections of prostitutes. Mid-Victorian feminists such as Josephine Butler viewed the CDA as state-sanctioned vice, and worked long and hard for their repeal, which came in 1886. See Judith Walkowitz, *Prostitution and Victorian Society: Women, Class, and the State* (Cambridge, 1980).

57. CWSS minutes, Jan. 24, 1918, Fawcett Library.

58. As quoted in *The Catholic Suffragist*, 15 Mar. 1917, 28–30.

59. Steven C. Hause has concluded that this was the case for French feminists in his article, "More Minerva Than Mars: The French Women's Rights Campaign and the First World War," in Higonnet et al., eds., *Behind the Lines*, 103.

Religion, Emancipation, and Politics in the Confessional Women's Movement in Germany, 1900–1933*

Ursula Baumann

In his famous 1844 essay on Georg Friedrich Hegel's *Philosophy of Right*, Karl Marx asserted that the critique of religion was the prerequisite for any critique, and emancipation from religion the foundation of all human liberation.[1] Although the philosophical underpinning of Marx's theses, which reduce religion to a mere phenomenon of projection and reflection, is disputable, certain historical developments—in particular the formation of the labor movement and the women's movement in Germany—seem to bear out his statement.

The early German women's movement, which evolved at the time when Marx published his essay in the period preceding the Revolution of 1848, was led by dissenters and women's associations attached to nonconformist religious movements. For these women, religious emancipation was most definitely a prerequisite for their engagement in feminist and liberal-democratic causes. Their critique of religion ranged from theological rationalism to pantheism and to a "religion of humanity" which sought to replace Christianity.[2] However, in the last third of the nineteenth century the link between religious emancipation and women's emancipation played only a very minor role in the German women's movement. Liberation from church dogma was no longer regarded as the foundation for women's legal, socioeconomic, and political emancipation, including equal educational and occupational opportunities, an end to discrimination in civil law, and full citizenship for women. This

---

*This is a revised version of a German article published in Tel Aviver Jahrbuch für Deutsche Geschichte (1992). For their comments on an early draft in English translated by Pamela Selwyn I am grateful to the participants of the Wiener Seminar at Tel Aviv University, 1991–92. Special thanks to Billie Melman for her constructive criticism. Marlene Schoofs took care of my linguistic problems and patiently corrected the worst of my "denglisch" sentences.

development also conforms, to some extent, to Marx's analysis in 1844, in which he concluded that the German critique of religion had already taken place. His description of the future historical process was also a program: "The critique of Heaven is transformed . . . into a critique of Earth, the critique of religion into that of law, the critique of theology into the critique of politics."[3] Indeed, compared with the 1840s, Wilhelmine society was characterized by a greater degree of secularization. Large sectors of both the middle and working classes had distanced themselves from the church and Christianity. Among the educated Protestant middle class, the main source of membership for the feminist movement, indifference to the church and traditional religion had defused much of the explosiveness of religious critique.

Nevertheless, we should not let this fact blind us to the considerable political and social influence that organized religion continued to exercise. Though secularization and de-Christianization affected ever greater segments of society from the 1870s on, a large portion of the population remained within the fold of the church. Women across the social spectrum were especially devoted churchgoers, so that one can speak of a "feminization of religion" in the nineteenth century that intensified in its last decades.[4] Women were also particularly affected by the power of the church. Well into the twentieth century, the churches zealously sought to protect religious norms regarding gender, which legitimated the relative placement in society of the sexes, with women almost invariably accorded a lower status than men. The Protestant and Catholic churches, as the two largest religious communities in Germany, played a decisive role in obstructing women's emancipatory efforts.

Against this background, the creation of a confessional-religious women's movement at the turn of the century is thus all the more remarkable. Until recently, this phenomenon has received comparatively little attention, mainly because feminist historians looking for the roots of the new women's movement have largely ignored the conservatively oriented church organizations. They have thereby failed to do justice to the historical significance of the confessional women's movement, which in quantitative terms was sometimes much more successful than secular feminism. Its influence, however, was felt in more than sheer numbers: On the one hand, the confessional women's movement contributed to the proliferation of emancipatory ideas among religious persons who could not be won over by secular feminism; but on the other hand, it sometimes had a problematic impact on secular feminism, impeding more radical aims such as the decriminalization of abortion. It is this ambivalent influence that makes the whole area of religious women's movements extremely interesting.[5]

ORGANIZATIONAL STRUCTURES AND MEMBERSHIP FIGURES

Among the many Protestant and Catholic women's organizations in the Kaiserreich and the Weimar Republic, only two, the German Protestant Women's League (*Deutsch-Evangelischer Frauenbund—DEF*), founded in 1899, and the League of Catholic Women (*Katholischer Deutscher Frauenbund—KDF*), founded in 1903, saw themselves as connected to the (secular) women's movement. The secular women's movement of the nineteenth century was the organizational response to a discussion that dated back to the late eighteenth century, usually known as the "Woman Question." This expression embodies the problematic nature that the age-old subordination of women had acquired for the new bourgeois society. On a general level, the aim of feminism or the women's movement—I use the two terms interchangeably—was to integrate women into civil society as equal members. The goal was not merely to right certain wrongs, such as women's lack of access to education, but rather to improve their lot more generally by overcoming their second-class status. Autonomy was a fundamental axiom for the women's movement, at once the final goal and organizational principle. Women were to bring about their own emancipation.

Deviating in several respects from this ideal type of secular feminism, both wings of the religious women's movement shared many of its goals.[6] Both the DEF and the KDF were, from the beginning, if to differing degrees, autonomous women's voluntary associations that stood outside the organizational structure of the church. Unlike the contemporary women's organizations under the aegis of the churches, such as the Protestant Women's Aid and the Catholic Young Women's and Mothers' Associations, the DEF and KDF had a female leadership. The DEF was particularly adamant in this regard, from the beginning relegating its statutory male board (composed mainly of clerics) to a purely advisory role.[7] As befitted Catholicism's more authoritarian structure, the Catholic women were more dependent upon the benevolence of their church in order to exist as an independent Catholic association. Thus the KDF suspended its activities almost completely for nine months after its founding in autumn of 1903 because the Church withheld official recognition. Only after some changes were made to the KDF's statutes were they approved by the cardinal responsible for the archdiocese of Cologne, the city where the organization had its headquarters. The new statutes stipulated that the League's ecclesiastical board would have not merely an advisory function but also voting authority.[8]

The two organizations also differed considerably in their patterns of growth, which mirrored the structural differences of Catholicism and Protestantism in Germany. Until World War I, DEF membership increased steadily. In 1914 there were 15,600 members in 134 local chapters. Growth slowed during the war years to 2,600 new members and three additional local groups. In 1919, membership fell somewhat, to 17,600, rising fairly continuously over the next decade to 33,000. In 1929, the DEF had 185 local groups. Compared to the KDF and the largest Church-run women's group, the Protestant Women's Aid, the DEF membership seems rather modest. Viewed as part of the bourgeois women's movement, however, the DEF managed to organize many more women than secular feminist organizations like the various women suffrage leagues, which counted only a few thousand members in the Kaiserreich. With forty thousand members in 1912, the KDF far outstripped its Protestant sister organizations before 1914, and the gap widened later. Unlike the DEF, the KDF grew disproportionately during and after the war. Membership passed the 110,000 mark in 1918, and the number almost doubled to 210,000 two years later, only to peak at 230,000 in 1922. By the end of the Weimar Republic, the figure decreased to 200,000, but the number of local groups continued to rise and had reached 1,300–1,400 by 1932.[9]

The reasons for the difference in membership figures must be sought first in the Catholic and Protestant women's movements' relationships to their respective churches, as well as in the different social-moral milieus in which each movement was embedded. Unlike the KDF, the DEF was only moderately successful in its initial goal of incorporating other Protestant women's associations. From 1910, the Catholic women's movement enjoyed extensive support from the Church.[10] The Protestant church, meanwhile, leant its support not to the DEF, but to the Protestant Women's Aid—founded in the same year—which quickly became the largest churchwomen's organization and in which male clerics held the most important leadership positions, at least until World War I. The Women's Aid devoted itself exclusively to parish work and, unlike the DEF, was most widespread in rural areas. The two organizations also had rather different social profiles. The mainly urban DEF recruited its members from the upper social strata. The fathers, husbands, and brothers of its adherents were mainly high-ranking bureaucrats, jurists, and churchmen. Members of the Women's Aid were more likely to come from the small-town lower-middle classes of artisans and shopkeepers. In highly industrialized regions with a confessionally mixed population, such as Westphalia, women from proletarian backgrounds also joined local chapters, although here, too, offices were reserved for the "better classes," particularly noblewomen. While the Women's Aid apparently attracted wives and mothers who did not work outside the home, the program of the DEF, with its emphasis on better educational and employment opportunities for women as part of a Christian answer to the "Woman Question," was attractive to many unmarried, salaried, and professional women.[11]

The KDF's social structure combined elements of both the DEF and the Women's Aid. In its first decade the KDF was mainly a middle-class urban movement. Apart from a few representatives of the Catholic nobility, the organization was dominated by the female relatives of higher civil servants, physicians, and politicians of the Center Party. From 1912, the KDF managed to penetrate other social groups, which led to its impressive growth during the war. While gaining more members from the lower-middle and working classes, the organization also increased its rural chapters, although the cities remained a strong base even in the late 1920s.[12] Like the Women's Aid, the KDF was mainly an organization of housewives because employed women from the working and lower-middle classes tended to be organized in special occupational church associations, while Catholic women represented only a tiny minority in the educated professions.

The social heterogeneity of the KDF (compared to the DEF and Women's Aid) was characteristic of the Catholic community, whose combination of religious, regional, political, and cultural traditions and socioeconomic way of life had no Protestant parallel. Protestantism had no forum for political action comparable to the Catholic Center Party, and the Protestant Church was prevented, by genuine theological considerations, from presenting itself as an authoritarian "institution of salvation" which sought the greatest possible influence over the daily lives of its flock. This was the function of the Catholic community, a tight network of parish, regional, and national associations which, together with the Catholic press and the Center Party, formed a social subsystem comparable to that of socialist workers' culture. This highly diverse milieu drew its inner cohesion largely from the fact that it had developed in opposition to the mainly Protestant liberal-bourgeois culture in Germany, and was thus the expression of an underprivileged minority.[13] Protestantism, as the religion of the majority (until 1945, three-fifths of the German population), which also was closely linked to the ruling elites, at least until 1918, was not a distinct social milieu. Rather, it was split both theologically and politically into conservative and liberal wings.[14]

PLATFORMS AND PROGRAMS BEFORE 1914

Until World War I, feminist discussions and activities concentrated on three main areas that were also central for the confessional women's movement: the "morality problem," which raised questions of sexual standards and gender relations; the so-called social question, which focused on the situation of wage labor; and the broad spectrum of demands for women's right to legal, economic, and political integration in civil society. Over the years, the DEF and KDF took up a number of feminist positions in all three areas, particularly in the fields of educational and social policy. After the turn of the century, the religious women's movement largely adopted the demands for women's admission to the universities, the hiring of women teachers for the upper classes of girls' secondary schools, and the reform of girls' education. The KDF, however, advocated a specifically "feminine" schooling for girls.[15]

Both wings of the religious women's movement were intensely involved in questions of sexual morality. The "morality problem" had a particular significance for the DEF. For the Protestant women's movement, the state regulation of prostitution, practiced in the Kaiserreich on the basis of §361.6 of the Imperial Penal Code, flagrantly violated the principle of a single moral standard for both sexes, which they saw as essential for the "religious and ethical renewal of national life." Regulation thus presented a double challenge to conscientious DEF members—as women and as Christians—which explains the importance the DEF accorded the "morality problem" as a "central issue for the entire women's movement."[16] In the beginning, the DEF's policy against regulation was in line with that of the Protestant men's social purity associations, which sought the criminalization of commercial vice. From 1904 on, however, the DEF joined forces with the Abolitionist Federation (active in Germany since 1899), and thus distanced itself openly for the first time from its spiritual fathers. Apparently they had reached the conclusion that the criminalization of prostitution would only undermine the struggle against the sexual double standard, since in practice it would only affect women, particularly those of the poorer classes. At the same time, the DEF rejected the Federation's liberal approach, which sought to separate the moral from the legal aspects of prostitution and to protect the private sphere from state intervention.[17] Nevertheless, the DEF's campaigns against regulation, and the confinement of prostitutes in state-sanctioned brothels, organized together with other women's associations on abolitionist principles, represent an important link between the Protestant and bourgeois women's movements. Of all the religious women's associations, the DEF expressed the most far-reaching position on the prostitution issue, insofar as they joined the moderates in the secular women's movement on the question of the regulation of prostitution. Both the KDF and the Jewish Women's League (founded in 1904) stopped short of demanding the abolition of regulation and limited themselves to social and charitable rescue work on behalf of "fallen" and endangered women.

The religious women's movement also increasingly turned its attention to the gradual loosening of "Victorian" sexual morality since the turn of the century. The postulate of sexual liberation, as expressed by parts of the radical wing of the secular women's movement, but mainly by the Federation for the Protection of Mothers (BfM) (founded in Berlin in 1905), was greeted with horror by the confessional women's movement. The BfM supported social recognition for unmarried mothers, legal equality for illegitimate children, and the easing of divorce laws. It also demanded access to contraceptives and the decriminalization of abortion as prerequisites for freely chosen motherhood. In its rejection of the "New Ethics," the religious women's movement found itself in accord with the "moderates" in the Federation of German Women's Associations (BDF). The Jewish Women's League (JFB) and the DEF joined them and managed to gain majority support in the BDF for their position on the "New Ethics" and especially for their rejection of the radicals' demand for the abolition of §218 of the anti-abortion law in 1908. The agreement between the religious women's movement and the secular "moderates" stemmed in large part from mutual mistrust of the idea of sexual freedom, for which they feared women would have to pay the final price. The demand for "moral self-restraint,"[18] which dominated the sexuality discussion of the Catholic, Protestant, Jewish, and "moderate" secular women's movements, can be interpreted as a strategy to defend women against male-dominated sexuality without renouncing the traditional gender order.

In contrast to the Protestant Women's Aid and the Catholic Mothers' Associations, with their traditional philanthropic activities at the parish level, the DEF and KDF oriented themselves more toward social policy. They were interested not merely in alleviating immediate suffering, but also in effecting structural change to eliminate the causes of social problems. The leadership of the DEF and KDF agreed that the "social question" was a structural consequence of industrialization, and not primarily of spiritual and moral decay.[19] Both Leagues sought to apply these principles by encouraging the professionalization of female social work and the self-help of working-class women, as well as by supporting social-policy initiatives. The DEF and KDF founded or supported working women's associations and tried to organize groups of women, such as home workers (*Heimarbeiterinnen*) and waitresses, who had been ignored by the trade unions.[20] Both supported the Christian trade unions, which were not very popular with the Protestant Church because they were mainly Catholic and sharply rejected by segments of the Catholic episcopate because they were officially interdenominational. Thus, the KDF was also affected by the so-called trade-union conflict, which weighed heavily on German Catholicism in the period before 1914.[21]

Alongside "self-help," state aid was to improve "the lot of the unpropertied classes" through a continuation of social legislation.[22] The DEF explicitly demanded the expansion of protective factory legislation for women, especially pregnant and nursing mothers, and the hiring of more female factory inspectors. In addition, it supported greater equality in employment, adopting the maxim "equal pay for equal work" and demanded active and passive voting rights in the commercial courts and trade boards. The KDF had a less-developed social-policy program, which can probably be attributed to the fact that the National Association for Catholic Germany (founded in 1890) and, of course, the Center Party itself, were both very active in the social-policy field. The conservative Protestant milieu was far behind in this regard, and the DEF, with its orientation toward the bourgeois women's movement and the Christian trade unions, represented one of the most progressive positions.

With the exception of proletarian feminism, which aspired to a socialist revolution, the secular women's movement's central aim was equal female participation in civil society. The most far-reaching demands for participation came in the political arena, with the call for women's suffrage from the 1890s. By 1908, when women gained the right to join political parties, the religious women's movement was confronted with the need to develop its own positions on women's suffrage. There were significant differences between the DEF and the KDF, which may be attributed to their divergent party-political attachments, as well as to the differing structures of the respective churches.

The Protestant women's movement focused its immediate attention on the possibility of equal participation in church activities. But the many petitions that the DEF sent to the various state and provincial synods between 1903 and 1918, demanding that they recognize women as equal members of the congregation, met with no success. It was not until after the Revolution of 1918–19, with the reform of the State-Church charters, that women were granted participation rights in the church. In 1908, the DEF published its position on political participation, which it was to retain unchanged until 1918.[23] The League, which perceived itself as representing the right wing of the bourgeois women's movement, was following power-political considerations. Their opposition to women's suffrage was motivated in large part by fears that it would increase the influence of the Social Democratic Party (SPD) and the Center Party. At the same time, the DEF explicitly claimed that there was no theoretical justification for excluding women from political participation. However, since the DEF did not distance itself too vigorously from women's suffrage, and indeed shared the BDF's demand for municipal voting rights, it encountered vehement disagreement, particularly in extremely reactionary Women's Aid circles, where all demands for women's church voting rights were also uncompromisingly rejected.[24] Dealing with the women's suffrage issue was less important in the Catholic arena. In contrast to Protestantism, where the teaching concerning the priesthood of all believers lent theological legitimacy to members' participation, the hierocratic character of Catholicism excluded any demands for suffrage within the Church. Thus, while Protestant clerics were confronted with demands for participation by female congregants, (who were much more active in church life than the men), their Catholic brothers were spared such bizarre requests and did not need to worry about relinquishing authority to female parish councils. Hence the entire issue of female participation, which had raised the suffrage question and caused so much controversy in Protestant church circles, was a non-issue for Catholics. The Church's reluctance to consider women as equal partners is demonstrated by the rejection of the KDF's 1908 petition to admit women to the annual Catholic conferences as full participants, a right they did not win until 1921.[25] Although German women finally received the right of political organization in May of 1908, the Catholic Center Party refused to admit women members.[26] But the Catholic clergy took into account the new situation created by the liberalization of the Association Law of 1908, to the extent that Michael Faulhaber (later Cardinal of Munich), declared at the annual Catholic meeting of 1909 that women's political participation was consistent with Catholic dogma. The Catholic Women's

League could therefore afford a benevolent neutrality on the suffrage question, but no more.[27] Significantly, the KDF never included the suffrage issue in its official platform.

WAR, REVOLUTION, AND THE DEVELOPMENT OF THE RELIGIOUS WOMEN'S MOVEMENT IN THE WEIMAR REPUBLIC

An examination of the activities of the Protestant and Catholic women's movements during World War I and in the Weimar Republic reveals both contrasting and kindred elements. While the movements differed widely in their relationship to the nation and the new state, there are similarities and connections in their positions on issues like the church and sexuality, and family and gender roles.

Until 1917, there were no substantial differences between the policies of the Protestant and Catholic women's movements regarding the war. Both Leagues competed in fulfilling their patriotic duties, without pausing to consider the problematic relationship between Christian ethics and war. Instead, both enthusiastically expressed faith in the "blessings of war," which were to stem the process of German society's "moral decline."[28] In 1917, though, social conflicts that had been set aside as part of a temporary war-effort truce (*Burgfrieden*) broke out anew, and the political fronts hardened. The Protestant Women's League clearly stood for an annexationist "war until victory" and opposed the policy of domestic reform advocated by those forces embarking on a democratization of the Constitution. The Catholic Women's League, by contrast, expressed a "longing for peace" in the September 1917 issue of its journal, implicitly referring to the Reichstag's July 19 peace resolution, which had passed with the votes of Social Democrats, Left-Liberals, and the Center Party, provoking the bitter opposition of the political Right. The KDF, however, also emphasized the need to stand fast and, like the DEF, expressed its devotion to the Empress and Crown Princess as late as October 1918.[29]

On November 12, 1918 the Government of National Deputies introduced women's suffrage in Germany by decree. Protestants reacted promptly; the same circles which only a short time before had loudly condemned any political participation by women now devoted their efforts to mobilizing women for the protection of the conservative interests against the revolutionary challenge and proclaimed that women's right to vote was a duty to vote. The DEF likewise adapted to the new political circumstances and worked side by side with its former enemies in the church to win women for the political Right. In a similar way, from the autumn of 1918, the KDF applied itself to organizing "the entry of Catholic women into politics" in support of the Center Party.[30]

It is doubtless rather ironic that precisely those political forces which had most vehemently opposed women's political equality profited most from women's votes.[31] In the elections to the constitutional National Assembly in 1919, in which 82.3 percent of women voters participated—not much less than the percentage of male voters—slightly more female than male votes went to the German National People's Party (DNVP), a trend that only increased in the course of the Weimar Republic. A glance at the Catholic Center, with its larger surplus of female votes, makes it clear that it was, above all, the religious component that won women voters for the Center and decidedly Protestant-Christian DNVP. The support of religious women's organizations, particularly the DEF and KDF, was of decisive importance. They not only did campaign work but also represented a significant recruiting ground for party functionaries.

The political differences between the two Leagues emerged most clearly in their responses to military defeat and revolution. Thus the November 1918 issue of the *Evangelische Frauenzeitung* contained an early version of the "stab-in-the-back" legend (according to which Liberals and Social Democrats were to blame for Germany's defeat), which was absent from the KDF's publications.[32] If we compare the two organizations' official statements after the revolutionary ninth of November, it is striking how quickly the KDF returned to business as usual. In a clear thrust against the now-ruling socialist parties, it called upon women to support the Center Party in the upcoming elections to the German National Assembly. The defeat and the abdication of the Emperor were passed off in a few short and sober sentences. By comparison, the reaction to socialist initiatives to introduce a separation of Church and State was harsh. Referring to the "most sacred feelings of the community of believers," the KDF issued a call to arms against this policy that had been initiated by the Prussian Ministry of Education and Cultural Affairs.[33] The Protestant women's movement also accorded the anti-socialist movement a high priority. A leading article that appeared in the December 1918 issue of the DEF journal *Evangelische Frauenzeitung*, entitled "What Now?" and written by DEF chairwoman Paula Müller (1865–1946), expressed the confusion with which the organization's leadership had reacted to the collapse of the Hohenzollern monarchy. The widespread shock felt by the Protestant elites in the wake of military defeat and the end of the Kaiserreich is palpable in her comment that: "We were so shaken by events that we moved about as if in an evil dream." In contrast to many others, including conservative circles, the Protestant women's movement's distress at the "toppling of the ruling house, the forced separation from our Empress," was sincere; their identification with the monarchy was, after all, religiously colored, since the Emperor was also the titular head of the church. Like conservative Protestantism more generally, the DEF was unable to overcome the trauma of 1918. The orientation toward the DNVP, initiated by the DEF leadership in 1918–19 (although it remained controversial among the membership), and the obsession with the notions of the "stab in the back" and the "war guilt lie," hindered the development of a positive attitude toward the Weimar Republic.

From the outset, the KDF had fewer problems adjusting, partly because Catholics, less emotionally attached to the Kaiserreich, also had more opportunities for high political office and influence within the new state. While the so-called national Protestantism of large segments of the churchgoing population had combined religious creed and German nationalism in an unholy alliance, German Catholicism was much less susceptible to nationalist sentiments. The detailed explanation that KDF chairwoman and Center Deputy Hedwig Dransfeld (1871–1925) published of her party's vote in favor of the Treaty of Versailles in the National Assembly may have been full of national pathos, but it was sustained by the rational patriotism that characterized the politics of the Catholic women's movement in the Weimar Republic.[34] They supported the League of Nations on principle, expressed pacifist sympathies, and in 1932 published an article in the League's journal on the need to "overcome nationalism" in the interest of "perfecting nations."[35]

Such positions would have been unthinkable in the DEF. There were, however, areas where the politics of the Protestant and Catholic women's movements overlapped. Thus, both Leagues voted unanimously "for the recognition of Christianity as the life force of the German people."[36] In practice, this meant that they fought all attempts on the part of the socialist parties to introduce a thorough French-style separation of Church and State. More specifically, both movements battled successfully for the maintenance of confessional religious education in nondenominational schools and for the continued existence of denominational primary schools, which constituted some eighty percent of the elementary schools in Germany in 1931.[37] The success of mass protests organized by the churches against the SPD's planned secularization program in 1918 and 1919 can be attributed not least to the work of confessional women's associations. Issues around the catchwords "family" and "morality" attracted a great deal of attention in both organizations. The KDF tended to combine its complaints over what it saw as moral decay with a critique of urban life. Berlin, in particular, was seen as a den of iniquity that represented, as Dransfeld explained in 1921, "the most dangerous source of infection for our nation's spiritual sickness."[38] Big cities, "places of cold reason and commercial calculation," where the rhythm and tempo of the machine penetrated every corner of life, became symbols of the secularization and industrialization that ran counter to the Catholic ideal of organic vitality.[39]

It is curious, given the widespread aversion to the metropolis among conservative Protestant cultural critics as well, that the subject is all but absent in the publications of the Protestant women's movement in stark contrast to the notoriously anti-urban Women's Aid.[40] The DEF was, nevertheless, also heavily disquieted by the "moral decline of the nation," even if the KDF's obsession with sexual license tended to be more pronounced.[41] Both Leagues deplored "the excesses of female fashion" and demanded a law to protect the young against trash and dirt, a law that passed in the Reichstag in 1926, signaling the increasing cooperation between the Catholic Center and the DNVP.[42] Probably around the same time, the DEF began a leaflet campaign against the supposed increase in female homosexuality, which it characterized as the "swamp flower" of an "aging culture."[43] It will come as no surprise that the two branches of the confessional women's movement joined forces against initiatives to repeal the anti-abortion law. The KDF was perhaps even more alarmed than the DEF by falling birth rates, which it attributed, above all, to women's "addiction to comfort" and the "fateful decline" in their "devotion to others."[44] From the mid-1920s on, the Protestant church, in contrast to the Catholic one, no longer officially condemned contraception.[45] Catholic intransigence on the issue of birth control, cemented by the papal encyclical *Casti connubi* of 1930, also affected the KDF's position on the planned reform of the divorce laws, which brought down the Center Party and the DNVP. Helene Weber (1881–1962), for example, a leading representative of the Catholic women's movement and member of the Reichstag for the Center Party, categorically rejected the proposed introduction of irretrievable breakdown of marriage as grounds for divorce.[46] The DEF, by contrast—here not entirely in line with the Protestant conservatives—considered this reform unavoidable, while at the same time condemning tendencies toward a "frivolous and irresponsible dissolution of marriage."[47]

On the marriage question, the DEF and KDF differed fundamentally in their attitudes toward gender relations. The KDF, for example, opposed the equality of husband and wife as set forth in Article

118 of the Constitution because it contradicted the Catholic doctrine of male supremacy in marriage. The fact that the KDF, following the party line, voted against the repeal of the marriage bar for
female civil servants shows the depth of Catholic difficulties with
the concept of equality.[48] The DEF welcomed the repeal of the marriage bar for women civil servants. They also did not publish any
statements opposing legal equality, which, after all, did not formally
conflict with Protestant dogma. In practical terms, though, this fundamental difference between the DEF and KDF had virtually no political consequences.

In the period after 1918, the Catholic and Protestant women's
movements lost the militant quality that, with varying intensity,
had characterized their actions and self-perception before the war.
Their partial opposition to traditional female roles in church and society seemed overturned by the revolutionary upheavals after 1918.
The opening of new spheres of activity and achievements coincided
with a far-reaching modernization crisis, which cast a shadow of
anxiety over emancipation for many women. In a 1929 article, Dran-
feld's successor, KDF Chairwoman Gerta Krabbel, described the developments in a way that applied equally to the DEF. The early
period of the confessional women's movement, she wrote, with its
impulse "to participate in the spiritual struggle for women's independence and freedom, to gain this freedom and at the same time
loyally to protect the faith and the community of the church . . . had
been a period of struggle and conquest." "Nowadays, however," she
lamented, everything was "completely different." "The period of
struggle is, by and large, over. Freedom has been won, everything is
possible. . . . Woman today is in the peculiar position of walking
new, untrodden paths at the same time as the place which was always her very own is threatened as never before."[49] This text reveals
the ambivalence many women experienced in view of the new situation after the war. Several unsettling developments—economic
downward mobility and insecurity of status, which affected the middle-class milieus of many DEF and KDF members, the growing fluidity of gender roles in the public and private spheres and the
acceleration in secularization deeply felt by contemporaries—led to
a strengthening of conservative elements in the confessional
women's movement. This conservatism was increased in the case of
the DEF by the fixation on the "national question," and in the case
of the KDF by the fear of the "masculinization" of women and the
widening gap between Catholic norms and actual sexual behavior.
Attachment to their respective confessional and party political
alliances also played a part in keeping religious women from self-

confidently taking the initiative and demanding improvements in their situation in church and society. Two examples may illustrate the practical implications of this process.

On the question of admitting women to church office, particularly the ministry, both the Protestant and Catholic women's movements reacted purely defensively. To be sure, the DEF supported the demand of the Federation of Protestant Women Theologians that the church create a special pastoral profession for women. Like the organized women theologians, however, the DEF emphasized that it did not seek full admission of women to the ministry. In 1927, women were admitted as vicars in some of the state churches, and the League, which had previously demanded women's equal participation in the congregation, made no further demands during the Weimar Republic, although they did not want to exclude for all time the possibility of women in the pulpit.[50] The KDF reacted more vehemently to those voices in Catholicism that saw no fundamental obstacle to women priests. With its assertion that admission to the priesthood could "never be part of the Catholic women's movement's program," the KDF was indeed far removed from any such "suffragette" aberrations.[51]

The second example, which concerns women's employment, is more complicated because, on this front, both wings of the religious women's movement were least ready to give up feminist interests. Ever since the founding of the Universal Association of German Women in 1865, female employment had been a central theme of the women's movement. The KDF devoted much energy to this issue during the Weimar Republic; in particular, professional Catholic women felt that they had to catch up with the Protestant-influenced secular women's movement.[52] The KDF presented some results of its debate at its tenth General Meeting in 1927, which was devoted to the theme "Women's Occupations and Women's Vocation." It is striking that almost every lecture emphasized employment outside the home not as a necessary evil, but rather as an improvement not only for women, but for the whole society, expressing Catholic women's new self-confidence, forged in confrontations with the widespread disapproval of employed women in the conservative religious milieu. Women identified with their work, and this was clearly not limited to the liberal professions. Factory workers and craftswomen also spoke at the congress, criticizing the "general devaluation of women's labor" and, in particular, the notion that paid employment was only a transitional phase in women's lives. The plenary passed a resolution demanding not only the expansion of social insurance and protective factory legislation for women (the latter

being traditional Center Party policy), but also, in light of contemporary "rationalization and mechanization," calling for more attention
to human needs in the organization of the economy.[53]

When it came to married women's employment, however, which
was coming increasingly under fire during the severe economic crisis at the end of the Weimar Republic, the Catholic spirit of affirmation was sadly lacking among Catholic women. The KDF was not
blind to problems in the campaign against two-wage families, but
believed it had to support a marriage bar for female civil servants
and did not hesitate to remind women of their "true duty," the "service of life." It legitimized all potential hardships in advance by re-
marking that "the right of the higher idea, the living realization of
marriage and family, takes precedence over the rights of the individual."[54] Accordingly, the KDF gave its full support to the law on the
status of female civil servants, passed by the Reichstag in May of
1932, which authorized the dismissal of married women.[55] The DEF
was no more critical of the new law, although it had expressed
"strong misgivings" only a year before.[56] Perhaps the uneasiness
many women felt can be extrapolated from the DEF's avoidance of
any commentary on the discriminatory legislation. Interestingly
enough, though, it was precisely the subject of women's employment that finally sparked the DEF to criticize the emerging National
Socialists.

The Religious Women's Movement and the Rise of National Socialism

Like their Protestant sisters, the Catholic women's movement was
late in its critical appraisal of National Socialism. Even after the
Nazis' electoral success of 1930, the KDF continued to concentrate
on the dangers of Bolshevism. It was not until after the elections of
July of 1932 that KDF spokeswomen warned against the "gaudy slogans of the 'Third Reich'" and a "new revolution" of those who denied women's abilities and desired only a "male-oriented state."
They urgently exhorted women not to succumb to the "restless-
ness" of the masses who "run longingly behind the Führer," an "illusory ideal."[57] Their appeal was not without success; according to
all election statistics, the Catholic population, and especially
Catholic women, were notably resistant to Hitler's party, which cannot be said for large strata of Protestants. Whereas until the 1930s
the NSDAP (National Socialist German Workers' Party) was elected
mainly by (Protestant) men, in 1932 and 1933 the party was somewhat more successful among Protestant women.[58] Thus it is perhaps

explicable that when it came to criticizing the National Socialists, it was not one of the leaders of the Protestant women's movement, but rather an unknown thirty-one-year old lawyer, Elisabeth Schwartzhaupt, who entered the fray.[59] In May 1932, the *Evangelische Frauenzeitung* published an article by her that vigorously attacked Nazi anti-feminism. Schwartzhaupt particularly criticized the threatened expulsion of women from paid employment and accused fascist ideologues of femininity of "disregarding women as persons and reducing them to a purely biological function."[60] Reactions to the publication of this article revealed that the DEF harbored not a few members of the NSDAP. The editorial board responded to their "stormy criticisms" in two ways: It noted that the article had not criticized the party as such, with its domestic and foreign policy platform, and it printed a statement by a NSDAP supporter attempting to demonstrate the compatibility between the Protestant women's movement and National Socialism. But for the traditional conservatives in the DEF leadership, this expression of sympathy for the Nazis was not to be the last word in the debate. In the next issue of their house organ, the longtime Deputy Chairwoman Countess Selma von der Groeben presented an unambiguously critical assessment of the National Socialist position on the "Woman Question." Her declaration in favor of the women's movement, which she defined as "woman's struggle for her external and inner independence," accorded with the better traditions of German Protestantism, which viewed the "emergence from self-imposed tutelage" as the divinely ordained task of all rational beings.[61] Groeben dissected statements on the subject by "the much-admired Führer" with gentle sarcasm. She ridiculed National Socialist campaign propaganda, mimicking their verbal style in order to refute them: "No, German woman, nobody, not even Hitler, can give you back the honor of German woman- and motherhood, German family life, true sisterhood, if you do not earn and protect it yourself. . . . If only National Socialism can do this for you, you are to be pitied." Trapped in their own reactionary tendencies, many conservative Protestant women who, like Groeben herself, praised the Nazis' "patriotic sentiments," realized only too late the inappropriateness of subtle irony as a response to the National Socialist threat.

CONCLUSIONS

The establishment of the German Protestant's Women's League and the League of Catholic Women was largely motivated by fear of competition from the influence of liberal and socialist emancipatory programs. At the same time, both organizations expressed the need of religious women to work at liberating themselves from clerical tutelage. Their relationship to secular feminism was thus characterized simultaneously by distance and identification, competition and solidarity. Thus, the religious women's movement in Imperial Germany developed in the space between "rebellion and reaction." This ambivalence between conservative models and emancipatory interests continued after 1918, with a shift—stronger among DEF women than among their Catholic sisters—toward a more reactionary position.

War, defeat, and revolution, which brought women the right to vote, also caused a substantial change in the character of the confessional women's movement. Whereas previously the DEF and KDF, as independent organizations, had distanced themselves from traditional churchwomen's groups, and the DEF had fought anti-feminist positions within German Protestantism, now both Leagues emphasized ties to their respective denominational and political milieus. The KDF, with its close ties to the Catholic Center Party, was more directly involved in party politics. The DEF increasingly supported the work of the Protestant-conservative German National People's Party. For both wings of the religious women's movement in the Weimar Republic, the "Woman Question" took a back seat to party loyalty and the preservation of church and conservative prerogatives. In regard to questions of sexual standards and gender relations, as well as to the whole process of secularization, the DEF adopted perhaps a slightly more liberal attitude than the KDF; nonetheless, similarities between the two movements outweighed differences in their religious orientations. Both confessional organizations diverged, however, on central issues regarding the attitude to the military defeat and the new political order, according to their adherence to different parties. While the KDF essentially supported the Weimar Republic, broad segments of the Protestant conservative middle class, which the DEF to a large extent represented, rejected or even openly opposed it.

The different development of the Catholic and Protestant women's movements between 1900 and 1933 cannot be attributed primarily to religious and theological differences, but rather arose from divergent social and political contexts. To return to Marx's statement quoted at the beginning of this essay: German feminism from its early beginnings in the 1840s, and with its confessional wings (the DEF and the KDF) from around 1900, may indeed demonstrate that religious emancipation—at least in its most basic version of an inherent critique of unquestioned religious authority—is a necessary, if not sufficient, condition for women's emancipation. However, social and political conditions often determine whether religious emancipation can develop. Moreover, a consideration of the confessional women's movement in the period between 1914 and 1933 seems to bear out the Marxist assertion that social and political interests govern religious discourse.

In retrospect, the increasingly divergent positions of Catholicism and Protestantism on "women's role in church and society" are remarkable. The theological conditions for Protestant women's advancement in the second half of the twentieth century, based on the autonomy of the laity and the grounding of faith in the subject's self-reflection, were already present in the nineteenth century. But the political orientation of conservative Protestantism in Germany erected a firm barrier to the development of an emancipatory potential which, in Hegelian terms, is inherent in the "Protestant principle." Compared with Protestants, Catholics were, and are, more confined by the authoritarian and hierarchical structure of their church: to this very day, Catholic women are still fighting for the admission of women to the ministry. However, during the Weimar Republic, the Catholic Women's movement represented without any doubt the more progressive alternative to the reactionary-nationalist narrow-mindedness of their Protestant counterparts.

In light of all these different historical experiences, the relationship between religion and politics turns out to be extremely variable. It may be best understood as a complex equation, whose parts stand in relation to each other, without being reducible to each other, and where the relative weight of each part is determined by concrete historical conditions and circumstances.

NOTES

1. Karl Marx, *Frühschriften*, ed. Siegfried Landschut (Stuttgart, 1971), 208.

2. For a detailed account, see Sylvia Paletschek, *Frauen und Dissens: Frauen im Deutschkatholizismus und in den freien Gemeinden* (Göttingen, 1990).

3. Marx, *Frühschriften*, 208–9.

4. See Hugh McLeod, "Weibliche Frömmigkeit—männlicher Unglaube? Religion und Kirche im bürgerlichen 19. Jahrhundert," in Ute Frevert, ed., *Bürgerinnen und Bürger. Geschlechterverhältnisse im 19. Jahrhundert* (Göttingen, 1989), 134–56.

5. See Doris Kaufmann, *Frauen zwischen Aufbruch und Reaktion. Protestantische Frauenbewegung in der ersten Hälfte des 20. Jahrhunderts* (Munich, 1988); Ursula Baumann, *Protestantismus und Frauenemanzipation in Deutschland 1850–1920* (Frankfurt/M., 1992); Michael Phayer,

Protestant and Catholic Women in Nazi Germany (Detroit, 1990), which includes a critical discussion of Claudia Koonz, *Mothers in the Fatherland: Women, the Family and Nazi Politics* (London, 1987); Lucia Scherzberg, "Die katholische Frauenbewegung," in Wilfried Loth, ed., *Deutscher Katholizismus im Umbruch zur Moderne* (Stuttgart, 1991); Irmtraud Götz von Olenhusen, *Frauen unter dem Patriarchat der Kirchen. Katholikinnen und Protestantinnen im 19. Jahrhundert* (Stuttgart, 1996); Marion A. Kaplan, *The Making of the Jewish Middle Class: Women, Family and Identity in Imperial Germany* (New York, 1991).

6. The "real" secular feminism in Germany also deviated in many respects from this "ideal type." As in other countries, the German secular women's movement was not at all unified. Nonetheless, despite harsh fights between "moderates" and "radicals," who often seemed to speak different languages, their differences often concerned questions of strategy rather than of content, while the moderate wing also aimed at women's full citizenship.

7. Already in 1899, the year the League was founded, the DEF's first chairwoman Gertrud Knutzen declared self-confidently that the new organization was "not a nursery school . . . in which the men must be teachers and the women children. We are most grateful for male advice, but we must act on our own." *Chronik der Christlichen Welt 9* (1899): 260.

8. *Fünfundzwanzig Jahre Katholischer Deutscher Frauenbund* (Köln, 1928), 21, 76.

9. *Evangelischer Frauenkalender 1910–1919*; Paula Müller-Otfried, *Dreissig Jahre Deutsch-Evangelischer Frauenbund* (Hannover, 1929); *Fünfundzwanzig Jahre Katholischer Deutscher Frauenbund*; Hildegund Becker, "Der Katholische Deutsche Frauenbund in der katholisch-sozialen Bewegung" (hereafter "KDF") (Freiburg, 1966; unpublished ms. at the Staatsarchiv Freiburg).

10. See Becker, "KDF."

11. Baumann, *Protestantismus*, 131ff., and Nancy R. Reagin, "Bourgeois Women, Local Politics, and Social Change: The Women's Movement in Hanover, 1888–1933," (Ph.D. diss., Johns Hopkins University, 1990), 233ff.

12. *Fünfundzwanzig Jahre*, 121.

13. See Wilfried Loth, "Soziale Bewegungen im Katholizismus des Kaiserreichs," *Geschichte und Gesellschaft* 17 (1991): 279–310; Loth extends his depiction to 1933 in his article "Integration and Erosion: Wandlungen des katholischen Milieus in Deutschland," in Loth, ed., *Deutscher Katholizismus*, 266–78.

14. See Gangolf Hübinger, *Kulturprotestantismus und Politik* (Tübingen, 1994).

15. Archive of the KDF, Cologne (hereafter AKDF), minutes of the executive meeting, Mar. 25, 1914.

16. Paula Müller, *Modernes Leben und sittliche Ideale* (Berlin and Lichterfelde, 1912), 12–13.

17. For the following, see also Baumann, *Protestantismus*, 157–66.

18. Hedwig Dransfeld's explanations in the KDF journal *Christliche Frau*

(hereafter *CF*) 3 (1904/05): 373. For the Protestant side, see for example "Verhandlungen des Evangelisch-sozialen Kongresses 1907," 374.

19. Paula Müller, *Die Beteiligung der Frau an den sozialen Aufgaben der Gegenwart* (Berlin and Lichterfelde, 1908); *CF* 5 (1906/07): 157.

20. Baumann, *Protestantismus*, 174–86; *Fünfundzwanzig Jahre*, 58–62.

21. Karl-Egon Klönne, *Der politische Katholizismus* (Frankfurt/M., 1985); Michael Schneider, *Die christlichen Gewerkschaften 1894–1933* (Bonn, 1982).

22. Paula Müller, ed., *Handbuch zur Frauenfrage* (Berlin and Lichterfelde, 1908), 86.

23. Ibid., 122–23.

24. See, for example, the Women's Aid's journal *Frauenhülfe* (Nov. 1912): 317ff.

25. Becker, "KDF," 41.

26. Amy K. Hackett, "The Politics of Feminism in Wilhelmine Germany, 1890–1918" (Ph.D. diss., Columbia University, 1976), 404.

27. See *CF* 5 (1906/07): 405–11; 6 (1907/08): 77–81.

28. *CF* 12 (1913/14): 343; *Evangelische Frauenzeitung* (hereafter *EFZ*) 22 (1914): 170.

29. AKDF, minutes of the executive meeting, Oct. 18, 1918.

30. *CF* 16 (1918): 177ff.

31. See Joachim Hoffmann-Götting, *Emanzipation mit dem Stimmzettel. 70 Jahre Frauenwahlrecht in Deutschland* (Bonn, 1986).

32. *EFZ* 19 (1918/19): 10.

33. *CF* 16 (1918): 177–85.

34. *CF* 17 (1919): 97–109, 149–54.

35. See for example *CF* 20 (1922): 31; 21 (1923): 69–72; 25 (1927): 384; 30 (1932): 209.

36. *EFZ* 20 (1919/20): 1.

37. Geoffrey G. Field, "Religion in the German Volksschule, 1890–1928," *Leo Baeck Institute Yearbook* 25 (1980): 53.

38. *CF* 19 (1921): 2.

39. *CF* 23 (1925): 101; 30 (1932): 33.

40. See Shelley Baranowski, "The Sanctity of Rural Life: Protestantism, Agrarian Politics, and Nazism in Pomerania during the Weimar Republic," *German History* 9 (1991): 1–22.

41. *EFZ* 32 (1930/31): 81.

42. Margret F. Stieg, "The 1926 German Law to Protect Youth against Trash and Dirt: Moral Protectionism in a Democracy," *Central European History* 23 (1990): 48.

43. Archive of the DEF, Hanover, V5.

44. *CF* 20 (1922): 125; 24 (1926): 93.

45. Cornelie Usborne, "The Christian Churches and the Regulation of Sexuality in Weimar Germany," in Jim Obelkevich et al., eds., *Disciplines of Faith: Studies in Religion, Politics and Patriarchy* (London, 1987), 105–6. For the context of birth control and population policy, see Cornelie Usborne, *The Politics of the Body in Weimar Germany* (London, 1992).

46. *CF* 26 (1928): 367–68.; 28 (1930): 6–7.

47. *EFZ* 30 (1928/29): 56; 29 (1927/28): 107.

48. *CF* 17 (1919): 168–69. and 17172.

49. *CF* 27 (1929): 143–44.

50. *EFZ* 28 (1926/27): 120.

51. *CF* 20 (1922): 31, 83ff.

52. *CF* 19 (1921): 184–85.

53. *CF* 25 (1927): 236–37.

54. *CF* 29 (1931): 73.

55. *CF* 30 (1932): 181–82.

56. *EFZ* 32 (1930/31): 31.

57. *CF* 30 (1932): 202. See also Laura Gellot and Michael Phayer, "Dissenting Voices: Catholic Women in Opposition to Fascism," *Journal of Contemporary History* 22 (1987): 91–114 (primarily about Austria).

58. This, however, does not justify the myth of women's responsibility for Hitler's success. For the most comprehensive research, see Jürgen W. Falter, *Hitlers Wähler* (Munich, 1991), 143ff., 169–93. An informative case study on Protestant women's attitudes toward the NS-System is Heide-Marie Lauterer, *Liebestätigkeit für die Volksgemeinschaft. Der Kaiserswerther Verband deutscher Diakonissenmutterhäuser in den ersten Jahren des NS-Regimes* (Göttingen, 1994).

59. For Schwartzhaupt's biography, see Jochen-Christoph Kaiser, ed., *Frauen in der Kirche. Evangelische Frauenverbände im Spannungsfeld von Kirche und Gesellschaft 1890–1945* (Düsseldorf, 1985), 141.

60. *EFZ* 33 (1931/32): 122–23.

61. *EFZ* 33 (1931/32): 136.

Ideological Crossroads

Feminism, Pacifism, and Socialism

Amira Gelblum

On the eve of World War I, Bertha von Suttner (1843–1914), the first woman to receive the Nobel Peace Prize (1905), called upon women to express their feelings concerning war:

> We won't be deterred by the accusation of being sentimentalists. We women have the right to show our feelings. Over the ages . . . we as mothers have had the privilege of hating war. . . . Let our hearts speak. . . .[1]

Suttner died a week before the assassination in Sarajevo, and it was left to the feminists who lived through the war to put their feminist and pacifist convictions to the test. A prevailing sentiment among feminists before the war had been that, as women and as mothers, it was natural for them to oppose war.[2] But the outbreak of World War I forced European feminists to clarify their position beyond general pacifist declarations. It also obliged them to articulate their definitions of masculinity and femininity when faced with the new division of labor in a society at war. Furthermore, they had to make a clear choice between nationalism—loyalty to their country—and internationalism—solidarity with women of all countries. In this essay I shall examine how these dilemmas were dealt with by two leading German feminists, Anita Augspurg (1857–1943) and Lida Gustava Heymann (1868–1943), and trace the transformation they underwent as a result of their experience of war and revolution.[3] Before the war they were liberal, equal-rights feminists. During the war they were ardent pacifists and among the founders of the Women's International League for Peace and Freedom (WILPF). After the war they moved from feminist pacifism toward socialism and elaborated a vision of a just and nonviolent society that would be governed by what they perceived as "feminine" values.

* * *

In the years leading to World War I, the bourgeois German women's movement was imbued with a vague notion of pacifism. Most feminists expressed their desire for peace and their rejection of war, having internalized traditional stereotypical images of women as nurturers and natural peacemakers. In their attempts to prove that women were worthy of equal rights, feminists often argued that women had a beneficial influence on society, including a pacifying effect. Alongside this essentialist feminist pacifism, other feminists called for pacifism based on the ideas of human rights and solidarity, internationalism, and the sanctity of life. This was the position adopted by radicals within the women's movement, whose leaders included Augspurg and Heymann. They followed the German feminist pacifist Margarethe Leonore Selenka (1860–1923) who, in 1889, had urged the organization of annual women's peace demonstrations all over the world, arguing that women's issues and peace issues were in essence part of the same struggle for "the rule of the law against the rule of force."[4] However, until 1914, there was very little pacifist activity within the women's movement, and the borderlines between essentialism and universalism, both in feminism and pacifism, were unclear. Both lines of argument were frequently used interchangeably, despite inherent logical contradictions.

With the outbreak of war, feminists were confronted with the dilemma of supporting the national cause or remaining loyal to their ideals of pacifism and internationalism. In these deliberations we find practical considerations as well as ideological ones. Would the "nation" reward "good citizenship" and patriotism? As soon became evident, most feminists—like the socialists—chose nationalism over internationalism and rushed to support their belligerent governments. Within the first months of war it became clear that only a minority would adhere to their prewar notion of pacifism and develop it as a central and integral part of their feminism, based on universal and/or essentialist grounds.

This minority, alongside the socialist feminists, has become a favored subject of research over the last two decades. Women's opposition to World War I has been documented and idealized in the search for origins and role models for present-day feminist pacifism. The war has thus become the pivotal point in the study of feminism and pacifism, while the interwar years have been examined mainly for the effect female suffrage had on feminism.[5] But the roots of postwar feminism lie in the prewar period, and the effect of the war on feminism can be fully comprehended only by examining the prewar and postwar period as a continuum. In the case of Germany it is also crucial to consider the impact of the November Revolution of 1918 on the development of feminist ideas between the two world wars.

* * *

Augspurg and Heymann were leading figures of the radical wing of the German bourgeois feminist movement (*Bund Deutscher Frauenvereine*—BDF) in the 1890s and founders of the German suffrage movement in 1902.[6] Their prewar activities encompassed the struggle for better education and professional opportunities for women and legal changes in the status of married women, and opposition to state regulation of prostitution, and culminated in the campaign for the vote. By the turn of the century, Augspurg and Heymann had become a couple, and they lived together until their death in exile in 1943. Since the Nazis confiscated and destroyed their private papers, there is very little source material concerning their personal life, and their biographer is therefore limited to studying their public and political writing and utterances.

They both came from an educated middle-class background and supported left-liberal parties. The couple's prewar feminism drew on the principles of individualism, equal rights, democracy, and universalism. They rejected the ideology of "separate spheres" and called for the inclusion of women in all walks of life, regarding political equality as a primary goal. Unlike feminists of the moderate wing within the BDF, who believed that women were essentially different from men and should therefore be given rights so that their unique female influence could be exerted in the public sphere, Augspurg and Heymann rejected the accepted gender division of labor in society and based their emancipation demands on the tradition of equal human rights.[7] Nonetheless, by 1910, they too began to speak of women's difference and uniqueness, notions that had hitherto been drawn on by the moderates; they no longer urged women to participate with men in political parties. It seems that the main reason for the shift toward essentialist and separatist attitudes was their disappointment with the left-liberal parties' refusal to include the demand for women's political rights in their manifestos.[8] Augspurg and Heymann strongly criticized "male politics" and attempted to develop a different, feminist definition of politics. Their call for separatist political action necessitated a theoretical foundation, which developed gradually as their feminism shifted away from liberal premises of human rights to a gendered value system. But it was not until World War I that these ideas germinated into a full-scale, feminist-pacifist ideology.

* * *

When the war broke out, feminists found themselves divided according to their positions on war and nationalism, but both camps sought to justify their stance by appealing to women in terms of their role as mothers. Thus, Gertrud Bäumer (1873–1954), leader of the BDF, argued that it was women's biology and vocation as mothers that obliged them to mobilize in aid of the war effort. At the other end of the political spectrum the Social Democrat Clara Zetkin (1857–1933) called upon women to oppose the "imperialist war" as mothers and wives.[9] The majority of organized women in Germany followed Bäumer's lead and, despite their professed abhorrence of war, regarded themselves as "mothers of the nation," thereby subordinating their feminism to nationalism. Thus the BDF mobilized women in support of the war effort on the home front in full cooperation with the civil and military authorities.[10]

Augspurg and Heymann, alongside other leading radicals such as Helene Stöcker (1869–1943) and Auguste Kirschhoff (1867–1940), chose the path of feminist pacifism. Distancing themselves from the nationalist war hysteria, the feminist pacifists remained true to the internationalist character of the prewar women's movement, having participated during the prewar years in international organizations such as the International Women's Suffrage Alliance and the International Abolitionist Federation.[11] Their priority continued to be international solidarity among women. Adhering to these principles, Augspurg and Heymann were to emerge from the experiences of the war with a clearly formulated feminist-pacifist theory. They came to understand war and society in terms of gender, identifying men with values and characteristics of power and aggression (the "male principle") and aspiring to a society based on the "female principle"— nurture, mutual aid, and nonviolence.

* * *

Writing their joint autobiography in exile in 1941, Heymann described her and Augspurg's first reaction to the news of the outbreak of war:

> Firstly: help can be obtained only from women. Secondly: We would not do any work that would directly support war-aims, such as hospital-service, nursing the wounded. To make the half-dead live and healthy in order to send them back to the same or worse suffering? No, we would not give in to such madness.[12]

Not only did they totally reject war, but they also spurned even the role of women in war as nurses. A closer look at the actual events of the time, however, raises doubts as to the veracity of this account. Augspurg and Heymann, together with the members of the small section of the suffrage movement that they headed at the time (*Deutscher Frauenstimmrechtsbund*—DFSB), immediately protested against the war and especially against the invasion of neutral Belgium. The consequences, however, were disastrous: mass desertion from the DFSB. At the same time, during the first few weeks of the war, Augspurg and Heymann did in fact opt for the traditional women's role in war: social work. The couple tried to repatriate children from occupied territories, send parcels to POWs, and help detained German women married to non-Germans. In any case, this line of action soon came to a halt when the authorities had all social work channeled through the Red Cross or the BDF.[13] Whether due to their own pacifist convictions or because of the authorities' restrictions, by mid-September 1914 Augspurg and Heymann had turned to political pacifist activity.

In a declaration considered to be the first antiwar propaganda in Germany during World War I, Heymann clearly distanced herself from the war and allied herself with women who opposed it:

> It is we, who took no part in the war, in the destruction, murder and slaughter . . . who are called upon to be the true carriers of culture in future. We, women, are not filled with hate of other nations. . . . We stretch out a hand to women of all nations, who think alike. . . .[14]

Augspurg and Heymann now began to develop the political principles of feminist pacifism, which they propagated in numerous pamphlets and articles. From the fundamental premise of total rejection of war as unjustifiable and unacceptable violence, they subsequently elaborated a gendered theory of pacifism based on the principles of internationalism and nonviolence. Both blamed war on "male politics." Peace could be obtained only by granting women of all nations political rights and engaging them in the reshaping of policies. Moreover, they believed that women were best qualified to promote internationalism: as a result of their long exclusion from politics, women had a different attitude toward the state than that of men, which made it easier for them to transcend nationalism and seek peace among the nations. Having already accepted the idea of "female uniqueness" before the war, Augspurg and Heymann were able to merge their feminism with pacifism. Childless themselves, they nevertheless constantly returned to a maternalist language that cast women as the "creators and cultivators of life," who must therefore "abhor war which destroys life," using the essentialist emphasis on the biological function of women in their call for a nonviolent society.[15]

Augspurg and Heymann were not alone in developing such ideas. Together with several other leading feminists (such as Alleta Jacobs, Holland; Rosika Schwimmer, Hungary; Jane Addams, USA; and Emmeline Pethick-Lawrence, Great Britain), who were disappointed with the women's movements' support of the war, the couple began planning an international women's peace conference. In a preparatory meeting held in Amsterdam in February of 1915, they formulated the aims of the conference: the peaceful settlement of international disputes and the parliamentary enfranchisement of women. The steering committee also decided to avoid the divisive issue of war guilt.[16]

The very fact that feminists of warring countries were planning an international conference in the midst of war encouraged Heymann to be more outspoken in her propaganda. In a pamphlet, of February 1915, she addressed women in an emotionally charged plea:

> Millions of men have remained in the field, they will never see their homeland again. . . . Europe's soil is filled with the stench of human blood. . . . No language is strong enough to describe the depth of human suffering. And the war goes on! Women of Europe, where is your voice? Are you strong only in patience and suffering? . . . Try at least to be true to your sex and with courage and might put a spoke in the blood-drenched wheels.[17]

Heymann's public address did not escape the notice of the authorities. The pamphlet's distribution was promptly forbidden. The press vehemently attacked the proposed peace conference and the BDF opposed it.[18] Nonetheless, preparations for the conference went ahead, and the German delegation numbering twenty-eight women (headed by Augspurg, Heymann, Stöcker, and Kirschhoff) left for The Hague.

The story of the Hague Congress (April 18 to May 1, 1915) has been told many times elsewhere.[19] The Congress, representing women from twelve warring and neutral countries (close to fifteen hundred participants), agreed upon a list of proposals to ensure future peace, including recognition of the right of self-determination, minorities' rights, abolition of secret diplomacy, the establishment of international courts to deal with disputes between nations, disarmament, freedom of trade, and education for peace. None of these ideas was original.[20] Although some references were made to the special plight of women in times of war, namely rape, the Congress's main novelty was in the fact that women had gathered to voice their opinions, which they felt could make a difference. The women at The Hague also linked their views on obtaining peace to their demand for full political citizenship as formulated in one of the Congress's key resolutions:

> Since the combined influence of the women of all countries is one of the strongest forces for the prevention of war, and since women can only have full responsibility and effective influence when they have

equal political rights with men, this International Congress of Women demands their political enfranchisement.[21]

Had it dispersed with declarations only, the Hague Congress would be etched in history as no more than a dramatic episode. But the Congress acted upon its resolutions. It sent delegations to both warring and neutral states, with specific propositions for peace negotiations, and these delegations were received by heads of states. More significant was the Congress's resolution to set up groups in all countries to work for peace and women's rights: Women's Committees for Permanent Peace (WCPP). The Congress also resolved to reconvene after the end of the war.[22] The delegates had thus established the framework for an international women's organization, eventually founded in 1919: the Women's International League for Peace and Freedom, which would advocate the concept of feminist pacifism during the interwar years.

Returning to Munich, Augspurg and Heymann called upon "German women and mothers" to wage a "war against war," and to: "join together" and work for a permanent peace. . . .

> We, mothers of all nations, who give life while we give up ourselves . . . we, the mothers of all nations are called upon to demand from the state, that the life we have created will not be spiritually corrupted and tortuously destroyed. . . . We want to help create peace through the means of moral, economic and political power.[23]

They established WCPP groups (*Frauenausschüsse für dauerenden Frieden*) in eighteen German cities, held meetings, set up pacifist libraries, distributed pamphlets, and signed petitions. As the BDF opposed this activity and all participants in the Hague Congress had been expelled from it, Augspurg and Heymann sought allies elsewhere. They cooperated with pacifist groups such as the German Peace Society (*Deutsche Friedensgesellschaft*) and the more radical New Fatherland Association (*Bund Neues Vaterland*). The basis for this cooperation was opposition to the war and the demand for peace without annexation and reparation. The military authorities were especially alarmed by the cooperation between feminist pacifists and Social Democrats. Augspurg and Heymann were subjected to restrictions ranging from censorship and limitations on holding public meetings to house searches and the expulsion of Heymann (who was a citizen of the state of Hamburg) from Bavaria (she remained in Munich in hiding).[24] The constraints on pacifist activity led the couple to a profound sense of isolation and failure, which may partially explain why they embraced the November Revolution of 1918 with such enthusiasm.

Unlike most bourgeois feminists, who either supported the Social Democratic Party (SPD)—by then no longer a revolutionary party—or expressed fear of a revolution, Augspurg and Heymann joined the November Revolution in support of Kurt Eisner (1867–1919), the Bavarian leader of the more radical revolutionary Independent Social Democratic Party (USPD). They had cooperated with Eisner during the war and regarded him as a true democrat as well as a pacifist. The term "socialism" no longer deterred them; they gave it their own idealistic interpretation. Indeed, the experience of the war had brought them to believe in the need for a different social and political order as the only way of preventing future wars and guaranteeing equal rights for all. After years of isolation and persecution they believed the November Revolution, which was nonviolent in its first stage, would fulfill all their dreams. Thus Augspurg and Heymann embraced the new socialist republic in Bavaria and offered their help in order to shape it in a "feminine spirit."[25] But after a few months of activity came the bitter disappointment: Eisner's assassination and the violent end of the Bavarian socialist republic. Nonetheless, their brief experience of the revolution drove Augspurg and Heymann to cross certain boundaries: They were now more sensitive to class issues than before 1914, and to their feminist pacifism they now added their own brand of socialism, not to be confused with Bolshevism, which both regarded as undemocratic and militaristic. Thus Augspurg and Heymann faced the newly formed Weimar Republic as socialists and pacifists, strongly critical of the victorious Social Democrats' use of force and reluctance to abolish Wilhelmine institutions such as the bureaucracy and the army.

* * *

Escaping the violent end of the November Revolution in Bavaria and the persecution that followed, Augspurg and Heymann traveled to Zurich in May 1919 to meet with feminist-pacifist WCPP members representing sixteen states. Many of them had endured political persecution for their antiwar activities. Some came from states devastated by the war and inflicted with hunger and political and social upheavals. These collective experiences found expression in the agenda of the Women's International League for Peace and Freedom.

WILPF was to be neither merely a women's organization campaigning for women's rights nor solely a pacifist organization seeking diplomatic means to settle disputes. WILPF's basic belief was that, without freedom (i.e., civil and human rights), there could be no peace, and that freedom could be maintained only in peace. Without eliminating the causes of war—political, social, economic, and psychological—there was no sense in calling for peace. These postwar feminists considered the policies of prewar pacifists, who had believed in solving interstate conflicts through diplomacy, as inadequate. The belief expressed at the Hague Congress in 1915 that the vote and women's participation in the decision-making process were sufficient to promote peace was also discarded. The founders of WILPF would no longer be satisfied with advancing women's rights and international agreements, but instead aimed at a fundamental change in society. Thus no topic—political, economic, or social—would escape their political scrutiny.[26]

Even before the Congress began its deliberations, it had protested against the terms of the Treaty of Versailles in a declaration sent to President Wilson. This was one of the first public responses to the treaty, criticizing it as unjust, undemocratic, and, most important, containing the seeds of a future war.[27] In its deliberations, the Congress addressed a wide range of topics concerning the outcome of the war, social justice, and the democratization of the proposed League of Nations. The Congress demanded the protection of minorities and an eight-hour workday, condemned racism and anti-Semitism, and composed a "Women's Charter," which was in fact a summary of prewar feminist demands: equal pay for equal work, equal education, and professional opportunities and the elimination of trade in women ("white slavery").[28]

There seems to have been wide agreement among the delegates to the Zurich Congress, who were all deeply moved by simply being together despite national barriers and the memories of the war. When Heymann rushed to embrace the French delegate, all the delegates stood up and took an oath: "I dedicate my life to the cause of peace."[29] In her concluding address, Heymann expressed the spirit of mission feminist pacifists shared:

> . . . these are no empty words, we women are capable of building a new world, but we must free ourselves of the idea that we want to build a world in the manner men have done. We want to build a world that is not based on lies, hate and force. We want to build a world based on love, justice and mutual understanding.[30]

Notwithstanding these demonstrations of solidarity, the Congress also witnessed the first signs of a rift that would plague interwar pacifist feminism.[31]

All participants agreed that the causes of war were rooted in the existing political, social, and economic order, namely in the capitalist economy and lack of full democratization. Divisions appeared when debating how far they were willing to go toward change. Augspurg and Heymann, in coalition with delegates from countries that had suffered most during the war and its aftermath (France,

Germany, Hungary, and Austria), urged support of workers' demands against the background of workers' uprisings in Hungary, Germany, and the Russian Revolution. These delegates believed that equality, peace, and nonviolence could be achieved only with a just distribution of resources, and that only in such a society could women find their liberation. The delegates from Great Britain, Holland, Scandinavia, and most U.S. delegates, whom Augspurg and Heymann called "the rightwing," were more cautious in their criticism of capitalism. Although they supported reform, these delegates opposed drastic measures both for ideological and pragmatic reasons.[32]

The second major divisive issue was the extent of active support for nonviolence, an issue that all feminist pacifists would face later when confronted with the rise of fascism and Nazism.[33] Until 1933, Augspurg and Heymann were identified as "radical pacifists" and demanded that WILPF members commit themselves totally to the principle of nonviolence in civil war as well as in a national-defensive war. Further debate arose in relation to WILPF's self-perception: whether it should serve as an idealistic vanguard or as a broadly based organization, even at the price of ideological compromise.[34] On this matter, too, Augspurg and Heymann—always in alliance with the French members—stood on the "radical" or "left" wing, as they were labeled within WILPF, vehemently opposing any ideological compromise.

Augspurg and Heymann had found their political and social home. Though they worked in Germany, it was the international organization that sustained them. As two of WILPF's "founding mothers," they held leading positions in its international bodies. In Zurich, Heymann was elected vice-president (a post she resigned in 1924, when she became honorary vice-president) and at least one of them was always on the International Executive Committee. In Germany they were the unofficial leaders of the German Section of WILPF.[35] They were always elected to the National Executive Committee, and jointly published the monthly *Die Frau im Staat*. There is hardly a pacifist petition or WILPF/German Section publication (except for local publications) that does not bear their signature. Without family ties and professional responsibilities, they were able to devote all of their energy and finances to their political work. Their correspondence with other WILPF members, especially with those in the WILPF office in Geneva, shows that Augspurg and Heymann devoted their whole life and financial resources to their politics, so much so that they were at times perceived as fanatics by some of their political colleagues.[36]

Their field of activity in the interwar period was strikingly different from before the war. Until 1914, Augspurg and Heymann had worked within the women's movement, but after the war they headed the most important women's organization within the *Deutsche Friedenskartell* (DFK), an umbrella organization for some thirty pacifist groups during the Weimar Republic. They regarded the women's movement (BDF) in the Weimar Republic as outdated and reactionary, believing that once women received political and civic rights, as under the Weimar constitution, the aims of a women's movement should change. The "post-vote dilemma" of what direction feminists should take after obtaining the vote troubled suffragists in many countries. Most feminists opted for maternalist politics and action within the evolving welfare state.[37] However, Augspurg and Heymann never followed that route. They paid little attention to the family and child care, emphasizing, rather, the need to expand women's participation in all spheres of life, demanding equal pay and job opportunities for women, and equal access to decision-making posts. Their banner was no longer "rights for women" but "women for peace and justice."[38]

Augspurg's and Heymann's political activity after the war was guided by a binary image of society and history governed either by the "male principle" (power, violence, competition, the pursuit of profit, exploitation) or the "female principle" (nurture, pacifism, mutual aid). They maintained that only a society governed by the "female principle" would bring an end to the use of force, to injustice and exploitation, and that it was up to women to bring about such a transformation. Augspurg and Heymann were not always clear on the question of whether women were naturally imbued with the "female principle" or acquired it through socialization. Although they continued to use essentialist terminology, both occasionally employed a universalist language, seeking historical and sociological explanations for identifying the "female principle" with women. Thus they claimed that although some men (such as their idol Goethe) had developed female values, most did not. Heymann, more than Augspurg, seems to have tried to develop a social and historical analysis based on women's particular life experience. Female values, she argued, were to be found mostly in women because they went through life caring for others and because by giving birth they developed a different attitude to life and to the "other":

> By creating a new human being, by physical contact with the child, by daily repetitive care and concern for the child until it matures both physically and spiritually, the mother has a different relationship to the child than the father. . . . The woman, as the source of life, judges

the efforts to create life differently than the man, and out of this different judgment and attitude her whole attitude to war that destroys life must be totally different from the man's. War destroys that which she has created, her work, the extension of herself . . . and thus women, just because they are women, will be the promoters of pacifism. Women of all nations, not only those who have given birth, but also spiritual mothers, all have the same attitude.[39]

Augspurg, who always tended to more poetic and extreme formulations, presented a binary model of the genders:

Man's violent reign has caused the suffering in the world, it is barren, deadly, it is negating like Ariman and Lucifer. . . . The essence of women will save the world, it is life-giving, it is creative and validating like Ormuzd.[40]

But both considered society's adoption of "feminine values" necessary for obtaining equality for women, as well as for the construction of a pacifist and just society.[41]

This binary theoretical model also served them in developing their own brand of socialism. From 1918, Augspurg and Heymann called themselves socialists, although they did not join any of the socialist or communist parties. Their socialism was based neither on an analysis of labor and market forces nor on the concept of class division, but rather on ethical voluntarism, individualism, direct democracy, and the just distribution of resources. Here again, they employed the theory of the two principles: capitalism as the embodiment of the male principle, of competition and exploitation, and socialism as the embodiment of the female principle, of mutual aid, sharing, and equality:

True Communism is a community of mutual aid in which each gives their best, where the belief in the good is kept alive. . . . Communism means that no one claims privileges and advantages. . . . Violence and Communism stand in total contradiction, the latter encompasses the principle of mutual aid, construction, while the former destroys and brutalizes.[42]

In their endeavor to implement the female principle in the political and social life of the Weimar Republic, Augspurg and Heymann commented and took a stand on all political events, such as the effects of the Treaty of Versailles, the French invasion of the Ruhr, the Great Inflation, unemployment, and the surge of right-wing extremism.[43] They propagated their views through publications, meetings, petitions, and various campaigns, either on their own (as WILPF) or in collaboration with other pacifist organizations. They demanded changes in school curricula so that children would learn not to glorify war. They opposed the sale of war toys[44] and organized cross-border activities with neighboring states to promote the spirit of internationalism.[45] They launched campaigns against the death penalty, against modern scientific (mainly chemical) warfare,[46] and in favor of disarmament.[47]

In their aim to promote pacifism, Augspurg and Heymann joined the campaign for adopting the Kellogg Agreement, which proposed delegitimizing the use of force to solve international disputes, and amending the German constitution accordingly.[48] They also joined the international campaign in support of conscientious objectors.[49] Both women believed that the most important tool in the struggle against war was a personal commitment not to take any part in war, whether aggressive or defensive. In a Lysistrata-style appeal, they called for a general strike by women to prevent war:

> It is up to us women and mothers, who have lived through the suffering and horrible experience of the World War, to strangle war from the start. War and peace lie in our hands when we are united. Without our will, without our willingness to fill in all the posts and maintain commerce, transport, and keep industry going at home, the cannons on the battlefield cannot fulfill their deadly work for one hour. Therefore, you women and mothers of all lands, join together and sign this oath and remain faithful to it when the time comes.[50]

Pacifism for Augspurg and Heymann was thus a moral and personal commitment. It was not merely a political ideal to be framed in international agreements, but also a crusade to cleanse society of its militaristic "male" mentality. The militarist spirit was embodied in the soldier and in military training—"the favorite playground of German men"—and Augspurg expounded the need to combat male adoration of force.[51]

The most important element in Augspurg and Heymann's pacifism was indeed their call for nonviolence on the personal, as well as the political, level, as epitomized by Mohandas K. Gandhi, whom they regarded as "a second Jesus":[52]

> People have often asked me what would I do if the cannons were directed at me, and were astonished by my reply: "I would let them fire at me." It is my deep conviction, that one should never use force to counter force. Force cannot be fought through force; it will be disarmed through an empty nothingness—a spiritual presence—or through human good.[53]

Nonviolence was not, however, about heroically facing death on the battlefield. In the difficult reality of the Weimar Republic it was not easy to adhere to the abstract declaration against any use of force when faced with daily violence on the streets, political assassinations, and confrontations with the growing Nazi movement. Public meetings became all too often the scene of brutal clashes, but the WILPF women refused to receive protection either from the police or from left-wing organizations, believing that it would lead only to more violence. Instead, they tried to deal with the violence by admitting only men who held tickets distributed in advance, by campaigning for an end to violence, and by demanding the enforcement of regulations forbidding citizens to carry arms.[54] Although Augspurg and Heymann, along with the other members of WILPF, vehemently criticized anti-Semitism, racism, and Nazism,[55] they nevertheless tenaciously and almost religiously clung to their belief in nonviolence and regarded their position not as a sign of weakness or incompetence, but rather as one of moral strength. Uncompromising on this issue, Augspurg and Heymann accused those pacifists who claimed they would use all means to defend the Republic against the Nazi danger of fighting violence with violence.[56]

Only after witnessing the atrocities of the Nazi regime from their exile in Switzerland (1933–1943) would Augspurg and Heymann express doubt in the absolute validity of the principle of nonviolence. Only then would they concede that "freedom" indeed might be a necessary prerequisite for achieving "peace" and that therefore there could even be a just war. Thus Heymann wrote on her deathbed:

> During these past years of total war we have probably all felt that there exists something higher than peace, namely freedom. Shouldn't we therefore call our International Women's League: the International Women's League for Freedom and Peace? Where freedom reigns peace will also be achieved. Long live freedom! This is my last greeting to my international colleagues.[57]

And so once again, events had caused a shift in their world view, forcing them to compromise their belief in absolute pacifism.

* * *

Augspurg and Heymann were often considered fanatical and uncompromising in their political work. Nevertheless, as we have seen, the turbulent events they lived through did induce them to modify their positions from time to time. Before World War I they had been liberal feminists campaigning for equal social, economic, and political rights for women. Bound to their class background, they had been unable to bring themselves to support the Social Democrats, who were the only party that supported their demands for full political equality. Party politics drove them to abandon the universalist premises of their emancipation demands and to adopt essentialist terminology. After the war and the revolution, they identified themselves as feminist pacifists and socialists, aspiring to construct a just and nonviolent world governed by "female" values. Later, the horrors of the Third Reich drove them to painfully relinquish their belief in absolute pacifism. In the end they emerged with a gendered pacifist-socialist vision, which, paradoxically for two such ardent feminists, led them to move beyond women's politics. Women were no longer the main object of their politics, but the means of bringing about the desired change in society: its feminization.

NOTES

The following abbreviations are used:

BAK - Bundesarchiv Koblenz
BayHstA - Bayerische Hauptstaatsarchiv
DFK - Deutsche Friedenskartell
BDF - Bund Deutscher Frauenvereine
FB - *Die Frauenbewegung*
FiS - *Die Frau im Staat*
IFFF - Internationale Frauenliga für Frieden und Freiheit (= WILPF)
Nl - *Nachlaß*
VF - *Völkerversöhnende Frauenarbeit*
WCPP - Women's Committees for Permanent Peace
WILPF - Women's International League for Peace and Freedom
WP - WILPF Papers
ZFS - *Zeitschrift für Frauenstimmrecht*

1. Bertha von Suttner's last letter to German women, published in *FB*, Aug. 1, 1914.
2. Richard J. Evans, "Women's Peace, Men's War," in idem, *Comrades and Sisters: Feminism, Socialism, and Pacifism in Europe, 1870–1945* (Sussex, 1987), 122–24.
3. I am currently writing a political biography of Anita Augspurg and Lida Gustava Heymann. For the relationship between feminism and pacifism during World War I, see my "Feminism and Pacifism: The Case of Anita Augspurg and Lida Gustava Heymann," *Tel Aviver Jahrbuch für deutsche Geschichte* 21 (1992): 207–25.
4. Margarethe Leonore Selenka quoted in Gisela Brinker-Gabler, ed., *Frauen gegen den Krieg* (Frankfurt a.M., 1980), 20; Anita Augspurg, "Die Internationale Friedenskundgebung," *FB*, Feb. 1, 1899, 25; Lida G. Heymann

and Anita Augspurg, *Erlebtes-Erschautes. Deutsche Frauen kämpfen für Freiheit, Recht und Frieden 1850–1940*, ed. Margrit Twellmann (Mannheim am Glan, 1972), 118–20.

5. See, for example, Bernice A. Carroll, "Feminism and Pacifism: Historical and Theoretical Connections," in Ruth Roach Pierson, ed., *Women and Peace* (London, New York, Sidney, 1987), 2–28; Evans, *Comrades and Sisters*; D. Kruse and Charles Sowerwine, "Feminism and Pacifism: 'Women's Sphere' in Peace and War," in A. Burns and N. Grieve, eds., *Australian Women: New Feminist Perspectives* (Melbourne, 1986), 42–43; Harrad Schenk, *Frauen kommen ohne Waffen. Feminismus und Pazifismus* (Munich, 1983); Sabine Hering and C. Wenzel, *Frauen riefen, aber man hörte sie nicht. Die Rolle der deutschen Frauen in der Internationalen Frauenfriedensbewegung zwischen 1892 und 1933* (Kassel, 1986); Sabine Hering, *Die Kriegsgewinnlerinnen. Praxis und Ideologie der deutschen Frauenbewegung im Ersten Weltkrieg* (Pfaffenweiler, 1990); Joanna Alberti, *Beyond Suffrage: Feminists in War and Peace 1914–1928* ((London, 1989); Susan Kingsley Kent, *Making Peace: The Reconstruction of Gender in Interwar Britain* (Princeton, 1993).

6. See, for example, Amy Hackett, "The Politics of Feminism in Wilhelmine Germany 1890–1918" (Ph.D. diss., Columbia University, 1976); Richard J. Evans, *The Feminist Movement in Germany, 1894–1933* (London, 1976); Barbara Greven-Aschoff, *Die bürgerliche Frauenbewegung in Deutschland 1894–1933* (Göttingen, 1981); Ute Frevert, *Frauen-Geschichte zwischen bürgerlicher Verbesserung und neuer Weiblichkeit* (Frankfurt a.M., 1986); Ute Gerhard, *Unerhört. Die Geschichte der deutschen Frauenbewegung* (Hamburg, 1990).

7. The terms "radical wing" and "moderate wing" (or respectively, "left wing" and "right wing") were used by feminists at the time. For the differences between the two groups, see for the radicals, Else Lüders, *Der "linke Flügel". Ein Blatt aus der Geschichte der deutschen Frauenbewegung* (Berlin, 1904); and for the moderates, Helene Lange, *Lebenserinnerungen* (Berlin, 1922), 223–26.

8. Heymann, *Wird die Mitarbeit der Frauen in den politischen Männerparteien das Frauenstimmrecht fördern?* (Gautzsch b. Leipzig, 1911); T. Wobbe, "Die Frauenbewegung ist keine Parteisache: Politische Positionen der Gemäßigten und Fortschrittlichen der bürgerlichen Frauenbewegung im Kaiserreich," *Feministische Studien* 2 (1986): 59. The left-liberal parties *Freisinnige Volkspartei, Freisinnige Vereinigung* and *Süddeutsche Volkspartei* united in 1910 into the *Fortschrittliche Volkspartei*.

9. See for example: Clara Zetkin, quoted in Brinker-Gabler, *Frauen gegen den Krieg*, 139–47; Evans, *Comrades and Sisters*, 130–43.

10. See, for example, Helene Lange, "Die Große Zeit und die Frauen," *Die Frau* 12 (Sept. 1914): 709–14; Gertrud Bäumer, "Nationaler Frauendienst," ibid., 714–15, and idem, *Der Krieg und die Frau* (Berlin, 1915).

11. Ute Gerhard, "National oder international. Die internationalen Beziehungen der deutschen bürgerlichen Frauenbewegung," *Feministische Studien* 2 (Nov. 1994): 34–52; Leila J. Rupp, "Constructing Internationalism:

The Case of Transnational Women's Organizations, 1888–1945," *American Historical Review* 99, no. 5 (Dec. 1994): 1571–660.

12. Heymann, *Erlebtes-Erschautes*, 121.

13. *FB*, Aug. 15, 1914, 124; Heymann and Augspurg, "Freiwillige Hilfsarbeit," *FB*, Sept. 1, 1914, 125–26; Heymann, "Aus der Tätigkeit des Bayerischen Vereins für Frauenstimmrecht während der Kriegszeit," *ZFS*, Aug. 15, 1915, 28; Heymann, "Pazifistische Frauen wärend der Kriegsjahre in Deutschland," *VF*, vol. 1 (Munich, 1920), 12–14.

14. Heymann, "Recht unter den Völkern-Frauenrecht," *FB*, Sept. 15, 1914, 129–130

15. Heymann, "Eine Frage: Frauen Europas, wann erschallt Euer Ruf?," *FB*, Feb. 1, 1915, 14; Heymann, "What Women Say About the War," *Jus Suffragii* 9, no. 3 (Dec. 1914): 207; BayHstA, MKr 1336; Heymann, "National-International," *ZFS* 2 (Feb. 1915); Heymann, "Zur Völkerbundfrage," *ZFS* 15/16 (Aug. 1918): 30–31; Heymann, *Frauenstimmrecht und Völkerverständigung* (Leipzig, 1919), 8, 15–18.

16. Heymann, "Bericht über die Vorbereitungen für einen internationalen Frauenkongress," *ZFS* 3 (Mar. 1915); Heymann, *Erlebtes-Erschautes*, 127–28; *International Congress of Women at The Hague, 28 April–1 May 1915* (The Hague, 1915), 33; "Call to the Women of all Nations," *Jus Suffragii* 9, no. 6 (Mar. 1915).

17. Heymann, "Eine Frage: Frauen Europas, wann erschallt Euer Ruf?," *FB*, Feb. 15, 1915, 14.

18. BayHstA: MKr 13366; Ludwig Quidde, *Der deutsche Pazifismus während des Weltkrieges 1914–1918*, ed. Karl Holl and Helmut Donat (Boppard, 1979), 110; BAK, Nl Quidde, 67.

19. For example, Jane Addams, Emily Green Balch, and A. Hamilton, *Women at the Hague* (New York, 1915); H. Ward, *A Venture in Goodwill* (London 1919), 1–33; Gertrude Bussy and Margaret Tims, *Pioneers for Peace: Women's International League for Peace and Freedom 1915–1965* (London, 1980), 17–24; Leila C. Costin, "Feminism, Pacifism, Internationalism and the 1915 International Congress of Women," *Women's Studies International Quarterly* 5 (1982): 301–15; Jo Vellacott, "Feminist Consciousness and the First World War," *History Workshop Journal* 23 (1987): 81–101.

20. Similar ideas had been raised in previous peace conferences. See Dieter Riesenberger, *Geschichte der Friedensbewegung in Deutschland* (Göttingen, 1985), 98–107; F. L. Carsten, *War against War: British and German Radical Movements in the First World War* (London, 1982), 18–24; Wilfried Eisenbeiss, *Die bürgerliche Friedensbewegung in Deutschland während des Ersten Weltkrieges* (Frankfurt a.M., 1980), 100–118.

21. *Towards Permanent Peace: A Record of the Women's International Congress Held in the Hague, April 28th–May 1st, 1915* (London, June 1915), 8; Emmeline Pethick-Lawrence, "The Bond of Faith," in ibid., 15.

22. International Committee of Women for Permanent Peace, *News Sheet*, no. 2 (Amsterdam, Aug. 1915); *International Frauenkongreß 1915*, 14.

23. BayHstA, MF 56840; Heymann, *VF* 1:22.

24. BayHstA, MK 19301a Nr. 11960/15, Nr. 101948; Quidde, *Der*

deutsche Pazifismus, 95–112, 165–72; Heymann, *ZFS*, 19/20 (Oct. 1917): 40–41; BAK, Nl Quidde 68, 69; BayHstA, MK 19301a, Nr. 106135/15, Nr. 11346/15; International Committee of Women for Permanent Peace, *News Sheet*, no. 3 (Amsterdam, Sept. 1915); BayHstA, MK 19301a Nr. 1853; MKr 13366 Nr. 68; MK 18007a (11.2.1917); Heymann, *Erlebtes-Erschautes*, 137–43; Eisenbeiss, *Die bürgerliche Friedensbewegung*, 138–43.

25. Heymann, *VF* 1:64; Heymann, *Erlebtes-Erschautes*, 159, 165–71; BayHstA, Arbeiter- und Soldatenräte 2; *FiS* (Feb. 1919): 9–10, 15–16; Heymann, "Kurt Eisner," *FiS* (Mar. 1919): 1–2; Staatsarchiv München, Stanw. 2428, 2077/2; *Stenographischer Bericht über die Verhandlungen des Kongresses der Arbeiter-, Bauern- und Soldatenräte vom 25. Februar bis 8. März 1919 in München* (Berlin, n.d.), 174, 179–80; Karl-Ludwig Ay, *Appelle einer Revolution. Dokumente aus Bayern zum Jahr 1918/19* (Munich, 1968), doc. 61; Christiane Sternsdorf-Hauck, *Brotmarken und rote Fahnen: Frauen der bayerischen Revolution und Räterepublik 1918/19* (Frankfurt a.M., 1989).

26. Rosa Manus to Aletta Jacobs, 7.1.1919, in WILPF Papers (original at Boulder University, Colorado; on microfilm at the UN Library, Geneva; hereafter WP): I:A:4 (1:168–69); Heymann to Jacobs, in WP: III:242 (65:217); for a list of participants at the Congress, see *Bericht des Internationalen Frauenkongreß, Zürich Mai 12–17, 1919* (Geneva, 1919), 445–46; Emily Green Balch, "Why Peace and Freedom," undated leaflet, quoted in Mercedes Randall, *Improper Bostonian: Emily Green Balch, Nobel Peace Laureate 1946* (New York, 1964), 271–72; Bussy and Tims, *Pioneers for Peace*, 207.

27. *Towards Peace and Freedom* (London, Aug. 1919), 18.

28. The Congress demanded that the Women's Charter be made part of the Versailles Treaty; see *Bericht der Internationalen Frauenkongreß, Zürich 1919*, 339–58; Irene Cooper Willis, "The Peace Terms," *Towards Peace and Freedom* (London, August 1919), 14–19; Ethel Snowden, *A Political Pilgrim in Europe* (London, 1921), 86–87; Jane Addams, *The Second Twenty Years at Hull-House* (New York, 1930), 146–48.

29. Florence Kelly to Mary Smith, 22.5.1919, letter quoted in A. D. Davis, *American Heroine: The Life and Legend of Jane Addams* (New York, 1973), 257; H. M. Swanwick, *I Have Been Young* (London, 1935), 318; Heymann, *Erlebtes-Erschautes*, 227; Randall, *Improper Bostonian*, 275–76.

30. *Towards Peace and Freedom*, 5.

31. Randall, *Improper Bostonian*, 308–311. Recently the term "transnationalism" has been applied to the WILPF; see Rupp, "Constructing Internationalism"; Jo Vellacott, "A Place for Pacifism and Transnationalism in Feminist Theory: The Early Work of the Women's International League for Peace and Freedom," *Women's History Review* 2, no. 1 (1993): 23–56.

32. *Report of the Third International Congress of Women, Vienna, July 10–17, 1921* (Geneva, n.d.), 98–103; International Executive Committee Protocol (hereafter IEC-Prot.), Freiburg, 6–12.9.1922, in WP: I:B:9 (9:6336–37); IEC-Prot., Swarthmore, W 25–29.4.1924 + 8.5.1924, in WP: I:B:11 (9:1228–38); Report of the Economy Committee, in *Report of the Sixth International Congress of WILPF, Prague, August 24–28, 1929*, 67; Economy

Committee Report, Eger 19–20.1929, in: WP: III:261 (66:532–56); IEC-Prot., Geneva, 4–8.9.1931, in WP: I:B:18 (10:950).

33. *Report of the Third International Congress of Women, Vienna, July 10–17, 1921,* 103–109, 146–50, 260; Randall, *Improper Bostonian,* 293–94; IEC-Prot., Innsbruck, 10–15.7.1925, in WP: I:B:12 (9:1414–22); IEC-Prot., Paris, 6–10.2.1926, in WP: I:B:13 (9:1611–65, 1672–75, 1682–83); *Report of the Fifth International Congress of Women, Dublin, July 8–15, 1926* (Geneva, n.d.), 184; Norman Ingram, *The Politics of Dissent: Pacifism in France, 1919–1939* (Oxford, 1991), 287–89.

34. Madeleine Doty, "Philosophers or Martyrs," *Pax International* (Mar. 1926); Augspurg, "Neither Philosophers nor Martyrs," ibid. (Apr. 1926).

35. According to their own reports, the German Section reached a total membership of 2,600 in 1920 and five thousand in 1926; see "German Section Report," WP: I:A:14 (1:647); Heymann, IFFF/Deutsche Zweig Bericht, Mai 1919 bis April 1921, in WP: I:B:6 (9:398); Gertrud Baer, "Aus der Arbeit 1924–1925 des Deutschen Zweiges der IFFF," *Friedens-Warte* (July 1925): 216–17; *Pax International* (Apr. 1926). Records of membership in the DFK show that membership fees were paid only by some two thousand in 1927; see Reinhold Lütgemeier-Davin, *Pazifismus zwischen Kooperation und Konfrontation. Das Deutsche Friedenskartell in der Weimarer Republik* (Cologne, 1982), 54.

36. Snowden, *A Political Pilgrim,* 83, described Augspurg as having "the expression of the religious fanatic." See also Auguste Kirschhoff quoted in H. Wottrich, *Auguste Kirschhoff. Eine Biographie* (Bremen, 1990), 189–90; Emily Green Balch quoted in Randall, *Improper Bostonian,* 441–42.

37. Seth Koven and Sonya Michel, "Womanly Duties: Maternalist Politics and the Origins of Welfare States in France, Germany, Great Britain, and the United States, 1880–1920," *American Historical Review* 95, no. 4 (Oct. 1990): 1076–1108; idem, eds., *Mothers of a New World: Maternalist Politics and the Origins of Welfare States* (London, 1993).

38. See, for example, Augspurg, "Die Wahlen," *FiS* (May 1920): 5–6; Heymann, "Frauenpolitik-Männerpolitik," *FiS* (July–Aug. 1920): 1–2; Heymann, "Der Mann im Staat," *FiS* (Feb. 1922): 4–6; Heymann, "Die weiblichen Abgeordneten im neuen Reichtage," *FiS* (July 1924): 10; Heymann, "Die 'verfassungmäßigen Rechte' der verheirateten Beamtin," *FiS* (Apr. 1926): 5–7; Heymann, "Schutz dem schwachen Geschlecht," *FiS* (Apr. 1927): 4–6; Heymann, "Freie Menschen," *FiS* (Jan. 1927): 1–2; "10 Jahre Frauenstimmrecht in Deutschland," *FiS* (Nov. 1928): 1–2; Heymann, "Frauen heraus!" *FiS* (Mar. 1930): 3. Augspurg and Heymann also paid little attention to the important campaigns at the time for abortion and birth control; see Atina Grossmann, *Reforming Sex: The German Movement for Birth Control and Abortion Reform, 1920–1950* (New York, 1995).

39. Heymann, *Frauenstimmrecht und Völkerverständigung* (Leipzig, 1919), 6–7.

40. Augspurg, "Die Zukunft," *FiS* (Jan. 1920): 2.

41. Heymann, "Die Frau", in K. Lenz and W. Fabian, eds., *Die Friedens-*

bewegung. Ein Handbuch der Weltfriedensströmungen der Gegenwart (Berlin, 1922), 93–96.

42. Heymann, "Kommunismus," *FiS* (Mar. 1922): 1–2.

43. For example: Augspurg, "Die Auslieferung der Schuldigen," *FiS* (Feb. 1920): 8; Heymann, "Praktische Pazifismus," *FiS* (Sept. 1920): 4; Pax Altra, "Das Ruhrgebiet," *FiS* (Feb. 1923): 1–2; "Offener Brief an die Arbeiter- und Beamtenschaft im besetzten Ruhrgebiet," *FiS* (Feb. 1923): 3; Anilid, "Reparationen," *FiS* (Mar. 1923): 1–3; "Friedensfront gegen Kriegsfront" leaflet quoted in *FiS* (Mar. 1923): 6–8.

44. Augspurg, "State Monopoly of Education," in *Report of the Third International Congress of Women, Vienna, July 10–17, 1921*, 31–34; IFFF/Bayern an Bayerische Staatsminister für Unterricht- und Kultus Herr Minister Matt, 20.12.1920, in WP: I:A:14 (1:690); Reinhart Bockhofer and Helmut Donat, "Kampf gegen Kriegsspielzeug," in Helmut Donat and Andreas Röpcke, eds., *"Nieder die Waffen—die Hände Gereicht!" Friedensbewegung in Bremen 1898–1958* (Bremen, 1989), 148–54; leaflet against war toys, in *VF* 2:27.

45. "Verständigung-Konferenz in Beuthen und Kattowitz, 6–8. Mai 1927," in WP: I:H:37 (34:331–32); Auguste Kirschhoff, "Deutsch-polnische Friedensarbeit," *Neue Generation* (Oct.–Nov. 1931): 194; Einladung zur Nordisch-Deutschen Konferenz in Flensburg, 24.–26. September 1926, in WP: III:251 (65:1975); "French and German Understanding," *Pax International* (Dec. 1925); Heymann, "Bäume des Friedens," *FiS* (Mar. 1926): 1–2.

46. Gertrud Woker, "Über Giftgase," *FiS* (Aug. 1923): 1–3; Frida Perlen, "Die neuen Kriegsmethoden und der Schutz der Zivilbevölkerung," *FiS* (Dec. 1928): 1–2. On the congress in Frankfurt a.M. on modern warfare, organized by WILPF (Frankfurt 4–6.1.1929) under the auspices of Albert Einstein, see Otto Nathan and Heinz Norden, eds., *Einstein on Peace* (New York, 1981), 93–94.

47. "Abrüstung," *FiS* (Nov. 1921): 1–2; Augspurg, "Der Panzerkreuzer," *FiS* (Sept. 1928): 1–2. An international petition was presented to the League of Nations with over eight million women's signatures on Feb. 6, 1932; see "Zur Abrüstung," *FiS* (Oct. 1931): 8–9; "Statement by the Disarmament Committee of the Women's International Organisations in relation to the Conference for the Reduction and Limitation of Armaments," in BAK: Nl Lüders, 150/10; *Pax International* (Mar. 1932).

48. Augspurg, "Der Mann im Staat - Die Frau im Staat," *FiS* (Oct. 1928): 1–2; IFFF/D.Z. an Reichstag und Regierung, 10.11.1928, in: BAK: R43 I/512 (D–809766); Lütgemeir-Davin, *Pazifismus zwischen Kooperation und Konfrontation*, 155–56.

49. "Kriegdienstgegner," *FiS* (Mar. 1921): 14–15; Heymann, "Militärdienst—Zivildienst," *FiS* (July–Aug. 1922): 1–3; Gruppe Revolutionären Pazifisten, "Protest gegen die beabsichtigte Wiedereinführung der allgemeinen Wehpflicht," quoted in Wolfgang Benz, ed., *Pazifismus in Deutschland. Dokumente zur Friedensbewegung, 1890–1939* (Frankfurt a.M., 1988), 202–203.

50. *VF* 2:27–28.

51. *Report of the Fourth International Congress, Washington, May 1–7* (Geneva, n.d.), 88.

52. Heymann, "Gewaltlose Revolution," *FiS* (Jan. 1922): 8–10; Augspurg, "Kann Gewaltlosigkeit sich durchsetzen?" *FiS* (Sept. 1924): 1–3; Mahatma K. Gandhi [sic], "Gewaltlosigkeit—Die größte Gewalt," *FiS* (Nov. 1926): 6.

53. *Report of the Third International Congress of Women, Vienna, July 10–17*, 56.

54. "Chronik," *FiS* (May 1932), 1; IFFF/D.Z. an Reichstag und Regierung, 10.11.1928, in BAK: R43 I/512 (D–809766); "Frauen gegen Gewaltpolitik," *VF* 6:14; Heymann, "S.O.S.," *FiS* (Jan. 1932): 1–2; Heymann, "Was tun? Ruhe bewahren - abwarten," *FiS* (Mar. 1933): 1–2; Heymann, *Erlebtes-Erschautes*, 192, 205, 207.

55. Leaflet against anti-Semitism, Stuttgart 1920, in WP: III:246 (65:931); L. Jannasch, "Schwarze Schmach—weiße Schmach," *FiS* (Nov. 1920): 1–4; Heymann, "Was ich in den besetzten Gebieten sah und hörte," *FiS* (Jan. 1921): 8–9; B. Baer, "Zum ersten internationalen Anti-Faschistenkongress," *FiS* (Apr. 1929): 2–3; Heymann, "Deutsche Debacle," *FiS* (Nov. 1930): 1–3; Heymann, "Nachkriegpsychose," *FiS* (Mar. 1931): 1–2; Heymann, "Chronik," *FiS* (May 1932): 1–2.

56. Heymann, "Gewaltpazifisten," *FiS* (Nov. 1923): 1–2.

57. WP: III:269 (66:1293).

THE POLITICS OF FEMALE NOTABLES IN POSTWAR EGYPT

BETH BARON

A week after unrest broke out in early March 1919 in Cairo, and had started to spread throughout the country, veiled elite Egyptian women "descended from their harems" onto the streets of the city, protesting the military suppression of demonstrations. The women marched down main thoroughfares of Cairo, but before they reached their final destination, they were surrounded by a cordon of British troops. Then, according to accounts, Huda Sha`rawi, a female notable who would later emerge as the leader of the feminist movement in Egypt, approached the soldiers and challenged them with the words: "We do not fear death, fire your rifle into my heart and make in Egypt a second Miss Cavell."[1] What an irony! Here we have an Egyptian woman evoking the memory of nurse Edith Cavell— who had been executed by the Germans in occupied Belgium for spying and had become a symbol of British patriotism—in the midst of a struggle to rid Egypt of the British occupation. Rather than look to the pantheon of ancient Arab or Egyptian female heroes cited in the Arabic press, Sha`rawi drew on the British war experience. Her cultural frame of reference, like that of many Westernized Egyptian notables, was European.

Since occupying Egypt in 1882, the British governed it indirectly and relied on male notables as intermediaries. Egyptian politics were guided in those decades by the group that Albert Hourani has called "urban notables," whose actions he has described as the "politics of notables."[2] Through their vast landholdings, the urban elite of Egypt had strong links to the countryside, but preferred life in the cities. According to Hourani, the influence of urban notables stemmed from two related factors: on the one hand, they had access to authority "to speak for society or some part of it at the ruler's court," while on the other hand they enjoyed independent "social power," which made them accepted and "natural" leaders and endowed them with an oppositional potential. Moreover, their links to the countryside enabled them to forge coalitions with rural notables toward this end.

Real authority in prewar Egypt, in any case, resided with the

British agent and consul-general, who more or less dictated to the Khedive, the representative of the Ottoman sultan (Egypt was still part of the Ottoman Empire). The notables thus played an ambiguous role, outwardly supporting the British occupation but quietly becoming the sounding boards of discontent. As the British began to rule more directly, the notables came to oppose the occupation more vocally. This position was reinforced by the declaration of a British protectorate over Egypt at the outset of World War I. At the moment of crisis after the war, the notables assumed the leadership of the rebellion against the British, and harnessed the agitation of peasants as well as the actions of workers to the nationalist cause. Fearful that popular violence might damage property and undermine the social order, they strove to contain it.[3]

Female notables chose this moment to become public political actors. This essay uses records from the British and U.S. archives, as well as Egyptian memoirs and periodicals, to examine gender and nationalist politics in an imperial outpost. It argues that a "politics of female notables" emerged after the war and, in part, out of it. Female notables, like their male counterparts, derived their power from their social position, which legitimized their authority and their claims to speak on behalf of the nation. The women examined here, who entered the political arena in the wake of the war, were mostly the wives and daughters of pashas and beys, through whom they had access to circles of power. Yet they were not just related to men of means: they often had large property holdings themselves, which gave them independent resources and links to the countryside.

A mythology has grown around what came to be known as the "ladies' demonstrations" of 1919, with participants earning such labels as "revolutionary gentlewomen."[4] The event has been elevated to an iconic national moment in Egyptian history and the national collective memory. However, the romance of revolution, and women's role in revolution, has overshadowed analysis of the political action of this group of women during and after the 1919 demonstrations, as well as the seeds for it in Egyptians' experiences of the war.

GENDERED EXPERIENCES OF THE WAR

The Egyptian Revolution of 1919 grew out of hardships encountered during the war and frustrated expectations for greater independence after it. With the exception of a brief Senussi occupation of the Western oases, and occasional air raids on Cairo, Egyptian territory west of the Suez Canal never became an arena of war. Yet it was an important staging ground: troops from all over the British Empire (Australia, New Zealand, Scotland, and India) gathered there to prepare for the Gallipoli and Palestine campaigns. Moreover, Egyptians were forced to provide labor and supplies for those campaigns. These contributions to the war effort went unrewarded with the denial of Egyptian demands for greater independence after the war.

Much more attention has been paid to the Revolution of 1919 than to the war that preceded, and in many ways precipitated, it. As a result, the war remains something of a historiographical hole, with historians tending either to discuss it summarily or bypass it altogether. Yet some background on the war years in Egypt and gendered experiences of the war are crucial to understanding why female notables participated in the revolution that erupted in its wake. Although the war experiences of peasant women and the urban elite were widely divergent, the war, albeit in different ways, transformed the lives of both groups. It also spurred notable women to speak in the name of all Egyptian women, though mostly on behalf of their own interests.

Shortly after a state of war was declared in Egypt, the British imposed martial law: newspapers were heavily censored, gatherings of five or more persons prohibited, and prominent male nationalists interned or deported to Malta. In December of 1914, a month after the Ottomans entered the war, the British declared Egypt a protectorate, thus severing her ties with the Ottoman Empire. Khedive Abbas Hilmi II (r.1892–1914), at the time in Istanbul, was replaced by his uncle, Prince Husayn Kamil (r.1914–1917). The latter became sultan, a title previously held by the Ottoman sovereign. Other symbols of state—flag, currency, stamps—were eventually altered. British officials had debated at length what status Egypt ought to have, and had settled on a protectorate, rather than a colony, as less offensive to Egyptians at a time when the British badly needed their cooperation.

Prior to the war, the most popular strain of Egyptian nationalism had emphasized Egypt's Islamic ties with the Ottoman Empire. Fearing that an attack on Egypt's eastern flank would stimulate an Egyptian uprising—as the Ottomans and Germans expected—the British selected the Suez Canal as the best position from which to repel an attack, and withdrew their troops from the Sinai Peninsula. Ottoman forces made two unsuccessful attempts to cross the Suez Canal, in February of 1915 and August of 1916. Moreover, the threatened uprising never materialized. Although some Egyptian army units even took part in the early defense of the canal, in May of 1917, well after the Ottoman threat had receded, Egyptians were disarmed.[5]

As the British pressed the campaign into Palestine in the spring of 1917, they increased their demands on Egyptians for labor and supplies. Camels and mules were requisitioned by the tens of thousands, along with fodder and grain to feed them. The heaviest burden came with the recruiting of Egyptians for the Labour Corps, the Camel Transport Corps, and similar units. When volunteers were not forthcoming, the government adapted the tactic of "administrative pressure." This was essentially conscription, though it was not labeled as such. It effectively reintroduced the *corvée*, a widely loathed system of collective forced labor that had been used for centuries in Egypt to dig and maintain irrigation canals (including the Suez Canal) and had been eliminated only a generation earlier.[6] In his memoirs, writer Salama Musa records seeing men in wartime "bound with thick ropes around their waists and put in a long row with their fellow victims, and marched like that to the village office, where they were confined in the room for the accused, to be consequently deported to Palestine." When village women came to him, weeping that men who worked his land had been detained, he obtained their release through a bribe. Yet later releases were rejected as he himself was threatened with conscription.[7]

From recruiting camps in Suhaj and Ruda Island, male Egyptians were sent, two thousand at a time, to base depots in the Canal Zone, where they were disinfected, clothed, equipped, and organized into gangs of fifty and companies of six hundred laborers. Most were sent to Palestine, but many also went to Mesopotamia, France, Italy, Salonika, and the Dardanelles to perform a number of labor-intensive tasks, including railway construction, bridge building, road making, laying pipelines, quarrying stone, draining malarial areas, loading ships, and digging trenches. From a pool of 3.2 million adult males in the Egyptian countryside, some 500,000 (according to British sources) to one or one and a half million (according to Egyptian historians) served in these corps. Although these were not frontline soldiers, they also suffered casualties from injury, disease, and death.[8]

The war also took its toll on women in the countryside. Fearing that *fellahin*, who had been unable to sell their cotton at the beginning of the war, would default on their taxes, government officials opened offices to accept women's gold jewelry—their chief investment—in lieu of banknotes.[9] In the following years, when the government conscripted men for the war effort, some of the women who were left behind complained to British officials of their lack of financial support. The government apparently allotted a lump sum of only three Egyptian pounds to care for families of recruits in the labor corps.[10]

During the war, women took to the fields in record numbers to tend to family crops. Although Egyptian censuses prove problematic for a number of reasons, including a tendency to undercount women, they do show important trends. The 1907 census listed a total of 2,258,005 male and 57,144 female agriculturalists.[11] By 1917, 1,897,103 men and 495,964 women were listed in the fields: a significant drop in the number of men and a nearly ninefold increase in the number of women. Ten years later, the number of men had surpassed earlier levels while the number of women listed had dipped only slightly.[12] The enormous increase in the number of women from 1907 to 1917 can be partially explained by greater efforts to document women's work and by natural population growth. But it mostly reflects the impact on female labor of the conscription of male peasants. The number of women engaged in labor in the fields surged and remained high through the twenties. Once in the fields, they seemed to stay there, and remained visible to census takers.

In contrast to rural women, urban elite women faced greater confinement in the home during the war. The preceding decades had been active ones for middle- and upper-class women who had explored a new range of educational, journalistic, and associational activities, which often had a nationalist tinge: women either legitimized their activities by linking them with the need for social reform on a national scale, or strove to disseminate nationalist ideas, adopting a new rhetoric in which they referred to themselves as "Mothers of the Nation."[13] The war forced a cutback in these new activities. Foreign travel was curtailed, and women who were abroad when war broke out in the summer of 1914 made their way home. A number of intellectual and educational societies initiated immediately before the war were disbanded. Some schools were taken over as hospitals or centers for refugees; few new initiatives in education were undertaken; and a number of women's journals folded due to the higher costs of production. Moreover, late in the war, one of the central figures in the fledgling women's movement, Malik Hifni Nasif (1886–1918), died in her early thirties. She was eulogized by Huda Sha'rawi, who strove to pick up her mantle. This is not to say that women's associational activities ground to a complete halt during the war—new organizations such as *Jam'iyyat al-Nahda al-Nisa'iyya* (the Society for Women's Awakening) were founded, and women learned nursing and practiced other skills to support the war effort—yet the pace of activities had slowed. Urban elite women did not necessarily suffer during the war, but they faced inconveniences, shortages, and higher prices. Moreover, the war provided them with new lessons in colonial politics and further familiarized them with the language of national determination.[14]

A great contrast exists between the war experiences of female peasants and that of notables. Yet both experienced increasing hostility toward the British occupation, which would find different expressions after the war, in peasant violence and notable protest. Eventually, female notables would step forward and, drawing on their social standing, would claim to speak on behalf of all Egyptians.

FROM WAR TO REVOLUTION

Egyptians regarded the protectorate as a temporary arrangement, and expected to gain independence after the war. However, British officials denied the Egyptian Wafd (Delegation) the opportunity to present their case in London. In March of 1919, when Wafd members were arrested and exiled, protests broke out in Cairo and then spread rapidly throughout the country. Egypt's movement for independence, which had stalled during the war, had resumed with vigor.

The psychological experience of mass protest is wonderfully described by the novelist Naguib Mahfouz in *Bayn al-Qasrayn* (*Palace Walk*), the first novel in a trilogy depicting the life of a middle-class Cairene family from 1917 to 1944. Mahfouz suggests what it may have felt like to be a young protestor in the streets of Cairo in 1919, and repeatedly uses the metaphor of water to describe the national collective. On the first day of the demonstrations, Fahmy, the middle son of the family and a law student, joined other students "surging" in a "formidable ocean." On the second day of protests, "Fahmy threw himself into the swarms of people with intoxicating happiness and enthusiasm, like a displaced person rediscovering his family after a long separation." The protests and Fahmy's participation continued. "Driven by his enthusiasm, he reached far-flung horizons of lofty sentiment. . . ."[15]

Much less interested in the political developments taking place, Fahmy's older brother Yasin, a government clerk, nonetheless later got caught up in celebrations of the release of the arrested head of the Wafd, Sa`d Zaghlul, and was "swept along by its swelling current and carried by its strong waves like a tiny, weightless leaf, fluttering everywhere." As he explained to his brother, "A man forgets himself in the strangest way when he's with so many people. He almost seems to become a new person." He remembers finding himself in "a swirling sea of people. There was an electric atmosphere of enthusiasm. Before I knew it, I forgot myself and merged with the stream. . . ."[16] Indeed, that was one of the central meanings of the drama of nationalist protest: the participant submerged himself in the mass, experienced symbolic death and rebirth, and emerged with a new identity—a loyal Egyptian, a nationalist. Collective action thus gave rise to a new collective identity.

Collective action also often draws new groups into politics, making new "political publics." Demonstrations reveal a great deal about how these groups are constituted, what their agendas are, and what messages they are attempting to convey to the broader public. In an innovative article on aspects of the 1920 Revolt in Syria, James Gelvin suggests how demonstrations can be analyzed as collective ceremonies that are used by certain groups in their attempts to define political community. He argues that "the ceremonies not only contain symbols, but the ceremony itself, in its entirety, acts as a symbol." Borrowing from Clifford Geertz and others, he elaborates a methodology by which ceremonies might be a "model of" reality and a "model for" reality at the same time, though components of the two are rarely equally balanced.[17] This approach seems an apt one for analyzing the women's demonstrations of March 1919.

SYMBOLS

The basic outlines of the story of the 1919 women's demonstrations in Egypt are well known, having been reconstructed from a limited number of British and Arabic sources. The first demonstration occurred on the morning of Sunday, March 16, and was followed by another a few days later. However, since the sources are rife with contradictions, making it almost impossible to produce a definitive detailed chronology, and because the symbolic components are more or less the same in any case, I will not make a great effort to distinguish between the protests, and instead will treat them almost as one.[18]

The demonstrations of 1919 are often depicted as being spontaneous. The marches of elite women, however, were planned in advance and well orchestrated. The circle around Huda Sha`rawi, a lead organizer, sent a delegation to the authorities to obtain permission for a protest. They returned empty handed, but later read in the daily al-Muqattam that permission had been granted. They only went ahead with their plan when they thought the action had been approved by colonial authorities. They then telephoned their friends (at the time, no doubt, telephones were limited to a small circle) to spread the word of the planned protest. Other advance preparations included the painting of banners, the penning of letters, and the signing of petitions. Although the Wafd reviewed at least one of these letters to give its stamp of approval, there is no evidence that the demonstrations themselves were planned by any group other than the participants.

On the morning of the march, women met at the home of Atiya Abu Asbu`a, which was located in Garden City near the central square of Midan Isma`iliyya (later renamed Midan al-Tahrir). Many government offices and foreign legations were located nearby, and affluent Cairenes lived in the area. The women discussed the route to be followed. The participants formed ranks or rows and marched in an orderly procession, as photographic evidence shows, with banners to the front. Some male students formed protective columns around the female protestors. The women walked on foot in these first marches, which was crucial to their effect. In later protests they often rode through the city in a procession of cars (driven by male chauffeurs).

The women wore the distinctive urban street dress of the elite: long black head scarves, white face veils, and black robes. This was a march of veiled women and thus had a certain aura of sanctity. Still, they shouted slogans and, on later occasions women from this cohort delivered speeches, sometimes veiled, at other times not veiled. The lists of names on the petitions signed by protestors reveal that these women indeed came from the highest strata of Egyptian society and were often the wives and daughters of pashas and beys, which is how they signed their names (the wife of . . . , the daughter of . . .). The lists also show that women often protested in the company of family members.

About two-thirds of the women who signed these petitions were married, although some married women, like Hidya Barakat (who later headed the charitable organization *Mabarrat Muhammad `Ali*), were still in their teens or early twenties. At least one, we are told, was a nursing mother. Others were students. Some participants were still alive on the fiftieth anniversary of the event and thus must have been relatively young in 1919. Huda Sha`rawi was about forty in 1919 and no doubt enjoyed a certain authority over more youthful demonstrators. Estimates of the number of participants ranged from 150 to 530, but three hundred is taken as a median figure. This was not a "surging sea," but a peaceful and ordered procession of limited size.

The event inverted the conventional gendered order, for here veiled women marched while men watched. Even more strikingly, women took center stage on major thoroughfares, commanding public space. Yet the procession remained segregated, with women moving in one space and male supporters in another.[19] In contrast, some female students mixed with men in the protests of 1919, while working-class and peasant women also occasionally engaged in the general unrest. The female "martyrs" came from these latter groups. Nonsegregated women, such as actresses, who were already accustomed to working with men, also joined men in their marches, but elite women hardly ever did. Although on a few occasions veiled women addressed crowds composed of male protestors, this did not necessarily involve their mixing with men, for most photographs taken on those occasions show the woman standing in a car or platform clearly above the crowd.

The closest they came to joining men occurred in a demonstration organized upon the release of Sa`d Zaghlul and other Wafd members from arrest in Malta on April 8, 1919. The order of march was fixed by profession or rank, with cabinet members and legislators in the lead followed by `ulama (religious leaders), judges, lawyers, doctors, government workers, army officers, workers, and students. Women brought up the rear: elite women rode in cars and women of lesser means sat on donkey carts.[20] The organizers no doubt intended to present a show of national unity to the foreign powers, but the ceremony also reflected and reinforced social divisions in Egyptian society.

In the demonstrations of late March and subsequent protests, elite women remained apart from men of their own classes as well as women of other classes. Women of different backgrounds had their own specific grievances and engaged in separate public action. In the countryside, peasant women used different tactics: they helped cut railroad lines, destroy telegraphs, and apparently participated in the murder of British officials trapped in railroad cars in the early hours of the unrest.[21] In the cities, prostitutes marched as well. "The ladies of the Wazza [an area where prostitutes lived in Cairo] paraded on carts in their gauds and their chemises, with music and the khankhan," wrote one Australian soldier in his memoirs.[22] The "ladies' demonstrations" were not intended to be a show of unity across class and moral boundaries. They were more a "model of" than a "model for" society. This did not discount cooperation among Coptic and Muslim women from the same strata, and in March of 1919 as well as in January of 1920, when the Women's Wafd was formed, Coptic and Muslim women of similar backgrounds worked together.

The women marching at the head of the procession in March carried Arabic and French placards with words in white on a black background. The banners read: "Long live supporters of justice, and freedom," "Down with oppressive tyrants and the occupation," "We protest the shedding of the blood of the innocent and the unarmed," "We demand complete independence," and so on. As they walked, they shouted slogans similar to those on their placards: "Long live freedom and independence!" and "Down with the protectorate!" Male Egyptians apparently responded enthusiastically to the demonstration, applauding and calling out their support, and the procession drew a large crowd, according to most accounts, with some women watching and ululating from windows.

The procession moved along Qasr al-Aini Street, the planned route, toward the foreign legations where the organizers had originally intended to deliver written protests. But those in front diverted the march in the direction of Sa'd Zaghlul's home, the focal point for Wafd meetings and political speeches, which became a symbolic site for the "national family" in the course of the revolution, acquiring the name *Bayt al-Umma* (House of the Nation). It is here that the main drama of the day unfolded. After declaring the demonstration illegal, British troops surrounded the marchers and Huda Sha'rawi spoke her words: "We do not fear death. . . ." The words, spoken in English (or, according to one source, in French), became a critical part of the memory of the event. The denouement came as a co-marcher, who feared that any harm to Huda would inspire the unarmed students to advance and thereby spark a bloodbath, restrained her. The ladies then stood or sat on curbstones for two to three hours as the "sun beat down" and the standoff dragged on. The confrontation ended in one of two ways, depending on the version and the day: either Sir Thomas Russell Pasha, British commander of the Cairo City Police, returned to call the women's carriages and allowed them to go; or the American consul-general intervened to the same end. As they returned home or shortly thereafter, the women presented their petitions to foreign legations.

The women's marches of 1919 quickly entered into the nationalist mythology, in part because they seemed so dramatic. In the eyes of observers, women had been catapulted from the private to the public sphere, from the harem to the street, virtually overnight. Yet women's actions should have come as less of a shock, for, as we have seen, elite women's lives had changed significantly in the previous three decades. Many of the participants had been educated, either at home by tutors or in state and foreign girls' schools. Literate Egyptian women formed the reading public of Arabic women's journals and other Egyptian and European periodicals. While the women's journals were primarily concerned with inculcating a cult of domesticity, they unwittingly helped to create a community of readers within national boundaries. Print culture was, no doubt, one factor in increasing their sense of national identity. In the press, in schools, and in societies, these women discussed the "woman question" and debated women's rights in the national context. They linked the issues of national liberation and women's advancement and expressed their growing national consciousness in a variety of cultural activities: teaching, writing, and volunteering.

The societies formed by these women—charitable, cultural, intellectual, and social—often augmented their sense of national community, for most espoused the goal cf Egyptian reform of one sort or another.[23] In their new societies, they also honed the organizational skills acquired in managing large households. Running meetings, giving speeches, and holding elections became familiar exercises. After that, organizing a demonstration seemed simple. The demonstrators also left written records, in the form of petitions and pamphlets, that document their demands and give insights into the politics of female notables. It is to these that we now turn.

TEXTS

When the British challenged the Wafd's authority to speak on behalf of all Egyptians, the Wafd began a drive to gain signatures on petitions (*tawkilat*) delegating it as the official representative of the nation. Although women were not approached to sign the *tawkilat*, elite women nevertheless adopted the tactic of the petition to express their political views. Delivering a petition to a foreign legation also became a central part of the ceremony of protest marches.

These petitions and similar texts produced in April by women in Alexandria reveal that their authors conceptualized Egyptian women as a collective and claimed, by virtue of their notable status, to speak for the whole group, for the female half of the political community. They would open with the phrase "In the name of the women of Egypt" and end with such signatures as "The Ladies of Egypt" and "The Egyptian Women."[24] Indeed, with their education and fluency in foreign languages, female notables were well positioned to act as spokeswomen. Moreover, as women of means they felt they were deserving of a certain respect, even as they protested. In an addendum to their original letter to the American diplomatic agency and consulate-general, they described how their demonstration had been thwarted: "Such is the treatment inflicted by the British troops occupying this country upon the ladies. This . . . shows clearly the persistence of the British in employing brute force even towards women."[25] As women, and women of the upper classes, they did not expect such "brute" treatment, and hoped the

Americans would agree that it was an outrage. Force, however, was relative: live ammunition was used on Egyptian crowds that included working-class women, some of whom died.

Early women's advocates carved out a special role for women as socializers and educators, calling themselves "Mothers of the Nation,"[26] while both male and female nationalists frequently invoked the metaphor of the nation-as-family as a device to build a sense of national community. Women demonstrating in 1919 strengthened this metaphor by presenting themselves as the female relations in this metaphoric family. They were "the mothers, sisters and wives of the victims massacred for the satisfaction of British ambitions."[27] The language of protest was both political and familial as the women constantly referred to themselves as "Egyptian mothers" and addressed others in family terms. The nation was thus a family writ large. It is significant, however, that despite their use of a feminine voice in these and other petitions, female demonstrators at this time refrained from raising particular feminist concerns or demands.[28]

Their petitions presented the case for Egyptian independence and protested the British military authorities' suppression of their public demonstrations. They objected, as they wrote, to the force used against Egyptian demonstrators, "who have done nothing more than claim the liberty and independence of their country, in conformity with the principles proclaimed by Dr. [President] Wilson and accepted by all belligerent and neutral nations." In particular, they condemned the "shooting down with machine guns [of] women and children, all absolutely unarmed; and this only because they had indulged in simple, pacific demonstrations of protest."[29] Here as elsewhere, appeals to the international community were based on Allied declarations made during the war. "We beg you to send our message to America and to President Wilson personally. Let them hear our call. We believe they will not suffer Liberty to be crushed in Egypt, that human Liberty for which you[r] brave and noble sons have died."[30]

Not to be outdone by women in Cairo, elite women in Alexandria produced a pamphlet of protest in April of 1919. The crescents and stars of the Egyptian flag (the Ottoman flag had only one star and crescent; the new Egyptian flag had three crescents and three stars) adorned the cover of the pamphlet sent to the American consul in that coastal city.[31] The authors spoke of the drama unfolding in Egypt. They began by invoking the past war, drawing on the language of self-determination propagated by the Allies during the war. "Impregnated with the principles of liberty and of justice that the Allied victory had assured," which included the "right to life and to independence," a peaceful but powerful movement made of all classes, groups, religions, and races was working for the realization of a national ideal. "Millions of human lives were sacrificed for the cause of this right and the defense of oppressed people. . . . Were these sacrifices in vain and have these agreements no further value?"[32]

The Alexandrian women argued that England had denied Egypt her right to exist: "Students, women, children and unarmed men were massacred because they reclaimed the liberty of their country." They spoke on behalf of those imprisoned, deported, and killed—their brothers. "If we raise our voice today it is not to cry but to appeal to the heart[s] of the women of Europe and of America, that all these injustices committed by England in Egypt are under the eyes of the civilized world."[33] Sixteen pages of signatures then followed, often inscribed both in Arabic and Latin letters (the text was in French). A few women gave their husband's profession (e.g., engineer, judge, lawyer, doctor, general prosecutor, chief of finances, head of the postal service) and title, which ranged from effendi to pasha. One woman gave her own profession as school director. Many were obviously from the same families, and there were Christians as well as Muslims.[34]

The petitions and pamphlets of female notables reveal a keen sense of political argumentation and politicization. The writers recalled the meaning of the past war and promises of self-determination to legitimize Egypt's right to independence, but they did not dwell on the direct burden of war in Egypt or the peasants' experiences of it. They spoke in familial terms as mothers, wives, and sisters, and of brothers and sons. They occasionally appealed to their female counterparts in Europe and America and claimed to speak on behalf of all Egyptian women. Yet they put forth no special claims for women. Rather, they critiqued British rule in a special voice.

Using a new language of protest, female notables thus carved out an autonomous political space. They claimed a legitimacy to speak for society—or at least the female half of it—because of their elite background and access to authority. The response to their marches and presentation of petitions shows that they indeed enjoyed a unique social power, which they duly capitalized on by organizing more formally.

POLITICAL ORGANIZATION

In 1919, students, peasants, and workers, who all had their own, disparate grievances, united behind the Wafd. Initially, the Wafd was a delegation of a few men deputized "by the nation" to speak on its behalf. These few men invited a few more to join, and the ranks of the inner circle grew. It was the exile of the core of the Wafd (Sa`d Zaghlul and others) that had sparked the 1919 Revolution. There were repeated exiles in the early 1920s for the British preferred to negotiate with a more malleable leadership, yet the Wafd was the only one with broad national support.

The Wafd remained an all-male organization; but in early January of 1920, a group of female notables gathered to form the Women's Wafd. Over a thousand women met at St. Mark's Church in Cairo to elect fifteen members to the Women's Wafd Central Committee. Huda Sha`rawi, whose husband was a founding member of the Wafd (but was among those who had quarreled with Zaghlul and left the Wafd), was named president even though she was not present at this meeting.[35] The Central Committee included Copts (vice-president Fahmi Bey Wissa and treasurer Habib Bey Khayyat) and mirrored the organization of the male Wafd in its show of national unity.[36]

At the first meeting of the Central Committee, the women composed a letter to Lord Milner, head of a Commission of Inquiry sent by the British government to Egypt to assess the political situation. In this letter they invoked the past war, in which millions of lives had been lost in defense of certain principles ("defending right and liberating the human race") but which England had of late compromised.[37] They then took to the streets, demonstrating in an orderly fashion and following a route that included Shepherd's Hotel (an international gathering spot), the Savoy Hotel, Opera Square, and the Palace. This was the Cairo of the elite. The women carried Egyptian flags and confronted, as in the past, British soldiers.[38]

The Women's Wafd proved instrumental in initiating and sustaining the boycott of British goods and merchants, launched in January of 1922. They went round shops in Cairo, urging shopkeepers to boycott British goods, organized women's committees in other cities and in the provinces, and convened meetings where women vowed to continue the boycott. As consumers of considerable means, notable women had economic clout and could shame others into boycotting British businesses. During the few months until Egypt was unilaterally declared an independent kingdom, the boycott proved effective. Subsequently, public support for the boycott seemed to diminish, though the women continued their vigilance against patrons of British stores.[39] Another group later tried to expand the boycott, urging the Egyptian government to participate.[40]

In early February of 1922, the Women's Wafd Central Committee met to discuss the appointment of a new prime minister and the formation of a new cabinet. In a prepared statement, they wrote that they wanted to publicize their decision "to oppose the formation of any Ministry before the return [from exile] of the venerable Leader [Sa`d Zaghlul] and his friends; the release of all political prisoners and the removal of the Martial Law; the abolition of the Press Censorship and the acknowledgement of the complete independence of Egypt and her Sudan."[41] However, British censors prevented publication of the Committee's statement, a step that was approved by the acting High Commissioner, indicating that the British regarded the Women's Wafd Central Committee as wielding some influence.[42] In March, the women again took to the streets, or rather their chauffeur-driven cars, to protest against the ministry that had eventually been formed, martial law, and the continuing exile of Zaghlul. In a demonstration that lasted two hours, the women went from consul-general to consul-general to deliver letters of protest.[43] The Women's Wafd, like its male counterpart, claimed to be the voice of the Egyptian nation—especially in the absence of exiled male leaders—and Ihsan Ahmed, the secretary of the Women's Wafd, wrote to High Commissioner Allenby on the nation's behalf. She noted "the urgency of taking quick steps in releasing the political prisoners, returning the exiles and allowing full freedom in the country."[44]

To what extent did urban female notables cooperate with women of other backgrounds, or strive to organize them? There is some evidence that they had ties with rural elites. Grace Thompson Seton, an American traveler, describes two "rich peasant" women she met in the early 1920s in the drawing room of Zaghlul's wife, Safiya Zaghlul, who was known as "Mother of the Nation." In contrast to the urban notable women, who dressed in Western style and spoke French, the rural women wore more traditional clothing and spoke only Arabic. One wore "astonishing quantities" of gold ornaments and had come to "offer her money and her heart to Egypt's cause." The other, who was also "weighted" with gold and had a very sizable income from her land, had come to support the circle of female nationalists around Safiya Zaghlul.[45] Female notables organized working-class women who learned sewing and other skills in the schools their charities sponsored. At a meeting convened by the Women's Wafd Central Committee to promote the boycott of British goods, girls from the workshop of Jam`iyyat al-Mar'a al-Jadida (the New Woman Society) sang nationalist songs.[46]

In Alexandria, Jam`iyyat Ummahat al-Mustaqbal (the Society of the Mothers of the Future) took inspiration from the Turkish leader Mustafa Kemal and hoped that Egypt would be equally as successful in pursuing independence. The Society's president,

Anisa al-Rashidi, sent a circular that called on Allah "to restore to Egypt 'her leader, Zaghloul Pacha,' to set at liberty Egyptian prisoners detained for political offences, and to save Egypt and the Sudan from oppression," and sent resolutions of the Society to the consuls of France, the U.S., and Italy.[47] The Society's secretary, Zaynab `Abd al-Hamid, later invited representatives from those same delegations, as well as other influential persons, to a ceremony to inaugurate the Society's school, which was under the patronage of the Egyptian Wafd.[48]

Women's organizations in provincial towns also proved active at this time. Because of their distance from the capital, members could not personally deliver pamphlets and petitions to foreign legations. They could, however, telegraph them. Women's organizations in the Delta (Tanta) and in Upper Egypt (Assyut) sent protests against British policy to various British newspapers as well as to British members of Parliament, the prime minister, and the speaker of the house of commons. A women's committee in Minya, another town in Upper Egypt, joined the provincial activists and sent a message of support to Sa`d Zaghlul, then in exile in Seychelles.[49] The activism of provincial women's organizations in the early 1920s points to the spread of nationalist sentiment among female elites as well as the links between Cairo and provincial centers. One should not forget that many female notables or their families owned land (Huda Sha`rawi's family owned large tracts of land in Minya) and often maintained residences close to their landholdings.

The British declared Egypt independent in 1922, reserving several points for negotiation. Then followed the drafting of a constitution and elections. The Wafd, which in the meantime had transformed itself into a political party, won an overwhelming majority of seats in the new Parliament due to its mass popularity. It governed for a few years but was blocked from power later in the decade amidst repeated Palace coups against parliamentary life and the Constitution. In telegrams to Great Britain, the Women's Wafd appealed in 1928 "to the sympathy of foreign public opinion to bear witness to the aggressive measures of the present anti-constitutional ministry [of Muhammad Mahmud]. . . ."[50] and protested against the decision of the British government to negotiate agreements with it, particularly over the distribution of Nile water, as an "unprecedented act of international injustice."[51]

In the 1920s, the Wafd split, and the Women's Wafd also witnessed the departure of several prominent members. Huda Sha`rawi left the Women's Wafd Central Committee in 1924. A year earlier, she had formed *al-Ittihad al-Nisa'i al-Misri* (the Egyptian Feminist

Union), and she continued to protest in the name of "Egyptian women" to American and other officials in an effort to address world public opinion.[52] In the early 1930s, female notables unified once again to oppose the increasingly dictatorial Sidqi regime. Women were driven in their cars through Cairo on several occasions, waving flags and shouting for the restoration of the Constitution and the resignation of the government. They presented themselves at the Ministry of the Interior, where they were turned away; and they held a demonstration in a garden adjacent to a home where the prime minister was being entertained. The British high commissioner denied that force had been used to break up some of the women's demonstrations, yet women sent notes protesting the use of British officers and constables to detain them. The letter was signed by sixty-five women, whose husbands or fathers, as indicated, were often doctors, beys, and pashas.[53]

If the British response to demonstrations by female notables was much the same as it had been twelve years earlier—fairly cautious because of their social status—the reaction of some Egyptians to women's demonstrations had changed in the interim. In the wake of the 1919 Revolution, poets and pamphleteers had praised them. By the early 1930s female notables such as Safiya Zaghlul and Huda Sha`rawi were no longer immune to being satirized in the cartoons of such weeklies as al-Kashkul.[54] Perhaps this was a sign of their political arrival. Or perhaps it was a sign that female notables had lost their special aura.

CONCLUSIONS

Before the war, women's nationalist activities had taken a cultural form as they channeled energy into enterprises intended both to reform women and to help the nation. These enterprises strengthened their sense of national community and prepared them for political action. Although the war subdued most activities, and female notables, like other nationalists, were quiescent, it also generated greater political awareness and higher expectations. After the war, women's nationalist expression acquired new political forms as women's public protests became a not uncommon sight. Female notables could not stand by as other groups actively protested. To have done so would have been to renounce any special claim to leadership.

Elite women took to the streets in 1919, a week into the unrest, becoming a new "political public." They wore the garb of privileged secluded women who worked neither in fields nor factories, nor in other people's homes. They communicated over the phone to plan their march, arrived to protest in cars (not on carts or on foot) and left in the same way. They marched toward symbols of power—foreign legations and Sa`d Zaghlul's home—speaking as much to the foreign community in English and French as to other Egyptians. They staged planned and orderly demonstrations in an effort to unseat the British colonial authority and to shore up the power of their own class. They did not march to popular quarters to walk hand-in-hand with working-class women in the hope of creating a new classless society; nor did they link arms with men to break gender boundaries and radically alter male-female relations. Their politics complemented the politics of the male elite and contrasted with the emerging mass politics of peasants and workers. It was, in short, notable politics with a feminine twist.

The "lady demonstrators" thus reinforced a hierarchical and segregated "model of" society. Yet they also presented a new "model for" society by carving out a public space for themselves. Herein lay the revolutionary potential of their demonstrations, for in spite of the plans and the order, there was a certain spontaneity to the marches, a liberation in taking to the streets, an exhilaration in shouting. These were women who earlier had not been able to walk in the streets without being harassed. Now they won admiration and respect when they marched for the nation. These were women who had never had the opportunity to engage in collective public action such as funeral marches or other public ceremonies. Now they gladly submerged themselves in the collective, and occasionally "lost their senses."[55] They emerged with a greater sense of solidarity and community, and with new identities: recollections of those heady days of March of 1919 would remain with them.

After 1919, female notables formed their own societies in the capital and in other cities and that comprised women from similar social backgrounds. They demonstrated separately, and penned their own petitions, pamphlets, telegrams, and letters. They also helped to orchestrate boycotts and other actions that drew on their skills and contacts. Theirs was a political revolt to unseat the British and to buttress the power of Egyptian notables. Yet, as the myth of women's role in the Revolution of 1919 grew stronger, the power of female notables weakened. With the declaration of Egypt's independence, the game changed, and Egyptian politicians struggled amongst themselves as well as with the British. Although segregation began to break down in the 1920s, the space for female notable politics narrowed. A few female notables (such as Safiya Zaghlul) wielded great influence, but most were excluded from party and parliamentary politics and got pushed to the sidelines, for they had no official capacity, no voting rights, and no right to run for office. They mostly turned their attention to creating a network of social services and agitating for women's rights. But those are other stories.

NOTES

1. `Abd al-Rahman al-Rafi`i, *Thawrat 1919* (Cairo, 1949; 3rd ed. 1968), 1:127; Huda Sha`rawi, *Mudhakkirat* (Cairo, 1981), 190. The texts of this line vary, for they are translated from English (or French) into Arabic and back, and remembered differently.

2. The concept of "urban notables" has been most broadly used to describe politics in the Fertile Crescent region. Afaf Lutfi al-Sayyid-Marsot, an Egyptian historian who was a student of Hourani, referred to the top echelons of urban society in Egypt as the *dhawat, bashawat*, or elite, and hesitated to call them notables, a term she explains was usually reserved for the rural group known as the *ayan*. I am using the term more generally. See Albert Hourani, "Ottoman Reform and the Politics of Notables," in *The Emergence of the Modern Middle East* (London, 1981), 36–66, reprinted in Albert Hourani et al., eds., *The Modern Middle East: A Reader* (Berkeley, 1993), 83–109, quote from p. 87; Afaf Lutfi al-Sayyid-Marsot, *Egypt's Liberal Experiment: 1922–1936* (Berkeley, 1977), 40–41.

3. Hourani, "Ottoman Reform and the Politics of Notables," 98, 88; Nathan J. Brown, *Peasant Politics in Modern Egypt* (New Haven, 1990), 212; Joel Beinin and Zachary Lochman, *Workers on the Nile* (Princeton, 1987), 89.

4. Afaf Lutfi al-Sayyid Marsot, "The Revolutionary Gentlewomen in Egypt," in Lois Beck and Nikki Keddie, eds., *Women in the Muslim World* (Cambridge, MA, 1978), 261–76.

5. On Egypt during the war, see Latifa Muhammad Salim, *Misr fi al-Harb al-`Alimiyya al-Ula* (Cairo, 1984); P. G. Elgood, *Egypt and the Army* (London, 1924); `Abd al-`Azim Ramadan, *Tatawwur al-Haraka al-Wataniyya al-Misriyya min Sanat 1918 ila Sanat 1936* (Cairo, n.d.), 66–82.

6. Elgood, *Egypt and the Army*, 314, 320; Brown, *Peasant Politics*, 196–203.

7. Salama Musa, *Tarbiyat Salama Musa* (Cairo, 1947), 131; trans. L. O. Schuman as *The Education of Salama Musa* (Leiden, 1961), 92.

8. U.S. Archives, State Department (hereafter SD) 883.22, Hampson, "Some of the Achievements of the Egyptian Labor Corps attached to General Allenby's Army in Palestine," Cairo, Mar. 31, 1919; *A Brief Record of the Advance of the Egyptian Expeditionary Force* (London, 1919) (hereafter *Egyptian Expeditionary Force*), 107–8; Brown, *Peasant Politics*, 198; Elgood, *Egypt and the Army*, 240–45.

9. Elgood, *Egypt and the Army*, 53.

10. *Egyptian Expeditionary Force.*

11. Egypt, Ministry of Finance, *The Census of Egypt Taken in 1907* (Cairo, 1909), 279.

12. Egypt, Ministry of Finance, *Ta`dad Sukkan al-Qatr al-Misri li-Sanat 1927* (Cairo, 1931), 279.

13. Beth Baron, "Mothers, Morality, and Nationalism in Pre-1919 Egypt," in Rashid Khalidi et al., eds., *The Origins of Arab Nationalism* (New York, 1991), 271–88.

14. Beth Baron, *The Women's Awakening in Egypt: Culture, Society, and the Press* (New Haven, 1994).

15. Naguib Mahfuz, *Bayn al-Qasrayn* (Cairo, n.d.), 341–42; Naguib Mahfouz, *Palace Walk*, trans. William Maynard Hutchins and Olive E. Kenny (New York, 1990), 359–60.

16. Mahfouz, *Palace Walk*, 479–80.

17. James L. Gelvin, "Demonstrating Communities in Post-Ottoman Syria," *Journal of Interdisciplinary History* 25, no.1 (1994): 23–44, esp. 24, 29–31.

18. The information below is drawn from al-Rafi`i, *Thawrat 1919* 1:126–130, 1:141–142; Ijlal Khalifa, *al-Haraka al-Nisa'iyya al-Haditha: Qissat al-Mar'a al-`Arabiyya `ala Ard Misr* (Cairo, n.d.), 151–60; Sha`rawi, *Mudhakkirat*, 187–91; *Musawwar*, no. 237 (Mar. 7, 1969): 42–47. In English, see John D. McIntyre, Jr., *The Boycott of the Milner Mission: A Study in Egyptian Nationalism* (New York, 1985), 127–55; Thomas Philipp, "Feminism and Nationalist Politics in Egypt," in Beck and Keddie, eds., *Women in the Muslim World*, 277–94; Margot Badran, *Feminists, Islam, and Nation: Gender and the Making of Modern Egypt* (Princeton, 1995), 74–80.

19. Gender rules were not suspended, as Badran has claimed. See her *Feminists, Islam, and Nation*, 74.

20. See Ahmad Shafiq, *Hawliyyat Misr al-Siyasiyya* (Cairo, 1926), 1:314–16; Badran, *Feminists, Islam, and Nation* 77; for a photo of working-class women riding on a donkey cart in a protest, see M. Sabry, *La Révolution Egyptienne* (Paris, 1919), 67.

21. Valentine Chirol, *The Egyptian Problem* (London, 1921), 168. Brown states that Chirol is alone in mentioning the extensive participation of rural women in the unrest (Brown, *Peasant Politics*, 249 n.33).

22. Hector Dinning, *Nile to Aleppo: With the Light-Horse in the Middle-East* (London, 1920), 266. In Alexandria as well, prostitutes joined nationalist processions. See McIntyre, *The Boycott of the Milner Mission*, 141.

23. Baron, *Women's Awakening*, chap. 8.

24. SD 883.00/130, Enclosure: The Egyptian Women to the American Diplomatic Agent and Consul-General, Cairo, Mar. 18, 1919; SD 883.00/135, Enclosure: Petition dated Mar. 20, 1919; SD 883.00/135, Enclosure: To the American Diplomatic Agent in Egypt, Cairo, Mar. 24, 1919.

25. SD 883.00/135, Enclosure: Petition dated Mar. 20, 1919.

26. Baron, "Mothers, Morality, and Nationalism."

27. SD 883.00/130, Enclosure: The Egyptian Women to the American Minister, Cairo, Mar. 18, 1919.

28. In later periods, Palestinian and other women participating in national movements would debate whether it was appropriate to raise the

issue of women's rights in the midst of a struggle, and some Algerian women would regret that they had not done so. See, for example, Marie-Aimée Helie-Lucas, "Women, Nationalism and Religion in the Algerian Liberation Struggle," in Margot Badran and Miriam Cooke, eds., *Opening the Gates* (Bloomington, 1990), 105–114.

29. SD 883.00/130, Enclosure: The Egyptian Women to the American Diplomatic Agent and Consul-General, Cairo, Mar. 18, 1919.

30. SD 883.00/135, Enclosure: To the American Diplomatic Agent in Egypt, Cairo, Mar. 24, 1919.

31. Like the flag of the Ottoman Empire, the flag of the protectorate was red. Independent Egypt adopted a green flag with one white crescent and three white stars in 1923. SD 883.015, Hampson to Secretary of State, Cairo, Apr. 30, 1919; SD 883.015/4, Ives to Secretary of State, Alexandria, Sept. 1, 1924; SD 883.015/12, Patterson to Secretary of State, Cairo, Dec. 18, 1948.

32. SD 883.00/165, Protestation des Dames Egyptiennes d'Alexandrie à Monsieur le Consul d'Amérique, Apr. 1919.

33. Ibid.

34. Ibid.

35. Marius Deeb, *Party Politics in Egypt: the Wafd and Its Rivals 1919–1939* (London, 1979), 67.

36. McIntyre, *The Boycott of the Milner Mission*, 145–46.

37. *Egyptian Gazette*, Jan. 20, 1920, quoted in ibid., 147.

38. Ibid., 147.

39. Grace Thompson Seton, *A Woman Tenderfoot in Egypt* (New York, 1923), 29–31, 35; Deeb, *Party Politics*, 68; Marsot, "Revolutionary Gentle-women," 271–72; Badran, *Feminists, Islam, and Nation*, 83–84.

40. FO 141/511/14083, "Resolutions Agreed upon by Egyptian Ladies," Cairo, Oct. 30, 1924.

41. FO 141/511/14083/3, Ihsan Ahmed, "Decision of the Women's Central Committee of the Delegation," Cairo, Feb. 1922.

42. FO 141/511/14083/4, Oriental Secretary to Monteith Smith, Cairo, Feb. 7, 1922.

43. Seton, *A Woman Tenderfoot*, 31.

44. FO 141/511/14083/13a, Ahmed to High Commissioner, Cairo, Apr. 20, 1923.

45. Seton, *A Woman Tenderfoot*, 35–36.

46. Badran, *Feminists, Islam, and Nation*, 83.

47. SD 883.00/427, Annisa al-Rashidi, "The Future-mothers' salutation to the Kemalist troops" (translation from Arabic), enclosure in letter from Maynard to Secretary of State, Alexandria, Sept. 19, 1922.

48. SD 883.00/429, Zaynab Abd al-Hamid, "The Egyptian Delegation at Alexandria," Alexandria, Sept. 29, 1922.

49. FO 141/511/14083/5, 6, and 10, Telegrams dated Feb. 9, 1922, Feb. 21, 1922, and May 23, 1922.

50. FO 141/511/14083/28, Women's Executive Committee, Cairo, Aug. 14, 1928; FO 141/511/14083/29, Ihsan Fahmy to Minister of Great Britain, Cairo, Aug. 14, 1928.

51. FO 141/511/14083, Esther Fahmy Weisa to Sir Austen Chamberlain, Cairo, May 8, 1929.

52. SD 883.00/510, Hoda Charaoui [sic] to Under-Secretary of State for Foreign Affairs, Cairo, Nov. 28, 1924.

53. FO 371/15405/1611, Stevenson to Henderson, Cairo, May 8, 1931; FO 371/15405/1673, Loraine to Henderson, Cairo, May 12, 1931.

54. See, for example, *al-Kashkul*, May 22, 1931, 16.

55. Sha`rawi, *Mudhakkirat*, 190.

PART IV
MOVING BOUNDARIES
WORK, GENDER, AND MOBILIZATION

Public Functions, Private Premises

Female Professional Identity and the Domestic-Service Paradigm in Britain, c.1850–1930*

Anne Summers

This paper is concerned with a particular sector of women's employment—the domestic sector—and, more specifically, with the relations of employment within that sector. It deals with the ways in which these relations shaped men's perceptions of women, and women's perceptions of each other. It seeks to show that not only the range of opportunities for employment, but also the longstanding assumptions underpinning the character of "women's work," remained remarkably stable over the best part of a century, despite the interruption of World War I. Structures and models of relationships that evolved in the Victorian and Edwardian periods in the apparently restricted sphere of the private household proved highly resilient to change when transplanted to very different contexts. These structures and relationships constitute the "domestic-service paradigm." The first half of this paper gives examples of the way it was transferred intact to female spheres of philanthropic and professional work in the Victorian and Edwardian periods; the second half advances the argument that even the exceptional circumstances of 1914–18, when women entered occupations hitherto confined to men, and participated in a national emergency in which many social conventions might have been expected to be discarded, did not seriously weaken the paradigm.

The Industrial Revolution of the eighteenth and nineteenth centuries, as is well known, created in Britain not only crowded slums but also a new middle class; dining rooms and gardens as well as factory floors.[1] If a single set of data were to be selected to illustrate the central importance of the nonindustrial, noncommercial sphere in

*Portions of this article have appeared in: "Sphère publique et sphère privée. L'identité professionelle féminine et le modèle du service domestique en Grand-Bretagne (1840–1920)," in Sextant, Revue du Groupe interdisciplinaire d'Etudes sur les Femmes (Université Libre de Bruxelles), no. 1 (Winter 1993/94), and are reproduced here by kind permission of the editors.

this period of economic and technological transformation, it would have to be the figures for female employment in domestic service. Although historians have recognized that women industrial workers in the nineteenth century constituted a relatively small proportion of the female workforce, they have tended to ignore domestic servants. Domestic service was the largest sector of female employment, and one that grew steadily. This development was so taken for granted by contemporaries that it was almost as invisible to them as the air they breathed—and just as indispensable! And for a long time this invisibility, rather than indispensability has, with few exceptions, communicated itself to historians concerned to explore the shifts and transformations in gender roles in nineteenth- and early twentieth-century Britain.[2]

It is not a paradox, but a direct consequence of industrialization that in 1841, when 1,815,000 women were listed by the census as "occupied," 358,000 of them worked in the textile industries, and 989,000 in domestic service; that in 1871, out of a total 3,650,000 occupied, 726,000 worked in the former sector, and 1,678,000 in the latter; and that in 1911, when the total was 5,413,000, the figures were 870,000 and 2,127,000 respectively.[3] What these figures demonstrate is that new patterns of comfortable living for the "nouveaux riches" of the expanding middle classes resulted in the expansion of *traditional* employment opportunities for the "toujours pauvres." The relatively crude figures quoted do not, of course, indicate such variables as size of employing firm or family, or number of staff per household or establishment; nor can they describe precisely the character of relations between employer and employee.[4] However, as the authors of the 1911 census report pointed out, "roughly one out of every three occupied single women is still a domestic servant."[5] The figures show us quite unequivocally that a great number of waged women undertook this form of employment, that a great number of unwaged women must have provided it or benefited from it, and indeed that a very large proportion of all women in Britain were in some way implicated in the practical work and the social relationships of domestic service.

World War I did not seriously modify this occupational landscape.[6] Although new employment opportunities indeed emerged for women after the war, the percentages of women employed outside domestic service, particularly in the manufacturing industries, remained negligible. In 1921, the number of female domestic servants dipped just below two million, but returned to prewar levels in 1931, when an increase in absolute numbers of sixteen percent was recorded. The census report for that year pointed out that the num-

ber of women in the occupational category "personal service" was
three times greater than that in any other female occupational
group, and that sixty-nine percent of the category (the next largest
subgroup, that of charwomen and office cleaners, constituted a mere
seven percent of the category!) consisted of live-in domestic service,
which represented 20.4 percent of the total "occupied" female population.[7] For a majority of women, therefore, whether they were giving the orders or taking them, domestic service provided a common
experience and a framework of interaction throughout the period
covered by this paper.

We might say, indeed, that women were "imprinted" with the
patterns of work and conduct embedded in this form of labor. If this
assumption is correct, we should not be surprised to see these patterns replicated where women chose, or were invited, to work outside the environment of the private home. We should expect to see
an extension of women's role in society conceived in terms that reflected or derived from previous traditions of work and responsibility; and for the customs, language, and practices of domestic service
to be transferred to other spheres. Before proceeding to specific case
studies, it is necessary to allude briefly to the context in which
"Woman's Mission"—the role of middle- and upper-class ladies in
social reform—was conceived in the nineteenth century, and the relation of "Woman's Mission" to the working practices of domestic
service.

WOMAN'S MISSION, NURSING, AND THE DOMESTIC-SERVICE PARADIGM

By the middle of the nineteenth century, many religious thinkers,
both male and female, considered the role of women as employers,
or "mistresses," of servants to be of crucial importance in a project
of social reconciliation and reform. The idea that Britain was not a
unitary society, but had become, in Benjamin Disraeli's widely used
term, "Two Nations" because of the increasing physical and social
distance between the different classes (especially in the cities) was a
cause of deep anxiety. In the growing cities and towns, prosperous
employers no longer lived "above the shop" and shared meals with
their workpeople, but moved themselves and their families out to
residences in the new suburbs; at the same time, the rapid increase
in the population of urban parishes placed many of the poor beyond
the effective reach of Christian pastoral care and teaching. By contrast, and in a simultaneous development, many women managers
of households were acquiring larger domestic staffs, developing close
residential contacts with their servants, and establishing personal

relationships across class barriers. They did not merely teach their employees their practical duties, but also disciplined their work patterns, modified their social behavior, and, frequently, supervised their religious observance.[8]

A lecture given to an audience of ladies around 1855 by an Anglican clergyman, the Rev. J. S. Brewer, illustrates the ambitious social expectations that could be invested in these "relations of employment." Brewer described the unemployed and destitute of London, who were obliged to become inmates of the workhouses set up under the Poor Laws, as belonging mainly to a class that

> . . . has never come into contact with the upper classes of society. They have not been domestic servants; they have been utterly removed in their sympathies, their training, their enjoyments, and their sorrows—in their whole lives, in short—from the upper ranks of society. . . . unwittingly, you are exercising in your own families a vast social and political power; you are educating the poor under you. . . . They carry into a lower and very extended circle the influence of your teaching and your training.[9]

On this occasion, the speaker was exhorting the ladies to extend their influence by visiting workhouses; but there were many other outlets for the exercise of "Woman's Mission." Clergy wives and daughters, and the (chiefly female) members of parish District Visiting Societies were already active in visiting the poor in their own homes, establishing thrift and sewing clubs for wives and mothers, and teaching their children in Sunday schools. The needs of the sick poor, both in their own homes and in hospitals, were claiming women's attention, especially during the cholera outbreaks of 1831–1832, 1848–1849, and 1854. Hospital conditions attracted the interest of reformers not because their standards of care were inadequate by the medical standards of their time—most were kindly, orderly, and publicly accountable institutions—but because they too offered scope for the exercise of influence across the class divide.[10] It was a Christian missionary project, rather than a medical one, that this clergyman envisaged around 1854:

> In the Hospital . . . the sick are in quiet and comfortable wards; the heart is already in some measure softened by the kindness received, and the mind is prepared to attend to the great concerns of eternity.[11]

This lecture was quoted with approval in a little book, *Hospitals and Sisterhoods*, published anonymously in 1854, the year of the outbreak of the Crimean War. Its author was Mary Stanley, a close friend of Florence Nightingale, who by the end of that year was processing applications from nurses to join Nightingale's expedition to Scutari.[12] Stanley argued that religious sisterhoods could enter hospitals to supervise the ordinary working nurses, ensure the proper physical care of poor patients, and see that no opportunity for salvation was neglected. She was particularly impressed by the example of the first Anglican nursing sisterhood, the St. John's Housing Training Institution for Nurses, which had been founded in 1848.[13]

The membership of St. John's House consisted of probationers and nurses, who received training for hospital and domiciliary care of the sick in return for wages, board, and lodging, and who were also expected to "assist in such domestic duties of the house as may be assigned to them," and of the Sisters, who supervised and helped to train the former. Sisters received no salary, and indeed paid for their own board and lodging. The constitution of St. John's House assumed that ladies were more spiritually motivated than working women, and that they were qualified to instruct the latter in nursing without themselves undergoing a period of formal probation; and it demonstrates a determined confusion of the notions of spiritual, social, and professional superiority.

Although the order was originally directed towards domiciliary care, it was seen as providing a model to be easily transposed to hospital wards where head nurses, or "sisters," supervised and were sometimes drawn from a higher social class than the ordinary nurses, or "ward maids." The latter often performed domestic as well as medical functions: as one surgeon expressed it, "the normal duties of a housemaid."[14] In 1856, St. John's House won an important contract to supply all the nursing and cleaning services of King's College Hospital, London, for a fixed annual sum; an additional contract was agreed with Charing Cross Hospital, London, in 1866.

The domestic service model of nursing organization appealed to some medical men because it appeared to guarantee the provision of reliable and disciplined auxiliaries. It proved, however, to have one important drawback. This was the Sisters' stipulation that they enjoy complete autonomy in their task of superintendence. As ladies, they were accustomed to powerlessness outside the private sphere, but to virtual independence within it. Now they claimed exactly the same rights over their nurses as they had exercised over domestic servants in their own homes; and their own unsalaried status may have strengthened their sense of identity in this respect. For a doctor to intervene between Sister and nurse would be as extraordinary as for a husband or father to give instructions to the cook or the washerwoman. The St. John's House Sisters considered themselves accountable, not to the doctors, but to the lay governors of the hospital. They refused doctors the right to hire, fire, or discipline nurses; they even forbade doctors to assign them their ward duties. In King's College, Charing Cross, and other hospitals nursed by sisterhoods, the wards rapidly became sites where male and female authorities competed for power.[15]

We might expect quite different conditions to attach to Florence Nightingale's penetration of the Army Medical Department. However, developments in military nursing after the commencement of the Crimean War in 1854 also followed this model of *imperium in imperio*. The female nurses were not an integral part of the war establishment. They were recruited by Nightingale and her female friends, and answerable to Nightingale and to those military medical officers who chose (and many did not) to call upon their services. They coexisted uneasily with the male ward orderlies of the Medical Staff Corps and other regiments, who were subordinate, not to medical men, but to ward sergeants and superior combatant officers. Nightingale herself deferred to the wishes of the medical officers, but enjoyed a wholly independent relationship with the Secretary of State for War (who was, indeed, a personal friend of many years' standing), to whom she reported directly.[16]

After the war, Nightingale was invited to draw up regulations for a permanent female corps. She undertook this task with the assistance of one of her wartime colleagues, Jane Shaw Stewart, a devout Anglican who was the daughter of a Scottish baronet. The new regulations, published in 1859 and implemented in 1861, stipulated that nurses were to be selected by a female superintendent-general. Neither appointments nor dismissals could occur without her sanction. Within individual hospitals, a female superintendent had the sole right to discipline nurses, and had to be consulted over any proposed changes in ward duties. Replicating Nightingale's wartime privileges, the superintendent-general's annual report was made not to the head of the Army Medical Department but, "over his head," directly to the Secretary of State for War.

In a strict sense, the separate female chain of command was a constitutional necessity. Before World War I, British soldiers enlisted, not in a national army, but in one of many local regiments, and they agreed to abide by the rules and punishments administered by regimental officers. Female nurses, having no regiment, needed disciplinary procedures devised outside the conventional framework. Nevertheless, the procedures arrived at were strikingly similar to those that the religious sisterhoods had introduced into civilian hospitals in London, and it is no coincidence that they were conceived by women of a comparable social background to the unsalaried Sisters of St. John's House.

Nightingale persuaded Shaw Stewart, much against the latter's own wishes and better judgment, to accept the first appointment as superintendent. Shaw Stewart argued that she was unsuitable, because her own social rank was higher than that of the average military-medical officer. The autonomous powers she would enjoy would provoke a hostile or jealous response; the only possibility of disarming such a response lay in appointing a woman closer to her male colleagues in social-class terms. The widow of an officer might be more successful than the daughter of a baronet. Shaw Stewart gave way to Nightingale only after exacting two conditions from the Secretary of State for War: that she should take office without a salary; and that all her nurses should be Anglicans. Although such a policy of religious discrimination applied nowhere else in the Army, her wish was granted, to Nightingale's own intense annoyance.

The years between 1861 and 1868, when Shaw Stewart held office, were for her something akin to time on the Cross. Her predictions of discord and rivalry, which to some extent may have been self-fulfilling, were borne out almost to the letter. The medical officers did all they could to marginalize her, and connived with the nurses to denounce her to the War Office, emphasizing, among other things, the high dismissal rate within the female service, which contrasted strongly with the greater tolerance extended by medical officers and ward sergeants to the peccadilloes of the male orderlies.

From an early stage, the superintendent and the medical officers engaged in disagreements over shared territory and separate space, which proved impervious to negotiation. Demarcation disputes between female nurses and male orderlies also multiplied. Both the military governor and the medical officers interpreted these conflicts in class terms. As early as 1863, the governor of Netley military hospital had informed the War Office that the post of superintendent "would be filled with greater advantage by a woman of the middle class."[17] When pressure from the governor, the medical officers, and the medical press resulted in a War Office inquiry and in Shaw Stewart's resignation, the *Medical Times and Gazette* declared:

> We should be glad to learn that the [vacant] appointment had been given to the widow of some deserving Medical or military officer possessing the necessary tact and knowledge, to whose income the salary attached to the office would be an acceptable addition.[18]

This wish was granted in November 1869, when Mrs. Jane Cecilia

Deeble, widow of an army medical officer, took over the post of superintendent of nurses. The medical officers had indeed succeeded in replacing an aristocrat with a woman of their own class; and her appointment coincided with the issue of modified hospital regulations, which began a process of eroding the autonomy of the female service. These culminated in 1885, when, in the most radical break with tradition, it was laid down that the director-general of the Army Medical Department alone would nominate superintendents and nurses from a list in his office, that no dismissal was to take place without his sanction, and that medical officers could recommend to their male superiors the suspension of a nurse from duty. The service's superintendent and its creator were equally appalled by these developments. Nightingale's fulminations against each stage of the new arrangements were couched as much in the language of class as of professionalism or gender. On hearing in 1883 that Director-General Sir Thomas Crawford had accepted Nightingale Training School "graduates" without requiring either written reference or interview, she drafted a furious note:

> Would Lady Crawford intrust you with the duty of selecting your housemaid or your cook? . . . how could the mistress of a household manage her household if she did not enquire personally into the character of her servants?[19]

The metaphor was revealing of her assumptions about the "relations of employment," and it also undermined the validity of her critique; for the administrative changes were designed precisely to subvert the domestic service model on which the nursing regulations had been based. At the same time that the Army Nursing Service underwent this remodeling, similar shifts were taking place in civilian nursing. Physicians' and surgeons' complaints against the principles of female segregation and superintendence had been gathering strength during the 1870s and 1880s. They demanded greater control over the training and supervision of nursing in their hospitals, and by and large lay managers acquiesced. New, secular nurse-training schools, controlled by male medics, grew up within some of the larger institutions. In 1885 the St. John's House sisterhood left King's College Hospital, and in 1889 it left Charing Cross.[20] The title "lady superintendent" reverted to the pre-reform "matron." Nightingale and the sisterhoods had perhaps been undone by their own success; certainly they had created a demand that they could not satisfy for a new species of refined and educated female employee, subordinate to male professionals, rather than to either "the lady of the house" or its overall master.

VOLUNTEER LADIES AND SALARIED WOMEN

While hospital nursing may offer the clearest example of a public function organized on the domestic service pattern, other areas of women's work in the nineteenth century show comparable features. The voluntary prison-visiting movement initiated by Elizabeth Fry in 1817 involved the care of "women" by "ladies." The latters' functions included making recommendations on the sanitation and cleaning of prisons; helping to rehabilitate discharged female prisoners, often by training them as domestic servants, and frequently taking them as such into their own homes; and supporting and periodically superintending the salaried female prison officers for whose appointment they had successfully campaigned.[21] In 1832, Elizabeth Fry had declared:

> I find a remarkable difference depending upon whether female officers are superintended by ladies or not. . . . One reason is, that many of the latter are not very superior women, not very high either in principle or habit, and are liable to be contaminated; they soon get familiar with the prisoners, and cease to excite the respect due to their office. . . .[22]

The respect accorded the lady visitor was due entirely to her external social standing, and had nothing to do with the official hierarchy within the prison itself. Permission to visit was, indeed, at the discretion of each prison governor, and might frequently be revoked; nevertheless it was well known that ladies could use the influence of their male connections to push for legislative change, and that in their philanthropic interventions they enjoyed a privileged relationship with "the master of the house." The rescue worker Susanna Meredith recalled in the 1890s that her visiting activities were arranged in agreement with the Home Secretary: "If I wanted to say anything, Sir George Grey said to me, 'You must publish nothing about this prison, but if you have anything to say you must come and say it to me,'" After the nationalization of the prison service in 1877, her activities were abruptly curtailed: "They altered the regulations without communicating with me. . . . I had previously nothing to do with anybody but the Home Secretary." She gave up prison visiting soon afterwards.[23]

Prison visiting by volunteer ladies did not cease after 1877; nor did the appointment of "ladies" within either army or civilian nursing services. The identification of professional with social authority died very hard indeed; and many of the new professional employments opened to women towards the end of the century were to be imprinted with the assumptions of the domestic sector. Celia

Davies and W. C. Dowling have documented the rise of ladies' "sanitary associations" in the mid-Victorian period: these paid for working women to go into the homes of the poor to give advice on domestic hygiene and infant care. But by 1900, when salaried health visitors were appointed by municipal authorities, (male) medical officers of health did not wish to recruit women of "the cottager type" for this work, but preferred ladies who were "patient and refined in manner." They could not conceive that instruction could be effectively communicated between women, except within the framework of a hierarchical social relationship.[24]

Helen Jones and Mary Drake McFeely have observed a similar phenomenon in the development of factory inspection as a profession for women after 1893. Although for almost fifteen years male and female trade unionists had been asking the Home Office to appoint female inspectors who were "not ladies, but practical working women," the official appointments which were finally made were of middle-class women.[25] By contrast, the male inspectorate was recruited from a wide social spectrum, and included former factory workers and trade unionists. Small wonder that the female inspectors could feel socially isolated and that Adelaide Anderson, "principal lady inspector," should have written in 1905 that no female inspector should be obliged to live and work away from her home base, on the grounds that she could "find no normal associates in, or through, her work."[26] Beatrice Webb had forseen the serious implications of this social anomaly. She wrote to one of the pioneers, Rose Squire, in 1896: "What I fear is, that if the level of Women Factory Inspectors is kept so uniformly high, there will be an organised movement to suppress them, from jealous males!"[27]

The female factory inspectorate had, indeed, commenced existence as a segregated and privileged chain of command in which a group of ladies based in London traveled throughout Britain to inspect the working conditions of factory women. They reported, not to senior local male inspectors, but to the principal lady inspector, who in turn was responsible directly to the chief inspector. This independence from the hierarchy of the male inspectorate was much resented, and localization was imposed on the female service by degrees; from 1921, although ladies continued to specialize in the inspection of the female workforce, their separate structure of reporting and seniority was abolished. Equal pay was not among the consequences of this equalization of conditions of employment.[28]

In 1896, Beatrice Webb had feared the jealousy of male factory inspectors; in 1919, when the founders of the wartime Women's Police Service asked for it to be placed on a permanent footing, this was refused on the grounds that educated women "would pin-prick the men."[29] How much had actually changed in the fifty years since Jane Shaw Stewart's ordeal in office? Male professionals remained jealous of their female colleagues, who so frequently came from a higher social stratum than theirs. While men expected to be recruited on grounds of objectively tested ability, women were being selected for reasons that were rarely put into print, or specified in official literature. Professional ladies appeared to enjoy a privileged position on this account, especially where they were employed within a segregated chain of command. But the privilege was very double-edged. Acceptance was dependent less on women's own achievements than on their family backgrounds: on their presumed capacity to manage and take care of lower-class women on behalf of male colleagues, employers, and society at large.

This fundamental asymmetry placed women outside the sphere of professional formation and promotion as it was perceived by men. Neither equality nor solidarity could develop between men and women in the same occupations, if they were selected according to such different criteria. The social impossibility of friendly meetings outside working hours on which Adelaide Anderson remarked was both a symptom and a cause of this fateful failure, and may have been at least as potent a source of male alienation as the prospect that female colleagues might drop out of the workforce in order to marry and have babies.[30]

There were equally damaging consequences for lower-class women from this state of affairs. Their aspirations to careers in the factory inspectorate or nursing or health visiting were frustrated not because of any proven lack of ability or expertise, but because of their presumed personal incapacity to communicate instructions or to exercise authority. In 1891, for example, the (female) head of the Army Nursing Service thought it perfectly reasonable to pass the following judgment: "Satisfactory report on all points. Not being a lady, is unfit for promotion" on one Annie Steele, who had given seven years' service and who promptly resigned.[31] If lower-class women suffered professional discrimination, and if the "ladies" did not take up the cudgels on their behalf, it is difficult not to see the ladies themselves as perpetrators as well as victims of the domestic service paradigm; and the question arises, how far did the paradigm compromise and vitiate campaigns by such ladies to widen educational and occupational opportunities for their own sex.

LADIES AND WOMEN IN THE WAR

A paradigm of relations of employment so deeply imprinted in the minds of both men and women was hardly likely to crumble at the outbreak of World War I, when large numbers of women made the transition from domestic to public employment, and/or from the civilian to the combatant sphere. It is particularly important to remember that women's participation in the war effort was, throughout, voluntary in character.[32] The organization of women's war service tended to place unsalaried ladies in positions of leadership, and often depended upon the labor of middle- and upper-class women for whom any wages or honoraria bore no relation to customary living expenses. There was an enormous gulf between them and women, of whatever social background, who had to work for a living. As will be seen, the former brought to their war work prewar assumptions—largely derived from domestic experience and philanthropic activities—concerning their relations both with women workers of lower classes and with male chains of authority, which were not always appropriate to the needs of the time.

Nursing: The work of nurses, especially those organized through the Voluntary Aid Detachments (VAD), is probably the most familiar aspect of British women's World War I service. Nurses were uniformed, performed physically arduous work under strict and hierarchical discipline, and sometimes came under enemy fire; they represented the most obvious female equivalent of battlefield service. Certainly theirs was at the time the most socially acceptable form of female participation. VAD work is also familiar because it was undertaken by literate and educated women for whom, unlike their professional nursing colleagues, war nursing was an exceptional episode on which they went voluminously into print after the war.[33] As their memoirs make clear, VADs frequently had as little respect for the regulation-bound professional nurses of Queen Alexandra's Imperial Nursing Service or the Territorial Force Nursing Service as Florence Nightingale had had for the official Army Medical Officers of the Crimean War.[34] Professional nurses, for their part, resented the VADs as amateurs who flirted with officers and undercut their own wages. All nursing staff kept their distance from the "General Service" VADs, who undertook a range of duties from laundering and cooking to clerical work.

Nursing VADs were usually paid £20 per annum, sometimes rising to £30, together with a small uniform allowance, and extra mess payments for those on foreign duty.[35] The somewhat elevated expectations of their social and economic background entertained by Katharine Furse, the VAD Commander-in-Chief, are indicated in her letter to each enlisted woman:

> Those of you who are paid can give to the Red Cross Society which is your Mother and which needs more and more money to carry on its great work.
>
> Those of you who are not paid are giving their best to their Mother Society and thus to the Sick and Wounded.[36]

In similar vein, the author of the wartime *General Service Hints for V.A.D. Members* pointed out that it was "recognised that the salary paid [to VADs] is rather a refund of out-of-pocket expenses than adequate remuneration for the service they give";[37] and the Gloucestershire County Director of the Red Cross reported in 1919:

> I wish to repeat what I have explained before, that we do not look on the small grant I have mentioned as a salary; it was merely an allowance which enabled a member to give us her services, who otherwise would have been obliged to seek work elsewhere, which, in every case, would have been far more remunerative than ours.[38]

This deliberate shunning of the word "salary," and emphasis on wartime employment as a species of *noblesse oblige*, rather than as a means to professional remuneration or the earning of a livelihood, or obedience to government imperatives, was wholly characteristic of the military-first-aid movement as a whole. Before the war, the VADs had been organized through two voluntary charitable organizations, the Red Cross and the Order of St. John, which continued to process training and applications for service after 1914.[39] The system began to break down under the weight of organizational rivalries, and was replaced by a centralized administration. However, Furse recalled that in 1917, when a Department of National Service was set up to streamline all such recruitment, "some of my colleagues in the Joint War Committee and V.A.D. Department . . . still strongly disapproved of the General Service scheme and of our co-operating with other services or the V.A.D.s being recruited through a Government Department as being *infra dig*."[40]

A similar set of attitudes seems to have permeated the Scottish Women's Hospitals (SWH), which were established in the face of initial official opposition by the suffragist Dr. Elsie Inglis. Their work was funded and overseen by voluntary management committees in London and Edinburgh. Ultimately the SWH were to make a virtue, if not a totem, of the independence that had originally been thrust upon them. From 1916, when official attitudes changed, a number of SWH medical officers chose to join the Royal Army Medical Corps. The SWH as a body, however, refused, despite the many dangers and difficulties of work in the field, to surrender their independent status and accept incorporation in the regular army service.

The SWH's most recent historian has shown why the medical officers might have been anxious to defect.[41] The hospital units employed many different grades of personnel, and the most junior, like the ladies of the committee, received no salary. Women from a moneyed stratum were, thus, frequently subordinated (in principle) to professionals whom they considered their social inferiors. While the clinical record of the units was impeccable, in the absence of official army regulations, social prejudices ran riot. There were units where unpaid orderlies with first-aid certificates despised the fully trained nurses, and where drivers of cars were insolent to medical officers. The administrator of the Girton and Newnham unit, a sister of General French, precipitated the resignations of four doctors before a headquarters ruling confirmed the authority of the Chief Medical Officer. The narrative of these squabbles indicates that male prejudice did not constitute the sole obstacle to the full development of women's professionalism in this period.[42]

Police Service: The history of the wartime Women's Police Service (WPS) illustrates several aspects of the domestic-service paradigm: the voluntary status of the work of "ladies," their assumption of a controlling and protective role vis-à-vis lower-class women, and their privileged relation to "the master of the house."[43] The group of women who founded the WPS in 1915 had strong connections to the prewar suffrage movement; however, for the commandant, Margaret Damer Dawson, the most formative prewar experience was almost certainly her work with the National Vigilance Association (NVA), which was founded to monitor and extend the provisions of the 1885 Criminal Law Amendment Act, itself a product of the agitation surrounding W. T. Stead's revelations of child prostitution in his *Pall Mall Gazette* articles on "The Maiden Tribute of Modern Babylon."[44] The NVA's volunteers, grouped in local branches, took on an extensive social caseload that included inaugurating prosecutions for sexual offenses against women and children. A subcommittee was established for the suppression of traffic in women, which worked with other organizations dedicated to the abolition of the so-called white slave trade.[45] In 1904 the NVA reported that it had mounted an intensive six-month vigil at ports and railway stations in order to befriend and warn young women seeking employment unaided, or responding to dubious advertisements. The report particularly thanked E. R. Henry, chief commissioner of the Metropolitan Police, for his encouragement of and cooperation with this scheme.[46]

After 1915, Margaret Damer Dawson, Mary Allen, Ellen Harburn, and others prevailed upon Chief Commissioner Henry to give them responsibility for training and providing women police constables for service in the capital and the provinces. Women police were rarely absorbed into local constabularies, but remained accountable, through their training committee, directly to the Chief Commissioner. The functions that they claimed for themselves, and that were initially willingly assigned to them, were the protection and control of women and girls during the many social dislocations imposed by wartime conditions. They were to curb indecent behavior in and around military camps, to supervise women and girls as they traveled round the country to take up new employments, and to continue this work of supervision when the women workers were installed in munitions factories.

Several former suffragists resigned from police work during the course of the war, appalled to find themselves "protecting" men from women and implementing a policy that almost invariably labeled women as the poisoners and corrupters of the male soldiery. Other policewomen felt and voiced their disquiet, but carried on with work that in many ways was simply a continuation of their prewar activities. The extent to which the women police were evenhanded in the matter of surveillance and arrests, together with the social and organizational distance that existed between them and their male colleagues, may well have contributed to their enforced disbandment at the end of 1918. Local police authorities showed no enthusiasm for building up their female forces after the war, and the WPS was bypassed when Women Police Patrols were established in London in 1919. However, an echo of the old "separation of spheres" was maintained by the appointment of a woman police superintendent who controlled the Patrols from New Scotland Yard. By 1923 this final vestige of segregation had been abolished, and the women were attached to their various divisions and police stations.[47]

Factory Work Inspection: The WPS were not the only ladies whose services were called upon when munitions production dictated the large-scale recruitment of female factory workers. The latter were overseen by a veritable army of voluntary and salaried ladies, working as factory inspectors or welfare supervisors, or through charitable committees assisting the workers' arrangements for lodging, food, and recreation. Indeed, throughout the war, women's industrial employment was treated as an abnormal and potentially dangerous social development that had to be subject to a battery of special controls. While the end product of women's factory production may have been identical to what would have been

required of a male workforce, the terms on which women were recruited, and the conditions under which they were employed, were
very different. Advertisements for female munition workers specified, as might advertisements for live-in domestic servants, that they
should be "of good character."[48] The wartime economy, indeed, propelled many former domestic servants into the factories; and the assumptions concerning this class of employee—that it was an object
of benevolence, instruction, and management—were not revised,
but were intensified with the transposition to a new workplace.

Laura Lee Downs has published a remarkable case study of female
welfare supervision at Armstrong-Whitworth's gun and gun-carriage
plant at Newcastle.[49] A Miss Jayne was appointed after the women
workers had been on strike, and was allowed to establish an *imperium in imperio* strikingly similar to that of Jane Shaw Stewart in
the army hospitals. Miss Jayne reported directly to the firm's managing director, Sir Percy Girovard, and established a vertical chain of
command, placing her own forewomen and overlookers (wherever
possible, selected from the few educated volunteers among the
women workers) alongside male charge hands and foremen. Foremen no longer had the freedom to hire, promote, or fire women
workers: Miss Jayne had to make the preliminary selection, or give
prior consent, in each case. She also had the power to transfer
women from one job to another for reasons of health or discipline.

It is indicative of the previous experience of such welfare supervisors that they considered that "the domestic servant is the best
type of worker: she is an early riser and has endurance."[50] The vali-
dation of their previous experience is implicit in an official report's
insistence that welfare supervisors should be "accustomed . . . by
habit and by social position . . . to supervising inferiors." That habit
was lacking in lower-class women, who were "uncertain of their
ability to control their equals."[51] The fact that working women were
capable of organizing, negotiating, and acting on their own initiative—as evidenced by their ability to initiate, maintain, and con-
clude a strike—could not be assimilated to the domestic-service
paradigm. Indeed, it so flatly contradicted the paradigm that it had to
be denied or ignored.

Even where a lady volunteer was politically biased towards the
cause of labor, there were deep ambiguities inherent in her role, as is
illustrated by a wartime recollection of Edith Picton-Turbervill. Picton-Turbervill, who came from a wealthy family, undertook both
missionary work in India and welfare work in munitions factories
under the aegis of the Young Women's Christian Association
(YWCA). At the end of the war she joined the Labour Party, and was

returned to Parliament as a Labour MP in 1929. She recalled in her memoirs:

> Lady Wantage came down with me to see one of the club-rooms and canteens which we had built for munition girls with her money near a factory. In spite of her age her energy was surprising. We met Margaret Bondfield outside the factory doing her Trade Union work amongst the girls during the dinner hour. I introduced her to Lady Wantage, and Lady Wantage was thrilled to meet and speak with a real live leader in the Trade Union world. I think she expected a fierce-looking revolutionary, and was delighted with the bright-eyed, high-coloured, charming Margaret Bondfield. Princess Alice was also there busy peeling potatoes in a canteen, so perhaps the presence of the Princess balanced the presence of a Trade Union official![52]

That most anomalous of creatures, the youthful female working outside the domestic sector and actually negotiating conditions for herself and her female peers, is here made to appear acceptable, and almost ladylike, to the benefactress who is her social "superior": not "fierce-looking," but "charming."

Most interestingly, Margaret Bondfield's own memoirs provide a rare instance of the reverse process: of working-class women commenting on the appearance and manner of a lady, and the latter's being "made over" in order to become acceptable to them:

> Mary [MacArthur] asked me to introduce Susan [Lawrence] to a factory-gate meeting. We went to the East End, where our branch members made a good crowd. But Susan's voice had not been trained for speaking to an East End audience, who treated her as a comic turn and roared with laughter. I felt ashamed of them, to treat a stranger so, but also felt that there was something to be said for the girls, who had never before heard that kind of voice. I reported to Mary that Susan had pluck to stick it out and complete her speech, but that unless she altered the tone of her voice and got control of it she would never hold a crowd. Susan *did* alter the tone, and did get voice control in a very short space of time, and could control crowds, inside and outside the Party, the L.C.C. and the House of Commons. That horrible experience made her "one of us."[53]

Susan Lawrence later became a Labour MP and Parliamentary Secretary to the Ministry of Health; Margaret Bondfield herself rose even higher, to become the first female cabinet minister and Privy Councillor in Britain. It is hard to dispute the contention that, even if the postwar feminist organizations could have maintained their élan and momentum after 1919, only the British labor movement

could have raised a working-class woman to a position of such emi-
nence in the interwar decades.

The almost poetic dénouement to the episode of women's munitions work came at the end of the war, when they were turned out of
the factories. They were denied unemployment compensation if
they refused any employment now offered them; what they were offered was domestic service. Rose Squire, the pioneer lady factory inspector, was assigned to the Department of Demobilisation and
Resettlement, where she and a staff of lady welfare supervisors managed to train and place over two thousand women for the domestic
sector.[54] The women welfare supervisors disappeared from the metalworking industries at the same time as their charges.[55]

* * *

It has perhaps not been sufficiently remarked that the coming of
peace in 1919 saw a reprise of the "single woman" debate, on which
so much ink had been spilt in the 1840s and 1850s.[56] The label "two
million surplus" was applied to all classes of women.[57] It was
bandied about on the basis of the terrible losses of potential husbands during the war; and, perhaps because of the high proportion of
casualties among the officer class, it was thought that many ladies
would now be engaged in a difficult search for employment. One of
several interwar writers on the subject of "the servant problem"
even prophesied that

> the domestic assistants of the future will be recruited from the same
> class that gave us our governesses, and will have to receive the same
> treatment; they will be educated women who are obliged to earn a
> livelihood, and who are unfitted, either by the type of their tempera-
> ment or lack of opportunities for training, to enter any of the learned
> professions.[58]

Other writers had only slightly more elevated ambitions for their fellow "educated women." In a 1923 essay on "The Moral Training of
Young Girls," the surgeon and obstetrician Mary Scharlieb expressed
her anxiety over the possible misuse of the independence that opportunities for employment outside the domestic sector offered the
young female worker. Wise superintendence was needed to prevent
her from going astray. She reminded her readers:

> During the Great War many ladies received an admirably practical
> training in domestic economics and also in the far more difficult tasks
> of moral supervision and "mothering." As Chief Welfare Workers, as
> Superintendents of Voluntary Aid Detachments, and in many similar

positions, women of good birth and breeding, and education, learned the very lessons that they might now once more turn to national account by mothering young women in various circumstances. Among these ladies are individuals who seem specially endowed with an intuitive appreciation of the wants and desires of working girls. . . . Some people talk of superfluous women. There are none. . . . We need the unmarried women as well as the married to be the spiritual mothers of the race. They are wanted in innumerable positions of trust and importance, such as those of teachers, doctors, nurses, welfare workers, inspectors of midwives, and of factories.[59]

Much has been made, in recent accounts of interwar feminism, of the use of a maternal paradigm by "new feminists" to justify a larger female participation in political life. The maternal model of women's citizenship, and "civic motherhood" as a concept which at the same time legitimated and restricted women's political agency, have been cited and discussed, but with very little reference to the variety of meanings contemporaries attached to the words "mother" and "maternal."[60] It needs to be remembered that terms relating to family and kin have often been borrowed and transformed within relations of employment and authority. Seniority within an institution or working practice has been endowed with the character of seniority within families. Those in authority tend to conceptualize their subordinates as more childlike than themselves. This was, not surprisingly, particularly marked in the case of domestic service in Britain, where married women were the principal employers of single girls, providing them with food and shelter at a stage in their lives when they could not have supported themselves outside a parental or quasi-parental home.

Pam Taylor has published an account of domestic service between the wars with the appropriate title "Daughters and Mothers—Maids and Mistresses," and has stressed that what was specific to this form of employment was "often a relation between an *older woman* of one class with a *younger woman* of another."[61] While not every "mistress" took injunctions to consider herself *in loco parentis* literally, the domestic-service paradigm nevertheless conferred the status of adulthood on the employer and that of childhood on the employee. Women of the servant-employing classes were pseudo-mothers; servants were pseudo-daughters. It is in this context that we should read Mary Scharlieb's references to "mothering." Concealed within her discourse of maternity was an unshakable class bias. The capacity for "moral supervision" was not derived from supposedly universal qualities such as biology and the caring instinct, but from "good birth, and breeding and education." The "mothers of the race" in Scharlieb's exhortation were never of the working classes.

Authority, management, control: these were the meanings encoded within the elaboration of "mothering" careers for middle- and upper-class women in nineteenth- and early twentieth-century Great Britain. The objects of these exercises in leadership were to be adult women of the working classes (though it should not be forgotten how great a part these watchwords also played in the elaboration of many theories of infant care). No matter how often biology might have been proclaimed as the destiny of most women, there were nevertheless several interpretations of maternity in this period, and they were filtered through many layers of everyday practice that are scarcely visible to late twentieth-century historians. Embodied in discourses of the maternal were the social relations and disciplines of middle- and upper-class households that are now, to all intents and purposes, extinct in the West. Few female readers of this book will have experienced the domestic and the institutional as did their predecessors. But until it is understood how far the domestic sector was, in the period of history we most associate with industrialization and modernization, the site of a system of hierarchical class relations, and until it is appreciated to what extent this system was extrapolated to every sector of the public domain occupied by women, we shall not arrive at a proper conception of the relationship between public and private spheres in the formation of modern female identities.

NOTES

1. See particularly Leonore Davidoff and Catherine Hall, *Family Fortunes: Men and Women of the English Middle Class 1780–1850* (London, 1987).

2. See, however, Leonore Davidoff, "Class and Gender in Victorian England: The Diaries of A. J. Munby and Hannah Cullwick," *Feminist Studies* 5 (1979); Edward Higgs, "Domestic Service and Household Production," in Angela V. John, ed., *Unequal Opportunities: Women's Employment in England 1800–1918* (Oxford, 1986).

3. Brian Redman Mitchell and Phyllis Deane, *Abstract of British Historical Statistics* (Cambridge, 1962), 60. The number of "unoccupied" women rose to 5,369,000 in 1841; 6,429,000 in 1871; and 11,375,000 in 1911.

4. On this question, see Higgs, "Domestic Service."

5. 1911 Census, *Preliminary Report*, 160.

6. Laura Lee Downs leaves this wider occupational context obscure in

her account of the expansion of women's employment opportunities in the engineering industries: *Manufacturing Inequality: Gender Division in the French and British Metalworking Industries, 1914–1939* (Ithaca, 1995), 191, 198, 229.

7. 1921 Census of England and Wales, *General Report*, 117, 126; 1931 Census of England and Wales, *General Report*, 151–52; comparable percentages are to be found in the 1921 Census for Scotland, *Preliminary Report*, vol. 3, pp. 19, 47, and the 1931 Census for Scotland, *Preliminary Report*, vol. 3, p. xvii.

8. Pamela Horn, *The Rise and Fall of the Victorian Servant* (Dublin, 1975); Mark Ebery and Brian Preston, *Domestic Service in Late Victorian and Edwardian England* (Reading, 1976); Anne Summers, "A Home from Home: Women's Philanthropic Work in the Nineteenth Century," in Sandra Burman, ed., *Fit Work for Women* (London, 1979).

9. F. D. Maurice, ed., *Lectures to Ladies on Practical Subjects* (Cambridge, 1855), 273–77.

10. On the charitable "voluntary hospitals," which treated only poor patients for most of the century (only in exceptional cases were middle- and upper-class patients treated away from their own homes), see John Woodward, *To Do the Sick No Harm* (London, 1974).

11. Anon. [M. Stanley], *Hospitals and Sisterhoods* (London, 1854), 4.

12. On Stanley's role in Crimean War nursing, see Anne Summers, *Angels and Citizens: British Women as Military Nurses 1854–1914* (London, 1988), chap. 2.

13. The following account of St. John's House is taken from its published regulations and annual reports, and R. Few, *A History of St. John's House* (London, 1884). See also Anne Summers, "The Costs and Benefits of Caring: Nursing Charities c. 1830–1860," in Jonathan Barry and Colin Jones, eds., *Medicine and Charity before the Welfare State* (London, 1991). On the sisterhood movement in general, see P. F. Anson, *The Call of the Cloister* (London, 1964).

14. J. F. South, *Facts Relating to Hospital Nurses* (London, 1857), 7, 9, 12. South was surgeon at St. Thomas's Hospital, where Nightingale later established her training school.

15. S. F. Holloway, "The All Saints Sisterhood at University College Hospital, 1862–1899," *Medical History* 3 (1959); S. A. Plotkin, "The Crisis at Guy's Hospital," *Guy's Hospital Gazette* 75 (1961).

16. The account which follows is taken from Summers, *Angels and Citizens*, unless otherwise stated.

17. Public Record Office, W.O. 33/20, Appendix C ff. 149–50, Wilbraham to Scott Robertson, Dec. 3, 1863.

18. *Medical Times and Gazette*, 1 Aug. 1868, 130.

19. BL Add. MS. 45772, ff. 51, 55. Notes by Nightingale, c. Dec. 1883.

20. Holloway, "The All Saints Sisterhood," 152; Plotkin, "The Crisis at Guy's Hospital," 45–50.

21. Frank Prochaska, *Women and Philanthropy in 19th Century England* (Oxford, 1980), 163–73; Lucia Zedner, *Women, Crime and Custody in*

Victorian England (Oxford, 1991); Anne Summers, "Elizabeth Fry and mid-19th Century Reform," in Richard Creese, W. F. Bynum and J. Bearn, eds., *The Health of Prisoners* (Amsterdam, 1995).

22. *Report from Select Committee on Secondary Punishments, PP* 1831–2 VII, 675.

23. *Report from the Departmental Committee on Prisons, PP* 1895 LVI, 246.

24. Celia Davies, "The Health Visitor as Mother's Friend: A Woman's Place in Public Health, 1900–1914," *Social History of Medicine* 1, no. 1 (1988): 46; see also W. C. Dowling, "The Ladies' Sanitary Association and the Origins of the Health Visiting Service" (M.A. thesis, London University, 1963).

25. Helen Jones, "Women Health Workers: The Case of the First Women Factory Inspectors in Britain," *Social History of Medicine* 1, no. 2 (1988): 167; Mary Drake McFeely, *Lady Inspectors: The Campaign for a Better Workplace 1893–1921* (Oxford, 1988), 14.

26. Jones, "Women Health Workers," 175.

27. Letter (copy) of Jan. 8, 1896, in Fawcett Library, London.

28. McFeely, *Lady Inspectors*, passim, and esp. chap. 18.

29. Mary S. Allen, *The Pioneer Policewoman* (London, 1925), 128.

30. This thesis may apply less directly to the teaching profession. The lack of support for female teachers' aspirations on the part of their male colleagues and fellow trade unionists is documented in Helen Corr, "Sexual Politics in the National Union of Teachers 1870–1920," in *History of Education Society Occasional Publications*, no. 8 (1987). Anecdotal evidence certainly suggests that male relatives of many middle- and upper-class women who entered state-sector teaching worked in far more prestigious professions, and that there may well have been a social gulf between them and their male colleagues.

31. Summers, *Angels and Citizens*, 109–10.

32. For recent insights into this topic, which particularly inform my paragraphs on World War I nursing, I am indebted to Krisztina Robert, Janet S. K. Watson, and David Silbey, who contributed papers on "Gender, Class, and Patriotism in Britain 1914–1918" at the annual meeting of the American Historical Association, Atlanta, Jan. 1996.

33. A useful bibliography of this enormous category of war memoir is to be found in Claire Tylee, *The Great War and Women's Consciousness* (London, 1990).

34. Cecil Woodham-Smith, *Florence Nightingale* (London, 1950), accurately conveys her subject's hostility to the Army Medical Department, to the point of perpetuating some of her calumnies: see W. H. Greenleaf, "Biography and the 'Amateur' Historian: Mrs. Woodham-Smith's *Florence Nightingale*," *Victorian Studies* 2 (1959): 190–202.

35. See, e.g., *The Red Cross in Gloucestershire during the War* (Gloucester, 1919), 28; Vera Brittain, *Testament of Youth* (London, 1978), 209; May Wedderburn Cannan, "Recollections of B.R.C. V.A.D. No. 12, Oxford University" (typescript P.360, Imperial War Museum), 16.

36. Katherine Furse, *Hearts and Pomegranates: The Story of Forty-Five Years, 1875 to 1920* (London, 1940), 334.

37. Mrs. Thornton Cook, *General Service Hints for V.A.D. Members* (London, n.d.), 4–5.

38. *The Red Cross in Gloucestershire*, 28.

39. Summers, *Angels and Citizens*, chap. 9.

40. Furse, *Hearts and Pomegranates*, 352–53.

41. Leah Leneman, *In the Service of Life* (Edinburgh, 1994).

42. Ibid., 20, 34, 53–55, 65, 73, 83, 105, 123, 135.

43. On the history of the WPS see Allen, *The Pioneer Policewoman*; Joan Lock, *The British Policewoman: Her Story* (London, 1979); Lucy Bland, "In the Name of Protection: The Policing of Women in the First World War," in Julia Brophy and Carol Smart, eds., *Women-in-Law* (London, 1985).

44. For a discussion of the agitation surrounding these revelations, see Judith R. Walkowitz, *City of Dreadful Delight: Narratives of Sexual Danger in Late-Victorian London* (London, 1992).

45. See, e.g., National Vigilance Association, annual reports, 1887, 1897.

46. National Vigilance Association, special report, 1904.

47. Bland, "In the Name of Protection," 35–39; Allen, *The Pioneer Policewoman*, 134–71, 181.

48. See, for example, the "small ads." section of the *Oxford Times* for 1915, where advertisements for male and female workers may be compared.

49. Downs, *Manufacturing Inequality*, 148–53.

50. Ibid., 161.

51. Ibid., 159.

52. Edith Picton-Turbervill, *Life is Good* (London, 1939), 119.

53. Margaret Bondfield, *A Life's Work* (London, 1949), 59–60.

54. McFeely, *Lady Inspectors*, 148–51; Gail Braybon and Penny Summerfield, *Out of the Cage: Women's Experiences in Two World Wars* (London, 1987), chap. 7.

55. Downs, *Manufacturing Inequality*, 13–14.

56. See Martha Vicinus, *Independent Women: Work and Community for Single Women, 1850–1920* (London, 1985). This "single-woman question" is not to be confused with the thesis of "compulsory heterosexuality" in the interwar period put forward by Sheila Jeffreys, *The Spinster and her Enemies* (London, 1985).

57. Billie Melman, *Women and the Popular Imagination in the Twenties: Flappers and Nymphs* (London, 1988), has analyzed the press debate around this slogan where voteless young women were concerned; for an example of how much middle-class women took the label to heart, see May Wedderburn Cannan, *Grey Ghosts and Voices* (Kineton, 1976), 145, 175–77, 187.

58. Violet M. Firth, *The Psychology of the Servant Problem* (London, 1925), 81.

59. Mary Scharlieb, "The Moral Training of Young Girls," in James Marchant, ed., *The Claims of the Coming Generation* (London, 1923), 124–26.

60. See, among others, Seth Koven and Sonya Michel, eds., *Mothers of the New World: Maternalist Politics and the Origins of Welfare States* (New York and London, 1993), passim; Susan Pedersen, *Family, Dependence and the Origins of the Welfare State: Britain and France 1919–1945* (Cambridge, 1993), also uses the term "maternalist feminism," e.g., p. 144). The term "maternalist" has yet to undergo the rigorous process of interpretation and definition to which the term "feminist" has been subjected.

61. Pam Taylor, "Daughters and Mothers—Maids and Mistresses: Domestic Service between the Wars," in John Clarke, Chas Critcher and Richard Johnson, eds., *Working-Class Culture: Studies in History and Theory* (London, 1979), 133 (emphasis in the original).

EMILY GOES TO WAR

EXPLAINING THE RECRUITMENT TO THE WOMEN'S ARMY AUXILIARY CORPS IN WORLD WAR I*

DORON LAMM

The WAAC was the largest among the women's voluntary, paramilitary organizations in wartime Britain. The waacs were predominantly working class with a conspicuous lower-middle-class element in the clerical section, and a famous handful of ambulance drivers who were mostly upper class. They were employed in army bases in Britain and France as cooks, secretaries, domestics, and drivers, thus releasing fit men for combat duty. According to the conventional view, the Great War generated social changes that were highly beneficial to women. Thus, the WAAC exemplify the retreat of military prejudice against women's service under the pressure of total war and its insatiable demand for manpower.[1] Researchers have since dismantled much of this argument. Although revisionists agreed that the army generated a strong demand for female labor, they were skeptical as to whether the attitudes and assumptions underpinning women's employment in the military genuinely changed.[2] This paper uses original data extracted from some six hundred service files of women who served in the WAAC, and combines economic and quantitative perspectives with those attentive to gender and class.[3] It contributes to the revision of the triumphalist interpretation of women's military service by showing that the expansion of the WAAC was precipitated by a massive wave of female unemployment that has hitherto escaped the attention of the Corps's historians. Indeed, many working-class women joined the WAAC only after more lucrative and emancipatory forms of

*I would like to thank Martin Van Creveld, Roderick Floud, Nachum Gross, Jonathan Marwil, Avner Offer, Dan Schultz, Dror Wahrman, the members of the Military Study Group at the University of Michigan, Ann Arbor, and the participants in the program on "European Women before and after World War I" at The Wiener Library, Tel Aviv University for their useful comments. My research was partly funded by a grant from the Institute for German History, Tel Aviv University.

women's war work had been eliminated. Considering the longer-term impact of the Great War on gender relations in Britain, this study suggests that, rather than the culmination of women's wartime penetration into male occupations, the growth of the WAAC represented the demise of their wartime integration, fore-shadowing the coming contraction in the range of women's employ-ment opportunities that characterized the 1920s.

By 1917, the British army suffered acute shortages of manpower. Working-class women regarded war work as a means to engage themselves in the war effort as well as to earn their living. They used their employment, increased earnings, skill, and patriotic sta-tus to negotiate and materialize the new spaces of autonomy created for them by the war.[4] Indeed, both the conventional historiography of women in World War I, and the critique put forward by revision-ist historians, identified a strong military demand for women, as well as strong motivations for military service on the part of work-ing-class women. In this essay, I seek to carry the discussion beyond the question of the army's intentions or the women's motivations, and into the study of their interaction in the course of recruitment. Figure 28 below provides us with the first indication that, contrary to conventional wisdom, the interaction between the army's de-mand and the choices made by active, independent women workers was complex and contradictory. It charts the monthly additions to the WAAC between the Army's famous "Great Call for Women" volunteers in February of 1917 and the armistice of November of 1918. With the exception of an initial, short-lived enthusiasm of March of 1917, recruitment for most of the first year was slow, fail-ing to gather momentum. Though numbers briefly rose in Septem-ber of 1917, they declined precipitously in October and did not fully recover before January of 1918. By contrast, the spring of 1918 revo-lutionized the WAAC. Between March and May of 1918, the number of new recruits quadrupled when compared to the preceding quarter, and the Corps more than doubled in size. Although monthly cohorts of fresh applicants were halved in the following quarter, (June–August of 1918) they were still larger than any of the pre-March of 1918 era. During the last three months of the war, recruitment prac-tically ceased.[5]

Figure 28 was compared to two independent sources in order to ensure that it does not document spurious fluctuations due to the sampling procedure. First, War Office figures of the monthly size of the WAAC's strength show that it increased by fifty percent in March of 1918.[6] The second, and more significant support comes from the Women's Land Army (WLA)—a rival of the WAAC aimed

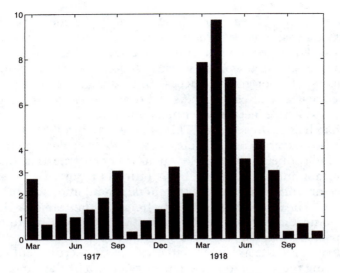

Figure 28: Recruitment to the WAAC by Month (000's)

at recruiting women workers for agricultural food production. Its data on recruiting indicates that both organizations expanded simultaneously: the WLA doubled its size between March and September of 1918.[7] The WAAC's rapid growth in the spring of 1918 was, therefore, indeed genuine.

Three factors determined the course of recruitment to the WAAC: the army's demand for women recruits, the general (non-military) demand for women workers, and the preferences of working women. None was wholly independent of the others, yet no simple correlation existed between them. Each proved dynamic over time, constantly altering the outcome of their interaction. How, then, should we explain the erratic growth of the WAAC? What retarded its growth during 1917? And how can we explain the dramatic upsurge in recruitment during the spring of 1917?

During Christmas of 1916, the War Office identified some twelve thousand jobs of non-combatant male soldiers in France as suitable for women.[8] The WAAC's first recruiting pamphlet stated that ten thousand women were needed at once (March of 1917), and a total of forty thousand by the close of 1917. Ultimately it took ten months to recruit the first ten thousand women, seven thousand of whom were already employed by the cookery section of the Women's Legion and were only transferred to the WAAC administratively. Only

in November of 1918, a year behind schedule, did the strength pass
the forty thousand mark.[9] Was it the army that reneged upon its initial goals? The records point to the contrary. Throughout 1917, the
government solicited women workers to join the WAAC with limited success. It met greater success in its search for well-paid and
better-educated clerical workers, who at the early stages of the
WAAC's existence (between February and June of 1917) constituted
more than half of the recruits. This did not satisfy a War Office hop-
ing to fill thousands of vacancies as well as to replace men in domestic and cookery jobs with low-paid women domestics. Between
the summer and the close of 1917, officials reported a persistent
shortage of women applicants in general, and domestic workers in
particular. The army then turned to Ireland—the traditional reservoir of domestic servants for the United Kingdom—in an attempt to
compensate for British scarcities, but to no avail.[10]

Traditionally, the army regulated voluntary recruitment of men
by adjusting the standard of age and physique to fit the supply of re-
cr.. s. Standards would be raised when volunteers were abundant
and low ered when they were scarce. Did the army undermine its
stated policy by setting women's standards for service too high—so
as to allow only a thin, selective group of women to join in 1917—
and then lower the standards in the spring of 1918? The evidence
suggests no such practice. Standards were hardly rigorous from the
outset, and there are also no indications of their sudden drop in early
1918. Take age, for example. If unofficial discrimination against
teenage recruits successfully turned them away, then its withdrawal
should have yielded a sudden increase in their numbers. But except
for the appearance of teenage clerks, in part due to a demand for female clerks in the headquarters of the U.S. Army in France, there
was never a significant rise in the share of 18–19-year-olds. In April
1918, the domestic section, then by far the largest in the Corps, grew
despite a decline in the proportion of teenagers among its new recruits. Further, according to the WAAC Sample medical standards
were low and not rigorously upheld. For example, poor eyesight and
poor teeth, major causes for disqualification among male recruits,
were also widespread among women recruits. Except for the most
severe cases, neither physical defect would have barred women from
service. Instead, waacs were encouraged to wear corrective lenses
and to use dentures. After April of 1918 recruiters may have upheld
dental standards: the proportion of recruits in need of immediate
treatment dropped from forty-six percent to thirty-five percent,
while the proportion of users of artificial dentures rose from fifteen
percent to twenty-two percent. Some applicants were even told to

extract all their carious teeth—in one case, as many as twelve—and acquire dentures at their own expense as a condition for their employment. Equally severe cases passed, fit for service, throughout 1917.[11] The standards of eyesight may have declined in 1918: more women who suffered from poor eyesight joined in the spring of 1918 than in the previous year: fifty-nine pecent versus forty-one percent respectively. On the other hand, a greater share among those suffering from impaired vision in 1918 wore glasses: twenty-seven percent versus seventeen percent, respectively. There is little in these fluctuations to suggest that they were anything more than coincidental. The only sound inference from these statistics would be a severe indictment of the state of health among British women, emanating from their appalling living conditions and particularly their poor nutritional status. The army, having to accept mass exemptions of unfit male conscripts, was more than willing to pay nominal attention to the physical health of the women who, as paid employees, substituted for them.

The recruiting problem came into the open in July 1917, when it was argued that the paucity of recruits threatened the WAAC's mission in France:

> Five hundred girl clerks are today unable to leave England [for France] and to release for the fighting line men who are now doing sedentary work, owing to the apathy of cooks, housemaids and scrubbers who have not responded to the National Service appeal to join the WAAC. Women are urgently needed to cook and perform household duties at the hostels where the clerical workers live.[12]

It was not the prospect of service overseas that kept working-class women from joining. Although the WAAC Sample reveals that some forty percent of all approved applicants joined for "Home Service" only, it confirms that there were twice as many fit volunteers for service abroad than members who ended up being sent to France. Indeed, the central recruiting problem of 1917 was to attract domestic servants. Administrators believed that domestic workers and unmarried middle-class women constituted two pools of potential WAAC recruits that had not been fully tapped. In mid-September of 1917, the War Office announced that "women will be required at the rate of at least 10,000 a month. . . . Domestic workers [are] the most urgently needed."[13] The Ministries of National Service and Labour had just reformed the recruiting system. They opened a permanent recruiting hut in Trafalgar Square amidst much publicity, issued posters and frequent press releases, and "systematically carried on [recruiting campaigns] by cinema displays and meetings."[14] Soon it became clear that these measures had failed to secure the army's demand for domestics.

Why, then, did domestic servants refrain from joining the WAAC? Sir Auckland Campbell Geddes, the newly appointed minister for National Service, blamed the failure on women's ignorance and indifference. Wearing the mantle of an altruistic and rational administrator, he criticized the cross-class collusion in favor of a cozy, yet inefficient, status quo:

> I know how divorced from understanding of the present situation many domestic servants are, but I appeal to all mistresses of large households to do their utmost to make it easy for their maids to join the WAAC. But not only domestic servants: I want the young women of that mass of middle-class homes who are doing no real war work . . . to come along and join up.[15]

This official frustration was echoed in the press:

> The WAAC is now ready to absorb an unlimited number of women . . . Where is the supply to come from? . . . It seems incredible that during the fourth year of the war thousands of women should be still content to make and buy and sell unnecessary articles when they might serve their country by . . . enrolling in the Women's army.[16]

Adam Kirkaldy, a contemporary economist, was closer to the truth. Although he shared the common belief that there was "still . . . a considerable reserve [of women] which ought theoretically to be drawn upon," he argued that the difficulty in recruiting stemmed not from women's apathy but from the conditions they were offered: "Unless compelled by actual need, women will not take employment where wages are low."[17]

Researchers have cast doubt on whether large reservoirs of unoccupied women still existed in Britain in 1917.[18] What is clear is that working-class women were not forthcoming, and that the problem lay primarily in the inferiority of the army's remuneration package for domestic workers. This was not simply a question of low monetary reward. Army wages were superior to the average civilian wage, but the army provided no career prospects and did not compensate for a loss of seniority and job security incurred by those who left good domestic and retail jobs. Teenage women whose seniority, income, and job security were particularly low were attracted to the WAAC in large numbers. Other domestics were reluctant to trade their job for an even lower grade of domestic work in army kitchens under military discipline. WAAC pay also compared poorly with the alternative pay offered by the munitions industries. During the first half of 1917, the war economy was still offering women plenty of "patriotic," yet lucrative, alternatives to sedentary, low-paid work. The munitions industry was booning: the proportion of women in national shell factories peaked at seventy-three percent in July of 1917. Woolwich Arsenal, for example, which had 9,484 women in 1916, employed 24,719 by the end of 1917. It is no surprise, therefore, that when an unskilled domestic servant wished to contribute to the war effort and receive fair compensation for her labor, she usually opted first for industry. The following examples represent a common pattern; Margaret and Ruth McG., daughters of a boilermaker from Durham, increased their weekly wages from 7s. and 5s. as living-out domestics to 39s. as cordite munitions workers in mid-1917. After losing their jobs in March of 1918, they joined the WAAC as assistant cooks, with their wages dropping to 10s. Similarly, Rosie A., a miner's daughter from Wigan, earned 17s. weekly in 1917 as a grocer's assistant, and 40s. in munitions, but only 31s. as a storewoman in the WAAC after she lost her job in industry.[19]

In contrast to working-class job seekers, skilled clerks had a narrower range of socially acceptable employment alternatives. Social convention did not permit them to earn more by simply taking on manual work in munitions. Clerical wages were also more rigidly standardized by formal education, efficiency certificates, and diplomas. The wages of shorthand typists, for example, were correlated with their speed: Ida C., who held a *Pitman's* shorthand certificate for fifty words per minute (WPM) earned 17s. 6d. weekly; Georgina B. with eighty to ninety words per minute received 22s. 6d.; and Evelyn T. R., with 120 words per minute (holder of the first Aberdeen Prize in shorthand writing) earned 36s. a week. Nonetheless, the war economy "disrupted" their civilian pay structure almost as drastically as it did that of non-clericals. Like most clerks who joined the WAAC, they had been employed by small, private businesses: a solicitor, an architect, and a photographer who could hardly afford to match government pay. Georgina's wages rose instantly by some sixty percent, from 22s. 6d. to 32s. plus overtime, and soon after to 37s. 6d. weekly; Ida and Evelyn, who joined later, received 43s. and 44s., respectively—raises ranging from twenty-two percent to 145 percent. In an exceptional case, where a shorthand typist suffered a slight decline in her money wage, she did not go to the WAAC from the private sector but from another government office.[20] Shirley Dex has shown that women clerks had a strong commitment to, and a conscious preference for, office work over semi-skilled and manual occupations. The tenacity with which they stayed in clerical occupations was particularly clear among the upwardly mobile who came from unskilled or semi-skilled backgrounds.[21] Given the social constraints upon skilled clerks' choice of employment, the WAAC offered them a suitable avenue for betterment—parallel to that which munitions work offered to general servants. It provided the fulfillment of putting their costly clerical education to use, and enabled them to remain on their professional trajectory. It may not have maximized their monetary wages, but it also did not tax their social status.

During 1917, while manual and domestic workers would have done their best economically by getting a job in munitions, clerical workers faced a strong incentive to join the WAAC. This phenomenon explains much of the War Office's difficulties in attracting sufficient applicants, as well as the Corps's predominance of clerks over domestics and manual workers. According to the WAAC Sample, by July of 1917, the Corps's workforce was seventy percent clerical, eighteen percent domestic, and twelve percent manual. In December of 1917, despite aggressive campaigns to recruit domestic staff, clerical workers still comprised forty-seven percent of the Corps, with domestics and manuals accounting for twenty-six percent each.

An improvement in enrollment, albeit weak and falling short of the requirements, was registered in the summer of 1917 following the authorization of Home Service. But then, after a record turnout in September, women almost ceased to apply. [Figure 28] This was a humbling setback to the new, energetic administrators who had just announced they were ready to deal speedily with the recruitment of ten thousand new waacs a month.[22] What was the reason for this setback? According to the latest official history of the Corps, a "scandal about the alleged licentiousness of the girls in France reached its height early in 1918; it was even affirmed that the WAACs were being recruited for army brothels. . . . As a result of the stories, the flood of WAAC applications slowed into a trickle."[23] This claim was first made by a commission that was appointed by the Minister of Labour to inquire into the "rumours"—as the scandal was referred to at the time.[24] But its report provided no evidence to substantiate this statement. War Office reports on the size of the WAAC also did not support it.[25] Judging by Figure 28, it is clear that prior to March of 1918 there had been hardly a "flood" of WAAC applications for the "rumours" to dry up. Yet the question remains whether the rumors either aborted or postponed an emerging wave of recruitment. In other words, what evidence do we have to support the claim that a backlash against women's service drove working-class women to relinquish a coveted opportunity for employment?

The early reactions of the recruiting authorities do not support this claim. There can be no doubt that the threat of a sex scandal was ever present in the administrators' minds.[26] The appearance of women in uniforms crystallized anxieties about changes in gender relations; the fact that these were working-class women added class condescension to male apprehensions. Men and women in authority were convinced that working-class women who served in close proximity to men had to be guided, protected, and closely controlled by middle- and upper-class women. And yet, a close scrutiny of the evidence shows that the same officials, who by October of 1917 were already anxious over the drop in recruitment, did not blame the rumors for the slowdown. Before the end of December they blamed it on the women's apathy and on past administrative inefficiency that had caused working-class women considerable aggravation and material loss. Their main objective was, therefore, to reassure potential candidates that enlistment was now speedy and that bureaucratic blunders were indeed a thing of the past.[27] They also did not blame the paucity of middle-class recruits on sexual allegations, but suspected that the choice of the Employment Bureau as the site for enrollment stigmatized the WAAC as a working-class organization. Middle-class women were promised that they would feel right in their element if they joined the WAAC as forewomen: "[you] would act in the same capacity as prefects. In fact, the whole organization was much like that of a boarding house of a large Public School."[28] Even the scheme to allow women to "enroll in the WAAC on the definite understanding that they may continue living in their houses" was not necessarily drafted in response to the allegations of a promiscuous lifestyle in France. It may well have been a genuine attempt to cater to women who preferred to stay at home. Indeed, it was common for wartime employers to compete aggressively for labor by offering working-class women a choice of wage/conditions packages.

Letters of reference written by employers, neighbors, or local community leaders on behalf of the waacs provide a rare, if indirect, glimpse of grass-roots confidence in the WAAC. These confidential notes contain no evidence that service in the army was perceived as detrimental to a working woman's morality. Many referees took great trouble to describe the women's character and qualifications honestly and accurately, whether or not their judgment was flattering. There would have been little reason to do so if one believed the army to be a corrupting environment fit for loose women. If the views of Mrs. Ben C., wife of a wine merchant, were representative, then a military job was, in fact, respected as a means for instilling discipline and inculcating respectability. "I know of no reason why she should not join," she wrote with regard to her maid. "Confidentially," she added,

BORDERLINES

"I would say I think she would do much better than in a private home, as she would have more supervision & discipline."[29]

"The rumours" were singled out as the major threat to the Corps's survival late in December or early in January. At that time, women leaders of charities and voluntary organizations had been scandalized, though not so much by the slanderous nature of the accusations as by what they believed was the Corps's lax supervision over the women's contacts with male soldiers.[30] Those who repudiated the allegations accrued political benefits. An official condemnation of "the slanders" appeared in the press on January 31, 1918. G. H. Roberts, a Labour member in the Cabinet, rebuked the allegations in a rally in the industrial north. In his capacity as the Minister of Labour, he was in charge of women's recruitment by the Employment Bureaus. Roberts was an embattled minister of a weak department searching for a cause. Just a couple of months earlier, he had been disowned by his local trades council for opposing British attendance at the Stockholm Peace Conference.[31] He turned the attack on the "malicious rumours" into the central theme of his addresses in recruiting rallies, carrying it to working-class constituencies and to the national press. He soon appointed a departmental committee of six women trade unionists and civil servants to investigate the allegations, ensuring that the issue would not disappear from the public eye for months to come. The Archbishop of Canterbury followed suit. During the war, the church's main effort with regard to the working class was directed towards women war workers. "The moral standard among these women [the waacs]" claimed the Primate, "was extremely high and control extremely good."[32]

The important thing to note is that well before these political figures reacted to the rumors, women had begun to apply for service in the WAAC at a rate that equaled the heyday of recruitment in 1917. More waacs joined in January of 1918 than in any previous month, and in February the flow of new recruits equaled that of the first enthusiastic rush of March of 1917, when the Corps was just initiated. Moreover, by the time the commission of inquiry published a report exonerating the waacs from the allegations in April of 1918, the largest increase in the history of the Corps had passed its peak. In other words, while it remains unclear whether the rumors in fact curbed the sluggish stream of working-class recruits between October and Christmas of 1917, it is obvious that the recovery of recruitment preceded all official attempts to counteract the allegations. In fact, it calls for an excessive stretch of the imagination to believe that thousands of young working-class women stipulated their recruitment upon the blessing of either the Archbishop of Canterbury or the Minister of Labour. Both the WAAC Sample and testimonies of waacs underscore the regularity and independence with which working-class women chose their jobs. At times, both the search and the selection were done in remarkable isolation and with little consultation;[33] on occasions, they decided contrary to parental advice;[34] and frequently, they either followed or joined forces with peers, friends, and acquaintances, especially when the choice of job entailed geographical migration or a move to a new line of employment.[35] When asked for their recollections of, and reaction to, the "slanders," ex-waacs discounted their impact, some were oblivious of these allegations altogether, and none mentioned them as a reason for either deferring enlistment or expediting discharge.[36] The decisions of working-class women to join the WAAC seem not to have been swayed dramatically either by the denigration and anxieties of their superiors with regard to their sexuality, or by their approval.

The reasons for the rise in the number of applications to the WAAC in 1918 are to be found in the change in the demand for women's work in the economy. The growth rate in replacement work—traditional men's work now executed by women—faltered during the latter half of 1917. Contemporaries noted that "in [munitions], as in industry generally, the employment of women was reaching its limit." Only seven thousand out of the ninety thousand new women who entered industry between April of 1917 and April of 1918 joined in the latter half of the year. The excess demand for women in lucrative munitions jobs that characterized the female labor market for almost two years all but disappeared.[37] Shortages in raw materials also worsened the relative position of women in the regional labor markets, as evident particularly in the case of textiles that had a high ratio of female labor.[38] In addition, the Board of Trade reported that the reduction of female labor in munitions was due "partly to the return of discharged soldiers." In fact, by late 1917, for the first time since 1915, men outnumbered women among new entrants to industry.[39] There were not yet signs of open, widespread female unemployment. But few new industrial openings were now available for them. Once again, it became difficult for women to leave low-paid, traditional jobs for well-paid war work or to replace one job in munitions with another. All of these factors explain much of the growth of the WAAC during January and February of 1918.

Women's employment in the second half of 1917 was characterized by stagnation. The dramatic flood of applicants to the WAAC that started in March of 1918 signified a general contraction in their opportunities. It followed a massive wave of layoffs of women munitions workers, which swelled the supply of women workers across the economy as a whole. At first, these women were hopeful of finding alternative, lucrative employment, and did not register at employment exchanges. "This was no doubt partly due to the desire for a holiday, but in many cases women were not willing to be transferred to occupations for which they had no training and where their earnings would be considerably lower."[40] As a result, signs of the new predicament were slow to travel from the shop floor to the national consciousness. Towards the end of February, the press reported that "considerable anxiety has been caused in some areas by the wholesale dismissal of women from munitions factories within the last few weeks." It was clear that both the extent and the causes of these redundancies were unusual:

> Several factories have been closed down completely, and it is stated that within a very short time . . . thousands of women have been thrown out of work in districts where they cannot readily be reabsorbed in other work of national importance. In one area . . . the local employment exchange is already unable to find work for the women on the books. . . . [N]one of the girls and women who are affected would raise any objection to losing their employment if they were, as has been stated elsewhere, being replaced by discharged soldiers. This, however, . . . is not the reason in most cases. . . . The fact is that a certain form of war work of an unskilled character is not now required.[41]

Answering for the government in Parliament, the junior Minister for National Service tried to play down the severity of the news by claiming that no more than eight thousand women had lost their jobs and that "openings for a considerable number of women [were available] in the Women Army Auxiliary Corps [and] in Agriculture. . . ." "The government," he added, "was considering the possibility of giving priority in employment on war work to these women."[42] Mary MacArthur, Chairman of the Women's Trade Union, was quick to respond, declaring that "the figures given by [the Minister] in the House of Commons were no reflection of the extent of the dismissals of the last few weeks."[43] According to her calculations, there would be forty thousand women unemployed by mid-April.[44] It was also clear that the problem was not isolated regionally but affected a diversity of localities nationwide. The government wasted no additional time disputing the facts. On March 1, it was stated that "The Ministry of Munitions recognize that they are faced with *a big employment problem* in consequence of the order of the War Cabinet for a reduction in the munitions program."[45] It estimated that "a certain amount of unemployment and hardship was inevitable."[46] The reasons given for this reduction were the existence of "enormous reserves" and the drop in demand for munitions due to the revolution in Russia.[47] Winston Churchill, Minister of Munitions, was unaccommodating. In meetings with labor representatives, he insisted that "the dismissals would continue," and that "it might also be practicable to lessen the hardship by reduction of working hours." The government, he added, was willing to "assist the women in obtaining employment in other forms of war work now open." New openings were almost exclusively available in the Women's Royal Air Force (WRAF), the Women's Land Army (WLA), the Women's Army Auxiliary Corps, and the Women's Royal Naval Service (WRNS).[48]

Of these organizations, only the WAAC and the WLA could truly absorb large numbers of munitions workers. The WRAF and the WRNS were small organizations with fewer than seven thousand members each.[49] They restricted their recruitment almost exclusively to middle-class women. The Land Army was of a similar size until mid-1917, and prided itself on a similar rigor of selection. But it was designed to expand as food production programs made headway in late 1917, and soon encountered considerable difficulties in securing the required number of recruits. Yet between March and July of 1918, its strength more than doubled.[50] The WAAC was by far the largest of these organizations and had continuously failed to secure its recruiting targets. It was the sudden influx of thousands of unemployed munitions workers into the labor market that enabled the WAAC to triple its strength between March and August of 1918.

Losing one's job was not a novel experience for working-class women, but it had always meant an immediate hardship. Sixteen hundred women from Leeds sent a telegram to the Ministry of Munitions asking "what steps were being taken to provide them with means to live." The women's union called for the unemployed to be given "a month's pay and free railway tickets home." Its demand "to give a subsistence allowance that would bring the girls money up to [one pound] a week . . . was refused." A few were entitled to 7s. in unemployment insurance. In one exceptional instance, three thousand Essex women did receive 23s. per week as unemployment benefit; but the Ministry of Munitions was quick to make clear that this did not constitute a precedent. For the great majority of the women the weekly income had now dropped from an average of some 35s. per week to nil. According to some reports "girls who had been dismissed . . . were turned out of their hostels and had nowhere to go when their notice had expired."[51]

Still, unemployed munitions workers fared better than other job-seeking women. The government promised to give them the first call upon vacancies in munitions work, and they enjoyed the relative advantage of having acquired experience in munitions factory work. Even with regard to problems such as limited bridging funds or the threat of losing their accommodation, they still fared better than low-paid civilian domestics who would be given the customary seven-day notice. Typically, domestic servants such as Florence C. M. would ask to expedite their recruitment: "I am leaving my situation next Saturday . . . and have only one week to find some more work." By contrast, Florence K. E., a munitions worker made redundant on January 10, applied for service only on March 1.[52] These advantages meant that munitions workers were better situated than the ordinary jobless along the various queues for jobs in the labor market. They would have encountered little difficulty if they chose to join the WAAC right away or return to traditional occupations, such as domestic service and laundry, where many had worked before. And they should have been more successful than others when they chose to avoid these options. On the other hand, a general servant who lost her job in 1918 could not realistically have aspired to leave domestic service for a job in industry, and must have felt a greater squeeze on superior positions in her own profession. As a result, the WAAC was able to grow rapidly, capitalizing on the swelling of the ranks of the unemployed, but without necessarily recruiting redundant munitions workers alone. More ex-munitions workers joined the WAAC during the first half of 1918 than either before or after, both in absolute and relative terms.[53] But domestic workers now constituted the majority among the recruits, and their proportion was constantly rising. If one accepts the description of the relative strength of these groups within the labor market, then the conclusion must be that a job in the WAAC was still considered an inferior choice of employment, attractive mainly to young general clerks, low-paid domestics, and a miscellany of unskilled women in traditional jobs.

Let us briefly consider two alternative explanations to the expansion of the WAAC in 1918, other than the rise of female unemployment. It has been suggested that the doubling of the WLA was largely due to the government's policy of increasing women's participation in the labor force by deliberately letting allowances paid to soldiers' families lag behind inflation.[54] This argument is consistent with mine in as much as both attribute the growth of the WAAC and the WLA to an increase in jobless women. It would be difficult, however, to attribute the sudden overflow in applicants to the gradual deterioration of the allowances. The latter was more likely to produce a gradual increase in new job seekers, not a sudden one. Another chal-

lenging proposition is that the German spring offensive of 1918 generated both a sharp rise in the military demand for manpower and a
wave of renewed patriotism, which conjointly enabled a dramatic expansion of the Corps. However, this hypothesis is incompatible with
the data regarding the timing of the growth of the WAAC. The surge
in applications to the WAAC started almost a month prior to the
spring offensive, at the time when the government had supposedly
been depriving the armies at the Western Front of fresh troops.[55] In
fact, recruitment to the WAAC was significantly heavier in the
weeks preceding the surprise German attack that started on March
21 than in the last third of the month.[56] The offensive may have
helped to retain the momentum in recruitment in later months, but
it cannot account for the surge in women's applications.

Having established the crucial role of unemployment in women's
recruitment to the WAAC, I shall proceed to place it in the gendered
and class-based contexts of the home-front mobilization during the
last year of the war. It was clear at the outset of 1918 that the labor
unrest of 1917 was waning. The new industrial calm was carefully
nurtured by various measures taken by the government. Labor, in its
turn, was committed more than ever to victory, and was willing to
accept painful measures if they were necessary for its attainment.[57]
Least palatable for labor was the issue of conscription: but it did not
resist the "combing-out" of men in growing numbers and of wider
age groups, so long as the government stopped short of industrial
conscription.[58] Munitions plants kept closing throughout the year,
including programs that employed men who were now more needed
as soldiers in France. As Churchill told his staff at the Ministry of
Munitions: "the War Office are blamed like Pharaoh of old, because
they will not let the people go. Our difficulty is we cannot let the
people stay. We have actually succeeded in discharging nearly a million persons, the bulk of whom did not want to go."[59] In contrast
with 1916 and 1917, few women were called to replace them. Given
the public's mood, there was little chance that a mass dismissal of
women workers from industry—let alone their transfer to "traditional jobs" in the WAAC—would have developed into a confrontation with the government. It is easy to imagine labor's uproar if male
unemployment had been relieved by conscription. But gender made
all the difference. A promise for a postwar reversal of the replacement of men by women in industry lay at the heart of labor's cooperation with the government over dilution throughout the conflict.
A demand for the reinstatement of the women in industry was not
even aired. It was impossible for a women's union to ask for the public's sympathy with a demand for increased benefits for women who

would have rather not joined the WAAC, while men were being called *en masse* with little regard for their age, marital status, or physical health.

Working-class women constituted an integral part of this consensus. Those who opted for the WAAC and the WLA in 1918 were neither leisurely ladies nor homemakers. Patriotism, remunerated work, and personal autonomy were inseparable in their mind. They had been wage earners for years and were now engaged in a search for new employment. Some had lost their jobs in industry. Others, most of whom were about to terminate their previous position, sought to replace low-paid, traditional jobs with higher-paying and less-"servile" ones that appealed to their patriotism and conferred social approbation. They could choose to join the WAAC immediately or wait for a better form of war work. They could also return to domestic service and laundry work. In short, by early 1918, women found that the WAAC, rather than extending dilution into the military sphere, now offered a temporary palliator of what was to become a contracting and segregated range of employment opportunities. Under these circumstances a job in the WAAC was attractive: wages, though lower than in most jobs in munitions, were still higher than the average pay in the private sector. They were even superior to the pay in the Land Army. The army wage was topped with war bonuses, laundry allowances, two weeks vacation, and medical care. Food was cheap, and rations were superior and plentiful. They could choose to serve while living at home, be posted somewhere else in Britain, or seek a position in France. True, much WAAC work was traditional domestic work, menial, and "feminine." But unlike domestic servants, waacs were neither at the beck and call of a mistress nor isolated in a small household. They worked with peers, wore military uniforms, and met men. They felt—just like women munitions workers, and maybe even more—that they too "were doing their bit." Thus, with a lukewarm commitment to service abroad, they chose to join the army. The Spring Offensive, with its ensuing tide of patriotism, did not cause the WAAC's rapid growth, though it probably helped to retain its momentum. More importantly, it successfully obscured the relationship between the ousting of women from wartime industry, and their employment in the military.

NOTES

1. Arthur Marwick, *Women at War 1914–1918* (London, 1977) is the chief interpreter of the WAAC as "a perfect paradigm" to the revolutionary power of Total War.

2. Jenny Gould, "Women's Military Services in First World War Britain," in Margaret Randolf Higonnet et al., eds., *Behind the Lines: Gender and the Two World Wars* (New Haven, 1987), 122–23. The "domestic-service paradigm" that Anne Summers develops in her article in this volume also captures central tenants in the views of officials who organized the women's paramilitary services. For a recent survey of the debate, see Martin Pugh, *Women and the Women's Movement in Britain 1914–1959* (London, 1992).

3. Hereafter WAAC Sample (WS). It was systematically drawn from some six thousand files, the remains of the original collection of WAAC files that was damaged during the Blitz on London. These files are at the disposal of the British Ministry of Defence. Each file held a number of official forms (e.g., Application Form, Physical Examination Form, and Reference Forms, that contained details on the social, economic, occupational, educational, and medical background of the women. Other forms recorded a woman's service history in the WAAC. Nonstandardized information was also included in correspondence between the WAAC and the woman or her family. A series of distributions—such as geographical, occupational, age, and marital status—did not reveal any bias that can be attributed to patterns of preservation. For a discussion on the representativeness of surviving files of male soldiers, see Doron Lamm, "British Soldiers of the First World War: Creation of a Representative Sample," *Historical Social Research* 13, no. 4 (1988): 55–98.

4. See, for example, Angella Woollacott, *On Her Their Lives Depend: Munition Workers in the Great War*, (Berkeley, 1994), 5–16.

5. The total number of recruits to the WAAC was estimated at about 57,000. Helen Gwynne-Vaughan, *Service with the Army*, (London, 1941), 42.

6. HMSO, *Statistics of the Military Effort of the British Empire during the Great War: 1914–1920*, (London, 1922), 205–6. This expansion is reported to have taken place between January and March of 1918, yet no data are given for February. War Office data on the size of the WAAC between February of 1917 and the armistice are fragmentary and should only be considered as rough estimates.

7. It rose from 7,665 to 16,000, respectively. P. E. Dewey, *British Agriculture in the First World War*, (London, 1989), 131.

8. Gwynne-Vaughan, *Service with the Army*, 11–12; Roy Terry, *Women in Khaki: The Story of the British Woman Soldier*, (London, 1988), 39; Katherine Furse, *Hearts and Pomegranates: The Story of Forty-Five Years, 1875 to 1920* (London, 1940), 548–49.

9. Terry, *Women in Khaki*, 39; Gwynne-Vaughan, *Service with the Army*, 42; HMSO, *Statistics of the Military Effort*, 205–6.

10. For example, *The Times*, July 30, Aug. 27, Sept. 1, Nov. 24, 1917.

11. WS # 71 Jenny L. A.; WS # 167 Evelyn H.; for 1917 recruits: WS # 206 Bridgetina L., "only four molars at all"; WS # 209 Barbara L., "10 carious"; WS # 151 Florie, H., "8 molars + premolars bad."

12. *The Times*, July 12, 1917.

13. Ibid., June 30, July 12, 17, Aug. 27, Sept. 1, 18, Nov. 13, 24, 26, 1917.

14. Ibid., Aug. 4, 13, 25, and 26, Sept. 18, 1917; Vera Brittain, *Testament of Youth* (1933; reprint n.p. Wideview Books, 1980), 453.

15. *The Times*, Nov. 19, 1917.

16. Ibid., Nov. 6, 1917.

17. Adam W. Kirkaldy, ed., *Industry and Finance: War Expedients and Reconstruction*, vol. 1 (London, 1918–20), 63.

18. Irene Osgood Andrews and Margarett A. Hobbs, *Economic Effects of the World War Upon Women and Children in Great Britain*, 2nd ed. (New York, 1921), 83; Deborah Thom, "Women and Work in Wartime Britain," in Richard Wall and Jay Winter, eds., *The Upheaval of War: Family, Work, and Welfare in Europe, 1914–1918* (Cambridge, 1988), 310.

19. WS # 230 Ruth McG.; # 231 Margaret McG; # 12 H. Rosie A.

20. WS # 33 Ida C.; # 90 Georgina B.; WS # 275, Evelyn T. R.; # 77 Agnes E. B.

21. Shirley Dex, *Women's Occupational Mobility* (London, 1987), 47–49, 58.

22. *The Times*, Aug. 4, Sept. 18, 1917.

23. Terry, *Women in Khaki*, 70.

24. *The Times*, Apr. 15, 1918.

25. HMSO, *Statistics of the Military Effort*, 205–6 and appendix 1.

26. Auckland Campbell Geddes, *Forging of a Family* (London, 1949), 256; Gwynne-Vaughan, *Service with the Army*, 49.

27. *The Times*, Nov. 6, 8, 1917. For past complaints, see, for example, ibid., Aug. 9, 10, 1917.

28. Ibid., Nov. 6, 1917.

29. WS # 100 Alice E. B.

30. Gwynne-Vaughan, *Service with the Army*, 50–51.

31. Rodney Lowe, "The Ministry of Labour, 1916–1919: A Still, Small Voice?" in Katheleen Burk, ed., *War and the State* (London, 1982), 111–12, 118, 125.

32. *The Times*, Feb. 6, 1917.

33. See, for example, Imperial War Museum, Department of Documents (hereafter IWM, DOD), 83/17/1, Miss O. M. Taylor.

34. IWM, Department of Sound Records (DSR), 7444/02, Anon.; IWM, DSR, 12307/2, Hall, Winifrie Amy.

35. IWM, DOD, Misc. 61 item 948, Mrs. O. Castle; IWM, DSR, 9731/02, Barker, Nora. IWM DSR, 8857/3, Parrott, Florence Mary.

36. IWM, DSR, 3137/02 Elsie J. Cooper; IWM, DOD, 83/17/1, Miss O. M. Taylor; IWM, DSR, 9731/2, Barker, Nora.

37. L. Grier and A. Ashley, *British Labour: Replacement and Conciliation 1914–1921*, (London, 1921), 19–20; Andrews, *Economic Effects*, 3; Kirkaldy, *Industry and Finance* 2:7, 9–10.

38. Dorothea M. Barton, "The Course of Women's Wages," *Journal of the Royal Statistical Society*, 82, no. 4 (July 1919): 517; Kirkaldy, *Industry and Finance* 2:7, 9.

39. Report on the Increased Employment of Women, *Parliamentary Pa-*

pers, 1919, xiv, Cd. 9164, pp. 5–6; Grier and Ashley, *British Labour*, 19–20; Kirkaldy, *Industry and Finance* 2:4.

40. HMSO, *The History of the Ministry of Munitions* (London, 1923), vol. 4, pt. 2, p. 79.

41. *The Times*, Feb. 22, 1918.

42. Ibid., Feb. 27, 1918. (My emphasis.)

43. Ibid., Feb. 28, 1918.

44. Ibid., Mar. 8, 1918.

45. Ibid., Mar. 1, 1918. (My emphasis.)

46. *The History of the Ministry of Munitions*, vol. 4, pt. 2, p. 78

47. *The Times*, Feb. 22, Mar. 1, 1918.

48. Ibid., Apr. 7, 14, 1918.

49. HMSO, *Statistics of the Military Effort*, 505; Furse, *Hearts and Pomegranates*, 372.

50. *The Times*, Feb. 6, 1918; Dewey, *British Agriculture*, 131–34; Pamela Horn, *Rural Life in England in the First World War* (New York, 1984), 134; Trevor Wilson, *The Myriad Faces of War: Britain and the Great War, 1914–1918*, (Cambridge, 1986), 720.

51. *History of the Ministry of Munitions*, vol. 4, pt. 2, pp. 79–80.

52. WS # 48 Florence C. M.; WS # 120 Florence K. E.

53. According to the WAAC Sample, the share of ex-munitions workers in the Corps rose from 10.5 percent during 1917 to sixteen percent early in 1918, then to eighteen percent between March and May and later dropped again to eleven percent.

54. Dewey, *British Agriculture*, 129.

55. The allegations that David Lloyd George, unsuspecting of a pending massive attack, starved Haig's army of manpower, and was thus responsible for the setbacks in the fighting, came up in the Maurice Affair. Wilson, *The Myriad Faces*, 550–51, 556, 558, 573–75.

56. According to the WS, eighty-two percent of the women joined before the German attack had started, and eighteen percent after, compared with an expected distribution of sixty-eight percent and thirty-two percent, respectively.

57. Alastair J. Reid, "Dilution, Trade, Unionism and the State in Britain during the First World War," in S. Tolliday, and J. Zeitlin, eds., *Shop Floor Bargaining and the State* (Cambridge, 1985), 46–74. José Harris, "Bureaucrats and Businessmen in British Food Control, 1916–1919," in Burk, ed., *War and the State*, 135–56. Wilson, *The Myriad Faces of War*, 654.

58. In April 1918, the age limits for the conscription of *men* were reduced to 17.5 years and raised to fifty-one (and in some cases to fifty-five) simultaneously. Medical standards for fighting units were also lowered. Winter, *The Great War and the British People*, 45–46; Wilson, *The Myriad Faces of War*, 566, 645.

59. Quoted in Thom, "Women and Work in Wartime Britain," 313.

Work, Gender, and Identity in Peace and War

France, 1890–1930

Françoise Thébaud

> The women of France responded to the call of their homeland in danger by giving all of their strength. Clad in overalls, they could be seen in the factories turning out mortar shells, melting down steel for cannons, making explosives. And in this atmosphere of death, amidst these hard tasks of men, so rough on their fragile arms, they contrived to remain women and retain all their charm.

"Responding to the call of the homeland," "hard tasks of men," "remain women": this commentary on "Victory's Working Woman," portrayed with a mortar shell in her left hand and a gun in her right hand on the cover of the illustrated weekly *J'ai Vu* of June 16, 1917, is a splendid introduction to the following discussion. First, it raises a number of questions concerning the relationship between war and social change, and between war and gender. Who were these women of the Great War, and what happened to them when the country no longer needed such a massive output of shells and cannons? How did their mass influx into the male sector of metalworking affect their female identity, and how did their contemporaries manage with the new situation? Was this kind of work really so novel and so temporary in its form, remuneration, and context?

This commentary, which is a typical example of the adulatory style of the period, suggests the need for a complex approach to the subject. Without repudiating the thesis I have developed elsewhere—that, on the whole, the Great War tended to accentuate divisions between the sexes[1]—I shall present it here in a more detailed and nuanced way through a study of women's work in France over a longer period. Since women's work is a massive area of life widely considered by the historiography, (for it entails both personal and family strategies on the one hand and collective and public policies on the other) it appears to be an excellent "observatory" from which to assess change and continuity beyond the framework of the war itself. It is of particular interest to attempt to define the various levels—material, institutional, symbolic—of change or continuity, and to trace the social, institutional, and mental mechanisms that allowed for certain transformations while preserving gender division. Thus, I shall consider women's and men's work from multiple perspectives: who does what and under what conditions; what are "women's work" and "men's work;" what self-awareness do they bestow; and what claims do they engender. Moreover, if the trilogy of "gender, race, and class," so much in use in the U.S., seems somewhat trite in France, it goes without saying that French working women were no more homogenous a group than were "the women of the Great War." Thus, while emphasizing what was specifically French as compared with other Western countries, I shall also note the diversity of women's circumstances, related to social class, age group, and place of residence.

SOCIAL HISTORY, WOMEN'S HISTORY, CULTURAL HISTORY

Even though the question of work has lost some of its importance, it has held a central place in France in the historiographical field of women's history, with successive methods of approach that can be defined as follows: a labor history of women's work, a women's history of work, and a gendered approach to work.

French historiography in the 1960s was predominantly economic and social. This was the era of the grand theories of quantitative economic history and social labor history. Women's history, which was marginal at the beginning of the 1970s, emerged as a result of some pioneering sociological works on labor and at first attached itself to this social history. It took as its first subject of study the question of women's work and the relations between women (whether workers or not) and the labor movement. The desire to demonstrate the trauma engendered by the Industrial Revolution, the exploitation of women workers, and the misogyny of workingmen underlay the conclusions this history reached, which made much of the dichotomy between a majority of women victims and a small minority of women rebels, strike leaders, and feminists.[2] Subsequently, the desire to shed light on all kinds of women's work extended the themes to include an analysis of housework and childcare and, in particular, to investigate those occupations that were said to be "suitable for women" but that also allowed women some measure of autonomy and, to a certain extent, sanctioned the right to work for the daughters of the middle classes. These studies thus relate to the twentieth century, considering both the professionalization of functions considered as naturally falling to the lot of women (welfare, care, education of young children) and the feminization of emerging sectors (the postal service, for example) or of sectors that were undergoing transformation (the electrical industry).[3] Finally, gender history, which in France began to develop only in the second half of the 1980s, emphasized the relations between the sexes and the cultural construction of the masculine and the feminine. It was an attempt to define family structures and production systems under the impact of sociological research and the belatedly translated book by Louise Tilly and Joan Scott,[4] and in particular to systematize and reevaluate existing knowledge by employing notions of the gendered division of labor, social and gender identity, and gendered legislation. At the same time, as a critique to this overly political social history, there emerged a longitudinal biographical approach to cohorts of workers of both sexes, which enabled an analysis of life courses and processes of mobility at the individual level.[5]

As many recent publications show, French historians have not held aloof from the current epistemological and political reflection on the practice of their discipline and their profession.[6] "Women's history," a generic term often used to designate all research on women and the relations between the sexes, has taken part in this reflection through an ongoing internal debate since its inception.[7] However, there is no irreducible opposition between those who practice—if we use Joan Scott's classification—women's history, gender history with the social science view of gender, or poststructuralist gender history. (Although poststructuralism is presented in the U.S. as a product of French thought, it has scarcely impinged on historical research in France).[8] Nor is there any controversy between social and cultural history, the latter seldom being used as the sole method of approach toward a phenomenon or a period.[9] If some historians, both men and women, express great distrust toward what they derisively term "discourse about discourse" and continue to research facts and the lived experience of men and women, others are also interested in language and gendered representations and do not disdain the empirical use of the contributions of the "turn to linguistics."[10] As my own personal development shows, I am open to all approaches, and I shall endeavor here to present a balanced picture of women's work in France from the end of the nineteenth century to the interwar period.

"WOMAN'S WORK," "WOMEN'S WORK," AND GENDER IDENTITY AT THE TURN OF THE CENTURY

Women's history, in a renewed critique of the source material, has focused on gendered representations of the construction of categories[11] and has decried the frequent underestimation of women's work, especially with regard to what was considered as mere assistance to an artisan husband or anything related to women's "menial tasks" that confined them to domestic work.[12] These jobs, such as boarding lodgers or washing other people's clothes, often done on an intermittent basis and thus accorded even less importance, are still little known to historians who have privileged the more visible figures of the laborer, the servant, and the employee. Nonetheless, census figures, such as they are, reveal that the rate of women's work in France was high as compared with neighboring countries. According to the 1906 census, thirty-six percent of French women worked (in Germany and Britain, the respective figures were twenty percent and twenty-six percent), which was almost thirty-eight percent (7.7 million) of the working population as a whole. There were two reasons for this high rate: on the one hand, industrialization in France was slow: this was still a predominantly rural country with a majority of small, independent farms and, in addition to 700,000 women agricultural workers, there were 2.5 million women who were married to farmers or ran farms themselves and whose tasks, necessary but auxiliary, were quite specific (in vine-growing country, for example, women neither sprayed the vines with copper sulphate nor cut them). On the other hand, France was the first Malthusian country, both chronologically and as regards the extent of the phenomenon: since 1870, demographic growth had been slow, and France needed working hands.[13] While Europe before 1914 had been an exporter of labor, France was obliged to welcome foreign workers and to set its women to work, including married women and those with children.

As they became increasingly numerous from the middle of the nineteenth century, women workers began to enter the secondary sector (where they numbered 2.5 million in 1906, which was one-third of the working population) in enterprises of varying size but on the average rather small, as was typical of France. A small minority worked in transport, chemicals, wood, stone, and metal works, many more in the paper, rubber, tobacco, and canning factories, while they dominated the textile and clothing industries, a long-standing female domain.[14] The gendered division of labor among the various sectors also existed within particular sectors. The ribbon industry of Saint-Étienne, which has been studied recently, and which developed after the munitions and textile factories, offers a good example of a women's trade, of a trade and way of life associated with women, as opposed to the masculine world of the mines.[15]

While men were in charge of the ribbon design and occupied the technical and managerial positions in the workshops and stores, women were assigned to certain stages of production (preparation of the silks and ribbon chain, folding), specific jobs that usually required no special skill. However, the electrification of weaving at the end of the nineteenth century reversed the relationship between the sexes at the loom, enhanced the value of the so-called feminine qualities (meticulousness and patience replaced physical strength), and blurred the borderlines between the masculine and the feminine: hence, perhaps, men's insistence both in memoirs written today and in written sources of that period, on grading skills and defining what was theirs—control of the technical aspects of production and the machinery.

Since women workers were generally unskilled or had skills that were not recognized even after a long apprenticeship (which was the case, for example, in ribbon weaving), and were hired in accordance with characteristics ostensibly linked to their sex, they were also underpaid. Women's wages, which were considered as supplementary pay, were, on average, half of men's, with great regional and sectoral differences. The poorest were those who worked at home—almost one million in 1906, at the height of this type of work in France—wearing themselves out at their sewing machines or needles, unprotected by any social legislation. The family workshop—usually a workshop family—was a particularly common phenomenon in France (the *canuts* of Lyon are well known) and offers an excellent site for studying the distribution of roles and tasks among men and women who worked alongside one another every day. In the city's trimmings (ribbon-weaving) industry, Mathilde Dubesset and Michelle Zancarini-Fournel have discovered female figures of devotion and submission to the head of the family: the eldest daughter practically obliged to remain single so as to assume her second job, that of devoted worker; the ever-busy mother-provider, a helper to whom the title of worker was denied by both the census and writers of memoirs. But these two historians have also pointed out the real power wielded by these mothers: they were the family's center of gravity and were often in charge of negotiations with the manufacturers. They were the ones who brought work and money to the household and, during their "errands," they could enjoy a few hours of freedom away from the confined atmosphere of the workshop.[16]

By the beginning of the twentieth century, the most feminized sector (forty percent) was the tertiary sector, where women still worked predominantly in domestic service and small businesses.[17] Nonetheless, with the development of the telephone and the typewriter, management found it difficult to resist the feminization of its personnel. As is shown in many satirical descriptions, office work was deemed less and less to be a man's job, except for design and executive posts. The gendered division of labor was, in fact, reinforced by specific frameworks for female labor, by the total removal of women workers from the domestic sphere to military-style workshops and factory-convents in the silk industry in the southwest of France.[18]

The new women's history at the end of the 1970s was surprised to discover the deep distrust of women's work on the part of the French labor movement before the war—a movement influenced more by Pierre Joseph Proudhon than by Marx. French workingmen and their organizations, which did not emerge until the Third Republic (an anarcho-syndicalist General Council of Labour (CGT), the very heterogenous French Section of the Workers' International (SFIO), with a slight Marxist-leaning Guediste tendency) feared competition from low-paid women and advocated the ideal of the mother in the home, educator of the little proletarian, who had to be protected from "mercenary" hands, the "[queen] bee" of the family beehive.[19] They jealously defended jobs that were considered masculine (wood, metals, printing)—"For men, wood and metal, for women, family and fabrics," a workers' report of 1867 declared[20]—as is shown by the 1913 Couriau Affair: When a couple of Parisian printers and union members, Emma and Louis Couriau, came to work in Lyon, the Lyon section of the Fédération du Livre rejected Emma's application for membership and expelled her husband for having allowed his wife to practice the profession and, under threat of a general strike, forced the company to fire the female intruder. The subject of much ridicule and even scandal at the time, this affair was discussed in the feminist and trade-union press, providing material of great value to the historian. Even if other equally glaring examples were not recorded, the debate that it aroused revealed the tenacity of a gendered image and gendered hierarchy of occupations, both in the mentality of the workingman and in public opinion in general.

The labor movement supported special legislation for the protection of women's and children's work, joining the demands of public-health workers and philanthropists who were slowly organizing themselves into pressure groups. Physicians and politicians who were concerned with the physical and "moral" health of the population demanded constraints on liberalism, both because of the vulnerability and lack of citizenship of women and children and for the sake of the supreme interests of the nation, and they succeeded in having protective laws passed in 1874 and 1892. The 1892 law was the first to distinguish between the sexes and not merely between ages. It banned night work for women, and limited their workday to eleven hours, in itself a considerable improvement. However, this legislation was badly implemented and subject to a large number of exemptions, applying only to factory work, which was not the main area of women's work. It thus failed to cover three-quarters of female labor, and it reinforced gender segregation, if only by giving credence to the notion that women were not really workers.[21] This attitude on the part of the labor movement, together with its male-oriented organization and methods of action, was one of the main reasons for the low percentage of women union members, who in 1911 constituted less than ten percent of unionized workers.[22]

But should one follow classic social history in perpetuating the terms of nineteenth-century discourse by treating women workers as marginal to the processes of industrialization and the formation of the working class? Should one not rather understand how these processes functioned in relation to the genesis of the marginalization of working women? Instead of seeking the technical and structural causes of the gendered division of labor and iterating the naturalist and pseudo-scientific contemporary arguments, Joan Scott proposes reading the history of women's work as a discursive construction of the gendered division of labor, a construction that by radically opposing women and work, reproduction and production, domestic work and paid employment, made the woman worker herself problematic.[23] "Workingwoman, an immoral word," wrote Jules Michelet, followed by Jules Simon (in *L'Ouvrière*, 1860), even before numerous trade unionists started singing the praises of the housewife and demanding a living wage for the family. This analysis of discourse is still much debated in France, where the reproach is often made that it underestimates reality and limits historical scope. It seems, however, extremely productive when used to demonstrate how ideas become converted through language into social realities. At the end of the nineteenth century, "men's work" and "women's work" were both opposing categories and opposing realities, and contemporaries considered this opposition to be "natural." Very significantly, the frontispiece of the *Guide de Saint-Étienne et ses environs*, published in 1908, shows a seated woman unwinding a ribbon, surrounded by a miner, recognizable by his lamp, and two metalworkers at their forge.[24] "Men's work," associated with the processing of hard materials (such as wood, or metals), with the exertion of physical strength (mining is a quintessentially male occupation), or the mastery of a technique (driving a train or printing, for example) was thus considered, above all, skilled work that was sufficiently well paid to support a family. In contrast, "women's work" was identified with badly paid, unskilled, menial tasks, and women's (outside) work was deemed to be a social problem that could only be resolved by a return to the home, or at least to pursuing work at home. Thus it was difficult—even impossible—for a woman to live alone, and the problems of women workers (e.g., wages, working conditions, child care) were seldom addressed, except by a few feminists.[25]

Women's work was, in fact, at the heart of a violent conflict between the labor and the feminist movements. Many teachers were prominent in the latter, women of modest condition but with education. The feminists propounded the idea that women were doubly oppressed—by capitalism and by men—and demanded gender equality in the workplace and independence of women through work. Like trade unionists, they denounced the passivity of women workers but sought to organize them either in autonomous structures—as did Marguerite Durand—or, like Hélène Brion, to make women's voices heard within the labor organizations.[26] They also encouraged the female "firsts"—such as the first women to obtain certain diplomas, or to enter a male profession—and proclaimed the right to work for daughters of the bourgeoisie, undermining the social and gendered reference to the mistress of the house as the "angel of the home." Indeed, under the influence of feminism, the education of girls, and foreign (notably American) examples, relations between the sexes began to change in many areas at the turn of the century: in law, work, and even sexuality.[27] Thus, after a fierce struggle by the feminists, a law passed in 1907 granted women the right to dispose freely of their pay, thus acknowledging to a certain extent that female labor had become commonplace.[28] However, it would take several decades for it to become accepted practice. These changes constituted the origin of a male identity crisis, which is better known than the way in which the identity of women as a whole was affected by the model that contemporaries referred to more and more, whether in praise or disparagement, as the "new woman."[29]

On the eve of World War I, between four hundred and six hundred girls sat for the male baccalauréat, a prerequisite for higher education and the liberal professions.[30] There were a few hundred women doctors, a few dozen women lawyers, and more and more teachers, nurses, and office workers. The CGT campaign for an English week (Saturday afternoons and Sundays off) implicitly recognized the need to reconcile work outside the home with household chores, and the debates aroused by the Couriau Affair led the CGT to launch a plan of action to organize women and to place the issue of women's work on the agenda of the next Congress (autumn of 1914). The war threw all of these issues into question.

"THERE IS STILL A HOUSEWIFE INSIDE THE WOMAN MAKING SHELLS"

It seems important to emphasize that women and men lived a different chronology of the war. While men rushed off to attack the enemy (who was, moreover, identified as feminine), believing their cause to be just, and victory imminent, the women who were left behind waited piously, made unemployed by the disorganization of the economy. They were taken care of by the state, which took the place of the mobilized husband, and were invited to serve in the most feminine of tasks—to feed, nurse, and comfort. When the war became bogged down, and the man sank into the mud of the trenches, sometimes falling victim to "female" diseases such as hysteria, women filled the void, assuming public responsibilities in order to operate the war machine, and soldiers' diaries as well as literature convey their fears of being dispossessed or betrayed, the feeling that they were making a sacrifice while women were benefiting. The war was certainly an exceptional period as far as women's work was concerned, if only for the phenomenon of replacement and the call for women workers within the munitions industry, but the degree of exception must be measured, the diversity of women's situations stressed, and the effects on identity examined.[31]

Whom and what does the term *female mobilization* include? While on August 7, 1914 Prime Minister Viviani used the male language of glory and national awakening to call on peasant women to complete the harvest and prepare for that of the following year, middle-class and well-to-do women and girls, accustomed to charitable work, busied themselves with comforting wounded civilians and soldiers. For many, however, this was a prelude to formative activism within a multitude of relief works or the Red Cross: military health services would employ seventy thousand volunteer nurses along with the thirty thousand paid ones. But for women workers and employees, the war—whose protracted nature the military and public authorities were late in realizing—meant, above all, material hardship that was hardly mitigated by the paltry allowance granted to mobilized women as of August 5. According to Ministry of Labor statistics, in August of 1914 the number of women workers in commerce and industry was only forty percent of the prewar figure, and in July of 1915 it was still less than eighty percent. They did not attain the prewar level until 1916, and exceeded it only by twenty percent at the end of 1917, the high point of women's employment, when women workers constituted forty percent of the labor force in these sectors as compared with thirty-two percent before the war.

The mobilization of French women was tardy, slow, and empirical, and remained limited; except in the countryside, the working world was not flooded by women. In the war factories, as a last resort after the hiring of civilians, the call-up of 500,000 workers instituted by the Dalbiez law, and the import of colonial and foreign men workers (in particular Chinese, Kabyles, and Indo-Chinese),

women munitions workers numbered 400,000 at the beginning of
1918—a quarter of the total labor force, and a third in the Paris region. However, as time went by, and the army claimed more and
more soldiers, women began to accomplish an increasing variety of
tasks—a real symbol of their penetration into traditionally male sectors. As in other industries, they apparently broke down the former
gendered division of labor. The January-February 1918 *Bulletin du
Ministère du Travail* noted that women workers, having been assigned tasks in accordance with their physical aptitudes, had
adapted to the most diverse kinds of work, and that "currently they
perform most of the operations either by machine or by hand, from
the moment the raw material arrives at the factory, until it is dis-
patched in the form of manufactured products." Thus women
kneaded the gingerbread dough or operated the machines that
crimped cans in the food industry, knotted threads in cotton and silk
mills, performed all the work in tanneries and dye works, and operated wood saws, planing machines, polishing tools, and even lino-
type machines in the male domain of printing. In Saint-Étienne,
people still remember the trimmings workers who, no longer able to
rely on their husbands for technical assistance, would get together
and sometimes spend the entire night trying to find out what was
wrong with their machine. Only the army resisted, not opening its
barracks and office jobs until the end of 1916, and then very spar-
ingly. France did not have a women's auxiliary corps, and could
imagine a woman soldier only as the bawdy figure appearing on numerous war postcards that depicted *poilues* sporting a very low
neckline, knickers, and boots.

The growth in the number of women workers, which was made
possible by an increase in the number of girls and women with families who went out to work, was accompanied by a partial transfer
from domestic work and traditionally female occupations—there
was a lasting depression in sewing and the clothing industry—to
rapidly growing sectors (e.g., metalworking and chemicals) or to
those that were essential to the life of the country (e.g., transport and
public and private services). This transfer engendered a sometimes
painful geographical mobility (both local and regional), but placed
women in highly visible posts endowed with patriotic value, which
were often better paid, especially in the war industry. However, the
high war wages were not widespread—the law instituting minimum
wages in the home-based clothing industry was finally voted upon
and promulgated on July 10, 1915 but was poorly implemented—and
this was just one of the difficulties women workers suffered.

While inflation—a new phenomenon that surprised and vexed

contemporaries—was sometimes compensated for by cost-of-living increments, wage inequality persisted. Thus, Mme. M., a shell maker in Renault from 1917 who was interviewed in the 1970s, cited the following exchange with a better-paid young man in the same workshop: "You don't make any more than I do, why do you earn more?" "You're a woman, it's natural." It was Munitions Minister Albert Thomas, a reformist socialist and advocate of the principle of equal pay for equal work, who made this inequality official in rates introduced from January of 1917.[32] His circulars pronounced it natural to deduct from women's wages "the cost price of all new tool modifications, work organization, supervision, and, in general, that part of additional costs entailed by the substitution of female labor for male labor." Somehow, women workers were to pay for the modernization of French industry. Indeed, the fact that less-experienced workers were being hired was exploited to establish more rational work methods that had been violently opposed by workers before the war. In the De Dion gun workshop, where the work was divided into forty-one operations remunerated by piece, lowering the rate of pay per piece provoked, in June of 1916, the first great women's strike in the war factories, after numerous conflicts in the textile and cloth industries. In the brand-new Citroën factory on the Quai de Javel, the workshops were made up of fourteen parallel sections, each producing four thousand shells daily, whose manufacture was begun at one end and finished at the other.[33] More than ever before, industrialists "discovered" female qualities—conscientiousness, meticulousness, aptitude for monotonous work—and employed women workers on mechanical production lines, in the manufacture of delicate articles and in inspection, after minimum training and under the supervision of foremen who did not eschew sexual harassment.

Women workers also suffered from the suspension of all social legislation and the difficult working conditions, especially in war factories.[34] Mentioned in all oral accounts—one of my interviewees had lost an eye in a cartridge factory—in trade-union journals, and in two long investigations carried out by women journalists hired as workers, the poor working conditions were mitigated from 1917 by a specific social policy with some measures benefiting women munitions workers and others, women workers in general.[35] These measures were not uniform, varying from one place to another, and included the establishment of canteens, welfare centers, or nursing rooms—the latter as a result of the Engerand law of August of 1917, which obliged all employers of over one hundred women to introduce such rooms to enable nursing mothers to feed their babies twice a day during work hours. These nursing rooms were little used and few in number—only twelve, for example, in the Paris region—and these efforts to reconcile work and motherhood could not conceal the fact that France remained behind the times as regards social protection for mothers, and would remain so for more than another decade. Nonetheless, the late introduction of female factory superintendents in charge of the physical and moral well-being of women workers—a prelude to gendered personnel management—was more lasting than in Great Britain, since it was inspired by pronatalist models.[36]

Could we say, then, that women experienced freedom in this period? During the war, young women from every milieu could find unhoped-for professional opportunities—with wages enabling some indulgences outside of paternal surveillance—or a rapid initiation into life's realities, as described in the memoirs of Louise Weiss and Clara Malraux.[37] But mothers of families of the urban lower classes were more likely to feel the extra burden of work and the difficulties of raising children alone, while peasant women, who replaced both the mobilized men and the requisitioned animals, as guardians of their property under the watchful eyes of the family saw all their hopes of reaching city lights dissipate.[38] How can one really know the deepest feelings of women workers who left no written record beyond occasional lines in trade-union papers in which they denounced their working conditions and sometimes expressed their pride in doing work previously reserved for men?[39] The few oral reports that I have managed to collect, which are of a retrospective nature, emphasize the hard work, the difficulties with male co-workers, and the gap, due to fear and misunderstanding, between female and foreign workers, but they draw up varying balance sheets, depending on each woman's marital and occupational circumstances: one acquired through her work the right to express an opinion; another quickly returned home under the pressure of a jealous husband. An analysis of the personal files of retired Parisian women workers enabled Catherine Omnès to challenge the hypothesis that the female labor force was unstable, and to stress the role played in their working lives by the wartime factory, which was where they acquired a professional identity.[40] But the young trade unions' Action Committee against the Exploitation of Women, led by the shirt and linen unions and by militants such as Hélène Brion, failed in its struggle for equal wages: in the workers' world, the war, rather than widening the opportunities that opened up in 1914, reinforced the militants' traditional hostility to female labor, contempt for the docile woman worker, and the male worker's attachment to hearth and home—attitudes sometimes tainted by hatred toward women who profited from the war and their husband's death.[41]

There is another level of analysis that seems to me to be important today: how did contemporaries interpret the upheavals caused by the war, how did they represent in images and words the upsurge and changes in women's work, and how did they adjust to them? Indeed, the praise for the "true" Frenchwoman was addressed more to the patriotic middle class than to women war workers. The latter sometimes elicited admiring amazement, but more often overt hostility that cited the intellectual and physical weakness of the female sex. Above all, they elicited fear that women would be "masculinized" (a term characteristic of the period),[42] and that sex differences would be blurred. Various means were employed to exorcise these fears, such as the use of reassuring metaphors, the adoption of the charming diminutive *munitionette*, which bore an uncanny resemblance to the term *midinette* (the Parisian seamstress, symbol of the prewar woman worker), or the foregrounding of the comforting figures of the military nurse or *marraine* (a woman who corresponded with soldiers at the front). While previously I was amused by these frequently used and curious metaphors ("to work at metal as at one's knitting," "to string the mortar shells like pearls," "puttering around") and touching descriptions (the *munitionettes* "have contrived to keep all their charm," "there is still a housewife inside the woman making shells"), I now view them as a form of verbal incantation, a means of affirming the temporary nature of the situation and the immutability of the borderlines between the genders. Similarly, instead of calling for competence, the official mobilization campaigns for women played on family relations (to save one's soldier-husband) and used a rhetoric of sacrifice which, by definition, relates to an exceptional situation. By contrast, the feminists, who wanted to use the war experience as a launching pad toward occupational and political equality, spoke in masculine terms of "the second front," "the fighting women on the home front," who answered the "nation's call." Instead of reacting to what may seem to be their "chauvinism," one can discern in this struggle over language a determination to bring about a shift in the definition of the sexes and to achieve women's integration into the nation. It is also significant that the cover of *La Vie féminine* of April 15, 1917 placed face to face, against a background of factory chimneys, a little *midinette* or milliner, with a hat box, and a big, strong *munitionette* in a man's work clothes.

This was an unequal struggle. As a logical result of the view that the war had been an interim period that was now over, the demobilization of women was brutal, especially for the war workers, and this violence seemed to have as much a psychological function as an economic one. It served, on the one hand, to reassure a masculine identity badly shaken during the four years of anonymous combat and, on the other, to obliterate the war and respond to the soldiers' ardent desire to restore the old world. Women's demobilization was accompanied by a questioning of their capacities and virulent criticism of the emancipated woman, the "enemy's dream," according to novelist Colette Yver who, in *Les Jardins du féminisme* (1920) as in her earlier *Les Cervelines* (1903) and *Princesses de science* (1907), reiterated that women could not, with impunity to themselves and society, be "autonomous beings." The demobilization also led to praise for the housewife, whom it was desired to transform into a professional, and a glorification of the mother—the first Mothers' Day was celebrated in Lyon in 1918—and her duty to repopulate the country, a goal that the July 31, 1920 law banning all birth-control propaganda aimed at promoting. But in a country that had lost ten percent of its male labor force (1.3 million soldiers killed, including 500,000 peasants) and which had 600,000 widows and many disabled, the widespread consensus in favor of women's remaining at home could not drown out the realistic voices that urged recognition of the inevitable need for women to work—even in industry—or the militant voices calling for women's emancipation. In the long history of women's work, the war could not be a mere parenthesis.

"FOR MEN, THE TOOL; FOR WOMEN, THE OFFICE CHAIR"

If the 1921 census showed an increase of 700,00 in the female labor force,[43] the ensuing years until 1968, except for 1946, showed a decline in female labor and in the feminization of work. As Jean-Louis Robert and I have pointed out, the war seems, therefore, to have reversed the nineteenth-century trend toward growth in the number of working women.[44] But this overall decline, albeit small in the interwar period, especially during the prosperous 1920s, must be analyzed more closely. It is, at least partially, primarily the result of statistics and the ideology they reflect. In order to avoid any ambiguity regarding the term "housewife" (meaning either "housekeeper" or "woman at home"), the 1926 census specified for the first time that "a woman who does not exercise any profession and only runs her own household will reply 'none.'"[45] Similarly, the method used for the census of women's work in agriculture often varied, as did their own perception of their work; the women who worked in

1921 were also those whom the separations that the war caused had made aware of the tasks they were fulfilling. On the other hand, the decline in women's work recorded from 1926 paralleled the decrease in the number of women working in agriculture, who nonetheless still constituted forty percent of working women in 1936, and whose role in running the farms increased as a result of the growing specialization in production and the shortage of hired help. The non-agricultural female working population increased slowly but surely (except for the economic crisis of the 1930s), and it is this sector that must be studied in detail in order to assess continuity and change.

Let us first consider traditionally female occupations. The decline in domestic employment (which before the war had been dubbed the "housemaid crisis") intensified during the 1920s, for such jobs were regarded as servile. Caricaturists poked fun at mistresses of the house taken aback by the demands of their maids and their far-from-domestic talents. Before collapsing during the 1930s crisis, the clothing industries, which, together with textiles, still constituted the foremost female branch of industry, enjoyed some prosperity, especially in the Paris region,[46] benefiting from the expanding market as a result of a monetary policy that favored the consumer-goods and export sectors. While work performed at home was still poorly protected, women were drawn to the workshops because of the contractual nature of the work relations instituted after the *midinettes'* strike in May of 1917, which led to a substantial improvement in wages, working conditions, and the training system. The latter, however, was oriented almost exclusively toward traditional trades, and thus tended to perpetuate the former gendered division of labor, which was reemerging in each sector. Thus, in the leather and fur industry, after the interlude of the war, women were once again excluded from skilled jobs, such as the cutting and preparation of skins.

Despite their resurgence after the war, these female industries were no longer the main providers of jobs for women. The relative, and eventually absolute, decline in women workers in these industries stood in marked contrast to the proportion of women—often former war workers—in the modern industries of metalworking, chemicals, electrical goods, and telephones. Thus, in the Seine region, work in metals became the second largest sector of employment for women, after clothing, with the proportion of women reaching 14.5 percent in 1921 (nine percent on the national level) and 17.4 percent in 1931, as against 7.4 percent in 1906 (three percent on the national level). This growth was a sign of continuity between the war and the 1920s, indicating that women fully participated in the economic changes of this decade, as emphasized in the somewhat peremptory title of Sylvie Zerner's article, "From Sewing to the Presses."[47] Despite trade-union opposition, the new methods of mass production and the rationalization of work entailed an increase in female labor in the factories, along with a new division of labor that assigned to women (a lesson that had been learned in the war) repetitive, unskilled jobs, mechanical, assembly-line jobs described so well by Simone Weil in *La Condition ouvrière*, and manual processing tasks. In this context, feminization did not do away with traditional gender disparities in terms of hierarchy and remuneration. Women were still excluded from managerial posts; even if they were equally skilled, they were mostly paid by piecework and therefore under pressure to produce more; and the wage gap between the sexes, which had been reduced during the war, widened immediately afterwards. Even in the mixed professions that emerged in the metalworking industries (about twenty out of the hundred or so listed), men were classified as "professionals," and women as "specialized workers."

Although French women were still without full civil rights, in 1925 they obtained the right to join a labor union without their husband's consent. However, the increasingly masculine imagery used by the unions since the Russian Revolution held little attraction for them, and they still constituted no more than 15 percent of the membership. While the development of Christian trade unions—the *Confédération française des travailleurs chrétiens* (CFTC) was established in 1919—reinforced working-class familialism, all workers' organizations remained in favor of special protection for women workers and welcomed, as did the beneficiaries, the maternity benefits included in the 1928 and 1930 laws on national insurance.[48] While all feminists supported social security for mothers, only a minority—members of the *Ligue française du droit des femmes* (LFDF), such as the attorney Andrée Lehman—opposed any other specific legislation governing women's work. But their defense of the universal right to work was tempered by their recognition of women's role as mothers, especially with reference to factory work. Does this mean that French feminism between the wars, haunted by the specter of the war's male violence and carnage, was weakened and divided, as was its British counterpart described by Susan Kingsley Kent?[49] From the outset, it was mostly in favor of populationist policies, and continued to propound the view that the sexes complemented one another. Above all, it mobilized for its main struggle—women's suffrage—in an old democracy that was hostile to political rights for women.[50]

"The prejudiced attitude that requires women to be excluded from certain jobs no longer exists," wrote the feminists Alice La Mazière and attorney Suzanne Grinberg in a 1917 guide on careers for women.[51] This type of book, which proliferated in the 1920s, advised women who were able to pursue lengthy studies to enter the liberal professions or engineering, and others to take up, besides office work, careers in commerce, the hotel and precision instrument industries, horticulture, and health. On a modest scale, private institutions initiated by militant feminists attempted to make up for the lack of adequate technical training for women, such as Valentine Thompson's hotel school; Louise Cruppi's École Rachel, which trained and placed women in three employment sectors (photographic retouching, electric-wire coiling, and artificial-limb polishing); and the school for nursemaids founded by the Association of Certificated Teachers. The kinds of work actually proposed, so strongly influenced by gender differentiation, belied the optimism that was asserted, but they also demonstrated that the war had shifted, both in deeds and in people's minds, the borderlines of the gendered division of labor. What was "women's work" after the traumatic experience of the war, when women had replaced men even in the hardest tasks? The voices heard at the time all wanted to steer women away from work requiring physical strength, toward the light and luxury industries and, above all, toward the services and office jobs. As the incisive Marcelle Capy wrote in a militant journal in November of 1918:

> Now that the war is over and the pretext of national defense is no longer valid, [now] that the world crushed by death, fire and ruin needs productive work, one must become organized to live. For men, men's work / For women, women's work / For men, heavy work, rough jobs / For women, sedentary work, clean jobs / For men, the tool / For women, the office chair. We have seen too many athletes cramped over account books and small women carting loads heavier than themselves. One must reverse the roles.

Economic development and the longer period of schooling for girls did indeed contribute to the increase of women workers, especially in executive positions, in the processing industry, as well as in the tertiary sector, which became the foremost provider of nonagricultural work for women.[52] This phenomenon tended to increase the number of wage earners—a gauge of autonomy—among nonagricultural working women (the proportion of such wage earners grew from thirty-three percent in 1906 to 52.6 percent in 1936) and to effect a partial transfer, which is difficult to express in figures, of female work from the working class to the middle and well-to-do classes. In fact, the feminization of the tertiary sector—more pronounced in banking, insurance, and administration than in commerce—along with the emerging health-care and social services (a diploma for nurses was established in 1922, for social workers in 1932),[53] enabled young women of the middle classes to practice a profession and obtain relative recognition of their right to work, even if they often paid for it by remaining single.[54] Despite the marriage boom that followed the armistice, and which reduced the effects of the demographic imbalance between men and women caused by the war—the proportion of unmarried women of this generation increased only slightly, from ten percent to 12.5 percent—women workers in some tertiary professions found it difficult to marry, not so much because of the burden of work or the call of a vocation as because of the virtual impossibility of finding a suitable partner. As one of the most radical French feminists, Madeleine Pelletier, explained in the 1920s, these young women refused to come down in the world by marrying a worker, while the men of their social background preferred women with better dowries, who stayed at home.[55]

For their part, well-to-do girls gravitated toward the liberal professions, where opportunities opened up for them as the result of the more egalitarian access to secondary and higher education: the establishment of the girls' baccalauréat in 1919, the equalization of male and female secondary education in 1924, and the opening of the great commercial and engineering schools. But these girls still confronted the sometimes tenacious resistance of institutions and the still-enduring view that science and intelligence were incompatible with the female sex.[56] Aware of being different from their mothers, these young women took for their models independent career women—Suzanne Lengden, Marie Curie, Colette, or the women attorneys whose defense of higher education for women had a general impact on the image of the working woman and her aptitudes. On the level of wages, inequality between the sexes remained the rule, but in the public service sector a breach was made—another result of the war—when equal salaries for men and women were instituted in primary schools in 1919, and in the postal service in 1928, as a result of a long struggle on the part of women employees.

The war thus renewed the old debate about work for the daughters of the middle and well-to-do classes and about the education they should receive at home and at school. In this sense, they were the principal beneficiaries of the war. "A prejudice is disappearing. . . . Girls of the middle class no longer want to depend on their fathers, and later their husbands, so as to be spared the cares of daily life," wrote the teacher Hélène Bureau in 1921 in her introduction to the *Guide pour le choix des carrières féminines*. As I already pointed out, such vocational guide manuals in fact codified the gendered division of labor and endowed it with the power of the written word; but they also popularized the notion that marriage was not the only career for women, that a profession was better than a dowry. Thus, it is striking that in this debate on these girls' futures, both opponents and advocates of work for women united in agreement on the same compromises, invoking the possible consequences of the war, reversals of fortune, and the risk of remaining single. The former spoke of women unfortunately obliged to work for their living; the latter of independent women capable of coping with the hazards of life. As Mary Louise Roberts noted in her cultural critique of the decade 1917-1927, the image of the "woman on her own" was indeed an attempt to negotiate between the disturbing symbol of change embodied in the "modern woman," "la garçonne," and the tradition represented in the figure of "the mother."[57] This was a compromise figure that enabled the debate on gender to advance within French society and allowed change to seep gradually into women's lives.

Did this figure of the single career woman, which, it should be recalled, was not a massive demographic phenomenon, mold the identity of French women in the 1920s? Did it enable them to resist familial and pronatalist propaganda that destined women for motherhood and demanded their constant presence at home,[58] as well as the injunctions of a society that was becoming medicalized and that located women at the heart of the fight against infant mortality? Perhaps—women's work in fact persisted, and the superintendents' reports expressed their astonishment at the determination of French women to work outside the home—but this figure certainly contributed also to making them accept the toll their work exacted: fewer children. While in 1919 the workday was limited to eight hours, before the introduction of the forty-hour week in 1936, and mothers were even better protected medically and socially,[59] French women had fewer and fewer children, and forty percent of the Parisian women workers in the interwar period whom Catherine Omnès studied had no children at all. The change, then, bears the mark of continuity inscribed in French Malthusianism of the period. Work and maternity are always in opposition; women cannot be mothers and workers at the same time. Thus, while the war shifted work structures and the gendered division of workers, at the same time it seems to have had a rather conservative effect on matters of identity.

Notes

1. Françoise Thébaud, "The Great War and the Triumph of Sexual Division," in *A History of Women*, vol. 5, *Toward a Cultural Identity in the Twentieth Century*, ed. Françoise Thébaud (Cambridge, MA, 1994), 21-75.

2. See Michelle Perrot's presentation in "Travaux de femmes dans la France du XIXe siècle," *Le Mouvement social*, no. 105 (Oct.-Dec. 1978); and Madeleine Guilbert, Nicole Lowit and Marie-Hélène Zylberberg-Hocquard, *Travail et condition féminine: Bibliographie commentée* (Paris, 1977).

3. See the special issue of *Le Mouvement social*, no. 140 (July-Sept. 1987), *Métiers de Femmes*, ed. Michelle Perrot.

4. Louise A. Tilly and Joan W. Scott, *Women, Work, and Family* (New York, 1978). The French version appeared in 1987 with an introduction that attenuated the economic and biological determinism of the original and called for research into cultural and political aspects.

5. See, for example, Catherine Omnès, "Marchés du travail et trajectoires personelles: Les ouvrières parisiennes de l'entre-deux-guerres" (Ph. diss., University of Paris X, 1993). This approach is also used by Mathilde Dubesset and Michelle Zancarini-Fournel to study the careers of women in the Maison Casino in the last chapter of their work, *Parcours des femmes: réalités et représentations: Saint-Étienne 1880-1995* (Lyon, 1993).

6. See *Passés recomposés: Champs et chantiers de l'Histoire*, Editions Autrement, Série Mutations, no. 150-151 (Jan. 1995); Bernard Lepetit, ed., *Les formes de l'expérience: Une Autre histoire sociale* (Paris, 1995); François Bédarida, ed., *L'Histoire et le métier d'historien en France 1945-1995* (Paris, 1995).

7. See Georges Duby and Michelle Perrot, eds., *Femmes et histoire* (Paris, 1993), which includes the proceedings of the conference held at the Sorbonne in November of 1992, following the publication of the five volumes of *Histoire des femmes*.

8. Joan W. Scott, "Women's History," in Peter Burke, ed., *New Perspectives on Historical Writing* (Cambridge, 1991).

9. An exception is Mary Louise Roberts's extremely interesting book, which is closely related to our subject, *Civilization without Sexes: Reconstructing Gender in Postwar France, 1917-1927* (Chicago, 1994). Susan Kingsley Kent's book, *Making Peace: The Reconstruction of Gender in Interwar Britain* (Princeton, 1993) seems to be the equivalent for Britain. See also Miriam Cooke and Angela Woollacott, eds., *Gendering War Talk* (Princeton, 1993), whose title is very indicative of current tendencies.

10. I recently attempted a synthesis of the history of women in France; See my *Ecrire l'histoire des femmes: Bilan critique et perspectives* (forthcoming, ENS Editions, 1996).

11. See Joan W. Scott, "Statistical Representations of Work: The Politics of the Chamber of Commerce. Statistique de l'industrie à Paris 1847-1848," in S. L. Kaplan and C. J. Koepp, eds., *Work in France* (Ithaca, 1986).

12. See Jean-Paul Burdy, Mathilde Dubesset, and Michelle Zancarini-Fournel, "Rôle, travaux, et métiers des femmes dans une ville industrielle:

Saint-Étienne 1900-1950," *Le Mouvement social*, no. 140 (July-Sept. 1987): 27-53.

13. The population grew from thirty-six million in 1872 to 39.5 million in 1911, then stagnated around forty million until 1946.

14. In 1906, the percentage of women in the working population was: fifteen percent in metallurgy, 5.5 percent in metal works, 6.5 percent in the timber industry, 11.9 percent in chemicals, 39.9 percent in textiles, and 85.9 percent in clothing.

15. Dubesset and Zancarini-Fournel, *Parcours de femmes*. See also Jean-Paul Burdy, *Le Soleil noir: Un quartier de Saint-Etienne, 1840-1940* (Lyon, 1989).

16. Dubesset and Zancarini-Fournel, *Parcours de femmes*.

17. 800,000 women, as against 150,000 men around the beginning of the century, despite complaints about the "maid crisis." See Geneviève Fraisse, *Essai sur le service domestique* (Paris, 1979); and Anne Martin-Fugier, *La Place des bonnes* (Paris, 1979).

18. Dominique Vanoli, "Les Ouvrières enfermées: Les Couvents soyeux," *Révoltes logiques*, no. 2 (spring–summer 1976).

19. See Marie-Hélène Zylberberg-Hocquard, *Féminisme et syndicalisme en France (Paris, 1978)*, and *Femmes et Féminisme dans le mouvement ouvrier français* (Paris, 1981); Michelle Perrot, "L'éloge de la ménagère dans le discours des ouvriers français au XIXe siècle," *Romantisme*, no. 13-14 (1976).

20. Cited in Michelle Perrot, "Le Syndicalisme français et les femmes: Histoire d'un malentendu," *Aujourd'hui* 66 (Mar. 1984): 44.

21. See Mary Lynn Stewart, *Women, Work, and the French State: Labour Protection and Social Patriarchy, 1879-1919* (Montreal, 1989); Leora Auslander and Michelle Zancarini-Fournel, eds., *Différence des sexes et protection sociale* (Vincennes, 1955).

22. See the pioneering work of the sociologist Madeleine Guilbert, *Les Femmes et l'organisation syndicale avant 1914: Présentation et commentaires des documents pour une étude de syndicalisme féminin* (Paris, 1966).

23. Joan W. Scott, "The Woman Worker," in *A History of Women*, vol. 4, *Emerging Feminism from Revolution to World War*, ed. Geneviève Fraisse and Michelle Perrot (Cambridge, MA, 1993).

24. Reproduced in Dubesset and Zancarini-Fournel, *Parcours de femmes*, 135.

25. Nonetheless, thirty-four percent of women aged fifteen to forty-nine, and 10.4 percent aged over fifty, were single in 1911.

26. Marguerite Durand (1864-1936), founder of *La Fronde* in 1897, the first daily to be entirely written, set, administered, and edited by women, bequeathed its archives to the city of Paris. The Marguerite Durand library is the only one in France that specializes in the history of women and feminism. The teacher Hélène Brion (1884-1962), trade unionist, socialist, but above all, feminist, failed in her efforts to make the cause of women heard in labor organizations and retired from public life after World War I. See her

1917 brochure, *La Voie féministe*, reprinted in 1978 with a preface by Huguette Bourchardeau.

27. See Michelle Perrot, "The New Eve and the Old Adam: Changes in French Women's Condition at the Turn of the Century," in Margaret Randolph Higonnet et al., eds., *Behind the Lines: Gender and the Two World Wars* (New Haven, 1987), 51-60.

28. On the pre-1914 feminist movement, see Laurence Klejman and Florence Rochefort, *L'égalité en marche: Le féminisme sous la Troisième République* (Paris, 1989).

29. See Annelise Maugue, *l'Identité masculine en crise au tournant du siècle* (Paris, 1987), and "L'Eve nouvelle et le vieil Adam," in *Histoire des femmes*, vol. 4.

30. Established in the 1870s, girls' secondary education awarded only a useless school-leaving certificate. The first girl to be awarded the baccalauréat was Julie Daubet in 1861.

31. There will henceforth be fewer references because the text is based on my own research cited earlier.

32. The degree of wage inequality was nonetheless reduced in comparison with previous rates and was also less than in neighboring countries.

33. On Citroën, see Sylvie Schweitzer, *Des Engrenages à la chaine: les Usines Citroën 1915-1935* (Lyon, 1982), and *André Citroën* (Paris, 1993).

34. Before the war, the workday had been limited to ten hours, there had been one day off per week, and women had not been allowed to work in factories at night.

35. The investigation by Marcelle Capy, feminist, pacifist, and libertarian, was published under the title "La Femme à l'Usine" in *La Voix des femmes*, Nov. 28, Dec. 5, Dec. 12, 1917 and Jan. 2, 1918. The investigation of the *Petit Parisien* by a "neutral journalist" appeared under the heading "Quinze jours comme ouvrière de la Défense nationale," July 19–21, 24, 27, 1916.

36. On the factory superintendents, see Annie Fourcaut, *Femmes à l'usine en France dans l'entre-deux-guerres* (Paris, 1982); and Laura Lee Downs, *Manufacturing Inequality: Gender Division in the French and British Metalworking Industries, 1914-1939* (Ithaca, 1995). The first group of women superintendents began training in 1917; 101 were working in 1928, and 191 in 1935.

37. Louise Weiss, *Mémoires d'une Européenne*, vol. 1, *1893-1919* (Paris, 1968); Clara Malraux, *Le Bruit de nos pas: Apprendre à vivre* (Paris, 1963).

38. Unpublished research has been carried out in several regions (e.g., Allier, Puy-de-Dôme, Gard, and Herault); some accounts describe the war in the countryside: Serge Grafteaux, *Mémé Santerre: Une vie* (Paris, 1975); Emilie Carles, *Une Soupe aux herbes sauvages* (Paris, 1977). See also letters and testimonies of mobilized peasants, for example, *Les Raisins sont bien beaux: Correspondance de guerre d'un rural* (Paris, 1977); *Les Carnets de guerre de Louis Barthas, tonnelier* (Paris, 1978). Rémi Cazals et al., *Années cruelles, 1914-1918* (Témoignages d'Audois, Atelier du gué, 1983).

39. I have not found any account by a woman factory worker. Louise

Délétang, who published her *Journal d'une ouvrière parisienne pendant la guerre* in 1935, did sewing at home along with her mother and sister.

40. Catherine Omnès, "Marchés du travail et trajectoires personelles."

41. See Jean-Louis Robert, *Les Ouvriers, La Patrie et la Révolution*, Annales littéraires de l'Université de Besançon, no. 592, 1995.

42. Before being popularized in France by Dr. Huot, the term was, it seems, used by the German physician A. von Moll in a 1912 treatise on sexology. See Cornelie Usborne, "Pregnancy is the Women's Active Service. Pronatalism in Germany in the First World War," in Richard Wall and Jay Winter, eds., *The Upheaval of War: Family, Work and Welfare in Europe, 1914-1918* (Cambridge, 1988), 389-416.

43. It also showed a corresponding decline in the male work force, a sign, taking deaths into account, of men's increased work. Obviously, these comparisons before and after the war must be carried out on equivalent territory and should exclude the population of Alsace-Lorraine.

44. Jean-Louis Robert, "Women and Work in France during the First World War," in Wall and Winter, eds., *The Upheaval of War*, 251-66. Françoise Thébaud, *La Femme au temps de la guerre de 14* (Paris, 1986).

45. Martine Martin, "Ménagère: une profession? Les Dilemmes de l'entre-deux-guerres," *Le Mouvement social*, no. 140 (July-Sept. 1987): 89-106.

46. See Omnès, "Marchés du travail et trajectoires professionelles."

47. Sylvie Zerner, "De la couture aux presses: l'Emploi féminin entre les deux guerres," *Le Mouvement social*, no. 140 (July-Sept. 1987): 9-26. See also idem, "Travail domestique et forme de travail: Ouvrières et employées entre la Première Guerre Mondiale et la grande crise" (Ph.D. diss., University of Paris X, 1985).

48. See Henry Hatzfeld, *Du pauperisme à la sécurité sociale* (Paris, 1971); Françoise Thébaud, *Quand nos grand-mères donnaient la vie: La maternité en France dans l'entre-deux-guerres* (Lyon, 1986); Gisela Bock and Pat Thane, eds., *Maternity and Gender Policies: Women and the Rise of the European Welfare States, 1880-1950s* (London, 1991). Some of the workers opposed the family allowances as an offense to the workers' dignity and a device to enable employers to put pressure on wages. Apart from protection of mothers, no special law to protect women workers was enacted in the interwar period. When companies instituted paid vacations before the 1936 law, the length of vacation was usually proportional to the length of employment.

49. Susan Kingsley Kent, "The Politics of Sexual Difference: World War I and the Demise of British Feminism," *Journal of British Studies* 27 (July 1988): 232-53; and idem, *Making Peace*.

50. On feminism in the interwar period, see Christine Bard, *Les filles de Marianne: Histoire des féminismes, 1914-1940* (Paris, 1995).

51. *Carrières féminines. Nouvelles écoles. Nouveaux métiers. Nouvelles professions* (Paris, 1917).

52. On male and female employees, see Delphine Gardey, "Un Monde en mutation, les employés de bureau en France (1892–1930), féminisation, mécanication, retionalisation," (Ph.D. diss., University of Paris 7, 1994).

53. See Yvonne Knibiehler, *Cornettes et blouses blanches, les infir-mières dans la société française 1880-1980* (Paris, 1984), and *Nous les as-sistantes sociales* (Paris, 1981).

54. See *Madame ou Mademoiselle: Itinéraires de la solitude féminine, 18e-20e siècles*, collected by Arlette Farge and Christiane Klapish-Zuber (Paris, 1984).

55. On Madeleine Pelletier see Klejman and Rochefort, *L'Égalité en marche*; Bard, *Les filles de Marianne*; Christine Bard, ed., *Madeleine Pel-letier (1874-1939): Logique et infortunes d'un combat pour l'égalité* (Paris, 1992); Charles Sowerwine and Claude Maignien, *Madeleine Pelletier, une féministe dans l'arène politique* (Paris, 1992); Felicia Gordon, *The Integral Feminist: Madeleine Pelletier 1874-1939. Feminism, Socialism and Medi-cine* (London, 1990). Pelletier analyzed spinsterhood in an undated brochure, *Le Célibat: Etat supérieur*.

56. There are few works in France on women students, scientists, or aca-demics. For a brief discussion, see Christophe Charle, *La République des universitaires, 1870-1940* (Paris, 1994).

57. See Roberts, *Civilization without Sexes. La Garçonne* is the title of a novel by Victor Margueritte, the first volume of the trilogy *La Femme en chemin*. It was an international success as soon as it appeared, and was much written about at the time and later. Anne-Marie Sohn, in "La Garçonne face à l'opinion publique: Type littéraire ou type social des années 20," *Le Mouvement social*, no. 80 (1972), has examined public opinion re-actions and shown that the figure of the *garçonne* was more a literary than a social reality. I have stressed in *Quand nos grand-mères donnaient la vie* that the novel is, as its author stated, "a fable of virtue" and   hero-ine undergoes a real redemption. For Annelise Maugue, *L'Identité mascu-line en crise*, the novel, which imbues the main male protagonist with an ideal chivalry and heralds the figure of the revolutionary, shows that the war revived ancient masculine myths. Roberts goes further in exploring the novel's symbolic role, which she compares to masculine war literature: the *garçonne* is a symbol of the cultural crisis, appeasing, through her own re-demption, cultural and sexual anxieties.

58. This propaganda took many forms, scored successes, and achieved the adoption of repressive legislation and inducements (financial and hon-orific). One of the main pronatalist movements, the *Alliance nationale con-tre la dépopulation*, received backing, especially in its fight against women's work, from women's Catholic associations such as the *Union féminine, civique et sociale* (UFCS), established in 1925. The latter participated in a 1937 international congress on "The Mother at Home, Worker for Human Progress," which distorted the meaning of the word *worker*.

59. See Thébaud, *Quand nos grands-mères donnaient la vie*.

CLASS, ETHNICITY, AND GENDER IN POST-OTTOMAN THESSALONIKI

THE GREAT TOBACCO STRIKE OF 1914

EFI AVDELA

In the spring of 1914, a tobacco workers' strike broke out in eastern Macedonia, just after the region and its multicultural center, Thessaloniki, were annexed by the Greek state as a result of the Balkan wars. This strike, in a trade that was central to the economy, lasted three weeks and involved more than thirty thousand men and women from the main ethnic groups in the region—Greeks, Jews, and Muslims. It occurred at a formative moment in the development of Greek national identity, when the relative positions of these three ethnic communities were being transformed as a result of the wars. In the transition from Ottoman multicultural coexistence to modern Greek national sovereignty, the Greeks, as victors, became integrated into a nation-state in which the Jews and Muslims now found themselves to be "aliens."[1]

My purpose here is to examine the relations among class, ethnicity, and gender in the upheavals of national wars, relations that have been previously ignored in the historiography of this much discussed event. The focus on class consciousness that permeates Greek labor history as well as the history of the strike has made historians overlook, or at least underestimate, the role of ethnicity and gender in these events, and incorporate the strike into the history of the Greek "national" labor movement. The strike has been viewed as the first large-scale class conflict in eastern Macedonia, transcending the prevailing climate of nationalism. Both its character and its outcome were seen as manifestations of a state policy that henceforth was to exploit the pretext of the national interest in order to stifle the growing class consciousness of the working masses. In this respect, historians have invariably reproduced the first interpretation of the strike presented by one of its leaders, Avraam Benaroya, sixteen years after the events.[2]

By introducing the concepts of gender and ethnicity into the analysis of the strike, I intend to highlight the centrality of work and public action to the construction of the gendered identity of tobacco workers, the different terms of reference used for the definition of masculinity and femininity, and changes brought about by the succession of wars in the gender and ethnic composition of tobacco workers. I shall attempt to display how the strike functioned as a theater where gender and ethnic tensions were related to class and national interests, and follow its incorporation into the process of Greek national domination of the area, in which ethnic diversity and women's agency were perceived as compromising factors. In this sense, I am here concerned with establishing a new basis on which known information is to be read differently and codified into a new narrative of the event, highlighting its "epoch-making" character with respect to the shifting relations among gender, ethnicity, and class.[3]

My intention of showing how the construction of Greek national predominance in eastern Macedonia suppressed ethnic and gender diversity in public action has dictated the choice of material. I draw principally on the Greek-language press of Thessaloniki, chiefly *Nea Alitheia* (New Truth), *Fos* (Light), and *Makedonia*, although I also take into consideration the Athenian press as well as that of the other ethnic communities of Thessaloniki.[4] These newspapers serve as types of discourse that—despite their differing starting points—progressively build up a shared "narrative of the nation,"[5] embedded in a coherent configuration of meanings through which the Greek community acquired its dominance. In this sense, the strike is analyzed on two levels: on the direct level of action, as expressed in hand-to-hand fighting on the streets of Thessaloniki between women strikers, women strikebreakers, and police, each ethnically distinct; and on the indirect level of newspaper discourse that ascribed a specific political meaning to the events, both shaping action and turning into action itself.

War and the Tobacco Trade

The tobacco workers strike of 1914 occurred at a crucial moment in modern Greek history, during the aftermath of the Balkan wars (1912–1913), which extended Greek sovereignty into parts of Macedonia that were inhabited by significant numbers of non-Orthodox populations—Muslims, Jews, Slavs, Armenians, and Vlachs. In particular, Thessaloniki was home to the most important Jewish community in the Balkans, as well as to the first workers' and socialist organization, the Workers' Socialist Federation (founded in 1909)—usually referred to simply as "the Federation"—a body that was officially multi-ethnic but in effect Jewish.[6] As national borders were not yet fixed in the area, Greece also nurtured hopes of expanding its sovereignty further into western Thrace and parts of Asia Minor.

1914, then, does not have the same meaning for Greece as it does for those countries that were to embark on World War I. Greece entered the war on the side of the Allies late in 1917, after Allied forces had been in Thessaloniki for two years and when Greece was on the brink of civil war. Yet this development constituted one phase in the ten-year state of war that started with the Balkan wars and ended with Greece's defeat in the Greco-Turkish War in 1922. This decade was marked by the irredentist and modernizing policy of the Liberal Eleftherios Venizelos and his opposition to King Konstantine concerning Greece's position in World War I, a dispute termed the *National Schism*: the King advocated that Greece should maintain her neutrality in the conflict, while Venizelos urged intervention on the side of the Entente. During this period, the country's borders were extended, and its population changed dramatically both in numbers and ethnic composition. Rent by internal antagonisms, diplomatic failures, and military defeats, Greece was to enter the interwar period after 1923 inundated by a million and a half refugees from Asia Minor.[7]

From the beginning of the century, the cultivation, marketing, and processing of tobacco leaves for export was the most important economic activity in eastern Macedonia.[8] The Balkan wars had a disruptive effect on the flourishing tobacco trade and caused unemployment and a high cost of living. These factors, along with movements of population due to hostilities in the region, dealt a blow to the relatively privileged status of tobacco workers.

The tobacco industry, which involved the seasonal (spring–autumn) industrial processing of the leaves of the tobacco plant, developed in the "port cities" of the tobacco-producing regions of eastern Macedonia and western Thrace, such as Thessaloniki and Kavala. The industry employed equal numbers of men and women and reflected the multicultural and multi-ethnic structure of the area, involving Jews, Greeks, and Muslims. The ethnic composition of the workforce varied in accordance with the ethnic structure of the population in each particular location: in Thessaloniki, most of the tobacco workers were Jews, while Muslims constituted approximately one-third of the workforce, and the Greeks were heavily outnumbered; in Serres, most of the workers were Greeks; in Kavala, Drama, and Xanthi (the latter under Bulgarian occupation after 1912) the Greeks also predominated, although there were significant numbers of Muslims and a few Jews. This situation began to change, however, with the shifts in population triggered by the Balkan wars. The Bulgarians were the first to leave the areas annexed by Greece immediately after 1913, followed by the Muslims, who in the years to come passed through Thessaloniki in a number of waves on their way to Turkey. After 1913 there is evidence that Greek employers systematically replaced their Jewish or Muslim workers with Greek-speaking refugees, especially in Thessaloniki.[9]

There was also a link between the ethnic and gender composition of the tobacco workforce in each area. While in Thessaloniki most of the workers were young girls, in Xanthi and Drama the processing and packing of tobacco leaves were primarily jobs for men. In Kavala, on the other hand, where the largest numbers of tobacco workers were to be found, the work was shared between the genders. This led to the establishment of a gendered division of labor, with the emergence of specialized jobs of the *dengçis* (for men) and the *pastaltzou* (for women), with a clear hierarchical relationship between them: the *dengçis* was responsible for processing the top-quality tobacco leaves, while the *pastaltzou* worked only with the poorer leaves. Wherever the presence of men in the tobacco industry was strong, women were subjected to restrictions—above all, they were not allowed to become *dengçides* (plural of *dengçis*).[10]

These restrictions were made statutory with unionization, which began while the area was still under Ottoman control: the International League of Kavala Tobacco Workers "Evdaimonia" (Prosperity), founded in 1908, was the first tobacco workers' union in the Balkans. Some of the unions were divided into branches according to the ethnic origins of their members, whereas other unions were completely identified with a distinct ethnic group. Although women formed a large part of the workforce, they were not admitted to the unions.

The Jewish tobacco workers were the most active group in self-unionization and were an important element of the Federation. The Greeks and Muslims, on the other hand, conformed to the highly nationalist atmosphere of the age, which militated against autonomous union organization and cooperation with "aliens." The Federation became highly active in organizing the tobacco workers of the entire area and, even before the Balkan wars began, extended its influence beyond the Jewish tobacco workers. Its role in masterminding the strike and in achieving the joint action of the Jewish and Greek tobacco workers was decisive. At the time of the strike, unionization was favored by the labor policy of the Greek Liberal government, aiming at regulating the labor market and at gaining the workers' support for its irredentist policy.[11]

THE TOBACCO STRIKE OF 1914

The Event

The tobacco strike was the most important of its kind in the area since the territorial annexation by the Greek state. A year earlier, the new conditions had enabled the formation of the first single regional tobacco workers' union and the formulation of joint demands. The strikers' demands were of three kinds: improved wages and working hours, statutory protection for the union's shopfloor activity, and institutionalization of the male privilege of occupying the senior position of *dengçis*. The strike broke out first in Kavala on March 24, soon spreading to Drama and Pravi (Eleftheroupoli), and reaching Thessaloniki on March 28.[12] If in the smaller towns (Pravi, Drama, and Kavala) most of the strikers were Greek, in Thessaloniki two-thirds of the strikers were Jews, while the rest were Greek; the Muslims who came out on strike in that city soon resumed their work: although they belonged to the local population, Muslim men were the least organized. The strike committee, composed of male representatives of all the unions, decided to base itself in Kavala.

During the course of the strike, Thessaloniki was the scene of fierce clashes among strikers, strikebreakers, and the police. These involved some interesting combinations of gender and ethnicity: as Jewish and Greek union men were engaged in negotiations with employers, with the mediation of the Greek authorities, Jewish women strikers were mobilized to confront the Muslim women strikebreakers and the Greek police who were protecting them. The clashes caused a furor in the city and started a sharp controversy in the local and metropolitan press. In response, the union leaders ordered the demobilization of the women and concentrated on the negotiations with the tobacco merchants and the state officials. Yet, as a result of these clashes, the Greek press began to express increasing suspicion, at first toward Jewish socialists—accused of anti-Greek action—and then toward the city's entire Jewish community.

The strike itself ended with partial satisfaction of the workers' demands and the signing of the first collective labor agreement ever to be concluded in Greece. Some months later, the authorities prosecuted and sentenced to internal exile three Jewish leaders of the Federation and of the tobacco workers, who had led the strike, on charges of anti-Greek activities.

A New Narrative

The strike should be seen both as a site of communal tensions and as a social event, with its own movements, sounds, and colors. The setting was Thessaloniki, where the Greek community was third in size after the Jewish and Muslim populations.[13] The ethnic structure of the city was clearly reflected in its spatial dimension: the center was occupied by the poor Jewish quarters, the tobacco factories, and a network of narrow alleys; around this, to the northwest, lived the Muslims, and to the east were the Greeks.[14] The crowds of strikers spread out gradually through the center. A colorful mass of people speaking different languages, wearing different clothes, set out from the Workers' Center, where the Jewish tobacco workers' union and the Federation also had their offices. The predominant color was red, which at that time had a complex range of connotations: for some it was the color of revolution, but for others it was the color of the Ottoman fez and the Ottoman flag, both symbols of national oppression.

The speeches were made in all three languages: Greek, Ladino (Jewish Spanish), and Turkish. The crowd consisted largely of men: on this first day of the strike, women were few. The demonstrators confirmed the decision to come out on strike and shouted their acclaim for the tobacco workers of Kavala "who have maintained and are still maintaining such a manly stance."[15] The adjective "manly" was far from coincidental, given that one of the main demands of the strikers was that no women should be made *dengçides*. The charter of the tobacco workers' union of Kavala had included this point as far back as its foundation in 1908: no women were to be admitted to the union, which was only for *dengçides*. The strikers' second demand, protection of the union's right to shopfloor activity, had as its objective (apart from organizing the workers) control over recruitment for the same purpose.

Two developments connected with the Balkan wars had permitted the unionized male tobacco workers to lay claim to the specialized job of *dengçis* as their self-evident and exclusive right throughout Macedonia: on the one hand, the emergence of the so-called yellow women workers, and on the other, the need for uniform trade organization.

The "yellow" women workers—a term that occurs repeatedly in accounts of the strike—were those who did not strike. These women, who were mainly Muslims, clashed with the Jewish women strikers. There was also mention of Greek women strikebreakers, but the Greek newspapers never referred to them as "yellow women," but rather as "refugees." Although the press also mentioned "Gypsies and Bulgarian women," whom the tobacco merchants enlisted "to do their work for them and reduce the Greek, Ottoman, and Israelite workers to poverty,"[16] the Muslim women clearly formed the majority of that category. These women appear, from all the evidence, to have belonged to the transient population of Muslim refugees created by the Balkan wars. In many cases, they came from Muslim tobacco-growing villages and were thus acquainted with the job of *dengçis*, which, while skilled, did not require a lengthy apprenticeship. Their presence in the city was merely a stopover on their road to Turkey, and they did not have links with the permanent Muslim population.[17]

The women strikebreakers, then, were Muslims and skilled workers. Their second attribute, skilled knowledge, made them a real threat not only to the strike, but also to the tobacco unions in general, partly on account of their lower wages but mainly because they undermined male predominance in the trade. The male *dengçides'* demand to exclude women was not simply economic in nature: it also had organizational and highly symbolic meanings involving their identity as males and workers. As recent studies have repeatedly shown, work is a decisive aspect of male identity, in spite of the fact that its significance changes over time, along with transformations in labor and politics. In fact, masculinity has often been defined by skill, and male workers have repeatedly defended their exclusivity in skilled jobs: the issue has been historically established as central to the process of formulating as male the identity of the worker and the work culture.[18]

As unionization of tobacco workers spread throughout Macedonia, the need to establish uniform terms of labor in every city as well as union hierarchy and representation became imperative: based on the model established in Kavala, the newly born tobacco workers' movement was made male right from the start. The injury caused to trade as a result of the Balkan wars, along with the movements of population, further complicated the situation and made any questioning of the exclusively male nature of their job still more menacing to the *dengçides*.

Significantly, skilled Muslim women strikebreakers were not confronted by male strikers. Instead, it was the "young Israelite women" workers who clashed with them. Even though they obeyed the union's instructions and came out on strike, these young Jewish women were not members of the union. Apart from their gender, the most striking characteristics of these strikers were their ethnicity and their youth: they wore the red armbands of the Federation and spoke Ladino, while the Muslim women were veiled and spoke Turkish. It seems likely that many of these Jewish girls were the daughters or sisters of tobacco workers. Yet, their active participation in the strike may have been influenced by their ethnic neighborhood networks even more than by family relationships—each ethnic group lived in its own neighborhood—as well as by the fact that they formed the majority of the tobacco workforce in the city. It was on the basis of a common ethnic identity that the leaders of the Federation mobilized Jewish women workers in order to neutralize the Muslim strikebreakers, whose gender and religion made them inaccessible to men outside their family.[19]

The Jewish women went out on the streets and defended the strike with all the means at their disposal. They were vividly pictured in the discourse of the press. These "harmless girls" were furiously beaten by the gendarmes "with their bayonets and rifle-butts" and shed their "gentle and pulsing blood" for the strike; they were the advance guard, those who "full of courage and determination, bare their breasts. They stand firm, and they exhort their menfolk to do the same."[20] In a sense, they were "our suffragettes," a description that contains all the ambiguous meanings of the period: the suffragettes were viewed by the press as women who, by demanding more rights, rejected their natural position and simulated that of men. The fluctuations in the newspapers' language betray a degree of puzzlement: these women who resembled men, who were pioneers or suffragettes, were going beyond accepted bounds. Even the attitude of the police toward the Jewish women strikers was judged by reference to the way the British police reacted to the Suffragettes.[21]

Women strikers, women strikebreakers, and the police thus confronted one another on the street, a public place that was seen as even more dangerous and unfit for women than the workplace.[22] When these two groups clashed with the Greek police, the confrontation had all the features of the clashes typical of old-style strikes: the movements, the sounds, the violence in words and actions, all made up "a psychodrama in which repressed tendencies could be released."[23] The women swore at each other, "pulled one another's hair," and "hit each other": the Jewesses tore the veils of the Muslim women—the ultimate insult to "their most delicate and sacred part"—and scratched "the face of a policeman with their nails." The Muslim women defended themselves with planks of wood, which they threw at their pursuers.[24]

The women gave to the strike an unprecedented degree of ferocity, which provided a pretext for vociferous opposition to it: it was now characterized as political rather than labor-related, meaning that its leaders were motivated by anti-Greek sentiments. This criticism was directly related to developments: the clashes had created tension between the city's Jewish and Muslim communities and caused concern in the politically dominant community, the Greeks. The restoration of order, undermined by the women's actions, called for the intervention of the men who were considered to be responsible for them, and more specifically of the religious leaders, Muslim and Jewish: the mufti intervened with the rabbi to protest over the ripping of the veils, while officials of the tobacco workers' union mediated to stop police violence. The clashes on the streets ended as a result of an official decision by the union to take the women strikers off the streets and to stop hindering the "yellow" women workers.[25]

From this moment on, the women were kept at a distance not only from public places but also from the public debate. Silence and invisibility were the price they had to pay for what was perceived as losing self-control, as violating commonly accepted borderlines. The fact that the women strikers followed the union's orders was not ignored. However, the violence of their actions was held by part of the press to be incompatible with the legitimate pursuit of the "workers' rights." Women were seen as dangerous because they did not know how to control their actions. Furthermore, since by nature they were as "fickle" as "politics" itself, today's female allies of the male tobacco workers could easily become tomorrow's opponents if the women's front, which now seemed divided, were united. The ironic tone of this comment scarcely hides the real concern with which the commentator noted the "frenzy" and "incredible manliness" of the women strikers.[26] The women were not directly blamed for the "acrimonious and fervid situation" which they had created. The blame was put rather on the males responsible for them: Jewish male workers, the leaders of the tobacco workers' union, and the Federation, all of whom allegedly nurtured "socialist ideas and outrageous suffragette attitudes," evils that "the perpetual foes of the Nation" had always promoted in the "New Lands" (that is, the territories annexed by Greece as a result of the Balkan wars).[27]

The women's public action was thus distorted by a logic that denied its autonomy and agency: in the eyes of the press they had acted under instigation from the male tobacco union, whose purpose they in fact served. Why, then, did the Jewish women strikers undertake to defend a strike that aimed to relegate them to a secondary position in the market for tobacco-processing labor? Mobilized through their ethnic and family networks, these young women—who most often worked in the factory only until their marriage—were actually defending the cultural patterns defining their gender and their ethnic identity at the workplace against the strikebreaking action of passing "foreigners." Yet, to the male unions, women's agency was acceptable only insofar as it served the union's own gender-specific interests. Their demobilization became vital as the relation of forces at play in the strike changed, and as the Greek nationalists used the pretext of disorderly women in order to discredit the union's leaders as anti-Greek. Showing restraint and responsibility in restoring the

patriarchal order, the unionized workers confirmed their right to demand male predominance in the trade's labor market.

DISCOURSE AS ACTION: NEGOTIATING THE MEANING OF THE STRIKE

As the women were forced to leave the forefront of the strike, the
scene of action shifted from the street to the newspaper columns in
the form of the new dispute that soon broke out: was the strike serving the workers' rights, or had it perhaps become "political," in the
sense that it questioned the legitimacy of the new Greek national
sovereignty?

The newspapers never contested the workers' right to strike,
which had been established by labor legislation introduced by the
Greek Liberal government in 1912. As a defender of the workers'
rights, the government was identified as progressive and socialist,
and through that identification each one of the three local newspapers laid claim to being socialist. The main feature of this "state socialism" was its patriotic character, as opposed to the international
socialism to which the Federation aspired.

In this context, the press at first welcomed the idea of shared
workers' interests beyond the bounds of race and religion, which the
strikers promoted. Yet this could not last for long. In multi-ethnic
Thessaloniki—where the Greek tobacco workers were in the minority and the number of Greek strikers was even smaller—the press
soon began to express the suspicion that those who defended the
joint interests of the workers regardless of race and religion were, in
fact, advocating internationalist socialism. In particular, those who
committed acts of violence in the name of those interests (especially
women), thereby disrupting the relations between the communities,
were denounced as seeking to undermine the recent and still-fragile
Greek sovereignty.

Nea Alitheia, for instance, interpreted the clashes as proof that in
Thessaloniki the strike had ceased to be labor-related, and that the
promotion of socialist demands was a pretext for anti-Greek action.
Avraam Benaroya—Federation leader, Jewish socialist, and Bulgarian
subject—was singled out as the mastermind behind this turn of
events.[28] As evidence, the paper cited the large number of foreigners
who participated in the strike, the widespread wearing of the fez, the
red kerchiefs, and the chanting of slogans from the Young Turks period. Its discourse very rapidly became generalized and shifted from
individual instigators to groups: the danger stemmed from the "foreign nationals" who were leading the strike, but above all from
those who were taking part in it in large numbers—the Jewish work-

ers, who allowed women to act in their place and who, as "rootless persons" themselves, were vulnerable to the teachings of the pro-Bulgarian socialists. Opposed to them was another category, which was an inverted image of the first: the Greek workers, who were Greeks first and workers second, Greeks with traditions that it was their duty to uphold, and who consequently had no place rubbing shoulders with people "who do not know what it means to have a country."[29]

The other newspapers, as well as the strikers themselves, refuted these accusations. Yet their replies were defensive and failed to transpose the debate to a different logic. The Jewish tobacco workers' union simply denied the charge that its members were influenced by Bulgarian *comitadjis*, while the Greek strikers protested their patriotism.[30]

As the days passed, the classifications in public discourse became more and more explicit in both the local and metropolitan press. Popular representations of sameness and difference, of "the self" and "the other," give a vivid picture of this process. The opposition was seen as one between real and false socialism: true socialism was Greek, patriotic, and manly; false socialism was foreign, rootless, and unrestrained—like the female nature. Soon the contrast between Greek patriots and rootless Jews became the key to the process of classification. This contrast led progressively to the complete denunciation of socialism, which was now identified with "the other" and thus became the main opponent of national interests.

The inverted images involved in the representations of identity gradually came to dominate the entire Greek press, in Athens as well as in Thessaloniki. The Greeks were described as patriots, with a motherland they loved, a religion they honored, and traditions they respected.[31] By contrast, the Jewish strikers were described as belonging to "foreign races," as "vipers" whom Greek Thessaloniki had been nursing for years. Such characterizations were further loaded with metaphors of gender: the Jewish workers were unrestrained, two-faced, and given to "indescribable garrulity."[32]

The discourse of the press became a form of action that ascribed a particular meaning to the strike, highlighting its ethnic dimension and contributing to the silencing of the women. When the strike ended, further occasions arose for renewed tension between the Greek and Jewish communities, such as the prosecution of three Jewish leaders of the Federation and the tobacco workers' union.[33] By this time, the entire local Greek press had acquired a common attitude: the newspapers emphasized the patriotic activities of the Greek workers and began to treat the entire Jewish community of

Thessaloniki as under suspicion of anti-Greek attitudes, especially when the community began to protest against the prosecutions of Jewish socialists and the attacks on Jewish newspapers.

This development did not reflect state policy on the issue. In the government's position, the emphasis was clearly placed on the distinction between "true" and "false" socialism, and the three labor leaders were being prosecuted "as bad citizens or, let us say, as bad socialists."[34] Venizelos, who was eager to gain both the confidence of the Jewish community of Thessaloniki and the support of the Jewish socialists for the promotion of his irredentist plans among European public opinion, overtly favored the formal organization of the Greek labor movement at the national level. In Thessaloniki, however, the "rootless" Jews represented a particular danger to the Greek community: it was not even possible to expel them. The distinction made by government policy between "true" and "false" socialism was not sufficient to quell local fears that the Jews, more than any other community, would threaten the legitimacy of the Greek national order from within.

The confrontation between Venizelos's Liberal government and the Jews of Thessaloniki was soon to emerge.[35] A significant turning point was reached during the period of the National Schism a year later, when the Jewish socialists refused to support Venizelos in his confrontation with the King over the position Greece should adopt in World War I, as well as regarding the foundation of the Socialist Workers' Movement of Greece and the General Confederation of Greek Labor in 1918 and 1919, respectively. Henceforth the contradiction became polarized between "healthy patriotism," on the one hand, and "unpatriotic elements" and "Benaroyas of various hues" on the other.[36]

THE AFTERMATH

The 1914 strike brought to the forefront a number of factors that were to be decisive in subsequent developments. With respect to the tobacco trade, the Balkan wars initially had negative effects on the cultivation and processing of the crop, due to hostilities in the area, refugee movements, and the departure of the Muslims. Yet with measures taken to facilitate the resettlement of a significant number of refugees as tobacco farmers in eastern Macedonia and western Thrace, the trade quickly picked up and prospered, and in the following years tobacco became Greece's chief export item.[37] Refugees were also settled in the urban "tobacco centers" of the area, disrupting the previous pattern of seasonal passage from farm to warehouse.[38] These developments finally established what was perceived as the sector's exclusively Greek identity: most of the Muslim workers were included in the exchanges of population in 1923 between Greece and Turkey, and after the early 1930s the Jews began to emigrate en masse to Palestine.[39]

Hellenization was related to the consolidation of the unions' structure. As the largest and one of the best-organized and most militant components of the Greek labor force, tobacco workers were able to negotiate their demands successfully and gain a relatively privileged position until the 1930s. In the representations that the union constructed of tobacco workers, their identity crystallized as Greek and male, while the women's solidarity with the union's demands was taken for granted, and women were elevated to the status of model workers in the militant myth. Yet, in practice their active participation in the decision-making process was still further restricted. At the same time, their growing presence in the workforce was increasingly perceived as a threat to the combativeness of the male workers and their radical ideology, despite their often active role in the strikes.[40]

Developments in the tobacco trade during the interwar period contributed to the focus on gender as the main factor generating conflict among tobacco workers. From the late 1920s, the steady trend within the international tobacco market toward cheaper leaves, combined with fluctuations in the crop's market prices and overproduction, led gradually to an extensive restructuring of the entire tobacco labor market that had a destabilizing effect on the situation of male workers. One of the most important developments related to this restructuring was the introduction of cheap processing methods employing mainly women, which made the by-now traditional distinction between *dengçides* and *pastaltzoudes* obsolete so that male unemployment increased significantly. In the 1930s, despite the fact that women were by then accepted as union members, the unions tried repeatedly to restrict their employment and to secure male predominance in numbers and wages.[41]

The tobacco workers' strike in eastern Macedonia in 1914 marked the beginning of a lengthy process in which the principal characteristics were to be the Hellenization and the masculinization of the dominant union representation in the trade, along with the actual feminization of its labor force. It was an "epoch-making" event in the sense that it symbolized the close links between nationalism and masculine predominance and marked the subsequent centrality of gender antagonism in the tobacco trade. The contradictions among class, ethnicity, and gender that permeated the clash are precise testimony to the fact that it occurred at a turning point in Greek history when ethnic and gender relationships were still fluid and negotiable; they also point to the direction in which the region and the social forces active within it were to develop during the following decades.

NOTES

1. The term *ethnic groups* is used in this paper to describe a group of individuals with a shared cultural identity in a given historical context where the group is faced with the problem of expressing this identity in political terms. The concept leaves open all the options regarding the content of that identity as well as the forms of its eventual political expression. In this respect it emphasizes the transitional character of the specific historical context to which the paper refers. It also highlights the ethnic dimension of religion in the specific place at the specific time. See Frederik Barth, *Ethnic Groups and Boundaries* (Boston, 1969); A. L. Epstein, *Ethos and Identity: Three Studies in Ethnicity* (London and Chicago, 1978); and Elisabeth Tonkin, Maryon McDonald, and Malcolm Chapman, *History and Ethnicity* (London and New York, 1989).

2. See the memoirs of Avraam Benaroya, *I proti stadiodromia tou ellinikou proletariatou* (The early career of the Greek proletariat) (Athens, 1975) (first published in installments in the newspaper *Tachydromos*, Thessaloniki, 1931), esp. 83–84. For subsequent references to the strike, see Yanis Kordatos, *Istoria tou ellinikou ergatikou Kinimatos* (History of the Greek labor movement) (Athens, 1956); G. B. Leon, *The Greek Socialist Movement and the First World War: The Road to Unity* (Boulder, CO, 1976); Antonis Liakos, *I Sosialistiki Ergatiki Omospondia Thessalonikis (Federasion) kai i Sosialistiki Neolaia. Ta katastatika tous* (The Socialist Workers' Federation of Thessaloniki [Federation] and the Socialist Youth Movement: Their charters) (Thessaloniki, 1985); and Center for Marxist Research, *I Sosialistiki Organosi Federasion Thessalonikis 1909–1918. Zitimata gyro apo ti drasi tis* (The Federation Socialist Organization of Thessaloniki: Some questions relating to its activity) (Athens, 1989).

3. Hayden White, "The Politics of Historical Interpretation: Discipline and De-Sublimation," in his *The Content of the Form: Narrative Discourse and Historical Representation* (Baltimore and London, 1987), 58–82. For the notion of an "epoch-making" event, see Jocelyn Létourneau, "La Mise en intrigue. Configuration historico-linguistique d'une grève célébrée: Asbestos, P.Q., 1949," *Recherches sémiotiques/Semiotic Inquiry* 12, nos. 1–2 (1992): 55.

4. These were the most important newspapers of Thessaloniki. All three more or less supported the policy of Eleftherios Venizelos's Liberal government (1910–1920), while at the same time adopting diverging positions on the question of Greek interests in the area. The Greek local press often reproduced information from the Jewish and Muslim newspapers as

well as from the Athens press. Only a very few issues of the Jewish and Muslim newspapers for 1914 still exist in Greek archives, and even these are exceptionally difficult to read: many of the former, such as *Avanti*, were published in *Rashi* (Ladino in Hebrew characters), while the latter, such as *Yeni Asr*, were in Arabic script.

5. Homi K. Bhabha, "Introduction: Narrating the Nation," in idem, *Nation and Narration* (Chicago, 1990), 1–7.

6. For the Federation, see Paul Dumont, "La Fédération Socialiste Ouvrière de Salonique à l'époque des guerres balkaniques," *East European Quarterly* 14, no. 4 (1980): 383–410; also references in note 2. For the Jewish community in Thessaloniki, see Rena Molho, "The Incorporation of the Jewish Community of Salonika into the Greek State (1912–1919)," *Middle Eastern Studies* 84, no. 4 (1988): 391–403.

7. M. S. Anderson, *The Eastern Question*, 7th edition (London, 1991); George Mavrogordatos, *Stillborn Republic: Social Coalitions and Party Strategies in Greece 1922–1936* (Berkeley, Los Angeles, and London, 1983).

8. John R. Lampe and Marvin R. Jackson, *Balkan Economic History, 1550–1950: From Imperial Borderlands to Developing Nations* (Bloomington, 1982); Lois Labrianidis, "Industrial Location in Capitalist Societies: The Tobacco Industry in Greece, 1880–1980," Ph.D. diss., London School of Economics and Political Sciences, 1982.

9. Leon, *The Greek Socialist Movement*; Donald Quataert, "Premières fumées d'usines," in Gilles Veinstein, ed., *Salonique 1850–1919: La "ville des Juifs" et le réveil des Balkans*, Autrement, Série Mémoires (Paris, 1992).

10. Paul Dumont, "The Social Structure of the Jewish Community of Salonica at the End of the Nineteenth Century," *Southeastern Europe/L'Europe du Sud-Est* 2 (1979): 44. For Kavala, see the report by G. Vaikos, vice-consul in Kavala, to the Greek Ministry of Foreign Affairs, Jan. 11, 1912, Archives of the Greek Ministry of Foreign Affairs [AGMFA], file AAK/B 1912, "Consulate of Thessaloniki and Xanthi, vice-consulate of Kavala" (in Greek).

11. Leon, *The Greek Socialist Movement*; Efi Avdela, "'To the Most Weak and Needy': Women's Protective Labor Legislation in Greece," in Ulla Wikander, Alice Kessler-Harris and Jane Lewis, eds., *Protecting Women: Labor Legislation in Europe, the United States, and Australia, 1880–1920* (Urbana, 1995).

12. The number of strikers was as follows: twenty thousand in Kavala, where tobacco workers from Xanthi and Komotini also gathered; five thousand in Drama; four thousand in Pravi; and three thousand in Thessaloniki. The tobacco workers of Serres did not strike.

13. The statistics concerning the ethnic composition of Thessaloniki— and of Macedonia as a whole—were an ideal battleground for confrontation between the opposing designs expressed by the various nationalisms of the area. As a result, it is extremely difficult to make even approximately accurate estimations. At any rate, according to the first Greek census in 1913, of the 157,889 inhabitants of Thessaloniki 61,439 were Jews, 45,889 Turks, and 39,956 Greeks, while there were also 6,263 Bulgarian's and 4,364 "oth-

ers" (Armenians and Westerners of various nationalities). See the articles by Rena Molho, "Le renouveau," and Kirki Georgiadou, "Les Grecs de Thessaloniki," in Veinstein, ed., *Salonique 1850–1918*, 65 and 121; also AGMFA, 1913, file A/5, "Statistical data concerning the population of the *vilayets* of Ioannina, Thessaloniki, Monastir and Adrianople" (in Greek).

14. *Topografia tis Thessalonikis tin epochi tis Tourkokratias, 1430–1912* (Topography of Thessaloniki under Turkish rule, 1430–1912) (Thessaloniki, 1983). This urban planning arrangement was to change radically after the great fire of 1917.

15. *Makedonia*, 29 Mar. 1914.

16. *Fos*, 2 Apr. 1914.

17. For Muslim refugees of the Balkan wars, see Public Record Office/Foreign Office, 371/1994/8949, Morgan (Salonica)—Lord Onslow, Feb. 28, 1914; and 286/580, Morgan (Salonica)—Louis Mallet (Constantinople), June 20 and July 20, 1914; also Carnegie Endowment for International Peace, *Report of the International Commission to Inquire into the Causes and Conduct of the Balkan Wars* (Washington, 1914).

18. See, among others, Patricia Cooper, *Once a Cigar Maker: Men, Women and Work Culture in American Cigar Factories, 1900–1919* (Urbana and Chicago, 1992); Joan Wallach Scott, "Work Identities for Men and Women: The Politics of Work and Family in the Parisian Garment Trades in 1848," in idem, *Gender and the Politics of History* (New York, 1988), 93–112; Paul Willis, "Masculinity and Factory Labor," in Jeffrey C. Alexander and Steven Seidman, eds., *Culture and Society: Contemporary Debates* (Cambridge, 1990), 183–95.

19. The male Muslim workers were not represented on their local strike committee and were the most reluctant to become involved in the strike: most of them returned to work on the second day, and we hear no more about them. There is evidence to suggest that their absence was the result of demographic changes related to the war: the male Muslim tobacco workers were largely members of the local population and not "passing migrants," as was the case with Muslim women. Yet, the two groups shared the status of the "defeated," and their position in the city was precarious.

20. Respectively, *Fos*, Mar. 30 and Apr. 1, 1914, and *Makedonia*, Mar. 29, 1914.

21. *Fos* Mar. 30 and 31, 1914; *Makedonia*, Mar. 31, 1914.

22. This was not the first occasion on which the women of Thessaloniki took to the streets. Commentators on the celebrations for the Young Turk Revolution in 1908 recorded as the most unexpected development the presence in the demonstration of women with their faces uncovered: Christian, Jewish, and even Muslim women, whose participation was, however, denounced as an affront to good morals. See Paul Dumont and François Georgeon, "La révolution commence à Salonique," in Veinstein, ed., *Salonique 1850–1918*, 237.

23. Michelle Perrot, *Jeunesse de la grève: France 1871–1890* (Paris, 1984), 14.

24. *Makedonia*, Mar. 30 and 31, 1914; *Fos*, Mar. 31, 1914; *Nea Alitheia*,

Apr. 3, 1914; and *Yeni Asr* as republished by *Nea Alitheia*, Apr. 4, 1914.

25. *Makedonia*, Mar. 29, 1914; *Fos*, Mar. 31, 1914; *Nea Alitheia*, Apr. 2, 1914.

26. *Nea Alitheia*, Apr. 4, 1914.

27. In the wording of the Athenian newspapers *Estia* and *Patris*, quoted in *Nea Alitheia*, Apr. 3 and 6, 1914, respectively.

28. *Nea Alitheia*, Apr. 1, 1914. For the activities of Benaroya before 1912, see Georges Haupt, "Introduzione alla storia della Federazione operaia socialista di Salonicco," *Movimento Operaio e Socialista* 18, no. 1 (1972): 99–112.

29. *Nea Alitheia*, Apr. 1 and 2, 1914, in reply to *Fos*, Mar. 31, 1914.

30. See letters of Greek tobacco workers from all over Macedonia and the protest from a Committee of Refugee Tobacco Workers, *Fos*, Apr. 2 and 3, 1914; and telegrams from tobacco workers' unions in eastern Macedonia and a protest signed by four hundred Greek tobacco workers of Thessaloniki, *Makedonia*, Apr. 4 and 5, 1914; reply from *Nea Alitheia*, Apr. 6, 1914.

31. *Nea Alitheia* , Apr. 3, 1914.

32. Respectively, *Proia* and *Patris*, quoted in *Nea Alitheia*, Apr. 6, 1914, and *Makedonia*, June 3, 1914. For the stereotype of the Jews as an out-group and of women as an "otherness" in Western thought, see Sander L. Gilman, *Difference and Pathology: Stereotypes of Sexuality, Race and Madness* (Ithaca and London, 1985).

33. The three prosecuted were Alverto Arditis, editor of the Federation's newspaper *Avanti*, Avraam Benaroya, secretary of the Federation, and Samouil Yonas, secretary of the Thessaloniki tobacco workers' union and head of the strike committee. The last two were sentenced to deportation. See *Makedonia*, May 27 and June 1, 5, 8, 13, and 14, 1914.

34. *Makedonia*, June 16, 1914.

35. Mavrogordatos, *Stillborn Republic*, 253–62.

36. Gunnar Hering, "'Epikindynoi sosialistai', 'ethnikofrona ergatika stoicheia', kai o 'afelis agrotis'. O Nomarchis tis Larisas kai to syndikalistiko kinima tou 1919" ("Dangerous socialists," "patriotic workers," and the "naive farmer." The Prefect of Larisa and the union movement of 1919), Symposium on Eleftherios Venizelos, *Praktika* (Proceedings) (Athens, 1988), 187–206.

37. Greek frontiers in Macedonia and Thrace were definitively drawn by the Treaty of Lausanne in 1923. See Douglas Dakin, *The Unification of Greece, 1770–1923* (London, 1972).

38. Mark Mazower, *Greece and the Inter-War Economic Crisis* (Oxford, 1991), 44, 59, 86–88.

39. The Nazi "cleansing operation" of 1943 spelled the end for those who had remained, and wiped out the entire Jewish community of Thessaloniki. See Raul Hilberg, *The Destruction of the European Jews* (1961; New York, 1985).

40. Developments in the various aspects of tobacco work in the interwar period, and their relation to gender and ethnicity, have been the subject of

my research in recent years, and of a book in progress. See Efi Avdela, "Paremvaseis tou kratous stin agora ergasias tin periodo tou Mesopolemou: i periptosi tis ellinikis biomichanias epexergasias kapnou" (State intervention in the labor market between the Wars: The case of the Greek tobacco-manufacturing industry), unpublished paper presented at the working group on Labour in Interwar Greece, held in January 1991 as part of the European Project on the Economic History of the Interwar Period.

41. For studies on the tobacco trade and tobacco work in the interwar period which, for all their merits, do not take gender into consideration, see Mazower, *Greece and the Inter-War Economic Crisis*; and Antonis Liakos, *Ergasia kai politiki stin Ellada tou Mesopolemou: To Diethnes Grafeion Ergasias kai i anadysi ton koikonikon thesmon* (Work and politics in interwar Greece: The International Labor Office and the emergence of social institutions) (Athens, 1993).

CONTRIBUTORS

Efi Avdela is Senior Lecturer at the Department of Education at the University of Athens, where she teaches courses in Greek History, the History of Gender and Labor history, and co-founder of the Greek feminist journal *Dimi*. She has published numerous essays on Greek feminism, women and labor in Greek history and on Gender studies in Greece.

Beth Baron is Associate Professor of History at City College, City University of New York. She is author of *The Women's Awakening in Egypt: Culture, Society and the Press* (New Haven, 1994) and co-editor of *Women in Middle Eastern History Shifting Boundaries in Sex and Gender* (New Haven, 1991).

Ursula Baumann is wissenschafliche Assistentin at the History Department at TU Berlin. She is the author of *Protestantismus und Frauenemanzipaztion in Deutschland 1850–1920* and of a number of essays on German feminism and religion. She is currently completing a history of suicide.

Ilana R. Bet-El received her PH.D. from University College London, on the cultural identity of British conscripts in World War I. She has been political analyst for the United Nations in Bosnia-Hercegovina, where she experienced the last war, mostly in Sarajevo. She is currently fellow at Green College, Oxford, researching and writing about various aspects of the international deployment in BiH.

Jacqueline deVries is Assistant Professor of History at Augsburg College, Minneapolis. She has published articles on suffragism and religion in Britain and is now writing a book on feminism, religion, and the politics of identity in Britain.

Amira Gelblum is teaching gender history at Tel Aviv University and has written on German feminism and pacifism. She is currently writing a biography of the German radical feminists and pacifists Anita Augspurg and Lida Gustava Heymann.

Fatma Müge Göçek is Associate Professor of Sociology and Women's Studies at the University of Michigan. She is author of *East Encoun-*

ters West: France and the Ottoman Empire in the Eighteenth Century (New York, 1988) and *Rise of the Bourgeoisie, Demise of Empire: Ottoman Westernization and Social Change. . .* and co-editor of *Reconstructing Gender in the Middle East: Tradition, Identity and Power* (New York, 1995).

Doron Lamm completes a PH. D. on conscription policies and gender in Britain in World War I. He teaches Hebrew literature at the University of Michigan.

Phyllis Lassner teaches writing and women's literature at North Western University. She is the author of *Elizabeth Bowen* (London, 1990) and *Elizabeth Bowen the Short Stories* (Boston, 1992).

Billie Melman is Professor of History at Tel Aviv University. She is the author of *Women and the Popular Imagination in the Twenties, Flappers and Nymphs* (London and New York, 1988) and *Women's Orients English Women and the Middle East 1718–1918* (Second edn., London and Ann Arbor, 1995) and of a number of essays on gender and colonialism, British nationalism, and Zionism.

Annabelle Melzer is Associate Professor of Drama at Tel Aviv University and has been Visiting Professor at Dartmouth College and Columbia University. She is the author of *Dada and Surrealist Performance* (New York, 1994) and editor of *Jean Giraudoux: The War Journals* (Forthcoming, Providence R.I. and Oxford).

Sonya Michel is Director of Women's Studies at the University of Illinois at Urbana-Champaign, ISA, where she teaches American and European women's and gender history. She is co-editor of *Behind the Lines: Gender and the Two World Wars* (New Haven, 1987) and *Mothers of a New World Maternalist Politics and the Origins of Welfare States* (New York, 1993). Her *Children's Interests/ Mothers' Rights: A History of Child care in the United States* is forthcoming from Yale. She is also a founding editor of the journal *Social Politics: International Studies in Gender, State and Society*.

Keren Petrone is Assistant Professor of History at the University of Kentucky at Lexington, where she teaches Russian history. She is writing a history of culture and politics in the Soviet Union during the 1930s.

Anne Summers is Curator of Manuscripts at the British Library, and a co-founder and co-editor of *History Workshop Journal*. She is the author of a number of articles on the history of nursing, and of *An-*

gels and Citizens British Women as Military Nurses 1854–1914 (London, 1988).

Pat Thane holds the Chair of Contemporary History at Sussex University, where she is Professor of Social Sciences and current Chair of the History Department. She has written a number of books and articles, mostly on the history of social welfare and of women in Britain, including the *Foundation of the Welfare State* (London, 1982), and co-edited *Maternity and Gender Policies: Women and the Rise of the European Welfare States, 1880–1950s* (London, 1991).

Françoise Thébaud is Professor of History at the University of Avignon. She is author of *La femme au temps de la guerre de 14* and *Quand nos grand-mères donnaient la vie: La maternité en France dans l'entre deux guerres*. She is editor of volume v of *A History of Women Toward a Cultural History of Women in the Twentieth Century*, (Cambridge Mass, 1994). She is founder and co-editor of *Clio, histoire, femmes et société*. Her *Ecrire l'histoire de femmes* is to appear shortly.

David Trotter is Quain Professor of English Language and Literature at University College London. His books include *Language and Subjectivity in Modern American, English and Irish Poetry* (Cambridge, 1984), *Circulation: Defoe, Dickens and the Economics of the Novel* (London, 1988) and *The English Novel in History* (London and New York, 1993). He is currently completing a book on mess in modern culture.

Martha Vicinus, Eliza M. Mosher Distinguished University Professor of English, Women's Studies and History at the University of Michigan, where she is also in her final year as Chair of the Department of English. She is writing a book on the formation of modern lesbian identities, 1780–1930, focusing on a range of communities of women in the English-speaking world. She is the author and editor of numerous essays and books on Victorian women and the history of sexuality, including *Independent Women: Life and Community for Single Women in Britain* (London, 1985), *Hidden from History: Reclaiming the Gay and Lesbian Past* (1989) and *Lesbian Subjects* (1996).

INDEX

Aaronsohn, Aaron, 130, 134, 135
Aaronsohn, Sara, 127, 130, 135–36
Abadam, Alice, 272
Abbéma, Louise, 169, 172
'Abd al-Hamid, Zaynab, 344
Abdülhamid II, Sultan, 48, 53
abortion, 291, 297
Abraham, A. J., 77, 86
Abraham, Moshe, 130
Actresses' Franchise League (AFL),
    179, 184, 187
actualities, see films, World War I
Adler, Alfred, 255
"The Advanced Lady" (Mansfield),
    201
Africans, see black colonial troops
agricultural settlements
    (moshavot), Palestine, 123–24,
    126–27, 133
agricultural work
    French women in postwar, 410–11
    French women in prewar, 400
    wartime mobilization of women,
    12, 378–79, 389, 405
Ahmad, Ihsan, 343
Aliens Act, 1905 (Great Britain), 39
Aliens Act, 1919 (Great Britain),
    248
Allatini, Rose, 196, 197–98
Allied Powers
    anti-German propaganda, 110
    in Turkish War of Independence,
    48–49, 52–54, 60–61, 62–63, 62
    (fig), 64
    see also specific countries
All Quiet on the Western Front
    (Remarque), 153
Al-Rashidi, Anisa, 344
Al-Sayyid-Marsot, Afaf-Lutfi, 9
America's Answer, 145

Anatolian Women's Society for
    National Defense, 52–53
Anatolia, see Turkish Republic
Anderson, Benedict, 8, 121
androgyny, 168–71, 174, 183
    see also female impersonation;
    male impersonation
Angelsey, Marquis of, 173, 175 (fig)
Anglican Church
    impacts of World War I, 273–76
    prewar feminism within, 266,
    267, 268–70
    women's ordination, 279
Anglo-Boer War (1899–1902), 30
anti-Semitism, see Jews
"A Organization" (espionage net-
    work), 123, 134, 135
Armenian genocide, 10, 134
Arncliffe-Sennett, Maud, 179
Atwood, Clare, 206
Augspurg, Anita
    background, 307, 309
    feminist pacifism of, 311–13,
    315–16, 317–21
    socialism of, 314, 316, 318
Australia, citizenship rights, 38, 42
Aztecs, flower war rituals, 231

Baden-Powell, Lord Robert, 79, 80,
    83
Bagnold, Enid, 246, 248–49
Balfour, Arthur, 39
Barakat, Hidiya, 336
Bar-Giora (self-defense organiza-
    tion), 126
Barker, Pat, ix, 13
Barney, Natalie, 174 (fig)
    background, 167–68
    Sarah Bernhardt's tragic heroes
    and, 169, 172–73, 176, 178

indifference to politics, 180, 187
The Battle and Fall of Warsaw, 147
The Battle of Przemysl, 148
Battle of the Somme, 147, 151
Bäumer, Gertrud, 310
Bayn al-Qasrayn (Mahfuz), 334–35
Beecham, Sir Thomas, 181
Belbeuf, Marquise de, 176
Belgium, as symbol of victimization, 10, 133, 221
Belkind, Sonya, 126
Benaroya, Avraam, 421
Ben-Tzvi, Rachel Lishanski, 127, 132
Ben-Yehuda, Baruch, 131, 132
Ben-Yehuda, Chemda, 128
Ben-Yehuda, Eliezer, 124, 127, 128
Ben-Yehuda, Ittamar, 127
Bernhardt, Sarah, tragic male roles, 169–72, 170–71 (fig), 173, 174–75, 177–78
Between the Acts (Woolf), 206
The Big Drive, 153–54
The Big Parade, 153
Birrell, Olive, 199
birthrates, declining, 30, 35, 297, 415
black colonial troops
    projection of sexuality on, 8, 214–15, 218, 221–33, 232 (fig)
    resistance by, 235–38
    in World War I, 7, 213, 219–21, 222–23 (fig), 233–35
Boer War (1899–1902), 30
Bondfield, Margaret, 369–70
Bone, Honor, 208–9
Bonheur, Rosa, 184
Borthwick, Jessica, 144
Bottome, Phyllis, 246, 254–55
Braybon, Gail, 5–6
Brenner, Yosef Chaim, 125
Brewer, Rev. J. S., 356
Brion, Hélène, 404, 408
Britain, *see* Great Britain
British army
    conscription vs. volunteerism, 30, 73–80, 82, 83–89

myths about, 78–79, 89
physical fitness, 30, 85
see also trench warfare; WAAC (Women's Army Auxiliary Corps)
British Empire, *see* colonialism; *specific countries*
British Nationality Act, 1948, 38, 43
British Nationality and Status of Aliens Act, 1914, 40, 41
Brooke, Rupert, 82
Brooks-Carrington, Bertram, 154
Brooks, Romaine, 168
Brownlow, Kevin, 145, 154
Brown, Mary Ann, 1–2
Bureau, Hélène, 415
Bussy, Dorothy, 168
Butler, Judith, 166

Cagan, Helga, 133
The Camera Man (Collins), 151
Canada, citizenship restrictions, 42
Capy, Marcelle, 413
Carpenter, Edward, 194, 195, 197, 206
Carrington, C. E., 77
cartoons, *see* political cartoons
Catholic Center Party (Germany), 293, 295
    pacifist sympathies, 294, 296
    social policy activism, 289, 292, 297, 299–300
Catholic Church
    British suffrage movement, 267, 268, 270–72, 277
    effects of World War I on British, 276–80
    German feminist group, *see* League of Catholic Women (KDF)
The Catholic Suffragist, 277
Catholic Women's League, *see* League of Catholic Women (KDF)
Catholic Women's Suffrage Society (CWSS), 268, 270–72, 276–80

Catholic Young Women's and Mothers' Associations, 287, 291

Cavell, Edith, 329

censorship, during World War I, 53–54, 143, 149, 312, 313, 331

Central Powers, *see specific countries*

Chankin, Alexandra, 133

chastushka (folk rhyme), 107–8, 109

Chesser, Elizabeth Sloan, 31

Children of No Man's Land (Stern), 200–201

chivalry, masculinity and, 79, 82

Christianity. *see* religion

Churchill, Winston, 389, 391

Church League for Women's Suffrage (CLWS) (later League of the Church Militant (LCM), 268–70, 274–76

The Church Militant, 275

cinematographers, 142–44, 146–48, 149–52, 153–55

citizenship
British, 14, 29, 32, 35–43, 82
Palestinian Jews and, 131, 132
of women in Turkey, 56, 67–68

class
British domestic service employment, 354, 355–56, 368, 371–72
in British feminist movement, 267, 271, 274–75, 277
British nursing supervision, 358–60, 363
Egypt during World War I and, 332, 333–34
Egyptian Revolution of 1919 and, 330, 336–37, 338–41, 343, 345
French professional women, 413, 414–15
gender identity and, 11
German feminist movement, 288–89, 292
Ottoman women's nationalism and, 49–53
rejection of gender roles in upper class, 163–65, 167–68

in Russian military culture, 97–98, 101, 102–3
in WAAC recruits, 380, 381–90, 392
World War I women's employment, 364, 366, 368–71, 405, 409

clerical workers, 380, 383–84, 401–2

Clermont-Tonnerre, Duchess of, 168

The Cleverest Woman in England (Meade), 203–4

clothing, *see* female impersonation; male impersonation

Colette, 168, 176, 414

Collins, Francis, 151

colonialism
citizenship restrictions, 32, 41–43
feminized symbolism of, 214–15, 219
French recruitment of soldiers, 233–35
native women, 218–19
World War I's effects on, 2, 7–8, 29–30
see also black colonial troops; *specific countries*

Commonwealth, *see specific countries*

comradeship, of World War I soldiers, 75, 86, 88–89, 100

confessional women's movement, *see* League of Catholic Women (KDF); Protestant Women's League (DEF)

"A Conjugal Episode" (Egerton), 200, 201

conscientious objectors, 75, 197–98
see also pacifism

conscription, during World War I, 30, 73–78, 82, 83–89, 332, 333

Conservative Party (Great Britain), restricting immigration, 39

Constantinople, 60, 61

The Constant Nymph (Kennedy), 246, 253–54

Contagious Diseases Acts (Great
    Britain), 10, 278
Corelli, Marie, 186
corvée (forced labor system), 332
Cossacks, 104
Council of the National Mission,
    273–74
courage, see heroes
Couriau, Emma, 402
Couriau, Louis, 402
cowardice, Russian poster represen-
    tations of, 104–10, 105–8 (fig),
    110 (fig)
Coward, Noel, 187
Crabier, Leon, 147
Craig, Edy, 184, 206
Crawford, Thomas, 360
Crawford, Virginia, 271
Creighton, Louise, 269
Crimean War, 358
Criminal Law Amendment Act
    (Great Britain), 366
cross-dressing, see female imper-
    sonation; male impersonation
Croy, Homer, 143
Culture and Imperialism (Said), 219
Curie, Marie, 414

Darrow, Margaret, 2, 3
Davidson, Randall T. (archbishop of
    Canterbury), 270, 273, 274
Dawson, Albert K., 148
Dawson, Margaret Damer, 366, 367
Day, Father Henry, 272
De Alberti, Leonora, 277
Dearmer, Mabel, 268
Dearmer, Percy, 268
Debora (language association), 128
Deeble, Jane Cecilia, 359–60
DEF, see Protestant Women's
    League (DEF)
Delarue-Mardus, Lucie, 168
dengçides (male tobacco workers),
    424, 425, 426, 427, 433
Denikin, Anton, 101
Denisov, Vl., 98
Derby Scheme, 83–84

Despised and Rejected (Allatini),
    197–98
Deutsche Friedenskartell (DFK),
    317
Diallo, Bakare, 234
DNVP, see German National Peo-
    ple's Party
documentary filmmaking, see
    films, World War I
domestic service (France), decline
    of, 411
domestic service (Great Britain)
    growth of, 354–55
    nursing combined with, 357,
        360
    paradigm defined, 353
    women as employers, 355–56
    World War I interruptions, 368,
        370, 390, 392
    in World War I WAAC, 377, 380,
        381–82, 384
Dominions, see colonialism; spe-
    cific countries
Downs, Laura Lee, 20, 368
Dransfeld, Hedwig, 296, 297
Durand, Marguerite, 404
Duse, Eleanora, 172

Ecksteins, Modris, 152
Edmonds, Charles, 77
education
    British state-mandated, 32, 34
    of Egyptian female notables,
        338–39
    of French women, 404, 413–14
    German feminist movement and,
        290, 296, 309
    of Jewish women in Palestine,
        124, 127, 128, 129
    of Ottoman women, 49, 50, 51
Egerton, George (Mary Chavelita
    Dunne), 200
Egypt
    British government in, 329–30
    feminism in, 330, 333, 335–41,
        342–47
    independence of, 344, 346

Revolution of 1919, 329, 330, 334–41, 343, 345
in World War I, 330–34
Eisner, Kurt, 314
Ellis, Havelock, 165, 194
employment, *see* labor; unemployment
Ercole, George, 143
Evangelische Frauenzeitung, 295, 301

factory workers/inspectors, 362, 367–70, 402, 407
see also munitions workers
families
    as cottage industry units, 401
    as primary social unit in Great Britain, 80
    as symbol of nationalism, 101, 121–22, 130, 340
    as symbol of Russian Empire, 95–97, 100–102, 110–15, 112–13 (fig)
    see also fatherhood; motherhood
fatherhood, in Russian military culture, 96–97, 99–104
Faulhaber, Michael, 293
Fawcett, Millicent Garrett, 276
Federation of German Women's Associations (BDF), 291, 293, 309, 310, 311, 312
Federation for the Protection of Mothers (BfM) (Germany), 291
Fehim, Münif, 54
Feinberg, Absalom, 125–26, 129, 134, 136, 137
Feinberg, Zila, 127, 129
female impersonation, 185, 186, 187
    by soldiers at front, 11, 216–17
femininity
    defined by sexologists, 164–65
    enemy associated with, 11, 60, 61–64, 61–63 (fig), 105–8, 106–8 (fig), 223 (fig), 232
    patriotism and, 81–82
    self-defense and, 126–27
    spirituality as quality of, 273

symptoms of shell shock and, 75, 405
see also gender identity
feminism
    effects of World War I on British, 194, 273–80
    in Egypt, 330, 333, 335–41, 342–47
    in France's labor movement, 404, 409
    gender identity and nationalism in, 8–9
    German pacifism and, 307–8, 309–10, 311–13, 315–16, 317, 318–21
    German secular, 285–87, 291, 292, 301–3, 309, 317
    in German Weimar Republic, 288, 294–300, 314, 317–20
    in Jewish Palestine, 129
    prewar British, 31, 193–94, 265–72
    soldier/volunteer myth and, 75
    in Turkish nationalist movement, 67
    see also League of Catholic Women (KDF); Protestant Women's League (DEF); suffrage movement
fiction, *see* literature
films, World War I
    certifying authenticity in, 146–48
    cinematographers, 142–44, 146–52, 153–55
    depicting Russian Jewish heroism, 114
    genuine vs. staged footage, 142, 144–46
    literature vs., 142, 151, 155
    women's roles, 149
First Aliya, 123, 130
First World War, *see* World War I
Fitzroy, A. T. (Rose Allatini), 196, 197–98
France
    antisuffragist women's groups, 267

colonial troops in World War I,
   see black colonial troops
gendered division of labor,
   399–404, 411, 413, 415
historiographical approaches to
   women's labor, 398–99
postwar women's paid labor,
   410–15
women's labor during World War
   I, 404–10
see also trench warfare
Freud, Sigmund, 165
front lines, see trench warfare
Fry, Elizabeth, 361
Furse, Katharine, 364–65
Fussell, Paul, 16, 17, 75, 141, 142

Galsworthy, John, 78
Gandhi, Mohandas K., 319
Garber, Marjorie, 166, 167
Geddes, Sir Auckland Campbell,
   382
Geertz, Clifford, 335
gender identity
   division of labor in France,
      399–404, 411, 413, 415
   effects of World War I on, 11–13,
      75, 76, 216–17, 409–10
   fictional portrayal of Jewish, 247,
      249, 254–56
   nationalism and, 7, 8–11, 74–84,
      121–37
   third sex (invert), 167, 172, 186,
      194–95, 197
   see also femininity; lesbians;
      masculinity
The Generation of Hope (youth
   organization), 124
German National People's Party
   (DNVP), 295, 296, 297
The German Side of the War, 145,
   146
Germany
   antisuffragist women's groups,
      267, 293, 294–95
   black colonial troops in, 229–31
   blame for World War I, 276–77

failure of wartime bureaucracy, 29
Protestant culture in, 289–90
rate of women working, 400
rise of National Socialism,
   300–301, 316, 320, 321
secularization in, 285–86, 297,
   298, 317
Weimar Republic era, 288,
   294–300, 314, 317–20
see also League of Catholic
   Women (KDF); Protestant
   Women's League (DEF)
Gideonites (self-defense organization), 123, 126, 132
Gilbert, Sandra, 75, 194, 195, 225
A Girl in the Karpathians (Dowie),
   202
Goetz medallion, 230–31, 230 (fig),
   233
Gökalp, Ziya, 67
Graves, Robert, 77
Great Britain
   army, see British army; WAAC
      (Women's Army Auxiliary
      Corps)
   citizenship rights, 14, 29, 32,
      35–43, 82
   expansion of state's role, 29,
      31–32
   gendered nationalism in, 7, 9,
      74–84
   Jewish immigration, 38–39
   occupation of Egypt, see Egypt
   rate of women working, 400
   use of colonial troops, 7–8
   welfare measures, 32–35
   see also domestic service (Great
      Britain)
Great War, see World War I
Greece
   annexation of Macedonia, 421–22
   Turkish War of Independence
      against, 60–61, 61–62 (fig),
      62–64, 423
   in World War I, 422–23
   see also tobacco industry (Mace-
      donia)

Green, Rev. F. M., 269, 275
Grinberg, Suzanne, 413
griots (chroniclers), of black troops, 234–38
Groeben, Selma von der, 301
Gubar, Susan, 194, 195

Hacivat (shadow-play figure), 54, 62 (fig), 64, 66 (fig), 67
Hague Congress (1915), 312–13
Hale, Alfred M., 77, 86
Hall, Radclyffe, 168
    fiction by, 180, 187, 193, 194–96, 201, 202, 208
    masculine clothing, 176–78, 177 (fig), 183
    suffrage movement and, 183
Hamilton, Cicely, 184, 196, 201, 202
Hamlet (Shakespeare), 169, 170 (fig), 172–73, 174 (fig), 176, 178
Hammill, Cicely Mary, *see* Hamilton, Cicely
The Happy Foreigner (Bagnold), 246, 248–49
Harari, Yehudit, 127
Ha-Shomer (self-defense organization), 126, 127
Hause, Steven, 5
health care
    as women's sphere, 356–57, 362
    see also nurses
Heart of Darkness (Conrad), 200
The Heart of a Woman (Tweedale), 200
Hebrew language, revival, 122, 123–24, 127–30, 132, 136–37
Hebrew Women's Union for Equal Rights in Eretz Israel, 129
Henry, E. R., 366–67
heroes
    backlash against, 153
    Sarah Bernhardt's tragic male, 169–72, 170–71 (fig), 173, 174–75, 177–78
    cinematographers as, 142–44, 146–48, 149–52, 153–55
    Russian portrayals of, 98, 99,

102–4, 107–9, 108 (fig), 110 (fig), 111–14, 112–13 (fig)
    volunteers as, 74, 75, 78
    women as, 56–60, 57–58 (fig), 135–36
Heroic France, 148
Heymann, Lida Gustava
    background, 307, 309
    feminist pacifism of, 311–13, 315–16, 317–21
    socialism of, 314, 316, 318
Higonnet, Margaret Randolph, 4, 13
Higonnet, Patrice, 4
Hinscliff, Claude, 268
Hinscliff, Gertrude, 268
Hirschenzohn, Chava, 128
Hirschfeld, Magnus, 226
Holland, Henry Scott, 268
homosexuality, *see* lesbians; male homosexuality
Hospitals and Sisterhoods (Stanley), 356
Hourani, Albert, 329
How Britain Prepared: The Retreat of the Germans, 148
How I Filmed the War (Malins), 151
How Motion Pictures are Made (Croy), 143
How the Vote Was Won, 179
Hungerheart (St. John), 206–8
Hunt, Violet, 199
Hynes, Samuel, 16, 142, 145

immigration
    of Jews to Palestine, 123, 127
    restrictions in Great Britain, 38–39
India, independence of, 30
Inglis, Elsie, 365
International Council of Women, 38
International Women's Suffrage Alliance, 38
Interplay (Harraden), 201
Ireland, independence of, 30, 42
Isenberg, Michael T., 145

Ismet Pasha, 57, 60, 62 (fig)

Jeffery, Gabrielle, 271
Jewish Women's League (JFB) (Germany), 291
Jews
    in British suffrage movement, 267
    citizenship rights, 14, 37, 39–41, 131, 132
    conflicts of loyalty during World War I, 122–23, 130–33
    education in Palestine, 124, 127, 128, 129
    Hebrew language revival, 122, 123–24, 127–30, 132, 136–37
    immigration to Great Britain, 38–39
    in interwar British fiction, 245–48, 249, 250–57
    rape as metaphor for persecution, 125–26, 133–35
    Russian heroic depictions of, 111–14, 113 (fig)
    self-defense organizations, 126–27
    Thessaloniki community, 422, 423, 431–32, 433
    in tobacco industry strike (Macedonia), 424, 425, 426–31
Joan of Arc, 184–85
Jones, Helen, 362
Journey to the End of the Night (Céline), 227

Kamil, Husayn, 331
Karagöz (shadow-play figure), 54, 62 (fig), 64, 66 (fig), 67
KDF, see League of Catholic Women (KDF)
Kellogg Agreement, 319
Kemal, Mustafa, 48–49, 66–67, 66 (fig), 343
Kendall, May, 271
Kennedy, Margaret, 246, 253–54
Kent, Susan Kingsley, 2, 265
Kidd, Alice, 270

Kirkaldy, Adam, 382
Kirschhoff, Auguste, 310, 312
Kleinschmidt, F. E., 150
Konstantine, King of Greece, 423, 432
Krabbel, Gerta, 298
Krafft-Ebing, Richard von, 164, 165, 194
Kriuchkov, Koz'ma, 100–101, 103–4

labor
    demobilization of women's, 246, 249, 370–72, 387–90, 410
    equal pay demands, 292, 315, 317, 407, 408, 414
    factory workers/inspectors, 362, 367–70, 402, 407
    gendered divisions in France, 399–404, 411, 413, 415
    in German religious women's movement, 299–300, 301
    historiographical approaches to women's, 398–99
    men's alienation from professional women, 359–60, 362–63, 367
    mobilization of women's, 11–13, 51–52, 363–72, 405
    in postwar France, 410–15
    social welfare programs protecting, 33–34, 292, 299–300, 402–3, 407–8, 412
    in wartime France, 404–10
    women's unpaid, 123, 356, 357, 359, 361, 364, 365, 366
    see also clerical workers; domestic service; munitions workers; nurses; WAAC (Women's Army Auxiliary Corps); wages
labor unions, see unions, labor
Labour Party (Great Britain), 34, 38, 368–70
La Condition ouvrière (Weil), 412
L'aiglon (Rostand), 169–71, 171 (fig), 172, 173–74, 175 (fig), 176
La Mazière, Alice, 413
LaVoy, Merl, 148

Lawrence, D. H., 206
Lawrence, Susan, 369
Lawson, Marie, 209
League of Catholic Women (KDF)
    membership, 288, 289
    organization structure, 287–88
    response to National Socialism,
        300
    social policy, 291–92, 293–95
    Weimar Republic era, 295–97
    in World War I, 294
League of the Church Militant
    (LCM) (earlier Church League
    for Women's Suffrage) (CLWS),
    268–70, 274–76
League of Nations, 38, 296, 315
Leed, Eric J., 75
Legge, Margaret, 202
Lengden, Suzanne, 414
lesbians
    emergence of subculture, 193–97
    German women's activism
        against, 297
    male impersonation as identity,
        163–64, 165–67, 168–69,
        172–73, 176–78, 184
    ménage à trois, 197, 206, 208–9
    suffrage movement identified
        with, 164, 182–84, 185–86
    see also literature
Les Cervelines (Yver), 410
Les Jardins du féminisme (Yver),
    410
Leverson, Ada, 202
Liberal Party (Great Britain)
    married women's citizenship
        rights, 37–38
    social welfare initiatives, 32, 34
    suffrage movement and, 178–79
liberty, women symbolizing, 56–57,
    57 (fig), 59
Lilienblum, Yehuda Leib, 125
Lilla (Lowndes), 195
literature
    families as symbols of national-
        ism, 101, 130
    Jewish Palestinian, 124, 125–26

Jews in British, 2, 245–48, 249,
    250–57
marriage as resolution, 198–200,
    247, 256
New Woman biographies, 208–9
New Woman novels, 193–94,
    195–96, 203
parallels between Jews and
    women, 245–47
Russian World War I, 99,
    100–101, 112–13
women's masculine attire as
    symbol, 198, 201–2, 207
World War I films vs., 142, 151,
    155
World War I memoirs, 74–75,
    133, 151, 364, 408
    see also specific titles
Lloyd George, David, 40
lost generation, 121
Love in a Mist (Birrell), 199
Love's Shadow (Leverson), 202
Lowell, Amy, 194
Lowndes, Marie Belloc, 195
lubki, see posters

MacArthur, Mary, 388
Macaulay, Rose, 246, 249–53
McDowell, J. B., 147
Macedonia, see tobacco industry
    (Macedonia)
McFeely, Mary Drake, 362
Mahfuz, Naguib, 334–35
A Maid of Mystery (Meade), 205–6
male homosexuality
    Sarah Bernhardt's cult status and,
        173–75
    comradeship in World War I and,
        75
    laws outlawing, 80
    sodomization of enemy, 11,
        231–33
male impersonation, 187
    Sarah Bernhardt's theatrical,
        169–72, 170–71 (fig), 173,
        174–75, 177–78
    fictional use of, 198, 201–2, 207

lesbian identity and, 163–64,
    165–67, 168–69, 172–73,
    176–78, 184
  suffragettes and, 179–80, 182
    (fig), 183
Malinowski, Bronislaw, 226
Malins, Geoffrey, 147, 151
Mangin, Charles, 221
Mansfield, Katherine, 201
marriage
  British citizenship rights and,
    35–38
  as German feminist issue, 291,
    297–98
  increase in postwar France, 414
  as literary resolution, 198–200,
    247, 256
  respectability and, 80, 84, 197
Marshal, Christabel (Christopher
    St. John), 197, 206–9
Marx, Karl, 285, 402
masculinity
  British military vs. public percep-
    tion of, 74, 85, 86–89
  cowardice and, 104–10, 105–8
    (fig), 110 (fig)
  enemy's lack of, 11, 60, 61–64,
    61–63 (fig), 104–10, 105– 8 (fig),
    110 (fig), 223 (fig), 232
  equating British volunteers with,
    74–84
  equating Russian heroism with,
    104, 108
  morality and, 79–80, 84
  in postwar Britain, 246–47
  war as epitome of, 4, 8, 141–42
  in women, see male imperson-
    ation
  World War I film portrayals,
    142–44, 146–48, 155
  Zionist models of, 124–27, 129,
    136–37
  see also gender identity; heroes
masturbation, 79, 80
Maternity and Child Welfare Act,
    1918 (Great Britain), 35
Meade, L. T., 196, 202–6

media, see films, World War I; polit-
    ical cartoons; posters
memory, collective, 74–75, 79, 125
Meredith, Susanna, 361
Meynell, Alice, 271, 277
Michelet, Jules, 403
Midwives Act, 1902 (Great Britain),
    34
Military Service Acts (Great
    Britain), 76, 83
misogyny, 226–31
Monnier, Adrienne, 168
Moor, Dmitrii, 103
morality
  British WAAC and, 384–87
  as German women's movement
    issue, 290–91, 296–97
  volunteerism as, 78–80, 81, 82, 84
  women's independence and,
    224–29, 366–68, 370–71,
    385–86
  as women's sphere, 64–65,
    273–74, 278–79, 355–56,
    371–72
  see also prostitution
Morel, E. D., 230
Morocco, 229, 235
moshavot (agricultural settlements),
    123–24, 126–27, 133
Mosse, George L., 4, 8, 16, 75, 100
motherhood
  British social welfare protecting,
    34–35
  femininity defined by, 164–65
  French glorification of, 410
  French social welfare protecting,
    407–8, 412, 415
  German social welfare protect-
    ing, 291, 292
  in Hebrew renaissance, 128, 129
  pacifism and, 309–10, 311,
    317–18
  as symbol of moral supervision,
    371–72
  as symbol of nation, 340
  as symbol of purity, 31, 56,
    64–68, 65–66 (fig)

Motion Picture News, 143
motion pictures, *see* films, World War I
Moving Picture World, 144, 148, 150
Müller, Paula, 295
munitions workers
  in France, 405–6, 407
  layoffs, 387–90, 391–92
  morality concerns for, 11, 367–68
  wages, 382–83, 407
Murrell, Christine, 208–9
Musa, Salama, 332
Muslims
  in Egyptian Revolution of 1919, 336, 337, 341
  Thessaloniki community, 421, 423
  in tobacco strike (Macedonia), 424, 425, 426–29
  see also Ottoman Empire
Mutual Weekly, 147

Nasif, Malik Hifni, 333
National Insurance Act, 1911 (Great Britain), 33, 40–41
nationalism
  ethno-linguistic, 7, 9
  families as symbols of, 101, 121–22, 130, 340
  gender identity and, 7, 8–11, 74–84, 121–37
  and German Protestantism, 296
  international competition nurturing, 30
  Jewish, 125–26
  in Ottoman Empire, 7, 10, 49–53, 67
  pacifism vs., 307–8, 309–10, 318–20
Nationality Acts (Great Britain), 14
National Socialism (Germany), 300–301, 316, 320, 321
National Vigilance Association (NVA), 366
Nevinson, Margaret Wynne, 268, 269

New Historicism, 194, 195
A Newnham Friendship (Stronach), 199
newsreels, *see* films, World War I
Nicholas I of Russia, 96
Nicholas II of Russia, 103
Nightingale, Florence, 358, 359, 360
Nihal, Şükufe, 52
Nili (espionage network), 123, 134, 135
NSDAP (National Socialist German Workers' Party), 300–301
nurses
  misogyny directed at, 226–28
  supervision of, 357–60, 363
  World War I organization of, 364–66, 405

office workers, *see* clerical workers
Ogden, Joan, *see* The Unlit Lamp (Hall)
Old Age Pensions Act, 1908 (Great Britain), 33, 37, 40, 41
Old Wine (Bottome), 246, 254–55
Omnès, Catherine, 408, 415
Ottoman Empire
  citizenship of Palestinian Jews, 130–33
  emergence of political cartoons, 53–55
  nationalism, 7, 10, 49–53, 67
  women in creation of Turkish Republic, 49–53
  women in political cartoons, 56–68, 57–58 (fig), 61–63 (fig), 65–66 (fig)
  see also Egypt; Turkish Republic

pacifism, 75, 197–98, 250–51, 296
  German feminism and, 307–8, 309–10, 311–13, 315–16, 317, 318–21
Packard, Roger, 148
Palace Walk, see Mahfuz
Palestine
  agricultural settlements, 123–24, 126–27, 133

British rule, 30
education of Jewish women, 124,
   127, 128, 129
Jewish citizenship, 131, 132
Palmer, Eva, 168
Pankhurst, Christabel, 180
Pankhurst, Emmeline, 180, 183,
   186
Pankhurst, Sylvia, 182–83
Parliamentary Recruiting Commit-
   tee (PRC), 81
pastaltzoudes (female tobacco
   workers), 424, 433
Pasternak, Leonid, 99
Pathway of the Pioneer (Wyllarde),
   199–200
patriotism, *see* nationalism
peace, women symbolizing, 56–57,
   58 (fig), 59
Péguy, Charles, 126
Pelletier, Madeleine, 414
Perrot, Michelle, 5
Pethick-Lawrence, Emmeline, 180,
   276
Philosophy of Right (Hegel), 285
*Photographic Activities of the
   Signal Corps, AEF, 1917–1918,*
   152
Picton-Turbervill, Edith, 368–69
Picture-Play Magazine, 148
Pogodin, Mikhail, 96
pogroms, 125
poilus, see soldiers
Polignac, Princess de, 168, 180
political cartoons
   asexual heroines, 56–60, 57–58
      (fig)
   emergence of, in Ottoman Em-
      pire, 53–55
   idealism vs. realism, 47–48, 55–56
   immoral women, 60–64, 61–63
      (fig)
   stolid mothers, 64–68, 65–66 (fig)
Poor Law (Great Britain), 32, 33
posters
   familial depictions in Russian
      wartime, 97, 100, 102

German enemies of Russia,
   102–6, 103 (fig), 105 (fig), 107
   (fig)
Great Britain's wartime use of,
   81–82, 83
multi-ethnic Russian, 110–15,
   112–13 (fig)
Russian heroism, 98–99, 102–5,
   106 (fig), 107–9, 108 (fig), 110
   (fig), 111–14, 112–13 (fig)
Turkish enemies of Russia,
   105–11, 107–8 (fig), 110 (fig),
   112 (fig)
Potterism (Macaulay), 246, 249–53
Pougy, Liane de, 172–73
poverty, in Great Britain, 32–35
Princesses de science (Yver), 410
prisons, women's volunteer work
   in, 361
propaganda
   emphasizing masculinity, 80–81
   enemy as effeminate in, 11, 60,
      61–62 (fig)
   labor mobilization through gen-
      der, 13
   see also films, World War I; polit-
      ical cartoons; posters
prostitution, 134, 174–76
   British women's activism
      against, 366, 367
   conceptions of British masculin-
      ity and, 80, 85–86
   German state regulation of,
      290–91, 309
   rumors of, in WAAC, 384–85
Protestants, *see* Anglican Church;
   Protestant Women's League
   (DEF)
Protestant Women's Aid
   (Germany), 287, 288–89, 291,
   293, 297
Protestant Women's League (DEF)
   membership, 288–90
   moral issues, 290–91, 297
   organizational structure, 287–88
   response to National Socialism,
      300–301

social policy and, 291–93,
291–93,
294–95
Weimar Republic era, 295–96
Proudhon, Pierre Joseph, 402
Puchachevsky, Nehama, 128

racial purity, women as guardians
of, 10–11, 31, 106
racism
British citizenship restrictions
and, 42–43
nationalism nurturing, 30
in Russian World War I posters,
106–10, 107–8 (fig)
toward French colonial troops,
221–24, 222–23 (fig), 226, 227,
228–29, 232 (fig)
WILPF's condemnation of, 315
The Rainbow (Lawrence), 206
rape, 217, 231, 312
as metaphor for Jewish persecution, 125–26, 133–35
The Rebellion of Esther (Legge), 202
Reichstadt, Duke of, 169–71, 171
(fig), 172, 173–74, 175 (fig), 176
religion
German feminism and, 285–87,
301–3
impacts of World War I on
British, 273–80
prewar British Anglican and
Catholic suffragists, 268–72
prewar British feminism and,
265–68
women employers teaching,
355–57
see also League of Catholic
Women (KDF); Protestant
Women's League (DEF)
Remarque, Erich Maria, 153
Report to Henrietta Szold (Feinberg), 134
ribbon industry (France), 400–401
Roberts, G. H., 386
Roberts, Mary Louise, 6, 415
Roman Catholic Church, *see*
Catholic Church

Rosenberg, Isaac, 77
Royden, A. Maude, 265, 273, 276
Rule, Albert L., 154
Russell, Sir Thomas, 338
Russia
effeminate portrayals of enemy,
11
military culture, 96–98, 99–104,
103 (fig)
multi-ethnic war propaganda,
110–15, 112–13 (fig)
patriarchal authority, 95–97
persecution of Jews, 125
propaganda promoting mobilization, 98–99
racial/gendered portrayals of
cowardice, 104–10, 105–8 (fig),
110 (fig)
Russo-Japanese War, 97

Sackville-West, Vita, 168, 194, 206
Said, Edward, 47, 219
St. Joan's International Alliance,
279
St. John, Christopher, 197, 206–9
St. John's Housing Training Institu-
tion for Nurses, 357–58, 360
Samuel, Herbert, 34
Sartre, Jean-Paul, 226
Savoy, Bert, 186
Scharlieb, Mary, 370–71
Schwartzhaupt, Elisabeth, 301
Scottish Women's Hospitals (SWH),
365–66
Scott, Joan Wallach, 12, 399, 403
Scouting for Boys (Baden-Powell),
79
Second Aliya, 127
Selenka, Margarethe Leonore, 308
Self Help, see Smiles
Senegalese troops, *see* black colo-
nial troops
sexology, 226
sexual identity defined, 164–65,
166, 176, 187
third sex classification, 167, 172,
186, 194–95, 197

The Sexual History of the World War (Hirschfeld), 226
sexuality
    Jewish nationalism and, 125–27
    in political cartoons, 55, 56–68, 57–58 (fig), 61–63 (fig), 65–66 (fig)
    of soldiers, 75, 85–86, 214–18, 221–33, 232 (fig)
    see also lesbians; male homosexuality
Sha'rawi, Huda
    in feminist movement, 333, 344–45
    in women's demonstrations, 329, 335, 336, 338, 342
Shaw, George Bernard, 206
Shaw Stewart, Jane, 358, 359
shell shock
    feminine symptoms of, 75, 405
    see also trench warfare
Shochat, Manya Vilboshevitz, 127
Showalter, Elaine, 75
The Siren (Meade), 204–5
Smiles, Samuel, 79
Smith, P. J., 154
Smith-Rosenberg, Carroll, 164
Smyth, Ethel, 166–67, 181 (fig), 187
    biography of, 208, 209
    as suffragette, 164, 180–84, 186
Smyth-Piggot, Blanche, 272
Social Democratic Party (SPD) (Germany), 293, 294, 295, 296, 314
socialism
    in German pacifist-feminist movement, 314, 316, 318
    German religious women's groups and, 295, 301–2
    in Greece, 422, 430
    nationalist focus during World War I, 308
social production, *see* labor
Society of the Mothers of the Future (Egypt), 343–44
sodomy, 11, 231–33
    see also male homosexuality

soldiers
    black colonial troops, *see* black colonial troops
    conscription, 30, 73–78, 82, 83–89, 332, 333
    films expressing experience, 152–53
    loss of identity in war films, 147–48
    masculinity equated with volunteer, 74–84
    myths about, 78–79, 85, 89
    paternalism toward Russian, 96–97, 99–104
    social distinctions between Russian officers and, 97–98, 101, 102
    theatrical performances, 215–17
    see also trench warfare; World War I
Somewhere in France, 147, 149
South Africa, 30–31, 42
Squire, Rose, 362, 370
Stanley, Mary, 356–57
Stein, Gertrude, 168, 194
Stern, G. B., 200
Stöcker, Helene, 310, 312
strikes, labor, 407
    see also tobacco industry (Macedonia)
Stronach, Alice, 199
suffrage
    British restrictions, 29, 37, 268, 274
    German women's, 294
suffrage movement
    Anglican Church and, 266–70, 274
    British Catholic women's activism, 267, 268, 270–72, 277
    French, 412
    German, 292–95, 309
    identified with lesbianism, 164, 182–84, 185–86
    Macedonian labor strike compared to, 428
    theatrics used by, 178–88

traditional femininity in, 201
   see also feminism
Suffragists Churchwoman's Protest
   Committee, 270
Suttner, Bertha von, 307

Tarn, Pauline, see Vivien, Renée
Taylor, Pam, 371
theatrics
   political, 178–88
   revealing sexual nature through,
      163, 165–66, 168–69, 172–78
   World War I frontline, 215–17
   see also female impersonation;
      male impersonation
Thessaloniki (Macedonia), see to-
      bacco industry (Macedonia)
Theweleit, Klaus, 227
Third Reich, see National Social-
      ism (Germany)
third sex (invert), 167, 172, 186,
      194–95, 197
Thomas, Albert, 407
Thompson, Donald, 146, 147, 149–50
Ticknor, Lisa, 185
Tilley, Vesta, 173
Tilly, Louise, 399
The Time Machine (Wells), 200
tirailleurs sénégalais, see black
      colonial troops
tobacco industry (Macedonia)
   ethnic/gender composition of,
      423–24, 432–33
   nationalist tensions in, 423,
      428–34
   strike, 424–26
   women strikebreakers, 426–28
Told by an Idiot (Macaulay), 253
travesti roles, see male imperson-
      ation
Treaty of Lausanne, 57, 58 (fig)
Treaty of Versailles, 14, 37, 296, 315
Trefusis, Violet, 168
trench scripts, 215–17
trench warfare
   filming, 143–44, 146, 147, 148,
      150, 154

gender identity and, 13, 75, 76,
      216–17
shell shock, 75, 405
survival issues, 74, 85, 86–89
   see also soldiers; World War I
"Triptych" (Sackville-West), 206
troops, see soldiers
Troubridge, Una, 178
Turkish Republic
   creation of, 48–49, 52–54, 423
   gendered citizenship rights, 56,
      67–68
   political cartoons and, 57, 57–58
      (fig), 59, 60–64, 61–63 (fig)
   see also Ottoman Empire
Türkiye, 55
The Turn of the Screw (James), 200
Tweedale, Violet, 200

Une femme m'apparut (Vivien), 168
unemployment
   in post-war Britain, 42–43
   women joining WAAC and,
      377–78, 387–90, 391–92
unions, labor
   in France, 402–3, 412
   in Germany, 292
   in Great Britain, 368–69, 389,
      391–92
   Macedonian tobacco workers,
      424, 425, 426, 429–30, 433
United Religious Leagues, 268
United States
   disillusionment in, 141
   filmmaking, 143, 144, 151–52,
      153
The Unlit Lamp (Hall), 193,
      195–96, 201, 202, 208

Vanbrugh, Violet, 187
Vartanyan, Hovsep, 53
venereal diseases, 10–11
Venizelos, Eleftherios, 423, 432
The Venus Model, 149
Vested Interests (Garber), 167
victims, women in war, 10, 133–35,
      136, 230

Vivien, Renée, 167, 168–69, 172
Voluntary Aid Detachments (VAD), 364–65
volunteers
    age and fitness standards, 380
    British conscripts vs., 30, 73–80, 82, 83–89
    Russian Jews as, 113–14
    women as unpaid, 356, 357, 359, 361, 364, 365, 366

WAAC (Women's Army Auxiliary Corps)
    clerical workers in, 380, 383–84
    domestic servants in, 377, 380, 381–82, 384
    morality issues, 384–87
    recruitment figures, 378–80, 379 (fig)
    unemployment contributing to growth, 377–78, 387–90, 391–92
Wafd
    in Egyptian revolution of 1919, 334, 336, 338, 339, 341–42, 344
    Women's Wafd, 337, 342–43, 344–45
wages
    equal pay demands, 292, 315, 317, 407, 408, 414
    for women in postwar France, 412
    for women in prewar France, 401
    World War I women's, 382–83, 406–7
Walby, Sylvia, 5
War As It Really Is, 146, 150
Warner, Marina, 89
Webb, Beatrice, 362
Weber, Helene, 297
Weber, Jean, 173
Weigle, Edwin, 146
Weil, Simone, 412
Weimar Republic, feminist groups in, 288, 294–300, 314, 317–20
welfare legislation, in Great Britain, 32–35

The Well of Loneliness (Hall), 180, 187, 194–95
Werfel, Franz, 10
Western Front, see soldiers; trench warfare
Wilde, Dolly, 168
Wilder, Frances, 195
William—An Englishman (Hamilton), 202
WILPF, see Women's International League for Peace and Freedom
Wings, 153
With the Russians at the Front, 150
women
    British anti-poverty measures, 32–35
    British citizenship rights, 35–38
    as guardians of racial purity, 10–11, 31, 106
    health care as sphere of, 356–57, 362
    as heroes, 56–60, 57–58 (fig), 135–36
    morality as sphere of, 64–65, 273–74, 278–79, 355–56, 371–72
    as symbol of liberty and peace, 56–57, 57–58 (fig), 59
    unpaid labor by, 123, 356, 357, 359, 361, 364, 365, 366
    as war victims, 10, 133–35, 136, 230
    see also lesbians; motherhood
Women's Aid (Germany), 287, 288–89, 291, 293, 297
Women's Army Auxiliary Corps, see WAAC (Women's Army Auxiliary Corps)
Women's Committees for Permanent Peace (WCCP), 313, 314
Women's Co-operative Guild, 34
Women's International League for Peace and Freedom (WILPF), 307
    Hague Congress (1915), 312–13
    philosophical principles, 314–16

Women's Land Army (WLA),
    378–79, 389, 390, 392
Women's Police Service (WPS), 11,
    362, 366–67
Women's Social and Political Union
    (WSPU), 180, 181, 182, 270
Woolf, Virginia, 206
Woollacott, Angela, 6, 9
The Workaday Woman (Hunt), 199
Workers' Socialist Federation
    (Macedonia), 422, 424, 427, 431
work, see labor
WRAF (Women's Royal Air Force),
    389
WRNS (Women's Royal Naval Ser-
    vice), 389

WSPU, see Women's Social and
    Political Union (WSPU)
Wyllarde, Dolf, 199

The Young Generation (youth orga-
    nization), 124, 131
Yourcenar, Marguerite, 168
Yver, Colette, 410

Zaghlul, Sa'd, 334–35, 337, 338,
    342, 343, 344
Zaghlul, Safiya, 343, 345, 346
Zetkin, Clara, 310
Zionism, construction of gender in,
    122, 123–27, 129, 136–37